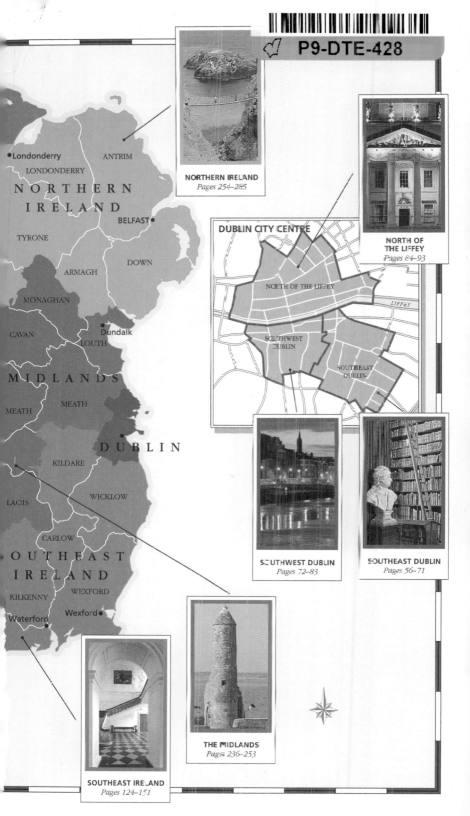

P9-DTE-428

Londonderry
LONDONDERRY
ANTRIM

NORTHERN
IRELAND

BELFAST

TYRONE

DOWN

ARMAGH

MONAGHAN

CAVAN

Dundalk

LOUTH

MIDLANDS

MEATH

MEATH

DUBLIN

KILDARE

WICKLOW

LAOIS

CARLOW

SOUTHEAST
IRELAND

WEXFORD

KILKENNY

Waterford   Wexford

NORTHERN IRELAND
Pages 254–285

DUBLIN CITY CENTRE

NORTH OF THE LIFFEY

LIFFEY

SOUTHWEST
DUBLIN

SOUTHEAST
DUBLIN

**NORTH OF
THE LIFFEY**
Pages 84–93

SOUTHWEST DUBLIN
Pages 72–83

SOUTHEAST DUBLIN
Pages 56–71

SOUTHEAST IRELAND
Pages 124–151

THE MIDLANDS
Pages 236–253

EYEWITNESS TRAVEL

IRELAND

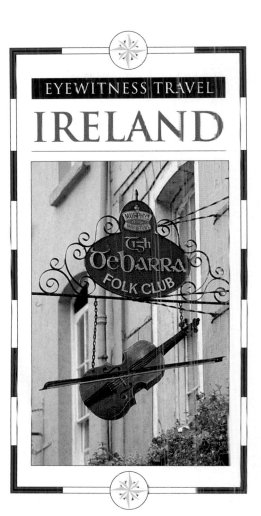

EYEWITNESS TRAVEL
IRELAND

MAIN CONTRIBUTORS:
LISA GERARD-SHARP AND TIM PERRY

LONDON, NEW YORK,
MELBOURNE, MUNICH AND DELHI
www.dk.com

PROJECT EDITOR Ferdie McDonald
ART EDITOR Lisa Kosky
EDITORS Maggie Crowley, Simon Farbrother, Emily Hatchwell, Seán
O'Connell, Jane Simmonds
DESIGNERS Joy FitzSimmons, Jaki Grosvenor,
Katie Peacock, Jan Richter
RESEARCHERS John Breslin, Andrea Holmes
PICTURE RESEARCHERS Sue Mennell, Christine Rista
DTP DESIGNERS Samantha Borland, Adam Moore

CONTRIBUTORS
Una Carlin, Polly Phillimore, Susan Poole, Martin Walters

PHOTOGRAPHERS
Joe Cornish, Tim Daly, Alan Williams

ILLUSTRATORS
Draughtsman Maps, Maltings Partnership, Robbie Polley

Reproduced by Colourscan, Singapore
Printed and bound in China by South China Printing Co. Ltd

First American edition 1995
12 13 14 15 10 9 8 7 6 5 4 3 2 1
Published in the United States by DK Publishing,
375 Hudson Street, New York, New York 10014

**Reprinted with revisions 1997, 1999, 2000, 2001, 2002,
2003, 2004, 2006, 2007, 2008, 2009, 2010, 2011, 2012**

Copyright 1995, 2012 © Dorling Kindersley Limited, London
A Penguin Company

Published in Great Britain by Dorling Kindersley Limited.

A catalog record for this book is available from the Library of Congress.

ISSN 1542-1554
ISBN 978-0-75668-411-2

FLOORS ARE REFERRED TO THROUGHOUT IN ACCORDANCE WITH EUROPEAN USAGE,
I.E., THE "FIRST FLOOR" IS THE FLOOR ABOVE GROUND LEVEL.

Front cover main image: Lake Kylemore, Connemara, County Galway

**The information in this DK Eyewitness Travel Guide
is checked regularly.**

Every effort has been made to ensure that this book is as up-to-date as
possible at the time of going to press. Some details, however, such as
telephone numbers, opening hours, prices, gallery hanging
arrangements and travel information, are liable to change. The
publishers cannot accept responsibility for any consequences arising from
the use of this book, nor for any material on third-party websites, and
cannot guarantee that any website address in this book will be a
suitable source of travel information. We value the views and
suggestions of our readers highly. Please write to:
Publisher, DK Eyewitness Travel Guides, Dorling Kindersley, 80 Strand,
London, Great Britain WC2R 0RL, or email: travelguides@dk.com.

CONTENTS

An evangelical symbol from the
Book of Kells *(see p64)*

INTRODUCING IRELAND

DUBLIN AREA BY AREA

Georgian doorway in Fitzwilliam
Square, Dublin *(see p68)*

IRELAND REGION BY REGION

Detail of the Chorus Gate at
Powerscourt (see pp134–5)

Grazing cows at Spanish Point near Mizen Head (see p167)

TRAVELERS' NEEDS

SURVIVAL GUIDE

Façade of a pub in Dingle (see p157)

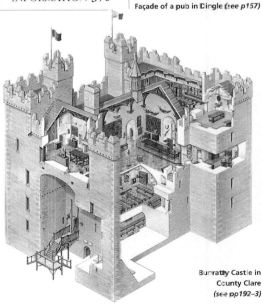

Bunratty Castle in
County Clare
(see pp192–3)

HOW TO USE THIS GUIDE

This guide helps you to get the most from your visit to Ireland. It provides both expert recommendations and detailed practical information. *Introducing Ireland* maps the country and sets it in its historical and cultural context. The seven regional chapters, plus *Dublin Area* by *Area*, contain descriptions of all the important sights, with maps, pictures and illustrations. Restaurant and hotel recommendations can be found in *Travellers' Needs*. The *Survival Guide* has tips on everything from the telephone system to transport both in the Republic and in Northern Ireland.

DUBLIN AREA BY AREA

Central Dublin is divided into three sightseeing areas. Each has its own chapter, which opens with a list of the sights described. A fourth chapter, *Further Afield*, covers the suburbs and County Dublin. Sights are numbered and plotted on an *Area Map*. The descriptions of each sight follow the map's numerical order, making sights easy to locate within the chapter.

Sights at a Glance lists the chapter's sights by category: Churches, Museums and Galleries, Historic Buildings, Parks and Gardens.

2 Street-by-Street Map
This gives a bird's-eye view of the key area in each chapter.

A suggested route for a walk is shown in red.

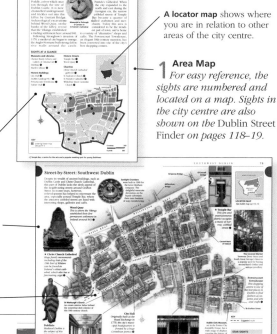

All pages relating to Dublin have red thumb tabs.

A locator map shows where you are in relation to other areas of the city centre.

1 Area Map
For easy reference, the sights are numbered and located on a map. Sights in the city centre are also shown on the Dublin Street Finder *on pages 118–19.*

Stars indicate the sights that no visitor should miss.

3 Detailed information
The sights in Dublin are described individually with addresses, telephone numbers and information on opening hours and admission charges.

Story boxes highlight noteworthy features of the sights.

IRELAND REGION BY REGION

Apart from Dublin, Ireland has been divided into seven regions, each of which has a separate chapter. The most interesting towns and places to visit in each area have been numbered on a Regional Map.

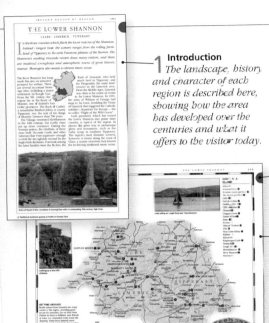

1 Introduction
The landscape, history and character of each region is described here, showing how the area has developed over the centuries and what it offers to the visitor today.

Each region of Ireland can be quickly identified by its colour coding, shown on the inside front cover.

2 Regional Map
This shows the road network and gives an illustrated overview of the whole region. All interesting places to visit are numbered and there are also useful tips on getting around the region by car and train.

Getting Around gives tips on travel within the region.

3 Detailed information
All the important towns and other places to visit are described individually. They are listed in order, following the numbering on the Regional Map. Within each town or city, there is detailed information on important buildings and other sights.

The Visitors' Checklist provides all the practical information you will need to plan your visit to all the top sights.

4 Ireland's top sights
These are given two or more full pages. Historic buildings are dissected to reveal their interiors. The most interesting towns or city centres are shown in a bird's-eye view, with sights picked out and described.

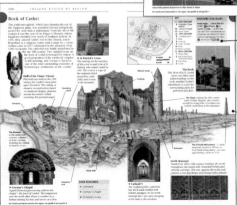

INTRODUCING
IRELAND

DISCOVERING IRELAND

Ireland's popularity as a tourist destination is ensured by its profound cultural heritage, breathtaking scenery and famously easy-going lifestyle. Much of the joy of travelling around Ireland is the warmth of the people; their welcome rarely

Bust of St Patrick

feels forced. Celtic ruins, medieval forts and stately homes dot the landscape, giving the island a certain majesty. The chapters in this guide have been divided into eight colour-coded regions, each incorporating counties of the Republic or Northern Ireland.

DUBLIN

- **Historic Trinity College**
- **Celtic treasures at the National Museum**
- **Superb theatre & pubs**

Cosmopolitan Dublin, with most of its attractions within easy walking distance, has much to offer the visitor. **Trinity College**, founded in 1592 by Queen Elizabeth I, allows access to its spectacular Old Library, which houses the medieval Book of Kells *(see pp62–4)*. The **National Museum** *(see pp66–7)*, just a few blocks from the college, offers a fascinating insight into Ireland's past, while the **National Gallery** *(see pp70–71)* (which is under refurbishment until 2013) presents excellent exhibitions.

Theatre in Dublin is top notch with plays by the Irish greats staged at venues such as the **Abbey** *(see p88)*, which was founded by WB Yeats.

The lively district of **Temple Bar** *(see p78)* offers a flavour of traditional Irish "craic", with a host of busy bars and

Crossing the River Liffey over Ha'penny Bridge, Dublin

The vivid greens surrounding the Killarney Lakes, County Kerry

restaurants. Keep in mind however that this city is far more expensive than anywhere else in the country.

SOUTHEAST IRELAND

- **Powerscourt**
- **Wicklow Mountains**
- **Fine beaches**

The "sunny southeast" is one of the most popular holiday regions in the country, with summer weather more reliable than elsewhere in Ireland. The port town **Rosslare** *(see p151)* boasts a fine 9.5-km (6-mile) beach and an excellent golf course nearby.

Located at the foot of the Great Sugar Loaf Mountain, the extensive grounds at **Powerscourt** *(see pp134–5)* are among the most beautiful in the country, with the stately Italian Garden cascading down landscaped terraces.

Glendalough *(see pp140–41)* in the Wicklow Mountains features the atmospheric ruins of a once flourishing monastic settlement established by St Kevin during the 6th century.

CORK & KERRY

- **Cork and the Blarney Stone**
- **Colourful fishing villages**
- **Lakes of Killarney**

This region, one of the country's most picturesque, has a long indented coastline which blends with the highest peaks in Ireland. Hundreds of miles of walking and cycling routes crisscross the area, including the celebrated **Ring of Kerry** *(see pp164–5)* which encircles the Iveragh Peninsula. The clear **Lakes of Killarney** *(see pp162–3)* are nestled into the lush hills of central Kerry and are one of the area's most popular holiday destinations.

Cork is a small, pretty city of riverside quays and winding alleys, enlivened by an exciting cultural buzz *(see pp174–7)*. Nearby, at the ruins of **Blarney Castle** *(see p171)*, visitors queue to kiss the Blarney Stone, said to bless them with the gift of the gab. To the east of Cork, the **Old Midleton Distillery** *(see p179)* offers tours and tastings that no whiskey drinker should miss.

THE LOWER SHANNON

- The rugged Burren
- Majestic Cliffs of Moher
- Early Christian settlements

The River Shannon runs through the region, dominated by barren limestone and we marshy land, before emptying into the sea. Few trees grow on the vast Burren, an atmospheric and otherworldy landscape (see pp186–8). The sudden 200-m (650-ft) drop of the Cliffs of Moher, shrouded in mist and battered by Atlantic gales, is one of the most dramatic stretches of coastline in the country (see p184). Built on a strategic hillock, the 5th-century Rock of Cashel was first a stronghold of the Munster kings and later of the Church (see pp196–7).

Poulnabrone Dolmen, perched on the limestone plateau of the Burren

THE WEST OF IRELAND

- Unspoilt Aran Islands
- Connemara National Park
- Galway's infectious charm

The West of Ireland is a region of contradictions, with farming areas, rugged coastlines and cosmopolitan towns. The Irish language (Gaelic) is still spoken in many areas and the region is a haven for traditional music and dancing. The Aran Islands (see pp214–15) offer a chance to experience unspoilt Ireland; island life has changed little in the last hundred years.
Connemara National Park (see p208) encompasses four of the Twelve Bens, which rise high above the surrounding heathland. This dazzling

Brightly painted shop fronts in the centre of Galway, West of Ireland

landscape provides habitats for peregrin falcons and semi-wild Connemara ponies.
Lively Galway is Ireland's fastest growing city, yet it somehow manages to retain much of its medieval charm (see pp210–11).

NORTHWEST IRELAND

- Deserted beaches and rugged coasts
- Prehistoric Celtic sites

Perched at the furthest reaches of the island, the northwest has remained isolated from events, retaining a large population of Gaelic speakers. The dramatic landscape includes the breathtaking cliffs of Slieve League, best visited at sunset when they are streaked with red (see p229). The large herd of deer is reason enough to visit Glenveagh National Park and Castle (see pp216–17) but there's also the stunning Lough Veagh and, just outside the park, the eerily forbidding valley, Poisoned Glen.

THE MIDLANDS

- Newgrange's ancient grave
- Ruins of Clonmacnoise

The pastures of the Midlands are the cradle of Irish civilization. Pre-dating the Celts, the mysterious passage graves of Newgrange were built around 3200 BC (see pp246–7). The once thriving monastery of Clonmacnoise is now in ghostly ruins (see pp250–51).
Elegant Birr (see p253) comprises a Georgian layout and beautifully restored houses.

NORTHERN IRELAND

- Giant's Causeway
- Magnificent lakeland
- Belfast's exciting nightlife

For many years, Northern Ireland has been associated with sectarian conflict. Finally visitors are rediscovering the region, which encapsulates the Mountains of Mourne (see p284) and Ireland's biggest lake, Lough Neagh (see p274).
Belfast (see pp276–9) is a fascinating city, where the political loyalties of its citizens are preserved in the murals of West Belfast. The Cathedral Quarter is a cultural hotspot, with culinary and architectural gems adorning its streets.
The Giant's Causeway (see pp262–3), a volcanic formation of basalt columns, is an unusual sight, which adds to the rugged beauty of the Causeway Coast (see p261).

The crumbling remains of Dunluce Castle in Northern Ireland

Putting Ireland on the Map

The island of Ireland covers an area of 84,430 sq km (32,598 sq miles). Lying in the Atlantic Ocean to the northwest of mainland Europe, it is separated from Great Britain by the Irish Sea. The Republic of Ireland takes up 85 per cent of the island, with a population of 4.5 million. Northern Ireland, part of the United Kingdom, has 1.8 million people. Dublin is the capital of the Republic and has good international communications.

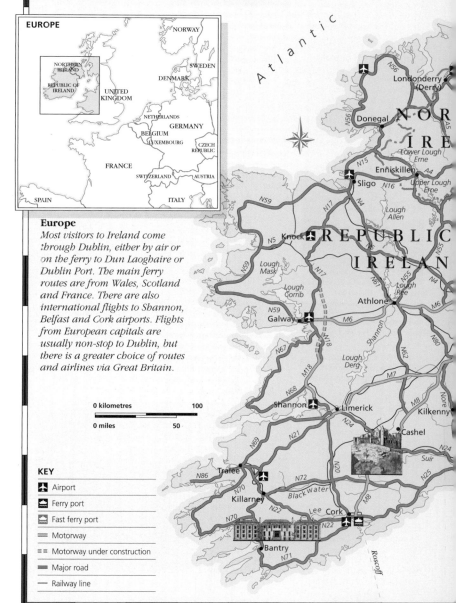

EUROPE

NORWAY
SWEDEN
DENMARK
NORTHERN IRELAND
REPUBLIC OF IRELAND
UNITED KINGDOM
NETHERLANDS
GERMANY
BELGIUM
LUXEMBOURG
CZECH REPUBLIC
FRANCE
SWITZERLAND
AUSTRIA
SPAIN
ITALY

Europe

Most visitors to Ireland come through Dublin, either by air or on the ferry to Dun Laoghaire or Dublin Port. The main ferry routes are from Wales, Scotland and France. There are also international flights to Shannon, Belfast and Cork airports. Flights from European capitals are usually non-stop to Dublin, but there is a greater choice of routes and airlines via Great Britain.

| 0 kilometres | 100 |
| 0 miles | 50 |

KEY

- ✈ Airport
- ⛴ Ferry port
- ⛴ Fast ferry port
- ▬ Motorway
- ▬ ▬ Motorway under construction
- ▬ Major road
- — Railway line

Atlantic Ocean

Londonderry (Derry)
Donegal
N O R
I R E
Lower Lough Erne
Enniskillen
Upper Lough Erne
Sligo
Lough Allen
N59
Knock
R E P U B L I C
I R E L A N
Lough Mask
Lough Corrib
Athlone
Lough Ree
Galway
Shannon
Lough Derg
Shannon
Limerick
Kilkenny
Cashel
Suir
Tralee
Killarney
Blackwater
Cork
Lee
Bantry
Roscoff
Nore

GREATER DUBLIN

Swords
Malahide
Dublin Airport
Finglas
Glasnevin
Marino
Howth
Royal Canal
Liffey
Lucen
Grand Canal
Kilmainham
Clondalkin
Rathmines
Ballsbridge
Dublin
Dublin Bay
Blackrock
Dundrum
Dun Laoghaire
0 km   5
0 miles   5

Greater Dublin
*Nearly one third of the Republic's population
lives in Dublin. The city centre has become
very congested, but access to the ports and
airport is relatively easy.*

SCOTLAND

Islay
Arran
Glasgow
Campbeltown
Troon

North   Channel

Ballycastle
Coleraine
Cairnryan
Stranraer
Larne

ENGLAND

THERN
LAND
Lough Neagh
Belfast
Armagh
Newry
Dundalk

Isle of Man
Douglas
Heysham
Fleetwood

OF

Irish   Sea

Manchester
Liverpool
Mostyn

Boyne
DUBLIN
Dun Laoghaire
Holyhead

Liffey

Barrow
Carlow
Slaney

Waterford
Wexford
Rosslare

Fishguard

WALES

St   George's   Channel

Roscoff/Cherbourg

Pembroke
Swansea
CARDIFF
Bristol

Bristol   Channel

A PORTRAIT OF IRELAND

Many visitors see Ireland as a lush green island, full of thatched cottages, pubs, music, wit and poetry. Like all stereotypes, this image of the country has a basis in truth and the tourist industry helps sustain it. The political and economic reality is, of course, rather less ideal, but the relaxed good humour of the people still makes Ireland a most welcoming place to visit.

Ireland, at least for the time being, is a divided island. History and religion created a North–South divide, with two hostile communities in the North. The IRA ceasefire of 1997 and the Good Friday Agreement brought new hope, however. John Hume of the SDLP and David Trimble of the Ulster Unionist Party were jointly awarded the Nobel Prize for Peace for their work in the peace process, and the inaugural meeting of the Northern Ireland Assembly took place on 1 July 1998.

Ireland has had more than its fair share of wars and disasters, culminating in the Great Famine of 1845–8, since when emigration has been part

Cathleen ní Houlihan, personification of Ireland

of Irish life. More people of Irish descent live in the USA than in Ireland itself. Suffering and martyrdom in the cause of independence also play an important part in the Irish consciousness. The heroine of WB Yeats's play *Cathleen ní Houlihan* inspires young men to lay down their lives for Ireland. Her image appeared on the first banknote issued by the newly created Irish Free State in 1922.

Yet, the Irish retain their easy-going attitude to life, with a young, highly educated population working hard to make its way in today's European Union. In the Republic, 43 per cent of the population is under 30.

Façade of Trinity College, Dublin, the Republic's most prestigious university

◁ Thatching a traditional cottage in Adare, County Limerick

Young first communicant in County Kerry

Despite its high birth rate, rural Ireland is sparsely populated. The Industrial Revolution of the 19th century barely touched the South and for much of the 20th century the Republic seemed an old-fashioned place, poorer than almost all its fellow members of the European Union.

ECONOMIC DEVELOPMENT

Tax breaks and low inflation have attracted foreign investment to the Republic and many multinationals have subsidiaries here. Ireland joined the single European currency in 1999, and the Republic enjoyed an economic boom from the mid-1990s to 2007. Since 2008, there has been an economic recession. Unemployment rates have soared, property prices have plummeted and the nation is saddled with debt.

An important industry for Ireland is tourism. The South receives over 5.5 million visitors a year and the North receives 1.4 million visitors.

Traditionally, Northern Ireland had far more industry than the

South, but during the 25 years of the "Troubles", old heavy industries, such as shipbuilding, declined and new investors were scared away. However, the election of members to the new Northern Ireland Assembly in June 1998 ushered in a new political and economic era for the North. For both parts of Ireland, geography is still a barrier to prosperity. Located on the periphery of Europe, the island is isolated from its main markets and thus saddled with high transport costs. Subsidies from the EU have helped improve infrastructure in the Republic.

RELIGION AND POLITICS

The influence of Catholicism is still felt but not to the extent that it once was. Irish Catholicism runs the gamut from missionary zeal to

Pavement artist on O'Connell Street, Dublin

simple piety. In recent years, attendance at Mass has dropped off considerably and some estimates now place attendance at less than 50 per cent. Moral conservatism is, however, still most evident in attitudes to abortion.

The election of liberal lawyer Mary Robinson as President in 1990, the first woman to hold the post, was seen as a sign of more enlightened times by many people, an attitude reinforced by the election of Mary McAleese as her successor in 1998. A new political climate has favoured the quiet spread

Traditional Irish dancing

Traditional farming: a field of haystacks overlooking Clew Bay, County Mayo

of feminism and challenged the old paternalism of Irish politics.

LANGUAGE AND CULTURE

Ireland was a Gaelic-speaking nation until the 16th century, since when the language has steadily declined. Today, however, the Republic is officially bilingual. Knowledge of Irish is a requirement for a career in the public sector, and one in three people on the island as a whole has some degree of competency.

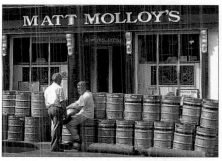

Connemara pony show

Irish culture, on the other hand, is in no danger of being eroded. The people have a genuine love of old folk legends and epic poetry and songs. Festivals, whether dedicated to St Patrick or James Joyce, pubs or oysters, salmon or sailing, are an important part of community life. Music is a national passion – from the rock of U2 and the pop of Westlife to the folk music of Clannad, the Chieftains and Mary Black.

Another national passion is horse racing. Ireland's breeders and trainers are masters of their

trade and enjoy astonishing international success for such a small country. Other sports are followed with equal intensity, including the traditional Irish pursuits of the Gaelic games and football.

Drinking also plays an important part in Irish culture: social life centres on the pub and the "craic" (convivial chat) to be enjoyed there. Unfortunately, the smoking ban and the recession have led to the closure of many pubs around the country, especially in rural areas. Although there is a concern that this may affect the traditional way of life, given the attachment to Guinness, gossip and music, this seems unlikely.

Matt Molloy's pub in Westport, County Mayo

The Landscape and Wildlife of Ireland

The landscape is one of the Ireland's greatest attractions. It varies from bogs and lakes in the central lowlands to mountains and rocky islands in the west. Between these two extremes, the island has abundant lush, green pastureland, the result of plentiful rainfall, but little natural woodland.

Corncrake

Parts of the far west, where the land is farmed by traditional methods, are havens for threatened wildlife, including the corncrake, which needs undisturbed hayfields in which to nest.

THE FAUNA OF IRELAND

Natterjack toad

Many animals (including snakes) did not make it to Ireland before the Irish Sea rose after the Ice Age. Other surprising absentees are the mole, weasel and common toad (the natterjack, however, can be seen). The wood mouse is the only small native rodent, but the once common red squirrel has now been virtually taken over by the grey.

ROCKY COASTS

Chough

The Dingle Peninsula *(see pp158–9)* is part of a series of rocky promontories and inlets created when sea levels rose at the end of the Ice Age. Cliffs and islands offer many sites for sea birds, with some enormous colonies, such as the gannets of Little Skellig *(pp164–5)*. The chough still breeds on cliffs in the extreme west. Elsewhere in Europe, this rare species of crow is declining in numbers.

Thrift *grows in cushion-like clumps, producing its papery pink flowerheads from spring right through to autumn.*

Sea campion *is a low-growing plant. Its large white flowers brighten up many a cliff top and seaside shingle bank.*

LAKES, RIVERS AND WETLANDS

Great crested grebe

This watery landscape around Lough Oughter is typical of the lakelands of the River Erne *(pp270–71)*. Rainfall is high throughout the year, which results in many wetlands, especially along the Shannon *(p185)* and the Erne. The elegant great crested grebe breeds mainly on the larger lakes in the north.

Water lobelia *grows in the shallows of stony lakes. Its leaves remain below the water, while the pale lilac flowers are borne on leafless stems above the surface.*

Fleabane, *once used to repel fleas, thrives in wet meadows and marshes. It has yellow flowers like dandelions.*

Grey seals *are a common sight in the waters off the Atlantic coast, feeding on fish and occasionally on sea birds.*

Otters *are more likely to be seen in the shallow seas off rocky coasts than in rivers and lakes, though they live in both habitats.*

Red deer *have been introduced into many areas, notably the hills of Connemara.*

Pine martens, *though mainly nocturnal, may be spotted in daytime during the summer.*

MOUNTAIN AND BLANKET BOG

Stonechat

As well as the raised bogs of the central lowlands (p252), much of Ireland's mountainous ground, particularly in the west, is covered by blanket bog such as that seen here in Connemara (pp206–209). On drier upland sites this grades into heather moor and poor grassland. The stonechat, which inhabits rocky scree and heathland, is a restless bird with an unmistakable white rump. It flits about, clipping and bobbing in pursuit of flies.

PASTURELAND

Rook

Rolling pastureland with grazing livestock, as seen here in the foothills of the Wicklow Mountains (pp138–9), is a very common sight throughout Ireland. The traditional farming methods employed in many parts of the island (particularly in the west) are of great benefit to wildlife. Rooks, for example, which feed on worms and insect larvae found in pasture, are very common.

Bog myrtle *is an aromatic shrub, locally common in Ireland's bogs. Its leaves can be used to flavour drinks.*

Bogbean, *a plant found in fens and wet bogland, has attractive white flowers splashed with pink. Its leaves were once used as a cure for boils.*

Meadow vetchling *uses its tendrils to clamber up grasses and other plants. It has clusters of pretty pale yellow flowers.*

Marsh thistle *is a common flower of wet meadows and damp woodland. It is a tall species with small, purple flowerheads.*

Architecture in Ireland

Window of an Irish cottage

Ireland's turbulent history has done incalculable damage to its architectural heritage. Cromwell's forces, in particular, destroyed scores of castles, monasteries and towns in their three-year campaign against the Irish in the mid-17th century. However, many fascinating buildings and sites remain, with Iron Age forts being the earliest surviving settlements. Christianity in Ireland gave rise to monasteries, churches and round towers; conflict between Anglo-Norman barons and Irish chieftains created castles and tower houses. The later landlord class built luxurious country mansions, while their labourers had to make do with basic, one-roomed cottages.

LOCATOR MAP

◻ Iron Age forts

◻ Round towers

◻ Tower houses

◻ Georgian country houses

IRON AGE FORTS

Ring forts (raths) were Iron Age farmsteads enclosed by an earth bank, a timber fence and a ditch to protect against cattle-raiders. Inside, people lived in huts with a souterrain (underground passage) for storage and refuge. Some were in use as late as the 17th century, but all you can usually see today are low circular mounds. In the west, stone was used for cahers (stone ring forts) and promontory forts (semi-circular forts built on cliff tops using the sea as a natural defence).

Thatched hut   **Entrance**   **Souterrain**

ROUND TOWER

Lookout window   **Conical roof**

Round towers, *often over 30 m (100 ft) tall, were built between the 10th and 12th centuries on monastic sites. They were bell towers, used as places of refuge and to store valuable manuscripts. The entrance, which could be as high as 4 m (13 ft) above ground, was reached by a ladder that was hauled up from the inside. Other moveable ladders connected the tower's wooden floors.*

Wooden floor

Moveable ladder

TOWER HOUSES

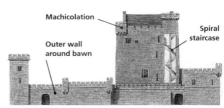

Machicolation

Outer wall around bawn

Spiral staircase

Tower House *were small castles or fortified residences built between the 15th and 17th centuries. The tall square house was often surrounded by a stone wall forming a bawn (enclosure), used for defence and as a cattle pen. Machicolations (projecting parapets from which to drop missiles) were sited at the top of the house.*

COTTAGE

One-roomed cottages, *thatched or slate-roofed, are still a common feature of the Irish landscape. Built of local stone with small windows to retain heat, the cottages were inhabited by farm workers or smallholders.*

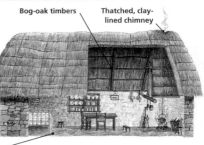

Bog-oak timbers   **Thatched, clay-lined chimney**

Clay floor

IRON AGE FORTS

1. Staigue Fort *p164*
2. Dún Aonghasa *p214*
3. Craggaunowen *p190*
4. Grianán of Ailigh *pp226–7*
5. Hill of Tara *p248*

ROUND TOWERS

6. Kilmacduagh *p212*
7. Ardmore *p145*
8. Clonmacnoise *pp250–51*
9. Devenish Island *p271*
10. Kilkenny *p144*
11. Glendalough *pp140–41*

TOWER HOUSES

12. Aughnanure Castle *p209*
13. Thoor Ballylee *pp212–13*
14. Knappogue Castle *p189*
15. Blarney Castle *p171*
16. Donegal Castle *p230*

GEORGIAN COUNTRY HOUSES

17. Strokestown Park House *pp218–19*
18. Castle Coole *p272*
19. Emo Court *p253*
20. Russborough House *pp132–3*
21. Castletown House *pp130–31*

The well-preserved round tower at Ardmore

GEORGIAN COUNTRY HOUSES

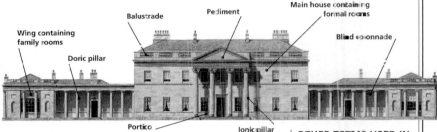

- Wing containing family rooms
- Doric pillar
- Balustrade
- Pediment
- Main house containing formal rooms
- Blind colonnade
- Portico
- Ionic pillar

Between the 1720s and 1800, *prosperous landlords commissioned palatial country mansions in the Palladian and Neo-Classical styles popular in England over that period. Castle Coole (above) has a Palladian layout, with the main house in the centre and a colonnade on either side leading to a small pavilion. The Neo-Classical influence can be seen in the unadorned façade and the Doric columns of the colonnades. Noted architects of Irish country houses include Richard Castle (1690–1751) and James Wyatt (1746–1813).*

STUCCO

Stucco (decorative relief plasterwork), popular in the 18th century, is found in many Georgian country houses as well as town houses and public buildings. The Italian Francini brothers were particularly sought after for their intricate stuccowork (notably at Castletown and Russborough) as was Irish craftsman Michael Stapleton (Trinity College, Dublin and Dublin Writers Museum).

Trompe l'oeil detail at Emo Court

Ceiling at Dublin Writers Museum

Stucco portrait at Castletown House

Stuccowork at Russborough House

OTHER TERMS USED IN THIS GUIDE

Beehive hut: Circular stone building with a domed roof created by corbelling (laying a series of stones so that each projects beyond the one below).

Cashel: Stone ring fort.

Crannog: Defensive, partly artificial island on a lake. Huts were often built on crannogs (*see p33*).

Curtain wall: Outer wall of a castle, usually incorporating towers at intervals.

Hiberno-Romanesque: Style of church architecture with rounded arches highly decorated with geometric designs and human and animal forms. Also called Irish-Romanesque.

Motte and bailey: Raised mound (motte) topped with a wooden tower, surrounded by a heavily fenced space (bailey). Built by the Normans in the 12th century, they were quickly erected in time of battle.

Tympanum: Decorated space over a door or window.

Literary Ireland

For a land the size of Ireland to have produced four Nobel prizewinners in Shaw, Yeats, Beckett and Séamus Heaney is a considerable feat. Yet it is not easy to speak of an "Irish literary tradition" as the concept embraces rural and urban experiences, Protestant and Catholic traditions and the Gaelic and English languages. Irish fiction today, as in the past, is characterized by a sense of community and history, a love of storytelling and a zest for language.

A first edition of Ulysses

WB Yeats – Ireland's most famous poet

The Blasket Islands, which provided inspiration for several writers

GAELIC LITERATURE

Irish literature proclaims itself the oldest vernacular literature in Western Europe, dating back to early monastic times when Celtic folklore and sagas such as the epics of Cúchulainn *(see p26)* were written down for the first time. The disappearance of Gaelic literature followed the demise, in the 17th century, of the Irish aristocracy for whom it was written. Gaelic literature has had several revivals. Peig Sayers is famous for her accounts of the harsh life on the Blasket Islands *(see p158)* in the early 20th century.

ANGLO-IRISH LITERATURE

The collapse of Gaelic culture and the Protestant Ascendancy led to English being the dominant language. Most literature was based around the privileged classes.

An early Anglo-Irish writer was satirist Jonathan Swift *(see p82)*, author of *Gulliver's Travels*, who was born in Dublin in 1667 of English parents. Anglo-Irish literature was strong in drama, the entertainment of the cultured classes, and owed little to Irish settings or sensibilities. By the 1700s, Ireland was producing an inordinate number of leading playwrights, many of whom were more at home in London. These included Oliver Goldsmith, remembered for his comedy *She Stoops to Conquer*, and Richard Brinsley Sheridan, whose plays include *The School for Scandal*. Near the end of the century, Maria Edgeworth set a precedent with novels such as *Castle Rackrent*, based on the class divide in Irish society.

Novelist Maria Edgeworth

The 19th century saw an exodus to England of Irish playwrights, including Oscar

Wilde, who entered Oxford University in 1874 and later became the darling of London society with plays such as *The Importance of Being Earnest*. George Bernard Shaw *(see p100)*, writer of *St Joan* and *Pygmalion*, also made London his home. This dramatist, critic, socialist and pacifist continued to write until well into the 20th century.

Playwright George Bernard Shaw

20TH-CENTURY WRITERS

In 1898, WB Yeats and Lady Gregory founded Dublin's Abbey Theatre *(see p88)*. Its opening, in 1904, heralded the Irish Revival, which focused on national and local themes. Playwright John Millington Synge drew inspiration from a love of the Aran Islands and Irish folklore, but the "immoral language" of his *Playboy of the Western World* caused a riot when first performed at the Abbey Theatre. Along with contemporaries, like Sean O'Casey and WB Yeats, Synge influenced subsequent generations of Irish

writers, including novelist
Seán O'Faolain, humorous
writer and columnist Flann
O'Brien, and hard-drinking,
quarrelsome playwright
Brendan Behan. The literary
revival also produced many
notable poets in the mid-20th
century such as the gifted
Patrick Kavanagh and Belfast-
born Louis MacNeice, often
considered to be one of the
finest poets of his generation.

The writer Brendan Behan enjoying the company in a Dublin pub

Caricature of protesters at Dublin's
Abbey Theatre in 1907

THREE LITERARY GIANTS

From the mass of talent to
emerge in Irish literature,
three figures stand out as
visionaries in their fields. WB
Yeats (see p233) spent half
his life outside Ireland but is
forever linked to its rural west.
A writer of wistful, melan-
choly poetry, he was at the
forefront of the Irish Revival,
helping forge a new national

cultural identity. James Joyce
(see p90) was another trail-
blazer of Irish literature – his
complex narrative and stream
of consciousness techniques
influenced the development
of the modern novel. Ulysses
describes a day in the life of
Joyce's beloved Dublin and
shaped the work of gener-
ations of writers. Bloomsday,
which is named after one of
the novel's characters, Leopold Bloom, is still celebrated
annually in the city. The last
of the three literary giants,
novelist and playwright
Samuel Beckett (see
p62), was another
of Dublin's sons,
though he later
emigrated to
France. His
themes of
alienation,
despair, and
the futility of
human existence pervade his
best-known plays, Waiting
for Godot and Endgame.

The poet Patrick Kavanagh
celebrating Bloomsday

CONTEMPORARY WRITERS

Ireland's proud literary
tradition is today upheld by
a stream of talented writers
from both North and South.
Among the finest are Cork-
born William Trevor, regarded
as a master of the short story.
Anne Enright (2007) and
John Banville (2005) are both
Man Booker prize winners.
Dubliner Roddy Doyle is
known for mining his
working-class origins in
novels such as The
Snapper and Paddy
Clarke Ha Ha Ha.
Other established
Irish writers are
Joseph O'Connor,
Cecelia Ahern and
Edna O'Brien. Out
of Ireland's con-
temporary poets,
the Ulster-born
writers Séamus Heaney and
Derek Mahon are considered
among the most outstanding.

IRELAND IN THE MOVIES

Ireland has long been fertile ground
for the world's film makers, and its
people have been the subjects of
major films, notably The Crying Game
(1992), In the Name of the Father (1994)
and Michael Collins (1996). Another
popular film was The Commitments
(1991). Filmed on location in and
around Dublin with an all-Irish cast, it
was based on a novel by Roddy Doyle.
The modern-day musical Once (2007),
is also set on the streets of Dublin.
The film achieved great critical acclaim,
winning an Oscar for best original song.

Cast of The Commitments, written by Roddy Doyle

The Music of Ireland

An Irish jig

Ireland is the only country in the world to have a musical instrument – the harp – as its national emblem. In this land, famous for its love of music, modern forms such as country-and-western and rock flourish, but it is traditional music that captures the essence of the country. Whether you are listening to Gaelic love songs that date back to medieval times or 17th- and 18th-century folk songs with their English and Scottish influences, the music is unmistakably Irish. Dance is an equally important aspect of Irish traditional music, and some of the most popular airs are derived from centuries-old reels, jigs and hornpipes. Nowadays these are mainly performed at *fleadhs* (festivals) and *ceilís* (dances).

Turlough O'Carolan *(1670–1738) is the most famous Irish harper. The blind musician travelled the country playing his songs to both rich and poor. Many of O'Carolan's melodies, such as* The Lamentation of Owen O'Neill, *still survive.*

Piano accordion

The *bodhrán* is a hand-held goatskin drum that is usually played with a small stick. It is particularly effective when accompanying the flute.

Flute

Two-row button accordion

John F McCormack *(1884–1945) was an Irish tenor who toured America to great acclaim during the early part of the 20th century. His best-loved recordings were arias by Mozart. Another popular tenor was Derry-born Josef Locke. A singer of popular ballads in the 1940s and '50s, he was the subject of the 1992 film* Hear My Song.

THE CURRENT MUSIC SCENE

Mary Black

Ireland today is a melting pot of musical styles. The resurgence of Irish traditional music has produced many highly respected musicians, such as the pipe-players Liam Ó Floin and Paddy Keenan from Dublin, while groups like the Chieftains and the Fureys have gained worldwide fame by melding old with new. Ireland is also firmly placed on the rock'n'roll map, thanks to singers such as Van Morrison in the 1970s and later bands like Thin Lizzy and the Boomtown Rats. The most famous rock band to come out of Ireland is Dublin's U2 who, in the 1980s, became one of the world's most popular groups. Other international successes include singers Enya, Mary Black, Sinéad O'Connor and Damien Rice; and bands like the Cranberries and the Corrs.

Bono of U2

Traditional Irish dancing *is currently enjoying renewed popularity. From the 17th century the social focus in rural areas was the village dance held every Sunday. From these gatherings, Irish dancing became popular.*

LIVE TRADITIONAL MUSIC

Wherever you go in Ireland, you won't be far from a pub with live music. For the Irish traditional musician, there are few set rules – the improvisational nature of the music means that no two performances of any piece are ever likely to be the same.

Violins, or fiddles, can either be tucked under the chin or held against the upper arm, shoulder or chest.

The New National Song—

ERIN Remember 1916

PRICE (2/-) NET

Published by
QUINN & COMPANY,
10 UPPER ABBEY ST.,
DUBLIN.

Irish folk songs, such as this one about the 1916 Easter Rising, tend to have a patriotic theme. But some of the most powerful songs have been written not just about the national struggle, but also about hardship, emigration and the longing for the homeland.

TRADITIONAL INSTRUMENTS

There is no set line-up in traditional Irish bands. The fiddle is probably the most common instrument used. Like the music, some instruments have Celtic origins – the uillean pipes are related to the bagpipes played in Scotland and Brittany today.

The melodeon *is a basic version of the button accordion. Both these instruments are better suited to Irish music than the piano accordion.*

The uillean pipes *are similar to bagpipes and are generally considered to be one of the main instruments in Irish traditional music.*

The harp *has been played in Ireland since the 10th century. In recent years there has been a keen revival of harp playing in Irish traditional music.*

The banjo *comes from the Deep South of the US and adds a new dimension to the sound of traditional bands.*

Tin whistle

Flute

The flute and tin whistle *are among the most common instruments used in traditional Irish music. The latter is often called the penny whistle.*

The violin *is called a fiddle by most musicians. The style of playing and sound produced varies from region to region.*

Ireland's Celtic Heritage

Stone carving on Boa Island

Ireland's rich tradition of storytelling embraces a folk heritage that abounds with myths and superstitions. Some stories have been in written form since the 8th century, but most originated over 2,000 years ago when druids passed on stories orally from one generation to the next. Like the Gaelic language itself, many of Ireland's legends have links with those of ancient Celtic races throughout Europe. As well as the heroic deeds and fearless warriors of mythology, Irish folklore is also rich in tales of fairies, leprechauns, banshees and other supernatural beings.

The formidable Queen Maeve of Connaught

Part of the 2,300-year-old Gundestrup Cauldron unearthed in Denmark, which depicts Cúchulainn's triumph in the Cattle Raid of Cooley

CUCHULAINN

The most famous warrior in Irish mythology is Cúchulainn. At the age of seven, going by the name of Setanta, he killed the savage hound of Culainn the Smith by slaying it with a hurling stick (one of the first times the sport of hurling is mentioned in folklore). Culainn was upset at the loss so Setanta volunteered to guard the house,

earning himself the new name of Cúchulainn, meaning the hound of Culainn.

Before he went into battle, Cúchulainn swelled to magnificent proportions, turned different colours and one of his eyes grew huge. His greatest victory was in the "Cattle Raid of Cooley" when Queen Maeve of Connaught sent her troops to capture the coveted prize bull of Ulster. Cúchulainn learned of the plot and defeated them

single-handedly. However, Queen Maeve took revenge on Cúchulainn by using sorcerers to lure him to his death. Today, in Dublin's GPO (see p89), a statue of Cúchulainn commemorates the heroes of the 1916 Easter Rising.

FINN MCCOOL

The warrior Finn McCool is the most famous leader of the Fianna, an elite band of troops chosen for their strength and valour and who defended Ireland from foreign forces. Finn was not only strong and bold but also possessed the powers of a seer, and could obtain great wisdom by putting his thumb in his mouth and sucking on it. When they were not at war, the Fianna spent their time hunting. Finn had a hound called Bran which stood almost as high as himself and is said to be the original ancestor of the breed known today as the Irish wolfhound. Many of the

FAIRIES, LEPRECHAUNS AND BANSHEES

The diminutive figure of the leprechaun

The existence of spirits, and in particular the "little people", plays a large part in Irish folklore. Centuries ago, it was believed that fairies lived under mounds of earth, or "fairy raths", and that touching one of these tiny figures brought bad luck. The most famous of the "little people" is the leprechaun. Legend has it that if you caught one of these, he would lead you to a crock of gold, but take your eyes off him and he would vanish into thin air. The banshee was a female spirit whose wailing presence outside a house was said to signal the imminent death of someone within.

A banshee with long flowing hair

Fianna possessed supernatural powers and often ventured into the life beyond, known as the Otherworld. Among these was Finn's son Ossian who was not only a formidable warrior, like his father, but was also renowned as a wise and knowledgeable poet. Through time, Finn has come to be commonly portrayed as a giant. Legend has it that he constructed the Giant's Causeway in County Antrim (see pp262–3).

A 19th-century engraving of Finn McCool dressed for battle

THE CHILDREN OF LIR

One of the saddest tales in Irish folklore involves King Lir, who so adored his four children that his stepmother was driven wild with jealousy. One day she took the children to a lake and cast a spell on them, turning them into white swans confined to the waters of Ireland for 900 years. However, as soon as she had done the deed, she became racked with guilt and bestowed upon them the gift of exquisite song. The

The children of King Lir being turned into white swans

king then decreed that no swan in Ireland should be killed – an act which is still illegal today. The end of the children's 900-year ordeal coincided with the coming of Christianity. They regained human form but were wizened and weak. They died soon afterwards, but not before being baptized.

SAINT BRENDAN

Brendan the Navigator, like many other 6th-century monks, travelled widely. It is known that although he lived in western Ireland he visited Wales, Scotland and France. It is likely, though, that his most famous journey is fictitious. This story tells of a shipload of monks who, after seven years of all kinds of strange encounters designed to test their faith, found the Land of Promise. It is essentially a Christian retelling of the common tales of the Celtic Otherworld. The Feast of St Brendan on 16 May is celebrated in Kerry by the climbing of Mount Brandon.

Engraving showing St Brendan and his monks encountering a siren

ORIGINS OF IRISH PLACE NAMES

The names of many of Ireland's cities, towns and villages today are largely based on ancient Gaelic terms for prominent local landmarks, some of which no longer exist. Here are just a few elements of the place names the traveller may come across.

The fort on the Rock of Cashel that gives the town its name

Ar, ard – *high, height*
Ass, ess – *waterfall*
A, ah, ath – *ford*
Bal, bally – *town*
Beg – *small*
Ben – *peak, mountain*
Carrick, carrig – *rock*
Cashel – *stone fort*
Crock, knock – *hill*
Curra, curragh – *marsh*
Darry, derry – *oak tree*
Dun – *castle*
Eden – *hill brow*
Innis, inch – *island*
Inver – *river mouth*
Isk, iska – *water*
Glas, glass – *green*
Glen, glyn – *valley*
Kil, kill – *church*
Lough – *lake, sea inlet*
Mona, mone – *peat bog*
Mor – *great, large*
Mullen, mullin – *mill*
Rath, raha – *ring fort*
Slieve – *mountain*
Toom – *burial ground*
Tul, tu agh – *small hill*

St Canice's Cathedral in Kilkenny (the town's name means "church of Canice")

The Sporting Year

All major international team sports are played in Ireland, but the most popular games are the two uniquely native ones of Gaelic football and hurling. Most of the big games, plus soccer and rugby internationals, are sold out well in advance. However, if you can't get a ticket you'll find plenty of company with whom to watch the event in pubs. Horse racing, with over 240 days of racing a year, attracts fanatical support. For those keen on participatory sports, there are also Ireland's famous fishing waters and golf courses *(see pp362–7)*.

The North West 200 *is the fastest motorcycle race in the world over public roads – held near Portstewart (see p260).*

Irish Football League Cup – Northern Ireland's final

Round-Ireland Yacht Race – held every two years

Four-day national hunt racing festival at Punchestown

The Irish Grand National *is a gruelling steeplechase run at Fairyhouse in County Meath.*

January	February	March	April	May	June

Irish Champion Hurdle, run at Leopardstown, County Dublin

The International Rally of the Lakes is a prestigious car rally around the Lakes of Killarney *(see pp162–3).*

Start of the salmon fishing season

The Six Nations Rugby Tournament, *between Ireland, Scotland, Wales, England, France and Italy, runs until April. Ireland play their home games at the Aviva Stadium, Dublin.*

KEY TO SEASONS

Hurling	
Gaelic football	
Flat racing	
National Hunt racing	
Rugby	
Association football	
Salmon fishing	
Equestrianism	

The Irish Open Golf Championship *is held at a different course each year and attracts a world-class field to courses such as Ballybunion in County Kerry.*

The Irish Derby, *Ireland's premier flat race, attracts many of Europe's best three-year-olds to The Curragh (see p129).*

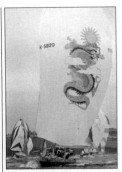

Cork Week *is a biennial regatta, organized by Royal Cork Yacht Club, where crews and boats of all classes meet and compete.*

The All-Ireland Football Final *is held at Croke Park in Dublin. The top two counties play for this Gaelic football championship. More people watch the game than any other event in Ireland.*

Greyhound Derby, run at Shelbourne Park, Dublin

Galway Race Week is one of Ireland's premier festival meetings and a popular social event.

The Dublin Marathon *is Ireland's foremost marathon event. It attracts a huge field including top-class athletes from around the world.*

July	August	September	October	November	December

Millstreet Indoor International showjumping event

Football Association of Ireland Cup – the Republic's football final

The Dublin Horse Show *is Ireland's premier horse show and a major event in the social calendar.*

All-Ireland Hurling Final at Croke Park, Dublin

THE GAELIC ATHLETIC ASSOCIATION

The GAA was founded in 1884 to promote indigenous Irish sport. Today, despite heavy competition from soccer, the most popular sport in Ireland remains Gaelic football. Its rules are somewhere between rugby and soccer, though it predates both games. In it, the ball can be carried and points scored over the goalpost. Another intriguing GAA game is hurling, a fast and physical field sport played with sticks and said to have originated in ancient Celtic times. Both games are played at parish and county level on a wholly amateur basis. The season ends with the All-Ireland finals, which draw large and passionate crowds to Dublin.

Camogie, a version of hurling played by women

THE HISTORY OF IRELAND

Ireland's relative isolation has cut it off from several of the major events of European history. Roman legions, for example, never invaded and the country's early history is shrouded in myths of warring Gods and heroic High Kings. Nevertheless, the bellicose Celtic tribes were quick to embrace Christianity after the arrival of St Patrick on the island in AD 432.

Until the Viking invasions of the 9th century, Ireland enjoyed an era of relative peace. Huge monasteries like Clonmacnoise and Glendalough were founded, where scholarship and art flourished. The Vikings failed to gain control of the island, but in 1169 the Anglo-Normans did. Many Irish chiefs submitted to Henry II of England, who declared himself Lord of Ireland. He left in 1172, and his knights shared out large baronies between themselves.

Matters changed when Henry VIII broke with the Catholic church in 1532. Ireland became a battleground between native Irish Catholics and the forces of the English Crown. Where

South Cross, Clonmacnoise

the Irish were defeated, their lands were confiscated and granted to Protestants from England and Scotland. England's conquest was completed with the victory of William of Orange over James II at the Battle of the Boyne in 1690. Repressive Penal Laws were put into place, but opposition to English rule continued.

The Famine of 1845 to 1848 was one of the bleakest periods in Irish history. Two million people died or emigrated, and many who stayed were evicted by English landlords. A campaign for Home Rule gathered strength, but it was 1920 before the Government of Ireland Act divided the island. The South became the Irish Free State, gaining full independence in 1937, while the North became part of the UK. In the 1970s, 1980s and much of the 1990s, Northern Ireland was a battleground, with both Loyalist and Republican paramilitary groups waging bombing campaigns. In 1998, the Good Friday Agreement was signed, paving the way for a new Northern Ireland Assembly and hopes of peace.

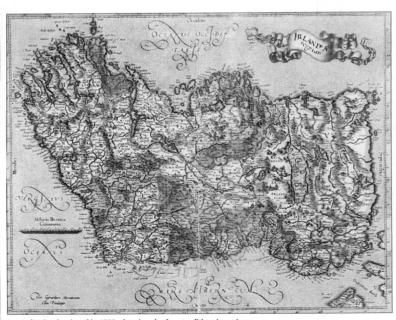

Map of Ireland, printed in 1592, showing the four traditional provinces

◁ *The Feast of St Kevin amid the Ruins of Glendalough by Joseph Peacock (1813)*

Prehistoric Ireland

Until about 9,500 years ago Ireland was uninhabited. The first people, who may have crossed by a land bridge from Scotland, were hunter-gatherers and left few traces of permanent settlement. The 4th millennium BC saw the arrival of Neolithic farmers and herdsmen who built stone field walls and

Early Bronze Age stone axe-head

monumental tombs such as Newgrange. Metalworking was brought from Europe around 2000 BC by the Bronze Age Beaker people, who also introduced new pottery skills. The Iron Age reached Ireland in the 3rd century BC along with the Celts, who migrated from Central Europe, via France and Britain, and soon established themselves as the dominant culture.

IRELAND C.8000 BC

▢ *Former coastline*

▢ *Present-day coastline*

The terminal discs were worn on the shoulders.

Dolmens or Portal Tombs
These striking megalithic tombs date from around 2000 BC. Legananny Dolmen in the Mountains of Mourne (see p284) is a fine example.

GLENINSHEEN GORGET
Many remarkable pieces of gold jewellery were created in the late Bronze Age. This gold collar dates from about 700 BC. The Iron Age Celts produced similarly fine metalwork and ornaments.

Three strands of ropework

Wooden Idol
This Iron Age fetish would have played a role in pagan fertility rites.

Celtic Stone Idol
This mysterious three-faced head was found in County Cavan. In Celtic religion the number three has always had a special significance.

Bronze Bridle Bit
Celtic chiefs rode into battle on two-horse chariots with beautifully decorated harnesses.

TIMELINE

c. 7500 BC First inhabitants of Ireland

Extinct giant deer or "Irish Elk"

5000-3000 Ireland covered by dense woodland dominated by oak and elm

2500 Building of Newgrange passage tomb *(see pp246–7)*

1500 Major advances in metalworking, especially gold

8000 BC	6000	4000	2000	1000

6000 Date of huts excavated at Mount Sandel, Co Londonderry; oldest known dwellings in Europe

3700 Neolithic farmers reach Ireland; they clear woods to plant cereals

2050 Beaker people (so-called for their delicate pottery vessels) reach Ireland at the beginning of Bronze Age

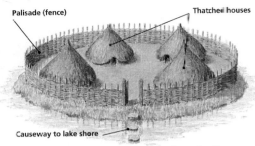

Palisade (fence) Thatched houses

Causeway to lake shore

Reconstruction of a Crannog

Originating in the Bronze Age, crannogs were artificial islands built in lakes. At first used for fishing, they soon developed into well-protected homesteads. Some remained in use up to the 17th century.

The raised bands on the collar were created by repoussé work, pushed through from the back. The delicate rope motifs were added from the front with a knife.

Bone Slip
(c.AD 50)
This may have been used for divination or for gambling.

Gold Boat
Part of a hoard of gold objects found at Broighter, County London-derry, the boat (1st century AD) was made as a votive offering.

WHERE TO SEE PREHISTORIC IRELAND

Prehistoric sites range from individual tombs such as Newgrange, Browne's Hill Dolmen (*see p141*) or Ossian's Grave to whole settlements, as at Céide Fields (*p204*) and Lough Gur (*p194*). The largest Stone Age cemetery is at Carrowmore (*p234*). Good reconstructions of prehistoric structures can be seen at Craggaunowen (*p190*). The National Museum – Archaeology in Dublin (*pp66–7*) houses the finest collection of artifacts, including wonderful gold objects from the Bronze Age.

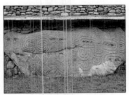

Newgrange (*pp246–7*) *is Ireland's finest restored Neolithic tomb. At the entrance lie huge spiral-patterned boulders.*

Ossian's Grave *is a court grave, the earliest kind of Neolithic tomb (p267). An open court stood before the burial mound.*

500 First wave of Celtic invaders	**500** Intertribal warfare; chieftains vie for title of *Ard Rí* (High King)	**AD 80** Roman general Agricola considers invasion of Ireland from Britain		**367** Roman Britain attacked by Irish, Picts and Saxons
750	**500**	**250**	**AD 1**	**AD 250**
Bronze goad decorated with birds		**250** Second wave of Celts, who bring La Tène style of pottery		*c. 150 Greek geographer Ptolemy draws up map and account of Ireland*

Bronze sword hilt imported from southern France

Celtic Christianity

Celtic Ireland was divided into as many as 100 chiefdoms, though these often owed allegiance to kings of larger provinces such as Munster or Connaught. At times, there was also a titular High King based at Tara (*see p248*). Ireland became Christian in the 5th century AD, heralding a golden age of scholarship centred on the new monasteries, while missionaries such as St Columba travelled abroad. At the end of the 8th century, Celtic Ireland was shattered by the arrival of the Vikings.

Monk illuminating a manuscript

IRELAND IN 1000

■ *Viking settlements*

□ *Traditional Irish provinces*

Ogham Stone
The earliest Irish script, Ogham, dates from about AD 300. The notches correspond to Roman letters, like a form of Morse code.

CELTIC MONASTERY
Monasteries were large centres of population. This reconstruction shows Glendalough (*see pp140–41*) in about 1100. The tall round tower served as a lookout for Viking raiders.

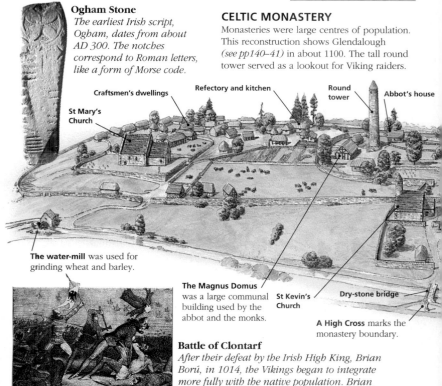

Craftsmen's dwellings

Refectory and kitchen

Round tower

Abbot's house

St Mary's Church

The water-mill was used for grinding wheat and barley.

The Magnus Domus was a large communal building used by the abbot and the monks.

St Kevin's Church

Dry-stone bridge

A High Cross marks the monastery boundary.

Battle of Clontarf
After their defeat by the Irish High King, Brian Ború, in 1014, the Vikings began to integrate more fully with the native population. Brian Ború himself was killed in the battle.

TIMELINE

400	500	600	700
430 Pope sends first Christian missionary, Palladius	**455** St Patrick founds church at Armagh	**563** St Columba (Colmcille), the first Irish missionary, founds monastery on Iona in the Hebrides	**664** Synod of Whitby decides that Irish Church should conform with Rome over date of Easter
	St Patrick		
432 Start of St Patrick's mission to Ireland	**c. 550** Beginning of golden age of Celtic monasticism	**615** St Columbanus dies in Italy after founding many new monasteries on the Continent	**c.690** *Book of Durrow* (*see p63*) completed

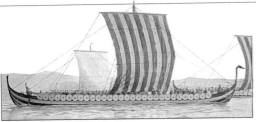

Viking Raids and Settlements

The first longships reached Ireland in 795. Though notorious for pillaging monasteries, the Vikings introduced new farming methods and coinage. They also founded walled cities such as Dublin, Waterford and Limerick.

Garryduff Gold Bird

Irish metalwork in the early Christian era was of very high quality. This gold ornament, possibly a wren, dates from around the 7th century AD.

Cathedral

Gatehouse

Guesthouse and stables

Monks' dwellings and barns

St Kieran's Church and other important churches were built of stone, but most buildings were wood.

The Crozier of the Abbots of Clonmacnoise

This 11th-century bishop's staff is decorated with an ornate silver casing. The incised patterns show Viking influence.

WHERE TO SEE EARLY CHRISTIAN IRELAND

Important early monastic sites besides Glendalough include Clonmacnoise and Devenish Island. Churches from this period can also be seen at Gallarus (see p.157), Clonfert (p213) and the Rock of Cashel (pp196–7), while High Crosses (p243) and round towers (p20) survive all over Ireland. Dublin's National Museum – Archaeology (pp66–7) has excellent ecclesiastical (and Viking) artifacts and Trinity College (pp62–4) houses the finest illuminated manuscripts.

Devenish Island has a fine 12th-century round tower and enjoys a peaceful setting on Lower Lough Erne (p271).

Clonmacnoise (pp250–51) lies on the east bank of the Shannon. This Romanesque doorway is part of the ruined Nuns' Church.

Viking silver brooch

795 First Viking invasion of coastal monasteries

841 A large Viking fleet spends the winter at Dublin

807 Work starts on Kells monastery (see p241)

967 Irish warriors sack Limerick and begin military campaign against Viking overlords

1014 High King Brian Ború of Munster defeats joint army of Vikings and the King of Leinster at Clontarf

999 Sitric Silkenbeard, the Viking king of Dublin, surrenders to Brian Ború

Viking coin

1156 Dermot McMurrough, King of Leinster, flees overseas

1134 Cormac's Chapel is built at Cashel (see pp196–7)

1142 Ireland's first Cistercian house founded at Mellifont (see p245)

800	900	1000	1100

Anglo-Norman Ireland

13th-century gold brooch

Anglo-Norman nobles, led by Richard de Clare (nicknamed Strongbow), were invited to Ireland by the King of Leinster in 1169. They took control of the major towns and Henry II of England proclaimed himself overlord of Ireland. In succeeding centuries, however, English power declined and the Crown controlled just a small area around Dublin known as the Pale (see p132). Many of the Anglo-Norman barons living outside the Pale opposed English rule just as strongly as did the native Irish clans.

IRELAND IN 1488

☐ Extent of the Pale

CARRICKFERGUS CASTLE

The first Anglo-Norman forts were wooden structures, but they soon started to build massive stone castles. Carrickfergus (see p275) was begun in the 1180s and by 1250 had acquired a keep and a gatehouse.

The keep contained a hall on the first floor and, above that, the lord's private apartments.

Guardroom

Storeroom

Stables

Bakery

Marriage of Strongbow
The King of Leinster gave his daughter to Strongbow for helping him regain his lands. Daniel Maclise's painting (1854) emphasizes Anglo-Norman power over the Irish.

Norman Weapons
These bows and arrows, unearthed at Waterford, may be relics of Strongbow's assault on the city in 1170.

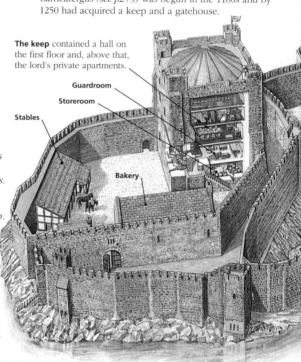

TIMELINE

1172 Pope affirms King Henry II of England's lordship over Ireland

1177 John de Courcy's forces invade Ulster

Dermot McMurrough, King of Leinster, who invited Strongbow to come to his aid

1318 Bruce killed in battle

1315 Scots invade Ireland; Edward Bruce crowned king

1200	1250	1300

1169 Strongbow's Anglo-Normans arrive at invitation of exiled King of Leinster, Dermot McMurrough

1224 Dominican order enters Ireland and constructs friaries

1260 Powerful Irish chieftain Brian O'Neill killed at the Battle of Down

1297 First Irish Parliament meets in Dublin

Richard II's Fleet Returning to England in 1399
*Richard made two trips to Ireland – in 1394 and 1399.
On the first he defeated Art McMurrough, King of Leinster,
and other Irish chiefs, but the second was inconclusive.*

WHERE TO SEE ANGLO-NORMAN IRELAND

The strength of Norman fortifications is best seen in the castles at Carrickfergus, Limerick (see p191) and Trim (p248) and in Waterford's city walls. Gothic cathedrals that survive include Dublin's Christ Church (pp80–81) and St Patrick's (pp82–3), and St Canice's (p249) in Kilkenny. There are impressive ruins of medieval Cistercian abbeys at Jerpoint and Boyle (p219).

Jerpoint Abbey (p145) *has a well-preserved 15th-century cloister decorated with carvings of curiously elongated figures.*

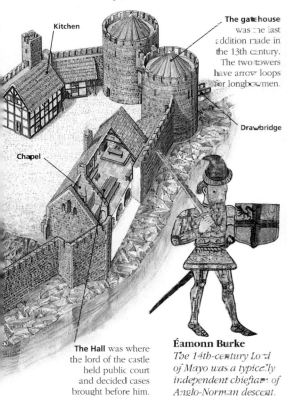

Kitchen

The gatehouse was the last addition made in the 13th century. The two towers have arrow loops for longbowmen.

Drawbridge

Chapel

The Hall was where the lord of the castle held public court and decided cases brought before him.

Éamonn Burke
*The 14th-century Lord
of Mayo was a typically
independent chieftain of
Anglo-Norman descent.*

Waterford's *Anglo-Norman
city walls include this sturdy
watchtower (pp146–7).*

---

*Great Charter Roll
of Waterford (1372)
showing portraits
of the mayors of
four medieval cities*

1394 King Richard II lands
with army to reassert control;
returns five years later but
with inconclusive results

1471 8th Earl of Kildare made Lord Deputy of Ireland

1496 Kildare regains Lord Deputy position

1491 Kildare supports Perkin Warbeck,
pretender to the English throne

| 1350 | 1400 | 1450 |

1366 Statutes of Kilkenny
forbid marriage between
Anglo-Normans and Irish

1348 The Black Death: one third
of population killed in three years

*English force (left)
confront Irish horse-
men on Richard II's
return expedition*

1487 Kildare crowns Lambert
Simnel, Edward VI in Dublin

1494 Lord Deputy
Edward Poynings forbids
Irish Parliament to meet
without royal consent

Protestant Conquest

Hugh O'Neill, Earl of Tyrone

England's break with the Catholic Church, the dissolution of the monasteries and Henry VIII's assumption of the title King of Ireland incensed both the old Anglo-Norman dynasties and resurgent Irish clans such as the O'Neills. Resistance to foreign rule was fierce and it took over 150 years of war to establish the English Protestant ascendancy. Tudor and Stuart monarchs adopted a policy of military persuasion, then Plantation. Oliver Cromwell was even more forceful. Irish hopes were raised when the Catholic James II ascended to the English throne, but he was deposed and fled to Ireland, where he was defeated by William of Orange (William III) in 1690.

IRELAND IN 1625

> Main areas of Plantation in the reign of James I

The first relief ship to reach Londonderry was the *Phoenix*. For three months English ships had been prevented from sailing up the Foyle by a wooden barricade across the river.

James II's army on the east bank of the Foyle attacks the ship.

Battle of the Boyne
This tapestry, from the Bank of Ireland (see p60), shows William of Orange leading his troops against the army of James II in 1690. His victory is still celebrated by Orangemen in Northern Ireland.

Silken Thomas Fitzgerald
Silken Thomas, head of the powerful Kildares, renounced his allegiance to Henry VIII in 1534. He was hanged along with his five uncles in 1537.

The artist's depiction of 17th-century weapons and uniforms is far from accurate.

TIMELINE

Henry VII	**1541** Henry VIII declared King of Ireland by Irish Parliament	*Sir Thomas Lee, an officer in Elizabeth I's army, dressed in Irish fashion*		**1585** Ireland is mapped and divided into 32 counties	**1592** Trinity College, Dublin founded
1500	**1525**	**1550**		**1575**	**1600**
1504 8th Earl of Kildare becomes master of Ireland after victory at Knocktoe	**1534** Silken Thomas rebels against Henry VIII **1539** Henry VIII dissolves monasteries	**1557** Mary I orders first plantations in Offaly and Laois		**1582** Desmond rebellion in Munster **1588** Spanish Armada wrecked off west coast	

The Siege of Drogheda
Between 1649 and 1652 Cromwell's army
avenged attacks on Protestant settlers with
ruthless efficiency. Here Cromwell himself
directs the gunners bombarding Drogheda.

The Walls of Derry have never been
breached by any attacker and many
of the original 17th-century gates and
bastions that withstood the siege of
1689 are still in place *(see pp.258–9)*

PLANTATION IRELAND

James I realized that force alone could
not stabilize Ireland. The Plantation
programme uprooted the native Irish and
gave their land to Protestant settlers from
England and Scotland. London livery
companies organized many of the new
settlements. The policy created loyal
garrisons who supported the Crown.

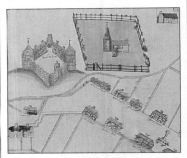

Bellaghy *in County Londonderry was settled*
by the Vintners Company. The map of the
neatly planned town dates from 1622.

St George's
flag

Ship Quay

Protestants emerge
from the besieged city
to greet the English
relieving force and to
engage the enemy

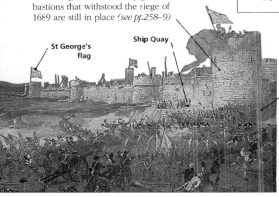

THE RELIEF OF DERRY *(1689)*

Some 20,000 Protestants were besieged for 105 days in
Londonderry by James II's forces. Thousands died from
starvation, until relief finally came from English warships.
This 18th-century painting by William Sadler II gives a
rather fanciful picture of the ending of the siege.

Loftus Cup
Adam Loftus,
Chancellor of
Ireland, used his
position to earn
his family. In 1593
he had the Great
Seal of Ireland
melted down and
made into this
silver-gilt cup.

1607 Flight of the
Earls: old Irish
leaders flee to
the Continent;
Plantation of Ulster

1632 Important Irish history,
The Annals of the Four Masters,
written by four Franciscan
friars from Donegal

Protestant
apprentice boys
closing the gates
of Derry before
the siege of 1689

1690 William of Orange defeats
James II at Battle of the Boyne;
James's army surrenders the
following year in Limerick

1625		1650	1675		1700

1603 Earl of Tyrone ends
eight years of war by signing
the Treaty of Mellifont

1641 Armed rebellion in
Ulster opposes Plantation

1649 Cromwell lands in
Dublin; razes Drogheda
and Wexford; Catholic
landowners transplanted
to far west

1688 James II,
deposed Catholic
king of England,
flees to Ireland
and raises army

1689 Siege of Derry

1695 Penal code
severely reduces rights
of Roman Catholics

Georgian Ireland

The Protestant ascendancy was a period of great prosperity for the landed gentry, who built grand country houses and furnished them luxuriously. Catholics, meanwhile, were denied even the right to buy land. Towards the end of the century, radicals, influenced by events in America and France, started to demand independence from the English Crown. Prime Minister Henry Grattan tried a parliamentary route; Wolfe Tone and the United Irishmen opted for armed insurrection. Both approaches ultimately failed.

Lacquer cabinet in Castletown House

IRELAND IN 1703

Counties where Protestants owned over 75 per cent of land

State Bedroom

The saloon, the Casino's main room, was used for formal entertaining. It has a magnificent parquet floor.

Stone lions by Edward Smyth (1749–1812)

The Irish House of Commons
This painting shows Irish leader Henry Grattan addressing the house (see p60). The "Grattan Parliament" lasted from 1782 to 1800, but was then abolished by the Act of Union.

The basement contains the servants' hall, the kitchen, pantry and wine cellar.

Surveyors
The 18th century saw work begin on ambitious projects such as the Grand Canal, new roads and Dublin's network of wide streets and squares.

TIMELINE

Jonathan Swift (1667–1745)

1713 Jonathan Swift appointed Dean of St Patrick's Cathedral *(see p82)*

1724 Swift attacks Ireland's penal code in *A Modest Proposal*

1731 First issue of the *Belfast Newsletter*, the world's oldest continually running newspaper

1731 Royal Dublin Society founded to encourage agriculture, art and crafts

1738 Death of Ireland's most famous harper, Turlough O'Carolan *(see p24)*

1742 First performance of Handel's *Messiah* given in Dublin

1751 Dublin's Rotunda Lying-In Hospital is first maternity hospital in the British Isles

| 1710 | 1720 | 1730 | 1740 | 1750 |

Linen Bleaching

Ulster's linen industry flourished thanks to the expertise of Huguenot weavers from France. The woven cloth was spread out in fields or on river banks to bleach it (see p268).

The Classical urns on the roof conceal chimneys.

The china closet was originally designed as a bedroom.

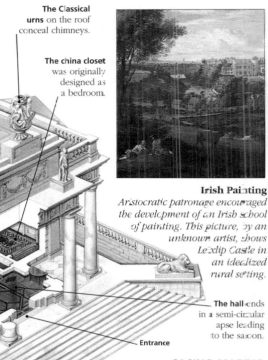

Irish Painting

Aristocratic patronage encouraged the development of an Irish school of painting. This picture, by an unknown artist, shows Leixlip Castle in an idealized rural setting.

The hall ends in a semi-circular apse leading to the saloon.

Entrance

CASINO MARINO

This frivolous summer house was built in the 1760s for the first Earl of Charlemont on his estate just north of Dublin *(see p100)*. Palladian architecture of this kind was popular among the Irish aristocracy, who followed 18th-century English fashions.

WHERE TO SEE GEORGIAN IRELAND

Dublin preserves many fine Georgian terraces and public buildings such as the Custom House *(see p88)* and the Four Courts *(p93)*. Around Dublin, the grand houses at Castletown *(pp130–31)*, Russborough and Powerscourt *(pp134–5)* are fascinating reminders of the lifestyle of the gentry. Other 18th-century country seats open to the public include Emo Court, Westport House *(pp204–05)* and Castle Coole *(p272)*.

Emo Court's *façade, with its plain Ionic portico, is by James Gandon, architect of many of Dublin's public buildings (p253).*

Russborough House *(p132) was built in 1741 by Richard Castle. Elegant niches with Classical busts flank the grand fireplace in the entrance hall.*

Guinness Brewery Gate

1782 Parliament gains greater degree of independence from Westminster

The Irish Volunteers, a local militia which pressed Parliament for reform

1798 Rebellion of Wolfe Tone's United Irishmen quashed

1760	1770	1780	1790

Custom House

1759 Arthur Guinness buys the St James's Gate Brewery in Dublin

1791 James Gandon's Custom House built in Dublin

1793 Limited emancipation for Irish Catholics

1795 Orange Order formed by Ulster Protestants

Famine and Emigration

Ration card from Famine period

The history of 19th-century Ireland is dominated by the Great Famine of 1845–8, which was caused by the total failure of the potato crop. Although Irish grain was still being exported to England, around one million people died from hunger or disease, with even more fleeing to North America. By 1900, the pre-famine population of eight million had fallen by half. Rural hardship fuelled a campaign for tenants' rights which evolved into demands for independence from Britain. Great strides towards "Home Rule" were made in Parliament by the charismatic politician Charles Stewart Parnell.

IRELAND IN 1851

▢ Areas where population fell by over 25% during the Famine

The ships that brought the Irish to America were overcrowded and fever-ridden, and known as "coffin ships".

Daniel O'Connell
Known as "The Liberator", O'Connell organized peaceful "monster rallies" of up to a million people in pursuit of Catholic emancipation. He was elected MP for Clare in 1828.

Castle Clinton was used for processing new arrivals to New York prior to the construction of the huge depot on Ellis Island.

The Boycotting of Landlords
In 1880, troops guarded the crops of Captain Boycott, the first notable victim of a campaign to ostracize landlords guilty of evicting tenants. His name later passed into the English language.

TIMELINE

Charles Bianconi's coach service, 1836

1815 First coach service begins in Ireland

1817 Royal Canal is completed

1838 Father Mathew founds temperance crusade – five million Irish take abstinence pledge and whiskey production is reduced by half

1845 Start of Great Famine, which lasts for four years

1800	1810	1820	1830	1840

1803 Uprising, led by Robert Emmet, is crushed after feared Napoleonic invasion of England fails to materialize

1800 Act of Union: Ireland legally becomes part of Britain

1828 After a five-year campaign by Daniel O'Connell, Catholic Emancipation Act is passed, giving a limited number of Catholics the right to vote

Father Mathew

Eviction of Irish Farmers
In the late 1870s, agricultural prices plummeted. Starving tenant farmers fell into arrears and were mercilessly evicted. Their plight spawned the Land League, which lobbied successfully for reform.

THE IRISH ABROAD

One result of the Famine was the growth of a strong Irish community in the USA. From the lowest rung of American society, the immigrants rose up the social scale and became rich by Irish Catholic standards. They sent money to causes back home, and as a well-organized lobby group put pressure on the American government to influence British policies in Ireland. A more militant group, Clan na Gael, sent veterans of the American Civil War to fight in the Fenian risings of 1865 and 1867.

New Yorkers *stage a huge St Patrick's Day parade, 17 March 1870.*

IMMIGRANTS ARRIVE IN NEW YORK
The Irish who survived the journey to America landed at Castle Garden in New York, seen here in a painting by Samuel Waugh (1855). Although mainly country people, most new arrivals settled in Manhattan, often enduring horrific living conditions.

The Irish were widely perceived as illiterate peasants in the USA and often met with a hostile reception.

Charles Stewart Parnell
A campaigner for the Land League and Home Rule, Parnell saw his political career ruined in 1890, when he was cited as co-respondent in a divorce case.

1853 Dublin Exhibition is opened by Queen Victoria		*Dublin Exhibition*	**1884** Founding of Gaelic Athletic Association, first group to promote Irish traditions	**1892** Second Home Rule Bill is defeated
		1877 Parnell becomes leader of the new Home Rule Party		
1850	**1860**	**1870**	**1880**	**1890**

1867 Irish-Americans return home to fight in a rising led by the Irish Republican Brotherhood, also known as the Fenians

1881 Parnell is jailed in Kilmainham Gaol, Dublin

1886 British PM Gladstone sponsors first Home Rule Bill but is defeated by Parliament

1848 Failure of the Young Ireland Uprising – a spontaneous response to insurrections elsewhere in Europe

1879–82 Land War, led by Michael Davitt's Land League, campaigns for the reform of tenancy laws

War and Independence

Irish Free State stamp of 1922

Plans for Irish home rule were shelved because of World War I; however, the abortive Easter Rising of 1916 inspired new support for the Republican cause. In 1919 an unofficial Irish Parliament was established and a war began against the "occupying" British forces. The Anglo-Irish Treaty of 1921 divided the island in two, granting independence to the Irish Free State, while Northern Ireland remained in the United Kingdom. There followed a civil war between pro-Treaty and anti-Treaty factions in the South.

IRELAND IN 1922

▨ *Northern Ireland*

☐ *Irish Free State*

The Unionist Party
Leader of the campaign against Home Rule was Dublin barrister Edward Carson. In 1913 the Ulster Volunteer Force was formed to demand that six counties in Ulster remain part of the UK.

The 1916 Service Medal, issued to all who fought in the Easter Rising, depicts, on one side, the mythical Irish warrior Cúchulainn.

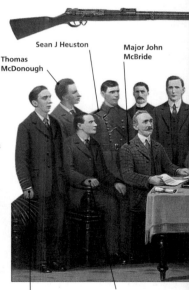

Sean J Heuston

Thomas McDonough

Major John McBride

William Pearse

Patrick Pearse, a poet, read the Proclamation of the Republic from the steps of the GPO on Easter Monday.

The Black and Tans
Named for their makeshift uniforms, these British troops – mostly demobbed World War I soldiers – carried out savage reprisals against the Irish in 1920–21.

TIMELINE

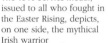

The Titanic

1913 General strike in Dublin

1912 Belfast-built *Titanic* sinks on her maiden voyage

1918 Sinn Féin wins 73 seats at Westminster; Constance Markievicz elected first woman MP

1916 Easter Rising quashed

1919 First meeting of the independent parliament (*Dáil Éireann*)

1905	1910	1915	1920

1905 Sinn Féin (We Ourselves) party founded

1904 Dublin's Abbey Theatre opens

1912 Edward Carson rallies Ulster Protestants; solemn covenant to defeat Home Rule signed by 471,414 people

Despatch bag carried by Constance Markievicz during Easter Rising

1920 Government of Ireland Act proposes partition of the island

1921 Anglo-Irish Treaty signed; de Valera resigns; southern Ireland plunged into civil war

The General Post Office, Easter 1916

What was supposed to be a national uprising was confined to 2,500 armed insurgents in Dublin. They managed to hold the GPO and other public buildings for five days.

This Mauser rifle, smuggled in from Germany in 1914, was used by rebels in the Rising.

Tom Clarke

James Connolly

Joseph Plunkett

Mementos of the Rising at Dublin's Kilmainham Gaol (*see p97*) include this crucifix made by a British soldier from rifle bullets.

EAMON DE VALERA (1882–1975)

After escaping execution for his part in the Easter Rising, American-born de Valera went on to dominate Irish politics for almost 60 years. The opposition of his party, Sinn Féin, to the Anglo-Irish Treaty of 1921 plunged the new Irish Free State into civil war. After forming a new party, Fianna Fáil, he became Prime Minister (*Taoiseach*) in 1932. De Valera remained in office until 1948, with further terms in the 1950s. Between 1959 and 1973 he was President of Ireland.

THE SHADOW OF THE GUNMAN

KEEP IT FROM YOUR HOME

VOTE FOR **CUMANN NA nGAEDHEAL**

LEADERS OF THE 1916 RISING

This collage portrait shows 14 leaders of the Easter Rising, who were all court-martialled and shot at Kilmainham Gaol. The brutality of their executions (the badly injured James Connolly was tied to a chair before being shot) changed public opinion of the Rising and guaranteed their status as martyrs.

Election Poster

Cumann na nGaedheal, the pro-Treaty party in the Civil War, won the Free State's first general election in 1923. It merged with other parties in 1933 to form Fine Gael.

1922 Irish Free State inaugurated; Michael Collins shot dead in ambush in Co Cork

Michael Collins (1890–1922), hero of the War of Independence, became chairman of the Irish Free State and Commander-in-Chief of the Army

1932 Fianna Fáil sweeps to victory in general election, and de Valera begins 16-year term as *Taoiseach* (Prime Minister)

1936 IRA proscribed by Free State Government

1939 Éire declares neutrality during World War II

1925	1930	1935

1923 WB Yeats wins Nobel prize for Literature

1925 GB Shaw also receives Nobel prize

1926 De Valera quits Sinn Féin; sets up Fianna Fáil (Soldiers of Destiny) party

1929 Work starts on River Shannon hydro-electric power scheme

1933 Fine Gael (United Ireland) party formed to oppose Fianna Fáil

1937 New constitution declares complete independence from Britain; country's name changes to Éire

Modern Ireland

Mary Robinson, Ireland's first woman President

Since joining the European Economic Community (now the EU) in 1973, the Irish Republic has done much to modernize its traditional rural-based economy. There have been social changes too and divorce has become legalised. Meanwhile, Northern Ireland has lived through more than 25 years of unrest. But recent peace agreements have brought new hope, especially since the inauguration in 1998 of the Northern Ireland Assembly. The power-sharing Sinn Féin and DUP government is addressing the final stumbling blocks of policing and justice.

1972 Bloody Sunday – British soldiers shoot dead 13 demonstrators in Derry. Northern Ireland Parliament is suspended and direct rule from Westminster imposed

1976 Organizers of the Ulster Peace Movement, Mairead Corrigan and Betty Williams, are awarded the Nobel Peace Prize in Oslo

1969 Violent clashes between the police and demonstrators in Belfast and Derry. British troops sent to restore order

1956 IRA launches a terrorism campaign along the border with Northern Ireland which lasts until 1962

1967 Northern Ireland Civil Rights Association is set up to fight discrimination against Catholics

NORTHERN IRELAND			
1945	1955	1965	1975
REPUBLIC OF IRELAND			

1949 New government under John A Costello. Country changes name from Éire to Republic of Ireland and leaves British Commonwealth

1955 Republic of Ireland joins United Nations

1959 Eamon de Valera resigns as *Taoiseach* (Prime Minister) and is later elected President

1973 The Republic joins the European Economic Community. Membership has given the country access to much-needed development grants

1947 Statue of Queen Victoria is removed from the courtyard in front of the Irish Parliament in Dublin

1963 John F Kennedy, the first American President of Irish Catholic descent, visits Ireland. He is pictured here with President Eamon de Valera

1969 Samuel Beckett, seen here rehearsing one of his own plays, is awarded the Nobel prize for literature, but does not go to Stockholm to receive it

1985 Barry McGuigan beats the Panamanian, Eusebio Pedroza, for world featherweight boxing title

1998 The Good Friday Agreement sets out proposed framework for self-government in Northern Ireland

1986 Bitter Loyalist opposition follows the previous year's signing by the British and Irish governments of the Anglo-Irish Agreement

2001 David Trimble resigns as first minister but is later re-elected. The beginning of a tortuous period of suspended talks and return to Westminster's direct rule

1987 IRA bomb explodes during Enniskillen's Remembrance Day parade, killing 11 people

1995 For the first time in 25 years, there are no troops on daylight patrols in Northern Ireland

2005 The IRA announces an end to its armed campaign, saying it will follow an exclusively democratic path

1994 IRA and Unionist cease-fires. Gerry Adams, Sinn Féin leader, allowed to speak on British radio and television

2010 The Democratic Unionist Party and Sinn Féin reach agreement to allow full transfer of police and justice powers from London to Belfast

		NORTHERN IRELAND
1985	**1995**	**2005**	**2015**
		REPUBLIC OF IRELAND

1982 Rising debt and unemployment lead to economic crisis and instability. Three elections are held in two years

2008 Padraig Harrington wins both the Open Championship and the PGA Championship

1994 Republic of Ireland football team reaches quarterfinals of World Cup in the USA. Here, Ray Houghton is congratulated on scoring the winning goal against Italy

1991 Mary Robinson becomes first female President of the Republic, succeeded by Mary McAleese in 1998

1979 Pope John Paul II visits Ireland and celebrates Mass in Dublin's Phoenix Park, in front of more than a million people

1988 Dublin's millennium is celebrated, boosting the city's image

2005 Foreign ministers of the European Union, unanimously, agree to make Irish an official language of the EU

2002 The single European currency, the euro replaces Irish punt notes and coins

1987 Dubliner Steven Roche wins the Tour de France, Giro d'Italia and World Championship in one incredible season

IRELAND THROUGH THE YEAR

Popular months for visiting Ireland are July and August, and Belfast no longer closes down in July for the marching season. June and September can be pleasant but never count on the weather, for Ireland's lush beauty is the product of a wet climate. Most tourist sights are open from Easter to September but have restricted opening hours or close in the low season. During spring and summer, festivals are

Ladies' Day at Dublin Horse Show

held in honour of everything from food to religion. A common thread is music, and few festivities are complete without musical accompaniment. Ireland is at its best during celebrations, so is an inspired choice for Christmas and New Year. Look out for the word *fleadh* (festival) but remember that the Irish are spontaneous: festivities can spring from the air, or from a tune on a fiddle. Festival dates may vary.

Dublin's annual parade to celebrate St Patrick's Day (17 March)

SPRING

St Patrick's Day is often said to mark the beginning of the tourist season. Later, the spring bank holiday weekend in May, when accommodation is in short supply, is celebrated with music in most places. After the quiet winter months, festivals and events start to become more common.

MARCH

St Patrick's Festival *(17 Mar)*. Five days of parades, concerts, céilí dances and fireworks in Dublin, and parades in all major towns around the country.
Horse Ploughing Match and Heavy Horse Show, Ballycastle *(17 Mar, see p266)*. A popular annual competition.
DLR Poetry Now Festival *(end Mar)*. Dún Laoghaire. Four day celebration of Irish poetry.

A St Patrick's Day float advertising Guinness

Feis Ceoil, Dublin *(end Mar)*. A classical music festival held at many different venues throughout the city.

APRIL

Pan Celtic Festival, Donegal *mid(-Apr, see p156)*. A lively celebration of Celtic culture, with music, dance and song.
Cork Choral Festival *(late Apr)*.

MAY

Belfast Civic Festival and Lord Mayor's Show *(mid-May, see pp276–9)*. Street parade with bands and floats.
Balmoral Show, Belfast *(mid-May)*. A three-day show with diverse events ranging from sheep-shearing competitions to dancing dogs and fashion shows.
"A Taste of Baltimore" Shellfish Festival *(end May, see p170)*.
Fleadh Nua, Ennis, *end May, see p189)*. Four days of traditional Irish music, songs and dance.

SUMMER

For the visitor, summer represents the height of the festive calendar. This is the busiest time of year for organized events, from music and arts festivals to lively local race meetings, summer schools and matchmaking festivals. Book accommodation if your plans include a popular festival.

Beach races at Laytown

JUNE

Kilkenny Cat Laughs *(end May–early Jun)*. Internationally renowned comedy festival.
County Wicklow Garden Festival *(May–Jul)*. Held at private and public gardens around the county, including Powerscourt *(see pp134–5)*.
Dublin Docklands Maritime Festival *(early Jun)*. Tall ships, street theatre, outdoor markets, concerts and events for all ages.
Women's Mini Marathon, Dublin City *(early Jun)*.
Bloomsday, Dublin *(16 Jun)*. Lectures, pub talks, readings, dramatizations and walks to celebrate James Joyce's greatest novel, *Ulysses*.

AVERAGE DAILY HOURS OF SUNSHINE

Hours

10
8
6
4
2
0

Jan Feb Mar Apr May Jun Jul Aug Sep Oct Nov Dec

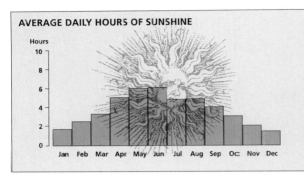

Sunshine Chart
The chart gives figures for Dublin, though conditions are similar around the country. The Southeast enjoys more sunshine hours than any other part of Ireland, while Northern Ireland receives marginally fewer hours of sun than the Republic.

Scurlogstown Olympiad Celtic Festival, Trim *(early Jun, see p248)*. Traditional Irish music, dance, fair and selection of a festival queen.

Music in Great Irish Houses *(mid-Jun)*. Classical music recitals in grand settings at various venues.

Castleward Opera, Strangford *(all month, see p284)*. Opera festival in the grounds of 18th-century stately home.

County Wexford Strawberry Festival, Enniscorthy *(end jun–early Jul, see p149)*. Craft fair, music, street theatre and, of course, strawberries.

JULY

Twelfth of July *(12 Jul, see p244)*. Members of the Orange Order march in towns across Northern Ireland to celebrate the Protestants' landmark victory over King James II's Catholic army in 1690.

Galway Arts Festival *(third & fourth weeks, see pp210–11)*. Processions, concerts, street theatre, children's shows and many other events in the medieval city centre. Followed

Steam-engine at Stradbally Rally (August)

Traditional sailing craft in the Cruinniú na mBác at Kinvara (August)

immediately by Galway's popular five-day race meeting.

Mary from Dungloe International Festival, Dungloe *(last week, see p228)*. Dancing, music and selection of "Mary", the beauty queen.

Lughnasa Fair, Carrickfergus Castle *(end Jul, see p275)*. A popular medieval-style fair.

Ballyshannon International Folk Festival *(end Jul or early Aug, see p231)* Three days of traditional Irish music.

O'Carolan Harp and Traditional Music Festival, Keadue, Co Roscommon *(end Jul or early Aug)*. Traditional music and dance celebrations.

AUGUST

Stradbally Steam-engine Rally, Co Laois *(early Aug)*. Many types of steam-engine join this rally.

Orangemen parading on the Twelfth of July

Galway Race Week, Co Galway *(early Aug)*. World renowned horse racing.

Dublin Horse Show *(first or second week)*. A premier showjumping competition and social event.

Puck Fair, Killorglin, Co Kerry *(mid-Aug, see p159)*. A wild goat is crowned "king" at this two-day-long traditional festival.

Blessing of the Sea *(second or third Sunday)*. Held in seaside towns all over Ireland.

Oul' Lammas Fair, Ballycastle *(mid-end Aug, see p266)*. A popular fair that is particularly famous for its edible seaweed.

Kilkenny Arts Week *(middle of the month, see pp142–3)*. A major arts festival including poetry, film and crafts.

Rose of Tralee Festival, *(end Aug, see p156)*. Bands, processions, dancing and selection of the "Rose".

Cruinniú na mBád, Kinvara *(mid-Aug, see pp211–12)*. Various types of traditional sailing craft take part in this "gathering of the boats".

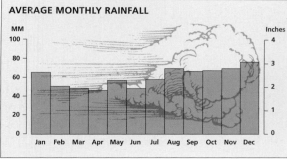

AVERAGE MONTHLY RAINFALL

MM   Inches
100 — 4
80 — 3
60 — 2
40 — 1
20
0 — 0

Jan Feb Mar Apr May Jun Jul Aug Sep Oct Nov Dec

Rainfall Chart
Ireland is one of the wettest countries in Europe, with rainfall distributed evenly through the year – the figures displayed here are for Dublin. The West has the heaviest annual rainfall, while the Southeast receives marginally less rain than other regions.

Galway Oyster Festival (September)

AUTUMN

Oysters and opera are the two big events in autumn. There are also festivals devoted to jazz, film and music. The October bank holiday weekend is celebrated with music in many towns.

SEPTEMBER

Heritage Week *(late Aug–early Sep)*. Events country-wide.
Laytown Beach Races, Co Meath *(first week of Sep)*. Horse races on the sand.
All-Ireland Hurling Final, Croke Park, Dublin *(first or second*

Sunday, see p29).
Lisdoonvarna Matchmaking Festival *(all month and first week of Oct, see p188).* Singles gather for traditional music and dance.
Waterford International Festival of Light Opera *(mid-Sep –early Oct, see p359).* Musicals and operettas at the Theatre Royal.
All-Ireland Football Final, Croke Park, Dublin *(3rd Sunday, see p29).* Gaelic football final.
Galway Oyster Festival *(end Sep, see pp210–11).* Oyster tastings at different venues.

OCTOBER

Octoberfest, Londonderry *(all month, see pp258–9).* Dance, poetry, film, comedy, theatre and music.
Cork Film Festival *(early Oct, see pp174–5).* Irish and international films.
Kinsale International Festival of Fine Food *(early Oct, see pp172–3).* Superb food served

All-Ireland Hurling at Croke Park, Dublin

in restaurants, hotels and pubs of Kinsale.
Ballinasloe Fair, Co Galway *(first week).* One of Europe's oldest horse fairs, staged amid lively street entertainment.
Dublin Theatre Festival *(first two weeks).* Features works by both Irish and foreign playwrights.
Wexford Opera Festival *(last two weeks in Oct, see p359).* A festival of lesser known operas.
Hallowe'en (Samhain) *(31 Oct).* An occasion celebrated all over the country.

Horse and trap at Lisdoonvarna fair

Cork Jazz Festival *(end Oct, see pp174–5).* An extremely popular festival, with music throughout the city.

NOVEMBER

Belfast Festival at Queen's, Queen's University *(last two weeks Oct, see pp276–9).* Arts festival featuring drama, ballet, cinema and all types of music from classical to jazz.
Éigse Sliabh Rua, Slieverue, Co Kilkenny *(mid-Nov).* Festival of local history and music with special guests and interesting talks.
Sligo International Choral Festival *(mid-Nov, see p234).* Choirs from around the world in concert and competition.

Traditional horse fair at Ballinasloe in County Galway (October)

AVERAGE MONTHLY TEMPERATURE

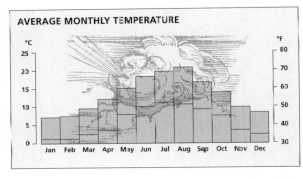

Temperature Chart
This chart gives the average minimum and maximum temperatures for the city of Dublin. Winter is mild throughout Ireland, except in the high mountain ranges, while the warmest summer temperatures are in the Southeast.

WINTER

Although a quiet time for festivals, there's a range of entertainment including musical and theatrical events. Christmas is the busiest social period and there are plenty of informal celebrations. There is also a wide choice of National Hunt race meetings *(see p28)*.

DECEMBER

Twelve Days of Christmas
(Dec). Dublin. A Christmas market with a vibrant festival atmosphere.
Leopardstown Races *(26 Dec, see p129)*. The biggest meeting held on this traditional day for racing. There are other fixtures at Limerick and Down Royal.
St Stephen's Day *(26 Dec)*. Catholic boys traditionally dress up as Wren boys (chimney sweeps with blackened faces) and sing hymns to raise money for charitable causes.

Young boys dressed up as Wren boys on St Stephen's Day

JANUARY

Salmon and Sea Trout Season
(17 Jan–end Sep, see pp362–3). Season begins for one of Ireland's most popular pastimes.

FEBRUARY

Jameson Dublin International Film Festival *(end Feb–early Mar)*. Films at various venues.
Belfast Musical Festival *(end Feb–mid-Mar)*. Young people take part in music (and speech and drama) competitions.
Six Nations Rugby Tournament, Aviva Stadium Dublin *(varying Saturdays Feb–Apr, see p28)*.

PUBLIC HOLIDAYS

New Year's Day (1 Jan)
St Patrick's Day (17 Mar)
Good Friday
Easter Monday
May Day (first Mon in May)
Spring Bank Holiday (Northern Ireland: last Mon in May)
June Bank Holiday (Republic: first Mon in Jun)
Twelfth of July (Northern Ireland: 12 Jul)
August Bank Holiday (first Mon in Aug).
Summer Bank Holiday (Northern Ireland: last Mon in Aug)
October Bank Holiday (last Mon in Oct)
Christmas Day (25 Dec)
St Stephen's Day (Republic: 26 Dec)
Boxing Day (Northern Ireland: 26 Dec)

Glendalough *(see pp140–41)* in the snow

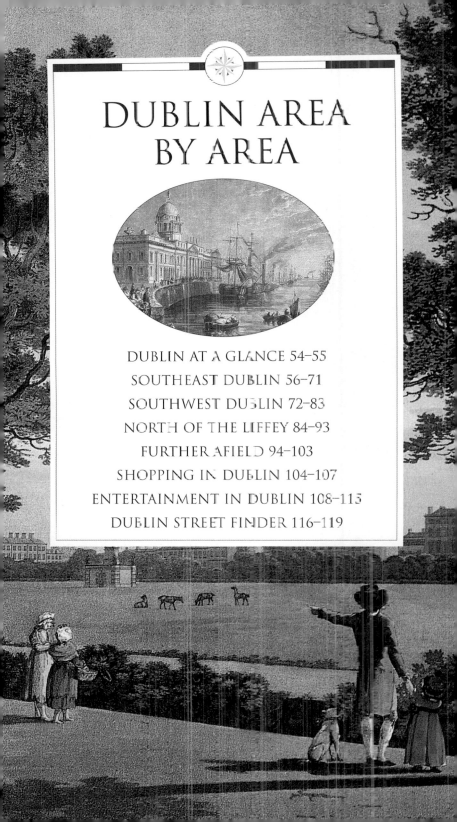

DUBLIN AREA
BY AREA

Dublin at a Glance

Ireland's capital has a wealth of attractions, most within walking distance of each other. For the purpose of this guide, central Dublin has been divided into three sections: *Southeast Dublin*, heart of the modern city and home to the prestigious Trinity College; *Southwest Dublin*, site of the old city around Dublin Castle; and *North of the Liffey*, the area around the imposing O'Connell Street. The map references given for sights in the city refer to the *Dublin Street Finder* on pages 118–119.

Christ Church Cathedral
was built by Dublin's Anglo-Norman conquerors between 1172 and 1220. It stands on high ground above the River Liffey. Much of the cathedral's present appearance is due to restoration carried out in the 1870s. (See pp80–81.)

NORTH OF THE LIFFEY
Pages 84–93

LIFFEY

SOUTHWEST DUBLIN
Pages 72–83

Dublin Castle *stands in the heart of old Dublin. St Patrick's Hall is part of the suite of luxury State Apartments housed on the upper floors on the south side of the castle. Today, these rooms are used for functions of national importance such as presidential inaugurations. (See pp76–7.)*

Saint Patrick's Cathedral
has a spectacular choir featuring banners and stalls decorated with the insignia of the Knights of St Patrick. The cathedral also holds Ireland's largest and most powerful organ, as well as memorials to Dean Jonathan Swift and prominent Anglo-Irish families. (See pp82–3.)

◁ **Stephen's Green (1796) by James Malton**

O'Connell Street, *Dublin's busiest thoroughfare, has a fine mix of architectural styles and a grand central mall punctuated with statues of famous Irish citizens and the 120-m (394-ft) Monument of Light spire. Just off O'Connell Street, on Moore Street, is a lively market. (See pp88–9.)*

The Custom House, *a classic Georgian public building by James Gandon, was built between 1781 and 1791. The sculpted heads on the keystones are personifications of the rivers of Ireland: the one shown above represents the River Foyle. (See p88.)*

Trinity College *is home to the Old Library which contains priceless illuminated manuscripts. These include the Book of Durrow which dates from the middle of the 7th century. (See pp62–4.)*

SOUTHEAST DUBLIN
Pages 56–71

The National Gallery *was opened in 1864. Housed on two floors, it holds an eclectic collection, particularly strong on Irish and Italian works. The gallery's most prized painting is Caravaggio's* The Taking of Christ. *The Millennium Wing has over 500 works on display. (See pp70–71.)*

0 metres	400
0 yards	400

National Museum of Ireland – Archaeology *has an impressive collection of artifacts dating from the Stone Age to the 20th century. The Ardagh Chalice (c.AD 800) is one of the many Celtic Christian treasures on display. (See pp66–7.)*

SOUTHEAST DUBLIN

Despite its location close to the old walled city, this part of Dublin remained virtually undeveloped until the founding of Trinity College in 1592. Even then, it was almost a hundred years before the ancient common land further south was enclosed to create St Stephen's Green, a spacious city park.

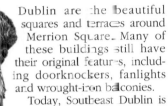

Georgian doorknocker in Merrion Square

The mid-18th century saw the beginning of a construction boom in the area. During this time, magnificent public buildings such as the Old Library at Trinity College, Leinster House and the Bank of Ireland were built. However, the most conspicuous reminders of Georgian Dublin are the beautiful squares and terraces around Merrion Square. Many of these buildings still have their original features, including doorknockers, fanlights and wrought-iron balconies.

Today, Southeast Dublin is very much the tourist heart of the city: few visitors can resist the lively atmosphere and attractive hops of Grafton Street. The area is also home to much of Ireland's cultural heritage. The National Gallery has a good collection of Irish and European paintings while the National Museum – Archaeology has superb displays of Irish Bronze Age gold and early Christian treasures.

SIGHTS AT A GLANCE

Museums, Libraries and Galleries
National Gallery pp70–71 12
National Library 8
*National Museum of Ireland –
Archaeology pp64–5* 7
National Wax Museum Plus 10
Natural History Museum 11
Royal Hibernian Academy 14

Historic Buildings
Bank of Ireland 1
Leinster House 9
Mansion House 5
Trinity College pp62–3 2

Historic Streets
Fitzwilliam Square 15
Grafton Street 3
Merrion Square 13

Churches
St Ann's Church 6

Parks and Gardens
St Stephen's Green 4

KEY

Street-by-Street *See pp58–9*	
Railway station	
DART station	
Luas stop	
Tourist information	

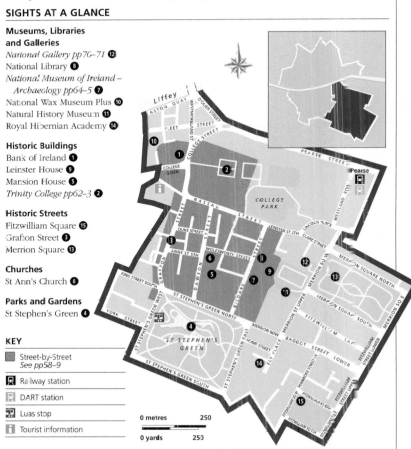

0 metres 250
0 yards 250

◁ **Marble bust of Jonathan Swift in the Old Library, Trinity College**

Street-by-Street: Southeast Dublin

The area around College Green, dominated by the façades of the Bank of Ireland and Trinity College, is very much the heart of Dublin. The alleys and malls cutting across busy pedestrianized Grafton Street boast many of Dublin's better shops, hotels and restaurants. Just off Kildare Street are the Irish Parliament, the National Library and the National Museum – Archaeology. To escape the city bustle many head for sanctuary in St Stephen's Green, which is overlooked by fine Georgian buildings.

To Dublin Castle

COLLEGE GREEN

Grafton Street
Brown Thomas department store is one of the main attractions on this pedestrianized street, alive with buskers and pavement artists ❸

Bank of Ireland
This grand Georgian building was originally built as the Irish Parliament ❶

Statue of Molly Malone (1988)

St Ann's Church
The striking façade of the 18th-century church was added in 1868. The interior features lovely stained-glass windows ❻

Mansion House
This has been the official residence of Dublin's Lord Mayor since 1715 ❺

Fusiliers' Arch (1907)

★ St Stephen's Green
The relaxing city park is surrounded by many grand buildings. In summer, lunch-time concerts attract tourists and workers alike ❹

For hotels and restaurants in this region see pp294–8 and pp324–8

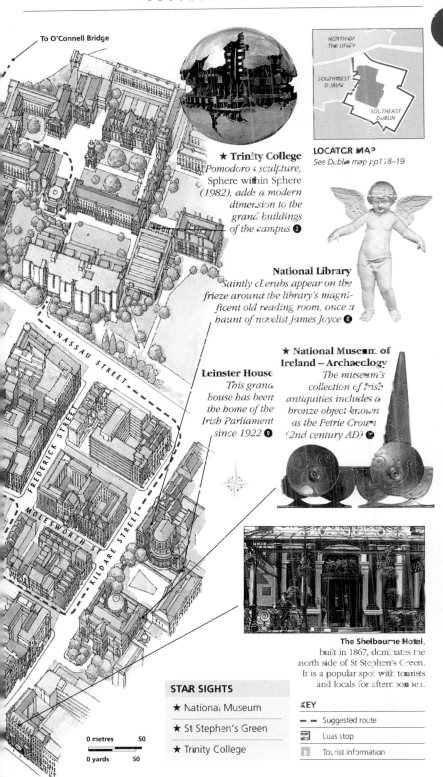

To O'Connell Bridge

See Dublin map pp118–19

NORTH OF
THE LIFFEY

SOUTHWEST
DUBLIN

SOUTHEAST
DUBLIN

LOCATOR MAP

★ **Trinity College**
Pomodoro's sculpture,
Sphere within Sphere
(1982), adds a modern
dimension to the
grand buildings
of the campus ❷

National Library
Saintly cherubs appear on the
frieze around the library's magni-
ficent old reading room, once a
haunt of novelist James Joyce ❽

★ **National Museum of**
Ireland – Archaeology
The museum's
collection of Irish
antiquities includes a
bronze object known
as the Petrie Crown
(2nd century AD) ❼

Leinster House
This grand
house has been
the home of the
Irish Parliament
since 1922 ❾

The Shelbourne Hotel,
built in 1867, dominates the
north side of St Stephen's Green.
It is a popular spot with tourists
and locals for afternoon tea.

STAR SIGHTS

★ National Museum

★ St Stephen's Green

★ Trinity College

KEY

- – Suggested route

🔲 Luas stop

🔳 Tourist information

0 metres   50

0 yards   50

Original chamber of the Irish House of Lords at the Bank of Ireland

Bank of Ireland ❶

2 College Green. **Map** D3. **Tel** 677 6801 ☐ 10am–4pm Mon, Tue & Fri, 10:30am–4pm Wed, 10am–5pm Thu, 11am–4pm Sat. ● public hols. **House of Lords** 📷 10:30am, 11:30am & 1:45pm Tue.

The prestigious offices of the Bank of Ireland began life as the first purpose-built parliament house in Europe. The original central section was started by Irish architect Edward Lovett Pearce and completed in 1739 after his death. Sadly, Pearce's masterpiece, the great octagonal chamber of the House of Commons (see p40), was removed at the behest of the British government in 1802. The House of Lords, however, remains gloriously intact, especially its coffered ceiling and oak panelling. There are also huge tapestries of the *Battle of the Boyne* and the *Siege of Londonderry*, and a splendid 1,233-piece crystal chandelier dating from 1788.
The east portico was added by architect James Gandon in 1785, with further

additions around 1797. After the dissolution of the Irish Parliament in 1800, the Bank of Ireland bought the building. The present structure was then completed in 1808 with the transformation of the former lobby of the House of Commons into a magnificent cash office and the addition of a curving screen wall and the Foster Place annexe.
At the front of the bank on College Green is a statue (1879) by John Foley of Henry Grattan (see p40), the most formidable leader of the old parliament.

Trinity College ❷

See pp62–3.

Grafton Street ❸

Map D4.

The spine of Dublin's most popular and stylish shopping district (see pp104–7) runs south from Trinity College to the glass St Stephen's Green Shopping Centre. At the junction with Nassau Street is a statue by Jean Rynhart of *Molly Malone* (1988), the celebrated street trader from the traditional song "Molly Malone". This busy pedestrianized strip, characterized by energetic buskers and talented

street theatre artists, boasts Brown Thomas, one of Dublin's finest department stores (see p104). In addition, there are plenty of recognisable high street retailers to tempt shoppers, including Monsoon, HMV and Oasis. There are also many excellent jewellers in Grafton Street. Number 78 stands on the site of Samuel Whyte's school, whose illustrious roll included Robert Emmet (see p77), leader of the 1803 Rebellion, and the Duke of Wellington.
Hidden along many of the side streets are quaint, traditional Irish pubs, catering to the weary shopper's need for a refreshment break.

St Stephen's Green ❹

Map D5. ☐ daylight hours. **Newman House** 85–86 St Stephen's Green. **Tel** 477 9810. ☐ Jun–Aug: 2–4pm Tue–Fri; Sep–May: by appt. ● public hols. 📷 📷 obligatory; tours start on the hour.

Royal College of Surgeons, which overlooks St Stephen's Green

Originally one of three ancient commons in the old city, St Stephen's Green was enclosed in 1664. The 9-ha (22-acre) green was laid out in its present form in 1880, using a grant given by Lord Ardilaun, a member of the Guinness family. Landscaped with flowerbeds, trees, a fountain and a lake, the green is dotted with memorials to eminent Dubliners, including Ardilaun himself. There is a bust of James Joyce (see p90), and a memorial by Henry Moore (1967) dedicated to WB Yeats (see pp232–3). At

Bronze statue of *Molly Malone* at the bottom of Grafton Street

Dubliners relaxing by the lake in St Stephen's Green

the Merrion Row corner stands a massive monument (1967) by Edward Delaney to 18th-century nationalist leader Wolfe Tone – it is known locally as "Tonehenge". The 1887 bandstand is still the focal point for free daytime concerts in summer.

The imposing Royal College of Surgeons stands on the west side. Built in 1806, it was commandeered by rebel troops under Countess Constance Markievicz in the 1916 Rising (see pp44–5) and its columns still bear the marks of bullets from the fighting.

The busiest side of the Green is the north, known during the 19th century as the Beaux' Walk and still home to gentlemen's clubs. The most prominent building is the refurbished venerable Shelbourne Hotel. Dating back to 1867, its entrance is adorned with statues of Nubian princesses and attendant slaves. It is well worth popping in for a look at the chandeliered foyer and for afternoon tea in the Lord Mayor's Lounge.

Situated on the south side is Newman House, home of the Catholic University of Ireland (now part of University College). Opened in 1854, its first rector was English theologian John Henry Newman Famous past pupils include Patrick Pearse, a leader of the 1916 Rising, former Taoiseach Eamon de Valera (see p45) and author James Joyce. Tours reveal some of the best

Georgian interior decor to survive in the city. The walls and ceilings of the Apollo Room and Saloon at No. 85 are festooned with intricate Baroque stuccowork (1739) by the Swiss brothers Paolo and Filippo Francini. The Bishops' Room at No. 86 is decorated with heavy 19th-century furniture.

The small University Church (1856) next door has a colourful, richly marbled Byzantine interior. Also on the south side of St Stephen's Green is Iveagh House, a town house once owned by the Guinness family and now the Department of Foreign Affairs.

Mansion House **⑤**

Dawson St. **Map** E4 ⬛ to the public.

Set back from Dawson Street by a neat cobbled forecourt, the Mansion House is an attractive Queen Anne-style building. It was built in 1710 for the aristocrat Joshua Dawson, after whom the street is named. The Dublin Corporation bought it from him five years later as the official residence of the city's Lord Mayor. The Round Room adjacent to the main building was built in 1821 for the visit of King George IV. The Dáil Éireann (see p65), which adopted the Declaration of Independence, first met here on 21 January 1919.

St Ann's Church **⑥**

Dawson St. **Map** E4. **Tel** 676 7727. ⬛ 10am–4pm Mon–Fri (also for Sun services at 8am, 10.45am & 6:30pm).

Founded in 1707, St Ann's striking Romanesque façade was added in 1868. Inside are colourful stained-glass windows, dating from the mid-19th century. The church has a long tradition of charity work: in 1723 Lord Newton left a bequest to buy bread for the poor. The original shelf for the bread still stands next to the altar.

Famous past parishioners include Wolfe Tone (see p41), who was married here in 1785, Douglas Hyde (see p45) and Bram Stoker (1847–1912), author of Dracula

Detail of window depicting Faith, Hope and Charity, St Ann's Church

Trinity College ❷

Trinity College coat of arms

Trinity College was founded in 1592 by Queen Elizabeth I on the site of an Augustinian monastery. Originally a Protestant college, it only began to take Catholics in numbers after 1970, when the Catholic Church relaxed its opposition to their attending. Among Trinity's many famous students were playwrights Oliver Goldsmith and Samuel Beckett, and political writer Edmund Burke. The college's lawns and cobbled quads provide a pleasant haven in the heart of the city. The major attractions are the Long Room and the Book of Kells Exhibition, housed in the Old Library.

★ Campanile
The 30-m (98-ft) bell tower was built in 1853 by Sir Charles Lanyon, architect of Queen's University, Belfast (see p278).

Reclining Connected Forms (1969) by Henry Moore

Dining Hall (1761)

Chapel *(1798)*
This was the first university chapel in the Republic to accept all denominations. The painted window above the altar is from 1867.

Parliament Square

Statue of Edmund Burke (1868) by John Foley

Main entrance

SAMUEL BECKETT (1906–89)

Nobel prizewinner Samuel Beckett was born at Foxrock, south of Dublin. In 1923 he entered Trinity, and later graduated with a first in modern languages and a gold medal. He was also a keen member of the college cricket team. Forsaking Ireland, Beckett moved to France in the early 1930s. Many of his major works such as *Waiting for Godot* (1951) were written first in French, and later translated, by Beckett, into English.

Statue of Oliver Goldsmith (1864) by John Foley

Provost's House (c. 1760)

Examination Hall
Completed in 1791 to a design by Sir William Chambers, the hall features a gilded oak chandelier and ornate ceilings by Michael Stapleton.

Library Square
*The red-brick building (known as the Rubrics) on
the east side of Library Square was built around
1700 and is the oldest surviving part of the college.*

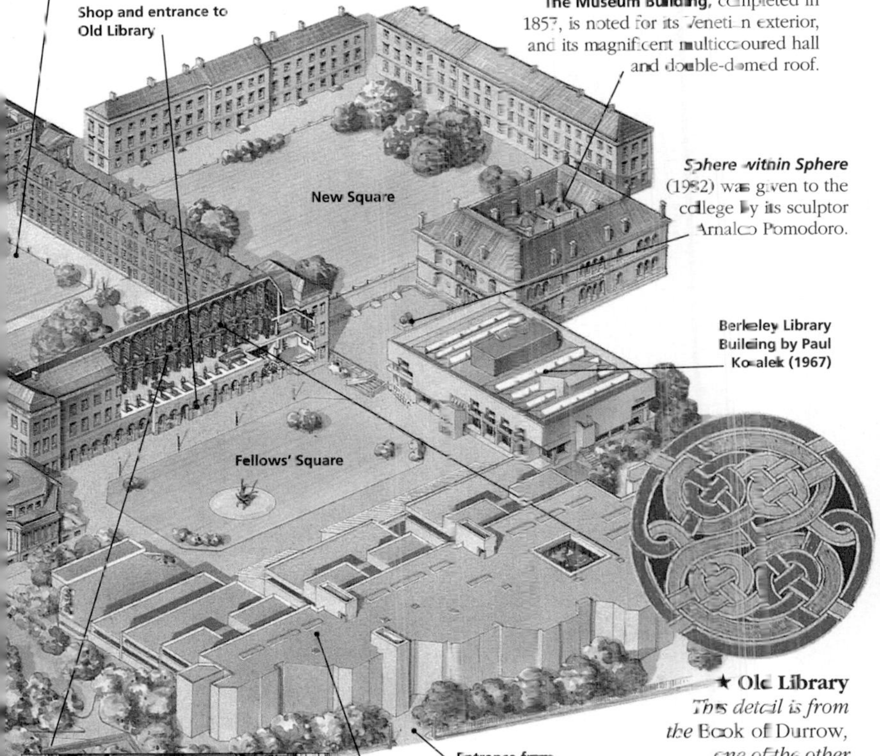

**Shop and entrance to
Old Library**

The Museum Building, completed in
1857, is noted for its Venetian exterior,
and its magnificent multicoloured hall
and double-domed roof.

New Square

Sphere within Sphere
(1982) was given to the
college by its sculptor
Arnaldo Pomodoro.

**Berkeley Library
Building by Paul
Koralek (1967)**

Fellows' Square

★ Old Library
*This detail is from
the Book of Durrow,
one of the other
magnificent illuminated
manuscripts housed in
the Old Library along
with the celebrated Book
of Kells (see p64).*

**Entrance from
Nassau Street**

The Douglas Hyde Gallery
was built in the 1970s to house
temporary art exhibitions.

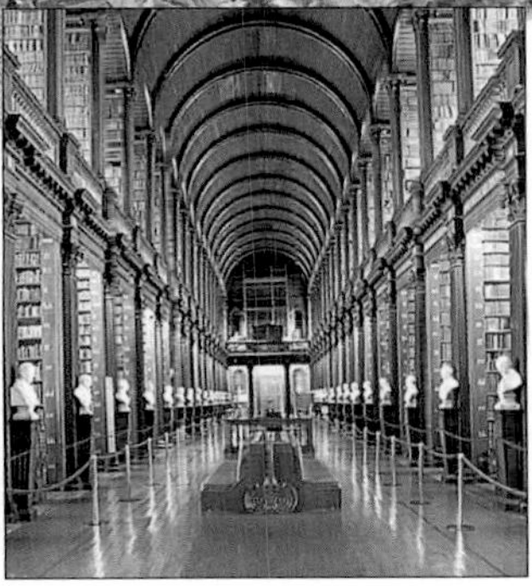

★ Long Room *(1732)*
*The spectacular Long Room
measures 64 m (210 ft)
from end to end. It houses
200,000 antiquarian
texts, marble busts of
scholars and the oldest
surviving harp in Ireland.*

STAR FEATURES

★ Campanile

★ Old Library

★ Long Room

The Book of Kells

The most richly decorated of Ireland's medieval illuminated manuscripts, the *Book of Kells* may have been the work of monks from Iona, who fled to Kells *(see p241)* in AD 806 after a Viking raid. The book, which was moved to Trinity College *(see pp62–3)* in the 17th century, contains the four gospels in Latin. The scribes who copied the texts also embellished their calligraphy with intricate interlacing spirals as well as human figures and animals. Some of the dyes used were imported from as far as the Middle East.

Pair of moths

Stylized angel

The Greek letter "X"

The symbols *of the four evangelists are used as decoration throughout the book. The figure of the man symbolizes St Matthew.*

The letter that looks like a "P" is a Greek "R".

The letter "I"

Interlacing motifs

Cat watching rats

A full-page portrait *of St Matthew, shown standing barefoot in front of a throne, precedes the opening words of his gospel.*

Rats eating bread could be a reference to sinners taking Holy Communion. The symbolism of the animals and people decorating the manuscript is often hard to interpret.

MONOGRAM PAGE

The most elaborate page of the book, this contains the first three words of St Matthew's account of the birth of Christ. The first word "XRI" is an abbreviation of "Christi".

The text *is in a beautifully rounded Celtic script with brightly ornamented initial letters. Animal and human forms are often used to decorate the end of a line.*

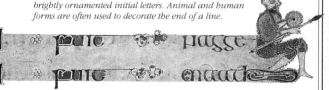

The magnificent domed Reading Room on the first floor of the National Library

National Museum of Ireland – Archaeology ❼

See pp66–7.

National Library ❽

Kildare St. **Map** E4. **Tel** 603 0200.
◯ 9:30am–9pm Mon–Wed,
9:30am–5pm Thu & Fri, 9:30am–1pm
Sat. ◯ public hols. **www**.nli.ie

Designed by Sir Thomas Deane, the National Library opened in 1890. It now contains first editions of every major Irish writer and a copy of almost every book ever published in Ireland. Its holdings also include manuscripts, prints, drawings, maps, photographs, newspapers, music, ephemera and genealogical material, all of which comprise the most outstanding collection of Irish documentary heritage in the world.

Visitors can browse in the famous Reading Room where distinguished Irish writers have studied, or explore the award-winning exhibitions.

For anyone with an interest in family history, the Genealogy Advisory Service is available free of charge to all personal callers.

The library also hosts an ongoing programme of events

including public lectures, poetry and music recitals, theatre, children's storytelling, public tours of exhibitions, family tours, creative workshops, and a lot more. Admission is free.

Leinster House ❾

Kildare St. **Map** E4. **Tel** 6 18 3000. ◯ groups by appt; foreign visitors to book through their own embassy. 📷 phone for details. **www**.oireachtas.ie

This stately mansion houses the Dáil and the Seanad – the two chambers of the Irish Parliament. It was originally

built for the Duke of Leinster in 1745. Designed by German-born architect Richard Castle, the Kildare Street façade resembles that of a large town house. However, the rear, looking on to Merrion Square, has the air of a country estate complete with sweeping lawns. The Royal Dublin Society bought the building in 1815. The government obtained a part of it in 1922 for parliamentary use and bought the entire building two years later.

Phone ahead to arrange a tour of the rooms, including the Seanad chamber with its heavily ornamented ceiling.

THE IRISH PARLIAMENT

The Irish Free State, forerunner of the Republic of Ireland, was inaugurated in 1922 (see p44), although an unofficial Irish parliament, the Dáil, had already been in existence since 1919. Today, parliament is made up of two Houses: the Dáil (House of Representatives) and Seanad Éireann (the Senate). The Prime Minister is the Taoiseach and the deputy, the Tánaiste. The Dáil's 166 representatives – Teachtaí Dála, known as TDs – are elected by proportional representation. The 60-strong Seanad is appointed by various individuals and authorities, including the Taoiseach and the University of Dublin.

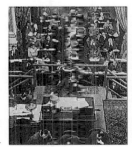

Opening of the first parliament of the Irish Free State – 1922

National Museum of Ireland – Archaeology ❼

Built in the 1880s, the National Museum of Ireland – Archaeology has a domed rotunda featuring marble pillars and a mosaic floor. The Treasury houses priceless items such as the Broighter gold boat *(see p33)*, while *Ór – Ireland's Gold*, an exhibition of Ireland's Bronze Age gold, has jewellery such as the Gleninsheen Gorget *(see pp32–3)*. The National Museum of Ireland consists of three other sites: Decorative Arts and History at Collins Barracks *(see p101)*, Country Life and Natural History *(see p68)*.

Egyptian Mummy
This mummy of the lady Tentdinebu is thought to date back to c.945–716 BC. Covered in brilliant colours, it is part of the stunning Egyptian collection.

★ Ór – Ireland's Gold
This is one of the most extensive collections of Bronze Age gold in Western Europe. This gold lunula (c.1800 BC), found in Athlone, is one of many pieces of ancient jewellery in this exhibition.

KEY TO FLOORPLAN

- ☐ Kingship and Sacrifice
- ☐ Ór – Ireland's Gold
- ☐ The Treasury
- ☐ Prehistoric Ireland
- ☐ Medieval Ireland
- ☐ Viking Ireland
- ☐ Ancient Egypt
- ☐ Ceramics and Glass from Ancient Cyprus
- ☐ Life and Death in the Roman World
- ☐ Temporary exhibition space
- ☐ Non-exhibition space

★ Bog Bodies
This preserved hand (c.600 BC) is one of the pieces in this fascinating exhibition of Iron Age bodies discovered in 2003.

Main entrance

GALLERY GUIDE
The ground floor holds The Treasury, Ór – Ireland's Gold exhibition, the Kingship and Sacrifice and the Prehistoric Ireland display. On the first floor is the Medieval Ireland exhibition, which illustrates many aspects of life in later medieval Ireland. Also on the first floor are artifacts from Ancient Egypt and from the Viking settlement of Dublin.

The domed rotunda, based on the design of the Altes Museum in Berlin, makes an impressive entrance hall.

The Treasury houses masterpieces of Irish crafts such as the Ardagh Chalice *(see p55)*.

First floor

Temporary exhibition space is located in the gallery of the second floor. Past exhibitions have included *Viking Ships* and *Finds from Irish Wetlands*.

VISITORS' CHECKLIST

Kildare St. Map E4. **Tel** 677 7444.
DART to Pearse Station, LUAS Green Line to St Stephen's Green. 10, 11, 13 and many other routes. 10am–5pm Tue–Sat, 2–5pm Sun. Good Fri & 25 Dec. ground floor only.
www.museum.ie

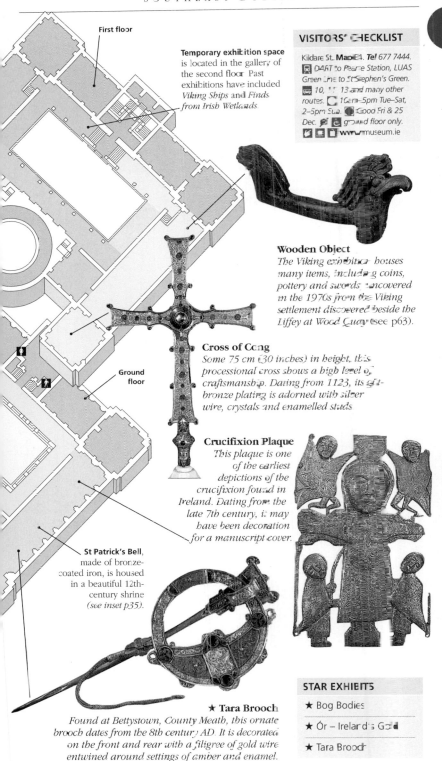

Wooden Object
The Viking exhibition houses many items, including coins, pottery and swords uncovered in the 1970s from the Viking settlement discovered beside the Liffey at Wood Quay (see p63).

Cross of Cong
Some 75 cm (30 inches) in height, this processional cross shows a high level of craftsmanship. Dating from 1123, its gilt-bronze plating is adorned with silver wire, crystals and enamelled studs.

Crucifixion Plaque
This plaque is one of the earliest depictions of the crucifixion found in Ireland. Dating from the late 7th century, it may have been decoration for a manuscript cover.

Ground floor

St Patrick's Bell, made of bronze-coated iron, is housed in a beautiful 12th-century shrine (see inset p35).

★ Tara Brooch
Found at Bettystown, County Meath, this ornate brooch dates from the 8th century AD. It is decorated on the front and rear with a filigree of gold wire entwined around settings of amber and enamel.

STAR EXHIBITS

★ Bog Bodies

★ Ór – Ireland's Gold

★ Tara Brooch

National Wax Museum Plus ⑩

The Armoury, Foster Place, College Green. **Map** D3. **Tel** 671 8373.
⬜ 10am–7pm daily. ⬤ 25 Dec.
🖼 🏠 🍴 🛍 **www**.wax museumplus.ie

This museum offers a modern take on the traditional wax-works museum, with displays over four floors that provide an interactive experience.

Visitors are taken on a journey through time with wax models of figures from Irish history, literature, music, film, science, politics and more. The Grand Hall is dedicated to stars of Irish rock music and film, such as U2 and Liam Neeson. International stars such as Madonna and Elvis also feature. In the Recording Studio, you can use the latest technology to make a music video.

A children's cinema and characters such as Harry Potter are the attractions in the Children's Fantasy World. The basement Chamber of Horrors is not for the faint-hearted.

The Wax Museum, located in the historical Armoury building

Natural History Museum ⑪

Merrion St. **Map** E4. **Tel** 677 7444.
⬜ 10am–5pm Tue–Sat, 2–5pm Sun.
⬤ Good Fri, 25 Dec. ♿ limited.
www.museum.ie

This museum was opened in 1857 with an inaugural lecture by Scottish explorer Dr David Livingstone. Inside the front door are three skeletons of

Georgian town houses overlooking Merrion Square gardens

extinct giant deer known as the "Irish elk". The ground floor houses the Irish Room, which is devoted to local wildlife. The upper floor illustrates the range of mammals inhabiting our planet. Among the most fascinating exhibits are the primates (monkeys, apes and lemurs) a Bengal tiger and skeletons of whales hanging from the ceiling.

National Gallery ⑫

See pp70–71.

Merrion Square ⑬

Map F4.

Merrion Square, one of Dublin's largest and grandest Georgian squares, was laid out by John Ensor around 1762.

On the west side are the impressive façades of the Natural History Museum, the National Gallery and the front garden of Leinster House *(see p65)*. However, they do not compare with the lovely Georgian town houses on the other three sides.

Many of the houses – now predominantly used as office space – have plaques detailing the rich and famous who once lived in them. These include the poet WB Yeats *(see pp232–3)*, who lived at No. 82. The playwright Oscar Wilde *(see p22)* spent his childhood at No. 1.

The attractive central park once served as an emergency soup kitchen, feeding the hungry during the Great Famine in the 1840s *(see p219)*. On the northwest side of the park stands the restored

Rutland Fountain. It was originally erected in 1791 for the sole use of Dublin's poor.

Royal Hibernian Academy ⑭

15 Ely Place. **Map** E5. **Tel** 661 2558.
⬜ 11am–5pm Mon & Tue, 11am–7pm Wed–Sat, 2–5pm Sun.
⬤ Christmas hols. ♿ **www**. royalhibernianacademy.ie

The academy is one of the largest exhibition spaces in the city. Through its touring exhibitions of painting, sculpture and other works, the institution challenges the public's understand of visual arts. This modern building, does, however, look out of place at the end of Ely Place, an attractive Georgian cul-de-sac.

Fitzwilliam Square ⑮

Map E5. **No. 29 Fitzwilliam St Lower**
Tel 702 6165. ⬜ 10am–5pm Tue–Sat, noon–5pm Sun & public hols.
⬤ Mon & 3 weeks at Christmas. 🖼
📷 🚫 ♿ limited, call in advance.
www.esb.ie/numbertwentynine

Dating from the 1790s, this was one of the last Georgian squares to be laid out in central Dublin. Much smaller than Merrion Square, it is a popular location for medical practices.

In the 1960s, sixteen town houses on Fitzwilliam Street Lower were torn down to make way for the headquarters of the Electricity Supply Board. The company has since tried to appease public indignation by renovating No. 29 as a Georgian showpiece home.

Dublin's Georgian Terraces

The 18th century was Dublin's Age of Elegance, a time of relative prosperity when the Irish gentry, keen not to appear as the poor relations of Britain, set about remodelling Dublin into one of the most elegant cities in Europe. Terraced town houses were built, forming handsome new streets and squares. During the 19th century the city's wealth declined,

Doorknocker, Merrion Square

forcing some middle-class families to divide their home into tenements. Many of Dublin's once grand streets slowly deteriorated. A century later the property boom of the 1960s threatened to rip out what was left of Georgian Dublin. Fortunately, much has survived and some of the city's finest architecture can be seen in Merrion Square and Fitzwilliam Square.

Playroom

Attic

The bedrooms were usually on the second floor, while the upper floors contained the servants' quarters and children's rooms.

Wrought-iron balconies *gave added prestige to the Georgian house Those still in place today are mostly later Victorian additions*

Lavish stuccowork *was an important way of showing an owner's wealth during the 18th century.*

The drawing room was always on the first floor. The high ceiling was decorated with the finest plasterwork.

Architrave

The dining room *was* normally on the ground floor.

The kitchen contained a huge cooking range which was fired by either coal or wood. The adjoining pantry was used to store the household's groceries.

The doorway *was usually crowned with a segmented fanlight. The principal decoration on the door itself was a heavy brass knocker.*

GEORGIAN TERRACED HOUSE

While Georgian streetscapes may appear uniform, close inspection reveals a diversity of styles in terms of detail such as fanlights, architraves and balconies. The hallways usually had stone floors and, facing the hall door, a staircase rising to the upper floors. Many of the town houses did not have gardens – the railed-off parks in the centre of the squares were reserved for residents only and served as such.

National Gallery of Ireland ⑪

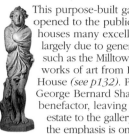

This purpose-built gallery was opened to the public in 1864. It houses many excellent exhibits, largely due to generous bequests, such as the Milltown collection of works of art from Russborough House *(see p132)*. Playwright George Bernard Shaw was also a benefactor, leaving a third of his estate to the gallery. Although the emphasis is on Irish art, the major schools of European painting are well represented. During the current major refurbishment of the historic Dargan and Milltown wings, the location of exhibits is subject to change.

The Houseless Wanderer by John Foley

★ **Pierrot**
This Cubist-style work, by Spanish-born artist Juan Gris, is one of many variations he painted on the theme of Pierrot and Harlequin. This particular one dates from 1921.

GALLERY GUIDE

The main entrance is through the lofty Millennium Wing on Clare Street. The gallery is undergoing major refurbishments until 2014/5, and this will result in changes to the presentation of the collection. Visitors are advised to call or email in advance to confirm whether and where specific exhibits will be displayed.

Mezzanine level

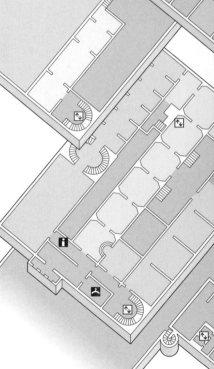

★ **For the Road**
The Yeats Museum houses works by Jack B Yeats (1871–1957) and his family. This mysterious painting reflects the artist's obsession with the Sligo countryside.

STAR PAINTINGS

- ★ The Taking of Christ
- ★ Pierrot
- ★ For the Road

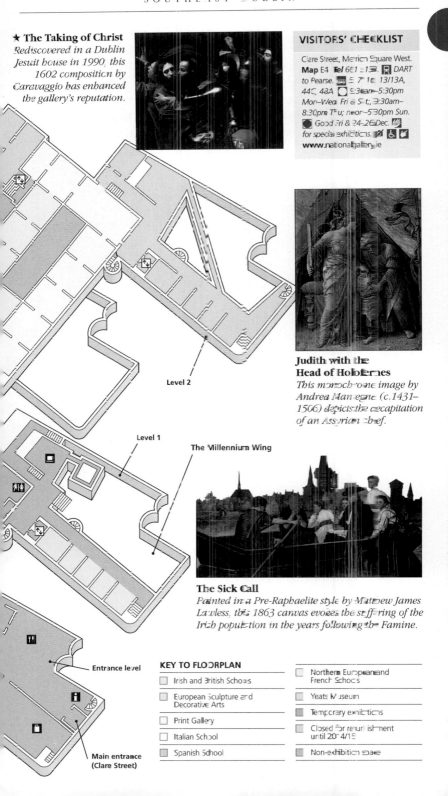

★ The Taking of Christ
Rediscovered in a Dublin Jesuit house in 1990, this 1602 composition by Caravaggio has enhanced the gallery's reputation.

VISITORS' CHECKLIST

Clare Street, Merrion Square West.
Map E4 **Tel** 661 5133. DART
to Pearse. 5, 7, 10, 13/13A,
44C, 48A Open 9:30am–5:30pm
Mon–Wed, Fri & Sat; 9:30am–
8:30pm Thu; noon–5:30pm Sun.
Closed Good Fri & 24–26 Dec.
for special exhibitions.
www.nationalgallery.ie

Level 2

Judith with the Head of Holofernes
This monochrome image by Andrea Mantegna (c.1431–1506) depicts the decapitation of an Assyrian chief.

Level 1

The Millennium Wing

The Sick Call
Painted in a Pre-Raphaelite style by Matthew James Lawless, this 1863 canvas evokes the suffering of the Irish population in the years following the Famine.

Entrance level

Main entrance (Clare Street)

KEY TO FLOORPLAN

- ☐ Irish and British Schools
- ☐ European Sculpture and Decorative Arts
- ☐ Print Gallery
- ☐ Italian School
- ☐ Spanish School
- ☐ Northern European and French Schools
- ☐ Yeats Museum
- ☐ Temporary exhibitions
- ☐ Closed for refurbishment until 2014/15
- ☐ Non-exhibition space

SOUTHWEST DUBLIN

The area around Dublin Castle was first settled in prehistoric times, and it was from here that the city grew. Dublin gets its name from the dark pool (*Dubh Linn*) which formed at the confluence of the Liffey and the Poddle, a river which once ran through the site of Dublin Castle It is now channelled underground and trickles out into the Liffey by Grattan Bridge. Archaeological excavations behind Wood Quay, on the banks of the Liffey, reveal that the Vikings established a trading settlement here around 841.

Following Strongbow's invasion of 1170, a medieval city began to emerge; the Anglo-Normans built strong defensive walls around the castle. A small

Memorial to Turlough O'Carolan in Saint Patrick's Cathedral

reconstructed section of these old city walls can be seen at St Audoen's Church. More conspicuous reminders of the Anglo-Normans are provided by the grand medieval Christ Church Cathedral and Ireland's largest church, Saint Patrick's Cathedral. When the city expanded to the north and east during the Georgian era, the narrow cobble streets of Temple Bar became a quarter of skilled craftsmen and merchants. Today this lively area of town bustles with tourists, and is come to a variety of "alternative" shops and cafés. The Powerscourt Townhouse, an elegant 18th-century mansion, has been converted into one of the city's best shopping centres.

SIGHTS AT A GLANCE

Museums and Libraries
Chester Beatty Library ❷
Dublinia and the Viking World ❽
Marsh's Library ⓬

Historic Buildings
City Hall ❸
Dublin Castle pp76–7 ❶
Powerscourt Townhouse ❹
Tailors' Hall ❿

Historic Streets
Temple Bar ❺
Wood Quay ❻

Churches
Christ Church Cathedral pp80–81 ❼
St Audoen's Church ❾
Saint Patrick's Cathedral ⑪
Whitefriar Street Carmelite Church ⑬

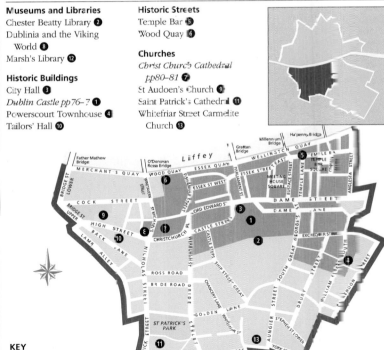

KEY

Street-by-Street map
See pp74–5

0 metres   250
0 yards   250

◁ Temple Bar district on the left side of the Liffey River

Street-by-Street: Southwest Dublin

Despite its wealth of ancient buildings, such as
Dublin Castle and Christ Church Cathedral,
this part of Dublin lacks the sleek appeal of
the neighbouring streets around Grafton
Street. However, redevelopment has helped
to rejuvenate the area, especially around
Temple Bar, where the attractive cobbled
streets are lined with interesting shops,
galleries and cafés.

Sunlight Chambers
were built in 1900 for
the Lever Brothers
company. The
delightful terracotta
decoration on the
façade advertises
their main business
of soap manufacturing.

Wood Quay
*This is where the Vikings
established their first
permanent settlement in
Ireland around 841* **⑥**

★ Christ Church Cathedral
*Huge family monuments
including that of the
19th Earl of Kildare
can be found in
Ireland's oldest cath-
edral, which also has a
fascinating crypt* **⑦**

St Werburgh's Church
An ornate interior hides behind
the somewhat drab exterior of
this 18th-century church.

City Hall
*Originally built as the
Royal Exchange in
1779, the city's muni-
cipal headquarters is
fronted by a huge
Corinthian portico* **③**

**Dublinia and the
Viking World**
*Medieval Dublin
and the Vikings are
the subjects of this
interactive museum,
located in the former
Synod Hall of the
Church of Ireland* **⑧**

★ Dublin Castle
*The Drawing Room, with its
Waterford crystal chandelier, is
part of a suite of luxurious rooms
built in the 18th century for the
Viceroys of Ireland* **①**

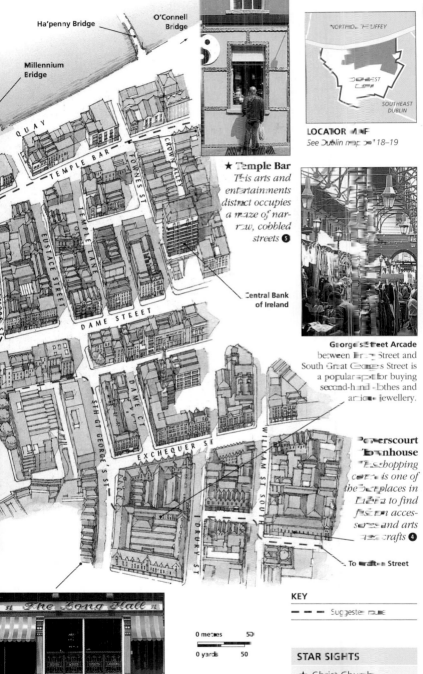

Ha'penny Bridge

O'Connell Bridge

Millennium Bridge

QUAY

TEMPLE BAR

CROWN ALLEY

TOWNES ST

TEMPLE LANE

EUSTACE STREET

DAME STREET

DAME CT

STH GT GEORGE'S ST

EXCHEQUER ST

DRURY ST

WILLIAM ST SOUTH

LOCATOR MAP
See Dublin map pp18–19

★ **Temple Bar**
This arts and entertainments district occupies a maze of narrow, cobbled streets ⑤

Central Bank of Ireland

George's Street Arcade between Drury Street and South Great George's Street is a popular spot for buying second-hand clothes and antique jewellery.

Powerscourt Townhouse This shopping centre is one of the best places in Dublin to find fashion accessories and arts and crafts ④

To Grafton Street

The Long Hall is a magnificent, old-fashioned pub with a great atmosphere. Behind the narrow room's long bar stands a bewildering array of antique clocks.

0 metres   50
0 yards   50

KEY

‒ ‒ ‒ Suggested route

STAR SIGHTS

★ Christ Church Cathedral

★ Dublin Castle

★ Temple Bar

Dublin Castle ❶

For seven centuries Dublin Castle was the seat of English rule, ever since the Anglo-Normans built a fortress here in the 13th century. All that remains of the original structure is the southeastern tower, now called the Record Tower. Following a fire in 1684, the Surveyor-General, Sir William Robinson, laid down the plans for the Upper and Lower Castle Yards in their present form. On the first floor of the south side of the Upper Yard are the luxury State Apartments, including St Patrick's Hall. These magnificent rooms served as home to the British-appointed Viceroys of Ireland.

St Patrick by Edward Smyth

Figure of Justice
Facing the Upper Yard above the main entrance from Cork Hill, this statue aroused much cynicism among Dubliners, who felt she was turning her back on the city.

★ **Throne Room**
This room is one of the grandest of the state apartments and contains a throne first installed for the visit of King George IV in 1821.

Wedgwood Room

Portrait Gallery

Bedford Tower (1761)

Entrance from Cork Hill

Entrance to State Apartments

Upper Yard

Bermingham Tower dates from the 13th century. It was turned into an elegant supper room around 1777.

Octagonal Tower (c.1812)

Record Tower (1226)

Entrance to Upper Yard

The treasury building constructed in 1717 is the oldest dedicate office block in Dublin.

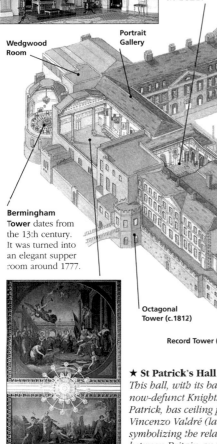

★ **St Patrick's Hall**
This hall, with its banners of the now-defunct Knights of St Patrick, has ceiling paintings by Vincenzo Valdré (late 1780s), symbolizing the relationship between Britain and Ireland.

The Chapel Royal was completed in 1814 by Francis Johnston. The 100 heads on the exterior of this Neo-Gothic church were carved by Edward Smyth.

ROBERT EMMET

Robert Emmet (1778–1803),
leader of the abortive 1803
rebellion, is remembered as
a heroic champion of Irish
liberty. His plan was to
capture Dublin Castle as a
signal for the country to rise
up against the Act of Union
(see p42). Emmet was
detained in the Kilmainham
Gaol and hanged, but the
defiant, patriotic speech he
made from the dock helped
to inspire future generations
of Irish freedom fighters.

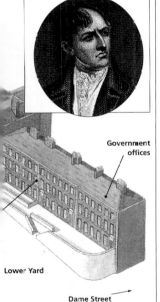

Government
offices

Lower Yard

Dame Street

STAR FEATURES

★ St Patrick's Hall

★ Throne Room

Manuscript (1874) from the Holy Koran written by calligrapher
Ahmad Shaikh in Kashmir, Chester Beatty Library

Chester Beatty
Library ❷

Clock Tower Building, Dublin Castle.
Tel 407 0750. 🕐 10am–5pm Mon–
Fri (Tue–Fri Oct–Apr), 11am–5pm Sat,
1pm–5pm Sun. 🔴 1 Jan, Good Fri,
24–26 Dec & public holidays. 🅿 ♿
ℹ️ **www**.cbl.ie

This world-renowned collection was named European
Museum of the Year in 2002.
It was bequeathed to Ireland
by the American mining mag-
nate and art collector Sir
Alfred Chester Beatty, who
died in 1968. This generous
act no doubt led to his
selection as Ireland's first
honorary citizen in 1957.

During his lifetime, Beatty
accumulated almost 300 copies
of the Koran, representing the
works of master calligraphers.
Also on display are 6,000-year-
old Babylonian stone tablets,
Greek papyri and biblical
material written in Coptic, the
ancient language of Egypt.

Treasures from the Far East
include a collection of Chinese
jade books – each leaf is made
from thinly cut jade, engraved
with Chinese characters which
are then filled with gold.
Burmese and Siamese art is
represented by the collection
of 18th- and 19th-century
Parabaiks, books of folk tales
with colourful illustrations on
mulberry leaf paper. The
Japanese collection includes
paintings, woodblock prints
and books and scrolls from
the 16th to 19th centuries.

One of the most beautiful
manuscripts in the western
European collection is the
Coëtivy Book of Hours, an
illuminated 15th-century
French prayer book.

City Hall ❸

Cork Hill, Dame St. **Map** C3. **Tel** 222
2204 🕐 10am–5.15pm Mon–Sat.
🔴 1 Jan, Good Fri & 24–26 Dec.
🚫 ♿ ℹ️ 📷

Designed by Thomas Cooley,
this imposing Corinthian-
style building was erected
between 1769 and 1779 as the
Royal Exchange. It was taken
over by Dublin Corporation
in 1852 as a meeting place for
the city council.

The building has been
restored to its original
condition and a permanent
multimedia exhibition, Dublin
City Hall – The Story of the
Capital, traces the evolution of
Dublin, from before the
Anglo-Norman invasion of
1170 to the present day.

City Hall from Parliament Street

Central courtyard of Powerscourt Townhouse Shopping Centre

Powerscourt Townhouse ❹

South Wi liam St. **Map** D4. *Tel* 671 7000. ◻ *10am–6pm Mon–Fri (8pm Thu), 9am–6pm Sat, noon–6pm Sun. See also **Shopping in Ireland** pp352–5.* **www**.pcwerscourtcentre.com

Completed in 1774 by Robert Mack, this grand mansion was built as the city home of Viscount Powerscourt, who also had a country estate at Enniskerry *(see pp134–5)*. Granite from the Powerscourt estate was used in its construction. Today the building houses one of Dublin's best shopping centres. Inside it still features the original grand mahogany staircase, and detailed plaster-work by Michael Stapleton.

The building became a drapery warehouse in the 1830s, and major restoration during

the 1960s turned it into a centre of specialist galleries, antique shops, jewellery stalls, cafés and other shop units. The enclosed central courtyard, topped by a glass dome, is a popular meeting place with Dubliners. The centre can also be reached from Grafton Street down the Johnson Court alley.

Temple Bar ❺

Map C3. **Temple Bar Information** *Tel* 677 2255. *Entertainment in Dublin* p114. **Project** 39 East Essex Street. *Tel* 881 9613. **Irish Film Institute** 6 Eustace Street. *Tel* 679 5744. 🎬 Diversions, (May–Sep). **www**.templebar.ie

Some of Dublin's best night spots, restaurants and unusual shops line these narrow, cobbled streets running between the Bank of Ireland *(see p60)* and Christ Church Cathedral. In the 18th century the area was home to many insalubrious characters – Fownes Street was noted for its brothels. It was also the birthplace of parliamentarian Henry Grattan *(see p40)*. Skilled craftsmen and artisans, such as clockmakers and printers, lived and worked around Temple Bar until post-war industrialization led to a decline in the area's fortunes.

In the 1970s, the CIE (the national transport authority) bought up parcels of land in this area to build a major bus depot. Before building, the CIE rented out, on cheap leases, some of the old retail and warehouse premises to

young artists and to record, clothing and book shops. The area developed an "alternative" identity, and when the development plans were scrapped the artists and retailers stayed on. Described by some cynics as the city's "officially designated arts zone", Temple Bar today is an exciting place with bars, restaurants, shops and several galleries. Stylish residential and commercial development is contributing further to the area's appeal.

Highlights include the **Project Arts Centre**, a highly respected venue for avant-garde performance art; and the **Irish Film Institute**, which shows art house and independent films, and has a popular restaurant/bar and shop.

Nearby Meeting House Square is one of the venues for Diversions, a summer programme of free outdoor concerts, theatre and film screenings. The National Photographic Archive and Gallery of Photography are also on the square and there is an excellent organic food market here on Saturdays, where you can sample oysters, salmon, cheese and other local produce.

The Temple Bar pub, established in 1840, located on Temple Bar

Wood Quay ❻

Map B3.

Named after the timber supports used to reclaim the land, Wood Quay has undergone excavations revealing the remains of one of the earliest Viking villages in Ireland *(see p79)*. The excavated area opened to public view in spring 2008.

Valuable and informative Viking artifacts can be seen at the Dublinia exhibition *(see p79)* and at the National Museum *(see pp66–7)*.

Strolling through the streets of Temple Bar

For hotels and restaurants in this region see pp294–8 and pp324–8

Former Synod Hall, now home to the Dublinia exhibition

Christ Church Cathedral ❼

See pp80–81.

Dublinia and the Viking World ❽

St Michael's Hill. **Map** B3. **Tel** 679 4611. ☐ Apr–Sep: 10am–5pm; Oct–Mar: 10am–4:30pm. ● 17 Mar & 23–26 Dec. 🎫 charge to enter Christ Church Cathedral via bridge. 🅰 **www**.dublinia.ie

The Dublinia exhibition covers the formative period of Dublin's history from the arrival of the Anglo-Normans in 1170 to the closure of the monasteries in the 1540s

(see p38). The exhibition is housed in the Neo-Gothic Synod Hall, which, up until 1983, was home to the ruling body of the Church of Ireland. The building and the hump-backed bridge linking it to Christ Church Cathedral date from the 1870s. Before Dublinia was established in 1993, the Synod Hall was used as a nightclub.

The exhibition is entirely interactive, encouraging the visitor to become an investigator of Dublin's past. Visitors enter via the basement where the Viking World exhibition tells the story of the notorious Scandinavian settlers. The exhibition continues on the ground floor, where a medieval city is depicted through life-size reconstructions including

a bustling market and the inside of a merchant's kitchen.

Major events in Dublin's history, such as the Black Death and the rebellion of Silken Thomas *(p39)* are also portrayed here as well as a large-scale model of Dublin circa 1500. An interactive archaeology room highlights excavations at nearby Wood Quay *(see p78)*.

The 60-m (200-ft) high St Michael's Tower offers one of the best vantage points for views across the city.

St Audoen's Church ❾

High St. Corn Market. **Map** B3. **Tel** 677 0088. ☐ May–Oct. 🎫

Tower of St Audoen's Church

Designated a national monument and open for visitors throughout the summer months, St Audoen's is the earliest surviving medieval church in Dublin.

The 15th-century name remains intact and the three bells date from 1423. The church stands in an attractive churchyard with well-maintained lawns and shrubs. To the rear of the churchyard, steps lead down to St Audoen's Arch, the only remaining gateway of the old city. Flanking the gate are restored sections of the 13th-century city walls.

Next door stands St Audoen's Roman Catholic Church, which was built in the 1840s. The two Pacific clam shells by the front door hold holy water.

THE VIKINGS IN DUBLIN

Viking raiders arrived in Ireland in the late 8th century and founded Dublin in 841. They built a fort where the River Poddle met the Liffey at a black pool (Dubh Linn), on the site of Dublin Castle. They also established a settlement along the banks of the Liffey at Wood Quay *(see p78)*. Much of their trade was based on silver, slaves and piracy.

Following their defeat by Brian Ború at the Battle of Clontarf in 1014 *(see p34)*, the Vikings integrated fully with the local Irish, adopting Christian beliefs. After Strongbow's Anglo-Norman invasion in 1170 *(see p36)*, the flourishing Hiberno-Viking trading community declined, and many were banished to a separate colony called Oxmantown, just north of the river.

Artist's impression of a Viking ship in Dublin Bay

Christ Church Cathedral ❼

Christ Church Cathedral was established by the Hiberno-Norse king of Dublin, Sitric "Silkbeard", and the first bishop of Dublin, Dunan. It was rebuilt by the Anglo-Norman archbishop, John Cumin in 1186. It is the cathedral for the Church of Ireland

Arms on Lord Mayor's pew

(Anglican) diocese of Dublin and Glendalough. By the 19th century it was in a bad state of repair, but was remodelled by architect George Street in the 1870s. The vast 12th-century crypt was restored in 2000.

★ **Medieval Lectern**
This beautiful brass lectern in the crypt's treasury, was hand-wrought during the Middle Ages. A matching lectern stands on the north side of the nave, in front of the pulpit.

Medieval stone carvings are on display in the north transept. Dating from about 1200, these exquisite Romanesque capitals feature a troupe of musicians and two human faces enveloped by legendary griffons.

Great Nave
The 25-m (68-ft) high nave has some fine early Gothic arches. On the north side, the original 13th-century wall leans out by as much as 50 cm (18 in) due to the weight of the roof.

Entrance

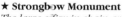

★ **Strongbow Monument**
The large effigy in chain armour is probably not Strongbow. However, his remains are buried in the cathedral and the curious half-figure may be part of his original tomb.

The bridge to the Synod Hall was added when the cathedral was being rebuilt in the 1870s.

STAR FEATURES

★ Crypt

★ Medieval Lectern

★ Strongbow Monument

For hotels and restaurants in this region see pp294–8 and pp324–8

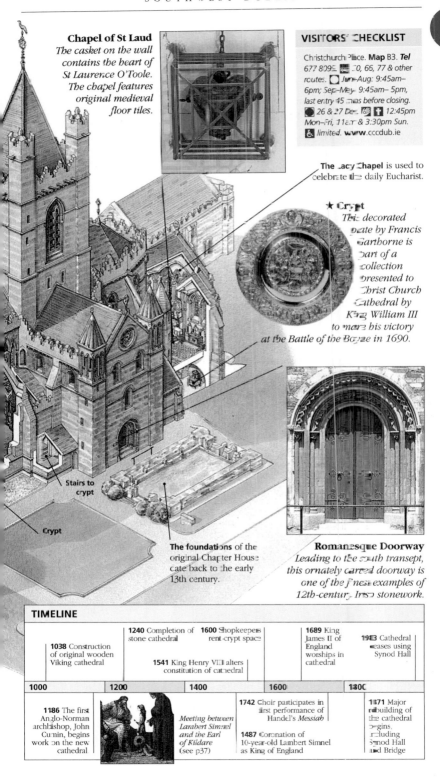

Chapel of St Laud
The casket on the wall contains the heart of St Laurence O'Toole. The chapel features original medieval floor tiles.

VISITORS' CHECKLIST

Christchurch Place. **Map** B3. **Tel** 677 8099. 50, 65, 77 & other routes. Jun–Aug: 9:45am–6pm; Sep–May: 9:45am–5pm, last entry 45 mins before closing. 26 & 27 Dec. 12:45pm Mon–Fri, 11am & 3:30pm Sun. limited. www.cccdub.ie

The **Lady Chapel** is used to celebrate the daily Eucharist.

★ Crypt
This decorated plate by Francis Garthorne is part of a collection presented to Christ Church Cathedral by King William III to mark his victory at the Battle of the Boyne in 1690.

Stairs to crypt

Crypt

The foundations of the original Chapter House date back to the early 13th century.

Romanesque Doorway
Leading to the south transept, this ornately carved doorway is one of the finest examples of 12th-century Irish stonework.

TIMELINE

1038 Construction of original wooden Viking cathedral

1186 The first Anglo-Norman archbishop, John Cumin, begins work on the new cathedral

1240 Completion of stone cathedral

1541 King Henry VIII alters constitution of cathedral

Meeting between Lambert Simnel and the Earl of Kildare (see p37)

1600 Shopkeepers rent crypt space

1742 Choir participates in first performance of Handel's *Messiah*

1487 Coronation of 10-year-old Lambert Simnel as King of England

1689 King James II of England worships in cathedral

1983 Cathedral ceases using Synod Hall

1871 Major rebuilding of the cathedral begins, including Synod Hall and Bridge

1000 · 1200 · 1400 · 1600 · 1800

Tailors' Hall ❿

Back Lane. **Map** B4. **Tel** *454 1786.*
⬚ *by appt only.* **www**.antaisce.org

Dublin's only surviving
guildhall preserves a
delightful corner of old
Dublin in an otherwise busy
redevelopment zone. Built in
1706, it stands behind a limestone arch in a quiet cobbled
yard. The building is the
oldest guildhall in Ireland and
was used by various trade
groups including hosiers,
saddlers and barber-surgeons
as well as tailors. It also
hosted political meetings –
Wolfe Tone addressed a
public United Irishmen rally
here before the 1798 rebellion
(see p41). The building closed
in the early 1960s due to
neglect, but an appeal by
Desmond Guinness saw it
refurbished. It now houses An
Taisce (the Irish National Trust).

**Façade of Tailors' Hall, home
of the Irish National Trust**

Saint Patrick's Cathedral with Minot's Tower and spire

Saint Patrick's Cathedral ⓫

Saint Patrick's Close. **Map** B4.
Tel *453 9472.* ⬚ *9am–5:30pm daily
(Nov–Feb: 9am–5pm Sat, 9am–3pm
Sun) – last admission 30 mins before
closing.* 🔲 *visiting restricted during
service times (9am & 5:30pm).* 📷
www.stpatrickscathedral.ie

Ireland's largest church was
founded beside a sacred well
where St Patrick is said to have
baptized converts circa AD 450.
A stone slab bearing a Celtic
cross and covering the well was
unearthed over a century ago.
It is now preserved in the west
end of the cathedral's nave.
The original building was
just a wooden chapel and
remained so until 1192 when
Archbishop John Comyn
rebuilt the cathedral in stone.

Over the centuries, Saint
Patrick's came to be seen as
the people's church, while the
older Christ Church Cathedral
(see pp80–81) nearby was
more associated with the
British establishment. In the
mid-17th century, Huguenot
refugees from France arrived
in Dublin, and were given the
Lady Chapel by the Dean and
Chapter as their place of worship. The chapel was
separated from the rest of the
cathedral and used by the
Huguenots until the late 18th
century. Today Saint Patrick's
Cathedral is the Anglican/
Episcopalian Church of
Ireland's national cathedral.

Much of the present building
dates back to work completed
between 1254 and 1270. The
cathedral suffered over the
centuries from desecration,
fire and neglect but, thanks to
the generosity of Sir Benjamin
Guinness, it underwent extensive restoration during the
1860s. The building is 91 m
(300 ft) long; at the western
end is a 43-m (141-ft) tower,
restored by Archbishop Minot
in 1370 and now known as
Minot's Tower. The spire was
added in the 18th century.

The interior is dotted with
busts, brasses and monuments.
A leaflet available at the front
desk helps identify them. The
largest, most colourful and
elaborate tomb was dedicated
to the Boyle family in the
17th century. Erected by
Richard Boyle, Earl of Cork, in
memory of his second wife
Katherine, it is decorated with
painted figures of his family,

JONATHAN SWIFT (1667–1745)

Jonathan Swift was born in Dublin and
educated at Trinity College *(see
pp62–3)*. He left for England in
1689, but returned in 1694 when
his political career failed. Back in
Ireland he began a life in the
church, becoming Dean of St
Patrick's in 1713. In addition to
his clerical duties, Swift was a
prolific political commentator –
his best-known work, *Gulliver's
Travels*, contains a bitter satire on
Anglo-Irish relations. Swift's personal
life, particularly his friendship with two
younger women, Ester Johnson, better known as Stella, and
Hester Vanhomrigh, attracted criticism. In his final years, Swift
suffered from Ménière's disease – an illness
of the ear which led many to believe him insane.

---

including his wife's parents. Other famous citizens remembered in the church include the harpist Turlough O'Carolan (1570–1738) *(see p24)* and Douglas Hyde (1860–1949), the first President of Ireland.

Many visitors come to see the memorials associated with Jonathan Swift, the satirical writer and Dean of Saint Patrick's. In the south aisle is "Swift's Corner", containing various memorabilia such as an altar table and a bookcase holding his death mask. A self-penned epitaph can be found on the wall on the southwest side of the nave. A few steps away, two brass plates mark his grave and that of his beloved Stella, who died before him in 1728.

At the west end of the nave is an old door with a hole in it – a relic from a feud which took place between the Lords Kilcare and Ormonde in 1492. The latter took refuge in the Chapter House, but a truce was soon made and a hole was cut in the door by Lord Kildare so the two could shake hands in friendship.

Marsh's Library ⑫

St Patrick's Close. **Map** 34.
Tel 454 3511 ☐ 9.30am–1pm & 2–5pm Mon & Wed–Fri, 10am–1pm Sat. ☐ Tue & Sun, 10 days at Christmas & public hols. ☑
www.marshlibrary.ie

The oldest public library in Ireland was built in 1701 for the Archbishop of Dublin, Narcissus Marsh. It was designed by Sir William Robinson, architect of much of Dublin Castle *(see pp76–7)* and the Royal Hospital Kilmainham *(see p97)*.

Inside, the bookcases are topped by a mitre and feature carved gables with lettering in gold leaf. To the rear of the library are wired alcoves (or "cages") where readers were locked in with rare books. The collection, from the 16th, 17th and early 18th centuries, includes irreplaceable volumes, such as Bishop Bedell's 1685 translation of the Old Testament into Irish and Clarendon's *History of the Rebellion*, with anti-Scottish margin notes by Jonathan Swift.

Statue of Virgin and Child in Whitefriar Street Carmelite Church

Whitefriar Street Carmelite Church ⑬

56 Aungier St. **Map** C4.
Tel 475 8821. ☐ 8am–7pm Mon & Wed–Sat, 8am–9pm Tue, 9:30am–7pm Sun & public hols.
www.carmelites.ie

Designed by George Papworth, this Catholic church was built in 1827. It stands alongside the site of a Medieval Carmelite foundation of which nothing remains.

In contrast to the two Church of Ireland cathedrals, St Patrick's and Christ Church, which are usually full of tourists, this church is frequented by city worshippers. Every day they come to light candles to various saints, including St Valentine – the patron saint of lovers. His remains, previously buried in the cemetery of St Hippolytus in Rome, were offered to the church as a gift from Pope Gregory XVI in 1836. Today they rest beneath the commemorative statue of St Valentine, which stands in the northeast corner of the church beside the high altar.

Nearby is a Flemish oak statue of the Virgin and Child, dating from the late 15th or early 16th century. It may have belonged to St Mary's Abbey *(see p93)* and is believed to be the only wooden statue of its kind to escape destruction when Ireland's monasteries were sacked at the time of the Reformation *(see p41)*.

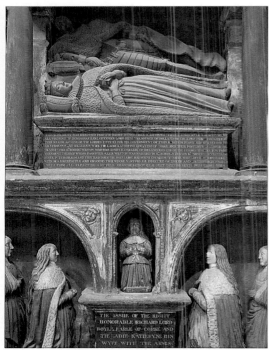

Carved monument (1632) to the Boyle family in St Patrick's Cathedral

NORTH OF THE LIFFEY

Dublin's northside was the last part of the city to be developed during the 18th century. The city authorities envisioned an area of wide, leafy avenues, but the reality of today's heavy traffic has rather spoiled their original plans. Nonetheless, O'Connell Street, lined with fine statues and monuments, is an impressive thoroughfare. This is where Dubliners come to shop and some of the adjacent streets, particularly Moore Street, have a colourful parade of stalls and street vendors offering cut-price tobacco.

Some public buildings, such as James Gandon's glorious Custom House and majestic Four Courts, together with the

Statue of James Joyce on Earl Street North

historic General Post Office (*see p89*), add grace to the area. The Rotunda Hospital, Europe's first purpose-built maternity hospital, is another fine building. Dublin's two most celebrated theatres, the Abbey and the Gate, act as a cultural magnet as do the Dublin Writers Museum and the James Joyce Cultural Centre, two museums dedicated to writers who lived in the city.

Some of the city's finest Georgian streetscapes are found in the north of the city. Many have been neglected for decades, but thankfully some areas, most notably North Great George's Street, are undergoing restoration.

SIGHTS AT A GLANCE

Museums and Galleries
Dublin Writers Museum ⑨
Hugh Lane Gallery ⑩
James Joyce Centre ⑤
National Leprechaun Museum ⑯
Old Jameson's Distillery ⑬

Historic Buildings
Custom House ①
Four Courts ⑮
King's Inns ⑪
Rotunda Hospital ⑦

Historic Streets and Bridges
Ha'penny Bridge ⑱
O'Connell Street ③
Smithfield ⑫

Theatres
Abbey Theatre ②
Gate Theatre ⑥

Churches
St Mary's Abbey ⑯
St Mary's Pro-Cathedral ④
St Michan's Church ⑭

Parks and Gardens
Garden of Remembrance ⑧

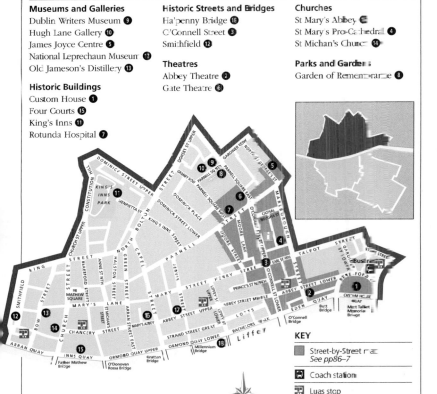

KEY
- Street-by-Street map *See pp86–7*
- Coach station
- Luas stop
- Tourist information

0 metres 250
0 yards 250

Street-by-Street: Around O'Connell Street

Throughout the Georgian era, O'Connell Street was very much the fashionable part of Dublin to live in. However, the 1916 Easter Rising destroyed many of the fine buildings along the street, including much of the

Detail of pavement mosaic, Moore Street

General Post Office – only its original façade still stands. Today, this main thoroughfare is lined with shops and businesses. Other attractions nearby include St Mary's Pro-Cathedral and James Gandon's Custom House, overlooking the Liffey.

James Joyce Cultural Centre
This well-restored Georgian town house contains a small Joyce museum ⑤

Parnell Monument (1911)

Gate Theatre
Founded in 1928, the Gate is renowned for its productions of contemporary drama ⑥

Rotunda Hospital
Housed in the Rotunda Hospital is a chapel built in the 1750s to the design of Richard Cassels. It features lovely stained-glass windows, fluted columns, panelling and intricate iron balustrades ⑦

Moore Street Market is the busiest of the streets off O'Connell. Be prepared for the shrill cries of the stall holders offering an enormous variety of fresh fruit, vegetables and cut flowers.

The Spire, an elegant stainless steel landmark rising to 120 m (394 ft).

The General Post Office, the grandest building on O'Connell Street, was the centre of the 1916 Rising.

James Larkin Statue (1981)

KEY

— Suggested route

🚉 Luas stop

ℹ Tourist information

0 metres   50

0 yards   50

STAR SIGHTS

★ Custom House

★ O'Connell Street

St Mary's Pro-Cathedral
Built around 1825, this is Dublin's main place of worship for Catholics. The plaster relief above the altar in the sanctuary depicts The Ascension ❹

LOCATOR MAP
See Dublin map pp 18–19

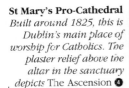

The statue of James Joyce (1990), by Marjorie Fitzgibbon, commemorates one of Ireland's most famous novelists. Born in Dublin in 1882, he catalogued the people and streets of Dublin in *Dubliners* and in his most celebrated work, *Ulysses*.

Abbey Theatre
Ireland's national theatre is known throughout the world for its productions by Irish playwrights, such as Sean O'Casey and JM Synge ❷

★ O'Connell Street
This monument to Daniel O'Connell by John Foley took 19 years to complete from the laying of its foundation stone in 1864 ❸

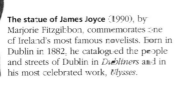

CUSTOM HOUSE QUAY

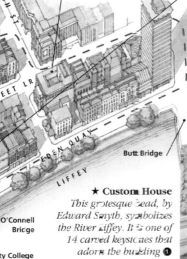

Butt Bridge

★ Custom House
This grotesque head, by Edward Smyth, symbolizes the River Liffey. It is one of 14 carved keystones that adorn the building ❶

O'Connell Bridge

To Trinity College

Illuminated façade of the Custom House reflected in the Liffey

Custom House ❶

Custom House Quay. **Map** E2 **Tel**
888 2000. ● closed to the public.

This majestic building was
designed as the Custom
House by the English
architect James Gandon.
However, just nine years after
its completion, the 1800 Act
of Union *(see p42)* transferred
the customs and excise
business to London, rendering
the building practically
obsolete. In 1921, supporters
of Sinn Féin celebrated their
election victory by setting
light to what they saw as a
symbol of British imperialism.
The fire blazed for five days
causing extensive damage.
Reconstruction took place in
1926, although further
deterioration meant that the
building was not completely
restored until 1991, when it reopened as government offices.
The main façade is made
up of pavilions at each end
with a Doric portico in its
centre. The arms of Ireland
crown the two pavilions and
a series of 14 allegorical
heads, by Dublin sculptor
Edward Smyth, form the
keystones of arches and
entrances. These heads
depict Ireland's main rivers
and the Atlantic Ocean.
Topping the central copper
dome is a statue of
Commerce, while the north

façade is decorated with
figures representing Europe,
Africa, America and Asia.
The best view of the building
is from the south of the Liffey
beyond Matt Talbot Bridge.

Abbey Theatre ❷

26 Lower Abbey St. **Map** E2. **Tel**
878 7222. ○ for performances only.
Box office ○ 10:30am–7pm Mon–
Fri. See also **Entertainment in
Dublin** p108. www.abbeytheatre.ie

Logo of the Abbey Theatre

The Abbey staged its first play
in 1904 with WB Yeats and
Lady Gregory as co-directors.
The early years of this much-
lauded national theatre
witnessed works by WB Yeats,
JM Synge and Sean O'Casey.
Many were controversial:
nationalist sensitivities were
severely tested in 1926 during
the premiere of O'Casey's *The
Plough and the Stars* when the

flag of the Irish Free State
appeared on stage in a
scene which featured a pub
frequented by prostitutes.
Today, the Abbey is
supported by the Arts Council
of Ireland/An Chomhairle
Ealaíon and its function is to
nurture new Irish writing and
artistic talent and produce an
annual programme of diverse,
engaging, innovative Irish and
international theatre.
Productions have included
work by Wilde, Beckett,
Shakespeare and Brecht, as
well as new plays by Marina
Carr, Tom Mac Intyre, Billy
Roche and Sam Shepard.

O'Connell Street ❸

Map D1–D2.

O'Connell Street is very
different from the original
plans of Irish aristocrat Luke
Gardiner. When he bought
the land in the mid-18th
century, Gardiner envisioned
a grand residential parade
with an elegant mall running
along its centre. Such plans
were short-lived. The construction of Carlisle (now
O'Connell) Bridge in 1790
transformed the street into the
city's main north-south route.
Also, several buildings were
destroyed during the 1916
Easter Rising and the Irish
Civil War. Since the 1960s

many of the old buildings have been replaced by the plate glass and neon of fast food joints, amusement arcades and chain stores.

A few venerable buildings remain, such as the General Post Office (1818), Gresham Hotel (1817), Clery's department store (1822) and the Royal Dublin Hotel, part of which occupies the street's only original town house.

A walk down the central mall is the most enjoyable way to see the street's mix of architectural styles and take a close look at the series of monuments lining the route. At the south end stands a massive monument to Daniel O'Connell (see p42), unveiled in 1882. The street, which throughout the 19th century had been called Sackville Street, was renamed after O'Connell in 1922. Higher up, almost facing the General Post Office, is an animated statue of James Larkin (1867–1943), leader of the Dublin general strike in 1913. The next statue is of Father Theobald Mathew (1790–1856), founder of the Pioneer Total

South end of O'Connell Street with monument to Daniel O'Connell

Abstinence Movement. At the north end of the street is the obelisk-shaped monument to Charles Stewart Parnell (1846–91), who was leader of the Home Rule Party and known as the "uncrowned King of Ireland" (see p43). The Dublin Spire sits on the site where Nelson's column used to be. It is a stainless steel, conical spire which tapers from a 3-m (10-ft) diameter base to a 10-cm (4-in) pointed tip of optical glass at a height of 120 m (394 ft), making it the city's tallest structure.

Statue of James Larkin (1981) in O'Connell Street

THE GENERAL POST OFFICE (GPO)

Built in 1818 halfway along O'Connell Street, the GPO became a symbol of the 1916 Irish Rising. Members of the Irish Volunteers and Irish Citizen Army seized the building on Easter Monday and Patrick Pearse (see p44) read out the Proclamation of the Irish Republic from its steps. The rebels remained inside for a week, but shelling from the British eventually forced them out. At first, many viewed the Rising unfavourably. However, as WB Yeats wrote, matters "changed utterly" and a "terrible beauty was born" when, during the following weeks, 14 of the leaders were caught and shot at Kilmainham Gaol (see p97). A museum has a copy of the 1916 Proclamation and accounts from the staff who were working that day. It also explores the influence of the post office in Ireland, and has a beautiful stamp collection.

Irish Life magazine cover showing the 1916 Easter Rising

St Mary's Pro-Cathedral ④

83 Marlborough St. **Map** D2. **Tel** 874 5441. ☐ 10am–6:45pm Mon–Fri 7:15pm. **Sat,** 8am–1:45pm & 5:30–7:45pm Sun. www.procathedral.ie

Dedicated in 1825 before Catholic emancipation (see p42), St Mary's backstreet site was the best the city's Anglo-Irish leaders were to allow a Catholic cathedral.

The façade, based on a Greek temple, has columns support a pediment with statues of St Mary, St Patrick and St Laurence O'Toole, 12th-century Archbishop of Dublin and patron saint of the city. Inside, one striking feature is the intricately carved high altar.

St Mary's is home to the famous Palestrina Choir, with which the great tenor John McCormack (see p40) began his career in 1904. The choir still sings on Sundays at 11am.

Austere Neo-Classical interior of St Mary's Pro-Cathedral

James Joyce Centre ❺

35 North Great George's St. **Map** D1.
Tel 878 8547. 🕒 10am–5pm Tue–
Sat, noon–5pm Sun. ⬤ 1 Jan, Good
Fri, 22–31 Dec & public hols. 🎟️ 📷
www.jamesjoyce.ie

This agreeable stop on the literary tourist trail is primarily a meeting place for Joyce enthusiasts, but is also worth visiting for its Georgian interior. The centre is in a 1784 town house which was built for the Earl of Kenmare. Michael Stapleton, one of the greatest stuccoers of his time, contributed to the plasterwork, of which the friezes are particularly noteworthy.

The centre's permanent and temporary exhibitions interpret and illuminate aspects of Joyce's life and work. Among the displays are biographies of real people on whom Joyce based his characters. Professor Dennis J Maginni, a peripheral character in *Ulysses*, ran a dancing school from this town house. Leopold and Molly Bloom, the central characters of *Ulysses*, lived a short walk away at No. 7 Eccles Street. The centre also organizes walking tours of Joyce's Dublin.

At the top of the road, on Great Denmark Street, is the Jesuit-run Belvedere College attended by Joyce between 1893 and 1898. He recalls his unhappy schooldays there in *A Portrait of the Artist as a Young Man*. The college's interior contains some of Stapleton's best and most colourful plasterwork (1785).

JAMES JOYCE (1882–1941)

Born in Dublin, Joyce spent most of his adult life in Europe. He used the city of Dublin as the setting for all his major works including *Dubliners*, *A Portrait of the Artist as a Young Man* and *Ulysses*. Joyce claimed that if the city was ever destroyed it could be recreated through the pages of *Ulysses*. However, the Irish branded the book pornographic and banned it until the 1960s.

Gate Theatre ❻

1 Cavendish Row. **Map** D1. 🕒 for
performances only. **Box office** *Tel*
874 4045. 🕒 10am–7pm Mon–Sat.
See also **Entertainment in Dublin**
pp108. www.gate-theatre.ie

Entrance to the Gate Theatre

Renowned for its staging of contemporary international drama in Dublin, the Gate Theatre was founded in 1928 by Hilton Edwards and Mícheál Mac Liammóir. The latter is now best remembered for *The Importance of Being Oscar*, his long-running one-man show about the writer Oscar Wilde *(see p22).* An early success was Denis Johnston's *The Old Lady Says No*, so-called because of the margin notes made on one of his scripts by Lady Gregory, founding director of the Abbey Theatre *(see p88).* Although still noted for staging new plays, the Gate's current output often includes classic Irish plays. Among the young talent to get their first break here were James Mason and a teenage Orson Welles.

Rotunda Hospital ❼

Parnell Square West. **Map** D1.
Tel 873 0700. www.rotunda.ie

Standing in the middle of Parnell Square is Europe's first purpose-built maternity hospital. Founded in 1745 by Dr Bartholomew Mosse, the design of the hospital is similar to that of Leinster House *(see p65).* German-born architect Richard Cassels designed both buildings, as well as Powerscourt Townhouse *(see p78)* and Russborough House *(see pp132–3).*

On the first floor is a beautiful chapel featuring striking stained-glass windows and exuberant Rococo plasterwork and ceiling (1755) by the German stuccoer Bartholomew Cramillion. The ceiling portrays the symbol of fertility and the virtues of faith, hope and charity. Nowadays, over 8,000 babies are born in the Rotunda Hospital every year.

Stained-glass Venetian window (c.1863) in Rotunda Hospital's chapel

Garden of Remembrance ⓽

Parnell Square. **Map** C1. ☐ *dawn-dusk daily.* **www**.heritageireland.ie

At the northern end of Parnell Square is a small park dedicated to the men and women who have died in the pursuit of Irish freedom. The Garden of Remembrance marks the spot where several leaders of the 1916 Easter Rising were held overnight before being taken to Kilmainham Gaol *(see p97)*. It was also where the Irish Volunteers movement was formed in 1913.

Designed by Daithí Hanly, the garden was opened by President Eamon de Valera *(see p45)* in 1966, to mark the 50th anniversary of the Easter Rising. In the centre of the garden's well-kept lawns is a cruciform pool. A mosaic on the floor of the pool depicts abandoned, broken swords, spears and shields, symbolizing peace. The focal point at one end of the garden is a large bronze sculpture by Oisín Kelly (1971) of the legendary *Children of Lir*, who were changed into swans by their stepmother *(see p27)*.

Children of Lir in the Garden of Remembrance

Gallery of Writers at Dublin Writers Museum

Dublin Writers Museum ⓽

18 Parnell Sq North. **Map** C1 **Tel** 872 2077. ☐ 10am–5pm Mon–Sat; (Jun–Aug. 10am–6pm Mon–Fri) 11am–5pm Sun & public hols (last adm: 45 mins before closing). ● 25 & 26 Dec. ♿ ☐ www.writersmuseum.com

Opened in 1991, the museum occupies a tasteful 18th-century town house. There are displays relating to Irish literature in all its forms from 300 years ago to the present day. The exhibits include paintings, manuscripts, letters, rare editions and mementoes of many of Ireland's finest authors. There are a number of temporary exhibits and a sumptuously decorated Gallery of Writers upstairs. The museum also hosts frequent poetry readings and lectures. A specialist bookstore, providing an out-of-print search service adds to the relaxed, friendly ambience.

Hugh Lane Gallery ⓾

Charlemont House, Parnell Square North. **Map** C . **Tel** 222 5550. ☐ 10am–6pm Tue–Thu, 10am–5pm Fri & Sat, 11am–5pm Sun. ● 24–26 Dec. www.hughlane.ie

Art collector Sir Hugh Lane donated his collection of Impressionist paintings to the Dublin Corporation in 1905, but the lack of a suitable location for them prompted Lane to begin transferring his gift to the National Gallery in London. The Corporation then proposed Charlemont House and Lane relented. However, before Lane's revised will could be witnessed, he died on board the *Lusitania (see p178)*. This led to a 50-year dispute which has been resolved by the Corporation and the National Gallery swapping the collection every five years.

Besides the Lane bequest of paintings by Degas, Renoir and Monet, the gallery has an extensive collection of modern Irish paintings and a sculpture hall with work by Rodin and others. An exciting addition is a bequest by John Edwards of the contents of Francis Bacon's renowned London studio. In 2009, the gallery celebrated Francis Bacon's centenary.

Beach Scene (c.1876) by Edgar Degas, Hugh Lane Municipal Gallery

Detail of wood carving (c.1724) at St Michan's Church

King's Inns ⓫

Henrietta St/Constitution Hill.
Map B1 ◐ *to the public.*

This classically proportioned public building was founded in 1795 as a place of residence and study for barristers. To build it, James Gandon chose to seal off the end of Henrietta Street, which at the time was one of Dublin's most fashionable addresses. Francis Johnston added the graceful cupola in 1816, and the building was finally completed in 1817. Inside is a fine Dining Hall, and the Registry of Deeds (formerly the Prerogative Court). The west façade has two doorways flanked by Classical caryatids carved by Edward Smyth. The male figure, with book and quill, represents the law.

Sadly, much of the area around Constitution Hill is less attractive than it was in Georgian times. However, the gardens, which are open to the public, are still pleasing.

Caryatid, King's Inns

Smithfield ⓬

Map A2.

Laid out in the mid-17th century as a marketplace, Smithfield used to be one of Dublin's oldest residential areas. However the two and a half acre space received a £3.5 million makeover with a well-designed pedestrian cobbled plaza. It is used as a venue for outdoor civic events and is lit by tall gas lighting masts. The traditional horse fair is still held here on the first Sunday of the month. The Lighthouse cultural cinema is a welcome addition to the area.

Old Jameson's Distillery ⓭

Bow St. **Map** A2. **Tel** 807 2355.
◯ 9am–6pm daily (last tour: 5:30pm).
● Good Friday, 25 & 26 Dec. 🎫 ▣
🍴 ▢ www.jamesonwhiskey.com

Proof of investment in the emerging Smithfield area is this large exhibition in a restored part of John Jameson's distillery, which produced whiskey from 1780 until 1971. A visit here starts with a video and further whiskey-related facts are then explained on a 40-minute tour. This takes you around displays set out as a working distillery, with different rooms devoted to the various stages of production.

The tour guides show how the Irish process differs from that of Scotch whisky: here the barley is dried with clean air, while in Scotland it is smoked over peat. The claim is that the Irish product is a smoother, less smoky tipple. After the tour, visitors can test this in the bar.

Sampling different brands at Old Jameson's Distillery

St Michan's Church ⓮

Church St. **Map** B3. **Tel** 872 4154.
◯ mid-Mar–Oct: 10am–12:45pm & 2–4:45pm Mon–Fri, 10am–12:45pm Sat; Nov–mid-Mar: 12:30–3:30pm Mon–Fri, 10am–12:45pm Sat. 🎫 ▣
▢ ♿ limited.

Largely rebuilt in 1685 on the site of an 11th-century Hiberno-Viking church, the dull façade of St Michan's hides a more exciting interior. Deep in its vaults lie a number of bodies preserved because of the dry atmosphere created by the church's magnesian limestone walls. Their wooden caskets, however, have cracked open, revealing the intact bodies, complete with skin and strands of hair. Among those thought to lie here are the brothers Henry and John Sheares, leaders of the 1798 rebellion *(see p41)*, who were executed that year.

Other less gory attractions include an organ (1724) on which Handel is said to have played. It is thought that the churchyard contains the unmarked grave of United Irishman Robert Emmet *(see p77)*, leader of the abortive 1803 Rising.

Four Courts ⓯

Inns Quay (public entrance: Morgan Place). **Map** B3. **Tel** 872 5555.
◯ 9:30am–12:30pm, 2–4:30pm Mon–Fri (when courts in session).

Completed in 1802 by James Gandon, this majestic public building was virtually gutted 120 years later during the Irish Civil War *(see pp44–5)*. The Public Records Office, with its irreplaceable collection of documents dating back to the 12th century, was also destroyed by fire.

By 1932, the main buildings were sympathetically restored using Gandon's original design. An imposing copper-covered lantern dome rises above the six-columned Corinthian portico, which is crowned with the figures of Moses, Justice, Mercy, Wisdom and Authority. This central section is flanked by two wings containing the four original courts. An information panel gives details about the building's history

The Ha'penny Bridge looking from Temple Bar to Liffey Street

St Mary's Abbey 16

Meetinghouse Lane. **Map** C2. *Tel 833 1618.* ◯ *call the office of public works on 086 606 2729 for opening times.* 📷 *www.heritageireland.ie*

Founded by Benedictines in 1139, but transferred to the Cistercian order in 1147, this was one of the largest and most important monasteries in medieval Ireland. As well as controlling extensive estates, the abbey acted as state treasury and meeting place for the Council of Ireland It was during a council meeting in St Mary's that "Silken Thomas" Fitzgerald *(see p38)* renounced his allegiance to Henry VIII and marched out to raise the short-lived rebellion of 1534. The monastery was dissolved in 1539 and during the 17th century the site served as a quarry.

All that remains today is the vaulted chamber of the Chapter House containing a model of how it would have looked 800 years ago.

National Leprechaun Museum 17

Twilft House. Jervis St. **Map** C2. *Tel 873 3899.* ◯ *9.30am–6.30pm daily (last adm 5:45pm).* 📷 ♿ 📷

This charming museum focuses on Irish myths and folklore, taking visitors inside Celtic culture to learn about leprechauns, fairies, banshees and other mythological creatures. Children will enjoy the lively storytelling by expert guides, but there is plenty to keep adults amused too.

Ha'penny Bridge 18

Map D3.

Linking the Temple Bar area *(see p78)* and Liffey Street, this high-arched cast-iron footbridge is used by thousands of people every day. It was built by John Windsor, an ironworker from Shropshire, England. One of Dublin's most photographed sights, it was originally named the Wellington Bridge. It is now officially called the Liffey Bridge, but is also known as the Ha'penny Bridge. Opened in 1816, the bridge got its better known nickname from the halfpenny toll that was levied on it up until 1919. Restoration work, which included the installation of period lanterns, has made the bridge even more attractive.

James Gandon's Four Courts overlooking the River Liffey

FURTHER AFIELD

There are many interesting sights just outside the city centre. The best part of a day can be spent exploring the western suburbs taking in the Museum of Modern Art housed in the splendid Royal Kilmainham Hospital and the eerie Kilmainham Gaol. Phoenix Park, Europe's largest city park, is a good place for a stroll and also has a zoo. Further north are the National Botanic Gardens, with over 20,000 plant species from around the world. Nearby is Marino Casino, one of Ireland's finest examples of Palladian architecture.

Candelabra at Malahide Castle

The magnificent coastline with its stunning views of Dublin Bay is easily reached by the DART rail network. It encompasses the towering promontory of Howth, while the highlights of the southern stretch are around Dalkey village and Killiney Bay. One of many Martello towers built as defences along this coast is known as the James Joyce Tower and houses a collection of Joyce memorabilia. To the northeast, a bit further from the city centre, is Malahide Castle, former home of the Talbot family.

SIGHTS AT A GLANCE

Museums and Galleries
Guinness Storehouse ❹
Irish Museum of Modern Art/
  Royal Hospital Kilmainham ❸
James Joyce Tower ⓮
Kilmainham Gaol ❷

National Museum of Ireland –
  Decorative Arts & History ❾
Shaw's Birthplace ❻

Parks and Gardens
Glasnevin Cemetery ❿
National Botanic Gardens ❺
Phoenix Park ❶

Historic Buildings
Casino Marino ❼
Dublin Docklands ❽
Malahide Castle ⓫

Towns and Villages
Dalkey ⓯
Dun Laoghaire ⓭
Howth ⓬
Killiney ⓰

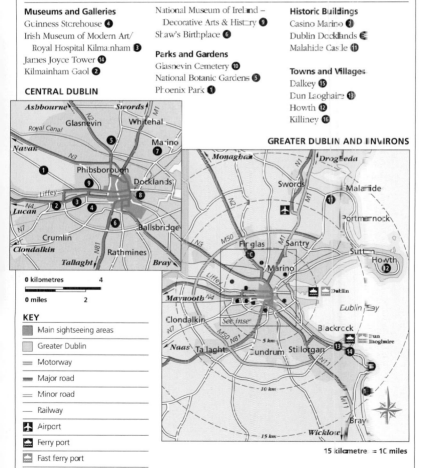

CENTRAL DUBLIN

GREATER DUBLIN AND ENVIRONS

KEY
- Main sightseeing areas
- Greater Dublin
- Motorway
- Major road
- Minor road
- Railway
- ✈ Airport
- Ferry port
- Fast ferry port

0 kilometres   4
0 miles   2

15 kilometres = 10 miles

◁ **Martello tower at Howth Head**

Phoenix Park ●

Park Gate, Conyngham Rd, Dublin 8.
▦ 10, 25, 26, 37, 38, 39 & many
other routes. ☐ 7am–11pm daily.
Phoenix Park Visitor Centre *Tel*
677 0095. ☐ Mar–Oct: 10am–6pm
daily; Nov–Feb: 9:30am–5:30pm Wed–
Sun. ▨ ☐ ⬛ ⬛ ground floor only.
www.phoenixpark.ie Zoo *Tel* 474
8900. ☐ Mar–Sep: 9:30am–6pm
daily; Oct: 9:30am–5:30pm daily;
Nov–Dec: 9:30am–4pm daily; Jan:
9:30am–4:30pm daily; Feb:
9:30am–5pm daily. (Last adm: 1 hr
before closing). ▨ ⬛ ⬛ ⬛
www.dublinzoo.ie

Just to the west of the city
centre, ringed by an 11-km
(7-mile) wall, is Europe's
largest enclosed city park.
The name "Phoenix" is said to
be a corruption of the Gaelic
Fionn Uisce, or "clear water".

The **Phoenix Column** is
crowned by a statue of the
mythical bird. Phoenix Park
originated in 1662, when the
Duke of Ormonde turned the
land into a deer park. In 1745
it was landscaped and opened
to the public.

Near Park Gate is the lakeside **People's Garden** – the
only part of the park which
has been cultivated. A little
further on are the **Zoological
Gardens**, established in 1830,
making them the third oldest
zoo in the world. The zoo is
renowned for the successful
breeding of lions, including
the one that appears at the
beginning of MGM movies.
The African Plains savannah
houses the larger residents.

In addition to the Phoenix
Column, the park has two
other conspicuous monuments.
The **Wellington
Testimonial**, a 63-m
(206-ft) obelisk, was
begun in 1817 and
completed in 1861. Its
bronze bas-reliefs were
made from captured
French cannons. The

**Pope John Paul II celebrating Mass
in Phoenix Park in 1979**

27-m (90-ft) steel **Papal Cross**
marks the spot where the pope
celebrated Mass in front of
one million people in 1979.
Buildings within the park
include two 18th-century
houses: **Áras an Uachtaráin**,
the Irish President's official
residence, for which 325 tickets
are issued every Saturday for a
free guided tour, and Deerfield,
home of the US Ambassador.
Ashtown Castle is a restored
17th-century tower house,
now home to the Phoenix
Park Visitor Centre.

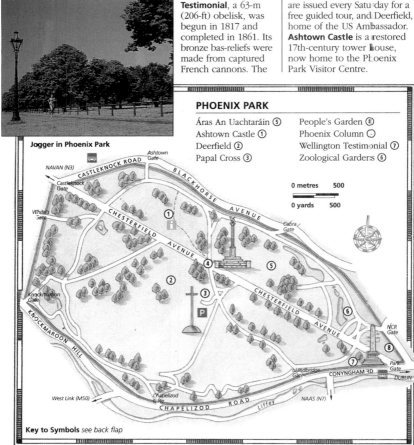

Jogger in Phoenix Park

PHOENIX PARK

Áras An Uachtaráin ⑤
Ashtown Castle ①
Deerfield ②
Papal Cross ③
People's Garden ⑧
Phoenix Column ④
Wellington Testimonial ⑦
Zoological Gardens ⑥

0 metres 500
0 yards 500

Key to Symbols *see back flap*

Restored central hall at Kilmainham Gaol

Kilmainham Gaol ❷

Inchicore Rd, Kilmainham, Dublin 8.
Tel 453 5984. 🚌 51B, 51C. 69, 73,
78A, 79. ⏰ Apr–Sep: 9:30am–6pm
daily; Oct–Mar: 9:30am–5:30pm Mon–
Sat, 10am–6pm Sun & public hols (last
adm: 1 hr before closing). ⚫ 24, 25
& 26 Dec. 📷 advanced booking
for groups. 🏪 🛍 ♿ limited.
www.heritageireland.ie

A long tree-lined avenue
runs from the Royal Hospital
Kilmainham to the grim, grey
bulk of Kilmainham Gaol. The
building was opened in 1796,
but was restored in the 1960s.
During its 130 years as a
prison, it housed many of
those involved in the fight for
Irish independence, including
Robert Emmet (see p77) and
Charles Stewart Parnell (p43).
The last prisoner held was
Eamon de Valera (p45), who
was released on 16 July, 1924.

The tour includes the chapel,
where Joseph Plunkett married
Grace Gifford just a few hours
before he faced the firing
squad for his part in the 1916
Rising (see pp44–5). The tours
end in the prison yard where
Plunkett's badly wounded

colleague James Connolly, unable to stand up, was strapped
into a chair before being shot.
You also pass the dank cells
of those involved in the 1798,
1803, 1848 and 1867 uprisings,
as well as the punishment cells
and hanging room. Among the
exhibits in the museum are
personal mementos of some
of the former inmates and
depictions of various events
which took place in the Gaol
until it closed down in 1924.

Part of the tour takes place
outside so dress accordingly.

Irish Museum of Modern Art - Royal Hospital Kilmainham ❸

Military Road, Kilmainham, Dublin 8.
Tel 612 9900. 🚆 Heuston Station.
🚌 51, 51B, 78A, 79, 79a, 90, 123.
Irish Museum of Modern Art
⏰ 10am–5:30pm Tue–Sat,
10:30am–5:30pm Wed, noon–
5:30pm Sun & public hols (last
adm: 5:15pm). ⚫ Good Fri & 24–26
Dec. 📷 🏪 🛍 ♿ limited. **Gardens**
open all year. **www**.imma.ie

Ireland's finest surviving 17th-
century building was laid out
in 1680, styled on Les Invalides
in Paris. It was built by Sir
William Robinson as a home
for 300 wounded soldiers – a
role it kept until 1927. When
it was completed, people were
so impressed by its Classical
symmetry that it was suggested it would be better used as
a campus for Trinity College.
The Baroque chapel has fine
carvings and intricate stained
glass. The plaster ceiling is a
replica of the original, which
fell in 1902. The Formal
Gardens, restored using many
of the 17th-century designs,
are now open to the public.

In 1991, the hospital's former
residential quarters became the
Irish Museum of Modern Art.
The collection includes a
cross-section of Irish and
international modern and
contemporary art. Works are
displayed on a rotating basis
and include group and solo
shows, retrospectives and
special visiting exhibitions.

The Royal Hospital Kilmainham

For hotels and restaurants in this region see pp294–8 and pp324–8

Drinking Guinness at a local pub

Guinness Storehouse ❹

St James's Gate, Dublin 8.
Tel 408 4800 🚌 7_A, 51B, 123.
🕐 9:30am–5pm (to 7pm Jul
& Aug) daily. 🔒 Good Fri, 24–26
Dec. 🅿🅰🅱🅲🅳
www.guinness-storehouse.com

The Guinness storehouse
is a development based in
St James's Gate Brewery, the
original house of Guinness,
now completely remodelled.
This 1904 listed building
covers nearly four acres of
floor space over seven floors
built around a huge pint glass
atrium. The first impression the
visitor has is of walking into a
large glass pint with light
spilling down from above and
a copy of the original lease
signed by Arthur Guinness
enshrined on the floor. The
Ingredients section is next
where visitors can touch, smell
and feel the ingredients
through interactive displays.
The tour continues into an
authentic Georgian anteroom
to "meet" Arthur Guinness
and see him at work. The
Brewing Exhibition is a noisy,
steamy and "hoppy" area
giving the impression of
brewing all around with full
explanation of the process.
The historical development of
Guinness cooperage is
accompanied by video
footage of the craft. Models
and displays tell the story of
Guinness transportation, the
appeal of Guinness world-
wide, and their popular
advertising campaigns. The
tour ends with a generous
tasting of draught Guinness in
the traditional Brewery Bar
and the rooftop Gravity Bar.

The Brewing of Guinness

Label from a Guinness bottle

Guinness is a black beer, known as
"stout", renowned for its distinctive
malty flavour and smooth creamy
head. From its humble beginnings over
200 years ago, the Guinness brewery
site at St James's Gate now sprawls
across 26 ha (65 acres). It is the largest
brewery in Europe and exports beers
to more than 120 countries throughout the world. Other famous brands owned by
Guinness include Harp Lager and Smithwick's Ale.

HOW GUINNESS IS MADE
The four main ingredients used to brew
Guinness are barley, hops, yeast and
water which, contrary to popular belief,
comes from the Wicklow Mountains
rather than the River Liffey.

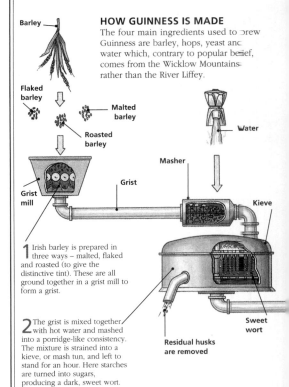

Barley

Flaked barley

Malted barley

Roasted barley

Grist

Grist mill

Water

Masher

Kieve

Sweet wort

Residual husks are removed

1 Irish barley is prepared in
three ways – malted, flaked
and roasted (to give the
distinctive tint). These are all
ground together in a grist mill to
form a grist.

2 The grist is mixed together
with hot water and mashed
into a porridge-like consistency.
The mixture is strained into a
kieve, or mash tun, and left to
stand for an hour. Here starches
are turned into sugars,
producing a dark, sweet wort.

Guinness
advertising has
become almost as
famous as the
product itself.
Since 1929,
when the first
advertisement
announced that "Guinness is
Good for You", poster and television advertising campaigns have
employed many amusing images
of both animals and people.

ARTHUR GUINNESS

Arthur Guinness

In December 1759, 34-year-old Arthur Guinness signed a 9,000-year lease at an annual rent of £45 to take over St James's Gate Brewery, which had lain vacant for almost ten years. At the time the brewing industry in Dublin was at a low ebb – the standard of ale was much criticized and in rural Ireland beer was virtually unknown, as whiskey, gin and poteen were the more favoured drinks. Furthermore, Irish beer was under threat from imports. Guinness started brewing ale,

but was also aware of a black ale called porter, produced in London. This new beer was so called because of its popularity with porters at Billingsgate and Covent Garden markets. Guinness decided to stop making ales and develop his own recipe for porter (the word "stout" was not used until the 1920s). So successful was the switch that he made his first export shipment in 1769.

Engraving (c.1794) of a satisfied customer

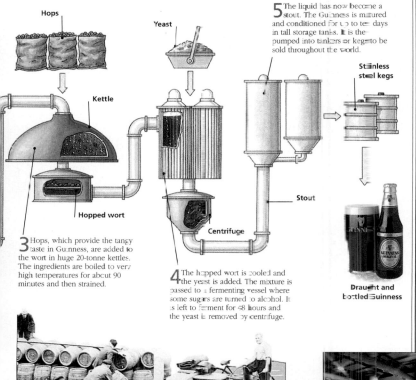

Hops

Yeast

Kettle

Hopped wort

3 Hops, which provide the tangy taste in Guinness, are added to the wort in huge 20-tonne kettles. The ingredients are boiled to very high temperatures for about 90 minutes and then strained.

Centrifuge

4 The hopped wort is cooled and the yeast is added. The mixture is passed to a fermenting vessel where some sugars are turned to alcohol. It is left to ferment for 48 hours and the yeast is removed by centrifuge.

5 The liquid has now become a stout. The Guinness is matured and conditioned for up to ten days in tall storage tanks. It is then pumped into tankers or kegs to be sold throughout the world.

Stainless steel kegs

Stout

Draught and bottled Guinness

The Guinness brewery *has relied heavily on water transport since its first export was shipped to England in 1769. The barges, which up until 1961 made the short trip with their cargo up the Liffey to Dublin Port, were a familiar sight on the river. Once at port, the stout would be loaded on to huge tanker ships for worldwide distribution.*

Steel kettles used in modern-day brewing

Giant water lilies in the Lily House, National Botanic Gardens

National Botanic Gardens ❺

Botanic Ave, Glasnevin, Dublin 9.
Tel 857 0309. 🚌 4, 13, 19, 19A, 83.
🕐 mid-Feb–mid-Nov: 9am–6pm
daily; mid-Nov–mid-Feb: 9am–
4:30pm daily. 🕐 25 Dec. 🔲 🍴
♿ 📷 groups on request.
www.botanicgardens.ie

Opened in 1795, the National
Botanic Gardens are Ireland's
foremost centre of botany and
horticulture. They still possess
an old-world feel, thanks to
the beautiful Palm House and
architect Richard Turner's
curvilinear glasshouses.
Turner was also responsible
for the Palm House at Kew
Gardens, London, and the
glasshouses at Belfast's
Botanic Gardens (see p278).

The 20-ha (49-acre) park
contains over 16,000 different
plant species. Particularly
attractive are the colourful
old-fashioned Victorian carpet
bedding, the rich collections
of cacti and orchids, renowned rose garden, and 30-m
(100-ft) high redwood tree.

The visitor centre houses a
restaurant, a display area with
exhibits relating to the history
and purpose of the gardens
and a lecture hall, which

hosts a programme of regular
talks and workshops. The
National Botanic Gardens
back onto the huge
Glasnevin or Prospect
Cemetery (see p101).

Shaw's Birthplace ❻

33 Synge St, Dublin 8.
Tel 475 0854. 🚌 16, 19, 122.
🕐 Jun–Aug: 10am–1pm & 2–5pm
Tue–Fri, 2–5pm Sat. 📷 🔲 **www**.
visitdublin.com

Playwright and Nobel Prizewinner George Bernard Shaw
was born in this house on 26
July 1856. In 1876 he followed
his mother to London. She had
left four years earlier with her
daughters, fed up with her
husband's drinking habits.
It was in London that Shaw

Kitchen at Shaw's Birthplace

met his wife Charlotte Payne-
Townsend. He stayed in
England until his death in 1950.

Inside the house visitors can
see the young Shaw's bedroom
and the kitchen where the
author remembered he drank
"much tea out of brown delft
left to 'draw' on the hob until
it was pure tannin". Although
there is little on Shaw's pro-
ductive years, the home gives
a fair idea of the lifestyle of a
Victorian middle-class family.

Casino Marino ❼

Cherrymount Crescent. **Tel** 833
1618. 🚉 DART to Clontarf. 🚌 20A,
20B, 27A, 42, 42C, 123. 🕐 May–
Oct: 10am–5pm daily. 📷 ♿
obligatory (last tour 45 mins before
closing). **www**.heritageireland.ie

This delightful little villa
(see pp40–41), designed by
Sir William Chambers in the
1760s for Lord Charlemont,
now sits in its own grounds at
Marino. Originally built as a
summer house for the Marino
Estate, the villa
survives although
the main house
was pulled down
in 1921. The
Casino is
acknowledged to
be one of the
finest
examples of
Neo-Classical
architecture
in Ireland.
Some
innovative
features were

Carved stone lion
at Marino Casino

used in its
construction, including
chimneys disguised as urns
and hollow columns that
accommodate drains. Outside,
four carved stone lion ,
thought to be by English
sculptor Joseph Wilton, stand
guard at each of the corners.

The building's squat
compact exterior conceals 16
rooms built on three floors
around a central staircase.
The ground floor comprises a
spacious hall and a saloon,
with beautiful silk hangings,
elaborate flooring and a
coffered ceiling. On the first
floor is the ostentatious State
Room and servant rooms.

A gilded chair on display at the National Museum of Ireland

Dublin Docklands ❽

www.dublindocklands.ie

Over three hundred years ago, most of the Docklands was underwater, with the exception of the small fishing hamlet of Ringsend. The area was redeveloped during the 1990s and 2000s and is one of the city's most exciting districts. Theatres, museums and the Dublin Wheel, which offers spectacular views over the city, as well as numerous cafés and restaurants, are all part of the attraction. The Docklands span both sides of the Liffey to the east of the city centre and are joined by the Samuel Beckett Bridge.

National Museum of Ireland – Decorative Arts & History ❾

Collins Barracks, Benburb St, Dublin 7. **Tel** 677 7444. 🚌 25, 25A, 66, 67, 90. ⬜ 10am–5pm Tue–Sat, 2–5pm Sun. ⬤ Good Fri & 25 Dec. 🎫 ♿ 📷

Close to Phoenix Park and just across the Liffey from the Guinness Brewery stands the wonderful decorative arts and history annexe of the National Museum *(see pp66–7)*. Its setting in the historic Collins Barracks is an inspired move. The massive complex was

commissioned by King William III in 1700, just ten years after victory at the Battle of the Boyne, and was the largest barracks in his domain, with accommodation for over 5,000 people. It was in use right up to the 1990s. After Irish independence the barracks was named for Michael Collins, the first commander-in-chief of the Irish Army.

The large central courtyard, measured at one hundred marching paces, is an object lesson in simplicity. In marked contrast to the grey institutional exterior, the museum's interior presents the exhibits in an innovative way using the latest technology, with interactive multimedia displays. Furniture, silver, glassware, ceramics and scientific instrument collections form the bulk of items on show in the South Block. In the West Block, however, visitors get an insight into the history, work and development of the National Museum. The Out of Storage exhibit brings together a wide array of artifacts from around the world, complemented by banks of interactive multimedia computers. One of the highlights of the museum is the Curator's Choice section where 25 unusual exhibits – such as an early hurling stick and ball – are displayed with the story of their cultural significance.

The north block holds a permanent exhibition, Soldiers and Chiefs, which explores Irish military history through the eyes of the average Irish soldier from 1550 to the late 1990s.

Glasnevin Cemetery ❿

Finglas Rd. **Tel** 830 1133. 🚌 13, 19, 19A, 40, 40A from Parnell St. ⬜ 8am–6pm daily. 🚶 2:30pm daily (lasts 90 minutes). **Museum Tel** 882 5500. ⬜ 10am–5pm Mon–Fri, 11am–5pm Sat & Sun. 🎫 🍴 🎁 ♿ **www**.glasnevinmuseum.ie

The largest cemetery in Ireland, Glasnevin covers more than 50 ha (124 acres) and contains over one million graves. Originally called Prospect Cemetery, Glasnevin was founded in 1832 after Daniel O'Connell *(see p42)* campaigned for a burial ground in which both Irish Catholics and Protestants could bury their dead with dignity.

The main part features high walls and watchtowers, intended to keep out body snatchers in the early 19th century. The St Paul's area across the road was added when more burial space was needed. Both cemeteries have a huge variety of monuments, from the austere high stones used until the 1860s, to the elaborate Celtic crosses of the nationalistic revival from the 1860s to the 1960s, to the plain marble of the late 20th century.

Glasnevin is a national monument and has a museum detailing its history and the people who are buried there. There are also daily walking tours offering interesting insights into the people whose final resting place it is, including Daniel O'Connell, Michael Collins, Éamon de Valera, Constance Markiewicz and Brendan Behan.

Glasnevin Cemetery, Dublin's largest cemetery

The oak-beamed Great Hall at Malahide Castle

Malahide Castle ⓫

Malahide, Cc Dublin. 🚇 and DART to Malahide. 🚌 42 from Beresford Place, near Busáras. **Tel** 846 2184. 🕐 Apr–Sep: 10am–5pm daily; Oct–Mar: 10am–5pm Mon–Sat, 11am–5pm Sun & public hols. 🚫 🎥 obligatory (last tours: 4:30pm). **www**.malahide castle.com **Fry Model Railway** 🕐 Apr–Sep: 10am–1pm, 2–5pm Tue–Sat. 1–5pm Sun & public hols. 🚫 ♿

Near the seaside dormitory town of Malahide stands a huge castle set in 100 ha (250 acres) of grounds. The castle's core dates from the 12th century but later additions, such as its rounded towers, have given it a classic fairy-tale appearance. The building served as a stately home for the Talbot family until 1973. They were staunch supporters of James II: on the day of the Battle of the Boyne in 1690 *(see p244)*, 14 members of the family breakfasted here; none came back for supper.

Guided tours take you round the castle's collection of 18th-century Irish furniture, the oak-beamed Great Hall and the impressively carved Oak Room. Part of the Portrait Collection, on loan from the National Gallery *(see pp70–71)*, can be seen here. It includes portraits of the Talbot family and other figures such as Wolfe Tone *(see p41)*.

In the old corn store is the Fry Model Railway, started in the 1920s by Cyril Fry, a local railway engineer. The 240 sq m (2,500 sq ft) exhibit contains models of Irish trains, miniatures of stations, streets and local landmarks such as the River Liffey and Howth Head.

Howth ⓬

Co Dublin. 🚇 DART. **Howth Castle grounds** 🕐 8am–sunset daily.

The commercial fishing town of Howth marks the northern limit of Dublin Bay. Howth Head, a huge rocky mass, has lovely views of the bay. A footpath runs around the tip of Howth Head, which is known as the "Nose". Nearby is Baily Lighthouse (1814). Sadly much of this area has suffered from building development.

To the west of the town is Howth Castle, which dates back to Norman times. The **National Transport Museum** in the grounds is worth a visit.

Ireland's Eye, an islet and bird sanctuary where puffins nest, can be reached by a short boat trip from Howth.

⚓ National Transport Museum
Tel 01 8320 427. 🕐 Sep–May: 2–5pm Sat, Sun & public hols; Jun–Aug: 10am–5pm Mon–Sat.

Dun Laoghaire ⓭

Co Dublin. 🚇 DART. **National Maritime Museum Tel** 280 0969. 🕐 May–Sep: 1–5pm Tue–Sun. **Comhaltas Ceoltóiri Éireann Tel** 280 0295. 🕐 music Wed & Sat; Céili Fri. **www**.comhaltas.ie

Ireland's major passenger ferry port and yachting centre, with its brightly painted villas, parks and palm

Baily Lighthouse on the southeastern tip of Howth Head

Yachts anchored in Dun Laoghaire harbour

trees, can sometimes exude a decidedly continental feel. Many visitors head straight out of Dun Laoghaire (pronounced Dunleary) but the town offers some magnificent walks around the harbour and to the lighthouse along the east pier. The villages of Sandycove and Dalkey can be reached via "The Metals" footpath which runs alongside the railway line.

In the 1837 Mariners' Church is the National Maritime Museum. Exhibits include a longboat used by French officers during Wolfe Tone's unsuccessful invasion at Bantry in 1796 *(see pp168–9)*.

Up the road in Monkstown's Belgrave Square is the Comhaltas Ceoltóirí Éireann, Ireland's main centre for traditional music and dance, with music sessions and *céilís* (dances).

James Joyce Tower **14**

Sandycove, Co Dublin. **Tel** 280 9265. ![] *DART to Sandycove.* ![] 59. ![] *Apr–Aug: 10am–1pm & 2–5pm Tue–Sat, 2–6pm Sun; Oct–Mar: open by prior request.* ![] ![]

Standing on a rocky promontory above the village of Sandycove is this Martello tower. It is one of 15 defensive towers erected between Dublin and Bray in 1804 to withstand a threatened invasion by Napoleon. One

hundred years later James Joyce *(see p90)* stayed here for a week as the guest of Oliver St John Gogarty, poet and model for the *Ulysses* character Buck Mulligan. Gogarty rented the tower for a mere £8 per year. Inside the squat 12-m (40-ft) tower's granite walls is a small museum with some of Joyce's correspondence, personal belongings, such as his guitar, cigar case and walking stick, and his death mask. There are also photographs and first editions of his works, including a deluxe edition (1935) of *Ulysses* illustrated by Henri Matisse.

The roof, originally a gun platform but later used as a sun-bathing deck by Gogarty, affords marvellous views of Dublin Bay. Below the tower is Forty Foot Pool, traditionally an all-male nude bathing spot, but now open to all.

Guitar at James Joyce Tower

Dalkey **15**

Co Dublin. ![] *DART.*

Dalkey was once known as the 'Town of Seven Castles', but only two of these now remain. They are both on the main street of this attractive village whose tight, winding roads and charming villas give it a Mediterranean feel.

A little way offshore is tiny Dalkey Island, a rocky bird sanctuary with a Martello tower and a medieval Benedictine church, both now in a poor state of repair. In summer the island can be reached by a boat ride from the town's Coliemore Harbour.

Killiney **16**

Co Dublin. ![] *DART to Dalkey or Killiney.*

South of Dalkey, the coastal road climbs uphill before tumbling down into the village of Killiney. The route offers one of the most scenic vistas on this stretch of the east coast, with views often compared to those across the Bay of Naples. Howth Head is clearly visible to the north, with Bray Head *(see p133)* and the foothills of the Wicklow Mountains *(see pp138–9)* to the south. There is another exhilarating view from the top of Killiney Hill Park off Victoria Road – well worth tackling the short steep trail for. Down below is the popular pebbly beach, Killiney Strand.

Shopfronts on the main street of Dalkey

SHOPPING IN DUBLIN

Dublin has two main shopping thoroughfares, each on either side of the River Liffey. On the north side, the area around Henry Street is where swanky department stores and small specialty shops beckon. The south side, especially trendy Grafton Street with its upmarket boutiques and shops, is reputed for its glamour and style. Yet, despite the wide choice of internationally known brands and retail chains found throughout

Sign from a specialty food shop

the city, the spirit of Dublin shines in the cheerful cacophony of its street markets, many of which stock a cornucopia of highly original Irish crafts and gifts. Dublin is also a haven for those searching for bargains and second-hand deals on everything from books and CDs to clothes and trinkets. There is something for everyone in this lively city, and the following pages will tell you where to start looking.

WHERE TO SHOP

Temple Bar has become a staple tourist destination. While the area is frequented by revellers at night, the area is a treasure trove of funky craft, design and souvenir outlets during the day.

Those who prefer a more relaxed and upmarket shopping experience should head for the Old City. To the west of Temple Bar, between Parliment and Fishamble Streets, it is home to sleek high-end designer stores and cosmopolitan cafés.

Dublin's rapid development has contributed to the growth of bustling markets in areas that used to be little more than wastelands. The first of these areas is the strip known as the Docklands, running along the shores of the Liffey, particularly on the north side, east of Custom House. New shops, restaurants and markets are opening up regularly. The Chq building

with its designer boutiques and specialist shops is the most recent addition.

Around Liffey Street, several old shopping areas have been regenerated. In contrast to just a few years back, Capel Street is now a thriving location, as is the impressive Bloom's Lane at the Millennium Bridge.

WHEN TO SHOP

Shopping hours are generally from 9am to 6pm, Monday to Saturday, and from 11am or noon to 6pm on Sundays. Many shops stay open until 9pm on Thursdays.

HOW TO PAY

Major credit cards such as Visa and MasterCard are accepted in almost all outlets. Sales tax or VAT is usually 21–25 per cent, which non-EU visitors can redeem at airports and ports. Redemption forms are available at points of purchase.

Brown Thomas department store

DEPARTMENT STORES

The best known department stores in Dublin are **Arnot's**, the city's oldest and largest, and **Debenhams**, both on Henry Street.

One of Dublin's oldest shops, **Clery's** on O'Connell Street, stocks everything from Irish-made gifts and clothing to internationally recognized branded goods. Prominent Irish retailer **Brown Thomas** is known for its upmarket wares with goods from the world's top designers.

There are also numerous Marks & Spencer shops, including branches on Grafton Street and Mary Street.

SHOPPING CENTRES

There are four main shopping centres in Dublin – three on the south side and one on the north. South of the Liffey are **Stephen's Green Centre** and the **Powerscourt Centre**.

Shoppers on busy Grafton Street

The colourful George's Street Arcade

Stephen's Green Centre is one of the largest enclosed shopping areas, with scores of shops under its roof. These include many craft and gift stores, clothing outlets and several fast food restaurants.

In an enclosed four-storey Georgian courtyard, the Powerscourt Centre is more upmarket and plush. It is home to many fine boutiques, restaurants and lovely antique shops. Also on the south side of the city is the **Dundrum Centre**.

On the north side of the river is the **Jervis Centre**, which houses many British chain stores as well as a number of popular Irish retailers.

MARKETS

On Dublin's north side, just off Henry Street, the famous and still-evolving Moore Street Market hosts a daily fruit and vegetable bazaar, replete with very vocal street vendors. The area has also become a hive of ethnic shops, where you can source anything from Iranian dance music CDs to tinned bok choi.

The wonderful **Temple Bar Food Market**, where you will find a wide range of organically produced items, is held every Saturday. A particularly popular stall sells delicious fresh oysters and wine by the glass – a great stop-off point for the weary shopper.

Quirky, quaint and unique, **George's Street Arcade** is open seven days a week and has many second-hand shops. It is a good place for records, books, Irish memorabilia and bric-a-brac, as well as funky clothing and accessories.

SOUVENIRS AND GIFTS

The most popular destination for souvenirs in Dublin is unsurprisingly found at the home of Ireland's most popular drink – the **Guinness Storehouse** (see pp98–9). The interactive tours of the storehouse are best rounded off with a visit to the gift shop, where a multitude of Guinness branded souvenirs and clothing can be bought.

Finely crafted pottery

Nassau Street has a concentration of fine tourist gift shops, such as **Heraldic Artists**, which assists visitors in tracing their ancestry. **Knobs and Knockers** specialize in a wide range of door accessories. For a more varied range of gifts on the same street, drop in to the **Kilkenny Shop**. This store stocks unique Irish ceramic wares, the famous Waterford crystal and many other handcrafted products.

Across the road, the gift shop at Trinity College sells university memorabilia and mementos of the *Book of Kells*, as well as many other souvenirs.

Rather less upmarket, **Carroll's Irish Gift Stores**, a chain of souvenir and clothing outlets, are difficult to miss while traversing the city. They stock a surfeit of kitschy leprechauns and other such amusing odds and ends.

FOOD AND WINE

Connoisseurs of fine wines and whiskies have many choices in Dublin. **Mitchell & Son** boasts a large shop in the financial services centre and an online delivery facility. The **Celtic Whiskey Shop** stocks a variety of Irish and Scotch whiskies, and the staff are very knowledgeable.

A number of gourmet food retailers add culinary character to the city. **Sheridans Cheesemongers** specialize in Irish farmhouse cheeses but stocks a wide array of other cheeses and foods too. **Butler's Irish Chocolate** tempts with exquisite handmade chocolates. For those craving fresh, caught Irish salmon, **Fallon & Byrne** on Exchequer Street is a good bet. They also sell an extensive range of organic and imported produce alongside a fine selection of wines, cheeses and charcuterie. Dublin's growing multi-culturalism has led to the proliferation of ethnic food stores, many of which can be found on Parnell Street and Moore Street on the north side, or around George's Street on the south side.

Sheridan's Cheesemongers' tempting display

FASHION

Although there are many elegant boutiques in Dublin, the most fashionable among them are clustered close to Dublin's "Fifth Avenue" – the smart Grafton Street area. **Costume**, with its wide range of Irish and international designer labels, is a popular destination for women's *haute couture*. You'll also find designers such as Roland Mouret, Temperley and Jonathan Saunders here.

Bargain hunters should head for the Temple Bar Old City fashion market, where many outlets sell uniquely Irish designs at reduced prices.

For classic menswear, **Louis Copeland** is Dublin's most famous tailor. For traditional clothing, stop at the Kilkenny Shop *(see p105)* or **Kevin & Howlin**. Both stock tweeds, Arans and other typically Irish clothing.

BOOKS

Given its rich literary heritage, it is not surprising that there are a number of specialist and interesting bookstores peppering Dublin's streets. Dawson Street is the top draw for booklovers, with the vast **Hodges Figgis** and small specialist shop **Murder Inc. Eason's**, on O'Connell Street, is a large bookstore. **Books Upstairs**, next to Trinity College, has a good selection of Irish titles. Antiquarian bookseller, **Cathach Books**, is Dublin's specialist provider of old Irish titles. The shop stocks an impressive selection of first editions and rarities. **Hughes & Hughes** often have book signings at their flagship store. **Chapters** has one of the city's largest second-hand sections.

MUSIC

The most concentrated area for record shops is in Temple Bar, where small stores stock everything from obscure electronica to indie and reggae. Fans of such music converge at **Borderline Records** as it caters to independent rock and metal tastes, with a range of both new and secondhand music.

For the best in hip-hop culture and dance music, pay a visit to **All City Records**. **HMV** on Grafton Street is the city's largest music store, with an extensive collection of music and film spanning all genres.

Most record shops in Dublin stock traditional Irish music, but **Celtic Note** on Nassau Street has one of the largest selections. The staff will gladly make recommendations. **McCullough Piggot** and **Opus II** on the South side, and **Waltons** on the North, are best for sheet music and traditional Irish instruments including accordions, uillean pipes and *bodhráns*.

ANTIQUES

One of Dublin's oldest antique retailers **Oman Antique Galleries** specializes in quality Georgian, Victorian and Edwardian furniture. **Clifford Antiques** offers both original and reproduction antique furniture, as well as decorative fireplaces. Its collection of bronze fountains and figures is unrivalled in the city. The eclectic collection at **Christy Bird** includes an array of salvaged and recycled furniture and pub fittings.

The Powerscourt Centre is also home to many antique dealers. Of these, **Delphi** is a specialist in Victorian and Edwardian period jewellery, and also stocks beautifully fragile Belleek porcelain antiques. **Windsor Antiques** is the best for antique watches, cuff links, brooches, diamond rings and other jewellery. For silver antiques, including Irish and English portrait miniatures from the 18th to the 20th century, visit **The Silver Shop**. For antique maps and prints, the Grafton Street area is a good hunting ground with the **Neptune Gallery** and **Antique Prints** nearby.

Located in one of the oldest areas of the city and near the historical Coombe, Francis Street offers a mish-mash of antique stores. Old clocks, second-hand furniture and loads of bric-a-brac line the streets, inviting visitors into shops that are almost antiques themselves.

Outside the city centre, **Beaufield Mews** specializes in porcelain and early 20th-century pictures, while **Q Antiques** in Dun Laoghaire stocks an interesting range of period lighting and furniture.

Those who wish to further explore vintage Irish treasures should consult the website and local listings for the **Antiques Fairs** that are held in the city at different times and locations throughout the year.

GALLERIES

The abundance of galleries and artists' workshops in Dublin make it a favourite destination of art lovers and collectors. Many galleries are located on Dawson Street, which runs parallel to Grafton Street. The prestigious **Apollo Gallery** flaunts a trendy pop sensibility and exhibits works by many of Ireland's best-known artists.

On Westland Row, the **Oisín Gallery** sells the work of some of Ireland's best young artists in its split-level exhibition space. Visitors may also visit **Whyte's Auction Rooms** to bid on international and Irish art. The catalogues are published online and can be consulted for those seriously interested in investigating Irish painting.

On Sundays, an outdoor art market is held at Merrion Square close to the museum quarter. Works of vastly varying quality are hung from the square's perimeter black railing, and in good weather, the colourful, impromptu exhibition makes for very enjoyable browsing.

The Temple Bar area is also home to many of the city's galleries, including the **Temple Bar Gallery and Studios**. It is one of the more modish, cutting-edge venues, housing the eclectic work of more than 30 Irish artists working in several mediums. Nearby, in the heart of Dublin's Left Bank, is the **Original Print Gallery** and the **Gallery of Photography**, which stocks an impressive collection of glossy art books. Despite its association with partying and drunken misconduct, the area is still deserving of its "cultural quarter" status.

DIRECTORY

DEPARTMENT STORES

Arnott's
12 Henry St. **Map** D2.
Tel 01 805 0400.
www.arnotts.ie

Brown Thomas
88–95 Grafton St. **Map**
D4. **Tel** 01 605 6666.
www.brownthomas.com

Clery's
18–27 Lower O'Connell
St. **Map** D2. **Tel** 01 878
6000. www.clerys.ie

Debenhams
54–62 Henry St. **Map** D2.
Tel 01 814 7200.
www.debenhams.com

SHOPPING CENTRES

Dundrum Centre
Dundrum. *Tel 01 299
1700.* www.dundrum.ie

Jervis Centre
125 Upper Abbey St.
Map C2. **Tel** 01 878
1323. www.jervis.ie

Powerscourt Centre
59 S William St. **Map** D4.
Tel 01 679 4144. www.
powerscourtcentre.com

Stephen's Green Centre
St Stephen's Green West.
Map D4. **Tel** 01 478 0888.
www.stephensgreen.com

MARKETS

George's Street Arcade
George's St. **Map** C4.
www.georgesstreet
arcade.ie

Temple Bar Food Market
Meeting House Sq,
Temple Bar. **Map** D3.
www.templebar.ie

SOUVENIRS AND GIFTS

Carroll's Irish Gift Stores
57 Upper O'Connell St.
Map A3. **Tel** 01 873 5709.
www.carrollsirishgifts.com

Guinness Storehouse
St. James's Gate. **Map** A3.
Tel 01 408 4800. www.
guinness-storehouse.com

Heraldic Artists
3 Nassau St. **Map** A3.
Tel 01 679 7020.
www.roots.ie

Kilkenny Shop
6–10 Nassau St. **Map** E4.
Tel 01 677 7066.

Knobs and Knockers
19 Nassau St. **Map** A3.
Tel 01 671 0288.

FOOD AND WINE

Butler's Irish Chocolate
24 Wicklow St. **Map** D4.
Tel 01 671 0591.

Celtic Whiskey Shop
27–28 Dawson St.
Map D4. **Tel** 01 675 9744.

Fallon & Byrne
11–17 Exchequer St.
Map D4. **Tel** 01 472 1010.

Mitchell & Son
Chq Building, IFSC.
Map D2. **Tel** 01 612 5540.

Sheridan's Cheesemongers
11 South Anne St.
Map D4. **Tel** 01 679 3143.

FASHION

Costume
10 Castle Market.
Map D4. **Tel** 01 579 4186.

Kevin & Howlin
31 Nassau St. **Map** E4.
Tel 01 677 0257.

Louis Copeland
39–41 Capel St **Map** C2.
Tel 01 872 1509.

BOOKS

Books Upstairs
36 College Green.
Map D3. **Tel** 01 679 6687.

Cathach Books
10 Duke St. **Map** D4.
Tel 01 671 8676.

Chapters
Ivy Exchange, Parnell St.
Map D2. **Tel** 01 872 3297.

Eason's
40 Lower O'Connell St
Map D2. **Tel** 01 858 3800.

Hodges Figgis
56–58 Dawson St.
Map D4. **Tel** 01 677 4754.

Hughes & Hughes
St Stephen's Green
Shopping Centre. **Map** D5.
Tel 01 478 3060. www.
hughesandhughes.ie

Murder Inc
15 Dawson St **Map** D4.
Tel 01 677 7570.

MUSIC

All City Records
4 Crow St, Temple Bar.
Map C3. **Tel** 01 677 2994.

Borderline Records
17 Temple Bar **Map** C3.
Tel 01 579 9097.

Celtic Note
12 Nassau St. **Map** E4.
Tel 01 670 4157.
www.celticnote.ie

Golden Discs
Jervis St. **Map** C2.
Tel 01 878 1063.
www.goldendiscs.ie

HMV
65 Grafton St. **Map** D4.
Tel 01 679 5334.
www.hmv.com

McCullough Piggot
11 S William St. **Map** D4.
Tel 01 577 3138. www.
mcculloughpiggot.com

Opus II
26 Sth Great George's St
Map C4. **Tel** 01 677 8571.

Waltons
2–5 N Frederick St. **Map**
D1. **Tel** 01 874 7805.
www.waltons.ie

ANTIQUES

Antiques Fairs
www.antiquefairsireland.
com

Antique Prints
16 South Anne St. **Map**
D4. **Tel** 01 671 9523.

Beaufield Mews
Woodlands Ave, Stillorgan,
Co Dublin. **Road map** D4.
Tel 01 288 0375. www.
beaufieldmews.com

Christy Bird
32 S Richmond St.
Tel 01 475 4049.

Clifford Antiques
7/8 Parnell St. **Map** D1.
Tel 01 872 5042.

Delphi
Powerscourt Centre.
Map D4. **Tel** 01 579 0331.

Neptune Gallery
41 E William St. **Map** D4.
Tel 01 671 7502.

Orran Antique Galleries
20/21 S William St.
Map D4. **Tel** 01 616 8991.

Q Antiques
76 York Rd Dun
Laoghaire, Co Dublin.
Road map D4.
Tel 01 280 1895.

The Silver Shop
Powerscourt Centre.
Map D4. **Tel** 01 679
4147. www.silver
shopdublin.com

Windsor Antiques
23D Powerscourt Centre.
Map D4.
Tel 01 670 5200.

GALLERIES

Apollo Gallery
51C Dawson St. **Map** D4.
Tel 01 671 2609.
www.apollogallery.ie

Gallery of Photography
Meeting House Sq,
Temple Bar. **Map** C3. **Tel**
01 671 4654.

Oisín Gallery
44 Westland Row. **Map**
F3. **Tel** 01 661 1315.

Original Print Gallery
4 Temple Bar. **Map** D3.
Tel 085 178 7447.

Temple Bar Gallery and Studios
5–9 Temple Bar. **Map** D3.
Tel 01 671 0073.

Whyte's Auction Rooms
38 Molesworth St.
Map D2.
Tel 01 676 2888.
www.whytes.ie

ENTERTAINMENT IN DUBLIN

Although Dublin is well served by theatres, cinemas, nightclubs and rock venues, what sets the city apart from other European capitals is its pubs. Lively banter, impromptu music sessions and great Guinness are the essential ingredients for an enjoyable night in any of the dozens of atmospheric hostelries here.

One of the most popular entertainment districts is the rejuvenated Temple Bar area. Along this narrow network of cobbled streets, you can find everything from traditional music in grand old pubs to the latest dance tracks in a post-industrial setting. The many pubs and venues around this area make the city centre south of the Liffey the place to be at night. The north side does, however, boast the two most illustrious theatres, the largest cinemas and the state-of-the-art O₂ arena, a converted 19th-century rail terminal beside the docks. It is now the venue for all major rock concerts and stage musicals, as well as a number of classical music performances.

Olympia Theatre façade

Buskers playing near Grafton Street in southeast Dublin

ENTERTAINMENT LISTINGS

Listings for clubs, cinemas, theatre and other entertainment can be found in most newspapers, such as the *Irish Times* and the *Irish Independent*, particularly on weekends. *Hot Press*, a national bimonthly newspaper covering both rock and traditional music, has comprehensive listings for Dublin. *The Evening Herald* is also a sound source of information for the latest concerts, movies and gigs. For bar and restaurant reviews, Try *The Dubliner* which is free with Thursday's Evening Herald.

BOOKING TICKETS

Tickets for many events are available on the night, but it is usually safer to book in advance. All the major venues take credit card payment over the telephone. **Ticketmaster** accepts phone bookings by credit card only for many of the major shows and events in and around Dublin, while **HMV** and **Dublin Tourism** (Suffolk Street) sell tickets for most of the top theatres and major rock gigs.

THEATRE

Ireland's national theatre, the **Abbey** (*see p88*), is the city's most popular venue, concentrating on major new productions as well as revivals of works by Irish playwrights such as Brendan Behan, Sean O'Casey, JM Synge and WB Yeats. The smaller Peacock Theatre downstairs features experimental works. Also on the north side, the **Gate Theatre** (*see p90*) is noted for its interpretations of well-known international plays, and the **Grand Canal Theatre** hosts West End musicals, ballet, opera and theatre productions. The **Samuel Beckett Theatre** is renowned for its sparse yet powerful productions. The main venue south of the Liffey, the **Gaiety Theatre**, stages a mainstream mix of plays, often by Irish playwrights. Some of the best fringe theatre and modern dance in Dublin can be seen at the **Project Arts Centre** in Temple Bar. **Smock Alley Theatre** hosts guest productions by experimental theatre groups, as well as student productions. **Bewley's Café Theatre** offers intimate lunchtime drama. The **Olympia Theatre** specializes in comedy and popular drama, and occasionally stages rock and Irish music concerts. Most theatres are closed on Sunday.

Every October, the **Dublin Theatre Festival** takes over all the city venues with mainstream, fringe and international plays.

Record shop and ticket office in Crown Alley, Temple Bar

Crowds enjoying the Temple Bar Blues Festival

CINEMA

The city's cinemas had a boost in the 1990s with the success of Dublin-based films such as *My Left Foot* (1989). Huge growth in the country's movie production industry followed, and hits like *Dancing at Lughnasa* (1998) and *Intermission* (2004) keep Ireland in the spotlight.

The **Irish Film Institute** showcases mostly foreign and independent films, along with a programme of lectures. It boasts two screens, as well as a bar and restaurant. **Screen**, close to Trinity College, and **The Lighthouse Cinema** in Smithfield have a repertoire of art house films.

The large first-run cinemas are all located on the north side. They usually offer tickets at reduced prices for afternoon screenings, and show late-night films on the weekend. The summer-long **Temple Bar Cultural Events** include open-air screenings, mainly in Meeting House Square. Tickets are available from Temple Bar Properties.

CLASSICAL MUSIC, OPERA AND DANCE

The **National Concert Hall** is served well by its resident orchestra, the RTÉ National Symphony Orchestra, which gives weekly performances. There are also impressive visiting international orchestras, such as the Berlin Philharmonic Orchestra. The popular venue caters for a wide range of musical tastes, with performances covering opera, jazz, dance, musicals, Irish folk and popular music among others.

The **Hugh Lane Gallery** *(see p91)* has regular Sunday lunchtime concerts. Other venues include the **Royal Hospital Kilmainham** *(see p97)*, **Bank of Ireland Arts Centre** and the **Royal Dublin Society (RDS)**. International opera is staged in **The O2**. Opera Ireland performs every April and November at the Gaiety Theatre. The programme at the **Grand Canal Theatre** on the city's south side includes opera and ballet productions

The Dubliner monthly magazine

ROCK, JAZZ, BLUES AND COUNTRY

Dublin has had a thriving rock scene ever since local band Thin Lizzy made it big in the early 1970s. U2's success acted as a further catalyst for local bands, and each night there's usually an interesting gig somewhere in the city. **Whelan's** is probably the most popular live venue. Since 1989, many famous names have performed on its stage. Temple Bar venue, **The Mezz**, hosts live music most nights of the week. Set on two floors, this place is always packed with dancers. Get there early if you want to find a good seat by the stage.

Eamonn Doran's in Temple Bar is another favourite for rock fans (and pizza lovers). Located in the same building is Di Fontaine's pizzeria, partly owned by Huey Morgan of the rock group, Fun Lovin' Criminals. Eamonn Doran's is a suitably grungy environment for visitors looking for an authentic Dublin rock experience.

The upstairs room at the likeable **International Bar** plays host to an acoustic session on Wednesday nights where singer/songwriters come to test themselves in public. There is also a Sunday afternoon traditional Irish music session that takes place between 1pm and 4pm. The **Ha'penny Bridge Inn** has folk and blues on Friday and Saturday nights.

Big names play at either **The O2** or, in summer at the local sports stadia. The **Olympia**, a Victorian theatre, hosts memorable concerts in extraordinary surroundings. Outside Dublin, Slane Castle hosts a big rock event most summers *(see p249)*.

Button Factory and **The Sugar Club** offer jazz, salsa, Latin and blues all year, and **The Academy** has live bands and DJs over four floors. Country music is popular in Ireland and plays at several Dublin pubs. Check entertainment listings for details.

Live rock band performing at the Sugar Club

TRADITIONAL MUSIC AND DANCE

To many Irish people, the standard of music in a pub is just as important as the quality of the Guinness. Central Dublin has a host of pubs reverberating to the sound of *bodhráns*, fiddles and uilleann pipes. One of the most famous is **O'Donoghue's**, where the legendary Dubliners started out in the early 1960s. The **Cobblestone** and the **Auld Dubliner** are also renowned venues. **Legends** at the Arlington Hotel combines Irish cuisine with nightly dance shows. **Johnnie Fox's**, in the Dublin mountains, is about 35 minutes by car from the city centre and has live music nightly.

PUBS AND BARS

Dublin's pubs are a slice of living history. These are the places where some of the best-known scenes in Irish literature have been set, where rebellious politicians have met, and where world-famous music acts have made their debuts. Today, it's the singing, dancing, talk and laughter that make a pub tour of Dublin an absolute must.

There are nearly 1,000 pubs inside the city limits. Among the best of the traditional bars are **Neary's**, popular with actors and featuring a gorgeous marble bar, the atmospheric **Long Hall**, and the friendly and chic **Stag's Head** dating from 1770.

Cosy snugs, where drinkers could lock themselves away for private conversation, were an important feature of 19th-century bars. A few remain, notably at the tiny, journalists' haunt of **Doheny & Nesbitt** and intimate **Kehoe's**.

The **Brazen Head** claims to be the city's oldest pub, dating back to 1198. The present pub, built in the 1750s, is lined with old photographs and dark wood panelling, and showcases traditional music sessions nightly. Every pub prides itself on the quality of its Guinness, though most locals acknowledge that **Mulligan's**, founded in 1782, serves the best pint in the city. **The Bull and Castle** serves a great variety of craft beers and is also known for good food.

The Grave Diggers is situated on the northern outskirts of the city in Phibsborough. Located next to a graveyard, this bar has more character than most, and it's worth the taxi ride just to see what a Dublin bar would have looked like hundreds of years ago. On summer weekends, the green outside fills with drinkers enjoying pints and chatting.

Grogan's bar, on William Street, is frequented by many of Dublin's bohemian characters. Part bar, part art gallery, it exhibits an array of paintings by local artists.

Café en Seine is influenced by a *belle époque* Parisian bar. Its interior is huge and cavernous, and the decor rich and alluring. At weekends, this bar heaves with Dublin's single thirty-somethings. Situated next door is **Ron Black's**, one of Dublin's more style-conscious bars, usually frequented by members of the film industry. Lofty ceilings, dark panelled walls and off-white furnishings set the mood for relaxed networking or enjoyable people-watching.

Grand Central is one of the very few bars on the city's main thoroughfare, O'Connell Street. Housed in a former bank, many of the original features have been retained. **Dakota** is a large and lively tapas and wine bar that draws a trendy young crowd. **The Welcome Inn** is a journey back to the 1970s; ow formica tables and vinyl stools complement the antiquated wallpaper. The young crowd can be rambunctious, depending on who has programmed the jukebox.

Dice Bar is a pseudo-dive bar with a dark interior of clashing blacks and reds. The music policy is a combination of rare rock 'n' roll and blues records.

Urban and cosmopolitan, **The Globe** is as popular during the day for coffee as it is at night. The crowd is a cool mix of musicians and city hipsters. Not unlike the Globe, but with a modern twist, **4 Dame Lane** is a slickly designed bar. At night it fills with a young crowd that loves the eclectic music. Two flaming torches mark the entrance.

Part of the sleek Morgan Hotel in Temple Bar, the beautifully designed **Morgan Bar** prides itself on serving outstanding cocktails. **The Market Bar** is one of the city's favourite gastro-pubs. Set in an old factory, high ceilings and red-brick walls lend this place a certain retro-industrial charm. Superb food is served throughout the day.

Small, comfy **Pete's Pub** has a reputation for quality pints and is considered by many to be the quintessential Dublin boozer.

GUINNESS TIME

A Guinness advertisement at a Dublin pub

French-style interior of the Café en Seine

Traditional façade of Doheny & Nesbitt

A LITERARY PUB CRAWL

Pubs with strong literary associations abound in Dublin, particularly around Grafton Street. **McDaid's**, an old pub with an Art Deco interior, still retains some of its bohemian air from the time when writers such as Patrick Kavanagh and Brendan Behan were regulars.

Davy Byrne's has a plusher decor than it did when Leopold Bloom dropped in for a gorgonzola and mustard sandwich in *Ulysses*, but it is still well worth paying a visit. These pubs, and others frequented by Ireland's most famous authors and playwrights, are featured on the excellent **Dublin Literary Pub Crawl**. The two-and-a-half-hour tours, which are led by actors, start with a beer in **The Duke**, and are by far the most entertaining way to get a real feel for the city's booze-fuelled literary heritage. Tours take place daily in summer, but are usually held only at weekends in winter.

NIGHTCLUBS

Dublin's clubs are continually revamping and relaunching, and variety remains the key in clubland, with plenty of massive superclubs and more intimate, laidback venues. The scene is somewhat curtailed, however, by the city's licensing laws. A nightclub licence allows a club to remain open until 2:30am – early by many major cities' standards. So Dublin clubbers start their night

early, often beginning at a pub. The **POD** complex houses four spaces, providing some of Dublin's most diverse offerings. **Crawdaddy** features live acts ranging from local hip-hop groups to international reggae stars. Next door is the ultra trendy **Lobby Bar**, featuring soul music and avant-garde design. Next to it is the original POD, where a trendy mix of cutting-edge sounds and attractive clubbers combine to produce an exclusive atmosphere. **Tripod** is a live music venue with balcony seating and private booths. Designed by Keith Hobbs as a multi-functional club, it plays host to a variety of live shows.

Copper Face Jacks is the most profitable nightclub of its size in Europe, notorious for its sweaty dancefloors, pop music and groups of single men and women looking for a good time. If the queues are too long there are several similar venues nearby.

Formerly Spirit, **The Academy** was opened in January 2008 and billed as a vibrant new music mecca. It plays music on four floors and is attempting to rival Whelans as a live music centre with a predilection for rock and pop acts as well as a range of DJs from all over the world.

Twisted Pepper, located next door to The Academy, is a music, art and entertainment space. It attracts a young and trendy crowd to its club nights, and also puts on gigs, film nights and comedy

shows. Art exhibitions are mounted in the café-bar, which serves great cocktails and a good range of beers. For those looking for laidback sophistication, Jo's is technically a wine bar and has a licence to stay open late.

Krystle, on Harcourt Street, running down St Stephen's Green, is the coolest nightclub in town. The large gastro pub and club sits on the north side of the River Liffey and its links with Irish rugby players and glamorous models have made it the place to be seen.

Ri-Ra, Irish for uproar, is one of Dublin's longest running nightclubs and has a different theme every night from hip-hop and house to funk, soul and reggae. An annexe to the ever popular Globe, Ri-Ra is packed with serious night owls, intent on dancing and having a ball, every night of the week.

Touted as Dublin's most prestigious night club, **Lillie's Bordello** has a luxurious, decadent atmosphere. The legendary VIP room has long been a favourite of Dublin's rich and famous, and regulars often rub shoulders with the entertainment elite.

Howl at the Moon is a smart club close to Merrion Square. It is spread across three floors and has outdoor areas including a heated, covered smoking area. The dress policy is smart-casual and over 23. Entry on Thursday and Friday nights is free and there are usually special promotions available on drinks prices.

An eclectic array of secondhand furniture and bric-a-brac decorates **Sheeban Chic**, one of Dublin's newest and trendiest hangouts. Enjoy a burger from their excellent food menu by day or dance to disco tunes by night.

The George is Dublin's premier gay venue, with club nights, karaoke and nightly drinks specials. Don't miss the infamous transvestite Bingo night on Sundays.

The Front Lounge has a more relaxed, gay-friendly vibe, with comfy chairs and great food. It is liveliest on Tuesday nights, when there is karaoke from 10pm.

DIRECTORY

BOOKING AGENTS

Dublin Tourism
Tourism Centre,
Suffolk St, Dublin 2.
Tel 01 605 7700.
www.visitdublin.ie

HMV
55 Grafton St. **Map** D4.
Tel 01 679 5334.
www.hmv.com

Ticketmaster
Tel 0818 719300.
www.ticketmaster.ie

THEATRE

Abbey Theatre
Abbey St Lower.
Map E2.
Tel 01 878 7222.
www.abbeytheatre.ie

Bewley's Café Theatre
Bewley's Café, 78
Grafton St. **Map** D4.
Tel 01 679 5720.
www.bewleyscafe
theatre.com

Dublin Theatre Festival
44 Essex St East.
Map C3.
Tel 01 677 8439.
www.dublintheatre
festival.com

Gaiety Theatre
King St South. **Map** D4.
Tel 01 677 1717.
www.gaietytheatre.com

Gate Theatre
Cavendish Row, Parnell
Sq. **Map** D1.
Tel 01 874 4045.
www.gate-theatre.ie

Grand Canal Theatre
Grand Canal Square,
Docklands.
Tel 01 677 7999.
www.grandcanal
theatre.ie

Olympia Theatre
Dame St. **Map** C3.
Tel 01 679 3323.
www.mcd.ie/olympia

Project Arts Centre
39 East Essex St.
Map C3.
Tel 01 881 9613.
www.project.ie

Samuel Beckett Theatre
Trinity College. **Map** E3.
Tel 01 896 1334.
www.tcd.ie

Smock Alley Theatre
SS Michael & John's
Church, Exchange St
Lower, Temple Bar.
Map C3.
Tel 01 679 9277.
www.smockalley.com

CINEMA

Cineworld Cinemas
Parnell St. **Map** C2.
Tel 1520 880 444.
www.cineworld.ie

Irish Film Institute
6 Eustace St, Temple Bar.
Map C3.
Tel 01 679 5744.
www.ifi.ie

The Lighthouse Cinema
Market Square,
Smithfield. **Map** B2.
Tel 01 879 7601.
www.lighthouse
cinema.ie

Screen
D'Olier St. **Map** D3.
Tel 01 672 5500.
www.screencinema.ie

Temple Bar Cultural Events
www.templebar.ie

CLASSICAL MUSIC, OPERA AND DANCE

Bank of Ireland Arts Centre
Bank of Ireland Arts
Centre, Foster Place,
College Green.
Map D3.
Tel 01 671 1488.
www.bankofireland.ie

Grand Canal Theatre
Grand Canal Square,
Docklands.
Tel 01 677 7999.
www.grandcanal
theatre.ie

Hugh Lane Gallery
Charlemont House,
Parnell Sq North.
Map C1.
Tel 01 222 5550.
www.hughlane.ie

National Concert Hall
Earlsfort Terrace.
Map D5.
Tel 01 417 0000.
www.nch.ie

Royal Dublin Society (RDS)
Ballsbridge.
Tel 01 668 0866.
www.rds.ie

Royal Hospital Kilmainham
Military Lane,
Kilmainham, Dublin 18.
Tel 01 612 9900.
www.modernart.ie

The O₂
East Link Bridge,
North Wall Quay.
Map D1.
Tel 01 819 8888.
www.theO2.ie

ROCK, JAZZ, BLUES AND COUNTRY

The Academy
57 Abbey St. **Map** C2.
Tel 01 877 9999.
www.theacademy
dublin.com

Button Factory
Curved St, Temple Bar.
Map E4.
Tel 01 670 9202.
www.buttonfactory.ie

Eamonn Doran's
Crown Alley,
Temple Bar, Dublin 2.
Map D3.
Tel 01 6799114.

Ha'penny Bridge Inn
42 Wellington Quay.
Map C3.
Tel 01 677 0616.

International Bar
23 Wicklow St. **Map** D3.
Tel 01 677 9250.
www.international-
bar.com

The Mezz
Eustace St, Temple Bar,
Dublin 2. **Map** C3.
Tel 01 670 7655.
www.mezz.ie

Slane Castle
Slane, Co Meath.
Tel 041 988 4400.
www.slanecastle.ie

The Sugar Club
8 Lower Leeson St.
Map E5.
Tel 01 678 7188.
www.thesugarclub.com

Whelan's
25 Wexford St.
Map E4 C5.
Tel 01 478 0766.
www.whelanslive.com

TRADITIONAL MUSIC AND DANCE

Auld Dubliner
Auld Dubliner, 24–25
Temple Bar. **Map** D3.
Tel 01 677 0527.

Cobblestone
77 King St North.
Map A2.
Tel 01 872 1799.
www.cobblestonepub.ie

Johnnie Fox's
Glencullen, Co Dublin.
Tel 01 295 5647.
www.jfp.ie

Legends
Arlington Hotel, Temple
Bar, 16–18 Lord Edward
St. **Map** C3.
Tel 01 670 8777.
www.arlingtonhotel
templebar.com

DIRECTORY

O'Donoghue's
15 Merrion Row.
Map E5.
Tel 01 660 7194.
www.odonoghues.ie

The Temple Bar
48 Temple Bar, Dublin 2.
Map C3.
Tel 01 672 5287.
www.thetemplebar
pub.com

PUBS AND BARS

4 Dame Lane
4 Dame Lane, Dublin 2.
Map C3.
Tel 01 679 0291.

Brazen Head
20 Bridge St Lower.
Map A3.
Tel 01 679 5186.
www.brazenhead.com

Café en Seine
40 Dawson St,
Dublin 2.
Map D4.
Tel 01 677 4567.
www.capitalbars.com

Dakota
9 S William St,
Dublin 2.
Map D4.
Tel 01 672 7690.
www.dakotabar.ie

Davy Byrne's
21 Duke St.
Map D4.
Tel 01 677 5217.
www.davybyrnes.com

Dice Bar
79 Queen St,
Dublin 7.
Map A2.
Tel 01 633 3936.

Doheny & Nesbitt
5 Lower Baggot St.
Map E5.
Tel 01 676 2945.

**Dublin Literary
Pub Crawl**
1 Suffolk St.
Map D3.
Tel 01 670 5602.
www.dublinpubcrawl.
com

The Bull and Castle
5-7 Lord Edward St.
Map C3.
Tel 01 475 1122.
www.bullandcastle.ie

The Duke
9 Duke St.
Map D4.
Tel 01 679 9553.

The Globe
11 S Great George's St,
Dublin 2.
Map C4.
Tel 01 671 1220.
www.globe.ie

Grand Central
Abbey St / O'Connell St
Dublin 1.
Map D2.
Tel 01 872 8658.

The Grave Diggers
Prospect Sq, Glasnevin,
Dublin 9.
Map D1.

Grogan's
15 S William St,
Dublin 2.
Map D4.
Tel 01 677 9320.
www.groganspub.ie

Kehoe's
9 S Anne St.
Map D4.
Tel 01 677 8312.

Long Hall
51 S Great George's St.
Map C4.
Tel 01 475 1590

The Market Bar
14a Fade St,
Dublin 2.
Map D4.
Tel 01 613 9094.
www.marketbar.ie

McDaid's
3 Harry St,
off Grafton St.
Map D4.
Tel 01 679 4395.
www.mcdaids.ie

Morgan Bar
The Morgan Hotel,
10 Fleet St, Dublin 2.
Map D3.
Tel 01 643 7000.
www.themorgan.com

Mulligan's
8 Poolbeg St.
Map E3.
Tel 01 677 5582.
www.mulligans.ie

Neary's
1 Chatham St.
Map D4.
Tel 01 677 8596.

Peter's Pub
1 Johnson's Place,
Dublin 2.
Map D4.

Ron Black's
38 Dawson St,
Dublin 2.
Map D4.
Tel 01 672 3231.
www.ronblacks.ie

Stag's Head
1 Dame Court,
off Dame Lane.
Map D4.
Tel 01 679 3687.

The Welcome Inn
13 Parnell St,
Dublin
Map D
Tel 01 874 3227.

NIGHTCLUBS

The Academy
Abbey St, Dublin 1.
Map C2
Tel 01 877 9999.

Copper Face Jacks
29-30 Harcourt St.
Map D5.
Tel 01 475 8777.
www.jackson-court.ie

Crawdaddy
Harcourt St.
Map D5
Tel 01 476 3374.
www.crawdaddy.ie

The Front Lounge
33-34 Parliament St.
Map C3.
Tel 01 670 4112.
www.thefrontlounge.ie

The George
89 Sth Great George's St.
Map C4.
Tel 01 478 2983.
www.thegeorge.ie

Howl at the Moon
718 Lower Mount St.
Map F4
Tel 01 634 5460.
www.howlatthemoon.ie

Joy's
Baggot St, Dublin 2.
Map F5
Tel 01 676 6723.
www.joysniteclub.com

Krystle
Harcourt St, Dublin 2.
Map D5
www.krystlenightclub.
com

Lillie's Bordello
Adam Court,
off Grafton St.
Map E4 D4.
Tel 01 679 9204
www.lilliesbordello.ie

POD, Lobby Bar
Harcourt St.
Map D5. Tel 01
475 3374
www.pod.ie

Ri-Ra
South Great George's
St, Dublin 2.
Map E3.
Tel 01 671 1220.
www.rira.ie

Shebeen Chic
4 Sth Great George's St.
Map C4.
Tel 01 679 9667.
www.shebeenchic.ie

Tripod
Harcourt St, Dublin 2.
Map D5.
Tel 01 476 3374.
www.pod.ie

Twisted Pepper
54 Middle Abbey St
Map D2
Tel 01 873 4038.
www.bodytonicmusic.
com

Dublin's Best: Entertainment

It's easy to pack a lot into a night out in Dublin. Most of the best nightspots are situated close to each other and, in the Temple Bar area alone, there are plenty of exciting haunts to try out. The city offers something to suit every taste and pocket: choose from world-class theatre, excellent concert venues, designer café-bars and lively or laid-back clubs hosting nights of traditional, country, jazz or rock music. Even when there is no specific event that appeals, you can simply enjoy Dublin's inexhaustible supply of great traditional pubs.

Gate Theatre
The Gate puts on both foreign plays and Irish classics such as Sean O'Casey's Juno and the Paycock. *(See p90.)*

Stag's Head
This gorgeous Victorian pub has a long, mahogany bar and has retained its original mirrors and stained glass. Located down an out-of-the-way alley, this atmospheric pub is well worth seeking out. (See p110.)

NORTH OF THE LIFFEY

SOUTHWEST DUBLIN

| 0 metres | 500 |
| 0 yards | 500 |

THE TEMPLE BAR AREA

It will take more than a couple of evenings to explore fully all that these narrow streets have to offer. Many of Dublin's best mid-priced restaurants are here, while modern bars sit next to traditional pubs hosting fiddle sessions. There are also theatres and the Irish Film Institute. Later, clubs play music ranging from country to the latest dance sounds.

MILLENNIUM BRIDGE

HA'PENNY BRIDGE

LIFFEY

WELLINGTON QUAY

ESSEX STREET EAST

TEMPLE BAR

THE AULD DUBLINER

project arts centre

SYCAMORE ST

MEETING HOUSE SQUARE

TEMPLE LANE

CROW ST

FOWNNES STREET

CROWN ALLEY

THE BAD ASS CAFE

COPE STREET

IFI Irish Film Institute

OLYMPIA

DAME STREET

| 0 metres | 100 |
| 0 yards | 100 |

Queuing for a concert in Temple Bar

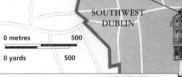

Street theatre events take place throughout the summer in Temple Bar. This actor is portraying George Bernard Shaw in a typical street performance.

Abbey Theatre

Despite recurring financial problems, Ireland's prestigious national theatre still manages to stage compelling new drama, such as An Ideal Husband *by Oscar Wilde. (See p88.)*

The O2

Beating in the heart of Dublin's docklands, the O2 is Ireland's top music venue. Custom built for music, the arena offers perfect sightlines and crystal clear acoustics that make every performance here special. (See p109.)

L I F F E Y

SOUTHEAST DUBLIN

McDaids

Playwright Brendan Behan (see p23) downed many a pint in this pub, which dates from 1779. Though firmly on the tourist trail, McDaid's retains its bohemian charm, and bars upstairs and downstairs provide space for a leisurely drink. (See p113.)

National Concert Hall

As Ireland's premier music venue, the National Concert Hall boasts a thrilling line up of national and international musicians in a broad range of events from traditional to opera, classical to jazz and weekly concerts by resident RTE National Symphony Orchestra. (See p109.)

Street Finder Index

KEY TO THE STREET FINDER

■ Major sight	🚌 Coach station	✝ Church
■ Place of interest	🚕 Taxi rank	☒ Post office
■ Railway station	🅿 Main car park	═ Railway line
🚇 DART station	ℹ Tourist information office	Pedestrian street
🚊 Luas stop	✚ Hospital with casualty unit	
🚍 Main bus stop	🚓 Police station	0 metres 200
		0 yards 200 1:11,500

KEY TO STREET FINDER ABBREVIATIONS

Ave	Avenue	E	East	Pde	Parade	Sth	South
Br	Bridge	La	Lane	Pl	Place	Tce	Terrace
Cl	Close	Lr	Lower	Rd	Road	Up	Upper
Ct	Court	Nth	North	St	Street/Saint	W	West

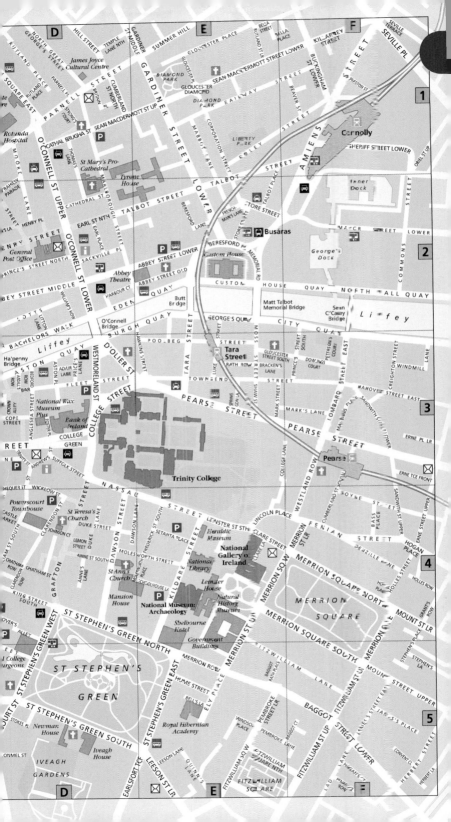

IRELAND REGION BY REGION

Ireland at a Glance

The lure of Ireland's much-vaunted Atlantic shores, from the wild coastline of Cork and Kerry to the remote peninsulas of the Northwest, is strong. However, to neglect the interior would be to miss out on Ireland's equally characteristic landscapes of lush valleys, dark peatlands and unruffled loughs. Most regions are rich in historic sights: from world-famous Neolithic sites in the Midlands to imposing Norman castles in the North and Palladian mansions in the Southeast.

Yeats Country is a charming part of County Sligo closely associated with WB Yeats. The poet was born here and is buried within sight of Ben Bulben's ridge. (See pp232–3.)

NORTHWEST IRELAND
(See pp220–35)

THE WEST OF IRELAND
(See pp200–219)

Connemara National Park *in County Galway boasts stunning landscapes in which mountains and lakes are combined with a dramatic Atlantic coastline. The extensive blanket bogs and moorland are rich in wildlife and unusual plants. (See p208.)*

Bunratty Castle
(See pp192–3)

The Rock of Cashel, *a fortified medieval abbey, perches on a limestone outcrop in the heart of County Tipperary. It boasts some of Ireland's finest Romanesque sculpture. (See pp196–7.)*

THE LOWER SHANNON
(See pp180–99)

CORK AND KERRY
(See pp152–79)

Bantry House
(See pp168–9)

The Lakes of Killarney, *flanked by the lush, wooded slopes of some of the country's highest mountains, are the principal attraction in the southwest of Ireland. (See pp162–3.)*

◁ Colourful Dingle High Street

The Giant's Causeway, *where ancient lava flows have been eroded to reveal columns of unnatural regularity, is Northern Ireland's most curious sight. According to local mythology, the rocks were placed here by a giant called Finn MacCool to enable him to walk across the sea to Scotland.* (See pp262–3.)

NORTHERN IRELAND
(See pp254–85)

Mount Stewart House, *a 19th-century mansion, is most renowned for its magnificent gardens. These were created as recently as the 1920s, but a colourful array of exotic plants has thrived in the warm microclimate enjoyed in this part of County Down.* (See pp282–3.)

Newgrange *(See pp246–7)*

THE MIDLANDS *(See pp236–53)*

SOUTHEAST IRELAND *(See pp124–51)*

Powerscourt *is a large estate in superb countryside on the edge of the Wicklow Mountains. Its grounds rank among the last great formal gardens of Europe. Originally planted in the 1730s, they were restored and embellished in the 19th century.* (See pp134–5.)

```
0 kilometres        50
0 miles        25
```

Kilkenny Castle *was for centuries the stronghold of the Butler dynasty, which controlled much of southeast Ireland in the Middle Ages. The last Norman fortress was remodelled during the Victorian period and still dominates Kilkenny – one of the country's most historic and pleasant towns.* (See pp142–3.)

SOUTHEAST IRELAND

KILDARE · WICKLOW · CARLOW · KILKENNY
WATERFORD · WEXFORD

Blessed with the warmest climate in Ireland, the Southeast has always presented an attractive prospect for settlers. Landscapes of gently rolling hills have been tamed by centuries of cultivation, with lush farmland, imposing medieval castles and great houses enhancing the region's atmosphere of prosperity.

The Southeast's proximity to Britain meant that it was often the first port of call for foreign invaders. Viking raiders arrived here in the 9th century and founded some of Ireland's earliest towns, including Waterford and Wexford. They were followed in 1169 by the Anglo-Normans (see pp36–7), who shaped the region's subsequent development.

Given its strategic importance, the Southeast was heavily protected, mostly by Anglo-Norman lords loyal to the English Crown. Remains of impressive castles attest to the power of the Fitzgeralds of Kildare and the Butlers of Kilkenny, who between them virtually controlled the Southeast throughout the Middle Ages. English influence was stronger here than in any other part of the island.

From the 18th century wealthy Anglo-Irish families were drawn to what they saw as a stable zone, and felt confident enough to build fine mansions like the Palladian masterpieces of Russborough and Castletown. English rule was not universally accepted, however. The Wicklow Mountains became a popular refuge for opponents to the Crown, including the rebels who fled the town of Enniscorthy after a bloody battle during the uprising against the English in 1798 (see p41).

This mountainous region is still the only real wilderness in the Southeast, in contrast to the flat grasslands that spread across Kildare to the west. To the east, sandy beaches stretch almost unbroken along the shore between Dublin and Rosslare in Wexford.

Traditional thatched cottages in Dunmore East, County Waterford

◁ Staircase hall with ornate 18th-century stuccowork in Castletown House, County Kildare

Exploring Southeast Ireland

The southeast has something for everyone, from busy seaside
resorts to quaint canalside villages, Norman abbeys and bird
sanctuaries. The Wicklow Mountains, the location of several major
sights such as the monastic complex of Glendalough and the
magnificent gardens of Powerscourt, provide perfect touring and
walking territory. Further south, the most scenic routes cut through
the valleys of the Slaney, Barrow and Nore rivers, flanked by
historic ports such as New Ross, from where you can explore
local waterways by boat. Along the south coast, which is more
varied than the region's eastern shore, beaches are interspersed
with rocky headlands, and quiet coastal villages provide good
alternative bases to the busy towns of Waterford and Wexford.
Further inland, the best places to stay include Lismore and
Kilkenny, which is one of the finest historic towns in Ireland.

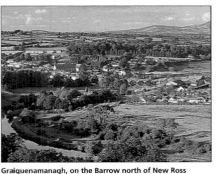

Graiguenamanagh, on the Barrow north of New Ross

SIGHTS AT A GLANCE

Ardmore ⑲
Avondale House ⑭
Bog of Allen Nature Centre ③
Bray ⑧
Brownshill Dolmen ⑮
Castletown House pp130–31 ①
Dunmore East ㉑
Enniscorthy ㉔
Glendalough ⑬
Hook Peninsula ㉒
Irish National Heritage Park ㉕
Jerpoint Abbey ⑰
Johnstown Castle ㉗
Kildare ⑤
Kilkenny pp142–3 ⑯
Killruddery House ⑨
Lismore ⑱
Monasterevin ④
Mount Usher Gardens ⑫
New Ross ㉓
Powerscourt pp134–5 ⑦
Robertstown ②
Rosslare ㉙
Russborough House ⑥

Saltee Islands ㉘
Waterford pp146–7 ⑳
Wexford ㉖
Wicklow Mountains ⑪

Tours
Military Road ⑩

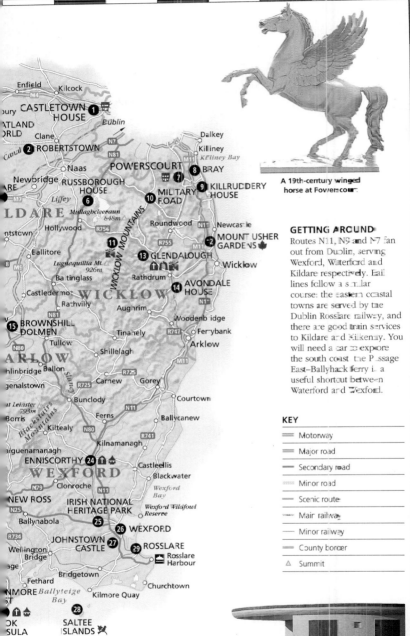

A 19th-century winged horse at Powerscourt.

Enfield
Kilcock
bury CASTLETOWN HOUSE ❶
ATLAND ORLD
Clane
Dublin
ROBERTSTOWN ❷
Naas
Newbridge RUSSBOROUGH HOUSE
ARE
Liffey
❻
POWERSCOURT ❼
Dalkey
Killiney
Killiney Bay
BRAY ❽
KILLRUDDERY HOUSE ❾
MILITARY ROAD ❿
LDARE
Mullaghcleevaun 848m
Hollywood
ntstown
Roundwood
MOUNT USHER GARDENS ⓯
Newcastle
Eallitore
WICKLOW MOUNTAINS
⓫
GLENDALOUGH ⓭
Wicklow
Lugnequillia Mt. 926m
Batinglass
Rathdrum
AVONDALE HOUSE ⓮
Castledermot
WICKLOW
Rathvilly
Aughrim
BROWNSHILL DOLMEN ⓯
Woodenbridge
Ferrybank
Tinahely
Arklow
Tullow
Shillelagh
ARLOW
hlinbridge Ballon
Carnew
Gorey
genalstown
Bunclody
Courtown
at Leinster 793m
Borris
Ferns
Ballycanew
Kilteally
Kilnamanagh
aiguenamanagh
ENNISCORTHY ㉔
WEXFORD
Castleellis
Blackwater
Clonroche
Wexford Bay
NEW ROSS
IRISH NATIONAL HERITAGE PARK ㉕
Wexford Wildfowl Reserve
Ballynabola
WEXFORD ㉖
JOHNSTOWN CASTLE ㉗
ROSSLARE ㉙
Wellington Bridge
Rosslare Harbour
age
Bridgetown
Fethard
NMORE Ballyteige Bay
Kilmore Quay
Churchtown
㉘
OK SULA
SALTEE ISLANDS

GETTING AROUND

Routes N11, N9 and N7 fan out from Dublin, serving Wexford, Waterford and Kildare respectively. Rail lines follow a similar course: the eastern coastal towns are served by the Dublin Rosslare railway, and there are good train services to Kildare and Kilkenny. You will need a car to explore the south coast; the Passage East–Ballyhack ferry is a useful shortcut between Waterford and Wexford.

KEY

═══	Motorway
───	Major road
───	Secondary road
⋯⋯	Minor road
───	Scenic route
═══	Main railway
───	Minor railway
───	County border
△	Summit

SEE ALSO

The seaside resort of Bray on the east coast

Castletown House ❶

See pp130–31.

Robertstown ❷

Road map D4. Co Kildare. 650.

Ten locks west along the Grand Canal from Dublin, Robertstown is a characteristic 19th-century canalside village, with warehouses and cottages flanking the waterfront. Freight barges plied the route until about 1960, but pleasure boats have since replaced them. Visitors can take barge cruises from the quay and the Robertstown Hotel, built in 1801 for canal passengers, is now used for banquets.

Near Sallins, about 8 km (5 miles) east of Robertstown, the canal is carried over the River Liffey along the **Leinster Aqueduct**, an impressive structure built in 1783.

Bog of Allen Nature Centre ❸

Road map D4. Lullymore, Co Kildare. *Tel* 045 860133. to Newbridge. to Allenwood. 9:30am–4pm Mon–Fri ltd. www.ipcc.ie

Anyone interested in the natural history of Irish bogs should visit The Nature Centre. Housed in an old farmhouse at Lullymore, 9 km (6 miles) northeast of Rathangan, it lies at the heart of the Bog of Allen, a vast expanse of raised bogland *(see p252)* that extends across the counties of Offaly,

The Robertstown Hotel in Robertstown

Laois and Kildare. An exhibition of flora, fauna and archaeological finds explores the history and ecology of the bog, while pre-booked guided walks across the peatlands introduce visitors to the bog's delicate ecosystem.

Stacking peat for use as fuel

Monasterevin ❹

Road map D4. Co Kildare. 3,000.

This Georgian market town lies west of Kildare, where the Grand Canal crosses the River Barrow. Waterborne trade brought prosperity to Monasterevin in the 18th century, but the locks now see little traffic. However, you can still admire the aqueduct, which is a superb example of canal engineering.

Moore Abbey, next to the church, was built in the 18th century on the site of a monastic foundation, but the grand Gothic mansion owes much to Victorian remodelling. Once the ancestral seat of the Earls of Drogheda, in the 1920s Moore Abbey became the home of the celebrated tenor, John McCormack *(see p24)*. It is now a hospital.

Kildare ❺

Road map D4. Co Kildare. 7,500. *Market House* 045 521240. Thu. www.kildare.ie

The charming and tidy town of Kildare is dominated by **St Brigid's Cathedral**, which commemorates the saint who founded a religious community on this site in 480. Unusually, monks and nuns lived here under the same roof, but this was not the only unorthodox practice associated with the community. Curious pagan rituals, including the burning of a perpetual fire, continued until the 16th century. The fire pit is still visible, as is the highest round tower that can be climbed in Ireland, which was probably built in the 12th

St Brigid's Cathedral and roofless round tower in Kildare town

Japanese Gardens at Tully near Kildare

century and has a Romanesque doorway. The cathedral was rebuilt in the Victorian era, but the restorers largely adhered to the 13th-century design.

🏠 St Brigid's Cathedral
Market Square. **Tel** 085 120 5920 ◐ May–Sep: daily. **Donation.** ♿

Environs
Kildare lies at the heart of racing country: the Curragh racecourse is nearby, stables are scattered all around and bloodstock sales take place at Kill, northeast of town.

The **National Stud** is a semi-state-run bloodstock farm at Tully, just south of Kildare. It was founded in 1900 by an eccentric Anglo-Irish colonel called William Hall-Walker. He sold his foals on the basis of their astrological charts, and put skylights in the stables to allow the horses to be "touched" by sunlight and moonbeams. Hall-Walker received the title Lord Waverree in reward for bequeathing the farm to the British Crown in 1915.

Visitors can explore the 400-ha (1,000-acre) grounds and watch the horses being exercised. Mares are generally kept in a separate paddock from the stallions. Breeding stallions wait in the covering shed: each one is expected to cover 100 mares per season. There is a special foaling unit where the mare and foal can remain undisturbed after the birth.

The farm has its own forge and saddlery, and also a Horse Museum. Housed in an old stable block, this illustrates the importance of horses in Irish life. Exhibits include the frail skeleton of Arkle, a famous champion steeple-chaser in the 1960s.

Sharing the same estate as the National Stud are the **Japanese Gardens** and **St Fiachra's Garden.** The Japanese Gardens were laid out in 1906–10 by Japanese landscape gardener Tassa Eida, with the help of his son Minoru and 40 assistants. The impressive array of trees and shrubs includes maple, bonsai, mulberry, magnolia, sacred bamboo and cherry. The gardens take the form of an allegorical journey through life, beginning with the Gate of Oblivion and leading to the Gateway of Eternity, a contemplative Zen rock garden.

St Fiachra's Garden covers 1.6 ha (4 acres) of woodland, wetland, lakes and islands, and features a Waterford Crystal Garden within the monastic cells.

♣ National Stud and Japanese and St Fiachra's Gardens
Tully. **Tel** 045 521617. ◐ mid-Feb– mid-Nov: 9:30am–5:30pm, mid-Nov– 22 Dec: 9:30am–5pm (las adm: 3pm). 🅿 ♿ ♿ National Stud only. 🖥 📷 www.irish-national-stud.ie

---

HORSE RACING IN IRELAND

Ireland has a strong racing culture and, thanks to its non-elitist image, the sport is enjoyed by all. Much of the thoroughbred industry centres around the Curragh, a grassy plain in County Kildare stretching unfenced for more than 2,000 ha (5,000 acres). This area is home to many of the country's studs and training yards, and every morning horses are put through their paces on the gallops. Most of the major flat races, including the Irish Derby, take place at the Curragh racecourse just east of Kildare. Other fixtures are held at nearby Punchestown – most famously the steeplechase festival in April/May – and at Leopardstown, which also hosts major National Hunt races (see pp28–9).

Finishing straight at the Curragh racecourse

Castletown House ❶

Built in 1722–29 for William Conolly, Speaker of the Irish Parliament, the façade of Castletown was the work of Florentine architect Alessandro Galilei and gave Ireland its first taste of Palladianism. The magnificent interiors date from the second half of the 18th century. They were commissioned by Lady Louisa Lennox, wife of William Conolly's great-nephew, Tom, who lived here from 1759. Castletown remained in the family until 1965, when it was taken over by the Irish Georgian Society. The state now owns the house and it is open to the public.

Conolly crest on an armchair

★ Long Gallery
The heavy ceiling sections and friezes date from the 1720s and the walls were decorated in the Pompeiian manner in the 1770s.

Green Drawing Room

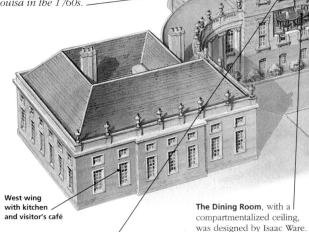

Red Drawing Room
The red damask covering the walls of this room is probably French and dates from the 19th century. This exquisite mahogany bureau was made for Lady Louisa in the 1760s.

West wing with kitchen and visitor's café

Boudoir Wall Paintings
The boudoir's decorative panels, moved here from the Long Gallery, were inspired by the Raphael Loggia in the Vatican.

The Dining Room, with a compartmentalized ceiling, was designed by Isaac Ware.

VISITORS' CHECKLIST

Road map D4. Celbridge, Co
Kildare **Tel** 01 628 8252.
57, 67A from Dublin.
mid-Mar–end-Oct:
10am–6pm Tue–Sun (est adm:
4:45pm). (limited)
obligatory **Summer concerts**.
www.castletown.ie

★ **Print Room**
*In this, the only intact 18th-century print room in Ireland,
Lady Louisa indulged her taste for Italian engravings. It was
fashionable at that time for ladies to paste prints directly on
to the wall and frame them with elaborate festoons.*

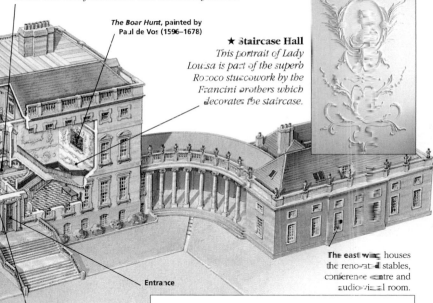

The Boar Hunt, painted by
Paul de Vos (1596–1678)

★ **Staircase Hall**
*This portrait of Lady
Louisa is part of the superb
Rococo stuccowork by the
Francini brothers which
decorates the staircase.*

The east wing houses
the renovated stables,
conference centre and
audio-visual room.

Entrance

The Entrance Hall is an
austere Neo-Classical room.
Its most decorative feature is
the delicate carving on the
pilasters of the upper gallery.

STAR FEATURES

★ Long Gallery

★ Print Room

★ Staircase Hall

CONOLLY'S FOLLY

This folly, which lies just
beyond the grounds of
Castletown House, provides
the focus of the view from
the Long Gallery. Speaker
Conolly's widow, Katherine,
commissioned it in 1740
as a memorial to her late
husband, and to provide
employment after a harsh
winter. The unusual structure
of superimposed arches
crowned by an obelisk is
from designs by Richard
Cassels, architect of Russborough House (*see p.132*).

Saloon in Russborough House with original fireplace and stuccowork

Russborough House ⑥

Road map D4. Blessington, Co Wicklow. **Tel** 045 865239. 🚌 65 from Dublin. ⬜ May–Sep: 10am–6pm daily; mid-Mar–Apr & Oct: 10am–6pm Sun & public hols. 🎫 🎥 obligatory. ♿ 📷 💻 www.russborough.ie

This Palladian mansion, built in the 1740s for Joseph Leeson, Earl of Milltown, is one of Ireland's finest houses. Its architect, Richard Cassels, also designed Powerscourt House (see pp134–5) and is credited with introducing the Palladian style to Ireland.

Unlike many grand estates in the Pale, Russborough has

survived magnificently, both inside and out. The house claims the longest frontage in Ireland, with a façade adorned by heraldic lions and curved colonnades. The interior is even more impressive. Many rooms feature superb stucco decoration, which was done largely by the Italian Francini brothers, who also worked on Castletown House (see pp130–31). The best examples are found in the music room, saloon and library, which are embellished with exuberant foliage and cherubs. Around the main staircase, a

Vernet seascape in the drawing room

riot of Rococo plasterwork depicts a hunt, with hounds clasping garlands of flowers. The stucco mouldings in the drawing room were designed especially to enclose marine scenes by the French artist, Joseph Vernet (1714–89). The paintings were sold in 1926, but recovered over 40 years later and returned to the house.

Russborough has many other treasures, including finely worked fireplaces of Italian marble, imposing mahogany doorways and priceless collections of silver, porcelain and Gobelin tapestries.

Such riches aside, one of the principal reasons to visit Russborough is to see the **Beit Art Collection**, famous for its Flemish, Dutch and Spanish Old Master paintings. Sir Alfred Beit, who bought the house in 1952, inherited the pictures from his uncle – also named Alfred Beit and co-founder of the de Beers diamond mining empire in South Africa. In 1974, 1986 and 2000 several masterpieces were stolen from the house. Most were later retrieved. More disappeared in another robbery in 2001, but were recovered. Only a selection of paintings is on view in the house at any one time, while others are on permanent loan to the National Gallery in Dublin

---

THE HISTORY OF THE PALE

The term "Pale" refers to an area around Dublin which marked the limits of English influence from Norman to Tudor times. The frontier fluctuated, but at its largest the Pale stretched from Dundalk in County Louth to Waterford town. Gaelic chieftains outside the area could keep their lands provided they agreed to bring up their heirs within the Pale.

The Palesmen supported their rulers' interests and considered themselves the upholders of English values. This widened the gap between the Gaelic majority and the Anglo-Irish, a foretaste of England's doomed involvement in the country. Long after its fortifications were dismantled, the idea of the Pale lived on as a state of mind. The expression "beyond the pale" survives as a definition of those outside the bounds of civilized society.

An 18th-century family enjoying the privileged lifestyle typical within the Pale

Bray's beachfront esplanade, with Bray Head in the background

(see pp 70–71). A self-guided interactive exhibition in the basement includes 3D photographs taken by Sir Alfred Beit in the 1920s and 1930s, as well as a selection of vinyl records and sheet music from the 1920s.

The west wing of the building was fully restored following a fire in 2010, and eight double bedrooms are now available to rent. Bookings can be made through the Irish Landmark Trust (www.irishlandmark.com).

Environs
The **Poulaphouca Reservoir**, which was formed by the damming of the River Liffey, extends south from Blessington. It is popular with watersports enthusiasts, while others enjoy the mountain views.

Powerscourt 7

See pp134–5.

Bray 8

Road map D4. Co Wicklow. 33,000. DART. Old Court House, Main St (01 286 7128). www.visitwicklow.ie

Once a refined Victorian resort, Bray is nowadays a brash holiday town, with amusement arcades and fish and chip shops lining the seafront. Its beach attracts large crowds in summer, including many young families. A more peaceful alternative is nearby Bray Head,

where there is scope for bracing cliffside walks. Bray also makes a good base from which to explore Powerscourt Gardens, the Wicklow Mountains and the coastal villages of Killiney and Dalkey *(see p103)*.

Killruddery House and Gardens 9

Road map D4. Bray, Co Wicklow. **Tel** 087 419 8574. **House** Jun–Sep: 1–5pm daily. **Gardens** 1 May–30 Sep: 9.30am–5pm daily; Apr & Oct: weekends only. outside main opening times, groups of 20–50 by appt only. limited. www.killruddery.com

Killruddery House lies just to the south of Bray, in the shadow of Little Sugar Loaf Mountain. Built in 1651, it has been the family seat of the Earls of Meath ever since, although the original mansion

was remodelled in an Elizabethan Revival style in the early 19th century. The house contains some good carving and stuccowork, but the real charm of Killruddery lies in the 17th-century formal gardens, regarded as the finest French Classical gardens in the country. They were laid out in the 1680s by a French gardener named Bonet, who also worked at Versailles.

The gardens, planted with great precision, feature romantic parterres, hedges and many fine trees and shrubs. The sylvan theatre, a small enclosure surrounded by a bay hedge, is the only known example of its kind in Ireland.

The Long Ponds, a pair of canals which extend 165 m (542 ft), once stocked fish. Beyond, a pool enclosed by two circular hedges leads to a Victorian arrangement of paths flanked by statues and hedges of yew, beech and lime.

View across the Long Ponds to Killruddery House

Powerscourt ⑦

The gardens at Powerscourt are probably the finest in Ireland, both for their design and their dramatic setting at the foot of Great Sugar Loaf Mountain. The house and grounds were commissioned in the 1730s by Richard Wingfield, the 1st Viscount Powerscourt. New ornamental gardens were completed in 1875 by the 7th Viscount, who added gates, urns and statues collected during his travels in Europe. The house was gutted by an accidental fire in 1974, but the ground floor has been beautifully renovated and now accommodates an upmarket shopping centre with an excellent restaurant and café.

Laocoön statue on upper terrace

Bamberg Gate
Made in Vienna in the 1770s, this gilded wrought-iron gate was brought to Powerscourt by the 7th Viscount from Bamberg Church in Bavaria.

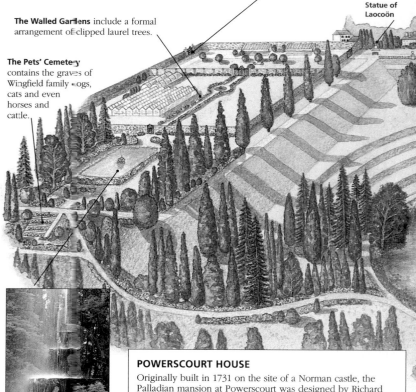

Statue of Laocoön

The Walled Gardens include a formal arrangement of clipped laurel trees.

The Pets' Cemetery contains the graves of Wingfield family dogs, cats and even horses and cattle.

Dolphin Pond
This pool, designed as a fish pond in the 18th century, is enclosed by exotic conifers in a lovely secluded garden.

POWERSCOURT HOUSE

Originally built in 1731 on the site of a Norman castle, the Palladian mansion at Powerscourt was designed by Richard Cassels, who was also the architect of Russborough House *(see p132)*. In 1974 a fire left the fine building a burnt-out, roofless shell. The Slazenger family, who now own the estate, have restored part of the house. It now includes a terrace café, speciality shops and audiovisual displays covering the history of the estate.

Powerscourt ablaze in 1974

★ The Perron
Leading down to Triton Lake is the Perron, a beautiful Italianate stairway added in 1874. Beside the lake, it is guarded by two statues of Pegasus – the mythical winged horse and emblem of the Wingfield family.

The Italian Garden is laid out on terraces which were first cut into the steep hillside in the 1730s.

Pebble Mosaic
Many tonnes of pebbles were gathered from nearby Bray beach to build the Perron and to make this mosaic on the terrace.

VISITORS' CHECKLIST

Road map D4. Enniskerry, Co Wicklow. **Tel** 01 204 6000.
185 from Bray DART station.
9:30am–5:30pm/dusk
Oct–Mar daily. 25 & 26 Dec.
www.powerscourt.ie

The Pepper Pot Tower was built in 1911.

★ Triton Lake
Made for the first garden, the lake takes its name from its central fountain, which is modelled on a 17th-century work by Bernini in Rome.

★ Japanese Gardens
These enchanting Edwardian gardens, created out of bogland, contain Chinese conifers and bamboo trees.

STAR FEATURES

★ Japanese Gardens

★ The Perron

★ Triton Lake

Powerscourt Gardens with Great Sugar Loaf Mountain beyond ▷

A Tour of the Military Road ⑩

Rare red squirrel

The British built the Military Road through the heart of the Wicklow Mountains during a campaign to flush out Irish rebels after an uprising in 1798 *(see p149)*. Now known as the R115, this road takes you through the emptiest and most rugged landscapes of County Wicklow. Fine countryside, in which deer and other wildlife flourish, is characteristic of the whole of this tour.

Powerscourt Waterfall ⑨
The River Dargle cascades 130 m (425 ft) over a granite escarpment to form Ireland's highest waterfall.

Glencree ①
The former British barracks in Glencree are among several found along the Military Road.

Sally Gap ②
This remote pass is surrounded by a vast expanse of blanket bog dotted with pools and streams.

Glenmacnass ③
After Sally Gap, the road drops into a deep glen where a waterfall spills dramatically over rocks.

Glendalough ④
This ancient lakeside monastery *(see pp140–41)*, enclosed by wooded slopes, is the prime historical sight in the Wicklow Mountains.

Great Sugar Loaf ⑧
The granite cone of Great Sugar Loaf Mountain can be climbed in under an hour from the car park on its southern side.

Lough Tay ⑦
Stark, rocky slopes plunge down to the dark waters of Lough Tay. Though it lies within a Guinness-owned estate, the lake is accessible to walkers.

Roundwood ⑥
The highest village in Ireland at 238 m (780 ft) above sea level, Roundwood enjoys a fine setting. Its main street is lined with pubs, cafés and craft shops.

Vale of Clara ⑤
This picturesque wooded valley follows the River Avonmore. It contains the tiny village of Clara, which consists of two houses, a church and a school.

TIPS FOR DRIVERS

Length: 96 km (60 miles).
Stopping-off points: There are several pubs and cafés in Enniskerry (including Poppies, an old-fashioned tearoom), and also in Roundwood, but this area is better for picnics. There are several marked picnic spots south of Enniskerry. (See also pp385–7.)

0 kilometers   5

0 miles   5

KEY

▬▬	Tour route
≈≈≈	Other roads
✲	Viewpoint

Map labels: DUBLIN, Enniskerry, Powerscourt, Glencree, R115, R760, Dargle, R755, R759, R115, Lough Dan, Vartry Reservoir, Annamoe, Glenmacnass, R756, Laragh, Avonmore, R755, Clara, RATHDRUM

Wicklow Mountains ⑪

Road map D4. 🚂 to Rathdrum & Wicklow. 🚌 to Enniskerry. Wicklow, Glendalough, Rathdrum & Avoca.
🏛 Rialto House, Fitzwilliam Square, Wicklow (0404 69117). **www.**
discoverireland.ie/eastcoast

Standing amid the rugged wilderness of the Wicklow Mountains, it can be hard to believe that Dublin is under an hour's drive away. The inaccessibility of the mountains meant that they once provided a safe hideout for opponents of English rule. When much of the southeast was obedient to the English Crown, within an area known as the Pale *(see p132)*, warlords such as the O'Tooles ruled in the Wicklow Mountains. Rebels who took part in the 1798 uprising *(see p41)* sought refuge here too. One of their leaders, Michael Dwyer, remained at liberty in the hills around Sally Gap until 1803.

The building of the **Military Road**, started in 1800, made the area more accessible, but the mountains are still thinly populated. There is little traffic to disturb enjoyment of the beautiful rock-strewn glens, lush forest and bogland where heather gives a purple sheen to the land. Turf-cutting is still a thriving cottage industry, and

you often see peat stacked up by the road. Numerous walking trails weave through these landscapes. Among them is the **Wicklow Way**, which extends 132 km (82 miles) from Marlay Park in Dublin to Clonegal in County Carlow. It is marked but not always easy to follow, so do not set out without a decent map. Although no peak exceeds 915 m (3,000 ft), the Wicklow Mountains can be dangerous in bad weather.

Hiking apart, there is plenty to see and do in this region. A good starting point for exploring the northern area is the picture-postcard estate village of **Enniskerry**. In summer, it is busy with tourists who come to visit the gardens at Powerscourt *(see pp134–5)*. From Laragh, to the south, you can reach Glendalough *(see pp140–41)* and the **Vale of Avoca**, where cherry trees are laden with blossom in the spring. The beauty of this gentle valley was captured in the poetry of Thomas Moore (1779–1852): "There is not in the wide world a valley so sweet as that vale in whose bosom the bright waters meet" – a reference to the confluence of the Avonbeg and Avonmore rivers, the so-called **Meeting of the Waters** beyond Avondale House *(see p141)*. Nestled among wooded

Bearnas na Diallaite **SALLY GAP**	
↑ Bealach Míleata **MILITARY ROAD**	✈
← Cleann Life **LIFFEY VALLEY**	↗
Bealach Fheartíre **VARTRY DRIVE** →	

Road sign in the Wicklow Mountains

Mount Usher Gardens, on the banks of the River Vartry

hills at the heart of the valley is the hamlet of Avoca, where the **Avoca Handweavers** produce colourful tweeds in the oldest hand-weaving mill in Ireland, in operation since 1723.

Further north, towards the coast near Ashford, the River Vartry rushes through the deep chasm of the **Devil's Glen**. On entering the valley, the river falls 30 m (100 ft) into a pool known as the **Devil's Punchbowl**. There are good walks around here, with fine views of the coast.

🏠 **Avoca Handweavers**
Avoca. **Tel** 0402 35105. 🅿 daily. 🌐
25 & 26 Dec. 🟦 🏠 www.avoca.ie

Mount Usher Gardens ⑫

Road map D4. Ashford, Co Wicklow.
Tel 0404 40205. 🚂 🚌 Ashford.
🕐 Mar–Oct: 10:30am–6pm daily.
🅿 🏠 🛍 open all year. 🚻 limited.
🍴 call to book. www.mount
ushergardens.ie

Set beside the River Vartry just east of Ashford are the Mount Usher Gardens. They were designed in 1868 by a Dubliner, Edward Walpole, who imbued them with his strong sense of romanticism.

The gardens contain many rare shrubs and trees, from Chinese conifers and bamboos to Mexican pines. The Maple Walk is glorious in autumn. The river provides the main focus, and amid the vegetation you can glimpse herons.

Colourful moorland around Sally Gap in the Wicklow Mountains

For hotels and restaurants in this region see pp299–302 and pp328–31

Glendalough ⓲

Road map D4. Co Wicklow. 🚌 *St Kevin's Bus from Dublin.* **Ruins** ⬚ *daily.* 📷 *in summer.* **Visitor Centre** **Tel** *0404 45325/45252.* ⬚ *daily.* ⬤ *23–30 Dec.* 📷

The steep, wooded slopes of Glendalough, the "valley of the two lakes", harbour one of Ireland's most atmospheric monastic sites. Established by St Kevin in the 6th century, the settlement was sacked time and again by the Vikings but nevertheless flourished for over 600 years. Decline set in only after English forces partially razed the site in 1398, though it functioned as a monastic centre until the Dissolution of the Monasteries in 1539 *(see p38)*. Pilgrims kept on coming to Glendalough even after that, particularly on St Kevin's Feast Day, 3 June, which was often a riotous event *(see p30)*.

The age of the buildings is uncertain, but most date from the 10th to 12th centuries. Many were restored during the 1870s.

View along the Upper Lake at Glendalough

The main group of ruins lies east of the Lower Lake, but other buildings associated with St Kevin are by the Upper Lake. Here, where the scenery is much wilder, you are better able to enjoy the tranquillity of Glendalough and to escape the crowds which inevitably descend on the site. Try to arrive as early as possible in the day, particularly during the peak tourist season. You enter the monastery through the double stone arch of the **Gatehouse**, the only surviving example in Ireland of a gateway into a monastic enclosure.

A short walk leads to a graveyard with a **Round Tower** in one corner. Reaching 30 m (100 ft) in height, this is one of the finest of its kind in the country. Its cap was rebuilt in the 1870s using stones found inside the tower. The roofless **Cathedral** nearby dates mainly from the

St Kevin's Kitchen

10th and 12th centuries and is the valley's largest ruin. At the centre of the churchyard stands the tiny **Priests' House**, whose name derives from the fact that it was a burial place for local clergy. The worn carving of a robed figure above the door is possibly of St Kevin, flanked by two disciples. East of here, **St Kevin's Cross** dates from the 8th century. Made of granite, it is one of the best preserved of Glendalough's High Crosses. Below, nestled in the lush valley, a minuscule oratory with a steeply pitched stone roof is a charming sight. Erected in the 11th century or even earlier, it is popularly known as **St Kevin's Kitchen;** this is perhaps because its belfry, thought to be a later addition, resembles a chimney. One of the earliest churches at Glendalough, **St Mary's**, lies across a field to the west. Some traces of

Remains of the Gatehouse, the original entrance to Glendalough

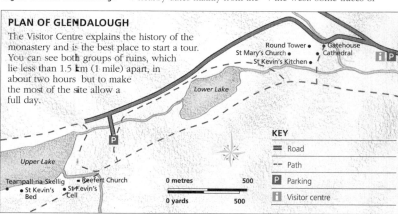

PLAN OF GLENDALOUGH

The Visitor Centre explains the history of the monastery and is the best place to start a tour. You can see both groups of ruins, which lie less than 1.5 km (1 mile) apart, in about two hours but to make the most of the site allow a full day.

Round Tower ●   ● Gatehouse
St Mary's Church ●   ● Cathedral
— St Kevin's Kitchen ●

Lower Lake

Upper Lake

Teampall-na-Skellig   ● Reefert Church
● St Kevin's   ● St Kevin's
Bed   Cell

0 metres   500
0 yards   500

KEY

═	Road
--	Path
P	Parking
i	Visitor centre

Round tower at Glendalough

moulding are visible outside the east window. Following the path along the south bank of the river, you reach the Upper Lake. This is the site of more monastic ruins and is also the chief starting point for walks through the valley and to a number of abandoned lead and zinc mines.

Situated in a grove not far from the Poulanass waterfall are the ruins of the **Reefert Church**, a simple nave-and-chancel building. Its unusual name is a corruption of *Righ Fearta*, meaning "burial place of the kings"; the church may mark the site of an ancient cemetery. Near here, on a rocky spur overlooking the Upper Lake, stands **St Kevin's Cell**, the ruins of a beehive-shaped structure which is thought to have been the hermit's home.

There are two sites on the south side of the lake which cannot be reached on foot but are visible from the opposite shore. **Teampall-na-Skellig**, or the "church of the rock", was supposedly built on the site of the first church that St Kevin founded at Glendalough. To the east of it, carved into the cliff, is **St Kevin's Bed**. This small cave, in reality little more than a rocky ledge above the upper lake, was apparently used as a retreat by St Kevin. It was from here that the saint allegedly rejected the advances of a woman by tossing her into the lake.

ST KEVIN AT GLENDALOUGH

St Kevin was born in 498, a descendant of the royal house of Leinster. He rejected his life of privilege, however, choosing to live instead as a hermit in a cave at Glendalough. He later founded a monastery here, and went on to create a notable centre of learning devoted to the care of the sick and the copying and illumination of manuscripts. St Kevin attracted many disciples to Glendalough during his lifetime, but the monastery became more celebrated as a place of pilgrimage after his death in around 618.

Colourful legends about the saint make up for the dearth of facts about him. That he lived to the age of 120 is just one of the stories told about him. Another tale claims that one day, when St Kevin was at prayer, a blackbird laid an egg in one of his outstretched hands. The saint remained in the same position until it was hatched.

Avondale House ⓮

Road map D4. Co Wicklow. **Tel** 0404 46111. 🚊 🚌 to Rathdrum. **House** ⭕ Easter–Oct. check website for days and times. ⬤ Good Fri & 23–28 Dec. ♿ 🚻 🎁 ☕ limited. **Grounds** ⭕ daily. www.coilteoutdoor.ie

Lying just south of Rathdrum, Avondale House is the birthplace of the 19th-century politician and patriot, Charles Stewart Parnell (*see p43*). The Georgian mansion is now a museum dedicated to Parnell and the fight for Home Rule.

The grounds are open to the public. Known as **Avondale Forest Park**, they include an impressive arboretum first planted in the 18th century and much added to

since 1900. There are some lovely walks through the woods, with pleasant views along the River Avonmore.

Brownshill Dolmen ⓯

Road map D4. Co Carlow. 🚊 🚌 to Carlow. ⭕ daily.

In a field 3 km (2 miles) east of Carlow, along the R726, stands a dolmen boasting the biggest capstone in Ireland. Weighing a reputed 100 tonnes, this massive stone is embedded in the earth at one end and supported at the other by three much smaller stones.

Dating back to 4000 BC, Brownshill Dolmen is thought to mark the tomb of a local chieftain. A path leads to it from the road.

Brownshill Dolmen, famous for its enormous capstone

Street-by-Street: Kilkenny ⑯

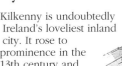

Kilkenny coat of arms

Kilkenny is undoubtedly Ireland's loveliest inland city. It rose to prominence in the 13th century and became the medieval capital of Ireland. The Anglo-Norman Butler family came to power in the 1390s and held sway over the city for 500 years. Their power has gone but their legacy is visible in the city's historic buildings, many of which have been restored. Kilkenny is proud of its heritage and every August hosts the Republic's top arts festival.

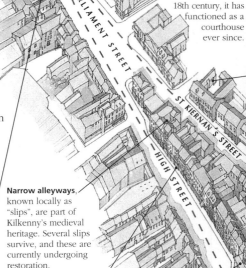

To Irishtown, St Canice's Cathedral

Grace's Castle was built in 1210 and later converted into a jail. Remodelled in the 18th century, it has functioned as a courthouse ever since.

PARLIAMENT STREET

ST KIERNAN'S STREET

HIGH STREET

Narrow alleyways, known locally as "slips", are part of Kilkenny's medieval heritage. Several slips survive, and these are currently undergoing restoration.

Marble City Bar

Tholsel (City Hall)

★ **Rothe House**
This fine Tudor merchant's house, built around two court-yards, is fronted by arcades once typical of Kilkenny's main streets. A small museum inside the house contains a display of local archaeological artifacts and a costume collection.

Butter Slip
The alley is named after the butter stalls that once lined this small market place.

View of the High Street
The 18th-century Tholsel, with its distinctive clock tower and arcade, is the main landmark on the High Street. Its elegant Georgian chamber is used by city councillors to this day.

STAR SIGHTS

★ Kilkenny Castle

★ Rothe House

Kyteler's Inn

This medieval coaching inn (see p346) is named after Dame Alice Kyteler, a 14th-century witch who once lived in the building. Like most of the pubs in the city, Kyteler's Inn sells Smithwick's beer, which has been brewed in Kilkenny since 1710.

VISITORS' CHECKLIST

Road map D4. Co Kilkenny.
26,000. Dublin Rd (056 772 2024) Bus Éireann (051 317 864). Shee Almshouse Rose Inn St (056 775 1500) **Rothe House Tel** 056 772 2853. Apr–Oct: 10:30am–5pm Mon–Sat, 3–5pm Sun; Nov–Mar: 10:30am–4:30pm Mon–Sat. 1–2pm Sat.

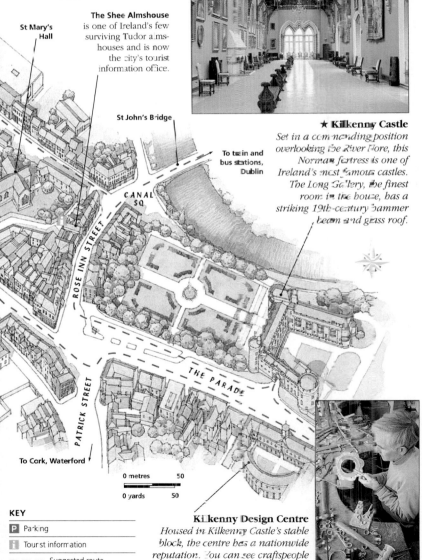

The Shee Almshouse is one of Ireland's few surviving Tudor alms-houses and is now the city's tourist information office.

St Mary's Hall

St John's Bridge

To train and bus stations, Dublin

CANAL SQ

ROSE INN STREET

THE PARADE

PATRICK STREET

To Cork, Waterford

★ Kilkenny Castle

Set in a commanding position overlooking the River Nore, this Norman fortress is one of Ireland's most famous castles. The Long Gallery, the finest room in the house, has a striking 19th-century hammer beam and glass roof.

0 metres 50
0 yards 50

KEY

P Parking

i Tourist information

- - - Suggested route

Kilkenny Design Centre

Housed in Kilkenny Castle's stable block, the centre has a nationwide reputation. You can see craftspeople in action and also buy their work.

Exploring Kilkenny

In a lovely spot beside a kink in the River Nore, Kilkenny is of great architectural interest, with much use made of the distinctive local black limestone, known as Kilkenny marble. A tour of the town also reveals many unexpected treasures: a Georgian façade often seems to conceal a Tudor chimney, a Classical interior or some other surprise.

The survival of the Irishtown district, now dominated by St Canice's Cathedral, recalls past segregation in Kilkenny. The area once known as Englishtown still boasts the city's grandest public buildings.

As a brewery city, Kilkenny is a paradise for keen drinkers, with at least 60 pubs to choose from.

Sign of the Marble City Bar on Kilkenny's High Street

♠ Kilkenny Castle

The Parade. **Tel** 056 770 4106.
⬤ daily. ⬤ Good Fri & Christmas.
🎦 □ 📷 🎦 obligatory. ⬤
limited. Queues are likely during the summer. www.kilkennycastle.ie

Built in the 1190s, Kilkenny Castle was occupied right up until 1935. The powerful Butler family (see p142) lived in it from the late 14th century, but because of the exorbitant running costs, their descendants eventually donated Kilkenny Castle to the nation in 1967. With its drum towers and

North side of Kilkenny Castle showing Victorian crenellations

solid walls, the castle retains its medieval form, but has undergone many alterations. The Victorian changes made in Gothic Revival style have had the most enduring impact.

Two wings of the castle have been restored to their 19th-century splendour and include a library, drawing room and the magnificent Long Gallery with its restored picture collection. The final phase of restoration is complete and includes a state-of-the-art conference centre, which is situated in one of the castle's 12th-century towers.

The castle grounds have diminished considerably over the centuries, but the French Classical gardens remain, with terraces opening onto a woodland walk and pleasant rolling parkland.

♠ St Canice's Cathedral

Irishtown. **Tel** 056 776 4971.
⬤ daily. 🎦 🛈 ⬤
www.stcanicescathedral.ie

The hilltop cathedral, flanked by a round tower, was built in the 13th century in an Early English Gothic style. It was sacked by Cromwell's forces in

1650, but has survived as one of Ireland's medieval treasures. Walls of the local Kilkenny limestone and pillars of pale limestone combine to create an interior of simple grandeur. An array of splendid 16th-century tombs includes the beautiful effigies of the Butler family in the south transept. It is worth climbing the tower for a fine view over Kilkenny.

♠ Black Abbey

Abbey St. **Tel** 056 772 1279.
⬤ daily. ⬤ www.kilkenny.ie

Lying just west of Parliament Street, this Dominican abbey was founded in 1225. Part of it was turned into a courthouse in the 16th century, but is once again a working monastery. The church has a fine vaulted undercroft, distinctive stonework, some beautiful stained-glass windows, and a 14th-century alabaster statue of the holy trinity.

Environs

Just north of the town lies **Dunmore Cave**, a limestone cavern with an impressive series of chambers, noted for its steep descent and curious rock formations.

Bennettsbridge, on the Nore 8 km (5 miles) south of Kilkenny, is famous for its ceramics. The Nicholas Mosse Pottery (see p357) specializes in colourful earthenware made from the local clay.

🎣 Dunmore Cave

Ballyfoyle. **Tel** 056 776 7726.
⬤ Mar–Oct: daily; Nov–Feb: Wed–Sun. 🎦 □ 🎦 obligatory. **www.**heritageireland.ie

Tomb of 2nd Marquess of Ormonde in St Canice's Cathedral

Jerpoint Abbey ⓱

Road map D5. Thomastown, Co
Kilkenny. *Tel* 056 772 4623. 🚆 🚌
to Thomastown. ☐ Mar–May &
mid-Sep–Oct: 9:30am–5pm daily;
Jun–mid-Sep: 9:30am–6pm daily;
Nov: 10am–4pm daily; Dec–Feb: by
appt only. 🎫 📷 ♿ **www.**
heritageireland.ie

On the banks of the Little
Arrige, just south of
Thomastown, Jerpoint Abbey
is one of the finest Cistercian
ruins in Ireland. Founded in
1160, the fortified medieval
complex rivalled Duiske
Abbey (*see p149*) in prestige.
Jerpoint flourished until the
Dissolution of the Monasteries
(*see p038–9*), when it passed to
the Earl of Ormonde.

The 15th-century cloisters
have not survived as
well as some earlier
parts of the abbey.
Despite this, they are
the highlight, with their
amusing sculptures of
knights, courtly ladies,
bishops and dragons.
The church itself is
well preserved. The
Irish-Romanesque
transepts date back to
the earliest period of
the Abbey's develop-
ment and contain
16th-century tombs
with exquisite stylized
carvings. The north
side of the nave has a
rich array of decorated
Romanesque capitals
and throughout the
abbey are tombs and
effigies of bishops. The
battlemented crossing tower
was added during the 1400s.

Burne-Jones window
in St Carthage's
Cathedral, Lismore

Stylized carving of saints on 16th-century tomb in Jerpoint Abbey

Lismore ⓲

Road map C5. Co Waterford.
🏘 1,500. 🚌 🛈 Lismore Heritage
Centre, Main St (058 54975). 🎁
craft shop. **www.**discoverlismore.com

This genteel riverside town is
dwarfed by **Lismore Castle**,
perched above the River
Blackwater. Built in
1185 but remodelled in
the 19th century, the
castle is the Irish seat
of the Duke of
Devonshire and is
closed to the public.
However, you can visit
the sumptuous
gardens, which include
a lovely riverside walk.
Lismore Heritage Centre
tells the story of St
Carthage, who founded
a monastic centre here
in the 7th century. The
town has two cathedrals
dedicated to him. The
Protestant **Cathedral of
St Carthage** is the
more interesting. It
dates from 1633 but
incorporates older
elements and was later altered
to suit the Neo-Gothic tastes
of the Victorians. It has fine
Gothic vaulting, and a
stained-glass window by the
Pre-Raphaelite artist, Sir
Edward Burne-Jones.

⚜**Lismore Castle
Gardens** *Tel* 058 54424.
☐ mid-Mar–Sep: 11am–4:45pm
daily. 🎫

Environs
From Lismore you can follow
a picturesque route through
the **Blackwater Valley** (*see
p177*). This runs from Cappoquin, in an idyllic woodland
setting east of Lismore, to the
estuary at Youghal (*see p179*).

Ardmore ⓳

Road map C5. Co Waterford.
🏘 450. 🚌 🛈 024 94444.

Ardmore is a popular seaside
resort with a splendid beach,
lively pubs, good cliff walks
and some interesting
architecture. The hill beside
the village is the site of a
monastery established in
the 5th century by St Declan,
the first missionary to bring
Christianity to this area.

Most of the buildings,
including the ruined **St
Declan's Cathedral**, date
from the 13th century. The
cathedral's west wall has
fine Romanesque sculptures,
arranged in a series of
arcades. The scenes include
The Archangel Michael
Weighing Souls in the upper
row, and below this The
Adoration of the Magi and
The Judgment of Solomon.

The adjacent round tower
is one of the best preserved
examples in Ireland, and rises
to a height of 30 m (98 ft). An
oratory nearby is said to mark
the site of St Declan's grave.

St Declan's Cathedral at Ardmore, with its near-perfect round tower

Waterford ⑳

Waterford city coat of arms

Waterford, Ireland's oldest city, was founded by Vikings in 914. Set in a commanding position by the estuary of the River Suir, it became southeast Ireland's main seaport. From the 18th century, the city's prosperity was consolidated by local industries, including the glassworks for which Waterford is famous. The strong commercial tradition persists today and Waterford's port is still one of Ireland's busiest. Following extensive archaeological excavations in the city centre, a new heart and atmosphere has been put into the old city with the creation of pedestrian precincts in the historic quarter and along the quays.

Reginald's Tower on the quayside

Cathedral Close, looking towards Lady Lane in the heart of the city

Exploring Waterford

The extensive remains of the city walls clearly define the area originally fortified by the Vikings. The best-preserved section runs northwest from the **Watch Tower** on Castle Street, although Reginald's Tower, overlooking the river, is the largest structure in the old defences. In The Reginald Bar you can see the arches through which boats sailed forth down the river; these sallyports are one of several Viking sections of the largely Norman fortifications.

Although Waterford retains its medieval layout, most of the city's finest buildings are Georgian. Some of the best examples can be seen on the Mall, which runs southwest from Reginald's Tower, and in the lovely Cathedral Square. The latter takes its name from **Christchurch Cathedral**, which

was built in the 1770s to a design by John Roberts, a local architect who contributed much to the city's Georgian heritage. It is fronted by a fine Corinthian colonnade. A grim 15th-century effigy of a rotting corpse is an unexpected sight inside. Heading down towards the river, you pass the 13th-century ruins of **Grey Friars**, often known as the French Church after it became a Huguenot chapel in 1693.

West along the waterfront, a Victorian clock tower stands at the top of Barronstrand Street. Rising above the busy shops is **Holy Trinity Cathedral**, which has a rich Neo-Classical interior. George's Street, which runs west from here, is dotted with period houses and cosy pubs. It leads to O'Connell Street, whose partially restored warehouses contrast with the shabbier buildings on the quay. In the summer, you can enjoy another view of the waterfront by taking a cruise on the river.

⚓ Reginald's Tower

The Quay. **Tel** 051 304220. ☐ Easter–mid-Sep: 10am–5pm daily; mid-Sep–Easter: 10am–5pm Wed–Sun. ◰
The Vikings built a fort on this site in 914 but it was the Anglo-Normans who, in 1185, built the stone structure seen today. With walls 3 m (10 ft) thick, it is said to be the first Irish building to use mortar, a primitive concoction of blood, lime, fur and mud. It is the oldest civic urban building in Ireland.

⛉ Waterford Museum of Treasures

The Granary, Merchants Quay. **Tel** 051 304500. ☐ Jun–Aug: 9am–6pm Mon–Sat, 11am–6pm Sun & public hols; Sep–May: 10am–5pm Mon–Sat, 11am–5pm Sun. ● 1 Jan & 25, 26 Dec. ◰ ♿ ⏍ 🛍 🚻 ℹ
This multi-award-winning interactive museum tells the story of Waterford from its Viking foundation to the late 19th century.

View of the city of Waterford across the River Suir

For hotels and restaurants in this region see pp299–302 and pp328–31

⛰ Waterford Crystal Visitor Centre

The Mall. **Tel** 051 332500. ☐ Nov–Feb: 9:30am–3:15pm Mon–Fri, Mar–Oct: 9am–4:15pm daily. ⬤ 24–27 Dec. 🅿 ♿ ✉ www.waterford visitorcentre.com

A visit to the Waterford Crystal Visitor Centre is highly recommended to learn about and observe the process of crystal-making.

The original glass factory was founded in 1783 by two

Craftsman engraving a vase at the Waterford Crystal Visitor Centre

brothers, George and William Penrose, who chose Waterford because of its port. For many decades their crystal enjoyed an unrivalled reputation, but draconian taxes caused the firm to close in 1851. A new factory and visitor centre was opened in 1947, just south of the city, and master blowers and engravers were brought from the Continent to train local apprentices. Competition from Tipperary and Galway Crystal had an effect in the early 1990s, but sales revived.

Following the closure in 2009 of the factories and visitor centre, a deal was brokered to secure the future of the glass in Waterford. While much of the glass manufacture now happens elsewhere, visitors can still observe the making of prestige pieces in a custom-built facility on the site of the grand old ESB building on the Mall. The centre offers tours that cover more than 225 years of glass-making and take in master craftsmen at work on individual pieces. A shop with the world's largest display of Waterford Crystal sells fine pieces engraved with the famous Waterford signature.

VISITORS' CHECKLIST

Road map D5. Co Waterford.
🏙 49,000. ✈ 10 km (6 miles) S.
🚉 Plunkett Station, The Bridge (051 873401). 🚌 The Quay (051 879000). 🛈 The Granary, Merchant's Quay (051 875823). www.discoverireland.ie/southeast 🎭 Int Festival of Light Opera (Sep).

Ballyhack Port, across Waterford Harbour from Passage East

Environs

The small port of **Passage East**, 12 km (7 miles) east of Waterford, witnessed the landing of the Normans in 1170 (see p36), but little has happened since. A car ferry links the village to Ballyhack in County Wexford, providing a scenic shortcut across Waterford Harbour as well as an excellent entry point to the Hook Peninsula (see p148).

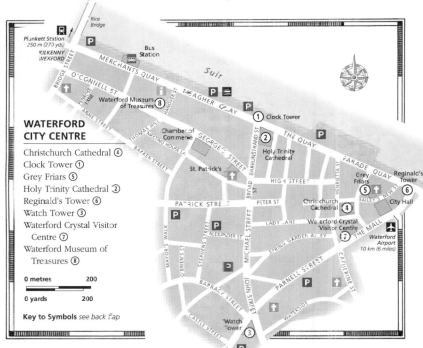

WATERFORD CITY CENTRE

Christchurch Cathedral ④
Clock Tower ①
Grey Friars ⑤
Holy Trinity Cathedral ②
Reginald's Tower ⑥
Watch Tower ③
Waterford Crystal Visitor Centre ⑦
Waterford Museum of Treasures ⑧

0 metres   200

0 yards   200

Key to Symbols see back flap

Dunmore East ㉑

Road map D5. Co Waterford.
🚶 *1,600.* 🚌

The appeal of Dunmore East, Waterford's most charming fishing village, lies chiefly in its red sandstone cliffs and bustling harbour. Paths run along the foot of the cliffs, but for the best views take the road that winds uphill from the beach, past tidy cottages and the ivy-clad Ship Inn to the Haven Hotel. A gate nearby leads to delightful gardens overlooking the fishing boats below. Climbing further, up steps cut into the rock, you are rewarded by views of the cliffs and noisy kittiwake colonies.

Busy fishing harbour at Dunmore East

Hook Peninsula ㉒

Road map D5. Co. Wexford.
🚌 to Duncannon. 🛥 from Passage East to Ballyhack (051 382480).
ℹ️ Fethard-on-Sea (051 397502).
www.hooktourism.com

This tapering headland of gentle landscapes scattered with ancient ruins and quiet villages is perfect for a circular tour. The "Ring of Hook" route begins south of New Ross at **Dunbrody Abbey**, the ruins of a 12th-century Cistercian church, but **Ballyhack** is another good place to start. Once a fortified crossing point into County Waterford, the town still has a ferry service to neighbouring Passage East *(see p147)*. **Ballyhack Castle**, built by the Knights Templar in about 1450, contains a small museum. About 4 km (2.5

miles) beyond is the small resort of **Duncannon**, with a broad sandy beach and a star-shaped fort, which was built in 1588 in expectation of an attack by the Spanish Armada.

The coast road continues south to **Hook Head**. Here is Europe's oldest working lighthouse, dating from 1172 and now with its own visitor centre. Paths skirt the coast famous for its fossils, seals and a variety of seabirds.

Just 2 km (1.5 miles) east is the village of **Slade**. A ruined 15th-century tower house, **Slade Castle**, presides over the harbour where fishing boats cluster around the slipways. The road proceeds along the rugged coastline, past the resort of Fethard-on-Sea and Saltmills to the dramatic ruin of **Tintern Abbey**. This 13th-century Cistercian foundation was built by William Marshall, Earl of Pembroke, in fulfilment of a vow made when his boat was caught in a storm off the coast nearby. Fields lead to an old stone bridge and views over **Bannow Bay**, where it is

thought the Normans made their first landing in 1169.

🏛 **Dunbrody Abbey**
Campile. **Tel** 051 388603.
◯ May–Sep: daily. 🎫 🗺 🛍 🚻 🖥

⛪ **Ballyhack Castle**
Ballyhack. **Tel** 051 389468.
◯ end-Jun–Aug: 10am–6pm daily.

🏛 **Tintern Abbey**
Tel 051 562 650.
🗺 mid-May–Sep: daily. 🎫 🖥

Norman lighthouse at Hook Head, on the tip of the Hook Peninsula

New Ross ㉓

Road map D5. Co Wexford. 🚶 *6,000.*
🚌 ℹ️ South Quay (051 421857).
🎭 Tue. **Galley Cruising Restaurants** The Quay (051 421723). ◯ Apr–Oct.

Lying on the banks of the River Barrow, New Ross is one of the oldest towns in the county. Its importance, now as in the past, stems from its status as a port. In summer there is much activity on the river, with cruises plying the Barrow, Nore and Suir rivers. Docked at South Quay is **The Dunbrody**, a full-scale reconstruction of a cargo

Castle ruins and harbour at Slade on the Hook Peninsula

For hotels and restaurants in this region see pp299–302 and pp328–31

ship that carried emigrants to the US and Canada during the famine. Traditional shopfronts line the streets, which rise steeply from the quayside. The **Tholsel**, now the town hall but originally a tollhouse, was occupied by the British during the 1798 rebellion (*see pp40–41*). Opposite, a monument to a Wexford pikeman commemorates the bravery of the Irish rebels who faced the British.

Nearby is **St Mary's** which, when founded in the 13th century, was the largest parish church in Ireland. A modern church occupies the site, but the original (now roofless) south transept remains, as do many medieval tombstones.

View over Enniscorthy and St Aidan's cathedral from Vinegar Hill

🏛 The Dunbrody
South Quay. **Tel** *051 425239.*
🔲 *daily.* 🖼 **www.dunbrody.com**

Environs
A popular trip up the meandering Barrow goes 15 km (10 miles) north to **Graiguenamanagh**. The main attraction of this market town is **Duiske Abbey**, the largest Cistercian church in Ireland. Founded in 1207, it has been extensively restored and now acts as the parish church. The most striking features include a Romanesque door in the south transept, the great oak roof and traces of a medieval pavement below floor level. There is also a cross-legged statue of the Knight of Duiske, which is one of the finest medieval effigies in Ireland.

Trips along the Nore River take you to **Inistioge**. Lying in a deep, wooded valley, this is an idyllic village, with neat 18th-century houses, a square planted with lime trees

and a ten-arched bridge spanning the Nore.

From Inistioge you can walk along the river or up to **Woodstock House Demesne**, a national park. Among the beech woods stands an 18th-century mansion, currently undergoing restoration.

On a hill 12 km (7.5 miles) south of New Ross, a large area of woodland is enclosed within the **John F Kennedy Park and Arboretum**. Founded in 1968, near the late president's ancestral home in Dunganstown (now **The Kennedy Homestead**), the 400-acre park boasts more than 4,500 types of tree and provides splendid panoramic views. There are marked paths and nature trails.

🏰 Duiske Abbey
Graiguenamanagh, Co Kilkenny.
Tel *059 972 4238.* 🔲 *Mon–Fri.* ♿

🌿 John F Kennedy Park and Arboretum
New Ross, Co Wexford. **Tel** *051 388171.* 🔲 *daily.* ⬛ *Good Fri & 25 Dec.* 🖼 ♿ 🔲 *May–end Sep.*
www.heritageireland.ie

The streets of Enniscorthy, on the banks of the River Slaney, are full of character and redolent of the town's turbulent

past. In 1798, Enniscorthy witnessed the last stand of the Wexford pikemen, when a fierce battle was fought against a British force of 20,000 on nearby **Vinegar Hill**. The events of that year are told in depth at the multimedia **National 1798 Visitor Centre.** Enniscorthy's other main sight is the Neo-Gothic **St Aidan's Cathedral**, designed in the 1840s by AWN Pugin (1812–52), better known for his work on London's Houses of Parliament.

Granaries, mills and potteries overlook the Slaney, including Carley's Bridge, founded in 1654 and still operational. Enniscorthy's historic pubs are another attraction. They include the Antique Tavern (*see p346*), which is hung with pikes used during the Battle of Vinegar Hill in 1798.

🏛 National 1798 Visitor Centre
Millpark Road. **Tel** *053 923 7596.*
🔲 *9:30am–5pm Mon–Fri, noon–5pm Sat (Jun–Sep: noon–5pm Sun).* 🖼 🔲 🔲 **www.1798centre.ie**

🏰 St Aidan's Cathedral
Main St. **Tel** *053 9235777.*
🔲 *9am–5pm daily.* ♿

The inland port of New Ross seen from the west bank of the River Barrow

View across the harbour to Wexford town

Irish National Heritage Park 25

Road map D5. Ferrycarrig, Co Wexford. **Tel** 053 912 0733.
◯ May–Aug: 9:30am–6:30pm (to 5:30pm Sep–Apr). ◖ week at Christmas. ◪ ◳ Mar–Oct. ▣ ⑴
Ⓖ www. nhp.com

Built on former marshland near Ferrycarrig, north of Wexford, the Irish National Heritage Park is a bold open-air museum. Trails lead through woods to replicas of homesteads, places of worship and burial sites, providing a fascinating lesson on the country's ancient history (see pp32–3).

Highlights include the Viking boatyard, complete with raiding ship and a 7th-century horizontal watermill.

Wexford 26

Road map D5. Co Wexford. ▨ 17,000. ▣ ▣ ➊ Quay Front (053 912 3111). www.discoverireland.ie/southeast

Wexford's name derives from *Waesfjord*, a Norse word meaning "estuary of the mud flats" It thrived as a port for centuries but the silting of the harbour in the Victorian era put an end to most sea traffic. Wexford's quays, from where ships once sailed to Bristol, Tenby and Liverpool, are now used mainly by a fleet of humble mussel dredgers.

Wexford is a vibrant place, packed with fine pubs and

Sign of a popular Wexford pub

boasting a varied arts scene. The town's singular style is often linked to its linguistic heritage. The *yola* dialect, which was spoken by early settlers, survives in the local pronunciation of certain words.

Wexford retains few traces of its past, but the Viking fishbone street pattern still exists, with narrow alleys fanning off the meandering Main Street. Keyser's Lane, linking South Main Street with The Crescent, is a tiny tunnel-like Viking alley which once led to the Norse waterfront. The Normans were responsible for Wexford's town walls, remnants of which include one of the original gateways. Behind it lies **Selskar Abbey**, the ruin of a 12th-century Augustinian monastery. King Henry II is said to have done penance here for the murder of Thomas à Becket in 1170.

Wexford also has several handsome buildings dating from a later period, including the 18th-century market house (now an arts centre), known as the **Cornmarket**, on Main Street. The nearby square, the **Bull Ring**, is of historic note: it was used for bull-baiting in Norman times and was the scene of a cruel massacre by Cromwell's men in 1649.

Wexford Opera Festival, held in October, is the leading operatic event in the country. It takes place at the state-of-the-art **Wexford Opera House** on the site of the old Theatre Royal. Aficionados praise the festival for its intimate atmosphere – both during

performances and afterwards, when artists and audience mingle together in the pubs: the Centenary Stores off Main Street is a favourite.

Environs
Skirting the shore just east of the town is **Wexford Wildfowl Reserve**. It covers 100 ha (250 acres) of reclaimed land and is noted for its geese: over a third of the world's entire population of Greenland white-fronted geese winter here between October and April.

The mudflats also attract large numbers of swans and waders. The birds can be viewed from hides and an observation tower. Another way to enjoy the region's wildlife is to take a boat trip up the Slaney River to **Raven Point** to see the seal colony.

▦ **Wexford Opera House**
High Street. **Tel** 053 912 2400. ▢
Ⓖ www.wexfordoperahouse.ie
✈ **Wexford Wildfowl Reserve**
Wexford. **Tel** 053 912 3129.
◯ daily. ◪ at weekends.
Boat Trips
Harbour Thrills, Seaview,
Murrintown. **Tel** 085 732 9787.

Johnstown Castle 27

Road map D5. Co Wexford. **Tel** 053 914 2888. ▣ ▣ to Wexford.
Gardens ◯ May–Sep: daily. ◖ 24 & 25 Dec. ◪

Façade of Johnstown Castle

Johnstown Castle, a splendid Gothic Revival mansion, lies amid gardens and woodland 6 km (4 miles) southwest of Wexford. In state hands since 1945, the castle is closed to the public. However, it is

Vast crescent of sand and shingle beach at Rosslare

possible to visit the **Irish Agriculture Museum** housed in the castle's farm buildings. Reconstructions illustrate traditional trades and there is an excellent exhibition on the Famine. There are also interesting exhibitions on traditional village crafts and country kitchens.

The real glory are the castle grounds, from the Italian garden to the lakes. Azaleas and camellias flourish alongside an array of trees including Japanese cedars and redwoods. The lakes are home to a wide range of waterfowl – mute swans, water hens, little grebes and heron.

Hidden among the dense woods west of the house lurk the ruins of **Rathlannon Castle**, a medieval tower house.

🏛 **Irish Agriculture Museum**
Johnstown Castle. **Tel** 053 914 2888. ☐ Nov–Mar: 9am–12:30pm, 1.30–5pm Mon–Fri; Apr–Oct: 9am–5pm Mon–Fri, 11am–4:30pm Sat, Sun & public hols. 🎟 ☐ ♿ limited. **www**.irishagrimuseum.ie

Saltee Islands ㉘

Road map D5. Co Wexford. 🚌 from Wexford to Kilmore Quay: Wed & Sat. 🚤 from Kilmore Quay. Apr–Sep (weather permitting). Tel 053 91 29637. **www**.salteeislands.info

These islands off the south coast of Wexford are a haven for sea birds. Great and Little Saltee together form Ireland's largest bird sanctuary, nurturing an impressive array, from gannets and gulls to puffins and Manx shearwaters. Great Saltee particularly is famous for its colonies of cormorants. It also has more than 1,000 pairs of guillemots and is a popular stopping-off place for spring and autumn migrations. A bird-monitoring programme is in progress, and a close watch is also kept on the colony of more than 100 grey seals.

The two uninhabited islands are privately owned, but visitors are welcome. Boat trips are run in fine weather from **Kilmore Quay**. These leave in late morning and return mid-afternoon.

Kilmore Quay is a fishing village built on Precambrian gneiss rock – the oldest rock in Ireland. Pretty thatched cottages nestle above a fine sandy beach and the harbour.

Rosslare ㉓

Road map D5. Co Wexford. 🚶 2,000. 🚇 🚆 📮 🚌 053 912 3111. **www**.rosslareharbour.ie

Rosslare replaced Wexford as the area's main port after the decline of the original Viking city harbour. The port is so active today that people tend to associate the name Rosslare more with the ferry terminal for France and Wales than with the town lying 8 km (5 miles) further north.

Rosslare town is one of the sunniest spots in Ireland and draws many holidaymakers. It boasts a fine beach stretching for 9.5 km (6 miles), lively pubs and an excellent golf course fringed by sand dunes. There are good walks north to Rosslare Point.

Environs
At Tagoat, 6 km (4 miles) south of Rosslare, **Yola Farmstead Folk Park** is a recreated traditional 18th-century village, with thatched roofs and a windmill.

🏛 **Yola Farmstead Folk Park**
Tagoat. **Tel** 053 913 2610. ☐ Mar, Apr & Nov: Mon–Fri; May–Oct: daily. 🎟 ☐ ♿ ♿

Colony of gannets nesting on the cliffs of Great Saltee Island

CORK AND KERRY

CORK · KERRY

Magnificent scenery has attracted visitors to this region since Victorian times. Rocky headlands jut out into the Atlantic and colourful fishing villages nestle in the shelter of the bays. County Kerry offers dramatic landscapes and a wealth of prehistoric and early Christian sites, whereas County Cork's gentle charm has enticed many a casual visitor into becoming a permanent resident.

Killarney and its romantic lakes are a powerful magnet for tourists, and so are Cork's attractive coastal towns and villages. Yet the region remains remarkably unspoiled, with a friendly atmosphere and authentic culture still alive in Irish-speaking pockets. There is also a long tradition of arts and crafts in the area.

This corner of Ireland used to be the main point of contact with the Continent. In the 17th century, in response to the threat of invasions from France and Spain, the English built a line of forts along the Cork coast, including the massive Charles Fort at Kinsale.

In the 19th century, the city of Cork was an important departure point for people fleeing from the Famine *(see p219)*, with Cobh the main port for emigrants to the New World. Cork's importance as a port has diminished, but it is still the Republic's second city with a lively cultural scene.

Poverty and temperament helped foster a powerful Republican spirit in the southwest. The region saw much guerrilla action in the War of Independence and the subsequent Civil War. In 1920, the centre of Cork city was burned in an uncontrolled act of reprisal by the notorious Black and Tans *(see pp4—5)*.

Kerry is known as "the Kingdom" on account of its tradition of independence and disregard for Dublin rule. The Irish recognize a distinctive Kerry character, with a boisterous sense of living life to the full. They also make Kerrymen the butt of countless jokes.

As well as the friendliest people in Ireland, the region has some of the finest scenery. Cork has lush valleys and a beautiful coast while Kerry is wilder and more mountainous. The islands off the Kerry coast appear bleak and inhospitable, but many were once inhabited. Remote, rocky Skellig Michael, for example, was the site of a 6th-century Christian monastery.

Puffins on the island of Skellig Michael off the coast of Kerry

◁ **Beach at Barley Cove near Mizen Head, County Cork**

Exploring Cork and Kerry

Killarney is a popular base with tourists for exploring Cork and Kerry, especially for touring the Ring of Kerry and the archaeological remains on the Dingle Peninsula. Despite the changeable weather, the region attracts many visitors who come to see its dramatic scenery and lush vegetation. As you pass through quiet fishing villages and genteel towns, such as Kenmare, you will always encounter a friendly welcome from the locals. For the adventurous there are plenty of opportunities to go riding, hiking or cycling. Cork city offers a more cosmopolitan atmosphere, with its art galleries and craft shops.

CARRIGAFOYLE CASTLE 1
Limeric
Ballybunnion
Tarbe
Ballylongfor
Ballyduff
Athea
R553
Listowel
Casben
Feale
Ballyheige
R556
N69
Abbeyfeale
Banna
Strand
ARDFERT CATHEDRAL 2
Kil
Ardfert
R551
Brosn
Brandon
Bay
Tralee
Bay
Fenit
TRALEE 3
Glananaruddery
Mountains
N21
Castleisla
Brandon Peak
953m
Castlegregory
Camp
Ballydesm
GALLARUS ORATORY 5
Slieve Mish Mountains
N22
Farranfore
R577
Ballyferriter
Anascaul
Castlemaine
K E R R Y
Dunquin
DINGLE AN DAINGEAN 4
6
Killorglin
KILLARNEY
DINGLE PENINSULA
Killorglin
7
Rathn
Great Blasket
Island
Dingle Bay
Glenbeigh
Laune
LAKES OF KILLARNEY 8
N70
Carrantuohil
1038m
Muckross
House
RING OF KERRY
Coomacarrea
772m
N71
Macgillycuddy's Reeks
Mangerton Mounta
838m
Cahirciveen
11
Kilgarvan
VALENTIA ISLAND 9
Knightstown
Inny
Derreendarragh
12 KENMARE
Balling
Portmagee
Sneem
N70
Ballinskelligs
Waterville
Kenmare Bay
Killabunane
Lauragh
Caha Mountains
Ballinskelligs Bay
Glengarriff
10
Scariff
Island
Ardgroom
R571
R574
GARINISH ISLAND 14
THE SKELLIGS
Eyeries
Adrigole
Bantry
16
Ballydonegan
13 Castletownbere
BANTRY BAY
15 BANTRY HOUSE
Dursey
Island
Bere
Island
Durrus
N71
The Bull
BEARA PENINSULA
Kilcrohane
Ballydehob
Skibbereer
Dunmanus Bay
R591
R592
R595
Toormore
MIZEN HEAD 17
Crookhaven
18 BALTIM
Barley Cove
Roaringwater Bay
Sherkin Isla
Cape Clear
Island

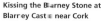

Kissing the Blarney Stone at Blarney Castle near Cork

GETTING AROUND

To explore the region a car is essential. The N22 connects Cork, Killarney and Tralee while the N71 follows the coastline via Clonakilty, Bantry and on to Killarney. In the more remote parts the road signs may only be written in Irish. Killarney is the base for organized coach tours of the area. The train service from Cork to Dublin is efficient, and trains also connect Killarney with Dublin and Cork, but you may have to change trains en route. Buses run throughout the region, but services to the smaller sights may be infrequent.

For additional map symbols see back flap

SIGHTS AT A GLANCE

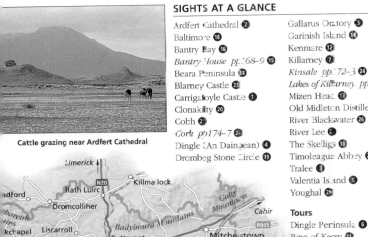

Cattle grazing near Ardfert Cathedral

KEY

━━ Motorway
━━ Major road
━━ Secondary road
┄┄ Minor road
━━ Scenic route
┅┅ Main railway
┄┄ Minor railway
━━ County border
▲ Summit

Newman's Mall in the quaint village of Kinsale

Ardfert Cathedral and the ruins of Teampall na Hoe and Teampall na Griffin

Carrigafoyle Castle ●

Road map B5. Co Kerry. 🚌 to Listowel.

High above the Shannon estuary, 3 km (2 miles) from Ballylongford, this 15th-century castle belonged to the O'Connor clan, who ruled much of northern Kerry. The English besieged or sacked it repeatedly but the body blow was delivered in 1649 by Cromwellian forces (see p39). The ruins include a keep and walled bawn, with romantic views of the estuary from the top of the tower.

Ruined keep of Carrigafoyle Castle

Ardfert Cathedral ●

Road map A5. Co Kerry. **Tel** 066 713 4711. 🔲 May–Sep: daily; rest of year on request. 🅿 ♿ **www.** heritageireland.ie

This complex of churches is linked to the cult of St. Brendan the Navigator (see p213), who was born nearby in 484 and

founded a monastery here in the 6th century. The ruined cathedral dates back to the 12th century and retains a delicate Romanesque door-way and blind arcading. The battlements were added in the 15th century. The south transept houses an exhibition of the history of the site. In the graveyard stand the remains of a Romanesque nave-and-chancel church, Teampall na Hoe, and a late Gothic chapel, Teampall na Griffin. The latter is named after the curious griffins carved beside an interior window.

A short walk away are the ruins of a Franciscan friary. It was founded by Thomas Fitzmaurice in 1253, but the cloisters and south chapel date from the 15th century.

Environs
Just northwest of Ardfert is **Banna Strand**. Irish patriot Roger Casement landed here in 1916 on a German U-boat, bringing in rifles for the Easter Rising (see pp44–5). He was arrested as soon as he landed and a memorial stands on the site of his capture. This beach was also used for the filming of David Lean's *Ryan's Daughter* (1970).

A 20-minute drive north of Ardfert, in the village of Ballyduff, stands the 28-m (92-ft) high **Ratoo Round Tower**. Dating from the 10th or 11th century, it was built as a lookout to warn of Viking attack. The tower is one of Ireland's finest and the last remaining one in Kerry.

Tralee ●

Road map B5. Co Kerry. 🏙 23,000. 🚌 🚆 🅸 Ashe Memorial Hall, Denny St (066 712 1288). 🔲 Fri. www.discoverireland.ie/southwest

Host to the renowned Rose of Tralee International Festival (see p49), Tralee has made great strides in promoting its cultural and leisure facilities. The town's main attraction is **Kerry County Museum**. Its theme park, "Kerry the King-dom", offers a show on Kerry scenery and a display of archaeological finds. The "Geraldine Experience" brings one back to medieval times.

The **Siamsa Tíre** National Folk Theatre of Ireland is a great ambassador for Irish culture. Traditional song and dance performances

Steam train on the narrow gauge railway between Tralee and Blennerville

take place here throughout the summer.

Just outside Tralee is the authentic **Blennerville Windmill**. Opposite the windmill is the Lee Valley Park, which has a nature reserve, visitor centre, activity lake and walking and cycling routes. The **Steam Railway** connects the park with Tralee along a narrow gauge track. The train also runs from Ballyard Station to the windmill.

⚲ Kerry County Museum
Ashe Memorial Hall, Denny St.
Tel *066 712 7777.* ⬤ *Nov–Apr:*
Tue–Sat; May–Oct: daily. ⬤ *1 week*
at Christmas. 🖼️ 🅰️ 🅰️ 🅰️

🎭 Siamsa Tíre
Town Park. ***Tel*** *066 712 3055.* ⬤
for performances May–Sep. 🖼️ 🅰️

⚲ Blennerville Windmill
Tel *066 712 1064.* ⬤ *Apr–Oct:*
daily. 🖼️ 🅰️ 🅰️

🚂 Steam Railway
Ballyard Station. ***Tel*** *066 712*
1064. ⬤ *Jun–Aug: daily.* 🖼️ 🅰️

Dingle ❹

Road map A5. Co Kerry. 🏘️ 2,000.
🚌 *Apr–Oct.* 🚆 *Strand St (066 915*
1188). 🚌 *Fri.* **www**.discoverire-and.
ie/southwest

This once remote Irish-speaking town is today a thriving fishing port and an increasingly popular tourist centre. Brightly painted craft shops and cafés abound, often with slightly hippy overtones.

Dingle Bay is attractive with a ramshackle harbour lined with fishing trawlers. Along the quayside are lively bars offering music and seafood. The harbour is home to Dingle's biggest star: Fungi, the dolphin, who has been a permanent resident since 1984 and can be visited by boat or on swimming trips. Other sea creatures can be seen at Ocean World, a great attraction with breathtaking underwater tunnels that bring visitors face to face with the local sea life.

Gallarus Oratory, a dry-stone early Christian church

Gallarus Oratory ❺

Road map A5. Co Kerry.
🚌 *to Dingle.* ***Tel*** *064 663 2402.*
⬤ *daily.* 🚆 *(Apr–Sep)*

Shaped like an upturned boat, this miniature church overlooks Smerwick Harbour. It was built some time between the 6th and 9th centuries and is the best-preserved early Christian church in Ireland. It represents the apogee of dry-stone corbelling, using techniques first developed by Neolithic tomb-makers. The stones were laid at a slight angle, allowing water to run off.

Fishing trawlers moored alongside the quay at Dingle

A Tour of the Dingle Peninsula ➏

Pub sign, Ballyferriter

The Dingle Peninsula offers some of Ireland's most beautiful scenery. To the north rises the towering Brandon Mountain, while the west coast has some spectacular seascapes. A drive around the area, which takes at least half a day, reveals fascinating antiquities ranging from Iron Age stone forts to inscribed stones, early Christian oratories and beehive huts. These are sometimes found on private land, so you may be asked for a small fee by the farmer to see them. Some parts of the peninsula – especially the more remote areas – are still Gaelic speaking, so many road signs are written only in Irish.

View from Clogher Head

Riasc (An Riasc) ⑦
This excavated monastic settlement dates from the 6th century. The enclosure contains the remains of an oratory, several cross-inscribed slabs and an inscribed pillar stone (see p243).

Ballyferriter (Baile an Fheirtéaraigh) ⑥
The attractions of this friendly village include the pastel-coloured cottages, Louis Mulcahy's pottery and a museum featuring the cultural heritage of the area.

Blasket Centre (Ionad an Bhlascaoid) ⑤
Overlooking Blasket Sound, the centre explains the literature, language and way of life of the inhabitants of the Blasket Islands. The islanders moved to the mainland in 1953.

Clogher Head

Dunquin (Dún Chaoin)

R559

Mount Eagle

Avonmore Sound

BLASKET ISLANDS

Ven (Ceann...

Vent...

DINGLE BAY

Dunmore Head (Ceann an Dúin Mhoir) ④
Mainland Ireland's most westerly point offers dramatic views of the Blaskets.

Slea Head (Ceann Sléibe) ③
As you round the Slea Head promontory, the Blasket Islands come into full view. The sculpture of the Crucifixion beside the road is known locally as the Cross (An Cros).

KEY

▬	Tour route
═	Other roads
❄	Viewpoint

0 kilometres   2

0 miles   1

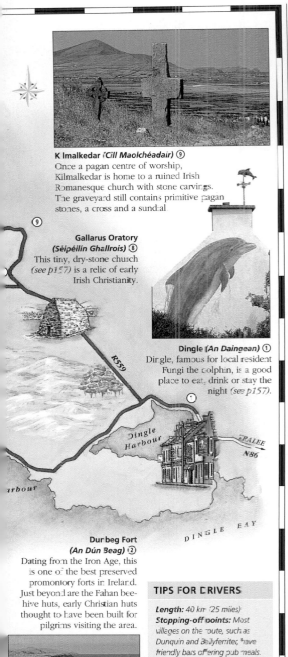

K Imalkedar (Cill Maolchéadair) ⑨
Once a pagan centre of worship,
Kilmalkedar is home to a ruined Irish
Romanesque church with stone carvings.
The graveyard still contains primitive pagan
stones, a cross and a sundial

**Gallarus Oratory
(Séipéilín Ghallrois)** ⑧
This tiny, dry-stone church
(see p157) is a relic of early
Irish Christianity.

Dingle (An Daingean) ①
Dingle, famous for local resident
Fungi the dolphin, is a good
place to eat, drink or stay the
night *(see p157).*

*Dingle
Harbour*

*TRALEE
N86*

DINGLE BAY

**Durbeg Fort
(An Dún Beag)** ②
Dating from the Iron Age, this
is one of the best preserved
promontory forts in Ireland.
Just beyond are the Fahan beehive huts, early Christian huts
thought to have been built for
pilgrims visiting the area.

TIPS FOR DRIVERS

Length: 40 km (25 miles)
Stopping-off points: Most
villages on the route, such as
Dunquin and Ballyferriter, have
friendly bars offering pub meals.
There are also many opportunities
to stop for a picnic. On the
winding coast road around Slea
Head stop only at the safe and
clearly marked coastal viewing
points. (See also pp385–7)

Jaunting cars waiting to take
visitors to sights around Killarney

Killarney ⑦

Road map B5. Co Kerry. 🛆 15,000.
🚌 🚆 ⓘ Beech Rd (064 6631633).
🌐 Fri. www.discoverireland.ie/
southwest

Killarney is often derided as
"a tourist town" but this has
not dented its cheerful atmosphere. The infectious Kerry
humour is personified by the
wise-cracking jarveys whose
families have run jaunting cars
(pony and trap rides) here for
generations. The town gets
busy in summer but has much
to offer, with shops open until
10pm in summer, several
excellent restaurants, and a
few prestigious hotels around
the lakes. From the town
visitors can explore the sights
around the Lakes of Killarney
(see pp162–3) and the surrounding heather-covered hills.

Environs
Overlooking the lakes and a
short drive from Killarney is
Muckross House, an imposing
mansion built in 1843 in
Elizabethan style. Inside, the
elegant rooms are decorated
with period furnishings. The
mansion is also home to the
Museum of Kerry Folklife. Next
to the house is the Walled
Garden Centre; the landscaped
gardens are particularly beautiful in spring when the rhododendrons and azaleas are in
bloom. The nearby Muckross
Traditional Farms portray
rural life in the 1930s and 40s.

🏛 **Muckross House**
6 km (3.5 miles) S of Killarney. **Tel**
064 667 0144. ⬜ Jul–Aug: 9am–
7pm daily, Sep–Jun: 9am–5:30pm
daily. ⬜ 25 Dec–2 Jan. ⬛ ⬛ ⬛ ⬛
⬛ ⬛ www.muckross-house.ie

Lakes of Killarney ⓫

Fruit of the strawberry tree

Renowned for its splendid scenery, the area is one of Ireland's most popular tourist attractions. The three lakes are contained within Killarney National Park. Although the landscape is dotted with ruined castles and abbeys, the lakes are the focus of attention: the moody water scenery is subject to subtle shifts of light and colour. The area has entranced many artists and writers including Thackeray, who praised "a precipice covered with a thousand trees ... and other mountains rising as far as we could see". In autumn, the bright red fruits of the strawberry tree colour the shores of the lakes.

Meeting of the Waters
This beauty spot, best seen from Dinis Island, is where the waters from the Upper Lake meet Muckross Lake and Lough Leane. At the Old Weir Bridge, boats shoot the rapids.

Long Range River

Torc Waterfall
The Owengarriff River cascades through the wooded Friars' Glen into Muckross Lake. A pretty path winds up to the top of this 18-m (60-ft) high waterfall, revealing views of Torc Mountain.

Muckross Lake

Dinis Island

Muckross Abbey was founded by the Franciscans in 1448, but was burnt down by Cromwellian forces in 1653.

Lough Leane

Killarney *(see p159)* is the main town from which tourists visit the sights around the lakes.

Innisfallen Island

N22 to Tralee *(see pp156–7)*

Ross Castle, built in the 15th century, was the last stronghold under Irish control to be taken by Cromwellian forces in 1653.

★ Muckross House
The 19th-century manor (see p159) enjoys a lovely location overlooking the lakes. Visit the wildlife centre for an introduction to the flora and fauna of the National Park.

Upper Lake

This narrow lake is the smallest of the three lakes. It flows into the Long Range River to the Meeting of the Waters.

Ladies' View gets its name from the delight it gave Queen Victoria's ladies-in-waiting when they visited the spot in 1861.

N71 to Moll's Gap and Kenmare (see pp164–6)

Upper Lake

Purple Mountain, 832 m (2,730 ft)

★ Gap of Dunloe

Glaciers carved this dramatic mountain pass which is popular with walkers, cyclists and horse riders. The route through the gap offers fabulous views of the boulder-strewn gorge and three small lakes.

Tomies Mountain, 735 m (2,411 ft)

Kate Kearney's Cottage was home to a local beauty who ran an illegal drinking house for passing travellers in the mid-19th century. It is still a pub today.

R562 to Killorglin (see pp164–5)

0 kilometres 2

0 miles 1

STAR SIGHTS

★ Gap of Dunloe

★ Muckross House

Lough Leane

The largest lake is dotted with un-inhabited islands and fringed with wooded slopes. Boat trips run between Ross Castle and Innisfallen.

VISITORS' CHECKLIST

Road map B5 Killarney, Co Kerry. ✈ Kerry (066 976 4644). 🚌 🚍 ℹ Killarney (064 663 1633). **National Park** Tel 064 663 1947 ☐ pedestrian access at all times, 8am–6pm (7pm Jul–Aug) for car access. www.killarney nationalpark.ie **Muckross House** Tel 064 667 0144. ☐ 9am–5:30pm (7pm Jul–Aug) daily. 🅿 ♿ 🚻 ☐ **Ross Castle** Tel 064 663 5851. ☐ mid-Mar–mid-Oct. daily. 🅿 ♿ obligatory. 🚢 from Ross Castle: **MV Pride of the Lakes** (087 236 4349): Apr–Sep (weather permitting); **The Lily of Killarney** (064 663 1068): Mar–Oct. **Kate Kearney's Cottage** Tel 064 664 4146. ☐ Easter–Oct: 9am–midnight daily; Nov–Easter 11am–9pm. 🚻 ☐

Valentia Island ⑨

Road map A5. Co Kerry. 🚌 to
Cahirciveen. 🏷 *May–Sep: Cahirciveen
(056 947 2589).* **www.**
discoverireland.ie/southwest

Although it feels like the mainland, Valentia is an island, albeit
linked by a cause-
way to Portmagee.
It is 11 km (7
miles) long
and

Stairway leading to Skellig Michael monastery

noted for its seascapes, water
sports, archaeological sites and
views from Geokaun Mountain.
Valentia is also popular for its
proximity to the Skellig Islands,
around 15 km (10 miles) southwest of the Iveragh Peninsula.
The **Skellig Experience
Centre**, near the causeway
linking Valentia to the mainland, houses an audiovisual
display about the construction
and history of the monastery
on Skellig Michael, the largest
of the Skellig Islands. Other
subjects covered include
sea birds and the
marine life around
the islands, a
reminder that
the Skellig cliffs
lie underwater for
a depth of 50 m
(165 ft). The centre
also operates
cruises around
the islands.
The main village
on Valentia

is **Knightstown**, which offers
accommodation, pubs and
superb views.

The first transatlantic cable
was laid from the southwest
point of the island to New-
foundland, Canada, in 1866.

> 🏛 **Skellig Experience Centre**
> Valentia Island. *Tel 066 947 6306.*
> ⏱ *varies, call ahead.* 📷 ♿

The Skelligs ⑩

Road map A6. Co Kerry. 🚢 *mid-
Mar–Oct: from Valentia Island.*
Tel 066 947 6306.

Skellig Michael, also known
as Great Skellig, is a UNESCO
World Heritage Site. This
inhospitable rock rising out of
the Atlantic covers an area of
17 ha (44 acres). Perched on
a ledge almost 218 m (714 ft)
above sea level and reached
by an amazing 1,000-year-old
stairway is an isolated early

A Tour of the Ring of Kerry ⑪

This long-established route around the
Iveragh Peninsula, which can be taken in
either direction, is always referred to as the
Ring of Kerry. Allow a day to see its
captivating mountain and coastal scenery,
dotted with slate-roofed fishing villages. Set
out early to avoid the mass of coach tours
which converge on the towns for lunch
and tea. There are interesting detours
across the spine of the peninsula.

Glenbeigh ③
Stop here to visit the Kerry
Bog Village, a cluster of
reconstructed cottages
dating from the 1800s.

Cahirciveen ④ The
main town on the
peninsula is home
to a unique
heritage centre.

Beach at Ballinskelligs

KEY

▬▬	Tour route
═══	Other roads
🛥	Boats to the Skelligs
🔆	Viewpoint

Little Skellig
Skellig Michael

Derrynane House ⑤
Dating from the 17th
century, the former
home of Daniel
O'Connell *(see p42)*
now houses a museum
featuring his memorabilia.

Staigue Fort ⑥
Set on a hill up a narrow track, this
Iron Age, dry-stone fort *(caher)* i
the best preserved in Ireland

Christian monastery. Monks settled for solitude on Skellig Michael during the 6th century, building a cluster of six corbelled beehive cells and two boat-shaped oratories. These dry-stone structures are still standing. The monks were totally self-sufficient, trading eggs, feathers and seal meat with passing boats in return for cereals, tools and animal skins. The skins were needed to produce the vellum on which the monks copied their religious manuscripts. They remained on this bleak island until the 12th century, when they retreated to the Augustinian priory at Ballinskelligs on the mainland.

Today the only residents on Skellig Michael are the thousands of sea birds which nest and breed on the high cliffs, including storm petrels, puffins and Manx

Gannets flying around the precipitous cliffs of Little Skellig

shearwaters. The huge breeding colonies are protected from predators by the sea and rocky shores.

Slightly closer to the mainland is Little Skellig. Covering an area of 7 ha (17 acres), the island has steep cliffs. Home to a variety of sea birds, it has one of the largest colonies of gannets (about 22,000 breeding pairs) in the world. Giant basking sharks, dolphins and turtles can also be seen

here. Except for a pier on Skellig Michael there are no proper landing stages on the islands. This is to discourage visitors from disturbing the wildlife, fragile plant cover and archaeological remains.

Atlantic gales permitting, there are boat tours around the islands. Private operators also run unofficial trips to the islands from Portmagee or Ballinskelligs during the summertime.

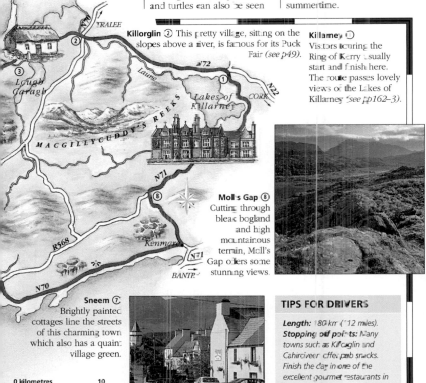

Killorglin ② This pretty village, sitting on the slopes above a river, is famous for its Puck Fair *(see p49).*

Killarney ① Visitors touring the Ring of Kerry usually start and finish here. The route passes lovely views of the Lakes of Killarney *(see pp162–3).*

Moll's Gap ⑧ Cutting through bleak bogland and high mountainous terrain, Moll's Gap offers some stunning views.

Sneem ⑦ Brightly painted cottages line the streets of this charming town which also has a quaint village green.

0 kilometres 10

0 miles 5

TIPS FOR DRIVERS

Length: 180 km (112 miles).
Stopping off points: Many towns such as Killorglin and Cahirciveen offer pub snacks. Finish the day in one of the excellent gourmet restaurants in Kenmare (see also pp385–7).

Lace making at Kenmare

Kenmare ⑫

Road map B5. Co Kerry. 🏛 *1,700.*
🚌 ℹ *May–Sep: Main St (064
664 1233).* 🛒 *Wed*
www.discoverireland.ie

This town, on the mouth of
the River Sheen, was founded
in 1670 by Sir William Petty,
Cromwell's surveyor general.
However, Kenmare's
appearance owes more to his
descendant, the first Marquess
of Lansdowne who, in 1775,
made it a model landlord's
town of neat stone façades
with decorative plasterwork.

Today Kenmare is renowned
for its traditional lace. During
the famine years, local nuns
introduced lace making to
create work for the women
and girls. Other attractions
include the fine hotels *(see
p304)* and gourmet restaurants
(see p333). The town is also

an excellent base for exploring
the Beara Peninsula and the
Ring of Kerry *(see pp164–5)*.

Set in a riverside glade off
Market Street is the **Druid's
Circle**, a prehistoric ring of
15 stones associated with
human sacrifice.

Beara Peninsula ⑬

Road map A6. Co Cork & Co Kerry.
🚌 *to Glengarriff (daily) &
Castletownbere (Mon, Wed, Fri &
Sun).* ℹ *Glengarriff (027 63084).*

Dotted with sparsely populated
fishing villages surrounded by
bleak moorland, this peninsula
is remote. It used to be a
refuge for smugglers, with the
Irish getting the better deal in
their exchange of pilchards for
contraband French brandy.

The peninsula offers some
spectacular scenery and wonderful walking country. From
the **Healy Pass**, which cuts a
jagged path across the spine of
the Caha Mountains, there are
some fine views of Bantry Bay
and the rugged landscape of
West Cork. To the west of the
pass is **Hungry Hill**, the highest
mountain in the Caha range
and popular with hill walkers.

Encircled by the Caha and
Slieve Miskish Mountains is
Castletownbere, the main town
on the peninsula. This sheltered port was once a haven for
smugglers, but is now awash
with foreign fishing trawlers.
McCarthy's Bar on Town
Square features an authentic
matchmaking booth, where

families used to agree marriage
terms until a generation ago.

West of Castletownbere
stands the shell of **Puxley
Mansion**, home of the Puxley
family who owned the mines
at nearby **Allihies**. Centre of the
copper-mining district until the
1930s, it is an interesting place,
with tall Cornish-style chimneys
and piles of ochre-coloured
spoil and is home to the
Allihies Copper Mine Museum.

From the tip of the peninsula
a cable car travels across to
Dursey Island, with its ruined
castle and colonies of sea birds.
Licensed to carry six passengers or one large animal at a
time, the cable car offers views
of Bull, Cow and Calf islands.

From the headland the R757
road back to Kenmare passes
through the pretty villages of
Eyeries, noted for its brightly
painted cottages and crafts,
and **Ardgroom**, a base for
exploring the scenic glacial
valley around **Glenbeg Lough**.

🏛 **Allihies Copper Mine
Museum**
Allihies. **Tel** *027 73218.* ⬜ *Apr–Oct:
daily; Nov–Mar: Mon–Fri.* 🎟 🎁 ♿

Garinish Island ⑭

Road map B6. Co Cork. 🚤 *from
Glengarriff (027 63116).* **Gardens Tel**
027 63040. ⬜ *Apr–Oct: daily.* 🎟 📷
♿ *limited.* **www.heritageireland.ie**

Also known as Ilnacullin, this
small island was turned into
an exotic garden in 1910 by
Harold Peto for Annan Bryce,

View of Caha Mountains from the Healy Pass, Beara Peninsula

For hotels and restaurants in this region see pp302–6 and pp331–4

Italianate garden with lily pool and folly on Garinish Island

a Belfast businessman. Framed by views of Bantry Bay, the gardens are landscaped with Neo-Classical follies and planted with subtropical flora. The microclimate and peaty soil provide the damp, warm conditions needed for these ornamental plants to flourish.

Exotic shrubberies abound especially during the summer. In May and June, there are beautiful displays of camellias, azaleas and rhododendrons. There is also a New Zealand fernery and a Japanese rockery, as well as a rare collection of Bonsai trees. A Martello tower, thought to be the first ever built, crowns the island and among the follies are a clock tower and a Grecian temple.

The centrepiece is a colonnaded Italianate garden, with a Classical folly and ornamental lily pool. Much of its charm resides in the contrast between the cultivated lushness of the garden and the glimpses of wild seascape and barren mountains beyond. An added attraction of the boat trip across to this Gulf Stream paradise is the chance to see cavorting seals in Bantry Bay.

Bantry House ⑮

See pp168–9.

Bantry Bay ⑯

Road map A6. Co Cork. 🚌 to Bantry and Glengarriff. 🛈 Mar–Oct: The Square, Bantry (027 50229). **www**.bantry.ie **Bamboo Park Tel** 027 63975. **w**www.bamboo-park.com

Bantry Bay encompasses the resorts of **Bantry** and **Glengarriff**. It is also a springboard for trips to Mizen Head and the Beara Peninsula.

Bantry nestles beneath the hills which run down to the bay. Just offshore you can see **Whiddy Island**, the original home of the White family, who moved to Bantry House in the early 18th century. Further along is **Bere Island**, a British base until World War II.

Glengarriff at the head the bay, exudes an air of Victorian gentility with its neatly painted shopfronts and craft shops. On the coast is the Eccles Hotel, a haunt of Queen Victoria and where George Bernard Shaw supposedly wrote *Saint Joan*.

Bamboo Park in Glengarriff is a unique, exotic garden with 30 different species as well as other tropical plants.

Mizen Head ⑰

Road map A6. Co Cork. 🚌 to Goleen. 🛈 Town Hall, North St, Skibbereen (028 21766).

Mizen Head, the most southwesterly tip of Ireland, has steep cliffs, often lashed by storms. In a lighthouse, **Mizen Head Visitors' Centre** is reached by a bridge. From the car park, a headland walk takes in views of cliffs and Atlantic breakers. The sandy beaches of nearby **Barley Cove** attract bathers and walkers; to the east is **Crookhaven**, a pretty yachting harbour. From here, a walk to **Brow Head** offers views of the lighthouse.

Mizen Head can be reached either from Bantry via Durrus or from the market town of **Skibbereen**, on the R592, via the charming crafts centre of **Ballydehob** and the village of **Schull**. Trips to Cape Clear Island (*see p170*) leave from Schull in the summer months.

🏛 Visitors' Centre
Mizen Head. **Tel** 028 35115. ◻ Mar–Oct: daily; Nov–mid-Mar: Sat & Sun. 🌐 🔒 🛗 limited. ◻ 🖥 www.mizenhead.ie

Rocky cliffs at Mizen Head

Bantry House ⑮

Bantry House has been the home of the White family, formerly Earls of Bantry, since 1739. The original Queen Anne house was built around 1700, but the north façade overlooking the bay was a later addition. Inside is an eclectic collection of art and furnishings brought from Europe by the 2nd Earl of Bantry. Highlights include the Aubusson tapestries made for Marie Antoinette on her marriage to the future Louis XVI. Guestrooms are available here on a Bed & Breakfast basis.

William and Mary clock in anteroom

North façade

The anteroom contains family mementos, china and a collection of 18th-century prints.

Loggia

To car park

Gobelin Room
The subject of this 18th-century Gobelin tapestry is The Bath of Cupid and Psyche. *The room also contains an early 19th-century piano.*

The Rose Garden, laid out in the early 18th century, is, in the words of the 1st Earl of Bantry, "a parterre after the English manner".

1ST EARL OF BANTRY (1767–1851)

Richard White, 1st Earl of Bantry, played a leading role in defending Ireland against an attempted invasion by Wolfe Tone and the United Irishmen *(see pp40–41)*. On 16 December 1796, Tone sailed from Brest in Brittany with a fleet of 43 French ships bound for Ireland. White chose strategic spots around Bantry Bay and mustered volunteers to fight. His efforts proved unnecessary as the French fleet was forced back by bad weather. Nonetheless, White was rewarded with a peerage by George III for his "spirited conduct and important services". In 1800 he was made Viscount Bantry, becoming Earl of Bantry in 1816.

★ Dining Room
This room is dominated by portraits of King George III and Queen Charlotte by court painter Allan Ramsay. The Spanish chandelier is decorated with Meissen china flowers.

★ Rose Room

The rose-coloured tapestries (c.1770) hanging in this room are thought to have been made for Marie Antoinette on her marriage to the Dauphin of France.

Entrance hall

Statue of Diana (1840)

South façade

Library

★ View of House and Bantry Bay

Bantry House enjoys a magnificent location overlooking Bantry Bay. This lovely view, from the terraces above the house, shows the harbour with Whiddy Island and the Caha Mountains beyond.

Italian Garden

Inspired by the Boboli Gardens in Florence, this garden encircles a pool decorated in Classical Grotesque style. It was designed in the early 1850s by the 2nd Earl.

STAR FEATURES

★ Dining Room

★ Rose Room

★ View of House and Bantry Bay

The steps, known as the "Staircase to the Sky", lead to a series of terraces with fabulous views over the house and across the bay.

Baltimore ⑱

Road map B6. Co Cork.
🏃 300 🚌 ⛴ to Sherkin Island
(087 911 7377); to Cape Clear
Island (028 39159).

Baltimore's most bizarre claim
to fame dates back to 1631
when more than 100 citizens
were carried off as slaves by
Algerian pirates. Now that the
threat of being kidnapped has
gone, this village appeals to
the yachting fraternity and
island-hoppers. Like neighbouring Schull and
Castletownshend, the town
bustles with summer festivals.
Overlooking the harbour is
a ruined 15th-century castle,
once the stronghold of the
O'Driscoll clan. Also worth a
visit are the seafood pubs,
including Bushe's Bar, an
atmospheric inn hung with
nautical memorabilia. Behind
the village, cliff walks lead to
splendid views of Carbery's
Hundred Isles – mere specks
on Roaringwater Bay. Baltimore
Beacon is an important marker
for boats in the bay.
A short ferry ride away is
Sherkin Island with its sandy
beaches in the west, ruined
15th-century abbey, marine
station and pubs. The ferry
ride to **Cape Clear Island** is
more dramatic, as the boat
weaves between sharp black
rocks to this remote, Irish-
speaking island, noted for its
bird observatory in the North
Harbour. There are spectacular
views of the mainland.

**Distinctive white beacon for boats
approaching Baltimore**

Drombeg Stone Circle, erected around the 2nd century BC

Drombeg Stone Circle ⑲

Road map B6. Co Cork. 🚌 to
Skibbereen or Clonakilty.

On the Glandore road 16 km
(10 miles) west of Clonakilty,
Drombeg is the finest of the
many stone circles in
County Cork. Dating
back to about 150
BC, this circle of 17
standing stones is 9.5
m (31 ft) in diameter.
At the winter solstice,
the rays of the setting
sun fall on the flat
altar stone which
faces the entrance to
the circle, marked by
two upright stones.
Nearby is a small stream
with a Stone Age cooking pit
(fulacht fiadh), similar to one
at Craggaunowen (see p190).
A fire was made in the hearth
and hot stones from the fire
were dropped into the cooking pit to heat the water. Once
the water boiled, the meat,
usually venison, was added.

**Sign for Clonakilty
black pudding**

Clonakilty ⑳

Road map B6. Co Cork.
🏃 5,500. 🚌 ℹ 25 Ashe Street
(023 8833226).

Founded as an English outpost
around 1588, this market town
has a typically hearty West
Cork atmosphere. The **West
Cork Regional Museum**, housed
in an old schoolhouse,
remembers the town's industrial heritage. A number of
quayside buildings, linked to
the town's industrial past, have
been restored. Particularly
pleasant is the Georgian
nucleus of Emmet Square.
Until the 19th century
Clonakilty was a noted linen
producer. Today, it is renowned for its rich black puddings,
handpainted Irish signs and
traditional music pubs. Near
the town centre is a
model village,
depicting the
town as it was in
the 1940s. Just
east of town is the
reconstructed **Lios-
na-gCon Ring Fort**,
with earthworks, huts
and souterrains (see
p20). A causeway
links Clonakilty to
Inchydoney beach.

🏛 **West Cork Regional
Museum**
Western Rd. **Tel** 023 883 3115.
◯ May–Sep: daily (except Mon
& Wed). ♿

🏠 **Lios-na-gCon Ring Fort**
Tel 023 8833226. ◯ by appt only;
call ahead. **www**.liosnagcon.com

Timoleague Abbey ㉑

Road map B6. Co Cork. 🚌 to
Clonakilty or Courtmacsherry. ◯ daily.

Timoleague Abbey enjoys a
waterside setting overlooking
an inlet where the Argideen
estuary opens into Courtmacsherry Bay. Founded around
the late 13th century, the
abbey is a ruined Franciscan
friary. The buildings have
been extended at various
times. The earliest section is
the chancel of the Gothic
church. The most recent

addition, the 16th-century tower, was added by the Franciscan Bishop of Ross. The friary was ransacked by the English in 1642 but much of significance remains, including the church, infirmary, fine lancet windows, refectory and a walled court-yard. There are also sections of cloisters and wine cellars In keeping with Franciscan tradition, the complex is plain to the point of austerity. Yet such restraint belied the friars' penchant for high living: the friary prospered on trade in smuggled Spanish wines, easily delivered thanks to its position on the then navigable creek.

Lancet window in ruined church at Timoleague Abbey

River Lee ㉒

Road Map B6. Co Cork 🚃 🚃 to Cork. 🛈 Cork (021 425 5100).

Carving a course through farm- and woodland to Cork city *(see pp174–7)*, the River Lee begins its journey in the lake of the enchanting **Gougane Barra Park**. The shores of the lake are linked by a causeway to **Holy Island,** where St Finbarr, the patron saint of Cork, founded a monastery. The Feast of St Finbarr, on 25 September,

signals celebrations that climax in a pilgrimage to the island on the following Sunday.

The Lee flows through several Irish-speaking market towns and villages. Some, such as **Ballingeary,** with its fine lakeside views, have good angling. The town is also noted for its Irish language college. Further east, near the town of Inchigeela, stand the ruins of **Carrignacurra Castle.** Further downstream lies the Gearagh, an alluvial stretch of marsh and woods which has been designated a wildlife sanctuary.

The river then passes through the Sullane valley, home of the thriving market town of **Macroom**. The hulk of a medieval castle, with its restored entrance, lies just off the main square. In 1654, Cromwell granted the castle to Sir William Penn. His son, who went on to found the American state of Pennsylvania, also lived here for a time.

Between Macroom and Cork, the Lee Valley passes through a hydroelectric power scheme surrounded by artificial lakes, water meadows and wooded banks. Just outside Cork, on the south bank of the river is **Ballincollig,** home to the fascinating Royal Gunpowder Mills museum.

Blarney Castle ㉓

Road Map E5. Blarney, Co Cork. **Tel** 021 438 5252. 🚃 to Cork. 🛈 daily. 🔲 24 & 25 Dec. 🅿 🛈 grounds only, no charge. 🛈 www.blarneycastle.ie

Visitors from all over the world flock to this ruined castle to see the legendary Blarney Stone. Kissing the stone is a long-standing tradition, intended to confer a magical eloquence. It is set in the wall below the castle battlements and, in order to kiss it, the visitor is grasped by the feet and suspended backwards under the parapet.

Little remains of the castle today except the keep, built in 1446 by Dermot McCarthy. Its design is typical of a 15th-century tower house *(see p20)*. The vaulted first floor was once the Great Hall. To reach the battlements you need to climb the 127 steps to the top of the keep.

The castle grounds offer some attractive walks, including a grove of ancient yew trees and limestone rock formations at Rock Close. **Blarney House,** a Scottish baronial mansion and the residence of the Colthurst family since the 18th century, is only open to the public from April to mid-June.

A short walk from the castle, Blarney has a pretty village green with welcoming pubs and some craft shops. The **Blarney Woollen Mills** sells garments and souvenirs.

Battlemented keep and ruined towers of Blarney Castle

Street-by-Street: Kinsale ㉔

Old office sign in Kinsale

For many visitors to Ireland, Kinsale heads the list of places to see. One of the prettiest small towns in Ireland, it has had a long and chequered history. The defeat of the Irish forces and their Spanish allies in the Battle of Kinsale in 1601 signified the end of the old Gaelic order. An important naval base in the 17th and 18th centuries, Kinsale today is a popular yachting centre. It is also famous for the quality of its cuisine – the town's annual Festival of Fine Food attracts food lovers from far and wide. As well as its many wonderful restaurants, the town has pubs and wine bars to cater for all tastes.

Desmond Castle was built around 1500. It is known locally as the "French Prison".

★ Old Market House
Incorporating the old courthouse, this museum includes a toll board listing local taxes for 1788.

Market Square

CHARLES FORT

The star-shaped fort is 3 km (2 miles) east of town in Summercove, but can be reached by taking the signposted coastal walk from the quayside, past the village of Scilly. The fort was built in the 1670s by the English to protect Kinsale harbour against foreign naval forces but, because of its vulnerability to land attack, was taken during the siege of 1690 by William of Orange's army. Nonetheless, it remained in service until 1922 when the British forces left the town and handed it over to the Irish Government. Charles Fort remains one of the finest remaining examples of a star-shaped bastion fort in Europe.

Walls and bastions of Charles Fort

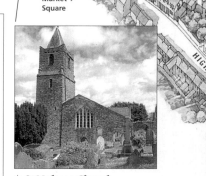

★ St Multose Church
This much-altered Norman church is named after an obscure 6th-century saint and marks the centre of the medieval town.

| 0 metres | | 50 |
| 0 yards | | 50 |

KEY

P	Parking
i	Tourist information
– – –	Suggested route

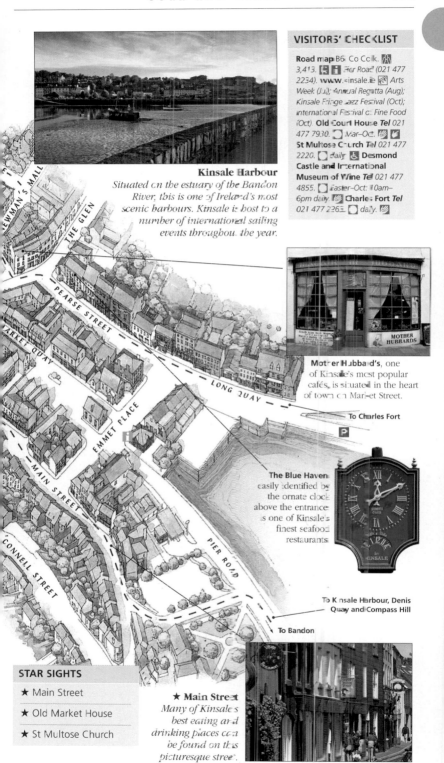

Kinsale Harbour
Situated on the estuary of the Bandon River, this is one of Ireland's most scenic harbours. Kinsale is host to a number of international sailing events throughout the year.

Mother Hubbard's, one of Kinsale's most popular cafés, is situated in the heart of town on Market Street.

To Charles Fort

The Blue Haven, easily identified by the ornate clock above the entrance, is one of Kinsale's finest seafood restaurants.

To Kinsale Harbour, Denis Quay and Compass Hill

To Bandon

★ Main Street
Many of Kinsale's best eating and drinking places can be found on this picturesque street.

Cork

Sign outside a Cork pub

Cork city derives its name from the marshy land on the banks of the River Lee – its Irish name *Corcaigh* means marsh – on which St Finbarr founded a monastery around AD 650. The narrow alleys, waterways and Georgian architecture give the city a Continental feel. Since the 19th century, when Cork was a base for the National Fenian movement (*see p43*), the city has had a reputation for political rebelliousness. Today this mood is reflected in the city's attitude to the arts and its bohemian spirit, much in evidence at the lively October jazz festival.

Clock tower and weather vane of St Anne's Shandon

🏠 St Anne's Shandon
Church St. **Tel** *021 450 5906.* ◻ *Mar–Oct: daily, Nov–Feb: Mon–Sat.* ● *25 Dec.* 🎫 ♿ *limited.*
This famous Cork landmark stands on the hilly slopes of the city, north of the River Lee. Built in 1722, the church has a façade made of limestone on two sides, and of red sandstone on the other two. The steeple is topped by a weather vane in the shape of a salmon. The clock face is known by the locals as the "four-faced liar" because, up until 1986 when it was repaired, each face showed slightly different times. Visitors can climb the tower and, for a small fee, ring the famous Shandon bells.

🧈 Cork Butter Museum
O'Connell Square. **Tel** *021 430 0600.* ◻ *Mar–Oct: 10am–5pm daily (to 5pm Jul–Aug).* 🎫 **www.corkbuttermuseum.ie**
This museum tells the story of Ireland's most important food export and the world's largest butter market. The exchange opened in 1770 and was where butter was graded before it was exported to the rest of the world. By

1892 it was exporting around 500,000 casks of butter a year. The exchange shut in 1924. Just next door is the Shandon Craft Centre where visitors can watch craft workers, such as crystal cutters and weavers, at work.

🏛 Crawford Art Gallery
Emmet Place. **Tel** *021 490 7855.* ◻ *10am–5pm Mon–Sat (to 8pm Thu).* ● *public hols.* ♿ 🍽 ▭ 🖥 **www.crawfordartgallery.ie**
The red brick and limestone building that houses Cork's major art gallery dates back to 1724. Built as the city's original custom house, it became a school of design in 1850. In 1884, a well-known art patron, William Horatio Crawford, extended the building to accommodate studios and sculpture and picture galleries.
The gallery houses some fine examples of late

St Fin Barre's Cathedral ⑪
GILL ABBEY ST   DEAN STREET

Cork Airport
6 km (4 miles) ✈

SIGHTS AT A GLANCE

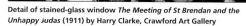

Detail of stained-glass window *The Meeting of St Brendan and the Unhappy Judas* (1911) by Harry Clarke, Crawford Art Gallery

19th- and early 20th-century Irish art including paintings by Jack Yeats. There are also three fine windows by Ireland's foremost stained-glass artist, Harry Clarke (1889–1931).

Another attraction is the small collection by British artists and international works by artists such as Joán Miró and Georges Rouault.

The gallery is well known for its excellent café, which serves lunches and delicious teas. The room is decorated with works of art from the collection.

Richly decorated apse ceiling of St Fin Barre's Cathedral

⛪ St Fin Barre's Cathedral

Bishop Street **Tel** 021 496 3387.
🕐 daily. 🌑 24 Dec–4 Jan. 📷 &
www.cathedral.cork.anglican.org
Situated in a quiet part of town, this cathedral is dedicated to the founder and patron saint of the city. Completed in 1870 to the design of William

Burges, it is an exuberant triple-spired edifice built in Gothic Revival style and decorated with stone tracery. Inside, the painted and gilded apse ceiling shows Christ in Glory surrounded by angels. The stained-glass windows below tell the story of Christ's life.

🏛 Cork City Gaol

Convent Avenue, Sunday's Well. **Tel**
021 430 5022. 🕐 daily. 📷 📹 &
🏠 📖 🏫 www.corkcitygaol.com
A pretty, 20-minute walk west of the city centre leads to the restored City Gaol, complete with its furnished cells. An exhibition traces the lives of individual inmates imprisoned here during the 19th and 20th centuries. Conditions were miserable and, for punishment, prisoners were made to run on a human treadmill that would normally be used to grind grain.

The Radio Museum Experience is also housed in this building and chronicles the development of radio in Ireland and across the world.

South Channel of the River Lee, looking towards Parliament Bridge

0 metres   250

0 yards   250

Exploring Cork

One of Cork's great attractions is that it is a city built on water. Its heart lies on an island between two arms of the River Lee, and many of today's streets were in fact once waterways lined with warehouses and merchants' residences. Although the Dutch canalside appearance has faded, picturesque quays and bridges remain. Steep lanes rise to the north and south of the central island to the city's 19th-century suburbs, offering wonderful views of the city and its fine buildings.

Selling fruit and vegetables at the English Market

The Quays

Although the river now plays only a minor part in the city's economy, much of Cork's commercial activity still takes place around the Quays (pronounced "kays" in the Cork accent). The South Mall, which covers an arm of the River Lee, was a waterway until the late 18th century. Boats were once moored at the foot of a series of stone steps, some of which are still intact today. These led to merchants' domestic quarters above. The arches below led to warehouses where goods were unloaded.

Near South Mall is **Parliament Bridge**, built in 1806 to commemorate the Act of Union (see p42). It is an elegant, single-arched bridge which is made mainly from limestone. Designed by William Hargrave, it replaced a bridge on the same site which was damaged by a flood in 1804. A short walk away, on Sullivan's Quay, is the Quay Co-Op, a popular vegetarian restaurant and meeting place.

National Monument, Grand Parade

From Sullivan's Quay an elegant footbridge, built in 1985, crosses the river to the south end of Grand Parade.

Grand Parade and St Patrick's Street

On Grand Parade, also once a waterway, stands the grandiose **National Monument**, recalling the Irish patriots who died between 1798 and 1867. Bishop Lucey Park, off Grand Parade, has a section of city walls and a fine gateway from the old cornmarket. Between St Patrick's Street and Grand Parade is the **English Market**, a covered fruit and vegetable market established in 1610. Bustling St Patrick's Street, the backbone of the city, was a waterway until 1800 when boats were moored under the steps of gracious houses such as the Chateau Bar (see p347). At the top of the street, near Patrick Bridge, is the **Father Mathew Statue**, a monument to the founder of the Temperance Movement.

Paul Street

Noted for its ethnic restaurants, chic bars, bookshops and trendy boutiques, Paul Street is the hub of the liveliest district in town. Just off Paul Street are the busy backstreets of Carey's Lane and French Church Street. In the early 18th century, Huguenots (French Protestants) settled in these streets and set themselves up as butter exporters, brewers and wholesale merchants. This area is Cork's equivalent to Dublin's Temple Bar (see p78).

Shandon Quarter

Crossing the Christy Ring Bridge to Pope's Quay, you will see on your left **St Mary's Dominican Church**, with its portico of Ionic columns topped by a huge pediment. John Redmond Street leads to the northern slopes of Cork, dominated by the spire of St Anne's Shandon (see p174) with its fine views of the city. To the northeast lies the lofty Montenotte district, once the epitome of Victorian gentility.

St Fin Barre's Quarter

South of the river, rising above the city, this area's distinctive landmark is St Fin Barre's Cathedral (see p175). Nearby is the ivy-clad **Elizabeth Fort**, a 16th-century structure which was converted into a prison in 1835 and later a *Garda* (police) station. A short walk to the east lies the **Red Abbey**, a 13th-century relic from an Augustinian abbey – the oldest building in Cork.

An attractive street in Cork

For hotels and restaurants in this region see pp302–6 and pp331–4

Environs

Some beautiful countryside surrounds the city of Cork, especially along the lush valley of the River Lee (see p171). The landscape of East Cork is much gentler than the wild, rocky coastline of West Cork and County Kerry, and the land is much more fertile. Many local attractions make good day trips and there are also plenty of opportunities for outdoor activities such as walking, riding and fishing.

♣ Blackrock Castle Observatory

Blackrock. **Tel** 021 435 7917. ◻
10am–5pm Mon–Fri; 11am–5pm Sat
& Sun. ● 1 Jan & 24–26 Dec. ◻
◻ ◻ ◻ ◻ www.bco.ie

On the banks of the River Lee, 1.5 km (1 mile) downstream from the city centre stands Blackrock Castle. Built in 1582 by Lord Mountjoy as a harbour fortification, the castle was destroyed by fire in 1827 and rebuilt in 1829. Welcoming schools and groups, it houses an exhibition on the cosmos. Further south at Carrigtwohill, near Fota Wildlife Park (see pp178–9), is Barryscourt Castle.

Blackrock Castle standing on the banks of the River Lee

♛ Barryscourt Castle

Carrigtwohill, Co Cork. **Tel** 021 488 2218. ◻ Jun–Sep: 10am–6pm daily.
◻ ◻ (obligatory).
www.heritageireland.ie
This castle was the seat of the Barry family from the 12th to 17th centuries. The building has been restored and has period fittings and furniture. It is a fine example of a 15th-century tower house with 16th-century additions

The 15th century tower house of Barryscourt Castle

and alterations. It is roughly rectangular with a four-storey tower house occupying the south-west corner. What makes Barryscourt stand out from most other tower house complexes is the 50-m (164-ft) long hall, which occupies the western section of the castle. Both the Great Hall and the Main Hall are open to the public and the keep houses an exhibition on the arts in Ireland from 1100 to 1600. The orchard has also been restored to an original 16th-century design and has a herb garden by the castle walls.

♣ Desmond Castle

Kinsale. **Tel** 021 477 4855.
◻ Easter–Oct: 10am–6pm daily (last adm: 5pm). ◻ ◻ www.
heritageireland.ie

Situated some 16 km (10 miles) south of Cork City, Desmond Castle was built by Maurice Bacach Fitzgerald, the ninth Earl of Desmond, in around 1500. A good example of an urban tower house, the castle consists of a keep with storehouses to the rear. It has spent time as an ordnance store, workhouse, customs house and prison. In 1938 it was declared a national monument.

The castle also houses the **International Museum of Wine**, which tells the story of wine in Ireland and has wine-related artifacts and antique wine bottles.

River Blackwater ㉖

Road Map B5. Co Cork.
◻ to Mallow ◻ to Fermoy, Mallow or Kanturk.

The second longest river in Ireland after the Shannon (see p185), the Blackwater rises in high bogland in County Kerry. It then flows eastwards through County Cork until it reaches Cappoquin, County Waterford, where it changes course south through wooded sandstone gorges to the sea at Youghal (see p179). Much of the valley is wooded, a reminder that the entire area was forested until the 17th century. The river passes some magnificent country houses and pastoral views. However, the region is best known for its fishing – the Blackwater's tributaries are filled with fine brown trout.

The best way to see the valley is to take the scenic Blackwater Valley Drive from Youghal to Mallow. The route passes through **Fermoy**, a town founded by Scottish merchant John Anderson in 1789. Angling is the town's main appeal, especially for roach, rudd, perch and pike. Further west is **Mallow**, a prosperous town noted for its fishing, golf and horse racing, and a good base for tours of the area. Detours along the tributaries include **Kanturk**, a pleasant market town with a castle, on the River Allow.

Weirs and bridge at Fermoy on the River Blackwater

Cobh ⑳

Road map C6. Co Cork. ⚑ *13,000.*
⚑ ⓘ *Cld Yacht Club (021 481 3301).*
www.cobhharbourchamber.ie

Cobh (pronounced "cove")
lies on Great Island, one of
the the three islands in Cork
Harbour which are now
linked by causeways. The
Victorian seafront has rows
of steeply terraced houses
overlooked by the Gothic
Revival **St Colman's Cathedral**.

Following a visit by Queen
Victoria in 1849, Cobh was
renamed Queenstown but
reverted to its original name
in 1922. The town has one of
the world's largest natural
harbours, hence its rise to
prominence as a naval base in
the 18th century. It was also a
major port for merchant ships
and the main port from which
Irish emigrants left for America.

Cobh was also a port of call
for luxury passenger liners. In
1838, the *Sirius* made the first
transatlantic crossing under
steam power from here. Cobh
was also the last stop for the
Titanic, before its doomed
Atlantic crossing in 1912. Three
years later, the
Lusitania was
torpedoed and
sunk by a German
submarine just
off Kinsale (*see
pp172–3*), south-
west of Cobh. A
memorial on the
promenade is
dedicated to all
those who died
in the attack.

IRISH EMIGRATION

Between 1848 and 1950 more than six million people
emigrated from Ireland – two and a half million of them
leaving from Cobh. The famine years of 1844–8 (*see p219*)
triggered mass emigration as the impoverished made
horrific transatlantic journeys in cramped, insanitary
conditions. Many headed for the United States and Canada,
and a few risked the long journey to Australia. Up until the
early 20th century, emigrants waiting to board the ships
were a familiar sight in Cobh. However, by the 1930s world
recession and immigration restrictions in the United States
and Canada led to a fall in the numbers leaving Ireland.

19th-century engraving of emigrants gathering in Cobh Harbour

🏛 **The Queenstown Story**
Cobh Heritage Centre. *Tel 021 481
3591.* ◯ *daily.* ⬤ *22 Dec–5 Jan.* ▨
🍴 ⬥ 🅿 **www**.cobhheritage.com
Housed in a Victorian railway
station, *The Queenstown Story*
is an exhibition detailing the
town's marine history. Exhibits
and audiovisual displays recall
the part Cobh played in Irish
emigration and the transportation of convicts. Between 1791
and 1853, 40,000 convicts
were sent to Australian penal
colonies in notorious "coffin
ships"; many prisoners
were also kept in

floating jails in Cork Harbour.
The exhibition also documents
Cobh's role as a port of call
for transatlantic liners.

Environs
North of Cobh is Fota Island,
with **Fota House and Gardens**.
This glorious Regency
mansion, surrounded by
landscaped gardens has a
19th-century arboretum with
rare trees and shrubs.

Also on the island, the **Fota
Wildlife Park** concentrates on
breeding and reintroducing
animals to their natural habitat.

Cobh Harbour with the steeple of St Colman's Cathedral rising above the town

For hotels and restaurants in this region see pp302–6 and pp331–4

The white-tailed sea eagle is one native species that has been saved from extinction in Ireland. The park boasts over 70 species, including giraffe, flamingo, and zebra. A train links the sections of the park.

🏠 Fota House and Gardens
Fota Island. *Tel* 021 481 5543.
⬜ May–Oct: daily; Nov–Apr: Sat & Sun. 🔲 💻 🚻

🦌 Fota Wildlife Park
Fota Island. *Tel* 021 481 2678. ⬜ daily. ⬤ 25 & 26 Dec. 🔲 ♿ 🍴 🚻

Old Midleton Distillery ㉘

Road map C5. Distillery Walk, Midleton, Co Cork.
Tel 021 451 3594. 🚌 to Midleton.
⬜ daily. ⬤ Good Fri & 24 & 25 Dec.
🔲 ♿ 🚻 🎦 🍴 in summer only.
www.toursjamesonwhiskey.com

A sensitively restored 18th-century distillery, Old Midleton Distillery is part of the vast Irish Distillers group at Midleton. Bushmills *(see p266)* is the oldest distillery in Ireland but Midleton is the largest, with a series of distilleries each producing a different whiskey, including Jameson.

The story of Irish whiskey is presented through audiovisual displays, working models and authentic machinery. A tour of the old distillery takes in the mills, maltings, still-houses, kilns, granaries and warehouses. Visitors can take part in whiskey tasting and try to distinguish between various brands of Irish, Scotch and bourbon whiskies. Highlights of the visit include the world's largest pot still, with a capacity of over 30,000 gallons, and the working water wheel.

Clock tower on the main street of Youghal

Youghal ㉙

Road map C5. Co Cork. 🚹 7,500.
🚌 🚆 ℹ️ Market House, Market Square (024 92447). **www.**youghal.ie

Youghal (pronounced "yawl") is a historic walled town and thriving fishing port. The town was granted to Sir Walter Raleigh by Queen Elizabeth I but later sold to the Earl of Cork. In Cromwellian times, Youghal became a closed borough – an English Protestant garrison town.

The picturesque, four-storey **Clock tower** was originally the city gate, but was recast as a prison. Steep steps beside the tower lead up to a well-preserved section of the medieval town wall and fine views across the Blackwater estuary. Through the tower, in the sombre North Main Street, is the **Red House**, a Dutch mansion built in 1710. Virtually next door are some grim Elizabethan almshouses and, on the far side of the road, a 15th-century tower, known as **Tynte's Castle**.

Nestling in the town walls opposite is **Myrtle Grove** (closed to the public), one of the few unfortified Tudor manor houses to survive in Ireland. It has a triple-gabled façade and exquisite interior oak panelling. Just uphill is the Gothic **Church of St Mary**. Inside are tomb effigies and stained-glass windows depicting the coats of arms of local families.

Grain truck (c.1940) at the Jameson Heritage Centre

THE LOWER SHANNON

CLARE · LIMERICK · TIPPERARY

*I*n the three counties which flank the lower reaches of the Shannon, Ireland's longest river, the scenery ranges from the rolling farmland of Tipperary to the eerie limestone plateau of the Burren. The Shannon's bustling riverside resorts draw many visitors, and there are medieval strongholds and atmospheric towns of great historic interest. The region also boasts a vibrant music scene.

The River Shannon has long made this area an attractive prospect for settlers. There are several important Stone Age sites, including a major settlement by Lough Gur. From the 5th century, the region lay at the heart of Munster, one of Ireland's four Celtic provinces. The Rock of Cashel, a remarkable fortified abbey in county Tipperary, was the seat of the Kings of Munster for more than 700 years.

The Vikings penetrated the Shannon in the 10th century, but Gaelic clans put up stern resistance. During the Norman period, the chieftains of these clans built Bunratty Castle and other fortresses that were impressive enough to rival the strongholds erected by the Anglo-Irish dynasties. Foremost among the latter families were the Butlers, the Earls of Ormonde, who held much land in Tipperary, and the Fitzgeralds, the main landowners in the Limerick area. From the Middle Ages, Limerick was often at the centre of events in the Lower Shannon. In 1691, the army of William of Orange laid siege to the town, heralding the Treaty of Limerick that triggered the Catholic nobility's departure for Europe – the so-called "Flight of the Wild Geese".

Lush grassland, which has turned the Lower Shannon into prime dairy country, is typical of the region. In places this gives way to picturesque glens and mountains, such as the Galty range in southern Tipperary. The region's most dramatic scenery, however, is found along the coast of Clare, a county otherwise best known for its thriving traditional music scene.

Ruins of Dysert O'Dea monastery in County Clare with an outstanding 12th-century High Cross

◁ Traditional musicians playing at Feakle in County Clare

Exploring the Lower Shannon

The central location of Limerick city makes it a natural focus for visitors to the region. However, there are many charming towns that make pleasanter bases, such as Adare, Cashel and also Killaloe, which is well placed for exploring the River Shannon. Most places of interest in Tipperary lie in the southern part of the county, where historic towns such as Clonmel and Cahir overlook the River Suir. County Clare's small villages are full of character and some, such as Doolin, are renowned for traditional music. The county is also home to Bunratty Castle and the Burren.

Looking up at the Cliffs of Moher

GETTING AROUND

Roads extend from Limerick into every corner of the region, providing good access for motorists; the car ferry from Tarbert in Kerry to Killimer, near Kilrush in Clare, is a convenient route across the Shannon. Trains from Limerick serve Cahir, Clonmel and Carrick, but in other areas you must rely on the bus network. This is rather limited, especially in County Clare, although buses to the Burren from Limerick pass the Cliffs of Moher. Some of the most popular sights, such as Bunratty Castle and the Burren, can be reached on bus tours from Limerick.

0 kilometres   20

0 miles   20

KEY

▬▬▬	Motorway
▬ ▬	Motorway under construction
▬▬	Major road
▬	Secondary road
▬▬▬	Minor road
▬	Scenic route
▬▬▬	Major railway
▬▬▬	Minor railway
▬▬	County border
△	Summit

Boats sailing on Lough Derg near Mountshannon

SIGHTS AT A GLANCE

Painted pub sign in Cashel

Looking south along the Cliffs of Moher, one of the most dramatic stretches of Ireland's west coast

The Burren **❶**

See pp186–8.

Cliffs of Moher **❷**

Road map B4. Co Clare. 🚌 *from Ennis, Galway & Limerick.* **Visitors' Centre Tel** 065 708 6141. ☐ *daily.* ● *24–26 Dec.* 🔓 📷 🛍 ♿ www.cliffsofmoher.ie

Even when shrouded in mist or buffeted by Atlantic gales, the Cliffs of Moher are breathtaking, rising to a height of 214 m (690 ft) out of the sea and extending for 8 km (5 miles). The sheer rock face, with its layers of black shale and sandstone, provides sheltered ledges where guillemots and other sea birds nest.

Well-worn paths lead along the cliffs. From the **Visitors' Centre**, northwest of Liscannor, you can walk south to **Hag's Head** in an hour. To the north, there is a three-hour coastal walk between **O'Brien's Tower** – a viewing point built for Victorian tourists – and Fisherstreet near **Doolin** *(see p188).*

Kilrush **❸**

Road map B4. Co Clare. 🏘 *2,800.* 🚌 🅹 *Frances St (065 905 1577).* ☐ *May–Sep*

With the addition of a marina and the promotion of Kilrush as a heritage town, the fortunes of this 18th-century estate town have been greatly revived.
Follow the well-marked walking trail starting from Market Square, which highlights the town's historic sights.

Environs
From Kilrush Marina, boats take visitors dolphin-spotting – the chances of seeing one of the 100 bottlenosed dolphins identified in the estuary are high. Boats also run to uninhabited **Scattery Island**, site of a medieval monastery. The ruins include five churches and one of the tallest round towers in the country.
The **Loop Head Drive** is a 27-km (17-mile) route which begins at the resort of Kilkee, west of Kilrush. It winds south past dramatic coastal scenery to Loop Head, from where you can enjoy superb views.

Glin **❹**

Road map B5. Co Limerick. 🏘 *600.* 🚌 *from Limerick.*

This village on the banks of the Shannon is the seat of the Knights of Glin, a branch of the Fitzgeralds who have lived in the district for seven centuries. Their first medieval castle is a ruin, but west of the village

Glin Castle, designed in the Gothic romance style, was built in 1780

stands their newer home, **Glin Castle**. Built in 1780, the manor succumbed to the vogue for Gothic romance in the 1820s, when it acquired battlements and gingerbread lodges. The castle has been used as a hotel, but is currently closed to the public.

Foynes **❺**

Road map B5. Co Limerick. 🏘 *650.* 🚌 *from Limerick.*

Foynes enjoyed short-lived fame in the 1930s and 1940s as the eastern terminus of the first airline passenger route across the Atlantic. **Foynes Flying Boat Museum** presents a detailed history of the seaplane service. The original Radio and Weather Rooms have transmitters, receivers and Morse code equipment. There is also a 1940s-style tea room and a full-sized replica of a B314 flying boat.

🏛 **Foynes Flying Boat Museum**
Aras Ide, Foynes. **Tel** 069 65416.
☐ *Mar–Oct: daily.* 🔓 📷 🛍 🅿 ♿
www.flyingboatmuseum.com

Environs
The historic town of **Askeaton**, 11 km (7 miles) east of Foynes, has a castle and Franciscan friary. The friary is particularly interesting, with a 15th-century cloister of black marble. In Rathkeale, 8 km (5 miles) south, **Castle Matrix** is a restored 15th-century tower house renowned for the fine library in the Great Hall.

⚜ **Castle Matrix**
Rathkeale. **Tel** 085 730 7760.
☐ *May–Sep: Sat–Thu.* 🔓

Fishing on Lough Derg, the largest of the lakes on the Shannon

River Shannon ❻

Road map B4, C4, C3. 🚏 to Limerick or Athlone 🚌 to Carrick-on-Shannon, Athlone or Limerick. 🛈 Arthur's Quay, Limerick (061 317522).
www.discoverloughderg.ie

The Shannon is the longest river in Ireland, rising in County Cavan and meandering down to the Atlantic. Flowing through the heart of the island, it has traditionally marked the border between the provinces of Leinster and Connaught. In medieval times, castles guarded the major fords from Limerick to Portumna, and numerous monasteries were built along the riverbanks, including the celebrated Clonmacnoise *(see pp250–51)*. Work began on the Shannon navigation system in the 1750s, but it fell into disuse with the advent of the railways. It has since been revived with the Shannon–Erne Waterway the latest stretch to be restored *(see p235)*.

There are subtle changes of landscape along the length of the river. South of **Lough Allen**, the countryside is covered with the drumlins or low hills typical of the northern Midlands. Towards **Lough Ree**, islands stud the river in an area of ecological importance which is home to otters, geese, grey herons and whooper swans. Continuing south beyond **Athlone** *(see p249)*, the river flows through flood plains and bog before reaching **Lough**

Grey heron on the Shannon

EXPLORING THE SHANNON

Carrick-on-Shannon is the main centre for boating on the upper reaches of the river, while Portumna and the atmospheric ports of Mountshannon and Killaloe are the principal bases for exploring Lough Derg.

Cruiser on the Shannon

KEY

🛈 Tourist information

🚢 Cruiser hire

🚤 Water-bus tour

Source of the Shannon
NORTHWEST IRELAND
Lough Allen
Shannon-Erne Waterway
Leitrim
Lough Key · Carrick-on-Shannon
Kilglass Lough
THE WEST OF IRELAND
Royal Canal
Lough Ree
THE MIDLANDS
🛈🚢🚤 Athlone
Grand Canal
Banagher 🚢🚤
🚤 Portumna
Lough Derg
🚤 Mountshannon · Dromineer 🚤
THE LOWER SHANNON
🛈🚢🚤 Killaloe · Ballina 🛈
Shannon Estuary · Limerick 🛈

0 km — 20
0 miles — 10

Derg, the biggest of the lakes on the Shannon. The scenery is more dramatic here, with the lough's southern end edged by wooded mountains. From **Killaloe** *(see p190)* the river gains speed on its rush towards **Limerick** *(see p191)* and the sea. The mudflats of the Shannon estuary attract a great variety of birdlife. The port of **Carrick-on-Shannon** *(see p235)* is the cruising centre of Ireland, but there are bases all along the river – especially

around Lough Derg, which is the lake most geared to boating. Water-buses connect most ports south of Athlone. If you hire a cruiser enquire about the weather conditions before setting out, particularly on Loughs Ree and Derg, which are very exposed. The calm stretch from **Portumna** *(see p213)* to Athlone is easier for inexperienced sailors.

Walkers can enjoy the Lough Derg Way, a signposted route around the lake. The woods by **Lough Key** *(see p219)* also provide good walking territory.

Athlone and the southern reaches of Lough Ree

The Burren ●

The word Burren derives from *boireann*, which means "rocky land" in Gaelic – an apt name for this vast limestone plateau in northwest County Clare. In the 1640s, Cromwell's surveyor described it as "a savage land, yielding neither water enough to drown a man, nor tree to hang him, nor soil enough to bury". Few trees manage to grow in this desolate place, yet other plants thrive.

Dark red helleborine

The Burren is a unique botanical environment in which Mediterranean and alpine plants rare to Ireland grow side by side. From May to August, an astonishing array of flowers adds splashes of colour to the austere landscape. These plants grow most abundantly around the region's shallow lakes and pastures, but they also take root in the crevices of the limestone pavements which are the most striking geological feature of the rocky plateau. In the southern part of the Burren, limestone gives way to the black shale and sandstone that form the dramatic Cliffs of Moher *(see p184).*

Grazing in the Burren
A quirk in the local climate means that, in winter, the hills are warmer than the valleys – hence the unusual practice in the Burren of letting cattle graze on high ground in winter.

FAUNA OF THE BURREN

The Burren is one of the best places in Ireland for butterflies, with 28 species found in the area. The birdlife is also varied. Skylarks and cuckoos are common on the hills and in the meadows, while the coast is a good place for razorbills, guillemots, puffins and other sea birds. Mammals are harder to spot. Badgers, foxes and stoats live here, but you are much more likely to see a herd of shaggy-coated wild goats or an Irish hare.

Turloughs are shallow lakes which are dry in summer but flood in winter, when they attract wildfowl and waders.

Spring gentian

The pearl-bordered fritillary, *one of a number of fritillaries found in the Burren, can be seen in no other part of Ireland.*

An Irish hare's *white and brown winter coat turns to reddish-brown in the summer.*

Whooper swans *from Iceland flock to the wetlands of the Burren in winter.*

The hooded crow *is easily identified by its grey and black plumage.*

Bloody Cranesbill
This striking plant, common in the Burren, is a member of the geranium family. It flowers in June.

Limestone Pavement
Glaciation and wind and rain erosion have formed limestone pavements with deep crevices known as "grykes". The porous rock is easily penetrated by rain-water, which has gouged out an extensive cave system beneath the rocky plateau.

Hawthorn is one of the few trees which manages to grow in the Burren, although the plants are usually twisted and stunted.

Exposed layers of limestone

Stone-built Burren cottage

Dry-stone wall

Limestone slabs, or "clints"

The hoary rock rose is one of several rare plants to grow abundantly in the Burren.

Holly trees can gain a foothold in the pavement, but grazing and wind restrict their growth.

Maidenhair fern thrives in the damp crevices of the Burren.

Mountain Avens
Normally a mountain plant, this flower grows here at sea level.

Exploring the Burren

If you are interested in the unique geology and natural history of the Burren, head for **Mullaghmore**, to the southeast of the area. This is one of the wildest parts of the plateau and reaches a height of 191 m (626 ft), with some of the best limestone pavements in the area.

A good place to begin a tour of the more accessible parts of the Burren is at the **Cliffs of Moher** (see p184). From here it is a short drive north to **Doolin**, near the port for the Aran Islands (see pp214–15). One of the world's largest free hanging stalactites is in Doolin Cave. The village is renowned for its traditional music; Gus O'Connor's pub (see p348) acts as a focus for music-lovers in the area. The coastal road runs north from Doolin to a desolate limestone outcrop at **Black Head**, while turning inland you will reach **Lisdoonvarna**. The Victorians developed the town as a spa, but it is now most renowned

Music shop in Doolin

for its colourful pubs and its matchmaking festival (see p50). To the north along the N67 lies **Ballyvaughan**, a fishing village dotted with slate-roofed cottages and busy with tourists in summer. It is well placed for reaching a number of sights. Nearby **Bishop's Quarter** has a sheltered beach with glorious views across a lagoon towards Galway Bay. **Aillwee Cave**, to the south, is just one of thousands of caves in the Burren. In the first, known as Bear Haven, the remains of hibernation pits used by bears are still visible.

Ruined forts and castles and numerous prehistoric sites dot the landscape. Just west of Aillwee Cave is **Cahermore Stone Fort**, with a lintelled doorway, and to the south

Gleninsheen Wedge Tomb, a style of grave which marks the transition between Stone and Bronze Age cultures. The more famous **Poulnabrone Dolmen** nearby is a striking portal tomb dating back to 2500–2000 BC. Continuing south you reach the ghostly shell of **Leamaneagh Castle**, a 17th-century mansion that incorporates an earlier tower house built by the O'Briens.

On the southern fringe of the Burren lies **Kilfenora**, a Catholic diocese which, by a historical quirk, has the Pope for its bishop. The village's modest cathedral, one of many 12th-century churches in the Burren, has a roofless chancel with finely sculpted capitals. Kilfenora, however, is more famous for its High Crosses: there are several in the graveyard. Best preserved is the Doorty Cross, with a carving of a bishop and two other clerics on the east face. Next door, the **Burren Centre** offers an excellent multicimensional exhibition giving information on the geology and fauna of the area and man's impact on the landscape.

Carved capital in Kilfenora Cathedral

Poulnabrone Dolmen in the heart of the Burren's limestone plateau

✳ **Aillwee Cave**
Ballyvaughan. **Tel** 065 7077036.
🕐 daily. 🏞 ✔ 🚻 🏠

🏛 **Burren Centre**
Kilfenora. **Tel** 065 7088030.
🕐 Mar–Oct. daily. 🏞 ♿ 🚻 🏠
www.theburrencentre.ie

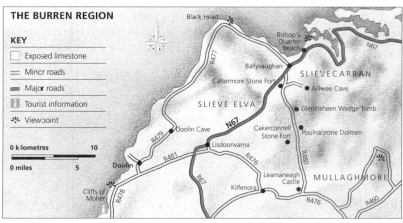

THE BURREN REGION

KEY

☐ Exposed limestone
═ Minor roads
▬ Major roads
ℹ Tourist information
✳ Viewpoint

0 kilometres   10
0 miles   5

Black Head
Bishop's Quarter Beach
N67
Ballyvaughan
Cahermore Stone Fort
SLIEVECARRAN
R477
Aillwee Cave
SLIEVE ELVA
Gleninsheen Wedge Tomb
R479
Doolin Cave
N67
Cakerconnell Stone Fort
Poulnabrone Dolmen
Lisdoonvarna
R480
Doolin
R481
R476
MULLAGHMORE
Leamaneagh Castle
R67
Kilfenora
R476
R460
Cliffs of Moher
R478

Dysert O'Dea ❼

Road map 4 B Corrofin, Co Clare.
🚌 from Ennis. **Tel** 065 683 7401.
🔲 May–Sep: daily. ▣

Dysert O'Dea Castle stands on a rocky outcrop 9 km (6 miles) north of Ennis. This tower house, erected in the 15th century, is home to the **Archaeology Centre** which includes a small museum and also marks the start of a trail around nearby historic sights. A map of the path, designed for both walkers and cyclists, is available in the castle.

Across a field from the castle is a monastic site said to have been founded by the obscure St Tola in the 8th century. The ruins are overgrown and rather worn, but the Romanesque carving above one doorway is still clear, and there is also an impressive 12th-century High Cross with a bishop sculpted on the east side (*see p243*).

Further south, the trail leads past the remains of two stone forts, a ruined castle and the site of a 14th-century battle.

Ennis ❽

Road map 4B. Co Clare. 🏘 25,000.
🚌 🛈 Arthur's Row (065 6828366).
www.visitennis.ie

Clare's county town, on the banks of the River Fergus, is a charming place with winding lanes that recall Ennis's medieval beginnings. The town is also renowned for its painted shopfronts and folk music festivals (known as *fleadh* in Gaelic). It abounds in "singing" pubs and traditional music shops.

15th-century Knappogue Castle, County Clare

Ennis can trace its origins to the 13th century and to the O'Briens, Kings of Thomond, who were the area's feudal overlords in the Middle Ages. The Franciscan friary that they founded here in the 1240s is now the town's main attraction. Dating from the 14th and 15th centuries, the ruined **Ennis Friary** is famous for its rich carvings and decorated tombs in the chancel – above all the 15th-century MacMahon tomb with its finely carved alabaster panels. Extensive conservation work is ongoing here.

Next door to the friary is a delightful 17th-century house, now Cruise's restaurant, and on the corner of nearby Francis Street stands the Queen's Hotel – featured in James Joyce's *Ulysses*. To the south, O'Connell Square has a *monument* to Daniel O'Connell (*see p42*), who was elected MP for Clare in 1828. He also gave his name to the town's main street, where, among the pubs and shops, you can spot a medieval tower, a Jacobean chimney stack and an 18th-century arch.

Finely carved Romanesque doorway at Dysert O'Dea

🛈 Ennis Friary
Abbey St. **Tel** 065 682 9100.
🔲 Easter–Oct: daily. ▣ &

Environs
The area around Ennis is rich in monastic ruins. Just 3 km (2 miles) south of the town is **Clare Abbey**, an Augustinian foundation set up by the O'Briens in 1189 but dating mainly from the 1400s.

Quin Franciscan Friary, set in meadows 13 km (8 miles) southeast of Ennis was also built in the 15th century, and incorporates the romantic ruins of a Norman castle. The well-preserved cloister is one of the finest of its kind in Ireland.

Knappogue Castle ❾

Road map 4B. Quin, Co Clare. **Tel** 061 360788. 🔲 May–Sep: opening hours vary, call ahead to check. 🅿 🏠 &
limited. ▪www.shannonheritage.com

A powerful local clan called the MacNamaras erected Knappogue Castle in 1467. Apart from a ten-year spell in Cromwellian times, it stayed in their hands until 1815. During the War of Independence (*see pp54–5*), the castle was used by the revolutionary forces.

Knappogue is one of Ireland's most charmingly furnished castles. The central tower house is original, but the rest is Neo-Gothic. Inside are fine Elizabethan fireplaces and linenfold wood panelling.

Medieval banquets are staged in the castle from April to October (*see p360*), with storytelling and singing.

Craggaunowen ❿

Road map B4. Kilmurry, Co Clare.
Tel 061 350788. ○ *mid-Apr–mid-Sep.* 🏷️ ♿ *(limited)* 🔲 🏠
www.shannonheritage.com

A woman in peasant costume spinning wool at Craggaunowen

The Craggaunowen Project, known as "Craggaunowen: the Living Past" and designed to bring Bronze Age and Celtic culture to life, is a shining example of a recreated prehistoric site. The centre was created in the grounds of Craggaunowen Castle in the 1960s by John Hunt, a noted archaeologist who had been inspired by his excavations at Lough Gur *(see p194)*. The "Living Past" experience is about the arrival of the Celts in Ireland and their farming and hunting methods.

In summer, people in costume sometimes act out particular trades, such as spinning or potting, or serve as guides. In addition there is a description of how communities lived in the ring fort, a typical early Christian homestead. You can also see a *fulacht fiadh*, a traditional hunter's cooking hole where meat was prepared.

The complex includes part of a *togher*, an original Iron Age timber road that was discovered in Longford. The most eye-catching sight, however, is the crannog *(see p33)*, a man-made island enclosing wattle and daub houses – a style of defensive homestead that survived to the early 1600s.

Another exhibit is a leather-hulled boat built in the 1970s by Tim Severin. He used it to retrace the route which legend says St Brendan took in a similar vessel across the Atlantic in the 6th century *(see p27)*.

Mountshannon ⓫

Road map C4. Co Clare. 🏘️ 240. 🛈
East Clare Heritage. **Tel** 061 921351.

This pretty village on the banks of Lough Derg *(see p185)* seems to have its back turned to the lake but is nevertheless a major angling centre. Solid 18th-century stone houses and churches cluster around the harbour, together with some good pubs.

Mountshannon is well placed for exploring the lake's western shores, with plenty of scope for walks and bicycle rides. Fishing boats are available for hire, and in summer you can go by boat to **Holy Island**, the site of a monastery founded in the 7th century. The ruins include four chapels and a graveyard of medieval tombs.

Bicycle hire and boat trips at Mountshannon

Killaloe ⓬

Road map C4. Co Clare. 🏘️ 950.
🚌 🛈 *May–Sep: Brian Ború Heritage Centre, The Bridge (061 360788).*
www.discoverkillaloe.ie

Killaloe, birthplace of Brian Ború (940–1014), High King of Ireland *(see p34)*, lies close to where the Shannon emerges from Lough Derg, and is the lake's most prosperous pleasure port. A 17th-century bridge separates Killaloe from its twin town of Ballina on the opposite bank. Ballina has better pubs, such as Goosers on the waterfront *(see p349)*, but Killaloe is the main boating centre *(see p365)* and offers more of historical interest.

Killaloe's grandest building is **St Flannan's Cathedral**, built around 1182. Its richly carved Romanesque doorway was once part of an earlier chapel. The church also has an ancient Ogham Stone *(see p34)*, unusual because the inscription is carved in both Nordic runes and Ogham. Outside stands St Flannan's Oratory, built around the same time as the cathedral.

The Brian Ború Heritage Centre, on the bridge, has an interesting exhibition on the history of Brian Ború and from here you can walk along a small section of the old Killaloe Canal. You can also arrange for local fishermen to take you out on the lake.

Bunratty Castle ⓭

See pp192–3.

Limerick 🄯

Road map B4. Co Limerick. 🏢 90,000.
🛫 *Shannon*. 🚌 🚍 🅸 *Arthur's*
Quay (061 317522). 🅿 *Sat.*
www.discoverlimerick.ie

The third largest city in the
Republic, Limerick was
founded by the Vikings. Given
its strategic point on the River
Shannon, it thrived under the
Normans, but later bore the
brunt of English oppression.
After the Battle of the Boyne
(see p244) the rump of the
defeated Jacobite army with-
drew here. The siege which
followed has entered Irish
folklore as a heroic
defeat, sealed by
the Treaty of
Limerick in 1691.
English treachery
in reneging on
most of the terms
of the treaty still
rankles. It is no
coincidence that
Catholicism and
nationalism are
strong in the city.

**Carved misericord in
St Mary's Cathedral**

Limerick has a
reputation for high
unemployment, crime and
general neglect. However, it is
fast acquiring a new image as
a commercial city, revitalized
by new industries and
restoration projects. Even so,
visitors may still have to dig a
little to appreciate its charm.

The city centre consists of
three historic districts. King's
Island was the first area to be
settled by the Vikings and was
later the heart of the medieval
city, when it was known as
Englishtown. It boasts
Limerick's two main landmarks,
King John's Castle and St Mary's
Cathedral. The old Irishtown,
south of the Abbey River, has
its fair share of drab houses
and shops, but also has its own

historic buildings and a pocket
of Georgian elegance in St
John's Square. Near here is
Limerick's most conspicuous
sight, St John's Cathedral, built
in 1861. Its 85-m (280-ft) spire
is the tallest in the country.

The most pleasant part of
Limerick in which to stroll is
Newtown Pery – a grid of
gracious Georgian terraces
focused on O'Connell Street.

♟ King John's Castle

Nicholas St. **Tel** 061 360288. ◯ *daily.*
◯ 24–26 Dec. 🎥 🅱 *limited.*
www.shannonheritage.com
Founded by King John in
1200, not long after the
Normans arrived,
this imposing
castle has five
drum towers
and solid
curtain walls.
Inside, the
castle is less
interesting
architecturally,
but it houses a
good audio-
visual exhibition
on the history of
the city. Ongoing
excavations have unearthed
pots and jewellery, and you
can also see Viking houses
and later fortifications.

Across the nearby Thomond
Bridge, the Treaty Stone marks
the spot where the Treaty of
Limerick was signed in 1691.

🄯 St Mary's Cathedral

Bridge Street. **Tel** 061 310293.
◯ 9:30am–4.30pm Mon–Fri, for
services only Sun. www.cathedral.
limerick.anglican.org
Built in 1172, this is the oldest
structure in the city. Except for
a fine Romanesque doorway
and the nave, however, little
remains of the early church.
The 15th-century misericords
in the choir stalls are the pride

**Characteristic Georgian doorway in
St John's Square**

of St Mary's, with superb
carvings in black oak of angels,
griffins and other creatures
both real and imaginary.

Nearby, George's Quay is a
pleasant street with restaurants
and outdoor cafés and good
views across the river.

🏛 Hunt Museum

Rutland St. **Tel** 061 312833.
◯ 10am–5pm Mon–Sat, 2pm–5pm
Sun. 🎥 *(free on Sun.* 🅷 🅿 🅱
www.huntmuseum.com
Located in the Old Customs
House, this fine museum has
one of the greatest collections
of antiquities in Ireland,
gathered by the archaeologist
John Hunt. The best exhibits,
dating from the Bronze Age,
include gold jewellery and
a magnificent shield. Among
the other artifacts are Celtic
brooches and the 9th-century
Antrim Cross.

🏛 Limerick Museum

Nicholas St. **Tel** 061-417826.
◯ 10am–1pm, 2:15–5pm Tue–Sat.
🌑 *for lunch, public hols & 7 days at
Christmas.* 🅱 www.limerick.ie
The city museum is in a fine
19th-century granary building.
Limerick's history and traditions
from lace- and silver-making
to rugby are on display.

View of Limerick showing Thomond Bridge across the Shannon and King John's Castle

Bunratty Castle & Folk Park ⓭

This formidable castle was built in the 15th century
by the MacNamaras. Its most important residents
were the O'Briens, Earls of Thomond, who lived
here from the early 16th century until the 1640s.
The present interior looks much as it did under
the so-called "Great Earl", who died in 1624.
Abandoned in the 19th century, the castle was
derelict when Lord Gort bought it in the 1950s,
but it has been beautifully restored to its
original state. The adjacent Folk Park reflects
19th century Irish rural and village life.
Bunratty is also famous for its
splendid medieval banquets.

The chimney is a
replica in wood of
the stone original.
It provided a vent
for the smoke
given off by the fire
in the centre of the
Great Hall.

★ North Solar
*This 17th-century German
chandelier is the most curious
feature in the Great Earl's private
apartments. The term "solar" was
used during the Middle Ages to
describe an upper chamber.*

The Murder Hole was
designed for pouring
boiling water or pitch on
to the heads of attackers.

Entrance

The basement, with
walls 3 m (10 ft) thick,
was probably used for
storage or as a stable.

North Front
*Bunratty Castle is unusual
for the high arches on both
the north and south sides of
the keep. However, the first-
floor entrance, designed to
deter invaders, was typical
of castles of the period.*

STAR FEATURES

★ Great Hall

★ Main Guard

★ North Solar

VISITORS' CHECKLIST

Road map 34. Bunratty, Co
Clare. **Tel** 051 360788.
Shannon. from Ennis,
Limerick. Shannon. Castle &
Folk Park. 9am–5:30pm daily
(last admission 4:30m). 24–26
Dec. to Folk Park.
Banquets see p360.
www.shannonheritage.com

★ Main Guard

*Now used for medieval-style
banquets, this was the room where
Bunratty's soldiers ate, slept
and relaxed. Music
was played to them
from the Minstrels'
Gallery, and a gate
in one corner gave
instant access to
the dungeons.*

South Solar

*The South Solar houses guest
apartments. The elaborately
decorated carved ceiling is
partly a reconstruction in
the late Tudor style.*

The Robing Room
was where the earls
put on their gowns
before an audience
in the Great Hall.
They also used it for
private interviews.

**A spiral
staircase** is
found in
each of the
four towers.

★ Great Hall

*This Tudor standard
was among the many
furnishings that Lord
Gort brought to the
castle. It stands in the
Great Hall, once the
banqueting hall and
audience chamber,
and still Bunratty's
grandest room.*

BUNRATTY FOLK PARK

A meticulous recreation of rural life in Ireland at
the end of the 19th century, this Folk Park began
with the reconstruction of a farmhouse which was
saved during the building of nearby Shannon Airport.
It now consists of a complete village, incorporating
shops and a whole range of domestic architecture
from a labourer's cottage to an elegant Georgian
house. Other buildings in the park include a farmhouse
typical of the Moher region in the Burren *(see p184)*
and a working corn mill. During the main summer
season, visitors can meet with various costumed
characters from the period

Main street of Bunratty Folk Park village

Typical thatched cottage in the village of Adare

Adare ⑮

Road map B5. Co Limerick. ☒ *2,000*.
🚌 🛈 *Heritage Centre, Main St*
(061 396666). ⭘ *daily.* **www.**
discoverireland.ie/shannonregion

Adare is billed as Ireland's
prettiest village. Cynics call it
the prettiest "English" village
since its manicured perfection
is at odds with normal notions
of national beauty. Originally a
fief of the Fitzgeralds, the
Earls of Kildare, Adare owes
its present appearance more
to the Earls of Dunraven,
who restored the village in
the 1820s and 1830s. The
village is a picture of neat
stonework and thatched roofs
punctuated by pretty ruins,
all in a woodland setting.

The tourist office is at the
Heritage Centre, which
includes a good exhibition on
Adare's monastic history. Next
door is the **Trinitarian Priory**,
founded by the Fitzgeralds in
1230 and over-restored by the
first Earl of Dunraven; it is now
a Catholic church and convent.
Opposite, by a stone-arched
bridge, is the Washing Pool, a
restored wash-house site.

By the main bridge, on the
Limerick road, is the **Augustinian Priory** which was
founded by the Fitzgeralds in
1316. Also known as Black
Abbey, this well-restored priory
has a central tower, subtle carvings, delightful cloisters and
a graceful sedilia – a carved
triple seat. Just over the bridge,
from where it is best viewed,
is **Desmond Castle**, a 13th-
century feudal castle set on
the banks of the River Maigue
– tickets are available from the
Heritage Centre (Jun–end Sep).

Nearby stands the main gate
to **Adare Manor**, a luxury hotel
and golf course *(see p307).*

Within its 900 ha (2,220 acres)
of parkland lie **St Nicholas
Church** and **Chantry Chapel**,
two evocative 12th-century
ruins. The graceful 15th-
century **Franciscan Friary**,
however, is surrounded by the
golf course, though it can be
seen clearly from the pathway.

In the heart of the village is
the elegant Dunraven Arms
Hotel *(see p306)* from where
the local hunt rides to
hounds. Some of the nearby
cottages, originally built by
the Earl of Dunraven in 1828
for his estate workers, have
been converted into pleasant
cafés and restaurants.

Lough Gur ⑯

Road map B5. Co Limerick.
Visitors' Centre *Tel 061 360788.*
⭘ *May–Aug: daily.* 📷 ♿ *limited.*
🖥 **www**.loughgur.com

This stone age settlement,
21 km (14 miles) south of
Limerick, was extensively inhabited in 3000 BC. Today the
horseshoe-shaped lough and
surrounding hills enclose an
archaeological park. All around
Lough Gur are standing stones
and burial mounds, including
megalithic tombs. One of the
most impressive sights is the
4,000-year-old **Great Stone
Circle**, just outside the park,
by the Limerick–Kilmallock
road. Excavations in the 1970s
unearthed rectangular, oval
and rounded Stone Age huts
with stone foundations. The

Colourfully painted shopfronts on Main Street in Adare

For hotels and restaurants in this region see pp306–9 and pp335–6

Façade of Cashel Palace Hotel

interpretive centre, which is housed in mock Stone Age huts on the site of the original settlement, offers a range of audiovisual displays, models of stone circles, burial chambers and tools and weapons.

As well as the various prehistoric sites scattered all over the Knockadoon Peninsula, there are two castle ruins from more recent times beside the lough – the 15th-century **Bourchier's Castle** and **Black Castle**, a 13th-century seat of the Earls of Desmond.

Roscrea ⓱

Road map C4. Co Tipperary. 🏠 4,600. 🚌 🚂 🛈 Heritage Centre, Castle St (0505 21850). ◷ Easter–Sep: daily. www.heritageireland.ie

This monastic town on the banks of the River Bunnow has an interesting historic centre. The 13th-century Anglo-Norman **Roscrea Castle** consists of a gate tower, curtain walls and two corner towers. In the courtyard stands **Damer House**, a Queen Anne-style residence with a magnificent staircase and Georgian garden. Just over the river lies **St Cronan's Monastery** with a High Cross, Romanesque church gable and a truncated round tower. There are remains of a 15th-century **Franciscan Friary** on Abbey Street and the renovated Blackmills now houses the St Cronan's High Cross and the **Roscrea Pillar**.

⛪ Roscrea Castle & Gardens
Castle Street. **Tel** 0505 21850.
◷ Easter–Sep: daily. 🏠 🛗 limited.
🖥 www.heritageireland.com

Holy Cross Abbey ⓲

Road map C5. Thurles, Co Tipperary. **Tel** 0504 43124. 🚌 🚂 to Thurles. ◷ 9am–8pm daily. 🏠 🎞 🛗 www.holycrossabbey.ie

Founded in 1169 by the Benedictines, Holy Cross was supposedly endowed with a splinter from the True Cross, hence its name. Now it has been restored, and the church is once again a popular place of worship and pilgrimage. Most of the present structure dates from the 15th century. It was built by the Cistercians, who took over the abbey in 1180. This gracious cruciform church, embellished with mullioned windows and sculpted pillars, is one of the finest examples of late Gothic architecture in Ireland.

Nearby, Farney Castle is the only round tower in Ireland that is occupied as a family home. It was built in 1495 and is currently the design studio and retail outlet of Irish international designer Cyril Cullen.

Crucifixion carving at Holy Cross Abbey

Cashel ⓰

Road map C5. Co Tipperary. 🏠 11,400. 🚌 🛈 Heritage Centre, Town Hall, Main St (062 62511). www.cashel.ie

The great attraction of the town is the magnificent medieval **Rock of Cashel** (see pp196–7). A private path leads to the rock from **Cashel Palace Hotel** (see p377), an opulent Queen Anne residence that was once the Bishop's Palace. Nearby, the remnant of a 12th-century castle has been turned into Kearney Castle Hotel. In the evening you can sample traditional Irish culture at the **Brú Ború Cultural Centre**. Named after Brian Ború, the 10th-century king of Munster (see pp44–5), the centre offers folk theatre, traditional music, banquets, and a craft shop. At the foot of the Rock is the 13th-century **Dominican Friary**. This austere sandstone church has a fine west door, a 15th-century tower and lancet windows. On farmland outside Cashel lie the scant remains of **Hore Abbey**, a 13th-century Cistercian foundation. The abbey was remodelled and a tower added in the 15th century, but the barrel-vaulted sacristy, the nave and chapter house are all original.

🎭 Brú Ború Cultural Centre
Cashel. **Tel** 062 61122.
◷ May–Sep: Mon–Sat; Oct–Apr: Mon–Fri. ⬛ 24 Dec–2 Jan. 🛗 🏠
www.bruboru.ie

⛪ Dominican Friary
Dominic Street. 🛗 limited.

Ruins of Hore Abbey (1272) with the Rock of Cashel in the background

Rock of Cashel

This rocky stronghold, which rises dramatically out of the Tipperary plain, was a symbol of royal and priestly power for more than a millennium. From the 4th or 5th century it was the seat of the Kings of Munster, whose kingdom extended over much of southern Ireland. In 1101, they handed Cashel over to the Church, and it flourished as a religious centre until a siege by a Cromwellian army in 1647 culminated in the massacre of its 3,000 occupants. The cathedral, which is subject to ongoing renovation, was finally abandoned in the late 18th century. A good proportion of the medieval complex is still standing, and Cormac's Chapel is one of the most outstanding examples of Romanesque architecture in the country.

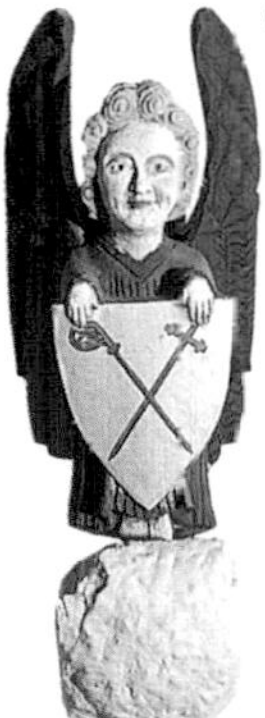

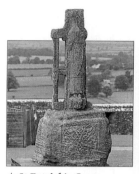

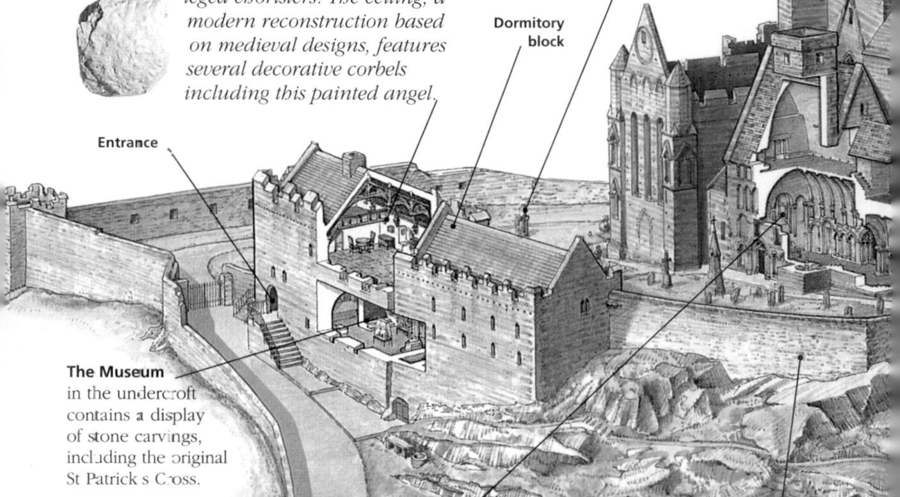

Hall of the Vicars' Choral
This hall was built in the 15th century for Cashel's most privileged choristers. The ceiling, a modern reconstruction based on medieval designs, features several decorative corbels including this painted angel.

★ St Patrick's Cross
The carving on the east face of this cross is said to be of St Patrick, who visited Cashel in 450. The cross is a copy of the original which stood here until 1982 and is now in the museum.

Dormitory block
Entrance
Outer wall
Limestone rock

The Museum in the undercroft contains a display of stone carvings, including the original St Patrick's Cross.

★ Cormac's Chapel
Superb Romanesque carving adorns this chapel – the jewel of Cashel. The tympanum over the north door shows a centaur in a helmet aiming his bow and arrow at a lion.

STAR FEATURES

- ★ Cathedral
- ★ Cormac's Chapel
- ★ St Patrick's Cross

For hotels and restaurants in this region see pp306–9 and pp335–6

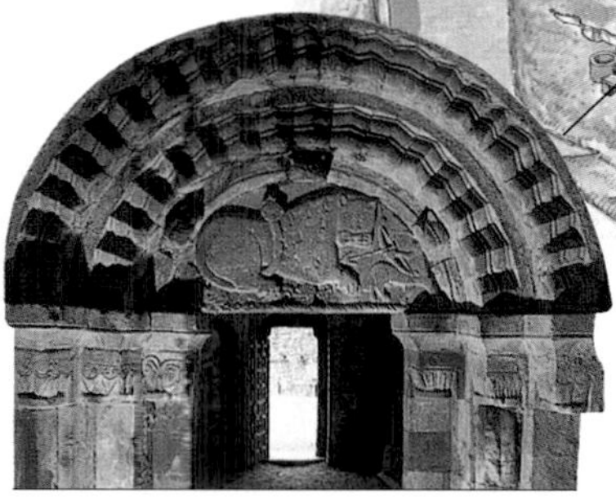

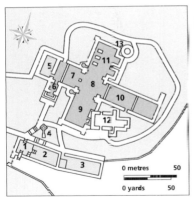

KEY

12TH CENTURY
4 St Patrick's Cross (replica)
12 Cormac's Chapel
13 Round tower

13TH CENTURY
6 Cathedral porch
7 Nave
8 Crossing
9 South transept
10 Choir
11 North transept

15TH CENTURY
1 Ticket office
2 Hall of the Vicars' Choral (museum)
3 Dormitory
5 Castle

0 metres 50
0 yards 50

VISITORS' CHECKLIST

Road map C5. Cashel. **Tel** 062 61437. to Thurles. to Cashel. daily. Early Jun–mid-Sep: 9am–7pm; mid-Mar–early Jun & mid-Sep–mid-Oct: 9am–5:30pm; mid-Oct–mid-Mar: 9am–4:30pm. 24–26 Dec.

The Rock
The 28-m (92-ft) round tower, the oldest and tallest building on the rock, enabled Cashel's inhabitants to scour the surrounding plain for potential attackers.

Round tower

Crossing

The Choir contains the 17th-century tomb of Miler Magrath, who caused a scandal by being both a Protestant and Catholic archbishop at the same time.

The O'Scully Monument, an ornate memorial erected in 1870 by a local landowning family, was damaged during a storm in 1976.

Graveyard

North Transept
Panels from three 16th-century tombs in the north transept are decorated with remarkable fresh and intricate carvings. This one, against the north wall, features a vine-leaf design and strange stylized beasts.

★ Cathedral
The roofless Gothic cathedral has thick walls riddled with hidden passages; in the north transept these are seen emerging at the base of the windows.

Athassel Priory ②⓪

Road map C5 8 km (5 miles) W of Cashel, Co Tipperary. ⊞ to Tipperary. ⬠ daily.

This ruined Augustinian priory is situated on the west bank of the River Suir. The tomb of William de Burgh, the Norman founder of the priory, lies in the church. Established in 1192, Athassel is believed to have been the largest medieval priory in Ireland until it burned down in 1447. The scattered monastic site conveys a tranquil atmosphere, from the gatehouse and church to the remains of the cloisters and chapter house. The church has a fine west doorway, nave and chancel walls, as well as a 15th-century central tower.

The ruins of Athassel Priory, on the banks of the River Suir

Glen of Aherlow ②①

Road map C5. Co Tipperary. ⊞ to Bansha or Tipperary. ℹ Coach Rd, on R663 8 km (5 miles) E of Galbally (062 56331) www.aherlow.com

The lush valley of the River Aherlow runs between the Galty Mountains and the wooded ridge of Slievenamuck. Bounded by the villages of **Galbally** and **Bansha**, the glen was historically an important pass between Limerick and Tipperary and a notorious hideout for outlaws.

Today there are opportunities for riding, cycling, rambling and fishing. Lowland walks follow the trout-filled river along the valley floor. More adventurous walkers will be tempted by the Galty range, which offers more rugged hill-walking, past wooded foothills, mountain streams, tiny corrie lakes and splendid sandstone peaks.

Cahir ②②

Road map C5. Co Tipperary. 🏠 2,100. ⊞ ⊞ ℹ Apr–Oct: Castle Street (052 744 1453). www.discoverireland.ie/southeast

Once a garrison and mill town, Cahir is today a busy market town. The pub-lined Castle Street is the most appealing area. It leads to the Suir River, Cahir Castle and the walk to the Swiss Cottage.

On the edge of town lies the ruined **Cahir Abbey**, a 13th-century Augustinian priory. Its fine windows are decorated with carved heads.

♣ Cahir Castle
Castle Street. **Tel** 052 744 1011. ⬠ daily. ⬛ 24–30 Dec. 🈸 🈂 ⬡ limited. www.heritageireland.ie
Built on a rocky island in the River Suir, Cahir is one of the most formidable castles in Ireland and a popular film set. This well-preserved fortress dates from the 13th century but is inextricably linked to its later owners, the Butlers. A powerful family in Ireland since the Anglo-Norman invasion, they were considered trusty lieges of the English crown and were granted the Cahir barony in 1375. Under their command, the castle was renovated and extended throughout the 15th and 16th centuries. It remained in the Butler family until 1964.

The castle is divided into outer, middle and inner wards, with a barbican at the outer entrance. The inner ward is on the site of the original Norman castle; the foundations are 13th-century, as are the curtain walls and keep. The restored interior includes the striking great hall, which dates largely from the 1840s, though two of the walls are original and the windows are 15th-century. From the ramparts there are views of the river and millrace.

⬛ Swiss Cottage
Ardfinnan Road, Cahir. **Tel** 052 744 1144. ⬠ Apr–Oct: daily. 🈸 🈂 obligatory.
The Swiss Cottage is a superb example of a *cottage orné*, a rustic folly. It was designed for the Butlers by the Regency architect John Nash in 1810. Here, Lord and Lady Cahir played at bucolic bliss, enjoying picnics dressed as peasants. Fashion dictated a

View across the unspoilt Glen of Aherlow

cottage orné should blend in with the countryside and all designs should be drawn from nature with nothing matching, so the windows and sloping eaves are all different. The beautifully restored cottage contains a tea room, gracious music room and two bedrooms.

The Swiss Cottage at Cahir, beautifully restored to its original state

Clonmel ㉓

Road map C5. Co Tipperary. 🚌 17,000. 🚉 🚍 🄸 *The Main Guard (052 612 2960).* **www.** discoverireland.ie

Set on the River Suir, Clonmel is Tipperary's main town. This Anglo-Norman stronghold was a fief of the Desmonds and eventually of the Butlers. Its prosperity was founded on milling and brewing. Today, Clonmel is a bustling, brash town with quirky architecture and lively nightlife.

The **Franciscan Friary** by the quays was remodelled in Early English style in Victorian times but retains a 15th-century tower and houses 16th-century Butler tomb effigies. Nearby is O'Connell Street, Clonmel's main shopping street, which is straddled by the West Gate, built in 1831. Visitors to **Hearn's Hotel** on Parnell Street can see memorabilia of

Clonmel's mock Tudor West Gate, spanning O'Connell Street

Charles Bianconi (1786–1875), including pictures of the horse-drawn coach service he established between Clonmel and Cahir. Eventually this developed into a nationwide passenger service.

Carrick-on-Suir ㉔

Road map C5. Co Tipperary. 🚌 5,500. 🚉 🄸 *Heritage Centre, Main St (051 640200).*

This small market town has a distinctly old-fashioned air. In the 15th century it was a strategic site commanding access west to Clonmel and southeast to Waterford, but after Tudor times the town sank into oblivion. Apart from Ormond Castle, there are few specific sights. However, you can stroll by the old waterside warehouses or shop in Blarney Woollen Mills *(see p354).*

⚜ Ormond Castle
Castle Park. **Tel** 051 640787. ◯ Jun–Sep: daily. 🎟 *obligatory.* 🚫 *limited.* www.heritageireland.ie
Although once a fortress, Ormond Castle is the finest surviving Tudor manor house in Ireland. It was built by the powerful Butler family, the Earls of Ormonde, who were given their title by the English crown in 1328. The castle has a gracious Elizabethan façade overlaying the medieval original; the battlemented towers on the south side sit oddly with the gabled façade and its mullioned and oriel windows.

The state rooms contain some of the finest decorative plasterwork in Ireland, while the Long Gallery extends to 30 m (100 ft). The Elizabethan

part of the castle was added by Black Tom Butler, the 10th Earl of Ormonde. On his death the Ormondes abandoned Carrick for Kilkenny *(see pp142–3).*

Intricate wood carving on a four-poster bed at Ormond Castle

Environs
In the churchyard at **Ahenny**, about 10 km (6 miles) north of Carrick, stand two magnificent High Crosses *(see p243).* Both are crowned by "caps" or "bishops' mitres" and have intricate cable, spiral and fret patterns.

At **Kilkieran**, 5 km (3 miles) north of Carrick, are three other interesting High Crosses, dating from the 9th century. The Plain Cross is unadorned but capped; the West Cross is profusely ornamented though weathered, the Long Shaft Cross has an odd design of stumpy arms on a long shaft.

THE WEST OF IRELAND

MAYO · GALWAY · ROSCOMMON

This is the heart of Connaught, Ireland's historic western province. The West lives up to its image as a traditional, rural, sparsely populated land, with windswept mountains and countryside speckled with low stone walls and peat bogs. Yet it also encompasses Galway, a vibrant university town whose youthful population brings life to the medieval streets and snug pubs.

The rugged Atlantic coastline of the West has been occupied for over 5,000 years. It is rich in prehistoric sites such as the land enclosures of Céide Fields and the ring forts on the Aran Islands. Evidence of the monastic period can be seen in the mysterious and beautiful remains at Kilmacduagh and Clonfert; and the region's religious associations still exert an influence, apparent in the pilgrimages to Knock and Croagh Patrick in County Mayo.

In medieval times the city of Galway was an Anglo-Norman stronghold, surrounded by warring Gaelic clans. After the Cromwellian victories of the 1640s, many Irish were dispossessed of their fertile lands and dispatched "to hell or to Connacht". Landlords made their mark in the 17th and 18th centuries, building impressive country houses at Clonalis, Strokestown Park and Westport. During the Great Famine, the West – especially County Mayo – suffered most from emigration. In spite of this, strong Gaelic traditions have survived in County Galway, which is home to the country's largest Gaeltacht (see p229), where almost half the population speaks Irish as a first language.

The bracken browns and soft violets of Connemara in the west of Galway and the fertile farmland, extensive bogs and placid lakes of County Roscommon are in striking contrast to the magnificent cliff scenery of the remote islands off the coast. This region is often shrouded in a misty drizzle or else battered by Atlantic winds and accompanying heavy downpours.

Summer is a time for festivities, such as the Galway Races in July and August, the Galway Arts Festival in July, traditional sailing boat races off Kinvara in August and the Galway Oyster Festival in September.

Swans by the quayside of the Claddagh area of Galway

◁ Typical Connemara landscape dominated by the peaks of the Twelve Bens

Exploring the West of Ireland

Galway city, Clifden and Westport make the best bases for exploring the region, with cosy pubs, good walks and access to the scenic islands. Connemara and the wilds of County Mayo attract nature lovers, while the islands of Achill, Aran, Clare and Inishbofin appeal to water-sports enthusiasts and ramblers. The lakes of counties Roscommon, Mayo and Galway are popular with anglers, and Lough Corrib and Lough Key offer relaxing cruises.

Decorative stuccowork in Westport House

SEE ALSO

- **Where to Stay** pp309–12

- **Restaurants, Cafés and Pubs** pp337–9 & 349–50

GETTING AROUND

The tiny airport near Rossaveal runs flights to the Aran Islands, which can also be reached by ferry from Rossaveal and Doolin (Co. Clare). Ferries run from Cleggan to Inishbofin and Roonagh near Louisburgh to Clare Island. There is no direct rail service between Galway and Westport but the towns are linked by buses. Bus Éireann runs services to Connemara from Galway and Clifden (via Oughterard or Cong) or the area can be explored on day-long coach tours from Galway or Clifden.

0 kilometres	20
0 miles	20

North Mayo Sculpture Trail

Broad Haven · Portlurin · Belderg · Ballycastle
Glenamoy · ① CÉIDE FIELDS · Killala Bay · Innisc
Belmullet · Barnatra · Killala
Carrowmore Lake
Bangor Erris · N59 · Bellacorick · Ballina
Crossmolina · Lough Conn · N57
Doohooma · Slieve Car 720m · FOXFOR ⑤
Blacksod Bay · Ballycroy · Nephin 806m · Pontoon · Lough Cuillin
Dooagh · R319 · ② ACHILL ISLAND · Cushcamcarragh 714m · R312 · Betra · R310
Doogort · N59 · Achill Sound · Lough Feeagh · Bellavary
Mulrany · Newport · Castlebar · ④ NATIONAL MUSEUM OF IRELAND COUNTRY
CLARE ISLAND ⑧ · Clew Bay · ③ WESTPORT
Roonagh Quay · Louisburgh · ⑦ CROAGH PATRICK · Ballintober · N84 · MAY
INISHTURK · Cregganbaun · N59
Mweelrea 819m · Asleagh · Lough Mask · Ballinro
INISHBOFIN ⑨ · KYLEMORE ABBEY · Leenane · Kilmaine · Neale
Cleggan · Letterfrack ⑪ · Maamturk Mountains · Maum · R345 · ⑬ CONG
⑫ CONNEMARA NATIONAL PARK · Maam Cross · LOUGH CORRIB · Headford
CLIFDEN ⑩ · Recess · Oughterard · Aughnanure Castle · Cloo ⑭
Alcock and Brown Memorial · Cashel · N59
Ballyconneely · R341 · Screeb · N59 · Moycullen
Roundstone · R340 · Carna · Kilkieran · R336 · GALWA
Lettermullan · Rossaveal · Spiddle
Inveran
North Sound · Galway Ba
Burrer
🏕 ARAN ISLANDS ⑯ · Kilronan · Ennis N67
South Sound

For additional map symbols see back flap

River valley at Delphi in northern Connemara

Colourful shopfronts lining
Quay Street, Galway

KEY

▭▭▭	Motorway
▭ ▭	Motorway under construction
▬▬▬	Major road
▬▬	Secondary road
▭▭▭	Minor road
▬▬	Scenic route
▬▬	Major railway
—	Minor railway
▬▬	County border
△	Summit

Céide Fields ❶

Road map B2. 8 km (5 miles) W of Ballycastle, Co Mayo. **Tel** 096 43325. ⬤ *Easter–end Oct: daily.* 📷 📱 📧 ♿ www.heritageireland.ie

Surrounded by heather-clad moorlands and mountains along a bleak, dramatic stretch of north Mayo coastline is Europe's largest Stone Age monument. Over 10 sq km (4 sq miles) were enclosed by walls to make fields suitable for growing wheat and barley, and grazing cattle. Remains of farm buildings indicate that it was an extensive community. The fields were slowly buried below the creeping bog formation, where they have been preserved for over 5,000 years.

Part of the bog has been cut away to reveal the collapsed stone walls of the ancient fields. The remains are simple but guides help visitors to find and recognize key features. Stone Age pottery and a primitive plough have been found in excavations. The striking, pyramid-shaped interpretative centre has a viewing platform overlooking the site, audiovisual presentations and displays on local geology and botany.

Environs

Scattered around the wilderness of the spectacular north Mayo coast from Ballina to the end of the Mullet peninsula is a series of sculptures forming the **North Mayo Sculpture Trail**. Created by 12 sculptors from three continents, the 15 works, often on a huge scale, are made from earth, stone and other natural materials, complimenting their surroundings. Additional sculptures are planned. They aim to highlight the coast's grandeur and enduring nature.

Achill Island ❷

Road map A3. Co Mayo. 👥 *3,000.* 🚌 *from Westport.* ℹ️ *098 47353.* www.achilltourism.com

Ireland's largest island, 22 km (13.5 miles) long and 19 km (12 miles) wide, is reached by a road bridge that can be raised for boats to pass. Achill offers moorland, mountains, rugged cliffs and long beaches, and is a popular spot for angling and water sports. There is evidence that the island was inhabited as many as 5,000 years ago.

For motorists, the best introduction is the **Atlantic Coast Drive**, a circular, signposted route from Achill Sound, by the bridge. The road goes to the island's southern tip, then north around the rest of Achill. Between Doeega and Keel in the southwest run the dramatic Minaun Cliffs and Cathedral Rocks. In the north a mountain overlooks Slievemore, abandoned during the Great Famine *(see p219).*

Westport ❸

Road map B3. Co Mayo. 👥 *6,000.* 🚆 🚌 ℹ️ *James Street (098 25711).* 🛒 *Thu.* www.discoverireland.ie/west

Westport is a neat town and has a bustling, prosperous air. In the 1770s, architect James Wyatt laid out the wide, tree-

The *Angel of Welcome* above the marble staircase at Westport House

lined streets, including the North and South Mall on either side of Carrowbeg River. The town originally traded in yarn, cloth, beer and slate, but industrialization and the Great Famine *(see p219)* brought a dramatic decline until the 1950s when new industry and visitors were attracted to the area.

Beyond the South Mall is Bridge Street, lined with cafés and pubs; the most appealing is Matt Molloy's *(see p350),* named after and owned by the flautist from The Chieftains.

Bog oak and silver bowl from Westport House

🏛 **Westport House**
Westport. **Tel** 098 27766. ⬤ *Apr–end Sep: daily.* 📷 📱 📧
www.westporthouse.ie

Just west of the town is the Carrowbeg estuary and Clew Bay. At the head of the bay stands Westport House, the seat of the Earls of Altamont, descendants of the Browne family, who were Tudor settlers. The town of Westport itself was started in the 1750s by John Browne, first Lord Altamont, to complement the house. Designed in 1732 by Richard Castle, and completed by James Wyatt in 1778, the limestone mansion stands on the site of an O'Malley castle. The mansion is privately owned by the Browne family, who are direct descendents of pirate Grace O'Malley. Its imposing interior is adorned with family portraits. The estate has a boating lake, miniature railway, museum, and a shop.

Bogwood centrepiece in Céide Fields interpretative centre

Statue of St Patrick at the foot of Croagh Patrick, looking out to Clew Bay

National Museum of Ireland – Country Life ❹

Turlough Park, Turlough, off the N5, 8 km (5 miles) east of Castlebar, Co Mayo. **Tel** 094 903 1751. ◯ 10am–5pm Tue–Sat, 2–5pm Sun. ⬛⬛⬛ ♿ www.museum.ie

Explore rural life in Ireland in this award-winning museum set in the grounds of Turlough Park. The collection focuses on the period from 1850–1950, when tenant farmers were struggling to become owners of the land they worked. The museum's exhibits illustrate the traditional way of country life while providing historical context of this difficult time. Four floors display fascinating artifacts, such as handcrafted harvest knots and wickerwork; spinning wheels and boats, and hand-operated machinery.

Foxford ❺

Road map B3. Co Mayo. ♿ 1,000. ◻ from Galway. ◻ Westport (098 25711).

This tranquil market town is known for good angling in nearby Lough Conn and for its woven rugs and tweeds. In the town centre is **Foxford Woollen Mills**, founded in 1892 by an Irish nun, Mother Arsenius (originally named Agnes). The thriving mill now supplies top fashion houses. An audiovisual tour traces the mill's history, and visitors can see craftspeople at work.

◻ Foxford Woollen Mills and Visitor Centre

St Joseph's Place. **Tel** 094 925 6104. ◯ daily. ◻ Good Fri, 24–26 Dec. ⬛⬛⬛ ♿ Exhibition Centre

Knock ❻

Road map B3. Co Mayo. ♿ 575. ◻ 15 km (9 miles) N of Knock. ◻ May–Sep: Knock (094 938 8193). www.discoverireland.ie

In 1879, two local women saw an apparition of the Virgin, St Joseph and St John the Evangelist by the gable of the Church of St John the Baptist. It was witnessed by 13 more onlookers and validated by the Catholic Church amid claims of miracle cures. Every year, over a million believers make the pilgrimage to the shrine, including Pope John Paul II in 1979 and Mother Teresa in 1993. Its focal point is the gable where the apparition was seen, which is now covered over to form a chapel. Nearby is the Basilica of Our Lady, a modern

Bottles of holy water for sale at the shrine in Knock

basilica and Marian shrine. **Knock Museum**, beside the basilica, portrays life in 19th-century rural Ireland. An Apparition section covers the background to the miracle.

⬛ Knock Shrine and Museum

Tel 094 938 8100. ◯ daily. ◻ 25 & 26 Dec ◻ (museum) ⬛ ♿ ◻ www.knock-shrine.ie

Croagh Patrick ❼

Road map E3. Murrisk, Co Mayo. ◻ from Westport. ◻ Westport (098 25711). ◻ www.croagh-patrick.com

Ireland's holy mountain, named after the national saint (see p281), is one of Mayo's best-known landmarks. From the bottom it seems cone-shaped, an impression dispelled by climbing to its flat peak. This quartzite, scree-clad mountain has a history of pagan worship from 3000 BC. However, in AD 441, St Patrick is said to have spent 40 days on the mountain fasting and praying for the Irish.

Since then, penitents, often barefoot, have made the pilgrimage to the summit in his honour, especially on Garland Friday and Reek Sunday in July. From the start of the trail at Campbell's Pub in Murrisk, where there is a huge statue of the saint, it is a two-hour climb to the top, at 765 m (2,510 ft). On Reek Sunday mass is celebrated on the peak in a modern chapel. A visitor centre has amenities for exhausted hikers.

Clare Island ❽

Road map A3. Co Mayo. 🚶 165.
⛴ from Roonagh Quay, 6.5 km
(4 miles) W of Louisburgh. **Tel** 098
25045 or 086 851 5003 (ferry
services). ℹ Westport (098 25711).

Clare Island is dominated by
two hills, and a square 15th-
century castle commands the
headland and harbour. In the
16th century the island was the
stronghold of Grace O'Malley,
pirate queen and patriot, who
held sway over the western
coast. Although, according to
Tudor state papers, she was
received at Queen Elizabeth I's
court, she stood out against
English rule until her death in
her seventies in 1603. She is
buried here in a tiny Cistercian
abbey decorated with medieval
murals and inscribed with
her motto: "Invincible on
land and on sea'

The island is dotted with Iron
Age huts and field systems as
well as promontory forts and
Bronze Age cooking sites
(see p170). Clare Island is rich
in bog flora and fauna, making
it popular with walkers. Animal
lovers come to see the seals,
dolphins, falcons and otters.

Environs
The mainland coastal village
of **Louisburgh** offers rugged

The ferry to Inishbofin leaving Cleggan Harbour

Atlantic landscape, sheltered
coves and sea angling. The
Granuaile Centre tells the story
of Grace O'Malley (*Granuaile*
in Gaelic) and has displays on
Mayo folklore and archaeology.

🏛 **Granuaile Centre**
St Catherine's Church, Louisburgh.
Tel 098 66341. ◻ Mon–Fri,
weekends by appt only. 📷 🎒 ♿

Inishbofin ❾

Road map A3. Co Galway. 🚶 200.
⛴ from Cleggan. ℹ Clifden (095
21163).

The name Inishbofin means
"island of the white cow".
This mysterious, often mist-
swathed island was chosen
for its remoteness by the
exiled 7th-century St Colman,
English Abbot of Lindisfarne.
On the site of his original
monastery is a late medieval
church, graveyard and holy

well. At the sheltered harbour
entrance lies a ruined castle,
occupied in the 16th century
by Spanish pirate Don Bosco
in alliance with Grace O'Malley.
In 1653 it was captured by
Cromwellian forces and used
as a prison for Catholic priests.
Inishbofin was later owned
by a succession of absentee
landlords and now survives
on farming and lobster-fishing.
Surrounded by reefs and
islets, the island's landscape is
characterized by stone walls,
reed-fringed lakes and hay
meadows, where the corn-
crake (see p18) can be seen,
or heard. Inishbofin's beaches
offer bracing walks.

Clifden ❿

Road map A3. Co Galway.
🚶 920. 🚗 ℹ Mar–end Sep:
Galway Road (095 21163). 🚌 Tue &
Fri. **www**.discoverireland.ie/west

Framed by the grandeur of
the Twelve Bens mountain
range and with a striking
skyline dominated by two
church spires, this early
19th-century market town
passes for the capital of the
Connemara region and is a
good base for exploring.
Clifden was founded in
1812 by John d'Arcy, a local
landowner and High Sheriff
of Galway, to create a pocket
of respectability within the
lawlessness of Connemara.
The family eventually went
bankrupt trying to bring
prosperity and order to the
town. The Protestant church
contains a copy of the Cross
of Cong (see p67).
Today craft shops have
taken over much of the town.
In the centre is the Square,
a place for lively pubs such
as EJ Kings (see p349).
Connemara is noted for its
sean nós (unaccompanied

Clifden against a backdrop of the Twelve Bens mountains

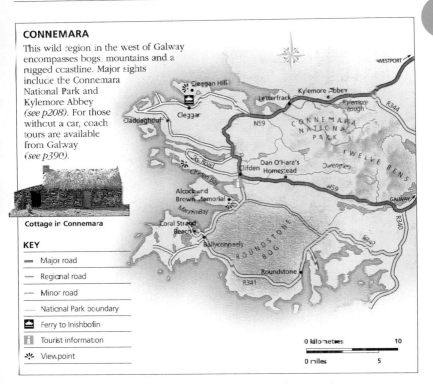

CONNEMARA

This wild region in the west of Galway encompasses bogs, mountains and a rugged coastline. Major sights include the Connemara National Park and Kylemore Abbey *(see p208)*. For those without a car, coach tours are available from Galway *(see p390)*.

Cottage in Connemara

KEY

—	Major road
—	Regional road
—	Minor road
	National Park boundary
🚢	Ferry to Inishbofin
ℹ	Tourist information
☀	Viewpoint

0 kilometres 10

0 miles 5

singing), but in Clifden, generally traditional music is more common.

Jutting out into **Clifden Bay** is a sand spit and beach, signposted from Clifden Square. South of Clifden, at the start of the Roundstone Road, is Owenglen Cascade where, in May, salmon leap on their way to spawn upstream.

Environs

The **Sky Road** is an 11-km (7-mile) circular route with stunning ocean views. The road goes northwest from Clifden and passes desolate scenery and the narrow inlet of Clifden Bay. Clifden Castle, John d'Arcy's Gothic Revival ruin, lies just off the Sky Road, as do several inlets.

The coastal road north from Clifden to Cleggan, via Claddaghduff, is spectacular, passing former smuggling coves. Cleggan, a pretty fishing village, nestles into the head of Cleggan Bay. From here boats leave for Inishbofin and Inishturk. **Cleggan Hill** has a ruined Napoleonic Martello tower and a megalithic tomb.

To the south of Clifden, the coastal route to Roundstone skirts a mass of bogland pitted with tiny lakes. The **Alcock and Brown Memorial** overlooks the bog landing site of the first transatlantic flight made by Alcock and Brown in 1919. Nearby is Marconi's wireless station, which exchanged the first transatlantic radio messages with Nova Scotia in 1907. The Ballyconneely area has craggy islands and the beautiful **Coral Strand Beach**. The village of **Roundstone** is best seen during the summer regatta of traditional Galway hookers *(see p211)*.

A short drive to the east of Clifden is **Dan O'Hara's Homestead**. In a wild, rocky setting, this organic farm recreates the tough conditions of life in Connemara before the 1840s. There is an audiovisual display on the history of Connemara.

🏛 **Dan O'Hara's Homestead**
Heritage Centre, Lettershea, off N59. *Tel* 095 21808. ◯ Apr–Oct: 9am–5pm daily. 🚗 📷 📖 🏠 ♿
www.connemaraheritage.com

View of the coast from the Sky Road

The imposing Kylemore Abbey on the shores of Kylemore Lough

Kylemore Abbey ⓫

Road map A3. Connemara, Co Galway. *Tel* 095 520□0. 🚌 *from Galway.* ◻ *daily.* 🚌 *Christmas.* ▨ *groups call to boc□.* **Walled garden** ◻ *daily.* ▨ 🍴 ▢ ♿ *ltd.* **www.** kylemoreabbeytourism.ie

Sheltered by the slopes of the Twelve Bens, this lakeside castle is a romantic, battlemented Gothic Revival fantasy. It was built as a present for his wife by Mitchell Henry (1826–1911), who was a Manchester tycoon and later Galway MP. The Henrys also purchased a huge area of moorland, drained the boggy hillside and planted thousands of trees as a windbreak for their new orchards and exotic walled gardens. After the sudden deaths of his wife and daughter, Henry left Kylemore and the castle was sold.

It became an abbey when Benedictine nuns fleeing from Ypres in Belgium during World War I, sought refuge here. For many years it was run by the nuns as a girls' boarding and day school. Visitors can view restored rooms in the abbey, as well as explore the grounds, a restaurant, craft shop, pottery studio and soapery.

There is also a restored Victorian walled garden in the grounds, featuring the longest double herbaceous borders in Ireland, a nuttery and a meandering streamside walk.

Connemara National Park ⓬

Road map A3. Letterfrack, Connemara, Co Galway. *Tel* 095 41325. **Park** ◻ *daily.* **Visitors' Centre** *Tel* 095 41323. ◻ *Mar–Oct: daily.* ♿ ▢ www.connemaranationalpark.ie

A combination of bogland, lakes and mountains makes up this National Park in the heart of Connemara. Within its more than 2,000 ha (5,000 acres) are four of the Twelve Bens, including Benbaun, the highest mountain in the range at 730 m (2,400 ft), and the peak of Diamond Hill. At the centre is the valley of Glanmore and the Polladirk River. Visitors come for the spectacular landscape and to glimpse the famous Connemara ponies.

Part of the land originally belonged to the Kylemore Abbey estate. In 1980 it became a National Park. There are traces of the land's previous uses all over the park: megalithic tombs, up to 4,000 years old, can be seen as well as old ridges marking former grazing areas and arable fields.

The park is open all year, while the Visitors' Centre near the entrance, just outside Letterfrack, is open only from March to mid-October. It features displays on how the landscape developed and was used and on local flora and fauna. There is also an audio-visual theatre and an indoor picnic area. Three signposted walks start from the Visitors' Centre. In summer there are guided walks, some led by botanists, and various children's activities. Climbing the Twelve Bens should be attempted only by experienced walkers equipped for all weather conditions.

CONNEMARA WILDLIFE

The blanket bogs and moorlands of Connemara are a botanist's paradise, especially for unusual bog and heathland plants. Birdlife is also varied with hooded crows, which can be recognized by their grey and black plumage, stonechats, peregrines and merlins – the smallest falcons in the British Isles. Red deer have been successfully reintroduced into the area and a herd can be seen in the National Park. Badgers, foxes, stoats and otters may also be spotted, as well as grey seals along the rocky coast.

The merlin *nests in old clumps of heather and feeds mainly on small birds.*

St Dabeoc's heath, *a pretty heather, grows nowhere else in Ireland or Great Britain.*

For hotels and restaurants in this region see pp309–12 and pp337–9

Cong ⑬

Road map B3. Co Mayo. 🚌 *350*.
🚉 ℹ️ Old Courthouse (094 954
6542). ◻ Mar–Oct: daily. **www.**
congtourism.com

This picturesque village lies
on the shores of Lough Corrib,
just within County Mayo. Cong
means isthmus – the village
lies on the strip of land
between Lough Corrib and
Lough Mask. During the 1840s,
as a famine relief project, a
canal was built linking the
two lakes, but the water
drained through the porous
limestone bed. Stone bridges
and stone-clad locks are still
in place along the dry canal.

Cong Abbey lies close to the
main street. The Augustinian
abbey was founded in the early
12th century by Turlough
O'Connor, King of
Connaught and High
King of Ireland, on the
site of a 6th-century
monastery estab-
lished by St Fechin.
The abbey has
doorways in a style
transitional between
Romanesque and
Gothic, stone carv-
ings and restored
cloisters. The Cross
of Cong, an ornate
processional cross
intended for the
abbey, is now in the National
Museum of Ireland – Country
Life (see p204) in Turlough.
The most fascinating remains
are the Gothic chapter house,
stone bridges and the monks'
fishing-house overhanging the
river – the monks had a system

**Carved 12th-century
doorway of Cong Abbey**

where a bell rang in the kitchen
when a fish took the bait.

Just south of Cong is **Ashford
Castle**, rebuilt in Gothic Revival
style in 1870 by Lord Ardilaun
of the Guinness family. One of
Ireland's best hotels (see p292),
its grounds can be visited by
boat from Galway and Oughterard. Cong was the setting for
The Quiet Man, the 1950s' film
starring John Wayne.

Lough Corrib ⑭

Road map B3. Co Galway. 🚌 from
Galway and Cong. ⛴ from Ought te-
rard, Cong and Wood Quay, Galway.
ℹ️ Main St, Oughterard (091
552808).

An angler's paradise, Lough
Corrib offers the chance to fish
with local fishermen for
brown trout, salmon,
pike, perch and eels.
Despite its proximity
to Galway, the lake
is tranquil, dotted
with uninhabited
islands and framed
by meadows, reed-
beds and wooded
shores. The water-
side is home to
swans and coots.
On **Inchagoill**, one
of the largest
islands, stand the
ruins of an early
Christian monastic settlement
and a Romanesque church.

The lake's atmosphere is best
appreciated on a cruise. From
Galway, the standard short
cruise winds through the
marshes to the site of an Iron
Age fort, limestone quarries

**View over Lough Corrib from the
shore north west of Oughterard**

and the battlemented Menlo
Castle. Longer cruises continue
to Cong or include picnics on
the islands.

Environs
On the banks of Lough Corrib,
Oughterard is known as
"the gateway to Connemara".
The village has craft shops,
thatched cottages and friendly
pubs. It is also an important
centre for golf, angling, hiking
and pony trekking. Towards
Galway City, **Brigit's Garden**
in Roscahill has 4.45 ha
(11 acres) of themed gardens.

About 4 km (2.5 miles)
southeast of Oughterard (off
the N59) is **Aughnanure Castle**.
This well-restored six-storey
tower house clings to a rocky
island on the River Drimneen.
The present castle, built by
the O'Flaherty clan, is on the
site of one dating from 1256.
The clan controlled West
Connaught from Lough
Corrib to Galway and the coast
in the 13th to 16th centuries.
From this castle the feuding
O'Flaherty chieftains held out
against the British in the
16th century. In 1585 Donal
O'Flaherty married the pirate
Grace O'Malley (see p206).
The tower house has an
unusual double bawn
(see p20) and a murder hole
from which missiles could be
dropped on invaders.

⚓ **Aughnanure Castle**
Oughterard. Tel 091 552214.
◻ Apr–Oct: daily. 🏛 ⬜
♿ limited. www.heritageireland.ie

Connemara ponies *roam semi-
wild and are fabled to be from
Arab stock that came ashore
from Spanish Armada wrecks.*

Fuchsias *grow profusely in the
hedgerows of Connemara,
thriving in the mild climate.*

Galway ⑮

Sign with Claddagh ring design

Galway is both the centre for the Irish-speaking regions in the West and a lively university city. Under the Anglo-Normans, it flourished as a trading post. In 1396 it gained a Royal Charter and, for the next two centuries, was controlled by 14 merchant families, or "tribes". The city prospered under English influence, but this allegiance to the Crown cost Galway dear when, in 1652, Cromwell's forces wreaked havoc. After the Battle of the Boyne (*see p244*), Galway fell into decline, unable to compete with east-coast trade. However, the city's profile as a developing centre for high-tech industry has been revived.

Inside The Quays seafood restaurant and pub

Houses on the banks of the Corrib

Exploring Galway

The centre of the city lies on the banks of the River Corrib, which flows down from Lough Corrib (*see p209*) widening out as it reaches Galway Bay. Urban renewal since the 1970s has led to extensive restoration of the narrow, winding streets of this once-walled city. Due to its compact size, Galway is easy to explore on foot, and a leisurely pace provides plenty of opportunity to stop off at its shops, pubs and historic sights.

Eyre Square

The redeveloped square encloses a pleasant plaza and park lined with imposing, mainly 19th-century, buildings. On the northwest of the square is the **Browne Doorway**, a 17th-century entrance from a mansion in Abbeygate Street Lower. Beside it is a fountain adorned with a sculpture of a Galway hooker boat. The **Eyre Square Centre**, overlooking the park, is a modern shopping mall built to incorporate sections of the historic city walls. Walkways link Shoemakers and Penrice towers, two of the 14 wall towers that used to ring the city in the 17th century.

Lynch family crest on Lynch's Castle

Latin Quarter

From Eyre Square, William Street and Shop Street are the main routes into the bustling "Latin Quarter". On the corner of Abbeygate Street Upper and Shop Street stands **Lynch's Castle**, now a bank, but still the grandest 16th-century town house in Galway. It was owned by the Lynch family, one of the 14 "tribes".

A side street leads to the **Collegiate Church of St Nicholas**, Galway's finest medieval building. The church, founded in 1320, was extended in the 15th and 16th centuries, but then damaged by the Cromwellians, who used it to stable horses. The west porch is from the 15th century and there are some finely carved gargoyles under the parapet.

Quay Street is lined with restaurants and pubs, including **The Quays** (*see p349*). Tí Neachtain is a town house which belonged to "Humanity Dick", an 18th-century MP who promoted laws against cruelty to animals. Today, it too is a restaurant and pub (*see p349*). Nearby are the Taibhdhearc and Druid theatres (*see p358*).

North Galway

The **Cathedral of St Nicholas** (1965), built of local limestone and Connemara marble, stands on the west bank. From here you can see Wood Quay, where Lough Corrib cruises start in the summer (*see p209*). **National University of Ireland**

Outside dining at one of the cosmopolitan cafés in Shop Street

GALWAY HOOKERS

Galway's traditional wooden sailing boats, featured on the city's coat of arms, were known as *pucans* and *gleotogs* – hookers in English. They have broad black hulls, thick masts and white or rust-coloured sails. Once common in the Claddagh district, they were also used along the Atlantic coast to ferry peat, cattle and beer. Hookers can be seen in action at the Cruinniú na mBác festival in Kinvara (*See p212*).

Small Galway hooker sailing by the old quays and Spanish Arch

Galway, further west, is a large campus with a 1849 Gothic Revival quad. Salmon Weir Bridge links the two banks. Shoals of salmon rest under the bridge on their way upstream to spawn.

The Old Quays

The **Spanish Arch**, where the river opens out, was built in 1584 to protect the harbour, then outside the city walls. Here, Spanish traders unloaded their ships. The old quays are a tranquil spot for a stroll down the Long Walk to the docks.

The Claddagh

Beyond the Spanish Arch, on the west bank of the Corrib, lies the Claddagh. The name comes from *An Cladach*, meaning "flat, stony shore". From medieval times, this fiercely independent fishing community beyond the city walls was governed by a "king", the last of whom died in 1954. The only remnants of this once close-knit, Gaelic-speaking community are Claddagh rings,

VISITORS' CHECKLIST

Road map B4. **To** Galway. 60,000. Carnmore, 11 km (7 miles, NE of Galway. Ceannt Station (091 561444). Ceannt Station (091 562000). The Fairgreen, Foster St (091 537 700). Sat & Sun. Galway Arts Festival (mic-Jul); Galway Races (late Jul–Aug).

betrothal rings traditionally handed down from mother to daughter (*see p356*).

Environs

Just west of the city is **Salthill**, Galway's seaside resort. The beaches at Palmer's Rock and Grattan Road are particularly popular with families in summer. A bracing walk along the promenade is still a Galway tradition.

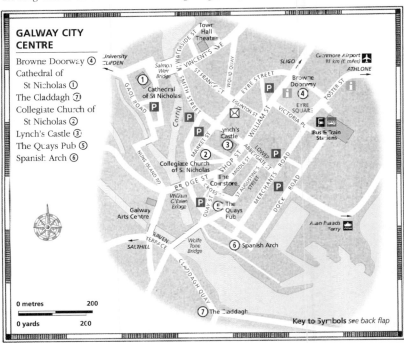

Spanish Arch on the site of the former docks

GALWAY CITY CENTRE

Browne Doorway ④
Cathedral of
St Nicholas ①
The Claddagh ⑦
Collegiate Church of
St Nicholas ②
Lynch's Castle ③
The Quays Pub ⑤
Spanish Arch ⑥

0 metres 200
0 yards 200

Key to Symbols *see back flap*

For hotels and restaurants in this region see pp309–12 and pp337–9

Mural in the centre of Kinvara depicting a shopfront

Aran Islands ⑯

See pp214–15.

Kinvara ⑰

Road map B4. Co Galway. 🚌 550.
🚌 🛈 *Galway (091 537700).*

One of the most charming fishing villages on Galway Bay, Kinvara's appeal lies in its sheltered, seaweed-clad harbour and traditional sea-faring atmosphere. From medieval times, its fortunes were closely linked to Kilmacduagh, the powerful monastery and bishopric upon which the village depended.

The pier is bordered by a row of fishermen's cottages. Kinvara remains a popular port of call for sailors of traditional Galway hookers *(see p211)* and is known for the Cruinniú na mBád (gathering of the boats) festival in August. Rambles include historical and nature trails. Bird-watchers may spot teal, curlews and oystercatchers by the shore.

Environs

North of Kinvara, on a promontory on the shore of Galway Bay, lies **Dunguaire Castle**. It is perched just beyond some quaint thatched cottages and a stone bridge. The castle is named after the 7th-century King Guaire of Connaught, whose court here was renowned as the haunt of bards and balladeers. Although the medieval earthworks survive, the present castle was built in the 16th century, a quintessential tower house *(see p20)* with sophisticated machicolations. The banqueting hall is still used for "medieval banquets" with Celtic harp music and the recital of Irish poetry.

⚓ Dunguaire Castle
Tel 061 360788. ◻ May–Sep:
daily. 🈲 🛈
www.shannonheritage.com

Kilmacduagh ⑱

Road map B4. Outside Gort on Corofin Rd, Co Galway. 🚌 to Gort. ◻ daily.

This monastic settlement is in a remote location on the borders of Counties Clare and Galway, roughly 5 km (3 miles) south-west of Gort. The sense of isolation is accentuated by the stony moonscape of the Burren

to the west *(see pp186–8)*. Reputedly founded by St Colman MacDuagh in the early 7th century, Kilmacduagh owes more to the monastic revival which led to rebuilding from the 11th century onwards.

The centrepiece of the extensive site is a large, slightly leaning 11th- or 12th-century round tower and a roofless church, known as the cathedral or Teampall. The cathedral is a pre-Norman structure, which was later remodelled in Gothic style, with flamboyant tracery and fine tomb carvings. In the surrounding fields lie the remains of several other churches that once depended on the monastery. To the northeast of the Teampall is the late medieval Glebe or Abbot's House, a variant of a 14th- or 15th-century tower house *(see p20)*.

Thoor Ballylee ⑲

Road map B4. Gort, Co Galway.
Ballylee Castle 🚌 to Gort. ◻ due to flood damage, call Galway Tourist Office on 091 537700 to check if open. 🈲 🛈 🚻 limited.

For much of the 1920s, this beguiling tower house was a summer home to the poet WB Yeats *(see pp22–3)*. Yeats was a regular visitor to nearby Coole Park, the home of his friend Lady Gregory (1852–1932), who was a cofounder of the Abbey Theatre *(see p88)*.

On one visit Yeats came upon Ballylee Castle, a 14th-century de Burgo tower adjoining a cosy cottage and a walled garden and stream. In 1902, both the tower and the cottage became part of the Gregory estate and Yeats bought them in 1916. From 1919 onwards, his family

Round tower and cathedral, the most impressive monastic remains at Kilmacduagh

divided their time between Dublin and their Galway tower. Yeats used the name Thoor Ballylee as the address using the Irish word for tower to "keep people from suspecting us of modern gothic and a deer park". His collection, *The Tower* (1928), includes several poems inspired by the house.

An audiovisual tour includes readings from Yeats's poetry, but the charm of a visit lies in the tower itself, with its spiral stone steps and views from the battlements over forest and farmland.

Environs

Just to the north of Gort is **Coole Park**, once the home of Lady Gregory. Although the house was demolished in 1941, the estate farm has been restored and the fine gardens survive. In particular, there is the "autograph tree", a spreading copper beech carved with the initials of George Bernard Shaw, WB Yeats, JM Synge *(see pp22–3)* and Jack Yeats *(see p70)*. In the farm buildings is an audiovisual display. The emphasis of the visitors' centre is on the life of Lady Gregory: it is the start of two sign-posted walks, one around the gardens and the other through beech, hazel, birch and ash woodland to Coole Lake.

> **✗ Coole Park**
> 3 km (2 miles) NE of Gort. *Tel 091 631804. Visitors' centre* ☐ *Easter–Sep: daily; park open all year.* ☐ ☐ *limited.* www.coolepark.ie

Thoor Ballylee tower house, the summer home of WB Yeats

Gentle hills and woodland by Coole Lake in Coole Park

Portumna ⑩

Road map C4. Co Galway. ☐ 1,200. ☐ ☐ *Galway (091 537700).* ☐ *Fri.*

Portumna is a historic market town with scattered sights, many of which have been restored. Situated on Lough Derg, it is a convenient base for cruising the River Shannon *(see p185)* and has a modern marina. **Portumna Castle**, built in the early 17th century, was the main seat of the de Burgo family. It boasts some elaborate interior stonework. Nearby is **Portumna Priory**. Most of the remains date from 1414 when it was founded by the Dominicans, but traces can also be found of the Cistercian abbey that was previously on the site. The de Burgo estate to the west of the town now forms **Portumna Forest Park**, with picnic sites and signposted woodland trails leading to Lough Derg.

> **♠ Portumna Castle**
> *Tel 090 974 1658.* ☐ *Apr–Sep and weekends in Oct.* ☐ ☐ ☐

Clonfert Cathedral ⑨

Road map C4. Clonfert, Co Galway. ☐ *daily* ☐

Situated near a bleak stretch of the Shannon bordering the boglands of the Midlands, Clonfert is one of the jewels of Irish-Romanesque architecture. The tiny cathedral occupies the site of a monastery, which was founded by St Brendan in AD 563, and is believed to be the burial place of the saint.

Although a great scholar and enthusiastic founder of monasteries, St Brendan is best known as the "great navigator". His journeys are recounted in *Navigatio Sancti Brendani*, written in about 1050, which survives in medieval manuscripts in several languages including Flemish, Norse and French. The text seems to describe a voyage to Wales, the Orkneys, Iceland and conceivably the east coast of North America. His voyage and his boat *(see p190)* have been recreated by modern explorers in an attempt to prove that St Brendan may have preceded Columbus by about 900 years.

The highlight of Clonfert is its intricately sculpted sandstone doorway. The round arch above the door is decorated with animal and human heads, foliage and symbolic motifs. The carvings on the triangular tympanum above the arch are of strange human heads. In the chancel, the 13th-century east windows are fine examples of late Irish-Romanesque art. The 15th-century chancel arch is adorned with sculptures of angels and a mermaid. Although Clonfert was built over several centuries, the church has a profound sense of unity.

Human heads carved on the tympanum at Clonfert Cathedral

Aran Islands ⑯

Jaunting car on Inishmore

Inishmore (Inis Mór), Inishmaan (Inis Meáin) and Inisheer (Inis Óírr), the three Aran Islands, are formed from a limestone ridge. The largest, Inishmore, is 13 km (8 miles) long and 3 km (2 miles) wide. The attractions of these islands include the austere landscape crisscrossed with dry-stone walls, stunning coastal views and several large prehistoric stone forts. In the 5th century, St Enda brought Christianity to the islands, starting a long monastic tradition. Protected for centuries by their isolated position, the islands today are a bastion of traditional Irish culture. Farming, fishing and tourism are the main occupations of the islanders.

Looking over the cliff edge at Dún Aonghasa

Clochán na Carraige is a large, well-preserved beehive hut *(see p21)*, probably built by early Christian settlers on the islands.

The Seven Churches
(Na Seacht dTeampaill)

Clochán na Carraige

Dún Eoghanachta

Dún Aengus
(Dún Aonghasa)

KILMURVY
(Cill Mhuirbhí)

N

I

S

H

M

O

R

E

Dún Eoghanachta is a 1st-century BC circular stone fort with a single wall terraced on the inside.

Na Seacht dTeampaill

The so-called Seven Churches make up a monastic settlement dedicated to St Brecan. Built between the 9th and 15th centuries, some are probably domestic buildings.

★ Dún Aonghasa

This Iron or Bronze Age promontory fort (see p20), has four concentric stone walls. It is also protected by a chevaux de frise, a ring of razor-sharp, pointed stone stakes.

ARAN TRADITIONS

Colourful Aran costume

The islands are famous for their distinctive knitwear *(see p354)* and for the traditional Aran costume that is still worn by some of the older generation: for women, a red flannel skirt and crocheted shawl; for men a sleeveless tweed jacket and a colourful knitted belt. From time to time you also see a *currach* or low rowing boat, the principal form of transport for centuries. Land-making, the ancient and arduous process of creating soil by covering bare rock with sand and seaweed, continues to this day.

Currach made from canvas coated in tar

FERRY ROUTES TO THE ARAN ISLANDS

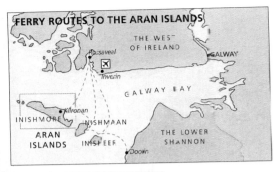

THE WEST OF IRELAND

Rossaveel

GALWAY

Inverin

GALWAY BAY

INISHMORE

Kilronan

INISHMAAN

ARAN ISLANDS

INISHEER

Doolin

THE LOWER SHANNON

VISITORS' CHECKLIST

Road map A4, 34. Co Galway.
200. ✈ from Connemara
Airport, Inverin (www.aerarann
islands.ie; 091 593034).
⛴ from Rossaveal:
Island Ferries
(www.aranislandferries.com;
091 568903); from Doolin:
Doolin Ferry Company
(www.doolinferries.com;
Easter–Oct only, 065 707 4455).
Ferries sail throughout the year;
some go to all three main
islands. Phone for details. Cars
cannot be taken to the islands.
From Kilronan, you can hire
bicycles and jaunting cars, or go
on minibus tours (099 61109).
ℹ Kilronan, Inishmore
(099 61263).
www.discoverireland.ie/ west

Kilmurvey Beach

The attractive sandy beach east of Kilmurvy offers safe swimming in a sheltered cove. The town itself is a quiet place to stay near a number of the island's most important sights.

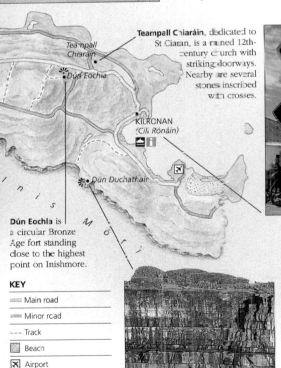

Teampall Chiaráin, dedicated to St Ciarán, is a ruined 12th-century church with striking doorways. Nearby are several stones inscribed with crosses.

Teampall Chiaráin

Dún Eochla

KILRONAN
(Cill Rónáin)

Dún Duchathair

Dún Eochla is a circular Bronze Age fort standing close to the highest point on Inishmore.

Inis Mór

KEY

▬▬	Main road
▬▬	Minor road
---	Track
▨	Beach
✈	Airport
⛴	Ferry service
ℹ	Tourist information
✱	Viewpoint

0 kilometres   2

0 miles   1

★ Kilronan

The Aran Islands' main port is a busy place, with jaunting cars (ponies and traps) and minibuses waiting by the pier to give island tours; bicycles can also be hired. Nearby, the fascinating Aran Heritage Centre is dedicated to the disappearing Aran way of life.

★ Dún Duchathair

Built on a headland, the Iron Age construction is known as the Black Fort. It has dry-stone ramparts.

STAR SIGHTS

★ Dún Aonghasa

★ Dún Duchathair

★ Kilronan

East wall and gatehouse at Roscommon Castle

Turoe Stone ㉑

Road map B4. Turoe Bullaun,
Loughrea, Co Galway. **Tel** 091 841580.
◯ mid-May–Aug: daily; Sep–mid-
May: Sat & Sun only. 🈂 🈺 🈲
www.turoepetfarm.com

The Turoe Stone stands at the
centre of the Turoe Pet Farm
and Leisure Park, near the
village of Bullaun (on the
R350). The white granite
boulder, which stands about
1 m (3 ft) high, dates back to
the 3rd or 2nd century BC. Its
top half is carved with curvilinear designs in a graceful
Celtic style known as La Tène,
also found in Celtic parts of
Europe, particularly Brittany.
The lower half has a smooth
section and a band of step-
pattern carving. The stone was
originally found at an Iron
Age ring fort nearby, and is
thought to have been used
there in fertility rituals.

The park around the Turoe
Stone is designed mainly for
children. The Pet Farm has
some small fields containing
farm animals and a pond with
several varieties of ducks and
geese. There is also a wooded

**The Celtic Turoe Stone carved
with graceful swirling patterns**

riverside walk with a nature
trail, outdoor and indoor
picnic areas, a tea room,
playground and two
supervised indoor play areas.

Roscommon ㉒

Road map C3. Co Roscommon.
🈁 3,500. 🈁 🈁 🈹 Jun–Sep:
Harrison Hall (090 662 6342). 🈁 Fri.
www.discoverireland.ie

The county capital is a busy
market town. In Main Street is
the former gaol, which had a
woman as its last executioner.
"Lady Betty", as she was
known, was sentenced to
death for the murder of her
son in 1780, but negotiated a
pardon by agreeing to
become a hangwoman. She
continued for 30 years.

South of the town centre,
just off Abbey Street, is the
Dominican Friary, founded in
1253 by Felim O'Conor, Lord
of Connaught. Set in the north
wall of the choir is a late 13th-
century effigy of the founder.

Roscommon Castle, an
Anglo-Norman fortress north
of the town, was built in 1269
by Robert d'Ufford, Lord
Justice of Ireland on land he
had seized from the
Dominican Friary, and rebuilt
11 years later after being destroyed by the Irish led by Hugh
O'Conor, King of Connaught.

Clonalis House ㉓

Road map B3. Castlerea, Co
Roscommon. **Tel** 094 962 0014. ◯
Jun–end Aug: 11am–5pm Mon–Sat.
🈂 🈯 🈹 limited. **www**.clonalis.com

This Victorian manor just
outside Castlerea is the ancestral home of the O'Conors,
the last High Kings of Ireland

and Kings of Connaught. This
old Gaelic family can trace its
heritage back 1,500 years. The
ruins of their gabled 17th-
century home are visible in
the grounds. On the lawn lies
the O'Conor inauguration
stone, dating from 90 BC.

The interior includes a
library of many books and
documents recording Irish
history, a tiny private chapel
and a gallery of family
portraits spanning 500
years. In the billiard room
is the harp once played by
Turlough O'Carolan (1670–
1738), blind harpist and last
of the Gaelic bards (*see p24*).

Strokestown Park House ㉔

Road map C3. Strokestown, Co
Roscommon. 🈁 **House, Pleasure
Gardens and Museum Tel** 071 963
3013. ◯ daily. 🈂 🈯 🈴 🈯 🈸
www.strokestownpark.ie

Strokestown Park House, the
greatest Palladian mansion in
County Roscommon, was
built in the 1730s for Thomas
Mahon, an MP whose family
was granted the lands by
Charles II after the Restoration.
It incorporates an earlier 17th-
century tower house (*see p20*).
The design of the new house
owes most to Richard Cassels,
architect of Russborough (*see
p132*). The galleried kitchen,
panelled stairwell and groin-
vaulted stables are undoubtedly
his work, tailoring Palladian
principles to the requirements
of the Anglo-Irish gentry.

The house stayed in the family's hands until 1979, when
major restoration began. In its
heyday, the estate included
ornamental parkland, a deer
park, folly, mausoleum and the

village of Strokestown itself. By 1979, the estate's original 12,000 ha (30 000 acres) had dwindled to 120 ha (300 acres), but the recreation of the Pleasure Gardens and the Fruit and Vegetable Garden have greatly increased the area.

Set in the stable yards, the **Famine Museum** uses the Strokestown archives to tell the story of tenants and landlords during the 1840s Famine. During the crisis, landlords divided into two camps: the charitable, some of whom started up Famine Relief schemes, and the callous, like the Mahons of Strokestown. Major Denis Mahon was murdered after forcing two-thirds of the starving peasantry off his land by a combination of eviction and passages in 'coffin ships' to North America. A section of the exhibition deals with continuing famine and malnutrition worldwide.

Boyle 🔵

Road map C3. Co Roscommon.
🏛 2,200. 🚌 🛈 Jun–Sep: King House (071) 966 2145). 🚌 Fri.
www.discoverireland.ie

County Roscommon's most charming town, Boyle is blessed with fine Georgian and medieval architecture. **Boyle Abbey** is a well-preserved Cistercian abbey founded in 1161 as a sister house to Mellifont in County Louth (see p245). It survived raids by Anglo-Norman barons and Irish chieftains, as well as the 1539 suppression of the monasteries. In 1659 it was

---

THE GREAT FAMINE

The failure of the Irish potato crop in 1845, 1846 and 1848, due to potato blight, had disastrous consequences for the people of Ireland, many of whom relied on this staple crop. More than a million died of starvation and disease, and by 1856 over two-and a half million had been forced to emigrate. The crisis was worsened by unsympathetic landlords who often continued collecting rents. The Famine had far-reaching effects: mass emigration became a way of life (see pp42–3) and many rural communities, particularly in the far west, were decimated.

Peasants queuing for soup during the Famine (1847)

---

turned into a castle. The abbey is still remarkably intact, with a church, cloisters, cellars, sacristy and even kitchens. The nave of the church has both Romanesque and Gothic arches and there are well-preserved 12th-century capitals. The visitors' centre in the old gatehouse has exhibits on the abbey's history.

King House, a Palladian mansion near the centre of town, is the ancestral home of the Anglo-Irish King family, later Earls of Kingston. Inside is a contemporary art gallery, and displays on such subjects as Georgian architecture and the mansion's restoration, the history of the surrounding area and the Connaught chieftains.

Carved capital in the nave at Boyle Abbey

🏛 **Boyle Abbey**
Tel 071 966 2604. 🕑 Easter–mid-Sep: 10am–6pm.

🏛 **King House**
Main St. **Tel** 071 966 3242. 🕑 Apr–Sep: Tue–Sat & public hols. 🍴 🚻
🅿 🚻 on request.

Environs
Lough Key is often called the loveliest lake in Ireland. The island-studded lake and surrounding woodland make a glorious setting for the **Lough Key Forest Park**. The 320-ha (790-acre) park formed part of the Rockingham estate until 1957, when Rockingham House, a John Nash design, burned down. The woods were added by 18th-century landlords.

The **Lough Key Experience** takes visitors on an audio journey through the 19th-century underground tunnels, up to the Moylurg viewing tower and along Ireland's first Tree Canopy Trail.

There are also several ring forts (see p20), a river jetty and an adventure playground providing entertainment for children of all ages.

🌳 **Lough Key Forest Park**
N4 8 km (5 miles) E of Boyle. **Tel** 071 967 3122. 🕑 Easter–Oct: daily; Nov–Mar: Fri–Sun. 🅿 🍴 📷 🚻

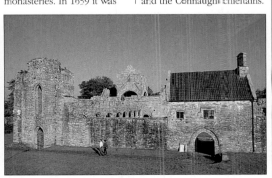

The gatehouse and remains of the nave at Boyle Abbey

NORTHWEST IRELAND

DONEGAL · SLIGO · LEITRIM

Towering cliffs, deserted golden beaches and rocky headlands abound along the rugged coast of Donegal, which incorporates some of Ireland's wildest scenery. To the south, Sligo is steeped in prehistory and Celtic myth, with its legacy of ancient monuments and natural beauty enriched by associations with the poet WB Yeats. By contrast, Leitrim is a quiet county of unruffled lakes and waterways.

In Celtic mythology Sligo was the power base of the warrior Queen Maeve of Connaught *(see p26)*, and the county's legacy of prehistoric sites shows that the area was heavily populated in Celtic times. Later, however, both County Sligo and neighbouring County Leitrim often seemed to be little affected by events taking place in the rest of Ireland. The Normans, for example, barely disturbed the rule of local Gaelic clans.

Donegal, on the other hand, was part of Ulster until 1921 and played an active role in that province's history. The O'Donnells held sway over most of Donegal in the Middle Ages, but they fled to Europe in 1607 following their ill-fated stand against the English alongside the O'Neills *(see p255)*. Protestant settlers moved on to land confiscated from the two clans, but they left much of Donegal and its poor soil to the native Irish, who lived there in isolation from the rest of Ulster. County Donegal remains one of the most remote parts of Ireland, and it is no coincidence that it boasts the country's largest number of Gaelic speakers. There is a wealth of traditions and culture to be found around the county and on islands such as Tory Island *(see p224)*.

While the beauty of Donegal lies mainly along the coast, Sligo's finest landscapes are found inland, around Lough Gill and among the sparsely populated Bricklieve Mountains.

The 19th-century interior of Hargadon's bar in Sligo town, with its original counter and stout jars

◁ View across to Falcarragh from Bloody Foreland in County Donegal

Exploring Northwest Ireland

The supreme appeal of Donegal lies in the natural beauty of its coast, with windswept peninsulas, precipitous cliffs and a host of golden beaches. There is a scattering of small seaside resorts which make good bases, and Donegal town is well placed for exploring the southern part of the county. The cultural heartland of the Northwest lies in and around Sligo, the only sizeable town in the region, from where you can reach several prehistoric remains and other historic sights. Further south, lovely scenery surrounds Lough Gill and the more remote Lough Arrow. In Leitrim, a county of lakes and rivers, the main centre of activity is the lively boating resort of Carrick-on-Shannon.

Procession during the Mary of Dungloe beauty contest in July

SEE ALSO

- *Where to Stay* pp312–14
- *Restaurants, Cafés and Pubs* pp339–41 & p35■

KEY

▬▬	Major road
—	Secondary road
┈┈	Minor road
～～	Scenic route
▬▬	Main railway
—	Minor railway
▬▬	National border
▬▬	County border
△	Summit

0 kilometres   20

0 miles   20

Map labels

Faisbtrabull
Malin Head
Ballyhillin
R242
Malin
Ballyliffin
Culdaff
Cardonagh
Gap of Mamore
Greencastle
Slieve Snaght 615m
R238
R238
Portsalon
R238
INISHOWEN PENINSULA
Moville

FANAD PENINSULA
PENINSULA
Lough Swilly
Buncrana
slough
Rathmullan
Rathmelton
Bridgend
Kilmacrenan
GRIANÁN AILIGH
Londonderry
N13
Belfast
Swilly
LETTERKENNY
N56
N14
Foyle
Lifford
St abane
orlar
N15
Castlefinn
Ballybofey
Finn
Omagh
Derg
LOUGH DERG
Pettigoe
47
ower
ough Erne
illen
illen
ins
Ballinamore
RIM
Carrigallen
R201
chill
nod
R198
ky
Longford

GETTING AROUND

The N56, linking Letterkenny and Donegal, provides access to much of the Northwest's best scenery, with minor roads branching off it around the coast's rocky peninsulas. A few buses serve this route, but travelling around without a car is easier further south, with buses running daily from Donegal along the N15 to Sligo via Ballyshannon. The rail network barely reaches the Northwest, though there are daily trains between Sligo and Carrick-on-Shannon.

Thatched cottage near Malin Head on Inishowen Peninsula

SIGHTS AT A GLANCE

View from Carrowkeel Bronze Age cemetery above Lough Arrow

Quartzite cone of Errigal, the highest of the Derryveagh Mountains

Tory Island ❶

Road map C1. Co Donegal. 🕮 175. 🚢 from Magherarcarty Pier near Gortahork and Bunbeg daily in summer. 074 953 5061, weather permitting in winter 074 953 1340).

The turbulent Tory Sound separates this windswept island from the northwestern corner of mainland Donegal. Given that rough weather can cut off the tiny island for days, it is not surprising that Tory's inhabitants have developed a strong sense of independence. Most of the islanders speak Gaelic and they even have their own monarch: the powers of this non-hereditary position are minimal, but the current incumbent is heavily involved in promoting the interests of his "subjects" and in attracting visitors to the island.

During the 1970s, the Irish government tried to resettle most of the islanders on the mainland, but they refused to move. Their campaign of resistance was led by Tory's school of Primitive artists. This emerged after 1968, inspired by a local man called James Dixon who claimed he could do better than a visiting English painter, Derek Hill. Since then, the school of artists has drawn a growing number of tourists; the **Dixon Gallery** opened in 1992 in the main village of West Town. There

are ruins of a monastery founded by St Columba *(see p34)* nearby, or else you can explore the island's dramatic cliffs and seabird rookeries.

🏛 **Dixon Gallery**
West Town. **Tel** 074 913 5011.
⭘ Easter–Sep: daily.

Bloody Foreland ❷

Road map C1. Co Donegal. 🚌 to Letterkenny.

Bloody Foreland, which gets its name from the rubescent glow of the rocks at sunset, boasts magnificent scenery. The R257 road skirts the coast around the headland, providing lovely views. The most scenic viewpoint is on the

north coast and looks across to the cliffs of nearby offshore islands, including Tory. A short distance further south, the tiny village of **Bunbeg** has a pretty harbour, but elsewhere the rocky landscape is spoiled by a blanket of holiday bungalows.

Derryveagh Mountains ❸

Road map C1. Co Donegal.

The wild beauty of these mountains provides one of the high spots of a visit to Donegal. Errigal Mountain, the range's tallest peak at 751 m (2,466 ft), attracts keen hikers, but the cream of the mountain scenery lies within **Glenveagh National Park**. Covering nearly 16,500 ha (40,000 acres), this takes in the beautiful valley occupied by Lough Veagh, and Poisoned Glen, a marshy valley enclosed by dramatic cliffs. The park also protects the largest herd of red deer in the country.

Glenveagh Castle stands on the southern shores of Lough Veagh, near the visitors' centre. This splendid granite building was constructed in 1870 by John Adair, notorious for his eviction of many families from the area after the Famine *(see p219)*. The castle was given to the nation in the 1970s by its last owner, a wealthy art dealer from Pennsylvania.

Shuttle buses whisk you up the private road to the castle from the visitors' centre. You can go on a guided tour of the sumptuous interior or just stroll

Glenveagh Castle overlooking Lough Veagh

Looking across to Dunfanaghy, gateway to the Horn Head peninsula

through the formal gardens and rhododendron woods. Trails weave all around the castle grounds; one path climbs steeply to reward you with a lovely view over Lough Veagh.

Glebe House and Gallery overlooks Lough Gartan 6 km (4 miles) south of the visitors' centre. This modest Regency mansion was the home of the painter, Derek Hill, who was also a keen collector The house reveals his varied tastes, with William Morris wallpapers, Islamic ceramics and paintings by Tory Island artists. The gallery contains works by Picasso, Renoir and Jack B Yeats among others.

Fountain at Glenveagh

The **Colmcille Heritage Centre**, less than a kilometre south, uses stained glass and illuminated manuscripts to trace the life of St Columba (Colmcille in Gaelic), who was born in nearby Church Hill in AD 521 *(see p34)*. A flagstone in Lacknacoo is said to mark the site of the saint's birthplace.

♣ **Glenveagh National Park and Castle**
Off R251, 16 km (10 miles) N of Churchill. **Tel** 074 913 7090. **Park & Castle** ☐ daily. 🚫 🅿 🚻 🛒 🚻 ltd. www.glenveaghnationalpark.ie

🏛 **Glebe House and Gallery**
Tel 074 913 7071. ☐ Easter & May–Sep: Sat–Thu. 🚫 🅿 limited. 🚫 🅿

🏛 **Colmcille Heritage Centre**
Tel 074 913 7306. ☐ Easter & May–Sep: daily. 🚫

Horn Head ❹

Road map C1. Co Donegal. 🚌 to Dunfanaghy from Letterkenny. 🛈 *The Workhouse, Dunfanaghy (074 913 6540). Jul & Aug: daily, Sep–Jun: Mon–Sat.* 🅿 🅿 www.dunfanaghy workhouse.ie

Carpeted in heather and rich in birdlife, this is the most scenic of the northern Donegal headlands, with lovely views of the sea and mountains. The appeal of the area is enhanced by **Dunfanaghy**, a delightful town with an air of affluence and Presbyterianism unusual in this area. The local beach, **Killahoey Strand**, offers excellent swimming.

Rosguill Peninsula ❺

Road map C1. Co Donegal.

Rosguill Peninsula juts out into the Atlantic Ocean between Sheephaven and Mulroy bays. The simplest way to see it is to follow the 11-km (7-mile) Atlantic Drive, a circular route which skirts the clifftops at the tip of the headland. Doe Castle,

5 km (3 miles) north of Creeslough village, is worth a visit as much for its setting on a promontory overlooking Sheephaven Bay as for its architectural or historical interest. It has been restored from the remains of a castle erected in the 16th century by the MacSweeneys, a family of Scottish mercenaries.

Fanad Peninsula ❻

Road map C1. Co Donegal. 🚌 to Rathmelton & Portsalon from Letterkenny

A panoramic route winds between the hilly spine and rugged coast of this tranquil peninsula. The eastern side is by far the most enjoyable and begins at **Rathmelton**, a charming Plantation town founded in the 17th century. Elegant Georgian homes and handsome old warehouses flank its tree-lined Main Street.

Further north, **Portsalon** offers safe bathing and great views from nearby Saldanha Head. Near **Doaghbeg**, on the way to Fanad Head in the far north, the cliffs have been eroded into arches and other dramatic shapes.

Doe Castle on Rosguill Peninsula, with its 16th-century battlements

A Tour of the Inishowen Peninsula ⑦

Inishowen, the largest of Donegal's northern peninsulas, is an area laden with history, from early Christian relics to strategically positioned castles and forts. The most rugged scenery lies in the west and north, around the the steep rock-strewn landscape of the Gap of Mamore and the spectacular cape of Malin Head, the northern-most point in Ireland. Numerous beaches dot the coastline and cater for all tastes, from the remote Isle of Doagh to the busy family resort of Buncrana. From the shores, there are views to Donegal's Derryveagh Mountains to the west and the Northern Ireland coast in the east. The Inishowen Peninsula can be explored by car as a leisurely day trip.

Tower on Banba's Crown, Malin Head

Carndonagh Cross ④
This 7th-century early Christian cross is carved with human figures and inter-lacing lines.

Gap of Mamore ③
The road between Mamore Hill and the Urris Hills is 250 m (820 ft) above sea level and offers panoramic views.

Dunree Head ②
On the headland, Dunree Fort overlooks Lough Swilly. It was built in 1798 to counter the threat of French invasion. Since 1986, it has been a military museum.

Buncrana ①
Buncrana has 5 km (3 miles) of sandy beaches and two castles. Buncrana Castle was rebuilt in 1718 and the intact keep of O'Doherty Castle dates from Norman times.

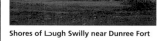

Shores of Lough Swilly near Dunree Fort

KEY

—	Tour route
=	Other roads
⁂	Viewpoint

Grianán Ailigh ⑦
At the neck of the Inishowen Peninsula, perched on a hilltop, stands this formidable circular stone fort. The solid structure that can be seen today is the result of extensive restoration in the 1870s.

Enjoying the views from the ramparts of the Grianán of Ailigh

Malin Head ⑤

This traditional cottage makes
a good stop for tea after
enjoying the superb Atlantic
views from Malin Head. At
the highest point, Banba's
Crown, stands a tower built
in 1805 to monitor shipping.

Greencastle ⑥

A resort and fishing port,
Greencastle is named after
the overgrown castle ruins
just outside town. Built in
1305 by Richard de Burgo,
Earl of Ulster, the castle
guarded the entrance to
Lough Foyle.

0 kilometres   5

0 miles   5

Grianán Ailigh ⑧

Road map C1. Donegal.
from Letterkenny or Londonderry.
Letterkenny (074 912 1160).

Donegal's most impressive
and intriguing ancient
monument stands just 10 km
(6 miles) west of the city of
Londonderry (see pp258–9) at
the entrance to the lovely
Inishowen Peninsula.

Overlooking Lough Swilly
and Lough Foyle, the circular
stone structure measuring
23 m (77 ft) in diameter, is
believed to have been built as
a pagan temple around the
5th century BC, although the
site was probably a place of
worship before this date. Later,
Christians adopted the fort:
St Patrick is said to have baptized Owen, founder of the
O'Neill dynasty, here in
AD 450. It became the royal
residence of the O'Neills, but
was damaged in the 12th century by the army of Murtagh
O'Brien, King of Munster.

The fort was restored in the
1870s. Two doorways lead
from the outside through 4-m
(13-ft) thick defences into a
grassy arena ringed by three
terraces. The most memorable
feature of the fort, however, is
its magnificent vantage point,
which affords stunning views
in every direction.

At the foot of the hill stands
an attractive church, dedicated
to St Aengus and built in 1967.
Its circular design echoes that
of the Grianán.

Letterkenny ⑨

Road map C1. Co Donegal.
17,500. Blaney Rd (074
912 1160). www.discoverireland.ie

Straddling the River Swilly,
with the Sperrin Mountains to
the east and the Derryveagh
Mountains (see pp224–5)

to the west, Letterkenny is
Donegal's largest town. It is
also the region's main
business centre, a role it took
over from Londonderry after
partition in 1921. The likeable
town makes a good base
from which to explore the
northern coast of Donegal
and, for anglers, is well
placed for access to the
waters of Lough Swilly.

Letterkenny has one of the
longest main streets in
Ireland, which is dominated
by the 65-m (215-ft) steeple
of **St Eunan's Cathedral**. A
Neo-Gothic creation built in
the late 19th century, it looks
particularly impressive when
floodlit at night. It contains
Celtic-style stonework, a rich
marble altar and vivid stained-
glass windows. **Donegal
County Museum** is located in
a former workhouse building.
It offers informative displays
on local history from the
Stone Age to the 20th century.
It also has a collection of
archaeological artifacts found
in Donegal, some of them
dating from the Iron Age.

☰ Donegal County Museum
High Rd. **Tel** 074 912 4613.
Mon–Sat (pm only Sat).
Christmas and public hols.

The imposing spire of St Eunan's
Cathedral in Letterkenny

Isolated cottage near Burtonport in the Rosses

The Rosses ⑩

Road map C1. Co Donegal.
🚉 to Dungloe or Burtonport from
Letterkenny. 🅸 (seasonal): Dungloe
(074 952 1297). ⛴ to Arranmore
from Burtonport (074 952 0532).

A rocky headland dotted
with more than 100 lakes,
the Rosses is one of the most
picturesque and unspoilt
corners of Donegal. It is also
a strong Gaeltacht area, with
many people speaking Gaelic.
    The hub of the Rosses, at
the southern end of the
headland, is **Dungloe**, a
bustling market town and
major angling centre.

Environs
There is a glorious sheltered
beach 8 km (5 miles) west of
Dungloe at **Maghery Bay**.
From here you can also walk
to nearby **Crohy Head**, an area
known for its caves, arches

and unusual cliff formations.
From the small fishing village
of Burtonport, 8 km (5 miles)
north of Dungloe, car ferries
sail daily to Donegal's largest
island, **Arranmore**. The rugged
northwest coast here is ideal
for clifftop walks, and from
the south coast you can enjoy
fine views across to the
Rosses. Most of Arranmore's
population of 700 lives in
Leabgarrow, where the
harbour is located.

Ardara ⑪

Road map C2. Co Donegal. 🏠 700.
🚉 from Killybegs or Donegal. 🅸
Donegal (074 972 1148). **www.**
discoverireland.ie/northwest

Ardara, the weaving capital of
Donegal, proliferates in shops
selling locally made tweeds
and hand-knitted sweaters.
Some larger stores put on dis-

plays of hand-loom weaving.
Ardara is also worth a stop for
its pubs, much loved for their
fiddle sessions.

Environs
A drive along the narrow
peninsula to **Loughros Point**,
10 km (6 miles) west of
town, provides dramatic
coastal views. Another
picturesque route runs
southwest from Ardara to
Glencolumbkille, going over
Glengesh Pass, a series of
bends through a wild,
deserted landscape.

Hand-loom worker in Ardara

Glencolumbkille ⑫

Road map B2. Co Donegal. 🏠 260.
🚉 from Killybegs. 🅸 Donegal (074
972 1148). **www.**glencolumbkille.ie

Glencolumbkille, a quiet,
grassy valley scattered with
brightly coloured cottages, feels
very much like a backwater, in
spite of the sizeable number
of visitors who come here.
    The "Glen of St Colmcille" is
a popular place of pilgrimage
due to its associations with the
saint more commonly known
as St Columba. Just north of
the village of Cashel, on the
way to Glen Head, is the
church where St Columba
worshipped: it is said that
between prayers the saint slept
on the two stone slabs still
visible in one corner.
    Another attraction here is
the **Folk Village Museum**,
which depicts rural Donegal
lifestyles through the ages. It
was started in the 1950s by a
local priest called Father James

Old irons at the Folk Village Museum in Glencolumbkille

For hotels and restaurants in this region see pp312–14 and pp339–41

Slieve League, the highest sea cliffs in Europe

Killybegs ⑭

Road map C2. Co Donegal. 🏚 1,700. 🚌 from Donegal. ℹ Donegal (074 972 1148). www.killybegs.ie

Narrow winding streets give Killybegs a timeless feel, which contrasts sharply with the industriousness of this small town. The sense of prosperity stems in part from the manufacture of the Donegal carpets for which the town is famous, and which adorn Dublin Castle (see pp76–7) and other palaces around the world.

Killybegs is one of Ireland's busiest fishing ports and the quays are well worth seeing when the trawlers arrive to offload their catch: gulls squawk overhead and the smell of fish fills the air. Trawlermen come from far and wide – so do not be surprised if you hear Eastern European voices as you wander around the town.

Trawler crew in Killybegs relaxing after unloading their catch

MacDyer. Concerned about the high rate of emigration from this poor region, he sought to provide jobs and a sense of regional pride, partly by encouraging people to set up craft cooperatives. There are regular craft demonstrations – such as spinning – at the museum and the folk village shop sells local wares.

There is plenty to explore in the valley, which is littered with cairns, dolmens and other ancient monuments. The nearby coast is lovely too, the best walks taking you west across the grassy foreland of **Malinbeg**. Beyond the small resort of Malin More, steps drop down to an idyllic sandy cove hemmed in by cliffs.

🏛 **Folk Village Museum**
Cashel **Tel** 074 973 0017. ⬜ Easter–Sep: daily. 🅿 🎫 📷 📱 ♿

Slieve League ⑬

Road map B2. Co Donegal. 🚌 to Carrick from Donegal or Killybegs.

One of the highest cliff faces in Europe, Slieve League is spectacular not just for its sheer elevation, but also for its colour: at sunset the rock is streaked with changing shades of red, amber and ochre. The 8-km (5-mile) drive to the eastern end of Slieve League from **Carrick** is bumpy but well worth enduring. Beyond Teelin, the road becomes a series

of alarming switchbacks before reaching **Bunglass Point** and Amharc Mor, the "good view". From here, you can see the whole of Slieve League, its sheer cliffs rising dramatically out of the ocean.

Only experienced hikers should attempt the treacherous ledges of **One Man's Pass**. This is part of a trail which climbs westwards out of Teelin and up to the highest point of Slieve League – from where you can admire the Atlantic Ocean shimmering 598 m (1,962 ft) below. The path then continues on to Malinbeg, 16 km (10 miles) west. During the summer, for a less strenuous but safer and equally rewarding excursion, pay a boat-owner from Teelin to take you out to see Slieve League from the sea.

THE IRISH GAELTACHTS

The term "Gaeltacht" refers to Gaelic-speaking areas of Ireland. Up to the 16th century, virtually the entire population spoke the native tongue. British rule, however, undermined Irish culture, and the Famine (see p219) drained the country of many of its Gaelic-speakers. The use of the local language has fallen steadily since. Even so, in the Gaeltachts 75 per cent of the people still speak it, and road signs are exclusively in Irish – unlike in most other parts of Ireland.

The Donegal Gaeltacht stretches almost unbroken along the coast from Fanad Head to Slieve League and boasts the largest number of Irish-speakers in the country. Ireland's other principal Gaeltachts are in Galway and Kerry.

Gaelic pub sign in Gaeltacht region

Donegal town, overlooked by the ruins of its 15th-century castle

Donegal ⓯

Road map C2. Co Donegal. 🚶 2,300.
🚌 🚉 *The Quay (✆4 972 1148).*
www.discoverireland.ie/northwest

Donegal means "Fort of the Foreigners", after the Vikings who built a garrison here. However, it was under the O'Donnells that the town began to take shape. The restored **Donegal Castle** in the town centre incorporates the gabled tower of a fortified house built by the family in the 15th century. The adjoining house and most other features are Jacobean – added by Sir Basil Brooke, who moved in after the O'Donnells were ousted by the English in 1607 (*see pp38–9*).

Brooke was also responsible for laying out the market square, which is known as the **Diamond**. An obelisk in the centre commemorates four Franciscan monks who wrote the *Annals of the Four Masters* in the 1630s, tracing the history of the Gaelic people from 40 days before the Great Flood up until the end of the 16th century. Part of it was written at **Donegal Abbey**, south of the market square along the River Eske. Built in 1474, little now remains of the abbey but a

few Gothic windows and cloister arches. About 1.5 km (1 mile) further on is **Donegal Craft Village**, a showcase for the work of local craftspeople.

Donegal town has some pleasant hotels (*see p313*) and makes a good base for exploring the southern part of the county.

> ♣ **Donegal Castle**
> Tirchonaill St. **Tel** 074 972 2405.
> ◻ *Mar–Oct: daily; Nov–Feb: Thu–Mon.* 🎫 📷 🚻 *limited.*

> 🏠 **Donegal Craft Village**
> Ballyshannon Rd. **Tel** 074 972 2225.
> ◻ *Apr–Sep: Mon–Sat; Oct–Mar: Tue–Sat.* 🚻 🚻 *limited.*

Lough Derg ⓰

Road map C2. Co Donegal. 🚢 *Jun–mid-Aug (pilgrims only).* 🚌 *to Pettigo from Donegal.* **www**.loughderg.org

Pilgrims have made their way to Lough Derg ever since St Patrick spent 40 days praying on one of the lake's islands in an attempt to rid Ireland of all evil spirits. The Pilgrimage of St Patrick's Purgatory began in around 1150 and still attracts thousands of Catholics every summer. Their destination is the tiny **Station Island**, close to Lough Derg's southern shore and reached by boat from a jetty

8 km (5 miles) north of the border village of Pettigo. The island is completely covered by a religious complex, which includes a basilica, built in 1921, and hostels for pilgrims.

The pilgrimage season runs from March to October. People spend three days on the island, eating just one meal of dry bread and black tea per day. Although only pilgrims can visit Station Island, it is interesting to go to the jetty to savour the atmosphere and get a good view of the basilica near the shore.

Rossnowlagh ⓱

Road map C2. Co Donegal. 🚶 55.
🚌 *from Bundoran & Donegal.*
🚉 *May–Sep: The Bridge, Bundoran (071 984 1350).*

Holiday-makers enjoying the fine sandy beach at Rossnowlagh

At Rossnowlagh, Atlantic waves break on to one of Ireland's finest beaches, drawing crowds of both bathers and surfers to this tiny place. Even so, the village remains far more peaceful than the resort of Bundoran, 14 km (9 miles) south. In addition, the cliffs at Rossnowlagh provide scope for exhilarating coastal walks. Away from the sea, you can visit the **Donegal Historical Society Museum**, housed in a striking Franciscan friary

Basilica on Station Island viewed from the shores of Lough Derg

For hotels and restaurants in this region see pp312–14 and pp339–41

Lissadell House dining room with Gore-Booth family portraits

Lissadell House ⑲

Road map E2. Carney, Co Sligo.
Tel 071 916 3150. 🚌 or 🚉 to
Sligo. 🔵 closed to the public.
www.lissadellhouse.com

A Greek Revival mansion built in the 1830s, Lissadell is famous more for its occupants than its architecture. It used to be the home of the Gore-Booths who, unlike some of the Anglo-Irish gentry, have contributed much to the region over the four centuries they have been in County Sligo. During the Famine *(see p219)*, Sir Robert charitably mortgaged the house to help feed his employees.

The most famous member of the Gore-Booth family is Sir Robert's granddaughter, Constance Markievicz (1868–1927), a leading nationalist who took part in the 1916 Rising *(see pp44–5)*. She was the first woman to be elected to the British House of Commons and later became Minister for Labour in the first Dáil. W B Yeats, who first visited the house in 1894, immortalized Constance and her sister, Eva, in one of his poems, describing them as "Two girls in silk kimonos, both beautiful, one a gazelle".

Built in grey limestone, the exterior of Lissadell House is rather austere. The interior, on the other hand, has an appealing atmosphere of faded grandeur, with copious memorabilia of the building's former occupants. The finest rooms are the gallery and the dining room, decorated with extraordinary full-length murals of the Gore-Booth family their famous butler Thomas Kilgallon, the gamekeeper, head woodman and a dog. Painted directly on to the wall, they were the work of Constance's husband, adventurer and self-styled "Count" Casimir Markievicz.

Lissadell House is now a private home and the building is not open to the public, although you can explore the paths skirting the seashore

built in the 1950s. The tiny but fascinating collection includes displays of Stone Age flints, Irish musical instruments and other local artifacts.

Rossnowlagh never fails to make the news in July, when it hosts the only parade to take place in the Republic by the Protestant organization, the Orange Order *(see p49)*.

🏛 **Donegal Historical Society Museum**
Tel 071 985 1342. 🔵 daily.

Ballyshannon ⑱

Road map C2. Co Donegal. 🏘
2,600. 🚌 from Bundoran & Donegal.

In Ballyshannon, well-kept Georgian homes jostle for space along hilly streets on the banks of the River Erne, near where it flows into Donegal Bay. This is a bustling town, full of character and off the main tourist track – though it gets packed during July's festival of traditional music, which is one of the best of its kind in the country.

The festival apart, Ballyshannon is most famous as the birthplace of poet William Allingham (1824–89), who recalled his home town in the lines "Adieu to Ballyshanny and the winding banks of the

Erne". He lies buried in the graveyard of St Anne's Church, off Main Street. There is a fine view over the river from here you can see the small island of **Inis Saimer** where, according to legend, Greeks founded the first colony in Ireland after the Great Flood. Beyond, you can glimpse a large Irish Army base: Ballyshannon's position on a

Mural of the family dog in Lissadell's dining room

steeply rising bluff overlooking the River Erne has always made the town a strategic military site.

About 1.5 km (1 mile) northwest of town lie the scant ruins of **Assaroe Abbey**, founded by Cistercians in 1184. A graveyard with some ancient burial slabs and headstones is all that remains. Nearby, two water wheels installed by the monks have been restored. **Water Wheels** has a small heritage centre as well as a café.

🏛 **Water Wheels**
Assaroe Abbey. **Tel** 071 985 1580.
🔵 mid-Apr–Sep: Sun only, (except Aug: daily). 🔲 🎁 ♿

A Tour of Yeats Country ⑳

Yeats tour sign

Even for people unfamiliar with the poetry of WB Yeats, Sligo's engaging landscapes are reason enough to make a pilgrimage. This tour follows a varied route, taking you past sandy bays and dramatic limestone ridges, through forest and alongside rivers and lakes. Lough Gill lies at the heart of Yeats country, enclosed by wooded hills crisscrossed by walking trails. In summer, boats ply the length of the lough, or you can head to one of the northwest's best beaches, at Rosses Point.

Ben Bulben ⑤
The eerie silhouette of Ben Bulben rises abruptly out of the plain. You can climb to the top, but go with great care.

Lissadell House ④
Yeats was a close friend of the Gore-Booth sisters who lived at Lissadell. The house is closed to the public *(see p231)*.

Drumcliff ③
Although he died in France, in 1948 Yeats's body was laid to rest in Drumcliff churchyard. The ruins of an old monastic site include a fine High Cross.

Rosses Point ②
Yeats and his brother used to spend their summers at this pretty resort. It stands at the entrance to Sligo Bay, and a steady flow of boats passes by.

Sligo ①
This town is a good place to begin a tour of Yeats country. It has many connections with the poet and his family, whose literary and artistic legacy has helped to inspire Sligo's thriving arts scene *(see p234).*

TIPS FOR DRIVERS

Length: 88 km (55 miles).
Stopping-off points: North of Sligo, the best choice of eating places is at Rosses Point, although there are good pubs in Drumcliff and Dromahair. Lough Gill provides most choice in terms of picnic spots.
Boat trips: visit www.inish.ie or www.roseofinnisfree.com. (See also pp385–7.)

KEY

— Tour route
= Other roads
⚓ Boat trips
☀ Viewpoint

DONEGAL
N15
⑤
Carney
Drumcliff Bay
③
Drumcl
②
Sligo Harbour
R291
N15
N16
①
Garavogue
R287
⑨
R284
N4
GALWAY

WB YEATS AND SLIGO

As a schoolboy in London, Yeats (*see p23*) longed for his native Sligo and as an adult he often returned here. He lovingly describes the county in his *Reveries over Childhood and Youth*, and the lake-studded landscape haunts his poetry. "In a sense", Yeats said, "Sligo has always been my home", and it is here that he wished to be buried. His gravestone in Drumcliff bears an epitaph he penned himself: "Cast a cold eye on Life, on death. Horseman pass by."

WB Yeats (1865–1939)

Parke's Castle viewed from across the calm waters of Lough Gill

Parke's Castle ㉑

Road map C2. 6 km (4 miles) N of Dromahair, Co Leitrim. **Tel** 071 916 4149. ☐ to ☐ to Sligo. ☐ Apr–mid-Sep 10am–6pm daily (last adm 5:15pm). ☐ ☐ limited. ☐ www.heritageireland.ie

This fortified manor house dominates the eastern end of Lough Gill. It was built in 1609 by Captain Robert Parke, an English settler who later became MP for Leitrim. It has been beautifully restored by the Office of Public Works using 17th-century building methods and native Irish oak.

Parke's Castle was erected on the site of a 16th-century tower house belonging to the O'Rourkes, a powerful local clan, and stones from this earlier structure were used in the new building. The original foundations and part of the moat were incorporated, but otherwise Parke's Castle is the epitome of a Plantation manor house (*see p39*). It is protected by a large enclosure or bawn, whose sturdy wall includes a gatehouse and two turrets as well as the house itself.

Among the most distinctive architectural features of Parke's Castle are the diamond-shaped chimneys, mullioned windows and the parapets. There is also a curious stone hut, known as the "sweathouse", which was an early Irish sauna. Inside, an exhibition and audiovisual display cover Parke's Castle and various historic and prehistoric sites in the area. There is also a working forge.

Boat trips around sights on Lough Gill that are associated with the poet, WB Yeats, leave from outside the castle walls.

Glencar Lough ⑥
'There is a waterfall ... that all my childhood counted dear', wrote Yeats of the cataract which tumbles into Glencar Lough. A path leads down to it from the road.

Parke's Castle ⑦
This 17th-century fortified manor house commands a splendid view over the tranquil waters of Lough Gill. It is a starting point for boat trips around the lough.

Isle of Innisfree ⑧
"There midnight's all a glimmer, and noon a purple glow", is how Yeats once described Innisfree. There is not much to see on this tiny island but it is a romantic spot. In summer, a boatman ferries visitors here.

Dooney Rock ⑨
A steep path leads from the road to Dooney Rock, from where glorious views extend over the lough to Ben Bulben. Trails weave through the surrounding woods and by the lake.

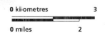

0 kilometres 3
0 miles 2

Hargadon's bar (see p350), one of Sligo town's most famous watering holes

🏛 **Sligo Abbey**
Abbey St. *Tel* 071 914 6406.
🕐 *Apr–mid-Oct: daily; mid-end*
Oct: Fri–Sun. 🅰 🅰

🏛 **Sligo County Museum**
Stephen St. *Tel* 071 914 1623.
🕐 *Tue–Sat daily (Oct–May: pm only).*

🏛 **Model Arts & Niland Gallery**
The Mall. *Tel* 071 9141405.
🕐 *Wed–Sun.* 🅰 🅰 🅰 🅰
www.modelart.ie

Sligo ㉒

Road map C2. ⌂ Sligo. 🏠 *20,000.*
✈ *071 916 828C.* 🅰 🅰 🛈 *Aras
Reddan. Temple S. (071 916 1201).*
🅰 *Fri.* **www**.discoverireland.ie/
northwest

The port of Sligo sits at the mouth of the River Garavogue, sandwiched between the Atlantic and Lough Gill. The largest town in the northwest, it rose to prominence under the Normans, being well placed as a gateway between the provinces of Ulster and Connaught. The appearance of Sligo today is mainly the result of growth during the late 18th and 19th centuries.

Sligo is perfectly situated for touring the ravishing countryside nearby, and it is also a good centre for traditional music. While at first sight it can seem a bit sombre, the town is thriving as the arts capital of northwest Ireland.

Sligo's link with the Yeats family is the main source of the town's appeal. WB Yeats (*see pp232–3*) Ireland's best-known poet, was born into a prominent local family. The Pollexfen warehouse, at the western end of Wine Street, has a rooftop turret from which the poet's grandfather would observe his merchant fleet moored in the docks.

The town's sole surviving medieval building is **Sligo Abbey**, founded in 1253. Some original features remain, such as the delicate lancet windows in the choir, but this ruined Dominican friary dates mainly from the 15th century. The best features are a beautifully carved altar and the cloisters. A short distance west from the abbey is O'Connell Street, with the town's main shops and Hargadon's bar – an old Sligo institution complete with a dark, wooden interior, snugs and a grocery counter. Near the junction with Wine Street, overlooking Hyde Bridge, is the Yeats Memorial Building. This houses the Yeats Society, who are dedicated to commemorating the life of the poet. The Yeats International Summer School is held here too: a renowned annual festival of readings and lectures on the poet's life and work.

Just the other side of Hyde Bridge is a statue of the poet, engraved with lines from his own verse. **Sligo County Museum** has Yeatsian memorabilia and local artifacts but the entire Niland Collection including the paintings by Jack B Yeats is in the **Model Arts & Niland Gallery** in The Mall. This outstanding centre also puts on temporary exhibitions of major Irish and international contemporary art.

Bronze statue of WB Yeats

Environs

Improbably set in the suburbs of Sligo, **Carrowmore Megalithic Cemetery** once held the country's largest collection of Stone Age tombs. Quarrying destroyed much, but about 40 passage tombs (*see pp246–7*) and dolmens (*see p32*) survive among the abandoned gravel pits, with some in private gardens and cottages.

The huge unexcavated cairn atop **Knocknarea** mountain dates back 5,000 years and is said to contain the tomb of the legendary Queen Maeve of Connaught (*see p26*). It is an hour's climb starting 4 km (2.5 miles) west of Carrowmore.

Tobernalt, by Lough Gill 5 km (3 miles) south of Sligo, means "cliff well", after a nearby spring with alleged curative powers. It was a holy site in Celtic times and later became a Christian shrine. Priests came here to celebrate Mass in secret during the 18th century, when Catholic worship was illegal. The Mass rock, next to an altar erected around 1900, remains a place of pilgrimage.

🏛 **Carrowmore Cemetery**
Tel 071 916 1534. 🕐 *Easter–Oct.* 🅰
🅰 www.heritageireland.ie

Altar by the holy well at Tobernalt, overlooking Lough Gill in Sligo

Lough Arrow ㉓

Road map C3. Co Sligo. 🚌 to
Ballinafad. 🚹 Jun–Sep: Boyle (071
966 2145). www.discoverireland.ie

People go to Lough Arrow to
sail and fish for the local
trout, and also simply to enjoy
the glorious countryside. You
can explore the lake by boat,
but the views from the shore
are the real joy of Lough
Arrow. A full circuit of the
lake is recommended, but for
the most breathtaking views
head for the southern end
around **Ballinafad**. This small
town lies in a gorgeous spot,
enclosed to the north and
south by the Bricklieve and
Curlew Mountains.

The **Carrowkeel Passage
Tomb Cemetery** occupies a
remote and eerie spot in the
Bricklieve Mountains to the
north of Ballinafad. The best
approach is up the single track
road from Castlebaldwin, 5 km
(3 miles) northeast of the site.

The 14 Neolithic passage
graves, which are scattered
around a hilltop overlooking
Lough Arrow, are elaborate
corbelled structures. One is
comparable with Newgrange
(see pp246–7), except that the
burial chamber inside this
cairn is lit by the sun on the
day of the summer solstice
(21 June) as opposed to the
winter solstice. On a nearby
ridge are the remains of Stone
Age huts, presumably those
occupied by the farmers who
buried their dead in the
Carrowkeel passage graves.

Passage tomb in Carrowkeel cemetery above Lough Arrow.

Carrick-on-Shannon ㉔

Road map C3. Co Leitrim.
🚶 3,000. 🚌 🚗 🚲 🚢 May–Sep: The
Old Barrel Store (071 962 0170).
www.leitrimtourism.com

The tiny capital of Leitrim,
one of the least populated
counties in Ireland (although
this is changing) stands in a
lovely spot on a tight bend of
the River Shannon.

The town's location by the
river and its proximity to the
Grand Canal were crucial to
Carrick's development. They
are also the main reasons for
its thriving tourist industry.
There is a colourful, modern
marina, where private boats
can moor in summer and
boats are available for hire.

Already a major boating
centre, Carrick has benefited
from the reopening of the
Shannon-Erne Waterway, one
end of which begins 6 km

(4 miles) north at Leitrim. The
channel was restored in a
cross-border joint venture
billed as a symbol of peaceful
cooperation between Northern
Ireland and the Republic.

Away from the bustle of
the marina, Carrick is an
old-fashioned place, with
19th-century churches and
convents, refined Georgian
houses and shopfronts. The
town's most curious building
is the quaint **Costello Chapel**
on Bridge Street, one of
the smallest in the world. It
was built in 1877 by local
businessman Edward Costello,
to house the tombs of himself
and his wife.

The Organic Centre ㉕

Road map C3. Rossinver, Co
Leitrim. Tel 071 985 4338. ◯ mid-
Mar–Oct: 10am–5pm daily. 🎫 🅿
♿ www.theorganiccentre.ie

Situated about 3.2 kilometres
(2 miles) from Rossinver on the
Kinlough Road, The Organic
Centre is a non-profit making
company that provides training, information and demonstrations of organic gardening,
cultivation and farming.

The centre is located on
a 7.7-ha (19-acre) site at
Rossinver in the unspoilt
countryside of the sparsely
populated North Leitrim. There
are display gardens for visitors
including a children's garden, a
taste garden and a heritage
garden. The Eco shop sells
seeds, cuttings and vegetables,
as well as books and kitchen
equipment. Some items can
also be bought online.

SHANNON-ERNE WATERWAY

This labyrinthine system
of rivers and lakes passes
through unspoiled border
country, linking Leitrim on
the Shannon and Upper
Lough Erne in Fermanagh. It
follows the course of a
canal which was completed
and then abandoned in
the 1860s. The channel
was reopened in 1993,
enabling the public to
enjoy both the Victorian
stonework (including 34
bridges) and the state-of-
the-art technology used to
operate the 16 locks.

Cruiser negotiating a lock on the
Shannon-Erne Waterway

THE MIDLANDS

CAVAN · MONAGHAN · LOUTH · LONGFORD
WESTMEATH · MEATH · OFFALY · LAOIS

The cradle of Irish civilization and the Celts' spiritual home, the Midlands encompass some of Ireland's most sacred and symbolic sites. Much of the region is ignored, but the ragged landscapes of lush pastures, lakes and bogland reveal ancient Celtic crosses, gracious Norman abbeys and Gothic Revival castles.

The fertile Boyne Valley in County Meath was settled during the Stone Age and became the most important centre of habitation in the country. The remains of ancient sites from this early civilization fill the area and include Newgrange, the finest Neolithic tomb in the country. In Celtic times, the focus shifted south to the Hill of Tara, the seat of the High Kings of Ireland and the Celts' spiritual and political capital. Tara's heyday came in the 3rd century AD, but it retained its importance until the Normans invaded in the 1100s.

Norman castles, such as the immense fortress at Trim in County Meath, attest to the shifting frontiers around the region of English influence known as the Pale *(see p132)*. By the end of the 16th century, this area incorporated nearly all the counties in the Midlands.

The Boyne Valley returned to prominence in 1690, when the Battle of the Boyne ended in a landmark Protestant victory over the Catholics *(see pp38–9)*.

Although part of the Republic since 1921, historically Monaghan and Cavan belong to Ulster, and the former retains strong links with the province. The rounded hills called drumlins, found in both counties, are typical of the border region between the Republic and Northern Ireland.

Grassland and bog dotted with lakes are most characteristic of the Midlands, but the Slieve Bloom Mountains and the Cooley Peninsula provide good walking country. In addition to Meath's ancient sites, the historical highlights of the region are monasteries like Fore Abbey and Clonmacnoise, this last ranking among Europe's greatest early Christian centres.

Carlingford village and harbour, with the hills of the Cooley Peninsula rising behind

◁ Temple Finghin round tower at Clonmacnoise monastery on the banks of the River Shannon

Exploring the Midlands

Drogheda is the obvious base from which to explore the Boyne Valley and neighbouring monastic sites, such as Monasterboice. Trim and Mullingar, to the southwest, are less convenient but make pleasanter places in which to stay. The northern counties of Monaghan, Cavan and Longford are quiet backwaters with a patchwork of lakes that attract many anglers. To the south, Offaly and Laois are dominated by dark expanses of bog, though there is a cluster of sights around the attractive Georgian town of Birr. For a break by the sea, head for the picturesque village of Carlingford on the Cooley Peninsula.

West doorway of Nuns' Church at Clonmacnoise

KEY

═══	Motorway
═══	Major road
───	Secondary road
┄┄┄	Minor road
───	Scenic route
┄┄┄	Main railway
────	Minor railway
▬▬▬	National border
═══	County border
△	Summit

GETTING AROUND

In the Midlands, there is an extensive network of roads and rail lines fanning out across the country from Dublin. As a result, getting around on public transport is easier than in most other areas. The Dublin–Belfast railway serves Dundalk and Drogheda, while Mullingar and Longford town lie on the Dublin–Sligo route. The railway and N7 road between Dublin and Limerick give good access to Laois and Offaly. For motorists, roads in the Midlands are often flat and straight but also potholed.

Enniskillen

Sligo
Blacklion

Mullan
Dowra
Swanlinbar
Derrynacreeve

Iron Mountains

Belt

DRUMLANE ②
Lough Oughter

R202

Cavan
Arvagh Bella

R198
Lough Gowna
N55

Kilc

Sligo

Newtown Forbes
R194
Granard

Shannon
Longford
N63

LONGFORD
TULLYNALLY CASTLE

Lanesborough
Ardagh
N4
Loug Derrave

Galway
CORLEA TRACKWAY ③
Royal Canal

Ballymahon

Lecarrow
R392
MULLINGAI

Lough Ree
N55
Ballymore
R390
WEST

N61
Lough Ennell
N5

ATHLONE ⑱
Moate
Rochfortbr

Galway
N62
KILBEGGAN ⑰ 血
M6

CLONMACNOISE ⑲
N80
TULLAN

Ferbane
⑳ DEW
Tullamo

Clonfert
Cloghan
Grand Canal
N52
Killeigh

Shannon
Banagher
Kilcormac
N8

Kilcormac
R421
Mountmelli

BIRR ㉑
R440
Kinnitty

Arderin 527m
㉒
SLIEVE BLOOM MOUNTAINS
Portl

N62
Shinrone

Roscrea
Borris in Ossory
LAO
Abbeyleix

M7
Thurles

Moneygall
M8
Durrow

Limerick
Toomyvara

Cashel

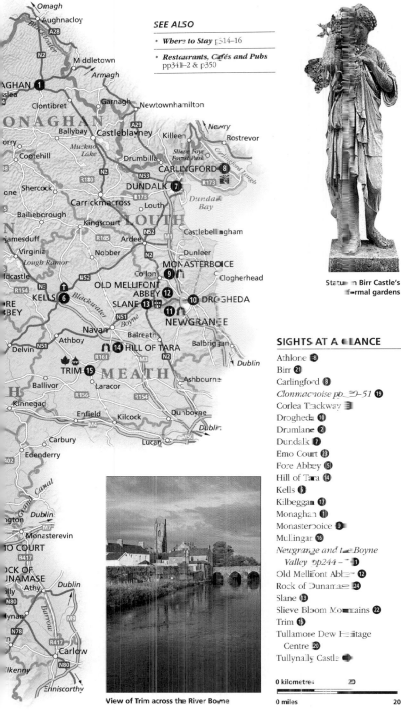

SEE ALSO

* *Where to Stay* p514–16

* *Restaurants, Cafés and Pubs*
pp341–2 & p350

Statue in Birr Castle's
formal gardens

SIGHTS AT A GLANCE

Athlone **⑱**
Birr **㉑**
Carlingford **⑧**
Clonmacnoise pp250–51 **⑲**
Corlea Trackway **㉓**
Drogheda **⑩**
Dramlane **②**
Dundalk **⑦**
Emo Court **㉓**
Fore Abbey **⑤**
Hill of Tara **⑭**
Kells **⑥**
Kilbeggan **⑰**
Monaghan **①**
Monasterboice **⑨**
Mullingar **⑯**
Newgrange and the Boyne
Valley pp244–5 **⑪**
Old Mellifont Abbey **⑫**
Rock of Dunamase **㉔**
Slane **⑬**
Slieve Bloom Mountains **㉒**
Trim **⑮**
Tullamore Dew Heritage
Centre **⑳**
Tullynally Castle **➡**

0 kilometres   20

0 miles   20

View of Trim across the River Boyne

Rossmore Memorial fountain in Monaghan

Monaghan ❶

Road map D2. Co Monaghan. 👥
6,000. 🚌 🛈 *Clones Rd (047 81122).*
www.monaghantourism.com

The spruce and thriving town
of Monaghan is the urban
highlight of the northern Midlands. Planted by James I in
1613 *(see p39)*, it developed
into a prosperous industrial
centre, thanks mainly to the
local manufacture of linen.
A crannog *(see p33)* off Glen
Road is the sole trace of the
town's Celtic beginnings.
  Monaghan centres on three
almost contiguous squares.
The main attraction in Market
Square is the 18th-century
Market House (now an arts
centre), a squat but charming
building with the original oak
beams still visible. To the east
lies Church Square, very much
the heart of modern Monaghan
and lined with dignified 19th-
century buildings, such as the
Classical-style courthouse. The
third square, which is known
as the Diamond, was the original marketplace. It contains
the **Rossmore Memorial**, a large
Victorian drinking fountain
with an ornate stone canopy
supported by marble columns.
  Do not miss the award-
winning **County Museum**, just
off Market Square, which tells
the story of Monaghan's linen
and lace-making industries.

The pride of its historical
collection is the Cross of
Clogher, an ornate bronze altar
cross which dates from
around 1400.
  The Gothic Revival Cathedral
of St Macartan perches on a
hilltop south of the town, from
where you can enjoy a fine
view over Monaghan.

🏛 County Museum
Hill St. *Tel 047 82928.* ⬜ *Mon–Sat.*
⬤ *public hols.* ♿ *limited.*

Drumlane ❷

Road map C3. 1 km (0.5 miles) S of
Milltown, Co Cavan. 🚌 *to Belturbet.*

Standing alone by the River
Erne, the medieval church
and round tower of Drumlane
merit a visit as much for their
delightful setting as for the
ruins themselves. The abbey
church, founded in the early
13th century but significantly
altered about 200 years later,
features fine Romanesque
carvings. The nearby round
tower has lost its cap but is
unusual for the well-finished
stonework, with carvings of
birds on the north side.

Corlea Trackway ❸

Road map C3. Kenagh, Co
Longford. *Tel 043 322 2386.* 🚌 *to
Longford.* ⬜ *Apr–Sep: 10am–6pm
daily (last adm: 45 mins before
closing).* 🅿 ✔ 🚻 ♿ *limited.*

The Corlea Trackway Visitor
Centre interprets an Iron Age
bog road built in the year
148 BC. The oak road is the
longest of its kind in Europe.
An 18 m (60 ft) length of preserved road is on permanent
display in a specially designed
hall to prevent the ancient
wood cracking in the heat.

Corlea Trackway

Authentic Victorian kitchen in Tullynally Castle

Environs

Just 10 km (6 miles) north of Corlea Trackway, **Ardagh** is considered the most attractive village in Longford, with pretty stone cottages gathered around a green. The River Shannon, Lough Ree, River Inny and Lough Gowna make Longford an angler's paradise. The "hot water" stretch at Lanesboro is famous for attracting coarse fish and canoeists head for the white water rush at Ballymahon.

Tullynally Castle ➍

Road map C3. Castle Pollard, Co Westmeath. **Tel** 044 966 1159.
🚌 to Mullingar. **Castle** ◻ to pre-booked groups only. 📷 obligatory. 🎟 **Tea rooms and gardens** ◻ May–Aug: 2–6pm Thu–Sun only. 🎫 🚻 ltd. 🅿 🛒
www.tullynallycastle.com

This huge structure, adorned with numerous turrets and battlements, is one of Ireland's largest castles. The original 17th-century tower house was given a Georgian gloss, but this was all but submerged under later Gothic Revival changes. The Pakenham family have lived at Tullynally since 1655. Thomas Pakenham now manages the estate.

The imposing great hall leads to a fine panelled dining room hung with family portraits. Of equal interest are the Victorian kitchen, laundry room and the adjacent drying room.

The 8,000-volume library looks out on to rolling wooded parkland, much of which was landscaped in the 1760s. The grounds include Victorian terraces, walled kitchen and flower gardens, and two small lakes.

Fore Abbey ➎

Road map C3. Fore, Castle Pollard, Co Westmeath. **Tel** 044 966 1780.
🚌 to Castle Pollard. ◻ daily.

The ruins of Fore Abbey lie in glorious rolling countryside about 8 km (5 miles) east of Tullynally Castle. St Fechin set up a monastery here in 630, but what you see now are the remains of a large Benedictine priory founded around 1200. Located on the northern border of the Pale (see p132), Fore Abbey was heavily fortified in the 15th century as protection against the native Irish.

The ruined church was part of the original Norman priory, but the cloister and refectory date from the 1400s. On the hill opposite lies St Fechin's Church, a Norman building said to mark the site of the first monastery. The tiny church nearby incorporates a 15th-century anchorite's cell.

Kells ➏

Road map D3. ◻ Meath.
🏛 5,500. 🚌 🛈 046 924 9336.
🌐 Dec–Jan. www.discoverireland
ie/eastcoast

Signposted by its Irish name, Ceanannus Mór, this modest town provides an unlikely backdrop to the monastery for which it is so famous.

Kells Monastery was set up by St Columba in the 6th century, but its heyday came after 806, when monks fled here from Iona. They may have been the scribes who illuminated the superb *Book of Kells*, now kept at Trinity College, Dublin (see p64).

The monastery centres on a rather gloomy 18th-century church beside which stands a decapitated round tower. There are several 9th-century High Crosses the South Cross is in the best condition.

Just north of the enclosure is **St Columba's House**, a tiny steep-roofed stone oratory, similar to St Kevin's Kitchen at Glendalough (see p140).

The Market Cross, a High Cross that once served to mark the entrance to the monastery, now stands outside the Old Courthouse. It was used as a gallows during the uprising in 1798 (see p41). The battle scene on the base is a subject rarely used in High Cross art.

Ruins of Fore Abbey, a medieval Benedictine priory

A fisherman's cottage on the Cooley Peninsula

Dundalk **7**

Road map D3. Co Louth. 👥 32,000. 🚌 🚂 ℹ Jocelyn St (042 933 5484). 🎣 Fri. www.discoverireland.ie

Dundalk once marked the northernmost point of the Pale, the area controlled by the English during the Middle Ages (see p132). Now it is the last major town before the Northern Irish border.

Dundalk is also a gateway to the magnificent countryside of the Cooley Peninsula. The **County Museum** is housed in an 18th-century distillery in the town. In three exhibition galleries it gives an imaginative history of the county, from the stone age to the present day.

🏛 **County Museum**
Jocelyn St. **Tel** 042 932 7056. 🕐 10am–5pm Tue–Sat. ⬤ 1 Jan, 25 & 26 Dec. 🎫 👥

Carlingford **8**

Road map D3. Co Louth. 👥 1,500. 🚌 ℹ Old Railway Station (042 937 3033). **Holy Trinity Heritage Centre** Dundalk St (042 937 3454). **Carlingford Adventure Centre** Tholsel St (042 937 3100). 🕐 10am–12:30pm, 2–4:30pm Mon–Fri. www.carlingford heritagecentre.com

This is a picturesque fishing village, located between the mountains of the Cooley Peninsula and Carlingford Lough. The border with Northern Ireland runs through the centre of this drowned river valley, and from the village you can look across to the Mountains of Mourne on the Ulster side (see pp284–5).

Carlingford is an interesting place to explore, with its pretty whitewashed cottages and ancient buildings clustered along medieval alleyways. The ruins of **King John's Castle**, built by the Normans to protect the entrance to the lough, still dominate the village. The **Holy Trinity Heritage Centre**, which is housed in a medieval church, traces the history of the port from Anglo-Norman times.

Carlingford is the country's oyster capital, and often holds an oyster festival in August, which draws a large crowd. The lough is a popular water sports centre too, and in summer you can go on cruises around the lough from the quayside where there is a marina.

The **Carlingford Adventure Centre** organizes walking tours, plus sailing, kayaking, canoeing and windsurfing.

Environs
A scenic route weaves around the **Cooley Peninsula**, skirting the coast and then cutting right through the mountains. The section along the north coast is dramatic: just 3 km (1.8 miles) northwest of Carlingford, in the **Slieve Foye Forest Park**, a corkscrew road climbs to give a gorgeous panoramic view.

The Tain Trail, which you can join at Carlingford, is a 30-km (19-mile) circuit through some of the peninsula's most rugged scenery, with cairns and other prehistoric sites scattered over the moorland. Keen hikers will be able to walk it in a day.

Monasterboice **9**

Road map D3. Co Louth. 🚌 to Drogheda. 🕐 daily.

Founded in the 5th century by an obscure disciple of St Patrick called St Buite, this monastic settlement is one of the most famous religious sites in the country. The ruins of the medieval monastery are enclosed within a graveyard in a lovely secluded spot north of Drogheda. The site includes a roofless round tower and two churches, but Monasterboice's greatest treasures are its 10th-century High Crosses.

Muiredach's High Cross is the finest of its kind in Ireland, and its sculpted biblical scenes are still remarkably fresh. They depict the life of Christ on the west face, while the east face, described in detail opposite, features mainly Old Testament scenes. The cross is named after an inscription on the base – "A prayer for Muiredach by whom this cross was made" – which is perhaps a reference to the abbot of Monasterboice. The 6.5-m (21-ft) West Cross, also known as the Tall Cross, is one of the largest in Ireland. The carving has not lasted as well as on Muiredach's Cross, but you can make out scenes from the Death of Christ. The North Cross, which is the least notable of the three, features a Crucifixion and a carved spiral pattern.

Detail from a tomb in Monasterboice graveyard

Round tower and West High Cross at Monasterboice

Ireland's High Crosses

High crosses exist in Celtic parts of both Britain and Ireland. Yet in their profusion and craftsmanship, Irish High Crosses are exceptional. The distinctive ringed cross has become a symbol of Irish Christianity and is still imitated today. The beautiful High Crosses associated with medieval monasteries were carved between the 8th and 12th centuries. The early crosses bore only geometric motifs, but in the 9th to 10th centuries a new style emerged when sculpted scenes from the Bible were introduced. Referred to as "sermons in stone", these later versions may have been used to educate the masses. In essence, though, the High Cross was a status symbol for the monastery or a local patron.

Pillar stones *inscribed with crosses, like this 6th-century example at Riasc (see p158), were precursors of the High Cross.*

Capstone, showing St Anthony and St Paul meeting in the desert

Tenon

MUIREDACH'S CROSS

Each face of this 10th-century cross at Monasterboice features scenes from the Bible, including the east face seen here. The 5.5-m (18-ft) cross consists of three blocks of sandstone fitted together by means of tenons and sockets.

The High Cross at Ahenny (see p199) *is typical of 8th-century 'ornamental' crosses. These were carved with interlacing patterns and spirals similar to those used in Celtic metalwork and jewellery.*

The Last Judgment shows Christ in Glory surrounded by a crowd of resurrected souls. The devil stands on his right clutching a pitchfork, ready to chase the damned souls into Hell.

Angle moulding

The ring served a functional as well as a decorative purpose, providing support for the head and arms of the stone cross.

Moses smites the rock to obtain water for the Israelites.

Adoration of the Magi

David struggling with Goliath

The Dysert O'Dea Cross (see p189) *dates from the 1400s and represents the late phase of High Cross art. It features the figures of Christ and a bishop carved in high relief.*

Socket

The Fall of Man *shows Adam and Eve beneath an apple-laden tree with Cain slaying Abel alongside. Both scenes are frequently depicted on Irish High Crosses.*

Base

Tenon

Drogheda ⑩

Road map D3. Co Louth.
🏠 30,000. 🚌 🚆 🛈 Mayoralty St
(041 983 7070). 🅰 Sat. www.
discoverireland.ie

In the 12th century, this Norman port near the mouth of the River Boyne was one of Ireland's most important towns. However, the place seems never to have recovered from the trauma of a vicious attack by Cromwell in 1649 (see p39), in which 2,000 citizens were killed. The town still has its original street plan and has a rich medieval heritage.

Little remains of Drogheda's medieval defences but **St Lawrence Gate**, a fine 13th-century barbican, has survived. Nearby, there are two churches called **St Peter's**. The one belonging to the Church of Ireland, built in 1753, is the more striking and has some splendid grave slabs. The Catholic church is worth visiting to see the embalmed head of Oliver Plunkett, an archbishop martyred in 1681.

South of the river you can climb Millmount, a Norman motte topped by a Martello tower. It provides a good view and is the site of the **Millmount Museum**, which contains interesting historical

Drogheda viewed from Millmount across the River Boyne

artifacts, including guns used in the War of Independence.

🏛 **Millmount Museum**
Millmount Square. **Tel** 041 983 3097. ◯ daily (Sun pm only). ● 7 days at Christmas. 📷 🎫 ♿ limited. www.millmount.net

Newgrange and the Boyne Valley ⑪

Road map D3. Co Meath. 🚆 to Drogheda. 🚌 to Slane or Drogheda. 🛈 Brú na Bóinne Interpretative Centre (041 988 0300). ◯ daily.

Known as Brú na Bóinne, the "Palace of the Boyne", this river valley was the cradle of Irish civilization. The fertile soil supported a sophisticated society in Neolithic times. Much evidence survives, in the form of ring forts, passage graves and sacred enclosures. The most important Neolithic monuments in the valley are three passage graves: supreme among these is **Newgrange** (see pp246–7), but **Dowth** and **Knowth** are significant too. The Boyne Valley also encompasses the Hill of Slane and the Hill of Tara (see p248), both of which are major sites in Celtic mythology. Indeed, this whole region is rich in

River Boyne near the site of the Battle of the Boyne

THE BATTLE OF THE BOYNE

In 1688, the Catholic King of England, James II, was deposed from his throne, to be replaced by his Protestant daughter, Mary, and her husband, William of Orange. Determined to win back the crown, James sought the support of Irish Catholics, and challenged William at Oldbridge by the River Boyne west of Drogheda. The Battle of the Boyne took place on 1 July 1690, with James's poorly trained force of 25,000 French and Irish Catholics facing William's hardened army of 36,000 French Huguenots, Dutch, English and Scots. The Protestants triumphed and James fled to France, after a battle that signalled the beginning of total Protestant power over Ireland. It ushered in the confiscation of Catholic lands and the suppression of Catholic interests, sealing the country's fate for the next 300 years.

William of Orange leading his troops at the Battle of the Boyne, 1 July 1690

associations with Ireland's prehistory. With monuments predating Egypt's pyramids, the Boyne Valley is marketed as the Irish "Valley of the Kings".

Newgrange and Knowth can only be seen on a tour run by **Brú na Bóinne Interpretative Centre** near Newgrange. The centre also has displays on the area's Stone Age heritage and a reconstruction of Newgrange.

Dowth
Off N51, 3 km (2 miles) E of Newgrange. to the public.
The passage grave at Dowth was plundered by Victorian souvenir hunters and has not been fully excavated. You cannot approach the tomb, but it can be seen from the road.

Knowth
1.5 km (1 mile) NW of Newgrange. as Newgrange (see pp246–7).
Knowth outdoes Newgrange in several respects, above all in the quantity of its treasures, which form the greatest concentration of megalithic art in Europe. Also, the site was occupied for a much longer period – from Neolithic times right up until about 1400.

Unusually, Knowth has two passage tombs rather than one. The excavations begun in 1962 are now complete and the site is open. The tombs can only be viewed externally to prevent further decay. Keep a lookout for the finely carved kerbstones. Visitors sign up for tours via Brú na Bóinne.

Ruined lavabo at Mellifont Abbey

Slane Castle in grounds landscaped by Capability Brown

Old Mellifont Abbey ⑫

Road map D3. Tullallen, Cullen, Co Louth. **Tel** 041 982 6459. to Drogheda. to Drogheda or Slane. May–Sep: 10am–5pm daily (last adm: 45 mins before closing).

On the banks of the River Mattock, 10 km (6 miles) west of Drogheda, lies the first Cistercian monastery to have been built in Ireland. Mellifont was founded in 1142 on the orders of St Malachy, the Archbishop of Armagh. He was greatly influenced by St Bernard who, based at his monastery at Clairvaux in France, was behind the success of the Cistercian Order in Europe. The archbishop introduced not only Cistercian rigour to Mellifont, but also the formal style of monastic architecture used on the continent. His new monastery became a model for other Cistercian centres built in Ireland, retaining its supremacy over them until 1539, when the abbey was closed and turned into a fortified house. William of Orange used Mellifont as his headquarters during

Glazed medieval tiles at Mellifont Abbey

the Battle of the Boyne in 1690. The abbey is now a ruin, but it is still possible to appreciate the scale and ground plan of the original complex. Little survives of the abbey church, but to the south of it, enclosed by what remains of the Romanesque cloister, is the most interesting building at Mellifont: a unique 13th-century octagonal lavabo where monks washed their hands in a fountain before meals. Four of the building's eight sides survive, each with a Romanesque arch. To the east of the cloister stands the 14th-century chapter house, with its impressive vaulted ceiling and medieval tiled floor.

Slane ⑬

Road map D3. Co Meath. 950.

Slane is an attractive estate village, centred on a quartet of Georgian houses. The Boyne flows through it and skirts **Slane Castle Demesne**, set in glorious grounds laid out in the 18th century by Capability Brown. The castle was damaged by fire in 1991 but reopened in 2001.

Just to the north rises the **Hill of Slane** where, in 433, St Patrick is said to have lit a Paschal (Easter) fire as a challenge to the pagan High King of Tara (see p248). The event symbolised the triumph of Christianity over paganism.

Newgrange

Tri-spiral carving on stone in chamber

The origins of Newgrange, one of the most important passage graves in Europe, are steeped in mystery. According to Celtic lore, the legendary kings of Tara *(see p248)* were buried here, but Newgrange predates them. Built in around 3200 BC, the grave was left untouched by all invaders until it was rediscovered in 1699. When it was excavated in the 1960s, archaeologists discovered that on the winter solstice (21 December), rays of sun enter the tomb and light up the burial chamber – making it the world's oldest solar observatory. All visitors to Newgrange and Knowth *(see pp244–5)* are admitted through the visitors' centre from where tours of the historic site are taken. Long queues are expected in summer and access is not always guaranteed.

Basin Stone
The chiselled stones in each recess would have contained funerary offerings and cremated human remains.

The chamber has three recesses or side chambers: the north recess is the one struck by sunlight on the winter solstice.

Chamber Ceiling
The burial chamber's intricate corbelled ceiling, which reaches a height of 6 m (20 ft) above the floor, has survived intact. The overlapping slabs form a conical hollow, topped by a single capstone.

CONSTRUCTION OF NEWGRANGE

The tomb at Newgrange was designed by people with clearly exceptional artistic and engineering skills, who had use of neither the wheel nor metal tools. About 200,000 tonnes of loose stones were transported to build the mound, or cairn, which protects the passage grave. Larger slabs were used to make the circle around the cairn (12 out of a probable 35 stones have survived), the kerb and the tomb itself. Many of the kerbstones and the slabs lining the passage, the chamber and its recesses are decorated with zigzags, spirals and other geometric motifs. The grave's corbelled ceiling consists of smaller, unadorned slabs and has proved completely water-proof for the last 5,000 years.

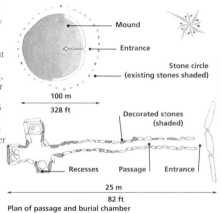

Mound

Entrance

Stone circle
(existing stones shaded)

100 m
328 ft

Decorated stones
(shaded)

Recesses   Passage   Entrance

25 m
82 ft
Plan of passage and burial chamber

VISITORS' CHECKLIST

Road map D3. 8km (5 miles) E
of Slane, Co Meath. **Tel** 041 988
0300. 🚉 🚌 Drogheda. 🚌 to
Drogheda & Drogheda to Brú na
Boinne visitors' centre. ⬜ May–
Sep: 9am–5.30pm (Jun–mid-Sep:
7pm) daily; Oct–mid-Mar: 9:30am–
5:30pm (Nov–Jan: 9am–5pm)
daily; last tour. 1 hr 45 mins before
closing. 🔴 24–27 Dec. 🚫 📷
inside tomb. ⬛ Brú na Boinne
visitors' centre only. 🎫 🍴 🛍

Restoration of Newgrange

Located on a low ridge north of the Boyne, Newgrange took more than 70 years to build. Between 1962 and 1975 the passage grave and mound were restored as closely as possible to their original state.

The standing stones in the passage are slabs of slate which would have been collected locally.

Passage
At dawn on 21 December, a beam of sunlight shines through the roof box (a feature unique to Newgrange), travels along the 19-m (62-ft) passage and hits the central recess in the burial chamber.

The retaining wall around the front of the cairn was rebuilt using the white quartz and granite stones found scattered around the site during excavations.

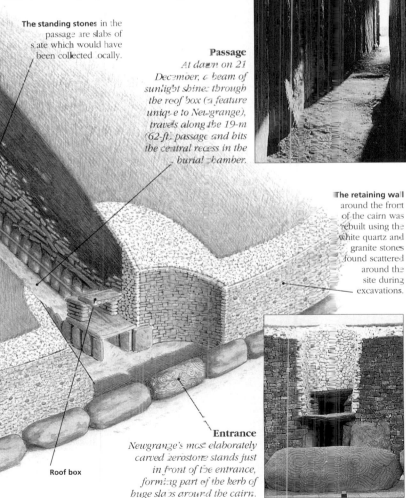

Roof box

Entrance
Newgrange's most elaborately carved kerbstone stands just in front of the entrance, forming part of the kerb of huge slabs around the cairn.

Trim Castle set in water meadows beside the River Boyne

Hill of Tara ⓮

Road map D3. Nr Killmessan Village, Co Meath. *Tel* 046 902 5903. to Navan. mid-May–mid-Sep:10am–6pm daily (last adm 1hr before closing). *Interpretative Centre.* www.heritageireland.ie

A site of mythical importance, Tara was the political and spiritual centre of Celtic Ireland and the seat of the High Kings until the 11th century. The spread of Christianity, which eroded the importance of Tara, is marked by a statue of St Patrick. The symbolism of the site was not lost on Daniel O'Connell (*see p42*), who chose Tara for a rally in 1843, attended by over one million people.

Tours from the Interpretative Centre take in a Stone Age passage grave and Iron Age hill forts, which, to the untutored eye, look like mere hollows and grassy mounds. Clearest is the Royal Enclosure, an oval fort, in the centre of which is Cormac's House containing the "stone of destiny" (*Liath Fáil*), fertility symbol and inauguration stone of the High Kings. Most moving, however, is the poignant atmosphere and views over the Boyne Valley.

Trim ⓯

Road map D3. Co Meath. 6,500. Castle St (046 943 7227). *Fri.* www.meathtourism.ie

Trim is one of the most pleasing Midlands market towns. A Norman stronghold on the River Boyne, it marked a boundary of the Pale

(*see p132*). The **Trim Visitor Centre** houses a multimedia exhibition on the town's history. It is also the starting point for a heritage trail, which takes in eight sites, including the town's two castles and two cathedrals.

The dramatic **Trim Castle** was founded in the 12th century by Hugh de Lacy, a Norman knight, and is one of the largest medieval castles in Europe. It makes a spectacular backdrop for films and was used in Mel Gibson's film *Braveheart* in 1995.

Over the river is **Talbot Castle**, an Augustinian abbey converted to a manor house in the 15th century. Just north of the abbey is **St Patrick's Cathedral**, which incorporates part of a medieval church with a 15th-century tower and sections of the original chancel.

From here the trail leads to the Saints Peter and Paul Cathedral further east.

A lovely walk leads from the castle along the River Boyne to Newtown Abbey.

Trim Castle
Tel 046 943 8619. Feb–Easter: 9:30am–5:30pm weekends; Easter–Oct: 10am–6pm daily; Oct: 9:30am–5:30pm daily; Nov–Jan: 9am–5pm weekends. obligatory. www.heritageireland.ie

Mullingar ⓰

Road map C3. Co Westmeath. 25,000. *Market Square* (044 934 8650). www.discover ireland.ie

The county town of Westmeath is a prosperous but unremarkable market town encircled by the Royal Canal

Aerial view of Iron Age forts on the Hill of Tara

(see p101), which with its 46 locks links Dublin with the River Shannon. The cost of building the canal bankrupted its investors and it was never profitable. Mullingar's main appeal is as a base to explore the surrounding area, but pubs such as Canton Casey's and Con's are a pleasant interlude.

Environs

The Dublin to Mullingar stretch of the Royal Canal has attractive towpaths for walkers, and fishing.

Just off the Kilbeggan road from Mullingar stands **Belvedere House**, a romantic Palladian villa overlooking Lough Ennel. The house, built in 1740 by Richard Castle, is decorated with Rococo plasterwork and set in beautiful grounds.

Shortly after the house was built the first Earl of Belvedere accused his wife of having an affair with his brother, and imprisoned her for 31 years in a nearby house. In 1760, the Earl built a Gothic folly – the Jealous Wall – to block the view of his second brother's more opulent mansion across the way. The Jealous Wall remains as does an octagonal gazebo and follies.

Charming terraces descend to the lake. On the other side of the house is a picturesque walled garden, enclosed by an arboretum and parkland.

🏛 Belvedere House
6.5 km (4 miles) S of Mullingar
Tel 044 934 9060. ☐ May–Aug: 9:30am–5:30pm (house), 9:30am–8pm (garden) daily; Mar–Apr & Sep–Oct 9:30am–6pm (house), 9:30am–7pm (garden) daily; Nov–Feb: 10am–4.30pm daily (house & garden). 🎥 ☐ 🚻 centre. **www**.belvedere-house.ie

The Jealous Wall at Belvedere House, near Mullingar

Athlone Castle below the towers of the church of St Peter and St Paul

Kilbeggan ⑰

Road map C4. Co Westmeath. 🏠 1,300. 🚌

Situated between Mullingar and Tullamore, this pleasant village has a small harbour on the Grand Canal. However the main point of interest is **Locke's Distillery**. Founded in 1757, it claims to be the oldest licensed pot still distillery in the world. Unable to compete with Scotch whiskey manufacturers, the company went bankrupt in 1954, but the aroma hung in the warehouses for years and was known as "the angel's share". The distillery reopened as a museum in 1987. The building is authentic, a solid structure complete with water wheel and inside steam engine. A tour traces the process of Irish whiskey-making, from the mash tuns to the vast fermentation vats and creation of wash (rough beer) to the distillation and maturation stages. At the tasting stage workers would sample the whiskey in the can pit room. Visitors can still taste whiskeys in the bar. Production restarted in 2007, with the results to go on sale in 2014.

Miniature whiskey bottles at Locke's Distillery in Kilbeggan

🏛 Locke's Distillery
Main Street. **Tel** 057 933 2134. ☐ daily. 🎥 🚻 🚻 ♿ 🛒 **www** lockesdistillerymuseum.ie

Athlone ⑱

Road map C3. Co Westmeath. 🏠 16,000. 🚌 🚍 🚉 Market Square (090 649 4630). 🛒 Sat.

The town owes its historical importance to its position by a natural ford on the River Shannon. **Athlone Castle** is a much-altered 13th-century fortress, which was badly damaged in the Jacobite Wars (see pp38–9). It lies in the shadow of the 19th-century church of St Peter and St Paul. The neighbouring streets offer several good pubs. Across the river from the castle, boats depart for Clonmacnoise (see pp256–51) or Lough Ree.

⚓ Athlone Castle
Visitors' Centre **Tel** 090 649 2912. ☐ May–Sep: daily; Oct–Apr: on request. 🎥 ♿ limited.

Environs

The Lough Ree Trail starts 8 km (5 miles) northeast of Athlone, at Glasson, and is a popular cycling tour that runs around the shores and into County Longford.

Clonmacnoise ⑲

This medieval monastery, in a remote spot by the River Shannon, was founded by St Ciarán in 545–548. Clonmacnoise lay at a crossroads of medieval routes, linking all parts of Ireland. Known for its scholarship and piety, it thrived from the 7th to the 12th century. Many kings of Tara and of Connaught were buried here.

Detail on a grave slab

Plundered by the Vikings and Anglo-Normans, it fell to the English in 1552. Today, a group of stone churches (temples), a cathedral, two round towers and three High Crosses remain.

Last Circuit of Pilgrims at Clonmacnoise
This painting (1838), by George Petrie, shows pilgrims walking the traditional route three times around the site. Pilgrims still do this every year on 9 September, St Ciarán's Day.

The Pope's Shelter was where John Paul II conducted Mass during his visit in 1979.

Cross of the Scriptures
This copy of the original 9th-century cross (now in the museum) is decorated with biblical scenes, but the identity of most of the figures is uncertain.

VISITING CLONMACNOISE

The Visitors' Centre is housed in three buildings modelled on beehive huts *(see p21)*. The museum section contains early grave slabs and the three remaining High Crosses, replicas of which now stand in their original locations. The Nuns' Church, northeast of the main site, has a Romanesque doorway and chancel arch.

KEY

1 South Cross	**7** Cathedral
2 Temple Dowling	**8** North Cross
3 Temple Hurpan	**9** Cross of the Scriptures
4 Temple Melaghlin	**10** Round Tower
5 Temple Ciarán	**11** Temple Connor
6 Temple Kelly	**12** Temple Finghin

0 metres   50
0 yards   50

Pilgrim path to Nuns' Church

Entrance

Pope's Shelter

To Visitors' Centre

VISITORS' CHECKLIST

Road map C4. 7 km (4 miles) N of Shannonbridge, Co Offaly. **Tel** 090 967 4195. 🚊 🚌 to Athlone, then minibus (090 647 4839/ 087 240 7706). 🚌 from Athlone. ◯ daily. Groups pre-book. ● 25 Dec. 📷 📹 in summer. 🚻 🛒 www.heritageireland.ie

Whispering Door

Above the cathedral's 15th-century north doorway are carvings of saints Francis, Patrick and Dominic. The acoustics of the doorway are such that even a whisper is carried inside the building.

The Tullamore Dew Heritage Centre, Co Offaly

Tullamore Dew Heritage Centre ㉖

Road map C4. Bury Quay, Tullamore, Co Offaly – access from Dublin–Galway N6 & Dublin–Cork N7 roads. **Tel** 057 932 5015. ◯ 9am–5pm Mon–Sat (to 6pm May–Sep) noon–5pm Sun. 📷 📹 🍴 🚻 🛒 🚻 www.tullamore-dew.org

The town of Tullamore and its most famous export, Tullamore Dew Whiskey, are intrinsically linked. It makes sense, therefore, that the Tullamore Dew Heritage Centre should attempt to explore not only the history of the Tullamore Dew brand but also that of the town itself.

The centre is housed in the original Tullamore Dew distillery dating back to 1897. Visitors can wander through the fascinating recreated working stations of the distillery, such as the malting, bottling, corking and co-operage areas as well as the warehouse where the old oak barrels filled with whiskey were left to mature.

The history of Tullamore town itself starts 9,000 years ago with the formation of the bog. The centre explains raised bogs and the different uses of peat. Here, too, visitors can chain themselves to stocks a public punishment of the day, fill a whiskey bottle by hand and see and touch various artifacts for themselves.

The tour ends in the on-site bar with a complimentary glass of whiskey or Irish Mist Liqueur both of which are on sale in the gift shop.

The **Round Tower** *(see p18)* is over 19 m (62 ft) high with its doorway above ground level.

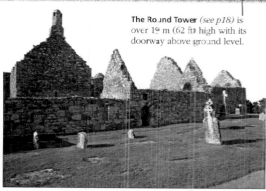

Temples Dowling, Hurpan and Melaghlin

Built as a family crypt, Temple Hurpan was a 17th-century addition to the early Romanesque Temple Dowling. The 13th-century Temple Melaghlin has two fine round-headed windows.

The Raised Bogs of the Midlands

Peatland or bog, which covers about 15 per cent of the Irish landscape, exists in two principal forms. Most extensive is the thin blanket bog found chiefly in the west, while the dome-shaped raised bogs are more characteristic of the Midlands – notably in an area known as the Bog of Allen.

Four-spotted chaser dragonfly

Although Irish boglands are some of the largest in Europe, the use of peat for fuel and fertilizer has greatly reduced their extent, threatening not only the shape of the Irish landscape but also the survival of a unique habitat and the unusual plants and insects it supports.

Unspoiled expanse of the Bog of Allen

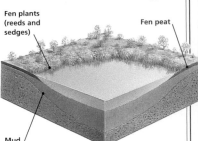

Peat cutters *still gather turf (as peat is known locally) by hand in parts of Ireland. It is then set in stacks to dry. Peat makes a good fuel, because it is rich in partially decayed vegetation, laid down over thousands of years.*

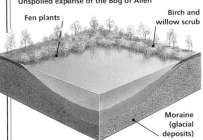

Fen plants

Birch and willow scrub

Moraine (glacial deposits)

8000 BC: *Shallow meltwater lakes that formed after the Ice Age gradually filled with mud. Reeds, sedges and other fen plants began to dominate in the marshy conditions which resulted.*

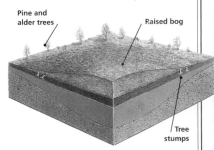

Fen plants (reeds and sedges)

Fen peat

Mud

6000 BC: *As the fen vegetation died, it sank to the lake bed but did not decompose fully in the waterlogged conditions, forming a layer of peat. This slowly built up and also spread outwards.*

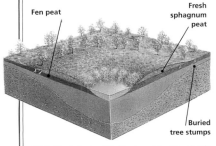

Fen peat

Fresh sphagnum peat

Buried tree stumps

3000 BC: *As the peat built up and the lake slowly disappeared, plant life in the developing bog had to rely almost exclusively on rainwater, which is acid. Fen plants could not survive in these acidic conditions and gave way to bog mosses, mainly species of sphagnum. As these mosses died, they formed a layer of sphagnum peat on the surface of the bog which, over the centuries, attained a distinctive domed shape.*

Pine and alder trees

Raised bog

Tree stumps

Present day: *Few raised bogs are actively growing today. Those that remain contain a fascinating historical record of the landscape. The survival of ancient tree stumps shows how well plants are preserved in peat.*

Sphagnum moss

Birr ㉑

Road map 4C. Co Offaly. 🚐 4,100.
🚌 ℹ May–Sep: Rosse Row (05791 20110).

Birr, a gentrified estate town, grew up in the shadow of the castle where the Earls of Rosse have resided for almost four centuries. It is famous for its authentic Georgian layout, with houses displaying original fanlights, door panelling and iron railings. Two particularly elegant streets are Oxmantown Mall, designed by the 2nd Earl of Rosse, and John's Mall. Emmet Square may have sold its Georgian soul to commerce, but Dooley's Hotel is still a fine example of an old coaching inn. Foster's bar, in nearby Connaught Street, is one of many traditional shopfronts to have been restored in Birr.

🏛 Birr Castle Demesne
Rosse Row. **Tel** 05791 20336.
Gardens ⬜ mid-Mar–Oct: 9am–6pm; Nov–mid-Mar: 10am–4pm.
🎟 ♿ 🅿 ℹ www.birrcastle.com

Birr Castle was founded in 1620 by the Parsons, later Earls of Rosse, and is still the family seat. They are most noted for their contribution to astronomy – a telescope, built by the 3rd Earl in 1845, was the largest in the world at the time. The 17-m (56-ft) wooden tube, supported by two walls, can be seen in the grounds, fully restored. The Historic Science Centre traces the family's work.

The castle is closed to the public, but the glory of Birr lies in its grounds, which are open. First landscaped in the 18th century, these are famous for their 9-m (30-ft),

An alcove in the front hall of Emo Court with the trompe-l'oeil ceiling

200-year-old box hedges and for the exotic trees and shrubs from foreign expeditions sponsored by the 6th Earl. The magnolias and maples are particularly striking. The gardens overlook the meeting of two rivers.

Slieve Bloom Mountains ㉒

Road map D4. Co Offaly and Co Laois.
🚌 to Mountmellick. ℹ May–Sep: Rosse Row, Birr (05791 20110).

This low range of mountains rises unexpectedly from the bogs and plains of Offaly and Laois, providing a welcome change in the predominantly flat Midlands. You can walk along the **Slieve Bloom Way**, a 30-km (19-mile) circular trail through an unspoiled area of open vistas, deep wooded glens and mountain streams. There are other marked paths too. Good starting points are **Cadamstown**, with an attractive old mill, and the pretty village of **Kinnitty** – both in the northern foothills.

Emo Court ㉓

Road map D4. 13 km (8 miles) NE of Portlaoise, Co Laois. **Tel** 05786 26573.
🚌 to Monasterevin or Portlaoise.
House ⬜ Easter–Sep: 10am–6pm daily (last adm: ½ hr before closing).
Gardens ⬜ daily. 🎟 ♿ limited.

Emo Court, commissioned by the Earl of Portarlington in 1790, represents the only foray into domestic architecture by James Gandon, designer of the Custom House in Dublin (*see p88*). The monumental Neo-Classical mansion has a splendid façade featuring an Ionic portico. Inside are a magnificent gilded rotunda and fine stuccowork ceilings.

Emo Court became the property of the Office of Public Works in 1994 but the previous owner is still resident on the grounds. These are adorned with fine statuary and include a lakeside walk.

Rock of Dunamase ㉔

Road map D4. 5 km (3 miles) E of Portlaoise, Co Laois. 🚌 to Portlaoise.

The Rock of Dunamase, which looms dramatically above the plains east of Portlaoise, has long been a military site. Originally owned by an Iron Age ring fort, the 13th-century castle which succeeded it is now more prominent – though it was virtually destroyed by Cromwellian forces in 1651. You can reach the battered keep by climbing up banks and ditches through two gateways and a fortified courtyard.

Rock of Dunamase viewed from Stradbally to the east

For hotels and restaurants in this region see pp314–16 and pp341–2

NORTHERN IRELAND

LONDONDERRY · ANTRIM · TYRONE
FERMANAGH · ARMAGH · DOWN

*N*orthern Ireland has sights from every era of Ireland's history as well as magnificently varied coastal and lakeland scenery. During the years of the "Troubles" it received fewer visitors than the Republic, however, now that there is a movement towards peace it is attracting the attention it deserves.

The province of Northern Ireland was created after partition of the island in 1921. Its six counties (plus Donegal, Monaghan and Cavan) were part of Ulster, one of Ireland's four traditional kingdoms. It was most probably in Ulster that Christianity first ousted the old Celtic pagan beliefs. In 432 St Patrick landed at Saul in County Down, later founding a church at Armagh, which is still the spiritual capital of Ireland.

The dominant political force in early Christian times was the Uí Néill clan. Their descendants, the O'Neills, put up fierce resistance to English conquest in the late 16th century. Hugh O'Neil, Earl of Tyrone, had some notable successes against the armies of Elizabeth I, but was defeated and in 1607 fled to Europe with other Irish lords from Ulster, in what became known as the "Flight of the Earls". Vacant estates were granted to individuals and companies, who planted them with English and Scottish Protestants (see p39). Many Plantation towns, such as Londonderry, preserve their 17th-century layout around a central square or "diamond". The arrival of new settlers meant that Irish Catholics were increasingly marginalized, thereby sowing the seeds of 400 years of conflict.

In the relative tranquillity of the 18th century, the Anglo-Irish nobility built stately homes, such as Mount Stewart House on the Ards Peninsula and Castle Coole near Enniskillen. Ulster also enjoyed prosperity in the 19th century through its linen, rope-making and ship-building industries.

Though densely populated and industrialized around Belfast, away from the capital the region is primarily agricultural. It also has areas of outstanding natural beauty, notably the rugged Antrim coastline around the Giant's Causeway, the Mountains of Mourne in County Down and the Fermanagh lakelands in the southwest.

Belfast's City Hall (1906), symbol of the city's civic pride

◁ Carrick-a-rede Rope Bridge, an unusual tourist attraction on the Causeway Coast

Exploring Northern Ireland

The starting point for most visitors to the province is its capital city, Belfast, with its grand Victorian buildings, good pubs and the excellent Ulster Museum. However, Northern Ireland's greatest attractions lie along its coast. These range from the extraordinary volcanic landscape of the Giant's Causeway to Carrickfergus, Ireland's best preserved Norman castle. There are also Victorian resorts, like Portstewart, tiny fishing villages and unspoiled sandy beaches, such as Benone Strand. Ramblers are drawn to the Mountains of Mourne, while anglers and boating enthusiasts can enjoy the Fermanagh lakelands of Lower Lough Erne.

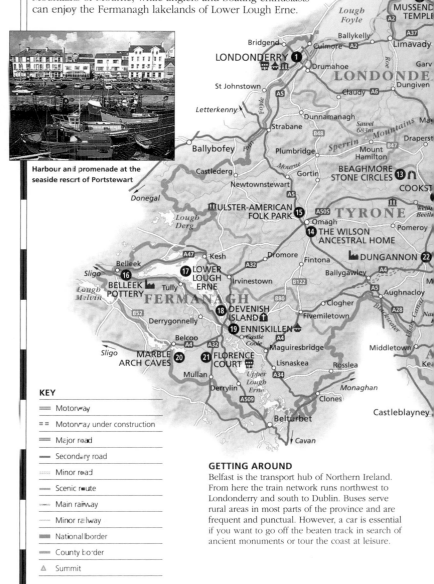

Harbour and promenade at the seaside resort of Portstewart

KEY

▬▬	Motorway
▪▪	Motorway under construction
▬	Major road
—	Secondary road
⋯⋯	Minor road
▬	Scenic route
▬▪	Main railway
—	Minor railway
▬	National border
▬	County border
△	Summit

Magilligan Pt   **PORTSTEW**
BENONE STRAND ②
Lough Foyle
MUSSEND ③
TEMPLE
A2
Ballykelly
A37
Bridgend   Culmore   A2   Limavady
LONDONDERRY ①
🏛 ⛪ 🏛
Drumahoe   Garv
LONDONDE
St Johnstown   A5   Claudy A6   Dungiven
Letterkenny
Dunnamanagh
Strabane   B48   Sperrin Mountains Ma
Ballybofey   Plumbridge   Mount Hamilton   Drapers
Castlederg   Gortin   **BEAGHMORE STONE CIRCLES** ⑬
Newtownstewart   A5   **COOKS**
Donegal
Lough Derg
🏛 **ULSTER-AMERICAN FOLK PARK** ⑮   A505   **TYRONE**   🏛 Welb Beetl
Omagh   Pomeroy
⑭ **THE WILSON ANCESTRAL HOME**
A47   Kesh   Dromore   Fintona   🏔 **DUNGANNON** ㉒
Belleek   A32   Ballygawley   A4
⑰ **LOWER LOUGH ERNE**   Irvinestown   B122   A5   Aughnacloy
Sligo   **BELLEEK POTTERY** ⑯   Tully   B80   Clogher   A28
Lough Melvin   **FERMANAGH**
Derrygonnelly   ⑱ **DEVENISH ISLAND**   Fivemiletown
⑲ **ENNISKILLEN**
Belcoo   Castle Coole
Sligo   **MARBLE ARCH CAVES** ⑳   ㉑ **FLORENCE COURT**   Maguiresbridge   Middletown
Mullan   Lisnaskea   Rosslea
Derrylin   A34
A509   Upper Lough Erne   Monaghan
Belturbet   Clones   Castleblayney
Cavan

GETTING AROUND

Belfast is the transport hub of Northern Ireland. From here the train network runs northwest to Londonderry and south to Dublin. Buses serve rural areas in most parts of the province and are frequent and punctual. However, a car is essential if you want to go off the beaten track in search of ancient monuments or tour the coast at leisure.

SIGHTS AT A GLANCE

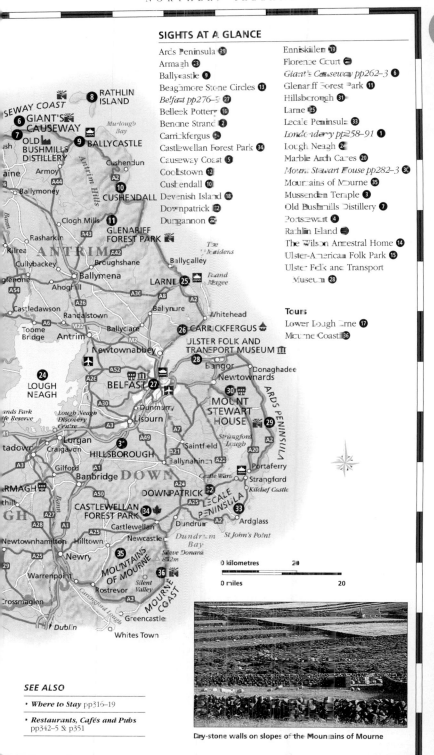

SEE ALSO

• *Where to Stay* pp316–19

• *Restaurants, Cafés and Pubs*
 pp342–5 & p351

Dry-stone walls on slopes of the Mountains of Mourne

Londonderry ❶

Carving on Shipquay Gate

St Columba founded a monastery here beside the River Foyle in 546. He called the place Doire or "oak grove", later anglicized as Derry. In 1613, the city was selected as a major Plantation project *(see pp38–9)*, organized by London livery companies. As a result, it acquired the prefix London, though most people still call it Derry. Although Derry suffered during the "Troubles", there have been a number of admirable heritage projects undertaken in the city.

★ **Tower Museum**
The excellent displays on local history in this museum include one on the mapping of the area during the reign of Elizabeth I.

Shipquay Gate

The Craft Village

First Presbyterian Church

Butcher's Gate

The Diamond
The war memorial in the Diamond or main square was erected in 1927. It was originally made for the city of Sheffield in England

MAGAZINE ST.

SHIPQUAY STREET

FERRYQUAY STREET

LINENHALL STR.

BISHOP STREET WITHIN

PUMP STREET

ARTILLERY STREET

LONDON

Court House

Bishop's Gate

The Playhouse

New Gate

★ **St Columb's Cathedral**
The nave's wooden ceiling dates from 1862. The corbels are carved with the heads of former bishops and deans.

KEY

🅿 Parking

— Suggested route

VISITORS' CHECKLIST

Road map C1. Co Londonderry.
107,000. ✈ 1 km (7 miles),
E. 🚆 Waterside, Duke St (028
7134 2228). 🚌 Foyle St (028
7125 2261). ℹ 44 Foyle St (028
7126 7284). 🎭 Walled City
Cultural Trail (Jul–Aug); Hallowe'en Festival (Oct). 🛍 Sat.

★ **The Guildhall**
This stained-glass window shows St Columba. Others feature incidents from the siege of Derry, including the Apprentice Boys shutting the city gates in 1688.

Ferryquay
Gate

To Craigavon Bridge
and River Foyle

0 metres   100

0 yards   100

STAR SIGHTS

★ The Guildhall

★ St Columb's Cathedral

★ Tower Museum

🔒 St Columb's Cathedral

London St. **Tel** 028 7125 7313.
☐ Mon–Sat. 📷 on request. ♿
www.stcolumbscathedral.org
Built between 1628 and 1633,
in "Planters' Gothic" style,
St Columb's was the
first cathedral to be
founded in the
British Isles after
the Reformation.
The interior was
extensively restored
in the 19th century.
A small museum in
the Chapter House
has relics from the
siege of 1689 *(see
pp38–9)*, including the
17th-century locks and
keys of the city. In the
vestibule is a hollow mortar
cannonball that was fired into
the city by James II's army. It
carried terms for capitulation,
but the reply of the Protestants within the walls was a
defiant "No surrender".

**Lock of city gate in
St Columb's Cathedral**

🏛 Tower Museum

Union Hall Place. **Tel** 028 7137
2411. ☐ 10am–4:30pm Tue–Sat.
📷 ♿ 🎧
Housed in O'Doherty Tower
(a replica of the original 16th-century building on this site),
the museum traces the history
of the city from its foundation
to the "Troubles" using
multimedia displays. Upstairs,
an exhibition about the 1688
Spanish Armada includes
artifacts from ships wrecked
in nearby Kinnagoe Bay.

⚓ The City Walls of Derry

Access from Magazine Street.
Derry is the only remaining
completely walled city in
Ireland and its fortifications
are among the best preserved
in Europe. The city walls rise
to a height of 8 m (26 ft) and

in places are 9 m (30 ft) wide.
Completed in 1618 to defend
the new merchant city from
Gaelic chieftains in Donegal,
the walls have never been
breached, not even during the
siege of 1689, when
7,000 out of a population of 20,000
perished from
disease or starvation.
Restoration work
means that it is
possible to walk right
around the walls. Just
outside the old
fortifications,
beyond Butcher's
Gate is the Bogside, a Catholic
area with famous murals that
depict recent events in
Northern Ireland's history.

🏛 The Guildhall

Guildhall Square. **Tel** 028 7137 7335.
☐ 9am–5pm Mon–Fri. ♿
Standing between the walled
city and the River Foyle, this
Neo-Gothic building was
constructed in 1890, but a fire
in 1908 and a bomb in 1972
both necessitated substantial
repairs. Stained-glass windows
– copies of the originals –
recount the history of Derry.
To the rear is Derry Quay,
from where Irish emigrants
sailed to America in the 18th
and 19th centuries.

Environs

The Peace Bridge, which
opened in the summer of
2011, provides foot and
cycle access across the River
Foyle. The bridge links the
city walls of Derry and the
Ebrington Centre, which is
being developed into an arts
and culture centre and
includes a 14,000-capacity
outdoor performance plaza
and a cinema.

The old walled city viewed across the River Foyle

Terraced houses behind the promenade at Portrush

Benone Strand ❷

Road map. D1 Co Londonderry.
ℹ️ *Benone Tourist Complex, 53
Benone Ave, Magilligan (028
7775 0555).* ⭕ *daily.*

The wide, golden sands of
Ireland's longest beach, also
known as Magilligan Strand,
sweep along the Londonderry
coastline for more than 10 km
(6 miles). The magnificent
beach has been granted EU
Blue Flag status for its
cleanliness. At the western
extremity of the beach is
Magilligan Point where a
Martello tower, built during
the Napoleonic wars, stands
guard over the entrance to
Lough Foyle. To get to the
point, renowned for its rare
shellfish and sea birds, you
have to drive past a military
training ground. There are
great views across to Donegal
from the Strand.

Mussenden Temple ❸

Road map. D1 Co Londonderry.
Tel *028 708 48728.* **Grounds**
⭕ *dawn–dusk daily (last adm 30
mins before closing).* **Temple**
⭕ *Mar–Oct: 10am–5pm daily.*
🏛️ *ltd.* www.nationaltrust.org.uk

The oddest sight along the
Londonderry coast is this
small, domed rotunda perched
precariously on a windswept
headland outside the family
resort of Castlerock. The
temple was built in 1785
by Frederick Augustus Hervey,
the eccentric Earl of Bristol
and Protestant Bishop of
Derry, as a memorial to his
cousin Mrs Frideswide
Mussenden. The design was
based on the Temple of Vesta
at Tivoli outside Rome.

The walls, made of basalt
faced with sandstone, open
out at the four points of the
compass to three windows
and an entrance. Originally
designed for use as a library
(or, as some stories go, an
elaborate boudoir for the
bishop's mistress), the structure is now maintained by the
National Trust and remains in
excellent condition.

The bishop allowed the local
priest to say Mass for his
Roman Catholic tenants in the
basement. The bishop's
former residence, the nearby
Downhill Castle, was gutted
by fire and is now little more
than an impressive shell.

The surrounding area offers
some good glen and cliff walks
and there are some magnificent
views of the Londonderry and
Antrim coastline. Below the
temple is Downhill Strand,
where the bishop
sponsored
horseback
races bet-
ween his
clergy.

Portstewart ❹

Road map D1. Co Londonderry.
👥 *8,000.* 🚆 *to Coleraine or Portrush.*
🚌 ℹ️ *Jul–Aug: Portstewart (028
7083 6396); Sep–Jun.: Coleraine (028
7034 4723).* www.northcoastni.com

A popular holiday destination
for Victorian middle-class
families, Portstewart is still a
family favourite today. Its
long, crescent-shaped seafront
promenade is sheltered by
rocky headlands. Just west of
town, and accessible by road
or by a cliffside walk, stretches
Portstewart Strand, a magnificent, long, sandy beach,
protected by the National Trust.

On Ramore Head, just to the
east, lies **Portrush**, a brasher
resort with an abundance of
souvenir shops and amusement
arcades. The East Strand is
backed by sand dunes and runs
parallel with the world-class
Royal Portrush Golf Links.
You can stroll along the beach
to White Rocks – limestone
cliffs carved by the wind and
waves into caves and arches.

To the south is **Coleraine**.
Every May, the North West 200
(see p28), the world's fastest
motorcycle road race, is run
between Portstewart, Coleraine
and Portrush, in front of
100,000
people.

Mussenden Temple set on a cliff-top on the Londonderry coast

Causeway Coast ❺

Road map D1. Co Antrim. 🛈 Giant's Causeway (028 2073 1855) **Carrick-a-rede Rope Bridge** Tel 028 2076 9839. ⭕ end Feb–Nov: daily, weather permitting. 🖼️ 🖵 🔣 &
www.nationaltrust.org.uk

The renown of the **Giant's Causeway** (see pp262–3), Northern Ireland's only World Heritage Site, overshadows the other attractions of this stretch of North Antrim coast. When visiting the Causeway, it is well worth investigating the sandy bays, craggy headlands and dramatic ruins that punctuate the rest of this inspirational coastline.

Approaching the Causeway from the west, you pass the eerie ruins of **Dunluce Castle** perched vulnerably on a steep crag. Dating back to the 13th century, it was the main fortress of the MacDonnells, chiefs of Antrim. Although the roof has gone, it is still well preserved, with its twin towers, gateway and some original cobbling intact.

Dunseverick Castle can be reached by road or a lengthy hike from the Causeway. It is a much earlier fortification than

The roofless ruins of 13th-century Dunluce Castle

Dunluce and only one massive wall remains. Once the capital of the kingdom of Dalriada, it was linked to Tara (see p248) by a great road and was the departure point for 5th-century Irish raids on Scotland.

Just past the attractive, sandy **White Park Bay,** a tight switch-back road leads down to the picturesque harbour of **Ballin-toy,** reminiscent – on a good day – of an Aegean fishing village. **Sheep Island,** a rocky outcrop just offshore, is a cormorant colony. Boat trips run past it in the summer.

Just east of Ballintoy is one of the most unusual and scary tourist attractions in Ireland the **Carrick-a-rede Rope Bridge.** The bridge hangs 25 m (80 ft) above the sea and wobbles and twists as soon as you stand on it. Made of planks strung between wires, it provides access to the salmon fishery on

the tiny island across the 20-m (65-ft) chasm. There are strong handrails and safety nets, but it's definitely not for those with vertigo. Further east along the coast ie **Kinbane Castle,** a 16th-century ruin with spectacular views.

🏰 **Dunluce Castle**
Tel 028 2073 1938. ⭕ daily. 🖼️ 📷 ▪ summer and by appt.
www.ni-environment.gov.uk

Fishing boats moored in the shelter of Ballintoy Harbour

Carrick-a-rede Rope Bridge

THE NORTH ANTRIM COASTLINE

KEY

═ Minor road	🅿 Parking
▬ Major road	🛈 Tourist information

Giant's Causeway · B146 · Dunseverick Castle · White Park Bay · Sheep Island · Carrick-a-rede Rope Bridge · Ballintoy · Kinbane Castle · B15 · Ballycastle · Dunluce Castle · Portballintrae · Bushmills · A2 · Portrush · A2 · B62 · B17 · B17 · B66 · B65 · B147 · B17 · A2 · B67 · Portstewart

0 kilometres 3
0 miles

Giant's Causeway 6

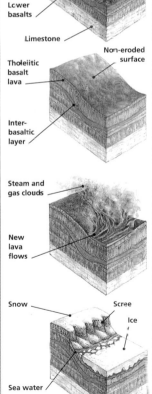

The sheer strangeness of this place and the bizarre regularity of its basalt columns have made the Giant's Causeway the subject of numerous legends. The most popular tells how the giant, Finn MacCool (see pp26–7), laid the causeway to provide a path across the sea to Scotland to engage in battle with a rival Scottish giant by the name of Benandonner. The Giant's Causeway

Chimney stacks

attracts many tourists, who are taken by the busload from the visitors' centre down to the shore. Nothing, however, can destroy the magic of this place, with its looming grey cliffs and shrieking gulls; paths along the coast allow you to escape the crowds.

Aird's Snout
This nose-shaped promontory juts out from the 120-m (395-ft) basalt cliffs that soar above the Giant's Causeway.

THE FORMATION OF THE CAUSEWAY

Hot lava

Wooded landscape

Valley

Lower basalts

Limestone

61 million years ago:
In a series of massive volcanic eruptions molten lava poured from narrow fissures in the ground, filling in the valleys and burning the vegetation that grew there.

Tholeiitic basalt lava

Non-eroded surface

Inter-basaltic layer

60 million years ago:
This layer of tholeiitic basalt lava cooled rapidly. In the process it shrank and cracked evenly into polygonal-shaped blocks, forming columnar jointing beneath the surface.

Steam and gas clouds

New lava flows

58 million years ago:
New volcanic eruptions produced further lava flows. These had a slightly different chemical composition from earlier flows and, once cool, did not form such well defined columns.

Snow

Scree

Ice

Sea water

15,000 years ago: At the end of the Ice Age, when the land was still frozen, sea ice ground its way slowly past the high basalt cliffs, eroding the foreshore and helping to form the Giant's Causeway.

Inter-basaltic layer

Shape of the Columns
Most columns are hexagonal, but some have four, five, eight or even ten sides. They generally measure about 30 cm (12 in) across.

Giant's Causeway and the North Antrim Coast

Millions of years of geological activity can be witnessed in the eroded cliffs flanking the Causeway. The striking band of reddish rock is the inter-basaltic layer, which formed during a long period of temperate climatic conditions. The high iron content explains the rock's rich ochre colour.

Middle Causeway

This section of the Middle Causeway is known as the Honeycomb. Like other unusual rock formations along the coast, it was christened by local guides during Victorian times.

Road

Little Causeway

GIANT'S CAUSEWAY TODAY

It has been estimated that 40,000 basalt columns extend from the cliffs down into the sea. Close to the shore, they have been eroded to form the Grand, Middle and Little Causeways.

Plant debris is trapped between the lava flows.

Lower basalts

Grand Causeway

Wishing Chair

Myth has it that this rocky seat was made for Finn MacCool when he was a boy, and that wishes made here will come true.

Visitors exploring the Giant's Causeway at low tide ▷

Old Bushmills Distillery ⑦

Road map D1. Bushmills, Co Antrim. **Tel** 028 2073 3218. 🚌 from Giant's Causeway & Coleraine. ◯ daily. ● 2 weeks at Christmas. Nov–Mar: Sat & Sun am. 🖾 🗹 obligatory. 🖺 🍴 🛓 limited. **www**.bushmills.com

The small town of Bushmills has an attractive square and a great river for salmon and trout fishing, but its main claim to fame is whiskey. The Old Bushmills plant on the edge of town prides itself on being the world's oldest distillery. Its Grant to Distil dates from 1608, but the spirit was probably made here at least 200 years before that.

In 2005 Bushmills became part of the Diageo Group, but its products have retained their own character. Most are a blend of different whiskeys; Old Bushmills, in contrast, is made from a blend of a single malt and a single grain.

The tour of the distillery ends with a whiskey sampling session in the 1608 Barn in the former malt kilns, which are also home to a small museum with old distilling equipment on display.

Whiskey barrel at Bushmills Distillery

Murlough Bay, on the coast facing Scotland to the east of Ballycastle

Rathlin Island ⑧

Road map D1. Co Antrim. 🚶 90. 🚢 daily from Ballycastle (028 2076 9299). 🛈 Ballycastle (028 2076 2024).

Rathlin is shaped rather like a boomerang – 11 km (7 miles) in length and at no point more than 1.6 km (1 mile) wide. The island is just a 50-minute boat ride from Ballycastle. About 90 people live on Rathlin Island, making a living from fishing, farming and tourism. Facilities are limited to a café, a pub, a guesthouse and a hostel. The fierce, salty Atlantic winds ensure that the landscape on Rathlin is virtually treeless.

High white cliffs encircle much of the island, and at craggy **Bull Point** on the westerly tip, tens of thousands of seabirds, including kittiwakes, puffins and razorbills, make their home. A local minibus service will take visitors to view the birds. At the opposite end of the island is **Bruce's Cave**, where, in 1306, Robert Bruce, King of Scotland, supposedly watched a spider climbing a thread. The spider's perseverance inspired the dejected Bruce to return and win back his kingdom.

Ballycastle ⑨

Road map D1. Co Antrim. 🚶 6,000. 🚌 🚢 to Campbeltown (Scotland). 🛈 Sheskburn House, 7 Mary St (028 2076 2024). 🎪 Ould Lammas Fair (end Aug), Apple Fair (end Oct). **www**.moyle-council.org

A medium-sized resort town, Ballycastle boasts a pretty harbour and a sandy beach. Near the seafront is a memorial to Guglielmo Marconi, whose assistant sent the first wireless message across water from here to Rathlin Island in 1898.

Ballycastle's Ould Lammas Fair, held in late August, is one of the oldest traditional fairs in Ireland, featuring stalls selling dulce (dried, salted seaweed) and yellowman (honeycomb toffee).

On the outskirts of town, the ruined 15th-century **Bonamargy Friary** houses the remains of Sorley Boy MacDonnell, former chieftain of this part of Antrim. Sections of the church, gatehouse and cloisters are well preserved.

IRISH WHISKEY

The word whiskey comes from the Gaelic *uisce beatha*, meaning water of life. Distillation was probably introduced to Ireland by monks from Asia over 1,000 years ago. Small-scale production became part of the Irish way of life, but in the 17th century, the English introduced a licensing system and started to close down stills. In the 19th century, post-famine poverty and the Temperance movement combined to lower demand. The result was that Scotch whisky (with no "e") stole an export march on the Irish, but thanks to lower production costs, improved marketing and the rise in popularity of Irish coffee, sales have increased around the world.

Poster showing the Old Bushmills Distillery beside the River Bush

Environs

Off the A2, 5 km (3 miles) east of town, a narrow scenic road starts to wind its way along the coast to Cushendall. First stop is **Fair Head**, where a poorly marked path meanders across heathery marshland to towering cliffs 200 m (650 ft) above the sea. From here there are stunning views of Rathlin and the islands off the Scottish coast.

To the lee side of the headland lies **Murlough Bay**, the prettiest inlet along the coast. This can be reached by road. Further to the southeast stands **Torr Head**, a peninsula that reaches to within 21 km (13 miles) of the Mull of Kintyre making it the closest point in Ireland to Scotland.

Carnlough Harbour a popular stop south of Cushendall

Cushendall ⑩

Road map D1. Co Antrim. 🚌 2,400. 🚍 ℹ️ 24 Mill St (028 2177 1180). 🕐 all year; Oct–June: mornings only. www.moyle-council.org

Three of the nine Glens of Antrim converge towards Cushendall, earning it the unofficial title of "Capital of the Glens". This attractive village has brightly painted houses and an edifice known as Curfew Tower, built in the early 19th century as a lock-up for thieves and idlers.

Environs

About 1.5 km (1 mile) north of the village stands **Layde Old Church**. It can be reached by a pretty walk along the cliffs. Founded by the Franciscans, it was a parish church from 1306 to 1790 and contains many monuments to the local chieftains, the MacDonnells.

Just over 3 km (2 miles) west of Cushendall, on the slopes of Tievebulliagh mountain, lies **Ossian's Grave**, named after the legendary warrior-poet and son of the giant Finn MacCool (see pp26–7). It is in fact a Neolithic court tomb: the area was a major centre of Stone Age toolmaking and axeheads made of Tievebulliagh's hard porcellanite rock have been found at a wide range of sites all over the British Isles.

Other attractive villages further south along the coast road include **Carnlough**, which has a fine sandy beach and a delightful harbour, and **Ballygally**, whose supposedly haunted 1625 castle is now a hotel (see p317).

Glenariff Forest Park ⑪

Road map D1. Co Antrim. **Tel** 028 2955 6000. 🕐 daily. 🅿️ for car park. 🅿️ ♿ www.forestserviceni.gov.uk

Nine rivers have carved deep valleys through the Antrim Mountains to the sea. Celebrated in song and verse, the Glens of Antrim used to be the wildest and most remote part of Ulster. This region was not "planted" with English and Scots settlers in the 17th century and was the last place in Northern Ireland where Gaelic was spoken.

Today the Antrim coast road brings all the glens within easy reach of the tourist. Glenariff Forest Park contains some of the most spectacular scenery. The main scenic path runs through thick woodland and wildflower meadows and round the sheer sides of a gorge past three waterfalls. There are also optional trails to distant mountain viewpoints. William Makepeace Thackeray, the 19th-century English novelist, called the landscape "Switzerland in miniature".

Glenariff Forest Park

Stone circle and stone rows at Beaghmore

Cookstown ⓬

Road map D2. Co Tyrone. ⓘ
11,000. 🚌 ℹ Eurnavon, Burn Road
(028 8676 9949). 🅿 Sat.
www.cookstown.gov.uk

Cookstown sticks in the
memory for its grand central
thoroughfare – 2 km (1.25
miles) long and perfectly
straight. The road is about
40 m (130 ft) wide
and, as you look
to the north, it
frames the bulky
outline of Slieve
Gallion, a prominent
mountain in the Sperrin
Mountains. A 17th-
century Plantation town
(see pp38–9), Cookstown
takes its name from its
founder Alan Cock.

**Ardboe
Cross**

Environs
The countryside around
Cookstown is rich in Neolithic
and early Christian monu-
ments. To the east on a
desolate stretch of Lough
Neagh shoreline, the **Ardboe
Old Cross** stands on the site
of a 6th-century monastery.
Although eroded, the 10th-
century cross is one of the best
examples of a High Cross *(see
p243)* in Ulster: its 22 sculpted
panels depict Old Testament
scenes on the east side and
New Testament ones on
the west. The **Wellbrook
Beetling Mill**, west of
Cookstown, is a relic
of Ulster's old linen
industry. "Beetling"
was the process of
hammering the cloth
to give it a sheen. Set
amid trees beside the
Ballinderry River, the mill
dates from 1768 and is a
popular tourist attraction.
The National Trust has
restored the whitewashed
two-storey building and its
water wheel. Inside,
working displays demonstrate
just how loud "beetling"
could be. From the mill,
there are pleasant walks
along the river banks.

🔒 **Ardboe Old Cross**
Off B73, 16 km (10 miles) E of
Cookstown.

🏭 **Wellbrook Beetling Mill**
Off A505, 6.5 km (4 miles) W of
Cookstown. **Tel** 028 8675 1735. 🔲
mid-Mar–Jun & Sep: Sat & Sun pm;
Jul–Aug: Thu–Tue pm (closed some
days). 🔳 www.nationaltrust.org.uk

Beaghmore Stone Circles ⓭

Road map D2. Co Tyrone. Off A505,
14 km (9 miles) NW of Cookstown.

On a stretch of open moorland in the foothills of the
Sperrin Mountains lies a vast
collection of stone monuments,
dating from between 2000
and 1200 BC. There are seven
stone circles, several stone
rows and a number of less
prominent features, possibly
collapsed field walls of an
earlier period. Their exact
purpose remains unknown,
though in some cases their
alignment correlates with
movements of the sun, moon
and stars. Three of the rows,
for example, are clearly aligned
with the point where the sun
rises at the summer solstice.

The individual circle stones
are small – none is more than
1.20 m (4 ft) in height – but
their sheer numbers make
them a truly impressive sight.
As well as the circles and
rows, there are a dozen
round cairns (burial mounds).
Up until 1945, the whole
complex, one of Ulster's
major archaeological finds,
had lain buried beneath a
thick layer of peat.

ULSTER'S HISTORIC LINEN INDUSTRY

The rise in Ulster's importance as a linen
producer was spurred on by the arrival from
France of refugee Huguenot
weavers at the end of the 17th
century. Linen remained a
flourishing industry for a
further two centuries, but
today it is produced only
in small quantities for the
luxury goods market.
Hundreds of abandoned
mills dot the former "Linen
Triangle" bounded by Belfast,
Armagh and Dungannon.
One of the reasons why the

**18th-century print, showing flax
being prepared for spinning**

material diminished in popularity was the
expensive production process: after cutting,
the flax had to be retted, or soaked,
in large artificial ponds so that
scutching – the separation
of the fibres – could begin.
After combing, the linen
was spun and woven
before being bleached
in the sun, typically in
fields along river banks.
The final stage was "beetling",
the process whereby the
cloth was hammered to
give it a sheen.

The Wilson Ancestral Home ⓮

Road map C2. 28 Spout Road, Dergalt, Strabane, Co Tyrone. **ℹ**
Tel 028 7138 4444. ☐ Jul–Aug: 2–5pm Tue–Sun (guided tour only). Visits at other times by arrangement.

Located 3 km (2 miles) southeast of Strabane, off the road to Plumbridge, is the ancestral home of US President Thomas Woodrow Wilson (1856–1924). Woodrow's grandfather, Judge James Wilson, left this house for America in 1807 at the age of 20. Today, a visit to the thatched white-washed house on the slopes of the Sperrin Mountains provides valuable insight into the history behind Ulster-American ties. The carefully-conserved rooms contain original furniture including curtained beds, kitchen utensils and farm implements. A portrait of James Wilson hangs over the traditional hearth fire.

Environs
Just outside the village of Newtownstewart, 12 km (7 miles) south of Strabane, is the medieval ruin of Harry Avery's Castle. This 14th-century Gaelic stone castle consisted of two storeys fronted by vast rectangular twin towers. These towers are still visible today.

Ulster-American Folk Park ⓯

Road map C2. Co Tyrone. **Tel** 028 8224 3292. ☐ from Omagh.
☐ opening times vary; call ahead or see website for more details. ⓰ **ℹ**
ℙ **&** www.folkpark.com

One of the best open-air museums of its kind, the Folk Park grew up around the restored boyhood home of Judge Thomas Mellon (founder of the Pittsburgh banking dynasty). The Park's permanent exhibition, called "Emigrants", examines why two million people left Ulster for America during the 18th and 19th centuries. It also shows what became of them, with stories of both fortune and failure, including the grim lives of indentured servants and the 15,000 Irish vagrants and convicts sent to North America in the mid-18th century.

The park has more than 30 historic buildings, some of them original, some replicas. There are settler homesteads including that of John Joseph Hughes, the first Catholic Archbishop of New York), churches, a schoolhouse and a forge, some with craft displays, all with costumed interpretative guides. There's also an Ulster streetscape a reconstructed

emigrant ship and a Pennsylvania farmstead. The farmhouse is based on one built by Thomas Mellon and his father in the early years of their life in America.

The Centre for Migration Studies assists descendents of emigrants to trace their family roots. Popular American festivals such as Independence Day and Hallowe'en are celebrated here and there is an Appalachian-Bluegrass music festival in early September.

Belleek Pottery ⓰

Road map C2. Belleek, Co Fermanagh. **Tel** 028 6865 9300. ☐ ☐ Jan–Feb: Mon–Fri, Mar–Oct: daily; Nov–Dec: Mon–Sat ☐ 1 Mar & Christmas. **ℹ** **&** **ℙ** **ℙ** www.belleek.ie

Worker at the Belleek factory making a Parian ware figurine

The little border village of Belleek would attract few visitors other than anglers were it not for the world-famous Belleek Pottery, founded in 1857. The company's pearly coloured china is known as Parian ware. Developed in the 19th century, it was supposed to resemble the famous Parian marble of Ancient Greece.

Belleek is now best known for its ornamental pieces of fragile lattice work decorated with pastel-coloured flowers. These are especially popular in the USA. Several elaborate showpieces stand on display in the visitors' centre and small museum. There's also a 20-minute audiovisual presentation on the company's history, a gift shop and ample parking space for tour buses.

Pennsylvania log farmhouse at the Ulster-American Folk Park

A Tour of Lower Lough Erne ⑰

Kingfisher

Fermanagh lakelands around Lower Lough Erne boasts a rich combination of both natural and historic sights. From pre-Christian times, settlers sought the security offered by the lough's forests and inlets. Monasteries were founded on several of its many islands in the Middle Ages, and a ring of castles recalls the Plantation era *(see p39)*. The lake is a haven for water birds such as ducks, grebes and kingfishers, and the trout-rich waters attract many anglers. Lough Erne is a delight to explore by land or by boat. In summer, ferries serve several islands, and cruisers are available for hire.

View across Lower Lough Erne

Boa Island ⑤
Two curious double-faced figures stand in Caldragh cemetery, a Christian graveyard on Boa Island. While little is known about the stone idols, they are certainly pre-Christian.

Castle Caldwell Forest ⑥ Castle Caldwell's wooded peninsulas are a sanctuary for birds, and you can watch waterfowl from hides on the shore. You may see great crested grebes, the common scoter duck and perhaps even otters.

Belleek ⑦
Northern Ireland's most westerly village, Belleek is famous for its pottery *(see p269)*.

Lough Navar Forest Drive ⑧
An 11-km (7-mile) drive through pine forest leads to a viewpoint atop the Cliffs of Magho, with a magnificent panorama over Lough Erne and beyond. Trails weave through the woods.

Tully Castle ⑨
A delightful 17th-century-style herb garden has been planted and is maturing well alongside this fortified Plantation house.

TIPS FOR WALKERS

Length: *110 km (68 miles).*
Stopping-off points: *Outside Enniskillen, the best places to eat are the pubs in Kesh and Belleek; in summer, a café opens in Castle Archdale Country Park. There are good picnic places all along the route of this tour, including at the Cliffs of Magho viewpoint.*
(See also pp385–7.)

KEY

▬	Tour route
⁓	Other roads
🛥	Boats to islands
🔆	Viewpoint

White Island ④

The Romanesque church on White Island has bizarre pagan-looking figures set into one wall. Of uncertain origin, they probably adorned an earlier monastery on this site. Ferries to the island leave from Castle Archdale Marina in summer.

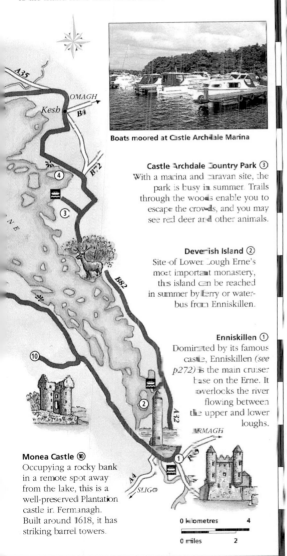

Boats moored at Castle Archdale Marina

Castle Archdale Country Park ③

With a marina and caravan site, the park is busy in summer. Trails through the woods enable you to escape the crowds, and you may see red deer and other animals.

Devenish Island ②

Site of Lower Lough Erne's most important monastery, the island can be reached in summer by ferry or water-bus from Enniskillen.

Enniskillen ①

Dominated by its famous castle, Enniskillen (see p272) is the main cruiser base on the Erne. It overlooks the river flowing between the upper and lower loughs.

Monea Castle ⑩

Occupying a rocky bank in a remote spot away from the lake, this is a well-preserved Plantation castle in Fermanagh. Built around 1618, it has striking barrel towers.

0 kilometres 4
0 miles 2

Beautifully constructed round tower on Devenish Island

Devenish Island ⑱

Road map C2. Co Fermanagh. 028 386 21588. Devenish Ferry (077 0255 287) from Trory Point, 5 km (3 miles) N of Enniskillen: Easter–Sep: daily for museum and tower. www.doeni.gov.uk/niea

St Molaise II, who had 1,500 scholars under his tutelage, founded a monastery on this tiny windswept island in the 6th century. Though raided by Vikings in the 9th century and burned in 1157, it remained an important religious centre up to the early 17th century.

Several fine buildings have survived, including **Teampall Mor** near the jetty. Built in 1225, this church displays the transition between Roman-esque and Gothic styles. On the highest ground stands **St Mary's Priory**, an Augustinian church that was erected in the 15th century. An intricately carved stone cross close by dates from the same period.

The most spectacular sight, however, is the 12th-century Round Tower, which stands some 25 m (82 ft) tall. From the high windows the monks could spot approaching strangers. It is perfectly preserved, and the five floors can be reached by internal ladders. Supporting the roof is an elaborate cornice with a human face carved above each of the four windows; this is a unique feature in an Irish round tower. A small museum cover both the history and architecture of the island, and contains a collection of anti-quities discovered at the site.

Enniskillen ⑲

Road map C2. Co Fermanagh.
🏠 15,000. 🚌 ℹ️ *Wellington Road
(028 6632 3110).* 🛒 *Thu.*
www.fermanaghlakelands.com

The busy tourist centre of
Enniskillen occupies an island
between Upper and Lower
Lough Erne. The town gained
fame for the wrong reason in
1987, when 11 people died in
an IRA bomb attack, but it
deserves a visit for its setting
and sights.

At the west end of town
stands **Enniskillen Castle**,
dating from the 15th century.
It houses **Fermanagh County
Museum** and the Inniskilling
Regimental Museum. Its most
stunning feature, however, is
the Watergate, a fairytale twin-
turreted tower, best admired
from the far bank of the river.
Further west, **Portora Royal
School**, founded in 1618,
counts among its old boys the
playwrights Oscar Wilde and
Samuel Beckett *(see pp22–3)*.

The **Cole Monument** stands
in a pretty Victorian park on
the east side of town. It is a tall
Doric column with a spiral

Enniskillen Castle seen from across the River Erne

staircase that can be climbed
for views of the lake country.

🏰 Enniskillen Castle
Tel 028 6632 5000. ⬜ *Jul & Aug:
10am–5pm Tue–Fri, 2–5pm Sat–Mon;
Apr–Jun & Sep-Oct: 10am–5pm Tue–
Fri, 2–5pm Mon & Sat; Nov–Mar:
10am–5pm Tue–Fri, 2–5pm Mon.* 🚫
⬛ *23 Dec–2 Jan.* 🅿️ ♿ *limited.*
www.enniskillencastle.co.uk

Environs

Just outside town, set in a park
with mature oak woodland
overlooking a lake, is **Castle
Coole**, one of the finest Neo-
Classical homes in Ireland. It
has a long Portland stone
façade, with a central portico
and small pavilions at each
end. The stone was shipped
from Dorset to Ballyshannon.
The first Earl of Belmore, who
commissioned the house in
the 1790s, was almost bankrupted by the cost of it. The
original design was by Irish
architect Richard Johnston, but
the Earl then commissioned a
second set of drawings by the
fashionable English architect
James Wyatt. The extravagant
Earl died, deep in debt, in
1802 and it was left to his son to
complete during the 1820s.

The glory of Castle Coole is
that almost all the house's
original furniture is still in
place. Family portraits from
the 18th century line the walls
of the dining room. In the
lavish State Bedroom there is
a bed made specially for King
George IV on the occasion of
his visit to Ireland in 1821,
though in the end he never
came here to sleep in it. One
of the finest rooms is the oval
saloon (or ballroom) at the
back of the house. The
furnishings may not be to
everyone's taste, but the
spacious oak-floored room
produces a magnificent effect
of unostentatious luxury.

🏛️ Castle Coole
Off A4, 2.4 km (1.5 miles) SE of Enniskillen. *Tel 028 6632 2690.* **House** ⬜
*mid-Mar–end May & Sep: 11am–5pm
Sat & Sun; Jun–Aug: 11am–5pm daily
(closed Thu in Jun).* 🚫 🅿️ ♿ ⬛
🌳 **Park** ⬜ *Mar–Oct: 10am–7pm
daily; Nov–Feb: 10am–4pm daily.*
www.nationaltrust.org.uk

The saloon at Castle Coole, with original Regency furnishings

Marble Arch Caves 20

Road map C2. Marlbank Scenic Loop Florence Court, Co Fermanagh. **Tel** 028 6634 8855. ☐ end Mar–Jun & Sep: 10am–4:30pm, Jul–Aug: 10am–5pm daily (phone first as bad weather can cause closure). 🎟 📷 obligatory. 📶 📷 www.marblearchcaves.net

The marble arch caves are cut by three streams which flow down the slopes of Cuilcagh Mountain, unite underground and emerge as the Cladagh River. Tours lasting 75 minutes consist of a boat ride into the depths of the cave complex and a guided walk that leads past stalagmites, calcite cascades and other curious limestone formations. The 9-m (30-ft) "Marble Arch" itself stands outside the cave system in the glen where the river gushes out from below ground.

The caves are very popular, so book ahead. It is best to ring to check the local weather conditions before setting out; the caves may be closed because of rain. Whatever the weather, bring a sweater and sensible walking shoes.

Boat trip through Marble Arch Caves

Florence Court 21

Road map C2. Co Fermanagh. **Tel** 028 6634 8249. **House** ☐ times vary: check National Trust website. 🎟 📷 obligatory. ♿ 📷 **Grounds** ☐ daily. 🎟 for car park. www.nationaltrust.org.uk

This three-storey Palladian mansion was built for the Cole family in the mid-18th century. The arcades and pavilions, which are of a later date than the main house, were added around 1770 by William Cole, first Earl of Enniskillen. The house features flamboyant Rococo plasterwork said to be by the Dublin stuccodore Robert West. Sadly however, not much of what you see today is original as most of the central block was seriously damaged by fire in 1955. Much of the furniture was lost, but the plasterwork was painstakingly recreated from photographs. The finest examples are in the dining room, the staircase and the small Venetian room.

Perhaps more spectacular than the mansion are the grounds, which occupy a natural mountain-ringed amphitheatre. There are many enjoyable walks around the house. One woodland trail leads to the famous Florence Court yew tree, whose descendants are to be found all over Ireland. Closer to the house is a walled garden where pink and white roses make an attractive sight in summer

Dungannon 22

Road map D2. Co Tyrone. 🚶 1,000. 🚌 🚊 Killymaddy Tourist Centre, Ballygawley Rd, 8 km (5 miles) W of town (028 3776 7259). 🏪 Thu. www.flavouroftyrone.com

Dungannon's hilly location made an ideal site for the seat of government of the O'Neill dynasty from the 14th century until Plantation (see pp.38–9), when their castle was razed. The town's **Royal School** is one of the oldest in Northern Ireland; it was chartered in 1608 by James I. Opened in 1614, it moved to its present site in 1789.

Once a major linen centre, this busy market town was also known for its glassmaking, as it was the base of the famous Tyrone crystal factory. The factory closed in 2010, however.

The Linen Green shopping centre in nearby Moygashel offers factory outlet shopping from brands such as Paul Costelloe and Anne Storey.

Florence Court, the former seat of the Earls of Enniskillen

View of Armagh dominated by St Patrick's Roman Catholic Cathedral

Armagh ㉓

Road map D2. Co Armagh.
🚊 15,000. 🚌 🚉 40 English St
(028 3752 1800). 🚲 Tue & Fri.
www.armagh.co.uk

One of Ireland's oldest cities,
Armagh dates back to the age
of St Patrick (see p281) and the
advent of Christianity. The
narrow streets in the city centre
follow the ditches that once
ringed the church, founded by
the saint in 455. Two cathedrals, both called **St Patrick's**,
sit on opposing hills. The
huge Roman Catholic
one is a twin-spired
Neo-Gothic building
with seemingly
every inch of
wall covered in
mosaic. The older
Anglican Cathedral
dates back to
medieval times. It
boasts the bones of
Brian Ború, the King of Ireland
who defeated the Vikings in
1014 (see pp34–5), and an
11th-century High Cross.

Armagh's gorgeous oval, tree-
lined Mall, where cricket is
played in summer is surrounded by dignified Georgian
buildings. One of these houses
the small **Armagh County
Museum**, which has a good
exhibition on local history. Off
the Mall **St Patrick's Trian** is a
heritage centre telling the
story of the city. It also has a
"Land of Lilliput" fantasy
centre for children, based on
Gulliver's Travels by Jonathan
Swift (see p82). The Armagh
Planetarium is on College Hill
in the **Observatory Grounds**,
from where there are splendid
views over the city.

**Skull of Barbary ape
from Navan Fort**

🏛 **Armagh County Museum**
The Mall East. **Tel** 028 3752 3070.
⭕ Mon–Sat. 🔵 some public hols.
🚲 by arrangement.
www.armaghcountymuseum.org.uk

🏛 **St Patrick's Trian**
40 English St. **Tel** 028 3752 1801.
⭕ daily. 🔵 25, 26 Dec. 🚲 🏛 🚲 🚲
www.visitarmagh.com

♣ **Observatory Grounds**
College Hill. **Tel** 028 3752 2928.
⭕ by appt only. Grounds open
Mon–Fri. **Planetarium Tel** 028
3752 3689. 🚲 for shows. 🚲 🚲
www.armaghplanet.com

Environs
To the west of
Armagh stands
Navan Fort, a
large earthwork
on the summit of
a hill. In legend,
Navan was Emain Macha,
ceremonial and spiritual
capital of ancient Ulster,
associated with tales
of the warrior
Cúchulainn (see p26). The
site may have been in use as
much as 4,000 years ago, but
seems to have been most
active around 100 BC when a
huge timber building, 40 m
(130 ft) across, was erected

over a giant cairn. The whole
thing was then burned and the
remains covered with soil.
Archaeological evidence indicates that this was not an act
of war, but a solemn ritual
performed by the inhabitants
of Emain Macha themselves.

Below the fort, the grass-
roofed **Navan Centre** interprets
the site. It is open to groups
outside of the main summer
season. One unexpected
exhibit is the skull of a
Barbary ape, found in the
remains of a Bronze Age
house. The animal must come
from Spain or North Africa,
evidence that by 500 BC Emain
Macha was already a place
with far-flung trading links.

🏛 **Navan Centre**
On A28 4 km (2.5 miles) W of Armagh.
Tel 028 3752 9644. ⭕ daily. 🚲
🚲

Lough Neagh ㉔

Road map D2. Co Armagh, Co
Tyrone, Co Londonderry, Co Antrim.

Legend has it that the giant
Finn MacCool (see pp26–7)
created Lough Neagh by
picking up a piece of turf and
hurling it into the Irish Sea, thus
forming the Isle of Man in the
process. At 400 sq km (153 sq
miles), the lake is the largest
in Britain. Bordered by sedgy
marshland, it has few roads
along its shore. The best
recreational areas lie in the
south: Oxford Island, actually
a peninsula, has walking
trails, bird lookouts and the
informative **Lough Neagh
Discovery Centre**. In the
southwest corner, a narrow-
gauge railway runs through
the bogs of **Peatlands Park**.

Navan Fort, the site of Emain Macha, legendary capital of Ulster

Hide for birdwatchers at Oxford Island on the southern shore of Lough Neagh

Salmon and trout swim in the rivers that flow from Lough Neagh. The lake is famous for its eels, with one of the world's largest eel fisheries at Toome.

⛪ Lough Neagh Discovery Centre
Oxford Island. Exit 10 off M1. **Tel** 028 3832 2205. ☐ daily. ● 24–26 Dec. ☑ ☒ 🍴 ☐ www. discoverloughneagh.com

🍂 Peatlands Park
Exit 13 off M1 **Tel** 028 3885 1102. Park ☐ daily. ● 25 Dec. **Visitors' centre** ☐ Easter-Oct: daily; Nov-Easter: Sun only. (Opening times vary, call ahead to check) ☒ www.peatlandsni.gov.uk

Larne ㉙

Road map D1. Co Antrim. 🖼 20,000. 🚍 🚂 🛈 Narrow Gauge Rd (028 2826 0088). www.larne.gov.uk

Industrial Larne is the arrival point for ferries from Scotland (*see pp382–4*). The town is not the finest introduction to Ulster scenery, but it lies on the threshold of the magnificent Antrim coastline (*see p267*).

The sheltered waters of Larne Lough have been a landing point since Mesolithic times – flint flakes found here provide some of the earliest evidence of human presence on the island – nearly 9,000 years ago. Since then, Norsemen used the lough as a base in the 10th century. Edward Bruce landed his Scottish troops in the area in 1315, and in 1914 the Ulster Volunteer Force landed a huge cache of German arms here during its campaign against Home Rule (*see pp44–5*).

Carrickfergus ㉖

Road map E2. Co Antrim. 🖼 42,000. 🚍 🚂 🛈 Antrim St (028 9335 8049) ☐ Apr-Sep: 10am-6pm, Oct-Mar: 10am-5pm. ● Thu. www.carrickfergus.org

Carrickfergus grew up around the massive castle begun in 1180 by John de Courcy to guard the entrance to Belfast Lough. De Courcy was one leader of the Anglo-Norman force which invaded Ulster following Strongbow's conquest of Leinster in the south (*see pp36–7*).

Carrickfergus Castle was shaped to fit the crag on which it stands overlooking the harbour. The finest and best-preserved Norman castle in Ireland, it even has its original portcullis (*see pp36–7*). Many changes have been made since the 12th century, including wide ramparts to accommodate the castle's cannons. Life-size model soldiers are posed along the ramparts. In continuous use up to 1928, the castle has

changed hands several times over the years. Under Edward Bruce, the Scots took it in 1315, holding it for three years. James II's army was in control of the castle from 1689 until General Schomberg took it for William III in 1690. William himself stayed here before the Battle of the Boyne (*see p244*) in 1690.

De Courcy also founded the pretty **St Nicholas' Church**. Inside are rare stained-glass work and a "leper window", through which the afflicted received the sacraments. Other attractions include the **Andrew Jackson Centre**, the ancestral home of the seventh president of the USA, and **Flame**, a museum based around a Victorian coal gasworks.

⚓ Carrickfergus Castle
Tel 028 9335 1273. ☐ daily. ● 9 am, 24–26 Dec. ☑ ☒ ☒ 📷 www.doeni.gov.uk/niea

⛪ Andrew Jackson Centre
2 Boneybefore. **Tel** 028 9335 8049. ☐ by appt only.

The massive Norman keep of Carrickfergus Castle

Belfast ㉗

Belfast was the only city in Ireland to experience the full force of the Industrial Revolution. Its ship-building, linen, rope-making and tobacco industries caused the population to rise to almost 400,000 by the end of World War I. The "Troubles" and the decline of traditional industries have somewhat damaged economic life, but regeneration projects, such as the Odyssey complex at Queen's Quay, and the development of the adjacent Titanic Quarter, are breathing new life into run-down areas and Belfast remains a friendly, handsome city.

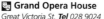

Red Hand of Ulster, Linen Hall Library

Mosaic in St Anne's Cathedral, showing St Patrick's journey to Ireland *(see p281)*

Interior of the Grand Opera House

🏛 Belfast City Hall

Donegall Square.
Tel 028 9027 0456.
📷 *call ahead for tour details.*

Most of Belfast's main streets radiate out from the hub of Donegall Square. In the centre of the square stands the vast rectangular Portland stone bulk of the 1906 City Hall. It has an elaborate tower at each corner and a central copper dome that rises to a height of 53 m (173 ft). Highlight of the tour of the interior is the sumptuous oak-panelled council chamber.

Statues around the building include a glum-looking Queen Victoria outside the main entrance and, on the east side, Sir Edward Harland, founder of the Harland and Wolff shipyard, which built the *Titanic*. A memorial to those who died when the *Titanic* sank in 1912 stands close by.

Detail of *Titanic* Memorial outside Belfast City Hall

🏛 Grand Opera House

Great Victoria St. **Tel** 028 9024 1919.
www.goh.co.uk

Designed by Frank Matcham, the renowned theatre-architect, this exuberant late-Victorian building opened its doors in 1894. The sumptuous interior, with its gilt, red plush and intricate plasterwork, was restored to its full glory in 1980. On occasions, bombings of the adjacent Europa Hotel disrupted business at the theatre, but it survives as a major venue for plays and theatre.

🏛 St Anne's Cathedral

Donegall St. **Tel** 028 9032 8332.
www.belfastcathedral.org

The Neo-Romanesque façade of this Anglican cathedral, consecrated in 1904, is not particularly impressive. The interior is far more attractive, especially the colourful mosaics executed by the two Misses Martin in the 1920s. The one covering the baptistry ceiling contains over 150,000 pieces. The wide nave is paved with Canadian maple and the aisles with Irish marble. Lord Carson (1854–1935), implacable leader of the campaign against Home Rule *(see p44)*, is buried in the south aisle.

ARMAGH

SANDY ROW
GREAT V
SHAFTESBURY SQUARE
UNIVERSITY ROAD
BOTANIC AVENUE
Bot Sta
UNIVERSITY STREET

⑦ Queen's Film Theatre
⑧ Ulster Museum   Queen's University
⑨ Botanic Gardens

STRANMILLIS ROAD
AGINCOURT AVENUE
P
STRANMILLIS EMBANKMENT
RIDGEWAY ST
ANNADALE EMBANKMENT
Ormeau Bridge
Lyric Theatre
ORMEAU ROAD

Giant's Ring
PARK ROAD

Key to Symbols *see back flap*

SIGHTS AT A GLANCE

0 metres   500
0 yards   500

For hotels and restaurants in this region see pp316–19 and pp342–5

VISITORS' CHECKLIST

Road map D2. Co Antrim. 500,000. George Best City Airport, 6.5 km (4 miles) E; Belfast International, 29 km (18 miles) NW. Central Station, East Bridge St (028 9066 6630); Great Victoria St Station (028 9066 6630). Europa Bus Centre, Great Victoria St, Lagarside Bus Centre, Oxford St (028 9066 6630). 47 Donegall Pl (028 9024 6609). www.goto belfast.com Balmoral Show (May) & Belfast City Carnival (Jun).

Entry both serve excellent lunches. In 1791, the United Irishmen, a radical movement inspired by the new ideas of the French Revolution was founded in a tavern on Crown Entry. Its most famous member was Wolfe Tone *(see pp.40–41)*.

Crown Liquor Saloon

Great Victoria St. **Tel** 023 9024 3187. daily. **www**.crownbar.com
Even teetotallers should make a detour to the tiled façade of this flamboyant Victorian drinking palace. The Crown, which dates back to the 1880s, is the most famous pub in Belfast. The lovingly restored interior features stained glass, marbling, mosaics and a splendid ceiling with scrolled plasterwork. The wooden snugs facing the long bar have their original gas lamps: the perfect place for a pint of Guinness or Bass and some Strangford Lough mussels.

In his determination to win, one cut off his own hand and threw it to the shore.

The Entries
The Entries are a series of narrow alleys between Ann Street and High Street. They feature some of the best pubs in the city, including White's Tavern *(see p351)*, reputedly the oldest bar in Belfast. McCracken's in Joy's Entry and the Morning Star on Pottinger's

Linen Hall Library
17 Donegall Square North. **Tel** 028 9032 1707. Mon–Sat. **www**.linenhall.com
Founded as the Belfast Society for Promoting Knowledge in 1788, the library has thousands of rare, old books. There is also extensive documentation of political events in Ireland since 1968 and a vast database of genealogical information. Even if you have no special reason for visiting the library, it is still worth going inside, if only for the delightful coffee shop and the vast selection of periodicals. There are also regular exhibitions. Above the library door you will see the Red Hand of Ulster, the emblem of the province. It is the subject of a gory legend about two Celtic heroes racing to see who would touch the land of Ulster first.

The ornate Victorian interior of the Crown Liquor Saloon

Exploring Belfast

Away from the city centre, Belfast has many pleasant suburbs to explore. The Queen's Quarter around Queen's University to the south of the city has two major attractions in the Ulster Museum and the Botanic Gardens. To the north, there are splendid views to be enjoyed from the heights of Cave Hill, while visitors interested in Belfast's industrial heritage will be keen to visit the Titanic Quarter, the old docks and the Harland and Wolff working shipyards.

Interior of the Victorian Palm House at the Botanic Gardens

🏛 Ulster Museum

Botanic Gardens. **Tel** 0845 608 0000.
◯ 10am–5pm Tue–Sun. & ▯ ▮
www.nmni.com/um
Founded in 1929 as the Belfast Municipal Museum and Art Gallery, the Ulster Museum reopened in 2009 following a £17-million refurbishment. Its 8,000 sq m (86,000 sq ft) of galleries house rich collections of art, local history, natural sciences and archaeology. Modern Irish art is particularly well represented, while the 6 m- (20 ft-) long Edmontosaurus dinosaur skeleton in the Window On Our World display tower is one of the museum's most popular exhibits.

In addition to its permanent exhibits, the museum has a changing programme of temporary exhibitions and events, several learning zones and plenty of opportunities for hands-on activities, including interactive areas where visitors can try on Victorian costumes and handle the skull of a two-headed calf.

🌿 Botanic Gardens

Botanic Ave. **Tel** 028 9032 4902.
◯ daily. **www**.belfastcity.gov.uk
Backing on to the university, the Botanic Gardens provide a quiet refuge from the bustle of campus. The 1839 Palm House is a superb example of curvilinear glass and cast-iron

work. The Tropical Ravine, or Fernery, is another fine piece of Victorian garden architecture. Visitors can look down from the balcony to a sunken glen of exotic plants.

🏫 Queen's University

University Rd. **Tel** 028 9097 5252
& ▯ ▮ **www**.qub.ac.uk
A 15-minute stroll south from Donegall Square, through the lively entertainment district known as the Golden Mile, leads to Northern Ireland's most prestigious university. The main building, designed by Charles Lanyon in 1849, bears similarities to Magdalene College, Oxford. A towered gateway leads to a colonnaded quadrangle.

🏛 W5

Odyssey, 2 Queen's Quay. **Tel** 028 9046 7700. ◯ daily (Sun: pm only). **www**.w5online.co.uk
W5, short for "whowhatwhere whenwhy", is an award-winning interactive museum, which presents science as an exciting process of discovery.

Large-scale metal sculpture outside the Ulster Museum

THE POLITICAL MURALS OF WEST BELFAST

Republican mural in the Falls Road

During the period of the "Troubles" (1968–1998), popular art played a conspicuous role in proclaiming the loyalties of Belfast's two most intransigent working-class communities, on the Protestant Shankill Road and the Catholic Falls Road. The gable walls of dozens of houses in these areas have been decorated with vivid murals expressing local political and paramilitary affiliations. Likewise, kerbstones on certain streets are

painted either in the red, white and blue of the United Kingdom or the green, white and gold of Ireland. Even with the successes of the current peace process, many are likely to remain. Some tourists make the journey out to West Belfast just to see the murals. The simplest way to do this is to pre-book a "Black Cab Tour" through the Belfast Welcome Centre. Call 028 9024 6609.

Protestant Loyalist mural

It has over 200 hands-on exhibits and experiments. Among many fascinating activities on offer, visitors can try working a replica of a Port of Belfast crane, sneak up on a butterfly, lift themselves up with pulleys, create an animated film or compose music on a laser harp.

Titanic Quarter
Queen's Road, Queen's Island
Tel 028 9076 6300
www.titanic-quarter.com

The doomed RMS *Titanic*, struck by an iceberg on its maiden voyage in 1912, was built in Belfast's docklands, and this area is now called the Titanic Quarter. The waterfront is being redeveloped, and space has been created for shops, restaurants, hotels and offices. Various walking, boat and bus tours provide an excellent way of exploring this vibrant area. Titanic Belfast, a new tourist attraction, has been built above the ship's slipway. The interactive exhibits guide visitors through the building of the *Titanic*, its fateful voyage and the discovery of the ship. The MV *Confiance* also houses an exhibition on Belfast's maritime and ship-building history.

Albert Memorial Clock Tower
Queen's Square.

One of Belfast's best-known monuments, today the clock tower leans slightly as a result of subsidence. Beyond it, facing the river, stands the Custom House (1854) by Charles Lanyon, architect of Queen's University.

Lagan Weir
Donegall Quay. **Tel** 028 9031 5304.

Belfast's once thriving harbour area can best be viewed from the footbridge alongside the Lagan Weir development. Five computer-controlled steel gates maintain a fixed water level, getting rid of the mud-banks produced by varying tide levels and allowing for angling and watersports along the river. At night, the weir is lit by gas-filter blue light that shimmers across the water.

There is a partly obscured view across to the giant yellow cranes – appropriately named Samson and Goliath – of the once-mighty Harland and Wolff shipyards.

The Weir has been fully revamped, including an upgrade of the hydraulic rams and dredging of the river.

Cave Hill
Antrim Rd, 6.5 km (4 miles) N of city.
Belfast Castle Tel 028 9077 6925.
daily. 25 Dec.
www.belfastcastle.co.uk **Belfast Zoo Tel** 028 9077 6277. daily
25 & 26 Dec.
www.belfastzoo.co.uk

It was on Cave Hill, next to MacArt's Fort (named after an Iron Age chieftain), that Wolfe Tone *(see p41)* and the northern leaders of the United Irishmen met in 1795 to pledge themselves to rebellion. The five artificial caves near the fort were carved out during the Neolithic period.

On the wooded eastern slopes of the hill stands the baronial pile of Belfast Castle, built in 1870. Previously home to the Earl of Shaftesbury, the castle now belongs to the city and houses a restaurant and a visitors' centre that interprets the area's history. A little further along the road past the castle is Belfast Zoo.

The unmistakable profile of Cave Hill above the roofs of Belfast

Giant's Ring
Off B23, 5 km (3 miles) S of city centre.

Little is known about this awe-inspiring prehistoric enclosure almost 200 m (660 ft) in diameter. It is surrounded by a grassy bank averaging almost 6 m (20 ft) in width and 4.5 m (15 ft) in height. Bones from a Stone Age burial were found under the dolmen in the centre. During the 18th century the ring was a popular venue for horse races.

Stormont
Newtownards Rd, 8 km (5 miles) SE of city centre. to the public by arrangement only.

Built between 1928 and 1932, at a cost of £1,250,000, Stormont was designed to house the Northern Ireland Parliament. The huge Anglo-Palladian mass of Portland stone and Mourne granite stands at the end of a majestic avenue, 1.6 km (1 mile) long, bordered by parkland. A statue of Lord Carson *(see p44)* stands near the front entrance.

Since the parliament was disbanded in 1972, the building has been used as government offices. Although it has been suspended on several occasions, the devolved Northern Ireland Assembly has sat here since the 1998 Agreement

Stormont in its parkland setting outside Belfast

Ulster Folk and Transport Museum 28

Road map E2. Cultra, near Holywood, Co Down. **Tel** 028 9042 8428. 🚉
🚃 ⬚ *Tue–Sun.* ● *Christmas period.* 🖾 *(free for the disabled).*
♿ 🖵 📷 www.uftm.com/uftm

This museum was set up following an act of parliament in 1958, to show the life and traditions of people in Northern Ireland. Demonstrations of traditional crafts, industries and farming methods are given.

The A2 road splits the folk museum from the transport section. This is dominated by a hangar that houses the Irish Railway Collection. The smaller Transport Gallery exhibits machinery made in Ulster, including a saloon carriage from the tram service that ran from Portrush to Giant's Causeway *(see pp262–3)*. Of particular note is a test model of the spectacularly unsuccessful De Lorean car, made in the early 1980s with a huge government subsidy. There's also a popular exhibit on another ill-fated construction – the *Titanic*. It's best to allow half a day to take in most of the attractions.

1883 tram carriage at the Ulster Folk and Transport Museum

Ards Peninsula 29

Road map E2. Co Down. 🚉 🚌 *to Bangor.* 🛈 *Newtownards (028 9182 6846).* www.ards-council.gov.uk

The peninsula – and some of Northern Ireland's finest scenery – begins east of Belfast at **Bangor**. This resort town has a modern marina and some well-known yacht clubs. A little way south is **Donaghadee**, from where boats sail to the three **Copeland Islands**, inhabited only by seabirds

Scrabo Tower, a prominent landmark of the Ards Peninsula

since the departure of the last human residents in the 1940s. The **Ballycopeland Windmill** (1784) is Northern Ireland's only working windmill and stands on the top of a small hill a little further south, near the town of Millisle.

Just across the peninsula is **Newtownards**. On a hill above the town is the pleasant and shady **Scrabo Country Park**. In the park stands the **Scrabo Tower**, built in 1857 as a memorial to the third Marquess of Londonderry.

Past the grounds of **Mount Stewart House** *(see pp282–3)* is the hamlet of Greyabbey, with its antique shops and Cistercian abbey ruins. Founded in 1193, **Grey Abbey** was used as a parish church until the 17th century. It is idyllically set in lush meadows by a stream and some of its features, particularly the finely carved west doorway, are well preserved.

On the tip of the peninsula, **Portaferry** overlooks the Strangford Narrows across from the Lecale Peninsula *(see p284)*. Portaferry's large aquarium, **Exploris**, displays

the diversity of life in the Irish Sea and Strangford Lough.

🏛 **Ballycopeland Windmill**
On B172 1.6 km (1 mile) W of Millisle. **Tel** 028 9181 1491. ⬚ Jul–Aug: Tue–Sun; winter on request. 🖾

🏛 **Scrabo Country Park**
Near Newtownards. **Tel** 028 918 1491. ⬚ daily. **Tower** ⬚ Easter–Sep: Sat–Thu or by appt.

🏛 **Grey Abbey**
Greyabbey. **Tel** 028 918 1491. ⬚ varies, call ahead. ♿

🏛 **Exploris**
Castle Street, Portaferry. **Tel** 028 4272 80€2. ⬚ daily. ● 24–26 Dec. 🖾
♿ 🖵 www.exploris.org.uk

Ballycopeland Windmill, which dates back to 1784

Mount Stewart House ③⓪

See pp282–3.

Hillsborough ③①

Road map D2. Co Down. 4,000. The Square (028 9268 9717). www.discovernorthernireland.com

Dotted with craft shops and restaurants, this Georgian town lies less than 16 km (10 miles) from Belfast. **Hillsborough Castle**, with its elaborate wrought-iron gates and coat of arms, is where visiting dignitaries to Northern Ireland normally stay.

Across from the 18th-century Market House in the town square is **Hillsborough Fort**. An artillery fort dating from 1650, it was remodelled in the 18th century for feasts held by the descendants of Arthur Hill, founder of the town.

⚓ Hillsborough Castle
Tel 028 9268 1309. May–Jun: Sat only (call to check times).

⚓ Hillsborough Fort
Access from town square or car park at Forest Park. *Tel* 028 9268 3285. daily. www.visitlisburn.com

Downpatrick ③②

Road map E2. Co Down. 19,000. 53a Market St (028 4461 2233). Sep–Jun: Mon–Sat; Jul–Aug: daily (Sun pm only). Sat.

Were it not for its strong links with St Patrick, Downpatrick would attract few visitors. The Anglican **Down Cathedral**, high on the Hill of Down, dates in its present form from the early 19th century – previous incarnations have been razed. In the churchyard is a well-worn 10th-century cross and the reputed burial place of St Patrick, marked by a 20th-century granite slab with the inscription "Patric".

Down County Museum, which is housed in the 18th-century Old County Gaol, features refurbished cells and exhibits relating to St Patrick, while close by is the **Mound of Down**, a large Norman motte and bailey.

Terraced houses in the town of Hillsborough

🏛 Down County Museum
English Street, The Mall. *Tel* 028 4461 5218. daily. Christmas; Sat & Sun am. www.downcountymuseum.com

Environs
There are several sights linked to St Patrick on the outskirts of Downpatrick. **Struell Wells**, believed to be a former pagan place of worship that the saint blessed, has a ruined church and 17th-century bath houses. Further out and to the north at **Saul**, near where St Patrick landed and began his Irish mission in 432, is a small memorial church.

The nearby hill of **Slieve Patrick** is an important place of pilgrimage and has a granite figure of the saint at its summit.

Not far from the banks of the River Quoile is the Cistercian **Inch Abbey**, founded by John de Courcy in about 1180. Its attractive marshland setting is more memorable than its remains, but it's worth a visit.

🏠 Inch Abbey
5 km (3 miles) NW of Downpatrick. daily. www.doeni.gov.uk/niea

---

THE LIFE OF ST PATRICK
Little hard information is known about St Patrick, the patron saint of Ireland, but he was probably not the first missionary to visit the country – a certain Palladius was sent by Pope Celestine in 431. Most stories tell that Patrick was kidnapped from Britain by pirates and brought to Ireland to tend sheep. From here he escaped to France to study Christianity. In 432, he sailed back to Ireland and in Saul, County Down, he quickly converted the local chieftain. He then travelled throughout the island convincing many other Celtic tribes of the truth of the new religion. The fact that Ireland has no snakes is explained by a legend that St Patrick drove them all into the sea.

19th-century engraving showing St Patrick banishing all snakes from Ireland

Mount Stewart House ⚠

This grand 19th-century house has a splendid interior, but it is the magnificent gardens which are the main attraction. These were planted only in the 1920s, but the exotic plants and trees have thrived in the area's subtropical microclimate. Now owned by the National Trust, Mount Stewart used to belong to the London-derry family, the most famous of whom was Lord Castlereagh, British Foreign Secretary from 1812 until his death in 1822.

Lord Castlereagh (1769–1822)

The Sunk Garden comprises symmetrical beds which in summer are full of rich blue, yellow and orange flowers, complemented by purple foliage.

Stone pergola

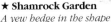

★ **Shamrock Garden**
A yew hedge in the shape of a shamrock encloses this topiary Irish harp and a striking flower-bed designed in the form of a red hand, emblem of Ulster.

The Music Room has a beautiful inlaid floor of mahogany and oak.

Italian Garden
The flowers in the Italian Garden, the largest of the formal gardens, are planted so that strong oranges and reds on the east side contrast with the softer pinks, whites and blues on the west.

Fountain

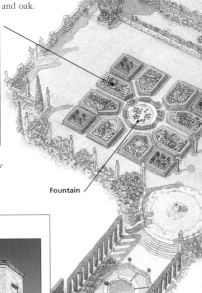

THE TEMPLE OF THE WINDS

This banqueting pavilion offers fantastic views over Strangford Lough and the Mourne Mountains beyond. It was built in 1785 by James "Athenian" Stuart, a renowned pioneer of Neo-Classical architecture, who took his inspiration from the Tower of the Winds in Athens. Restored in the 1960s, the building's finest features are the spiral staircase and the upper room's plasterwork ceiling and exquisite inlaid floor.

The Spanish Garden is framed by a neat arcade of clipped cypress trees.

For hotels and restaurants in this region see pp316–19 and pp342–5

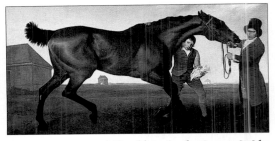

★ Hambletonian by George Stubbs
This picture of the celebrated racehorse at Newmarket, painted in 1799, hangs halfway up the main staircase.

VISITORS' CHECKLIST

Road map E2. 3 km (2 miles) N of Greyabbey, Co Down. **Tel** 028 4278 8387 from Belfast. **House** Mar–Oct: daily. **Temple** Apr–Oct: 2–5pm Sun & public hols. **Gardens** Mar–Oct: daily. **Lake** all year. in house. www.nationaltrust.org

Entrance
The Dining Room contains 22 chairs used at the Congress of Vienna (1815) and was given to Lord Castlereagh in recognition of his role in the talks.
The Chapel, converted from a sitting room in 1884, is still used by the Londonderry family

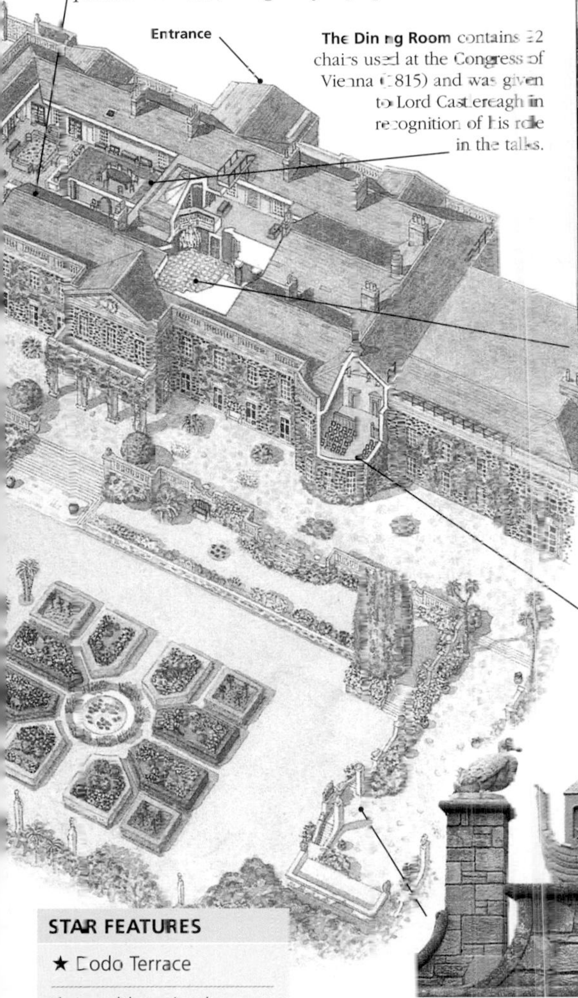

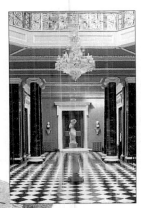

Entrance Hall
The most austere room in the house, this hall features Ionic stone pillars which have been painted to resemble green marble. It is lit by an impressive glass dome.

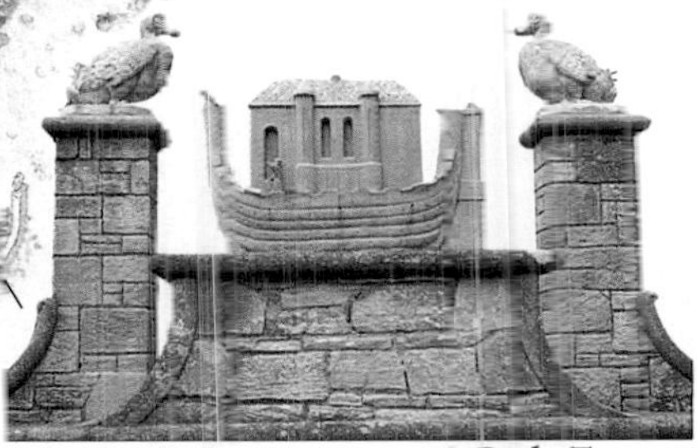

★ Dodo Terrace
The stone dodos and ark on this terrace relate to the Ark Club, a social circle set up by Lady Londonderry in London during World War I. Each member was given an animal nickname.

STAR FEATURES

- ★ Dodo Terrace
- ★ Hambletonian by George Stubbs
- ★ Shamrock Garden

Lady Bangor's Gothic boudoir in Castle Ward on the Lecale Peninsula

Lecale Peninsula ㉝

Road map E2 Co Down. 🚌 to Ardglass. 🏛 Downpatrick (028 4461 2223). www.discovernorthern ireland.com

A good way to get to this part of County Down is to take the car ferry from Portaferry on the Ards Peninsula to Strangford. Just outside this tiny port is **Castle Ward**, the estate of Lord and Lady Bangor, who seemed to argue about everything – including the design of their 18th-century mansion. His choice, Palladian, can be seen at the front, while her favourite Gothic style influences the garden façade. Likewise, the interior is a mix of Classical and Gothic fantasy. Look out for Lady Bangor's cluttered boudoir, with its extravagant fan-vaulted ceiling based on Henry VIII's chapel in Westminster Abbey. Around the grounds are trails, gardens, play areas and a farm-yard with a working corn mill.

About 4 km (2.5 miles) south of Strangford, the A2 passes **Kilclief Castle**, dating from the 15th century, one of the oldest tower houses *(see p20)* in Ireland. The road continues to **Ardglass**, now a small fishing village but once Ulster's busiest harbour. A cluster of castles was erected between the 14th and 16th centuries to protect the port, of which six remain.

St John's Point, 6 km (3.5 miles) southwest of Ardglass, offers a sweeping panorama over Dundrum Bay.

⛪ Castle Ward
On A25, 2.5 km (1.5 miles) W of Strangford. **Tel** 028 4488 1204. **House** ◯ mid-Mar–Oct: 11am–5pm daily. 🏷 ♿ ▢ ▢ **Grounds** ◯ daily. www.nationaltrust.org.uk

Castlewellan Forest Park ㉞

Road map D2. Main St, Castlewellan, Co Down. **Tel** 028 4377 8664. ◯ 10am–sunset daily. 🏷 for car park.

The outstanding feature of Castlewellan Forest Park, in the foothills of the Mourne Mountains, is its magnificent arboretum. This has grown far beyond the original walled garden, begun in 1740, and now comprises hothouses,

dwarf conifer beds and a rhododendron wood.

Elsewhere in the park are a 19th-century Scottish baronial-style castle (now a conference centre), a lake and pleasant woodlands; these are at their most colourful in autumn.

Mountains of Mourne ㉟

Road map D2. Co Down. 🚌 to Newry. 🚌 to Newcastle. 🏛 10–14 Central Promenade, Newcastle (028 4372 2222). www.downdc.gov.uk

These mountains occupy just a small corner of County Down, with no more than a dozen peaks surpassing 600 m (2,000 ft), and yet they attract thousands of visitors each year.

Only one road of any size, the B27 between Kilkeel and Hilltown, crosses the Mournes, making this ideal territory for walkers. A popular but tough trail runs from **Newcastle**, the main gateway to the area, up to the peak of **Slieve Donard**: at 848 m (2,781 ft), this is the highest mountain in the range. Part of the route follows the **Mourne Wall**, which was erected in 1904–22 to enclose the catchment area of the two reservoirs in the **Silent Valley**.

Over 20 short hikes are to be enjoyed in the area. These range from easy strolls around Rostrevor Forest to rather more arduous treks up Slieve Muck and other Mourne peaks. Tourist information centres will have details.

Some 35 km (22 miles) north of Newcastle, the **Legananny Dolmen** *(see p32)* is one of the finest and most photo-graphed ancient sights in the country.

Rounded peaks of the Mountains of Mourne

A Tour of the Mourne Coast 36

Newcastle, where, in the words of the 19th-century songwriter Percy French, "the Mountains of Mourne sweep down to the sea", makes a good base from which to explore this area. Driving up and down the dipping roads of the Mournes is one of the highlights of a trip to Northern Ireland. Along the coast, the Mourne Coastal Route drive skirts between the foothills and the Irish Sea, providing lovely views and linking a variety of fishing villages and historic castles. Heading inland, you pass through an emptier landscape of moorland, purple with heather. The Silent Valley, with a visitors' centre and well-marked paths, is one of the areas that have been developed especially for tourists

Dundrum ②
The town is overlooked by the ruins of a Norman castle, and from the nearby bay you can see the mountains rising in the distance.

Tollymore Forest Park ③
This attractive park is dotted with follies like the Gothic Gate that formed part of the original 18th-century estate.

Spelga Dam ④
There are stunning views north from the Spelga Dam over the Mourne foothills.

Newcastle ①
A popular resort since the early 19th century, Newcastle has a promenade overlooking a sweeping, sandy beach.

Rostrevor with Slieve Martin behind

Silent Valley ⑦
The valley is closed to traffic, but you can walk to the top of Ben Crom Mountain from the car park, or in summer go by bus.

Rostrevor ⑤
This tranquil and leafy Victorian resort nestles below the peak of Slieve Martin, on the shores of Carlingford Lough.

Green Castle ⑥
Erected in the 13th century, Green Castle lies at the end of a single-track road on a rocky outcrop at the entrance to Carlingford Lough.

TIPS FOR DRIVERS

Length: 85 km (53 miles).
Stopping-off points: Newcastle has the biggest choice of pubs and restaurants. Dundrum, Annalong, Kilkeel and Rostrevor all have pubs, and a café opens in the Silent Valley in summer. The Spelga Dam and Tollymore Forest Park are good picnic spots. (See also pp385–7.)

0 kilometres 5

0 miles 3

KEY

▬▬	Tour route
===	Other roads
☀	Viewpoint

TRAVELLERS' NEEDS

WHERE TO STAY

Whether you are staying in exclusive luxury or modest self-catering accommodation, one thing you can be certain of in Ireland is that you'll receive a warm welcome. The Irish are renowned for their friendliness. Even in big corporate hotels, where you might expect the reception to be more impersonal, the staff go out of their way to be hospitable. The choice is enormous: you can stay in an elegant 18th-century country house, a luxurious (or slightly run-down) castle, a Victorian town house, an old-fashioned commercial hotel, a cosy village inn, or on a working farm. For the hardier visitor there are good hostels, plenty of trailer and camping sites, or even your own horse-drawn caravan. We give details here of the types of accommodation available, tourist board ratings and the choices for house or apartment rental. Our listings on pages 294–319 recommend over 300 hotels around the country – all places of quality, ranging from simple bed-and-breakfast to unashamed luxury accommodation. Fáilte Ireland (the Irish Tourist Board) and the Northern Ireland Tourist Board both publish comprehensive guides.

Waterford Castle doorman

Entrance hall of the Delphi Lodge *(see p311)* in Leenane

HOTELS

At the top of the price range there are a handful of expensive, luxury hotels in castles and stately country houses. Magnificently furnished and run, they offer maximum comfort, delicious food and a wide range of sports facilities – either owned by the hotel or available close by. Salmon-fishing, fox-hunting and shooting can be arranged as well as riding, golf, sailing and cycling.

If your priority is a full range of indoor facilities, such as a gym, sauna and pool, the modern hotel chains will best cater to your needs. **The Doyle Collection** and **The Tower Hotel Group** offer this standard of accommodation in the Republic, as does **Hastings Hotels** in Northern Ireland. However, these establishments can sometimes lack the charm and individuality of privately run hotels.

Coastal resort hotels usually offer a range of sports activities or can advise you on the best places to go. In smaller towns, the main hotel is often the social centre of the area. Some hotels offer reduced rates for stays of two nights or longer.

The shamrock symbols of both the Northern Ireland Tourist Board and Fáilte Ireland are displayed by hotels (and other forms of accommodation) that have been inspected and officially approved.

COUNTRY HOUSE ACCOMMODATION

Visitors wishing to stay in a period country home and sample authentic Irish country life can contact a specialist organization called **Hidden Ireland**. However, this type of accommodation may not suit everybody, as the houses are not guesthouses, hotels or bed-and-breakfast establishments, but something quite different. You should therefore not expect the same facilities and service usually found in a hotel, such as a swimming pool, elevators, televisions, porters and room service. Instead, the experience is a very intimate one; guests dine together with their host and hostess as if at a private dinner party. Many of the houses have been in the same family for hundreds of years and the history attached to them can be fascinating. Prices reflect the type of house and the standard of accommodation, but all offer excellent value for money and

The entrance to the Shelbourne Hotel in Dublin

◁ **Murphy's Pub, Dingle**

Bar at the Hunter's Hotel (see p301) in Rathnew, County Wicklow

a first-hand experience of an aspect of the Irish way of life.

There are many other private residences that also take paying guests. Two useful publications, *Friendly Homes of Ireland* and *Ireland's Blue Book*, provide listings and information and are available from tourist offices and bookshops. Tourist boards throughout Ireland also supply listings and make reservations.

GUESTHOUSES

Most guesthouses are found in cities and large towns. They are usually converted family homes and have an atmosphere all of their own. Most offer a good-value evening meal and all give you a delicious full Irish breakfast (see p322). Top-of-the-range guesthouses can be just as good, and sometimes even better, than hotels. You will see a much more personal side of a town or city while staying at a guesthouse. If you are looking for anonymity, however, a guesthouse may not suit you – both the proprietor and your fellow guests are likely to try and draw you into conversation.

There are plenty of good guesthouses to choose from in the Dublin area and the prices are usually reasonable. **The Irish Hotels Federation** publishes a useful booklet with guesthouse listings that cover the whole of Ireland including Dublin. The Northern Ireland Tourist Board publishes its own

similar booklet, called *Where to Stay in Northern Ireland*. This includes a comprehensive list of approved guesthouses which is updated annually. However, it is hard to beat personal recommendations you might receive from fellow guests.

Bedroom at Enniscoe House (see p310), Crossmolina in County Mayo

PRICES

Room rates advertised in both Northern Ireland and the Republic are inclusive of tax and service. In general, prices in the Republic are on a par with the North. Hotel rates can

vary by as much as 40 per cent depending on the time of year. Many hotels often have large discounts. Country house rates also vary a great deal according to the season. Guesthouse prices are influenced by their proximity to tourist sights and public transport. For those on a tight budget, farmhouse accommodation represents excellent value for money, though the cheapest option is self-catering in a rented cottage (see p290).

TIPPING

Tipping in Ireland is a matter of personal discretion but is not common practice, even at the larger hotels. Tasks performed by staff are considered part of the service. Tipping is not expected, for example, for carrying bags to your room or for serving drinks. However, it is usual to tip the waiting staff in hotel restaurants: the standard tip is around 10 per cent and anything over 15 per cent of the bill would be considered generous.

BOOKING

It is wise to reserve your accommodation during the peak season and public holidays (see p5), particularly if your visit coincides with a local festival or major sporting event (see pp28–9). Fáilte Ireland can offer advice and make reservations through its nationwide accommodation service; the Northern Ireland Tourist Board runs a similar service. Central reservation facilities are available at the hotel chains that have been listed here.

Façade of the Londonderry Arms (see p318) in Carnlough, County Antrim

A bed-and-breakfast on the River Corrib in Galway

BED-AND-BREAKFAST ACCOMMODATION

Ireland has the reputation for the best B&Bs in Europe. You will never be far from a place to stay, even in the remotest spots. Your welcome will always be friendly and the food and company excellent. Even if the house is no architectural beauty the comfort and atmosphere will more than compensate. Not all bedrooms have bathrooms *en suite*. When one is available, you may have to pay a little extra, but considering the inexpensive rates, the surcharge is negligible.

The Irish swear by their B&Bs and many stay in them by choice rather than suffer the impersonality and prices of the mainstream hotels; frequent visitors to Ireland agree. The **Ireland Bed and Breakfast Network** will provide details of bed-and-breakfast accommodation throughout Ireland. The **Town and Country Homes Association** covers the Republic.

FARMHOUSES

Farmhouse vacations are a popular tradition in Ireland. **Irish Farmhouse Holidays Ltd** has a list of farmhouses in the Republic that take paying guests. You can stay for one night or longer and they

make an excellent base for touring the countryside. As with most things in Ireland, it is the hospitality and friendliness of the people that makes staying on a farm so memorable. You get a feel of rural Ireland with its rich agricultural heritage, and the families are determined you will enjoy every moment of your stay.

HOUSE AND APARTMENT RENTALS

Vacations spent in rental houses are an increasingly popular option in Ireland and there are properties to rent all over the country. You are likely to have more choice in the south and west as these areas have traditionally attracted the majority of tourists. Fáilte Ireland has a small section in its accommodation guide, but local tourist offices have lists

of apartments and houses to rent in their area. Accommodation can range from quaint, stone cottages and converted barns to more modern, purpose-built bungalows. All will generally have adequate facilities, with simple but comfortable furnishings, modern kitchen equipment and televisions.

The properties available through the popular organization **Rent an Irish Cottage** are built in traditional style with whitewashed walls inside and out, and painted roofs and windows; the decor is also traditional – simple and attractive. Locations are generally superb; the only possible criticism is, if you wanted to be "away from it all", they are built in clusters of about ten.

At the other end of the scale, you could rent a castle or country house, furnished with paintings and antiques. In some cases, the properties are fully staffed. A company called **Elegant Ireland** has a selection of such properties. **Irish Landmark Trust Ltd** has a range of stunning accommodation in castles, lighthouses and gate lodges.

CAMPING, TRAILERS AND MOTOR HOMES

A list of fully inspected camping and trailer parks is given in the Fáilte Ireland accommodation guide. Many of the camp sites and parks offer additional facilities – these might include a shop, restaurant or café/snack bar, an indoor games room, laundry, tennis court and minature golf course. The standard and

A farmhouse in Clonakilty, County Cork

A traditional painted horse-drawn caravan

condition of these facilities will vary but you can be reliably guided by the tourist board's star ratings: four-star parks have an extensive range of facilities with a high standard of management; three-star parks have good facilities and management; two-star parks offer limited facilities and good management and the one-star parks have the minimum facilities required for registration with Fáilte Ireland. A complete list of approved camping sites in the North is produced by the Northern Ireland Tourist Board.

If you want to experience the Irish countryside at a more leisurely and relaxing pace, it is possible to hire a traditional horse-drawn caravan. One of the best companies specializing in this type of trip is **Kilvahan Caravans**, which is based at Portlaoise in the Midlands.

YOUTH HOSTELS

There are 26 youth hostels registered with **An Óige** (the Irish Youth Hostel Association), set in some wonderfully scenic areas of Ireland in buildings ranging from castles to military barracks. Accommodation is generally provided in simple dormitories with comfortable beds and basic cooking facilities. You can only use these hostels if you are a member of An Óige or another youth

organization affiliated to the International Youth Hostel Federation. Charges vary according to the standard of accommodation, location and season. Northern Ireland is covered by the **Youth Hostel Association of Northern Ireland** which has eight registered hostels.

Independent Holiday Hostels of Ireland publishes a guide to a host of independent hostels, and places such as universities offer similar inexpensive accommodation. Tourist boards have recommendations or check booking websites such as www.hostelworld.com.

DISABLED TRAVELLERS

A fact sheet for disabled visitors can be obtained from tourist offices, Dublin Tourism, and Fáilte Ireland, and in their main accommodation guide there is a symbol for wheelchair accessibility. A similar symbol is used in the accommodation listings in this book (see pp294–319). The Citizens Information Board (see p372) is another body that offers information on accommodation for the disabled.

The annual publication *Holidays in the British Isles* caters specifically for the disabled traveller and covers Northern Ireland. There is also a guide, with comprehensive listings, available from the Northern Ireland Tourist Board entitled *Accessible Accommodation*.

Fáilte Ireland sign for approved accommodation

Typical bed-and-breakfast sign in Pettigo, County Donegal

DIRECTORY

An Óige (Irish YHA)
61 Mountjoy St, Dublin 7.
Tel 01 830 4555.
www.anoige.ie

Elegant Ireland
Box No. 1087, Dublin 8.
Tel 01 473 2505. www.elegant.ie

Hastings Hotels
1066 House, Upper Newtownards d, Belfast.
Tel 028 3047 1066.
www.hastingshotels.com

Hidden Ireland
P. O. Box 31, Westport, Co Mayo.
Tel 01 662 7166 or 098 66650.
www.hiddenireland.com

Independent Holiday Hostels of Ireland
PO Box 11772, Fairview, Dublin 3. *Tel* 01 836 4700.
www.hostels-ireland.com

Ireland Bed and Breakfast Network
www.bnb.ie

Irish Farmhouse Holidays Ltd
Belleek Rd, Ballyshannon, Co Donegal. *Tel* 071 982 2222.
www.irishfarmholidays.com

Irish Hotels Federation
13 Northbrook Rd, Dublin 6.
Tel 01 497 6459. www.ihf.ie

Irish Landmark Trust Ltd
25 Eustace St, Dublin 2.
Tel 01 670 4733
www.irishlandmark.com

Kilvahan Caravans
Coolrain, Co Laois.
Tel 05787 35178. www.horse drawncaravans.com

Rent an Irish Cottage
51 O'Connell St, Limerick.
Tel 061 411109
www.rentacottage.ie

The Doyle Collection
Pembroke Rd, Dublin 4.
Tel 01 607 0000.
www.doylecollection.com

Tower Hotel Group
Tower Hotel Group, FBD House, Naas Rd, Dublin 12.
Tel 01 428 2400.
www.towerhotelgroup.com

Town and Country Homes Association
Belleek Rd, Ballyshannon, Co Donegal. *Tel* 071 982 2222.
www.townandcountry.ie

YHA Northern Ireland
22–32 Donegall Rd, Belfast. *Tel* 028 9032 4733. www.hini.org.uk

Ireland's Best: Hotels

The hotels featured here are a selection from our lists of recommended places to stay on pages 294–319. They give an indication of the very best that Ireland has to offer, ranging from private establishments which are members of the Hidden Ireland group *(see p288)* to the efficiency and luxury of five-star hotels and the romance of historic castles. All are impressive places, both for their setting and the buildings themselves.

Harvey's Point
This unique, country hotel enjoys a fabulous location on the shores of Lough Eske. (See p313.)

Delphi Lodge
The atmosphere at this comfortable, well-run fishing lodge is extremely relaxing. The River Delphi and nearby loughs provide plenty of sport. (See p311.)

NORTHWEST IRELAND

Ashford Castle
This huge Gothic-style edifice is set on the shores of Lough Corrib. The standard of service is impeccable and the food is excellent. (See p310.)

THE WEST OF IRELAND

Adare Manor
Set in a large estate beside one of the prettiest villages in the country, this luxurious hotel occupies a magnificent Victorian Gothic mansion. (See p307.)

THE LOWER SHANNON

CORK AND KERRY

Bantry House
The spacious library in this 18th-century house looks out on to the gardens. Many of the bedrooms enjoy superb views of Bantry Bay. (See pp168–9 and p302.)

Everglades Hotel
This imposing hotel sits on the banks of the River Foyle, a short drive from the wild beaches of County Donegal and the stunning Sperrin Mountains. (See p319.)

NORTHERN
IRELAND

THE
MIDLANDS

Hunter's Hotel
Cobbled courtyards, paddocks and a magnificent garden are only a few of the attractions of this friendly and comfortable inn. The building dates back to 1720, and is owned and run by the fourth generation of the Hunter family. (See p301.)

SOUTHEAST
IRELAND

Roundwood House
This fine, small Palladian house is set in chestnut and beech woods. The Slieve Bloom Mountains are close by and you can fish and play golf locally. The lovely rooms are filled with antiques, books and pictures and the atmosphere is one of relaxed informality. (See p316.)

0 kilometres 50

0 miles 25

Waterford Castle
The ultimate in "getting away from it all", this 15th-century castle sits on a beautifully located island in the estuary of the River Suir. The hotel is reachable only by its own private ferry. (See p302.)

Choosing a Hotel

These hotels have been selected for their good value, facilities and location. They are listed by region, starting with Dublin, and then by price. Price bands for Northern Ireland are given on pages 317 and 319. Map references refer either to the Dublin Street Finder on pages 116 and 117, or the road map on the inside back cover.

DUBLIN

SOUTHEAST DUBLIN Baggot Court Townhouse
€

92 Lower Baggot St, Dublin 2 **Tel** *01 661 0246* **Fax** *01 661 0253* **Rooms** *17* **Map** *F5*

A comfortable and relaxing stay is guaranteed at this historical Georgian townhouse, which is renowned for its friendly and helpful service and its excellent cooked breakfasts. Baggot Court is a short walk from Grafton Street. Complimentary Wi-Fi and parking. **www.baggotcourt.com**

SOUTHEAST DUBLIN Harcourt Hotel
€€

60 Harcourt St, Dublin 2 **Tel** *01 478 3677* **Fax** *01 475 2013* **Rooms** *104* **Map** *D5*

Just off St Stephen's Green, Harcourt Hotel boasts a central location. Though the interior is unremarkable, bedrooms are modern and well equipped. There is a popular nightclub, D-Two, situated in the basement of the hotel which is a draw for late-night revellers. **www.harcourthotel.ie**

SOUTHEAST DUBLIN Leeson Hotel
€€

27 Leeson St Lower, Dublin 2 **Tel** *01 676 3380* **Fax** *01 661 8273* **Rooms** *20* **Map** *E5*

Close to St Stephen's Green, this cheerfully decorated hotel is spread across two Georgian buildings. The ambience is relaxed and informal, and service is of a high quality. Its bar, Kobra, is elegant with wood furnishings and is open on Fridays and Saturdays. Bedrooms are tidy and comfortable, if on the small side. **www.theleesonhotel.com**

SOUTHEAST DUBLIN Russell Court
€€

21–25 Harcourt St, Dublin 2 **Tel** *01 478 4066* **Fax** *01 478 1576* **Rooms** *42* **Map** *D5*

Jolly and welcoming, Russell Court is a good choice for younger clientele. Bedrooms are neat and service is modest. The hotel's main attraction is the exclusive Krystle night club and Bojangles for the 30-plus. At the rear, Dicey's Garden is a popular beer garden. Trams pass at the front of the hotel. **www.russellcourthotel.ie**

SOUTHEAST DUBLIN Stauntons on the Green
€€

83 St Stephen's Green, Dublin 2 **Tel** *01 478 2300* **Fax** *01 478 2263* **Rooms** *54* **Map** *D5*

Beside the Ministry of Foreign Affairs, this guesthouse offers cosy and modest accommodation in three terraced Georgian houses. While all bedrooms are reasonably equipped and en suite, those to the rear are quieter, with views of the private garden and Iveagh gardens. Valet-serviced parking available. **www.thecastlehotelgroup.com**

SOUTHEAST DUBLIN Trinity Lodge
€€

12 South Frederick St, Dublin 2 **Tel** *01 617 0900* **Fax** *01 617 0999* **Rooms** *23* **Map** *E4*

Close to Grafton Street and a stone's throw from Trinity College, this Georgian town house enjoys one of the best locations in town. Though traditional in style, it is furnished with modern conveniences. Warmly-coloured en suite bedrooms are well maintained. **www.trinitylodge.com**

SOUTHEAST DUBLIN The Alexander Hotel
€€€

Merrion Square, Dublin 2 **Tel** *01 607 3700* **Fax** *01 661 5663* **Rooms** *102* **Map** *F4*

The Alexander is a comfortable, contemporary hotel near the museums and Georgian area of Merrion Square and a short stroll from Grafton Street. An attractive stone tower at the front of the building gives suites a circular living area. Rooms are larger than average. **www.ocallaghanhotels.com**

SOUTHEAST DUBLIN Buswells
€€€

25 Molesworth St, Dublin 2 **Tel** *01 614 6500* **Fax** *01 676 2090* **Rooms** *67* **Map** *E4*

Comprising five Georgian town houses, this slightly old-fashioned hotel has been in operation since 1882. It has a central location beside government buildings and on a street renowned for high-level commercial art galleries. The sophisticated interior is decorated in warm colours. Frequented by political figures. **www.quinnhotels.com**

SOUTHEAST DUBLIN The Cliff Townhouse
€€€

22 St Stephen's Green, Dublin 2 **Tel** *01 638 3939* **Fax** *01 638 3900* **Rooms** *9* **Map** *D4*

Set in a Georgian house overlooking St Stephen's Green, this charming and intimate boutique hotel is stylishly furnished with antiques and quality reproduction pieces. Each of the bedrooms is individually designed with comfort and character in mind. The sophisticated restaurant serves outstanding food. **www.theclifftownhouse.com**

Key to Symbols *see back cover flap*

SOUTHEAST DUBLIN Davenport

Merrion Square, Dublin 2 **Tel** *01 607 3500* **Fax** *01 661 5663* **Rooms** *115*

€€€
Map F4

Close to the National Gallery, this hotel lies in the heart of Georgian Dublin. The Neo-Classical façade dates from 1863. Mahogany, brass and marble furnishings give it the feel of a gentleman's club. Ample bedrooms are well appointed with warmly coloured decor. There's a fitness suite. **www.ocallaghanhotels.com**

SOUTHEAST DUBLIN The Fitzwilliam Hotel

St Stephen's Green, Dublin 2 **Tel** *01 478 7000* **Fax** *01 478 7878* **Rooms** *138*

€€€
Map D5

This Conran-designed hotel is ideally located at the top of Grafton Street, near shopping, bars and restaurants and opposite the St Stephen's Green park. Guestrooms have CD players and high-speed broadband. Restaurants in the hotel include the Michelin-starred Thornton's Restaurant. **www.fitzwilliamhoteldublin.com**

SOUTHEAST DUBLIN Kilronan House

70 Adelaide Rd, Dublin 2 **Tel** *01 475 5266* **Fax** *01 478 2841* **Rooms** *15*

€€€

Situated on a leafy street near St Stephen's Green, around the corner from the National Concert Hall, this listed town house dates from 1834. Still retaining its Georgian character, it offers modern comforts, including orthopaedic beds. Delicious breakfasts with home-made breads. Friendly hosts. **www.kilronanhousehotel.com**

SOUTHEAST DUBLIN Molesworth Court Suites

Molesworth Court, Schoolhouse Lane, Dublin 2 **Tel** *01 676 4799* **Fax** *01 676 4982* **Rooms** *12*

€€€
Map E4

Tucked away in a quiet lane off the fashionable Molesworth Street, this four-star hotel comprises 12 purpose-built, self-contained apartments and penthouses. Equipped with modern conveniences, rooms are clean and cosy. Service is friendly. Enclosed parking is provided. Good value for families. **www.molesworthcourt.ie**

SOUTHEAST DUBLIN Mont Clare

Merrion Square, Dublin 2 **Tel** *01 607 3800* **Fax** *01 661 5663* **Rooms** *74*

€€€
Map F4

Though not as grand as its sister hotel, the Davenport opposite, Mont Clare enjoys a good location and is traditionally furnished. Well-appointed bedrooms are air conditioned and tastefully decorated. The sizeable and popular bar serves carvery lunches. Guests may visit the gym across the road. **www.ocallaghanhotels.com**

SOUTHEAST DUBLIN Number 31

31 Leeson Close, Leeson St Lower, Dublin 2 **Tel** *01 676 5011* **Fax** *01 676 2929* **Rooms** *21*

€€€
Map E5

Reputedly the most stylish guesthouse in the city, this elegant Georgian house is more of a boutique hotel than a B&B, with individually decorated, luxurious bedrooms. The Coach House features a collection of original art and a sunken seating area. Award-winning breakfasts are served in the plant-filled conservatory. **www.number31.ie**

SOUTHEAST DUBLIN The Stephen's Green Hotel

2 St Stephen's Green, Dublin 2 **Tel** *01 607 3600* **Fax** *01 661 5663* **Rooms** *99*

€€€
Map D5

This smart contemporary hotel on St Stephen's Green incorporates two restored Georgian houses and is fronted by a large glass atrium. The hotel is modern and comfortable, with attractive features such as a restored Georgian library. It is a short stroll to shopping and nightlife around Grafton Street. **www.ocallaghanhotels.com**

SOUTHEAST DUBLIN Stephen's Hall Premier Hotel

14–17 Leeson St Lower, Dublin 2 **Tel** *01 638 1111* **Fax** *01 638 1122* **Rooms** *30*

€€€
Map E5

Close to St Stephen's Green, Stephen's Hall Hotel provides suites, which include an attached kitchen. Its proximity to the vibrant city centre makes it an ideal base from which to explore Dublin's main sights. This is a very good-value family option. Underground parking is available. **www.premiersuitesdublin.com**

SOUTHEAST DUBLIN The Merrion

Merrion St Upper, Dublin 2 **Tel** *01 603 0600* **Fax** *01 603 0700* **Rooms** *142*

€€€€
Map E4

In the heart of Georgian Dublin, the Merrion is an elegant and stylish oasis with open log fires, opulent interiors and a collection of Irish art and period antiques. It's a landmark hotel, comprising four listed town houses from the 1760s, sensitively restored to their original grandeur. Guests can use the excellent Tethra Spa. **www.merrionhotel.com**

SOUTHEAST DUBLIN The Shelbourne Hotel

27 St Stephen's Green, Dublin 2 **Tel** *01 663 4500* **Fax** *01 661 6006* **Rooms** *265*

€€€€
Map E4/5

This elegant and stylish hotel, built in 1824, is a Dublin landmark. Sitting in an excellent location overlooking St Stephen's Green and near the museums, Merrion Square and the Georgian district, it provides five-star luxury while retaining its historic charm. Its bar is popular with well-heeled Dubliners. **www.theshelbourne.ie**

SOUTHEAST DUBLIN Westbury Hotel

Grafton St, Dublin 2 **Tel** *01 679 1122* **Fax** *01 679 7078* **Rooms** *205*

€€€€
Map D4

Enjoying possibly the most convenient location in the city, the Westbury is only seconds from Dublin's main shopping street. The first-floor lobby of this smart, ritzy, yet traditionally-styled hotel, is a popular meeting place for afternoon tea. Underground parking comes with valet service. There's also a small gymnasium. **www.doylecollection.com**

SOUTHEAST DUBLIN Westin Hotel

College Green, Dublin 2 **Tel** *01 645 1000* **Fax** *01 645 1234* **Rooms** *163*

€€€€
Map D3

Two 19th-century landmark buildings and part of the former Allied Irish Bank were reconstructed to create this sizeable hotel, across the street from Trinity College. Well-appointed bedrooms are furnished to a high standard. The beds are very comfortable. The former vaults of the bank are now a bar, the Mint. **www.thewestindublin.com**

SOUTHEAST DUBLIN Conrad Hotel

Earlsfort Terrace, Dublin 2 **Tel** *01 602 8900* **Fax** *01 676 5424* **Rooms** *191*

Map *D5*

Opposite the National Concert Hall, this international-style hotel is geared towards business people. The decor is tasteful and the atmosphere airy. Bedrooms are fitted out in a contemporary style with light-wood furnishings and comfortable beds. The higher floors have good views. **www.conradhotels.com**

SOUTHWEST DUBLIN Avalon House

55 Aungier St, Dublin 2 **Tel** *01 475 0001* **Fax** *01 475 0303* **Rooms** *70*

Map *C4*

One of the longest established hostels in the city, the centrally located Avalon House provides cheap and cheerful accommodation in a restored redbrick Victorian building. Dorm rooms are clean, with pine and tile floors, high ceilings and an open fire. Popular with young, independent travellers. There's a café in the front. **www.avalon-house.ie**

SOUTHWEST DUBLIN Blooms Hotel

Anglesea St, Dublin 2 **Tel** *01 671 5622* **Fax** *01 671 5997* **Rooms** *100*

Map *D3*

On the fringes of bustling Temple Bar and close to Trinity College, Blooms Hotel's location is its main selling point. Although unremarkable inside, it has a striking modern exterior. Compact bedrooms are adequate, but those at the front are preferable. There's live music in the busy Vat House Bar, while Club M is a popular nightclub. **www.blooms.ie**

SOUTHWEST DUBLIN Central Hotel

1–5 Exchequer St, Dublin 2 **Tel** *01 679 7302* **Fax** *01 679 7303* **Rooms** *70*

Map *D5*

Established in 1887, this three-star hotel is aptly named, given its convenient location, very close to Grafton Street. Equipped with modern facilities, it retains a somewhat old-fashioned atmosphere, with traditional, yet cosy, decor and a relaxing library. Bedrooms are neat, functional and reasonably priced. **www.centralhotel.ie**

SOUTHWEST DUBLIN Jury's Inn Christchurch

Christ Church Place, Dublin 8 **Tel** *01 454 0000* **Fax** *01 454 0012* **Rooms** *182*

Map *B4*

Opposite Christ Church Cathedral, in the old Viking centre of Dublin, this modern hotel lies within walking distance of Temple Bar and the city centre. Rooms are neat and well equipped. Bathrooms are adequate, if a little on the small side. Prices charged per room prove particularly good value for families. **www.jurysinns.com**

SOUTHWEST DUBLIN Temple Bar Hotel

Fleet St, Dublin 2 **Tel** *01 612 9200* **Fax** *01 677 3088* **Rooms** *129*

Map *D3*

Its location in the heart of Temple Bar – a lively area, with several pubs and restaurants – makes this modern hotel popular for stag and hen parties. Bedrooms are clean and adequate, if a little on the small side and lacking in character. Multi-storey parking nearby. **www.templebarhotel.com**

SOUTHWEST DUBLIN Grafton Capital Hotel

Lower Stephen's St, Dublin 2 **Tel** *01 648 1221* **Fax** *01 648 1122* **Rooms** *75*

Map *D4*

Located in the centre, this modern hotel with a Georgian façade offers neat and well-furnished accommodation at reasonable prices. Bedrooms provide all modern facilities. The popular bar, also a casual dining restaurant and nightclub, features live music. Business facilities are available and there is parking nearby. **www.graftoncapitalhotel.com**

SOUTHWEST DUBLIN Radisson Blu Royal Hotel

Golden Lane, Dublin 8 **Tel** *01 898 2900* **Fax** *01 898 2909* **Rooms** *150*

Map *C4*

This modern luxury hotel is in a quiet street in the heart of old Dublin, within walking distance of the city centre, Dublin Castle and Trinity College. Rooms and bathrooms are spacious and guests can use a fitness centre and swimming pool nearby. There is also a business centre. **www.radissonblu.ie/royalhotel-dublin**

SOUTHWEST DUBLIN Clarence Hotel

6–8 Wellington Quay, Dublin 2 **Tel** *01 407 0800* **Fax** *01 407 0820* **Rooms** *49*

Map *C3*

Overlooking the River Liffey, this 1852 Dublin landmark was bought by the rock band U2 in 1992 and has acquired cult status. With original wood-panelling in arts and crafts style, and luxuriously furnished rooms, this old establishment successfully combines contemporary cool and comfort. **www.theclarence.ie**

SOUTHWEST DUBLIN Morgan Hotel

10 Fleet St, Dublin 2 **Tel** *01 643 7000* **Fax** *01 643 7060* **Rooms** *120*

Map *D3*

In the heart of Temple Bar, this self-styled boutique hotel is contemporary in design with clean lines and uncluttered public spaces. Minimalistic bedrooms have beech wood furnishings, cotton linen and CD systems. The ambience is relaxing, though rooms overlooking the street can be noisy. There's a fine Morgan bar. **www.themorgan.com**

SOUTHWEST DUBLIN Brooks

59–62 Drury St, Dublin 2 **Tel** *01 670 4000* **Fax** *01 670 4455* **Rooms** *98*

Map *D4*

This immaculately maintained boutique hotel, excellently located just minutes from Grafton Street, has a club-like feel, welcoming ambience and enjoys a great reputation. It was built in 1997 and remodelled in 2003 with contemporary flourishes and warm colours, though the decor is tastefully traditional. **www.brookshotel.ie**

NORTH OF THE LIFFEY The Belvedere Hotel

Parnell Square, Great Denmark St, Dublin 1 **Tel** *01 873 7700* **Fax** *01 873 7777* **Rooms** *92*

This comfortable hotel is located 100 metres (110 yards) away from the top of O'Connell Street. The bedrooms have power showers and free broadband access. There is also a bar, bistro and entertainment on site. It is not advisable to walk alone in the area at night. **www.belvederehotel.ie**

NORTH OF THE LIFFEY Hotel Isaacs
€€ Map E2

Store St, Dublin 2 **Tel** *01 813 4700* **Fax** *01 836 0390* **Rooms** *103*

Conveniently located opposite the bus station, and within walking distance of many bars and restaurants, this three-star hotel is furnished in a contemporary style. Bedrooms are relaxing, if modest. A European-style café-bar serves light lunches. There's also an Italian restaurant, Il Vignardo. **www.isaacs.ie**

NORTH OF THE LIFFEY Jury's Inn Parnell Street
€€ Map D2

Moore Street Plaza, Parnell St, Dublin 1 **Tel** *01 878 4900* **Fax** *01 878 4999* **Rooms** *253*

Located just off O'Connell Street, this hotel offers good value for money and is an ideal base from which to explore the north side of the city. Rooms are modern and neat. The Innfusion Restaurant serves reasonably priced breakfasts and dinners daily. **www.jurysinns.com**

NORTH OF THE LIFFEY Cassidy's Hotel
€€€ Map D2

Cavendish Row, Upper O'Connell St, Dublin 1 **Tel** *01 878 0555* **Fax** *01 878 0687* **Rooms** *113*

This hotel is conveniently located at the top of O'Connell Street, opposite the Gate Theatre, in three adjoining red-brick Georgian town houses. The generously proportioned rooms have been modernized, while retaining some period features. Spacious bedrooms are all en suite, with contemporary furnishings. **www.cassidyshotel.com**

NORTH OF THE LIFFEY Clarion IFSC
€€€ Map F2

International Financial Service Centre, North Wall Quay, Dublin 1 **Tel** *01 433 8800* **Fax** *01 433 8801* **Rooms** *180*

Overlooking the River Liffey, in the heart of the financial district, this hotel is as popular with tourists as with business travellers. Public spaces are bright, airy and minimalist in style. A short stroll from the centre, it offers well-designed and decent accommodation. **www.clariondublincity.com**

NORTH OF THE LIFFEY Gresham Hotel
€€€ Map D1

23 O'Connell St Upper, Dublin 1 **Tel** *01 874 6881* **Fax** *01 878 7175* **Rooms** *288*

One of Dublin's oldest and best-known hotels, the Gresham is a popular rendezvous spot with ever-lively public areas. It has pleasant furnishings that combine classic and contemporary styles. The bedrooms are well equipped and cheerfully decorated. This is a good business hotel. **www.gresham-hotels.com**

NORTH OF THE LIFFEY The Morrison
€€€ Map C3

Ormond Quay, Dublin 1 **Tel** *01 887 2400* **Fax** *01 874 4039* **Rooms** *138*

Located on the quay overlooking the river, this luxurious contemporary hotel was built in 1999, with John Rocha as design consultant. The interior is a mix of high ceilings, dark woods, pale white walls, dim lighting, handcrafted Irish carpets and original art. Bedrooms have a modern design. There's a stylish restaurant, Halo. **www.morrisonhotel.ie**

FURTHER AFIELD Bewley's Hotel
€€

Merrion Rd, Ballsbridge, Dublin 4 **Tel** *01 668 1111* **Fax** *01 668 1999* **Rooms** *304*

This magnificent roderick building, formerly a school, is part of the reliable Bewley's chain of hotels. Comfortably furnished in a contemporary style, it has big and well-equipped bedrooms. Arguably the best value hotel in Dublin. The Brasserie is a popular restaurant. **www.bewleyshotels.com**

FURTHER AFIELD Deer Park Hotel
€€ Road Map D3

Howth, Co Dublin **Tel** *01 832 2624* **Fax** *01 839 2405* **Rooms** *69*

This hotel is set in the grounds of Howth Castle on Howth Head and has beautiful sea views. It is surrounded by parkland golf courses and there is a transport museum in the castle grounds. It is a short walk to the fishing village of Howth, with its marina and great seafood restaurants. **www.deerpark-hotel.ie**

FURTHER AFIELD Glenogra Guesthouse
€€

64 Merrion Rd, Ballsbridge, Dublin 4 **Tel** *01 668 3661* **Fax** *01 668 3698* **Rooms** *12*

This stylish and award-winning guesthouse provides pleasant and good-value B&B accommodation in this leafy, up-market area of Dublin. The owners create a welcoming atmosphere for their guests. Bedrooms are well appointed and the breakfast is good. **www.glenogra.com**

FURTHER AFIELD Grand Canal Hotel
€€

Grand Canal St, Ballsbridge, Dublin 4 **Tel** *01 646 1000* **Fax** *01 646 1001* **Rooms** *142*

This spacious and modern hotel has comfortable rooms and friendly staff. The on-site pub, Gasworks, fuses the old and new. There's also a restaurant, EPIC. It is in a convenient location between Trinity College and Landsdowne Road. **www.grandcanalhotel.com**

FURTHER AFIELD Herbert Park Hotel
€€

Ballsbridge, Dublin 4 **Tel** *01 667 2200* **Fax** *01 667 2595* **Rooms** *153*

Overlooking the park from where it derived its name, this big contemporary hotel is bright. to furnish the interiors include polished granite, Irish abstract art, Irish furniture and gla appointed and stylishly designed. **www.herbertparkhotel.ie**

FURTHER AFIELD The Red Bank

6–7 Church St, Skerries, Co Dublin **Tel** *01 849 1005* **Fax** *01 849 1*

On the premises of a former bank, in the heart of the village furnished rooms with good facilities. The award-winning in seafood. Warm hospitality is guaranteed. Dublin

FURTHER AFIELD Royal Marine Hotel   €€

Marine Rd, Dun Laoghaire, Co Dublin **Tel** *01 230 0030* **Fax** *01 230 0029* **Rooms** *228*   **Road Map** *D4*

This landmark hotel is in the port town of Dun Laoghaire on Dublin Bay, and ideally located for the ferry terminal and marina as well as for sightseeing in South Dublin and Wicklow. The hotel has hosted many heads of state, royalty and celebrities, including Queen Victoria, Frank Sinatra, Laurel & Hardy and Charlie Chaplin. **www.royalmarine.ie**

FURTHER AFIELD Sandymount Hotel   €€

7 Herbert Rd, Ballsbridge, Dublin 4 **Tel** *01 614 2000* **Fax** *01 660 7077* **Rooms** *168*

Formally the Mount Herbert, the Sandymount Hotel is located in a residential area just a stone's throw from the Aviva Stadium. A terrace of interconnecting houses is decorated with modern furnishings, and the en suite bedrooms are equipped with good facilities. The hotel has secure parking and private gardens. **www.sandymounthotel.ie**

FURTHER AFIELD Tara Towers Hotel   €€

Merrion Rd, Booterstown, Dublin 4 **Tel** *01 269 4666* **Fax** *01 269 1027* **Rooms** *111*

South of the city centre, this three-star hotel is situated on the coast road. Dun Laoghaire is a 15-minute drive away. Ambience is relaxed and service modest. Bedrooms are comfortable and spacious, if rather basic in decor. There's a traditional restaurant on site. Well-serviced bus route and nearby DART station. **www.taratowers.com**

FURTHER AFIELD Aberdeen Lodge   €€€

53–55 Park Ave, Ballsbridge, Dublin 4 **Tel** *01 283 8155* **Fax** *01 283 7877* **Rooms** *17*

The luxurious suburb of Ballsbridge is home to this lodge boasting large rooms; some with four-poster beds and whirlpool spas. Guests can dine outside and also enjoy a hot tub. The expansive and well-manicured gardens provide an oasis of calm in the city. There is complimentary parking and Internet access. **www.aberdeen-lodge.com**

FURTHER AFIELD Blake's Townhouse   €€€

50 Merrion Rd, Ballsbridge, Dublin 4 **Tel** *01 668 8324* **Fax** *01 668 4280* **Rooms** *32*

This impeccably designed hotel in desirable Ballsbridge offers luxurious, ultra-modern rooms. Breakfast comes highly recommended, but the icing on the cake is the superb Austrian-themed spa and wellness centre, which boasts a choice of saunas, an ice room, herbal steam baths and a heated outdoor pool. **www.blakeshotelandspa.com**

FURTHER AFIELD Butlers Town House   €€€

44 Landsdowne Rd, Ballsbridge, Dublin 4 **Tel** *01 667 4022* **Fax** *01 667 3960* **Rooms** *20*

Luxuriously furnished in a country-house style, the Georgian Butlers Town House offers four-star accommodation. There are individually designed bedrooms with Egyptian cotton sheets. Good breakfast is served in the Conservatory Restaurant, which features an all-day menu, making this more of a small hotel than a B&B. **www.butlers-hotel.com**

FURTHER AFIELD Clontarf Castle   €€€

Castle Ave, Clontarf, Dublin 3 **Tel** *01 833 2321* **Fax** *01 833 0418* **Rooms** *111*   **Road Map** *D3*

This historic castle dates back to 1172 and the hotel offers guests a warm and cosy atmosphere. Not far from the city centre and Dublin airport, it is also ideally located for sightseeing in North County Dublin and a short drive from the fishing village of Howth. **www.clontarfcastle.ie**

FURTHER AFIELD Fitzpatrick Castle Hotel   €€€

Killiney, Co Dublin **Tel** *01 230 5400* **Fax** *01 230 5430* **Rooms** *113*   **Road Map** *D4*

This family-owned hotel is set in an 18th-century castle in the plush seaside suburbs of Dalkey and Killiney. The hotel has plenty of character, rooms are spacious and facilities include a swimming pool, gym, sauna and Jacuzzi. It is adjacent to Killiney Hill park which has excellent walks, forests and sea views. **www.fitzpatrickcastle.com**

FURTHER AFIELD Grand Hotel   €€€

Malahide, Co Dublin **Tel** *01 845 0000* **Fax** *01 816 8225* **Rooms** *203*

This lovely seaside Dublin town has been home to "The Grand" since 1835. The hotel has survived the years as a four-star destination. The Palm Court Carvery, Coast Restaurant and Ryan's Bar provide wide-ranging options. The leisure centre includes a pool, steam room, sauna and Jacuzzi. **www.thegrand.ie**

FURTHER AFIELD Dylan   €€€€€

Eastmoreland Place, Dublin 4 **Tel** *01 660 3000* **Fax** *01 660 3005* **Rooms** *44*

This boutique hotel located close to the Aviva Stadium boasts a plush interior with sumptuous rooms, each of which ~~~ been individually designed. Dine in the hotel's elegant but informal restaurant or sip cocktails in the luxurious bar ~~~ww.dylan.ie

~~~FIELD Four Seasons   €€€€€

~~~*lsbridge, Dublin 4* **Tel** *01 665 4000* **Fax** *01 665 4099* **Rooms** *197*

~~~essfully combines period-style elegance with contemporary comfort. Generously ~~~opulently decorated with deep-pile rugs and rich furnishings. Bedrooms are large ~~~e Ice Bar is a magnet for the fashionistas. **www.fourseasons.com**

~~~ & Golf Links   €€€€€

~~~*846 2442* **Rooms** *138*   **Road Map** *D3*

~~~lly owned this house with a lovely beachside location. It ~~~e excellently furnished, with views of the sea or the ~~~ose to Dublin Airport. **www.portmarnock.com**

SOUTHEAST IRELAND

ARTHURSTOWN Dunbrody Country House Hotel & Cookery School

Arthurstown, Co Wexford **Tel** 051 389 600 **Fax** 051 389 601 **Rooms** 22 Road Map C5

This Georgian manor is set in 80 ha (200 acres) of rolling parkland, close to the ferry at Ballyhack linking Wexford and Waterford. Kevin Dundon is one of Ireland's best known chefs and the accommodation is country house elegance in an extended building that leaves a lasting impact on guests. **www.dunbrodyhouse.com**

ASHFORD Ballyknocken House

Ashford, Glenealy, Co Wicklow **Tel** 0404 44627 **Fax** 0404 44696 **Rooms** 7 Road Map D4

A romantic 19th-century Victorian farmhouse on an organic farm, this long-established guesthouse and cookery school is furnished in country-house style. The on-site dining room features wholesome Irish cooking. Breakfasts are delicious. The location is ideal for walkers wishing to explore the Wicklow Mountains. **www.ballyknocken.com**

ATHY Coursetown House

Stradbally Rd, Athy, Co Kildare **Tel** 059 863 1101 **Fax** 059 863 2740 **Rooms** 4 Road Map D4

This 200-year-old farmhouse is set in the centre of a 260-acre arable farm. Attractions include a superb natural history library and beautifully maintained gardens. Bedrooms vary in size but all are thoughtfully decorated in a country-house style. Delicious breakfasts feature pancakes and seasonal fruits. Pets are allowed. **www.coursetown.com**

AUGHRIM Meath Arms Country Inn

Aughrim, Co Wicklow **Tel** 0402 36463 **Rooms** 10 Road Map D4

Located in the centre of a pretty village is this charming country inn that has been run by the Phelan family since 1728. It offers cosy accommodation, beautiful views and makes a relaxing, friendly base from which to explore the Garden County. The Grainstore restaurant serves excellent meals and there's a beer garden. **www.meatharms.com**

BALLYMACARBRY Clonanav Farm Guesthouse

Ballymacarbry, Co Waterford **Tel** 052 613 6141 **Fax** 052 613 6294 **Rooms** 10 Road Map C5

Traditionally furnished, this three-star bungalow farmhouse and dry fly-fishing centre is situated on a working farm in the Nire valley. Rooms are en suite and there are log and peat fires. Savour the excellent Irish breakfast. Attractions include an on-site hard tennis court and wild brown trout fishing on river and stream. **www.flyfishingireland.com**

CAPPOQUIN Richmond House

Cappoquin, Co Waterford **Tel** 058 54278 **Fax** 058 54988 **Rooms** 10 Road Map C5

This delightful Georgian house is owned by the Deevy family, celebrated for its genuine warm hospitality. Set in peaceful parkland it is charmingly decorated with antiques. Each of the bedrooms is a blend of Georgian splendour and modern comfort. Relish the excellent award-winning, country-house cooking. **www.richmondhouse.net**

CARLOW Barrowville Town House

Kilkenny Rd, Carlow **Tel** 059 914 3324 **Fax** 059 914 1953 **Rooms** 7 Road Map D4

Standing on its own mature grounds, this three-star listed Regency house is just a few minutes' walk from the town centre. It is immaculately maintained and well furnished with antiques, with an open fire in the lovely drawing room. Bedrooms vary in size, though all have good bathrooms. Superb breakfasts. **www.barrowville.com**

CASTLEDERMOT Kilkea Lodge Farm

Castledermot, Co Kildare **Tel** 059 914 5112 **Fax** 059 914 5112 **Rooms** 4 Road Map D4

Set in 70 ha (180 acres) of rolling parkland, this farmhouse has been in the same family since 1740. It's popular with racegoers, as the Curragh, Punchestown and Naas racecourses are all within easy reach. It offers warm hospitality with open fires. There's also an equestrian centre holding regular courses and a golf course nearby. **www.kilkealodgefarm.com**

THE CURRAGH Martinstown House

The Curragh, Co Kildare **Tel** 045 441 269 **Fax** 045 441 203 **Rooms** 4 Road Map D4

This charming Gothic-style cottage ornée, idyllically set on a farm in mature woodland and gardens offers old-fashioned hospitality and unassuming elegance. Each bedroom has its own character and fresh flowers. Hens, goats, sheep and horses create a delightful pastoral setting. **www.martinstownhouse.com**

DUNGARVAN Cairbre House

Abbeyside, Dungarvan, Co Waterford **Tel** 058 42338 **Rooms** 4 Road Map C5

This beautiful Georgian guesthouse was built in 1819 by the Duke of Devonshire. The location is idea, with wonderful views of the Colligan River and the Comeragh Mountains. There is also a private rose garden for guests to enjoy. Dungarvan village is less than ten minutes' walk away. **www.cairbrehouse.com**

DUNGARVAN Clonea Strand Hotel

Dungarvan, Co Waterford **Tel** 058 45555 **Fax** 058 42880 **Rooms** 59 Road Map C5

The main attraction of this large, modern three-star resort hotel is its location beside a lovely 3-km (2-mile) Blue Flag beach. Bedrooms are en suite, most have sea views. Leisure facilities include a 20-metre (65-ft) indoor heated pool and bowling alley. Good facilities for children makes it ideal for families. Live Irish music in the bar. **www.clonea.com**

DUNGARVAN Powersfield House
11 大 W €€

Ballinamuck, Dungarvan, Co Waterford **Tel** 058 45594 **Fax** 058 45550 **Rooms** 6   **Road Map** C5

This mock-Georgian house has been stylishly decorated with antiques and rich fabrics. The Powers are ebullient hosts, with a flair for creating bright and relaxing interiors as well as imaginative cooking. Delicious breakfasts and dinner can be arranged for residents. A cooking school is on the premises. **www.powersfield.com**

DUNLAVIN Rathsallagh House
11 W €€€€

Dunlavin, Co Wicklow **Tel** 045 403 112 **Fax** 045 403 343 **Rooms** 29   **Road Map** D4

Just one hour's drive from Dublin, this country house is set in 215 ha (530 acres) of peaceful parkland. It is comfortably furnished with open fires and has a relaxed atmosphere. Service is professional and courteous, and the buffet breakfast is one of the best in Ireland. Excellent restaurant and lovely gardens. Not suitable for children. **www.rathsallagh.com**

DUNMORE EAST Strand Inn
11 大 Y W €€

Dunmore East, Co Waterford **Tel** 051 383 174 **Fax** 051 383 756 **Rooms** 16   **Road Map** D5

Located right on the Blue Flag beach in Dunmore East, most of the Strand Inn's rooms boast balconies overlooking the water. Accommodation is bright, airy and modern, with a seaside feel. The inn also has one of the South East's finest seafood restaurants, while the bar hosts live music during the summer. **www.thestrandinn.com**

ENNISCORTHY Salville House
11 W €€

Enniscorthy, Co Wexford **Tel & fax** 053 923 5252 **Rooms** 5   **Road Map** D5

Standing on a hilltop overlooking the River Slaney, this 19th-century house offers comfort and friendly hospitality. Ample rooms have lovely views over the wooded countryside. Dinner is available by prior arrangement in a gracious dining room serving award-winning country cooking. Guests can bring their own wine. **www.salvillehouse.ie**

ENNISCORTHY Ballinkeele House
11 大 W €€€

Enniscorthy, Co Wexford **Tel** 053 913 8105 **Fax** 053 913 8468 **Rooms** 5   **Road Map** D5

This elegant manor house has been the ancestral home of the Maher family since 1840. It is set in 140 ha (350 acres) of mature parkland, game-filled woods, ponds and lakes. Rooms are well proportioned and the original furniture very well preserved. The place is known for its good home cooking as well as painting courses. **www.ballinkeele.ie**

ENNISKERRY Summerhill House Hotel
11 大 Y W €€€

Enniskerry, Co Wicklow **Tel** 01 286 7928 **Fax** 01 286 7929 **Rooms** 88   **Road Map** D4

Opposite the magnificent Powerscourt Estate in the rolling hills of County Wicklow, this friendly hotel is set in its own tree-filled grounds. Rooms are spacious, comfortable and many offer beautiful views of Bray Head. It is a short walk to the village. The hotel is a popular choice for wedding receptions. **www.summerhillhousehotel.com**

FERRYCARRIG Ferrycarrig Hotel
11 大 Y W €€€

Ferrycarrig, Co Wexford **Tel** 053 912 0999 **Fax** 053 912 0982 **Rooms** 102   **Road Map** D5

With sweeping vistas across the River Slaney, this modern hotel is furnished in a smart, contemporary style. A calm and airy atmosphere prevails. Staff are very friendly and competent. Well-equipped bedrooms offer lovely views. There's an excellent health and fitness club, with a 20-metre (65-ft) pool. **www.ferrycarrighotel.ie**

GOREY Marlfield House
11 大 W €€€€

Gorey, Co Wexford **Tel** 053 942 1124 **Fax** 053 942 1572 **Rooms** 19   **Road Map** D5

One of Ireland's leading country houses, this Regency-style mansion is luxuriously furnished with antiques, fine art, crystal chandeliers and marble fireplaces. Secluded amid woodland and beautifully maintained gardens, it is a haven of tranquility. Opulent bedrooms feature fresh flowers and marble bathrooms. **www.marlfieldhouse.com**

INISTIOGE Cullintra House
大 €€

The Rower, Instioge, Co Kilkenny **Tel** 051 423 614 **Rooms** 6   **Road Map** D5

A 200-year-old farmhouse, set in beautiful woods and farmland, this cat lovers' paradise is a cosy guesthouse with log fires. The host is an accomplished cook and offers leisurely breakfasts until noon. Tasty food, using only local produce, is served for candlelit dinners. The farm is an animal and bird sanctuary. **www.cullintrahouse.com**

KILKENNY Butler House
大 W €€€

16 Patrick St, Kilkenny **Tel** 056 776 5707 **Fax** 056 776 5626 **Rooms** 13   **Road Map** C4

This Georgian town house is an integral part of the Kilkenny Castle estate. Decor is contemporary, with period features such as marble fireplaces and plasterwork ceilings. Bedrooms are large and relatively snug. Excellent breakfasts are served in the refurbished stables of the castle, which now houses the Kilkenny Design Centre. **www.butler.ie**

KILKENNY Langton House Hotel
11 Y W €€€

69 John St, Kilkenny **Tel** 056 776 5133 **Fax** 056 776 3693 **Rooms** 34   **Road Map** C4

This is a friendly boutique-style hotel in the centre of medieval Kilkenny and is full of character and charm. Food and service is excellent and the hotel bars have won a number of awards. Kilkenny Castle and the River Nore are a short stroll from the hotel. **www.langtons.ie**

MACREDDIN The BrookLodge Hotel & Wells Spa
11 大 Y W €€€

Macreddin Village, Co Wicklow **Tel** 0402 36444 **Fax** 0402 36580 **Rooms** 90   **Road Map** D4

Built on the site of a deserted village in a Wicklow valley, this hotel complex is decorated in a contemporary, yet elegant country-house style with open fires and large airy spaces. The hotel is an organic food pioneer with several dining options and Actons Country Pub serves excellent pints from its own microbrewery. **www.brooklodge.com**

Key to Price Guide *see p 294* **Key to Symbols** *see back cover flap*

MAYNOOTH Carton House

Maynooth, Co Kildare **Tel** 01 505 2000 **Fax** 01 651 7703 **Rooms** 165

Road Map D4

This glorious former residence of the Duke of Leinster has been adapted to offer every modern luxury, while retaining the character and grandeur of Richard Castle's 1740 design. The accommodation is plush and elegant, and there are extensive grounds, sports facilities and a golf course. The Linder Tree Restaurant is excellent. **www.cartonhouse.com**

RATHNEW Hunter's Hotel

Rathnew, Co Wicklow **Tel** 0404 40106 **Fax** 0404 40338 **Rooms** 16

Road Map D4

A 1720 coaching inn, now in the fifth generation of the Hunter family, Hunter's offers old-fashioned comfort and charm. Surrounded by picturesque gardens along the banks of the river and decorated with chintzy furnishing, it exudes a traditional and relaxing atmosphere. Country-house cooking uses fresh local produce. **www.hunters.ie**

RATHNEW Tinakilly Country House & Restaurant

Rathnew, Co Wicklow **Tel** 0404 69274 **Fax** 0404 67806 **Rooms** 47

Road Map D4

This classical Victorian-Italianate mansion, 48 km (30 miles) south of Dublin, was built by Captain Halpin, who laid the first telegraph cable linking Europe and America. Standing on lovely Victorian gardens, the house is furnished with elegant antiques. Bedrooms decorated in period style feature modern comforts. Fine dining. **www.tinakilly.ie**

ROSSLARE Kelly's Resort Hotel

Rosslare, Co Wexford **Tel** 053 913 2114 **Fax** 053 913 2222 **Rooms** 118

Road Map D5

A reliable, family-run hotel overlooking an expansive sandy beach, Kelly's is cosy if lacking in character. It boasts an extensive collection of art. Many of the bedrooms have sea views; some have balconies. Its vast choice of leisure facilities, two popular restaurants and a supervised creche make it an ideal location for families. **www.kellys.ie**

STRAFFAN Kildare Hotel & Country Club

Straffan, Co Kildare **Tel** 01 601 7200 **Fax** 01 601 7297 **Rooms** 92

Road Map D4

Originally built in the 17th century, the Kildare has since been luxuriously renovated to become a five-star hotel, with an air of French elegance. Well-furnished rooms have been styled individually. The restaurants are excellent. Facilities include two 18-hole championship golf courses, health spa, tennis, river fishing and coarse fishing. **www.kclub.ie**

THOMASTOWN Ballyduff House

Thomastown, Co Kilkenny **Tel** 056 775 8488 **Rooms** 3

Road Map D5

Overlooking the River Nore, this charming 18th-century manor house is a haven of tranquility, done up in a country-house style. Bedrooms are large, with pretty views over the river or garden. There are beautiful walks as well as salmon and trout fishing. Woodstock Gardens are nearby. Open March to October. **www.ballyduffhouse.com**

THOMASTOWN Mount Juliet Estate

Thomastown, Co Kilkenny **Tel** 056 777 3000 **Fax** 056 777 3019 **Rooms** 57

Road Map D5

Set within a large country estate, Mount Juliet offers opulent rooms and suites and has elegance and quality in abundance. The estate is a nature and golf lovers paradise, incorporating an 8-hole championship golf course, as well as horse riding, fishing, archery facilities, a health club and luxury spa. **www.mountjuliet.ie**

TULLOW Mount Wolseley Hotel

Tullow, Co Carlow **Tel** 059 918 0100 **Fax** 059 915 2123 **Rooms** 143

Road Map D4

A delightful golf and spa resort hotel, Mount Wolseley has an 18-hole championship golf course as well as a spa, pool and leisure club. Rooms are bright and airy and amenities local to this rural retreat include everything from forest walks and mountain hiking trails to canoeing and hang gliding. **www.mountwolseley.ie**

WATERFORD Athenaeum House Hotel

Christendom, Ferrybank, Waterford **Tel** 051 833 999 **Fax** 051 833 977 **Rooms** 29

Road Map D5

This is a chic and comfortable Georgian house which overlooks the city yet has the feel of the country. There are beautiful river views, hospitality is relaxed and the restaurant has won awards for its cuisine. It is also convenient for Waterford train station. **www.athenaeumhousehotel.com**

WATERFORD The Fitzwilton Hotel

Bridge St, Waterford City, Waterford **Tel** 051 345 900 **Fax** 051 878 650 **Rooms** 88

Road Map D5

A smart and modern four-star hotel in Waterford city, many of the Fitzwilton's bedrooms have floor-to-ceiling windows with city views. Restaurant Chez K provides excellent dining and the hotel's location in the city centre is ideal for shopping and exploring. **www.fitzwiltonhotel.ie**

WATERFORD Foxmount Country House

Passage East Rd, off Dunmore Rd, Waterford **Tel** 051 874 308 **Fax** 051 854 906 **Rooms** 4

Road Map D5

A 15-minute drive from Waterford city, Foxmount is an imposing, yet peaceful and welcoming, 18th-century country house and working dairy farm. Appealing bedrooms overlook the valley on one side of the house and the farmyard on the other. The Kent family are warm hosts. Delicious home baking. **www.foxmountcountryhouse.com**

WATERFORD Sion Hill House & Gardens

Ferrybank, Waterford City **Tel** 051 851 558 **Fax** 051 851 678 **Rooms** 4

Road Map D5

George and Antoinette Kavanagh are enthusiastic hosts in their hillside manor house which is surrounded by award-winning gardens with over 20,000 daffodils and more than 400 species of roses. The rooms are well proportioned and are decorated with beautiful antique furniture. **www.sionhillhouse.ie**

WATERFORD Waterford Castle
🖥 🍴 👤 📺 W €€€€

The Island, Ballinakill, Waterford **Tel** *051 878 203* **Fax** *051 879 316* **Rooms** *19*　　　　**Road Map** *D5*

Dating from the 15th century, this luxury hotel lies on a private 310-acre island, 5 km (3 miles) outside Waterford city. Reached by a private car ferry, the Castle mixes old-world elegance with modern comfort. Good fine-dining choices as well as an 18-hole golf course and tennis. **www.waterfordcastle.com**

WEXFORD Maple Lodge
👤 W €€

Castlebridge, Wexford **Tel** *053 915 9195* **Rooms** *4*　　　　**Road Map** *D5*

The hosts at Maple Lodge are renowned for their friendly hospitality. The guesthouse is a modern build, but the bright and spacious rooms are elegantly decorated with traditional furnishings. The hotel is located in the village of Castlebridge, which has a range of decent pubs and restaurants. **www.maplelodgewexford.com**

WEXFORD McMenamin's Townhouse
👤 W €€

6 Glena Terrace, Spawell Rd, Wexford **Tel** *053 914 6442* **Rooms** *4*　　　　**Road Map** *D5*

This late-Victorian redbrick B&B is highly rated and within walking distance of the town centre and only 25 minutes' drive from the Rosslare ferry. Nicely decorated bedrooms are equipped with modern facilities. Some rooms have four-poster beds. Seamus and Kay McMenahin are friendly and helpful hosts. **www.wexford-bedandbreakfast.com**

CORK AND KERRY

BALTIMORE Baltimore Bay Guest House
🍴 👤 🍸 €€

The Waterfront, Baltimore, Co Cork **Tel** *028 20600* **Fax** *028 20495* **Rooms** *13*　　　　**Road Map** *B6*

This guesthouse, overlooking the harbour, is run by Youen Jacob, the younger son of celebrated restauranteur Youen. Airy bedrooms provide modern facilities and some have views over the sea and Sherkin Island. Well-chosen antiques add character to this contemporary house. There's a great restaurant on site. **www.youenjacob.com**

BALTIMORE Casey's
🍴 👤 🍸 W €€€

Baltimore, Co Cork **Tel** *028 20197* **Fax** *028 20509* **Rooms** *14*　　　　**Road Map** *B6*

The serenity of the location, overlooking a natural harbour and the Ilen River Estuary, is matched by the quiet elegance of the rooms. Seafood is brought in fresh from the sea and the West Cork region provides farm-fresh produce. Lobster and mussels are specialities. **www.caseysofbaltimore.com**

BANTRY Bantry House
🍴 👤 €€€

Bantry, Co Cork **Tel** *027 50047* **Fax** *027 50795* **Rooms** *8*　　　　**Road Map** *B6*

An 18th-century stately home, Bantry House has a wonderful collection of period furniture. The current owner is the ninth generation of his family to live in this grand home. Restful bedrooms look out over the pretty gardens. Climb the monumental stone "Stairway to the Sky" for stunning views. Open March to October. **www.bantryhouse.ie**

BANTRY Ballylickey Manor House
🍴 🏊 👤 €€€€

Bantry Bay, Co Cork **Tel** *027 50071* **Fax** *027 50124* **Rooms** *14*　　　　**Road Map** *B6*

Built over 300 years ago by Lord Kenmare as a shooting lodge, this delightful manor stands in award-winning gardens and parkland. It has a romantic setting, surrounded by mountains and moorland. The furnishings are luxurious and bedrooms are cosy. Delicious food. Outdoor heated swimming pool. **www.ballylickeymanorhouse.com**

CARAGH LAKE Ard na Sidhe
🍴 €€€

Caragh Lake, Co Kerry **Tel** *066 976 9105* **Fax** *066 976 9282* **Rooms** *18*　　　　**Road Map** *A5*

Housed in a Victorian-style building dating to 1913, Ard na Sidhe offers deluxe accommodation by Caragh Lake. The rooms are furnished with antiques and overlook the lake or the countryside. The award-winning gardens lead down to the lake where boating is available. Open May to October. **www.ardnasidhe.com**

CARAGH LAKE Carrig Country House
🍴 W €€€

Caragh Lake, Co Kerry **Tel** *066 976 9100* **Fax** *066 976 9166* **Rooms** *17*　　　　**Road Map** *A5*

Set in woodland and timeless gardens full of rare plants close to the water's edge, this extended family-run Victorian house exudes a relaxed atmosphere. There are open fires and antiques, and bedrooms are large and snug. Lakeside restaurant features trout and Kerry lamb. The area is a leading golfing destination. **www.carrighouse.com**

CASTLELYONS Ballyvolane House
🍴 👤 W €€

Castlelyons, Co Cork **Tel** *025 36349* **Fax** *025 36781* **Rooms** *6*　　　　**Road Map** *C5*

Surrounded by extensive gardens and parkland, this 1728 house was remodelled in the Italianate style in the 1800s, as seen in the classical pillared hall, with a baby grand piano. There are open fires and elegant furnishings. Large bedrooms feature period furniture. Trout lake and salmon fishing are arranged. **www.ballyvolanehouse.ie**

CASTLETOWNSHEND Bow Hall
📺 👤 W €€

Main St, Castletownshend, Co Cork **Tel** *028 36114* **Rooms** *3*　　　　**Road Map** *B6*

In the heart of the picturesque village of Castletownshend stands Bow Hall, a 17th-century house offering stylish accommodation and warm service. Overlooking well-maintained gardens, it is decorated in Shaker style, with interesting collectables. **dvickbowhall@eircom.net**

Key to Price Guide *see p294* **Key to Symbols** *see back cover flap*

CLONAKILTY O'Donovan's Hotel

🔲 🍴 🎿 🎦 W   €€

Clonakilty, Co Cork **Tel** 023 883 3250 **Fax** 023 883 3883 **Rooms** 20   **Road Map** B6

This traditional hotel, in the centre of the vibrant market town, is owned by the fifth generation of the O'Donovan family. Though old-fashioned, with a modest decor, it has a friendly ambience. There's a fully licensed restaurant as well as a bar featuring live music. Sheltered coves and sandy beaches are close by. **www.odonovanshotel.com**

CLONAKILTY Inchydoney Island Lodge & Spa

🔲 🍴 🎿 🎿 🎦 W   €€€€

Clonakilty, West Cork **Tel** 023 883 3143 **Fax** 023 883 5229 **Rooms** 67   **Road Map** B6

This is a contemporary hotel and spa set on a peaceful island joined to the mainland by a causeway. It overlooks a stunning beach and is near the picturesque village of Clonakilty. The luxury resort is popular for spa breaks and many of the rooms have sea views. **www.inchydoneyisland.com**

CORK Garnish House

🔲 W   €€

Western Rd, Cork **Tel** 021 427 5111 **Fax** 021 427 3872 **Rooms** 30   **Road Map** C5

Five minutes' walk from the city centre, Garnish House is a comfortable guesthouse, furnished in warm colours. Hot home-baked scones with tea and coffee on arrival reflects the gracious hospitality of the Lucey family. Bedrooms, all en suite, some with Jacuzzis, include modern facilities. B&B only. **www.garnish.ie**

CORK Jury's Inn Cork

🔲 🍴 🎿 🎦 W   €€

Anderson's Quay, Cork **Tel** 021 494 3000 **Fax** 021 427 6144 **Rooms** 133   **Road Map** C5

This three-star hotel, with a fixed-price room rate, is located in the heart of Cork city and overlooks the River Lee. Reasonably priced bedrooms are en suite with regular modern facilities and can accommodate up to two adults and two children. Room service is not available. Breakfast is an extra charge. **www.jurysinns.com**

CORK Lancaster Lodge

🔲 🎿 W   €€

Lancaster Quay, Western Rd, Cork **Tel** 021 425 1125 **Fax** 021 425 1126 **Rooms** 48   **Road Map** C5

This modern, purpose-built four-storey guesthouse is located within five minutes' walk of the city centre. The interior is contemporary in design, with light wood furnishings. Bedrooms are spacious and well appointed. Bathrooms are intelligently designed. Excellent breakfasts are provided. **www.lancasterlodge.com**

CORK Maryborough House Hotel

🔲 🍴 🎿 🎿 🎦 W   €€€

Maryborough Hill, Douglas, Cork **Tel** 021 436 5555 **Fax** 021 436 5662 **Rooms** 93   **Road Map** C5

The 18th-century core building stands at the heart of this hotel, which has been extended significantly. There are 10 ha (24 acres) of ornate gardens and woodland. Bedrooms are large and contemporary, with well-designed bathrooms. Only 10 minutes' drive from the airport and the city centre. Good leisure facilities. **www.maryborough.com**

CORK Hayfield Manor Hotel

🔲 🍴 🎿 🎿 🎦 W   €€€

Perrott Ave, College Rd, Cork **Tel** 021 434 5900 **Fax** 021 431 6839 **Rooms** 88   **Road Map** C5

A member of the Small Luxury Hotels of the World, this delightful hotel is set amid gardens. Though opened in 1996, it has the feel of a fine period house. Elegant furnishings are of a high standard. Generously proportioned and thoughtfully designed bedrooms come with good bathrooms. Excellent leisure facilities. **www.hayfieldmanor.ie**

COURTMACSHERRY Travara Lodge

€€

Courtmacsherry, Co Cork **Tel** 023 8846493 **Rooms** 6   **Road Map** C5

This early-Victorian terraced building, in a cheerful seaside village, overlooks Courtmacsherry Bay. A former captain's house, then a gentleman's residence, it is now a guesthouse with attractive, cosy furnishings. Simple and tasty meals are served using fresh local produce. Staff are friendly and helpful. **www.travaralodge.com**

DINGLE The Captain's House

🎿   €€

The Mall, Dingle, Co Kerry **Tel** 066 915 1531 **Fax** 066 915 1079 **Rooms** 9   **Road Map** A5

So called because the host was a former captain in the merchant navy, this hotel is approached via a small footbridge over the River Mall and a pretty garden. The interior comprises antiques and nauticalia, collected by Captain Jim Milhenc on his travels. An open turf fire and a warren of cosy rooms create a warm ambience **captigh@eircom.net**

DINGLE Greenmount House

€€

Upper John St, Dingle, Co Kerry **Tel** 066 915 1414 **Fax** 066 915 1974 **Rooms** 14   **Road Map** A5

Five minutes' walk from the centre of Dingle, this modern B&B offers lovely accommodation and wonderful views of the town and harbour. Many of the well-equipped bedrooms are junior suites with sitting rooms and balconies. Decor features floral furnishings and wooden floors. Award-winning breakfasts. **www.greenmount-house.com**

DINGLE Dingle Skellig Hotel & Peninsula Spa

🔲 🍴 🎿 🎿 🎦 W   €€€

Dingle, Co Kerry **Tel** 066 915 0200 **Fax** 066 915 1501 **Rooms** 113   **Road Map** A5

With a modest exterior, this four-star hotel enjoys a wonderful seaside location on the fringes of Dingle. It is particularly ideal for families, with neat and adequately furnished bedrooms. The airy interiors make the most of the sea views. Excellent leisure facilities are available along with the Peninsula Spa. **www.dingleskellig.com**

DINGLE Emlagh House

🔲 🎦 W   €€€

Dingle, Co Kerry **Tel** 066 915 2345 **Fax** 066 915 2359 **Rooms** 10   **Road Map** A5

A few minutes' walk from the heart of Dingle, this luxurious guesthouse is set in peaceful landscaped gardens. It is furnished in a tasteful country-house style with Irish art, though a contemporary feel prevails. Bedrooms are cosy, ample and decorated with flower themes. Most of them have harbour views. **www.emlaghhouse.com**

DINGLE PENINSULA Gorman's Clifftop House & Restaurant

€€

Glaise Bheag, Ballydavid, Co Kerry **Tel & Fax** 066 915 5162 **Rooms** 9   **Road Map** A5

This guesthouse is beautifully located in the Gaeltacht area, overlooking the Atlantic. Open log fires, pottery lamps and locally handmade tapestries create a relaxed feel. Bedrooms are furnished in handmade waxed pine and natural fabrics. The hosts are friendly and the breakfasts superb. **www.gormans-clifftophouse.com**

FOTA ISLAND Fota Island Resort

€€€

Fota Island, Co Cork **Tel** 021 467 3000 **Fax** 021 488 3713 **Rooms** 131   **Road Map** C6

This is a stunning resort set on a tranquil island in East Cork, just 15 minutes from Cork City. It includes a hotel, a championship golf course and a luxury spa in a beautiful setting. There is a selection of restaurants. Fota Wildlife Park and Fota House and Gardens are both on the island. **www.fotaisland.ie**

GOLEEN Fortview House

€€

Gurtyowen, Toormore, Goleen, Co Cork **Tel & Fax** 028 35324 **Rooms** 3   **Road Map** B6

Situated on a working farm, this farmhouse is elegantly furnished with country pine. Bedrooms feature antiques and cast-iron and brass beds. Help with milking the cows, or stroll across the grounds. Generous breakfasts. Dinner for guests is by arrangement. Self-catering cottages available for hire. Open Mar–Nov. **www.fortviewhousegoleen.com**

KENMARE Hawthorn House

€€

Shelbourne St, Kenmore, Co Kerry **Tel** 064 6641035 **Fax** 064 6641932 **Rooms** 8   **Road Map** B5

Modestly decorated, yet immaculately kept, this family-run B&B is welcoming and restful. Generous hospitality can be expected. En suite bedrooms are cheerfully painted and furnished in pine. Mary O'Brien, the lively and warm-hearted host, prepares a lovely breakfast. **www.hawthornhousekenmare.com**

KENMARE O'Donnabhain's Bar & Guesthouse

€€

Kenmare, Co Kerry **Tel** 064 664 2106 **Fax** 064 664 2312 **Rooms** 10   **Road Map** B5

This family-run guesthouse and gastro bar offers guests warm hospitality combined with fine food and drink, making it a popular venue for both locals and visitors alike. Rooms are bright and spacious, with contemporary furnishings, and there is a guest lounge and free Wi-Fi access. Off-street parking is available. **www.odonnabhain-kenmare.com**

KENMARE Sea Shore Farm Guesthouse

€€

Tubrid, Kenmare, Co Kerry **Tel & fax** 064 664 1270 **Rooms** 6   **Road Map** B5

Beautifully situated overlooking the Beara Peninsula, the O'Sullivan's guesthouse is just 1.6 km (1 mile) west of the heritage town of Kenmare. The rooms are spacious and comfortably furnished and the views are stunning. The nearby Glen Inchaquin Park has several walks along lakes, mountain streams and woodland. **www.seashorekenmare.com**

KENMARE Park Hotel Kenmare

€€€€€

Kenmare, Co Kerry **Tel** 064 664 1200 **Fax** 064 41402 **Rooms** 46   **Road Map** B5

In a stunning setting overlooking the gardens to Kenmare Bay, this 1897 hotel is one of Ireland's finest. The luxurious style and antique furnishings add to the plush ambience. Bedrooms are individually decorated. There's a world-class destination spa and an 18-hole golf course on site. Exceptional service. **www.parkkenmare.com**

KENMARE Sheen Falls Lodge

€€€€€

Kenmare, Co Kerry **Tel** 064 664 1600 **Fax** 064 41386 **Rooms** 66   **Road Map** B5

Across the river from town, this five-star waterside hotel set in 120 ha (300 acres), has garnered a reputation as one of the best in the country since it opened in 1991. Lavishly decorated, the classic and modern furnishings create a grand yet restful ambience. There's an equestrian centre as well as salmon fishing on site. **www.sheenfallslodge.ie**

KILLARNEY Earls Court House

€€

Woodlawn Junction, Muckross Rd, Killarney, Co Kerry **Tel** 064 663 4009 **Fax** 064 663 4366 **Rooms** 30 **Road Map** B5

A five-minute walk from the heart of Killarney, this luxury 4-star award-winning hotel is superbly maintained. Open fire, antiques, tasteful furnishings and fresh flowers create a relaxed atmosphere. Neat bedrooms are generously proportioned. Excellent breakfast is served. **www.killarney-earlscourt.ie**

KILLARNEY Aghadoe Heights Hotel and Spa

€€€€

Lakes of Killarney, Co Kerry **Tel** 064 663 1766 **Fax** 064 663 1345 **Rooms** 74   **Road Map** B5

This award-winning five-star resort is in a stunning setting with panoramic views over the Lakes of Killarney. Service is top class, rooms are luxurious and comfortable and the outstanding restaurant has also won awards. A great place to escape and unwind. **www.aghadoeheights.com**

KILLARNEY Hotel Dunloe Castle

€€€€

Killarney, Co Kerry **Tel** 064 664 4111 **Fax** 064 664 4583 **Rooms** 102   **Road Map** B5

This modern hotel stands in lovely subtropical gardens, with its award-winning collection of rare plants and flowers, by the ruins of the 13th-century castle. Rooms are large and well appointed. Facilities feature an on-site equestrian centre, indoor tennis courts and fishing on the River Luane. **www.thedunloe.com**

KILLARNEY Hotel Europe

€€€€

Killarney, Co Kerry **Tel** 064 667 1300 **Fax** 064 663 2118 **Rooms** 187   **Road Map** B5

A huge five-star resort hotel with stunning views of the Lakes of Killarney and the nearby mountains, Hotel Europe is excellently maintained. It has large open rooms and elegant furnishings. Bedrooms, too, are well proportioned and those on the lakeside enjoy wonderful views. There are several golf clubs adjacent to the hotel. **www.theeurope.com**

Key to Price Guide *see p294* **Key to Symbols** *see back cover flap*

KILLARNEY Killarney Park Hotel

Killarney, Co Kerry **Tel** 064 663 5555 **Fax** 064 663 5266 **Rooms** 68   **Road Map** B5

Set in its own grounds but in the centre of Killarney town, this elegant hotel has the best of both worlds. Hospitality is warm and facilities include a swimming pool and an outdoor hot tub. Rooms either overlook the hotel gardens and the mountains beyond, or face the town. **www.killarneyparkhotel.ie**

KINSALE Blindgate House

Blindgate, Kinsale, Co Cork **Tel** 021 477 7858 **Fax** 021 477 7868 **Rooms** 11   **Road Map** B6

Set in its own gardens, this purpose-built house boasts inspiring interiors and a bright and airy atmosphere. Excellent breakfasts include fresh juices, farmhouse yogurts, cheeses and fresh fish as well as the full Irish. Contemporary in style, the en suite bedrooms are uncluttered. Closed late-Dec–Mar. **www.blindgatehouse.com**

KINSALE Carlton Hotel Kinsale

Rathmore Rd, Kinsale, Co Cork **Tel** 021 470 6000 **Fax** 021 470 6001 **Rooms** 110   **Road Map** B6

Set in its own wooded grounds, with 36 ha (90 acres) of parkland and beautiful views over Oysterhaven Bay, the Carlton is a tranquil place to stay just outside Kinsale. Facilities include a pool, a kids' club and a luxury spa with beautiful views. **www.carltonkinsalehotel.com**

KINSALE Old Bank House

11 Pearse St, Kinsale, Co Cork **Tel** 021 477 4075 **Fax** 021 477 4296 **Rooms** 17   **Road Map** B6

Situated right in the centre of town, this used to be a working branch of the Munster and Leinster Bank. Now it is a well-run guesthouse, offering excellent accommodation. Bedrooms are spacious and decorated in a country-house style with good bathrooms. Some enjoy picturesque views of the town. **www.oldbankhousekinsale.com**

KINSALE Acton's Hotel

Pier Rd, Kinsale, Co Cork **Tel** 021 477 99 00 **Fax** 021-4772231 **Rooms** 73   **Road Map** B6

This is a comfortable, friendly hotel in Kinsale set beside the seafront, overlooking the harbour and with its own gardens. It is convenient for the village and also for sightseeing in the area. Rooms are tastefully decorated and superior rooms have lovely views over the harbour and marina. **www.actonshotelkinsale.com**

KINSALE Old Presbytery

43 Cork St, Kinsale, Co Cork **Tel** 021 477 2027 **Fax** 021 477 2166 **Rooms** 6   **Road Map** B6

High-quality accommodation is provided at this charming Georgian guesthouse. The atmosphere is restful and oozes character. Pretty bedrooms have antique brass beds and simple pine country furniture. Some rooms have a Jacuzzi or balcony. Breakfasts are a treat. The penthouse suite sleeps up to five guests. **www.oldpres.com**

KINSALE Trident Hotel

World's End, Kinsale, Co Cork **Tel** 021 477 9300 **Fax** 021 477 4173 **Rooms** 75   **Road Map** B6

This hotel has a great location, set beside the bay, with lovely views of the harbour. The Executive rooms all have king-sized beds and sea views. The restaurant, Pier One, shifts between generous bistro and à la carte menus, dominated by locally caught seafood. **www.tridenthotel.com**

KINSALE The Harbour Lodge

Scilly, Kinsale, Co Cork **Tel** 021 477 2376 **Fax** 021 477 2675 **Rooms** 9   **Road Map** B6

This four-star waterfront guesthouse provides well-maintained accommodation. Bedrooms are large and well furnished. Some have balconies with views of the harbour. Very good breakfasts are served. The Spinnaker restaurant next door serves a delicious surf 'n' turf. **www.harbourlodge.com**

LISTOWEL Allo's Town House and Restaurant

41–43 Church St, Listowel, Co Kerry **Tel** 068 22880 **Fax** 068 22803 **Rooms** 3   **Road Map** B5

Just off the main square of the market town, this hotel combines modern comforts with old-world charm. Stylishly decorated bedrooms feature period furniture. Bathrooms are furnished in distinct Connemara marble. The hosts are friendly. No breakfast is served, but there is a lovely on-site bar and bistro with good vegetarian options.

LISTOWEL Listowel Arms Hotel

Listowel, Co Kerry **Tel** 058 21500 **Fax** 068 22524 **Rooms** 42   **Road Map** B5

Situated in a quiet corner of the main square, this historic three-star hotel is renowned as the venue for the annual Listowel Writers' Week, held in June. It has modern comforts but without losing any of its character. The on-site restaurant serves traditional cuisine. **www.listowelarms.com**

LITTLE ISLAND Radisson Blu Hotel & Spa Cork

Ditchley House, Little Island, Cork **Tel** 021 429 7000 **Fax** 021 429 7101 **Rooms** 129   **Road Map** C6

This chic and elegant hotel is just 10 minutes outside Cork city. Set in 4 ha (9 acres) of landscaped gardens, it offers a mix of old world charm and contemporary design. Facilities include a luxury spa with a hydrotherapy treatment pool and a fitness centre, as well as the stylish bar and restaurant. **www.radissonblu.ie/hotel-cork**

MACROOM Gougane Barra Hotel

Gougane Barra, Ballingeary, Macroom, West Cork. **Tel** 026 47069 **Fax** 026 47059 **Rooms** 26   **Road Map** B6

Hidden away in Gougane Barra National Forest Park and beside the source of the River Lee and the tranquil Gougane Barra Lake, this small family-run hotel offers a peaceful nature haven. There are plenty of outdoor activities including forest walks and wildlife spotting in the national park. **www.gouganebarrahotel.com**

MALLOW Longueville House
Mallow, Co Cork **Tel** *022 47156* **Fax** *022 47459* **Rooms** *20*   **Road Map** *B5*

Set in a large wooded estate in the heart of the Blackwater Valley, this historic Georgian mansion has classically proportioned rooms with plasterwork ceilings and sumptuous family antiques. The Presidents' Restaurant is an award-winning eatery and there is a period conservatory. Beautiful walks. **www.longuevillehouse.ie**

MIDLETON Barnabrow House
Barnabrow, Cloyne, Midleton, Co Cork **Tel & Fax** *021 465 2534* **Rooms** *19*   **Road Map** *C6*

Barnabrow is romantically set in rolling parkland, enjoying beautiful views over nearby Ballycotton Bay. A tranquil house, it is stylishly decorated and features African furniture. Bedrooms are generously proportioned; some are in restored buildings to the rear of the house. There's an on-site crafts shop. **www.barnabrowhouse.ie**

SCHULL Corthna Lodge Guesthouse
Airhill, Schull, Co Cork **Tel** *028 28517* **Rooms** *6*   **Road Map** *B6*

This charming guesthouse is within walking distance of Schull village and harbour. Rooms are comfortable and well-appointed, and an excellent breakfast is included in the price of the room. The landscaped gardens have a sun patio, outdoor hot tub and barbecue area for guests to use. **www.corthna-lodge.net**

SHANAGARRY Ballymaloe House
Shanagarrry, Co Cork **Tel** *021 465 2531* **Fax** *021 465 2021* **Rooms** *30*   **Road Map** *C6*

Perhaps Ireland's best-known country house, restaurant and cookery school, the elegantly furnished Ballymaloe House is surrounded by a large expanse of farmland and gardens. Bedrooms are tastefully decorated. The restaurant is nationally renowned. Staff are professional and courteous. There's a good craft shop on site. **www.ballymaloe.ie**

SKIBBEREEN West Cork Hotel
Ilen St, Shibbereen, Co Cork **Tel** *028 21277* **Fax** *028 22333* **Rooms** *34*   **Road Map** *B6*

Built in 1900, West Cork Hotel has a wonderful location on the banks of the river. It has been refurbished in a tasteful contemporary style. Self-sufficient bedrooms are equipped with modern facilities. Those at the back overlook the river. There is an on-site restaurant and bar. **www.westcorkhotel.com**

SNEEM Tahilla Cove Country House
Sneem, Co Kerry **Tel** *064 6645204* **Fax** *066 4445104* **Rooms** *9*   **Road Map** *A6*

This friendly guesthouse is spread over two houses and surrounded by mature oak forest and garden, which sweep down to the water's edge. Neatly furnished bedrooms vary, but all are en suite and most enjoy views of the mountains or the sea. The Waterhouse family is hospitable. Good country cooking. **www.tahillacove.com**

SNEEM Parknasilla Hotel
Parknasilla, Sneem, Co Kerry **Tel** *064 6675600* **Fax** *064 6645323* **Rooms** *83*   **Road Map** *A6*

Surrounded by 160 ha (300 acres) of subtropical parkland, this Victorian hotel commands a stunning position overlooking Kenmare Bay. Elegant antiques, fine art and fresh flowers create a relaxed ambience. It also has an excellent spa. The elegant Pygmalion restaurant is good. **www.parknasillahotel.ie**

WATERVILLE The Old Cable House
Waterville, Co Kerry **Tel** *066 947 4233* **Rooms** *6*   **Road Map** *A6*

There are wonderful views of the Atlantic from this Victorian style house owned by Alan and Margaret Brown. The emphasis here is on a warm welcome and a comfortable stay. The hotel is located in one of the most beautiful areas of Ireland, with the Ring of Kerry nearby as well as Waterville golf club. **www.oldcablehouse.com**

WATERVILLE The Smugglers Inn
Cliff Rd, Waterville, Co Kerry **Tel** *066 947 4330* **Rooms** *14*   **Road Map** *A6*

This cliff-top inn offers stunning views – relax in the spacious, first-floor sitting room and enjoy the wondrous sea vistas. The hotel is in close proximity to the world-famous Waterville Golf Links club. The rooms are pleasant and homely. **www.the-smugglers-inn.com**

THE LOWER SHANNON

ABBEYFEALE Fitzgerald's Farmhouse & Equestrian Centre
Mount Marian, Abbeyfeale, Co Limerick **Tel** *068 31217* **Fax** *068 31558* **Rooms** *6*   **Road Map** *B4*

Situated on the Kerry/Limerick border, this is an ideal retreat for children. There's an animal sanctuary and riding centre, with sheep, goats, guinea fowl, hens and over 30 horses. Ride cross-country on the beach or enjoy a more leisurely trek. Delightful nature-trail. Friendly and very hospitable, with open fire. **www.fitzgeraldsfarmhouse.com**

ADARE Dunraven Arms
Adare, Co Limerick **Tel** *061 605 900* **Fax** *061 396 541* **Rooms** *89*   **Road Map** *B5*

Established in 1792, in one of Ireland's most picturesque villages, this inn has retained its atmosphere and character and grown into a luxurious country-house hotel. With its open fires, antique furniture and friendly staff, it is renowned for its exemplary Irish hospitality. Bedrooms are beautifully furnished. **www.dunravenhotel.com**

Key to Price Guide *see p 294* **Key to Symbols** *see back cover flap*

ADARE Adare Manor Hotel & Golf Resort

Adare, Co Limerick Tel 061 605 200 Fax 061 396 124 Rooms 62

Road Map B5

Set in 360 ha (900 acres), on the banks of the River Maigue, this Neo-Gothic mansion dates from 1720 and was the former home of the Earls of Dunraven. High-ceilinged rooms with period features are luxuriously furnished and overlook formal gardens and an impressive golf-course. Elegant bedrooms and health spa. www.adaremanor.com

ARDFINNAN Kilmaneen Farmhouse

Newcastle, Arafinnan, Co Tipperary Tel & Fax 052 6136231 Rooms 3

Road Map C5

This 200-year-old award-winning farmhouse is situated on a working dairy farm in a garden setting. The hosts are pleasant and the ambience is relaxed. Surrounded by the mountains and close to the River Suir, it makes an ideal base for a walking or fishing holiday. Good home cooking. Dinner by arrangement. www.kilmaneen.com

BALLINDERRY Kylenoe House

Ballinderry, Nenagh, Co Tipperary Tel 067 22015 Fax 067 22275 Rooms 3

Road Map C4

Close to Lough Derg, this 200-year-old stone house stands on farm and woodland. It is furnished in a country-house style with antiques and open fires, creating the ambience of a welcoming home and a peaceful retreat. Award-winning breakfasts. Dinner available if requested

BALLYVAUGHAN Hylands Burren Hotel

Ballyvaughan, Co Clare Tel 065 707 7037 Fax 065 707 7131 Rooms 30

Road Map B4

In the heart of Ballyvaughan village, this traditionally styled family-run hotel dates from the 18th century. Bedrooms are neat and simple. Informal and cheerful atmosphere with turf fires and live Irish music in the bar. Food available all day. Its location, on the edge of the Burren, makes it a popular spot. www.hylandsburren.com

BANSHA Lismacue House

Bansha, Co Tipperary Tel 062 54106 Fax 062 54055 Rooms 5

Road Map C5

A member of the Hidden Ireland group, this classically proportioned Irish country house dates back to 1813. Set in 80 ha (200 acres) it is approached by an avenue of lime trees. Ornate interiors with period furniture make it an elegant and peaceful retreat, within view of the Galtee Mountains. Trout fishing on the estate. www.lismacue.com

BORRISOKANE Coolbawn Quay

Coolbawn, Nenagh, Borrisokane, Co Tipperary Tel 067 28158 Fax 067 28152 Rooms 48

Road Map C4

There is a variety of lakeshore suites, village rooms and cottages scattered around this lakeside marina. Boats are also available for transient sailors. Facilities include a spa which overlooks Lough Derg, a small and intimate bar and a country dining room. The breakfasts are tasty, in particular the homemade muesli. www.coolbawnquay.com

BUNRATTY Bunratty Castle Hotel

Bunratty, Co Clare Tel 061 478 700 Fax 061 364 891 Rooms 144

Road Map B4

Just 8 km (5 miles) from Shannon Airport, this Georgian hotel is situated in its own grounds, opposite the historic Bunratty Castle and folk-park, and has good-sized, modern bedrooms. Kathleen's Bar serves lunch and dinner, and there's also an Italian restaurant. www.bunrattycastlehotel.com

CASHEL Hill House

Palmer Hill, Cashel, Co Tipperary Tel 062 51277 Rooms 5

Road Map C5

This delightful Georgian house, built in 1710, is steeped in history and character. It has the extra dimension of a fabulous view of the famed Rock of Cashel. Breakfast is outstanding, with freshly baked bread and scones, fruit, cereal and a traditional Irish "fry". www.hillhousecashel.com

CASHEL Cashel Palace Hotel

Main St, Cashel, Co Tipperary Tel 062 62707 Fax 062 61521 Rooms 20

Road Map C5

Originally a bishop's palace, this beautiful Queen Anne-style house, dating from 1730, is set in its own grounds in the centre of Cashel town. The large, elegant rooms overlook tranquil gardens to the rear and the Rock of Cashel. The Bishop's Buttery restaurant serves lunch and dinner. A peaceful retreat. www.cashel-palace.ie

CLONMEL Minella Hotel

Clonmel, Co Tipperary Tel 052 612 2388 Fax 052 612 4381 Rooms 90

Road Map C5

Overlooking the River Suir, the four-star Minella Hotel has been gradually expanded from the original 1863 house. Great racing enthusiasts, the Nallens have carried this equine theme throughout the hotel, with stables nearby. Traditional Irish food is served. There is a leisure centre with swimming pool and outdoor hot tub. www.hotelminella.ie

COROFIN Fergus View

Kilnaboy, Corofin, Co Clare Tel & Fax 065 683 7606 Rooms 6

Road Map B4

This good-value guesthouse has small but nice bedrooms, furnished with information packs on the surrounding areas. Breakfasts include locally sourced and home-grown produce. A well-maintained garden stretches down to the River Fergus. Open March to October. www.fergusview.com

DOOLIN Ballinalacken Castle Country House

Doolin, Co Clare Tel 065 707 4025 Rooms 12

Road Map B4

A 15th-century castle stands beside this country house, which features antique furniture, welcoming rooms and a warm fire for those cold winter days. Choose a room overlooking the sea. Quality local seafood and meat dishes are served up in the grand restaurant dining room. www.ballinalackencastle.com

ENNIS Newpark House

Ennis, Co Clare **Tel** *065 682 1233* **Fax** *065 682 1233* **Rooms** *6*   **Road Map** *B4*

W thin walking distance of the town, this historic house is surrounded by lovely old lime, beech and oak trees. Peaceful and nicely decorated bedrooms vary in size, but are all convenient and en suite. The Barron family can give genealogical advice on tracing your family roots. **www.newparkhouse.com**

ENNIS The Old Ground

Ennis, Co Clare **Tel** *065 682 8127* **Fax** *065 682 8112* **Rooms** *103*   **Road Map** *B4*

This ivy clad hotel dates back to the 18th century. It is located centrally in one of Ireland's most energetic towns. The Poets Corner is a traditional bar with Irish music from Thursday to Sunday night. The O'Brien Room is a quality restaurant, drawing in a good mix of locals and tourists. **www.flynnhotels.com**

GLEN OF AHERLOW Aherlow House

Glen of Aherlow, Co Tipperary **Tel** *062 56153* **Fax** *062 56212* **Rooms** *29*   **Road Map** *C5*

Situated in the middle of a pine forest in the Glen of Aherlow Nature Park, this hotel offers good accommodation with views of the Galtee Mountains. Forest walks and fishing are popular pursuits, while cycling and horse-riding are available close by. Well-equipped self-catering lodges with open fires are also available. **www.aherlowhouse.ie**

GLIN Old Castle House

Glin, Co Limerick **Tel** *068 34963* **Rooms** *4*   **Road Map** *B5*

Set in the picturesque village of Glin, this charming old-style bed and breakfast is set in its own gardens beside the ruins of the Old Castle and rooms have river or castle views. Meals can be served on the riverside terrace. This is a relaxed and comfortable place to stay. **www.oldcastlehouse.com**

KILKEE Stella Maris Hotel

Kilkee, Co Clare **Tel** *065 905 6455* **Fax** *065 906 0006* **Rooms** *19*   **Road Map** *B4*

Situated in the centre of the vibrant town of Kilkee, this family-run hotel is both relaxed and friendly. With open log fires, it provides a warm welcome on a winter's day and its coastal position makes it popular with summer visitors. Bedrooms are bright and airy. There is a traditional Irish food restaurant. **www.stellamarishotel.com**

KILMALLOCK Flemingstown House

Kilmallock, Co Limerick **Tel** *063 98093* **Fax** *063 98546* **Rooms** *5*   **Road Map** *B5*

This 250-year-old farmhouse is set on a working farm. The original house has been extended and now offers well-maintained accommodation, warm hospitality and laid-back atmosphere. Breakfasts are a treat and include home-made bread and cheeses. Dinner can also be arranged. **www.flemingstown.com**

LAHINCH Moy House

Lahinch, Co Clare **Tel** *065 708 2800* **Fax** *065 708 2500* **Rooms** *9*   **Road Map** *B4*

With its breathtaking sea views across Liscannor Bay, towards the Cliffs of Moher, this 1820s house is the area's most luxurious hotel, furnished with rugs, antiques and elegant fabrics. Well-appointed bedrooms overlook the sea. The 6 ha (15 acres) of grounds include a fruit orchard and an organic vegetable garden. **www.moyhouse.com**

LIMERICK Woodfield House

Ennis Rd, Limerick **Tel** *061 453 022* **Fax** *061 326 755* **Rooms** *26*   **Road Map** *B4*

This pleasant, three-star family run house is traditional in style. Bedrooms are smartly coordinated and well equipped with modern facilities. Located just outside Limerick en route to Ennis, the city centre and major sights are easily accessible. Woodies Steakhouse is a good restaurant on the premises. **www.woodfieldhousehotel.com**

LIMERICK The Clarion Hotel

Steamboat Quay, Dock Rd, Limerick **Tel** *061 444 100* **Fax** *061 444 101* **Rooms** *158*   **Road Map** *B4*

Overlooking the River Shannon, this modern 17-storey hotel is reputedly the tallest in Ireland. Clean-lined and contemporary in style, it uses modern colours and walnut panelling. Well-appointed bedrooms. The Sinergie restaurant has an excellent waterfront location. On-site health and fitness club. **www.clarionhotellimerick.com**

LIMERICK No 1 Perry Square

1 Perry Square, Limerick **Tel** *061 402 402* **Fax** *061 313 060* **Rooms** *20*   **Road Map** *B4*

A smart and stylish boutique hotel, No 1 Perry Square is set in a terrace of Georgian houses in the city's Georgian area. The building has been lovingly restored, with many original architectural features. There is an excellent restaurant and there is also a holistic spa in the basement. **www.oneperrysquare.com**

LOOP HEAD Anvil Farm Guesthouse

Kilbaha, Loop Head, Co Clare **Tel** *065 905 8018* **Fax** *065 905 8331* **Rooms** *5*   **Road Map** *B4*

This tastefully decorated cliff-top farmhouse is located on the beautifully unspoilt Loop Head. En suite bedrooms are cosy. It's an ideal base to explore the remote area, with dolphin-watching, walking, angling, diving, pony-trekking and bird-watching. Good home cooking. Open March to October. **www.westclare.com**

NENAGH Ashley Park House

Ardcroney, Nenagh, Co Tipperary **Tel & fax** *067 38223* **Rooms** *7*   **Road Map** *C4*

This lovely 18th-century country house is set in woodland and gardens, on the shores of Lough Ourna. Elegantly furnished, it exudes an air of old-fashioned charm and comfort. Bedrooms have views of the lake and beyond to the Slieve Bloom Mountains, and boast brass beds. A separate one-bedroom cottage is available. **www.ashleypark.com**

Key to Price Guide *see p294* **Key to Symbols** *see back cover flap*

NEWMARKET-ON-FERGUS Carrygerry House

Newmarket-on-Fergus, Co Clare **Tel & fax** 061 360 500 **Rooms** 11   Road Map B4

Only 10 minutes from Shannon Airport, this late-18th-century house is set in a peaceful rural setting and overlooks the Shannon and Fergus estuaries. It is furnished in a relaxed country-house style, with open fires. Tasty farm breakfasts are served. There's a pleasant restaurant serving home cooking. **www.carrygerryhouse.com**

NEWMARKET-ON-FERGUS Dromoland Castle

Newmarket-on-Fergus, Co Clare **Tel** 061 368 144 **Fax** 061 363 355 **Rooms** 99   Road Map B4

This is one of Ireland's finest hotels. Its grand elegance, with lush furnishings, antiques and crystal chandeliers, is enhanced by the picture-postcard scenery of the surrounding estate. Bedrooms are luxurious. Just 13 km (8 miles) from Shannon Airport. **www.dromoland.ie**

THURLES Inch House

Bouladuff, Thurles, Co Tipperary **Tel** 0504 51261 **Fax** 0504 51754 **Rooms** 5   Road Map C4

This stately Georgian house is set in 100 ha (250 acres) of rich farmland. Large, high-ceilinged rooms are nicely furnished. The William Morris-style drawing room has a beautiful plasterwork ceiling and stained-glass windows. There's an award-winning restaurant on site which is open from Tuesday to Saturday nights. **www.inchhouse.ie**

THE WEST OF IRELAND

ACHILL ISLAND Bervie

Keel, Achill Island, Co Mayo **Tel** 098 43114 **Fax** 098 43407 **Rooms** 14   Road Map A3

Formerly a coastguard station, this low-lying beachside house has a wicker gate opening onto the sand. Warm hospitality and a turf fire await. Bedrooms are compact and en suite. Afternoon tea with freshly baked scones are a treat. Evening meals are served primarily for residents. **www.bervie-guesthouse-achill.com**

ACHILL ISLAND Gray's Guest House

Dugort, Achill Island, Co Mayo **Tel** 098 43244 **Rooms** 15   Road Map A2

Comprising several houses in the small village of Dugort, this long-established guesthouse has been known for its warm hospitality since 1970. It is somewhat rambling, with different areas varying in decor. Bedrooms offer old-fashioned comfort. Afternoon tea and dinner served. Open Easter to October.

ARAN ISLANDS An Dún Guest House

Inis Meain, Aran Islands, Co Galway **Tel & Fax** 099 73047 **Rooms** 5   Road Map B4

This welcoming guesthouse is located at the foot of Conner's Fort on Inismeain, the most traditional of the three Aran Islands. It is run by the Faherty family. All of the en suite bedrooms have great scenic views and there's a mini sauna. **www.inismeainaccommodation.com**

ARAN ISLANDS Kilmurvey House

Kilronan, Aran Islands, Co Galway **Tel** 099 61218 **Fax** 099 61397 **Rooms** 12   Road Map B4

On the west side of the island, at the foot of Dun Aonghasa, this 150-year-old stone house is close to the glorious beach of Kilmurvey Bay. En suite bedrooms have great views and there are comfortable sitting rooms. Ideal base for cycling or walking. **www.kilmurveyhouse.com**

ARAN ISLANDS Man of Aran Cottage

Kilmurvey, Inishmore, Aran Islands, Co Galway **Tel** 099 61301 **Fax** 099 61324 **Rooms** 2   Road Map B4

Renowned for its starring role in the film of the same name, this delightful cottage offers limited but good accommodation. Situated beside Kilmurvey beach, it is surrounded by wildflowers and a vegetable garden. Only one room is en suite. Open March to October. Evening meals are available for guests. **www.manofarancottage.com**

BALLINA The Ice House Hotel

The Quay, Ballina, Co Mayo **Tel** 096 23500 **Fax** 096 23598 **Rooms** 32   Road Map B2

This design hotel, based in a restored country house, is set beside the River Moy Estuary at the Quay in Ballina and floor-to-ceiling windows in the spacious rooms allow for beautiful views. There is also a spa with its own gardens and outdoor hot tubs. The breakfast menu offers a great range of delicious options. **www.icehousehotel.ie**

BALLYCONNEELY Emlaghmore Lodge

Ballyconneely, Co Galway **Tel** 095 23529 **Fax** 095 23860 **Rooms** 4   Road Map A3

This small, secluded period fishing lodge, situated halfway between Roundstone and Ballyconneely, is furnished with antiques and family portraits. Uncluttered bedrooms enjoy beautiful views. Go fly-fishing in the river running through the garden. Evening meals are available for guests. **www.emlaghmore.com**

CARRICK-ON-SHANNON Hollywell Country House

Carrick-On-Shannon, Co Leitrim **Tel & Fax** 071 962 1124 **Rooms** 4   Road Map C3

Tom and Rosaleen Maher are the hosts at this period house with its own river frontage and calming views of the River Shannon. There is a warm welcome waiting for you here and a pervading relaxed atmosphere. The breakfast is a delight, ranging from freshly baked bread to Irish pancakes with maple syrup.

CASHEL BAY Zetland House
Cashel Bay, Co Galway **Tel** 095 31111 **Fax** 095 31117 **Rooms** 22   **Road Map** A3

Originally built in the 19th century as a sporting lodge, this stylish country-house hotel is a quiet retreat. It commands an enviable position overlooking Cashel Bay and is surrounded by woodland gardens and flowering shrubs. Inside, peaceful rooms are furnished with antiques and exude an easy-going atmosphere. Superb cooking. **www.zetland.com**

CASHEL BAY Cashel House
Cashel Bay, Co Galway **Tel** 095 31001 **Fax** 095 31077 **Rooms** 30   **Road Map** A3

This renowned country house, set in sprawling gardens and woodland, enjoys excellent views of Cashel Bay. Previous guests included Charles de Gaulle and his wife. Patrons are attracted by the quiet comfort of the antique-furnished rooms, with their log fires and fresh flowers, and the excellent cooking. **www.cashel-house-hotel.com**

CASTLEBAR Breaffy House Hotel & Spa
Castlebar, Co Mayo **Tel** 094 902 2033 **Fax** 094 902 2276 **Rooms** 127   **Road Map** B3

Situated on the outskirts of Castlebar town, this hotel dates back to 1890, but it has been substantially modernized, while retaining the flavour of an old country house. Bedrooms are neat and well appointed. Very good leisure facilities as well as a health spa are available. **www.breaffyhousehotel.ie**

CASTLECOOTE Castlecoote House
Castlecoote, Co Roscommon **Tel** 0906 663 794 **Fax** 0183 30666 **Rooms** 5   **Road Map** C3

Surrounded by pastoral countryside and overlooking the River Suck, this fine Georgian house stands on the grounds of a medieval castle. The lavish interior comprises stucco ceilings, marble fireplaces and portraits by Sir Joshua Reynolds. Delightful bedrooms. Games room, tennis courts and croquet on site. **www.castlecootehouse.com**

CASTLEREA Clonalis House
Castlerea, Co Roscommon **Tel & Fax** 094 962 0014 **Rooms** 4   **Road Map** C3

Set in a 700-acre wooded estate, this impressive Victorian-Italianate mansion is the ancestral home of the O'Connors of Connacht, descendants of Ireland's last high kings. Rich in history, with a wonderful library, heirlooms include the famous Carolan's harp. Rooms are vast and well furnished. Country home cooking. **www.clonalis.com**

CLIFDEN Dolphin Beach Country House
Lower Sky Rd, Clifden, Co Galway **Tel** 095 21204 **Fax** 095 22935 **Rooms** 9   **Road Map** A3

This charming beachside house, with its own private cove, is bright and stylish, with a friendly atmosphere. Bedrooms are spacious, with antique furniture and crisp bed linen and there is delicious home cooking in the dining room overlooking the bay (guests only). **www.dolphinbeachhouse.com**

CLIFDEN The Quay House
Beach Rd, Clifden, Co Galway **Tel** 095 21369 **Fax** 095 21608 **Rooms** 14   **Road Map** A3

Built on the quayside in 1820 for the harbour master, The Quay House is now possibly the oldest building in Clifden. Seasoned hosts Paddy and Julia Foyle have an innate sense of worldly style, evident in the sumptuous and quirky rooms. Delicious breakfasts are served in the conservatory. **www.thequayhouse.com**

CLIFDEN Abbeyglen Castle Hotel
Sky Road, Clifden, Connemara, Co Galway **Tel** 095 21201 **Fax** 095 21797 **Rooms** 49   **Road Map** A3

This historic castle in Connemara dates back to 1832. Set in its own grounds, it has stunning views of the Twelve Bens Mountains and the sea, and is within walking distance of the village of Clifden. The restaurant is top class and bedrooms are full of character. **www.abbeyglen.ie**

CONG Ashford Castle
Cong, Co Mayo **Tel** 094 954 6003 **Fax** 094 954 6260 **Rooms** 83   **Road Map** B3

Ireland's most luxuriously grand castle hotel is romantically set in 140 ha (350 acres) of beautiful parkland, lakes and landscaped gardens. Dating back to the 13th century, its lavish interiors feature dark wood panelling, an armoury, fine art, antiques and beautiful fireplaces. Formal yet very peaceful atmosphere. **www.ashford.ie**

CROSSMOLINA Enniscoe House
Castlehill, near Crossmolina, Co Mayo **Tel** 096 31112 **Fax** 096 31773 **Rooms** 6   **Road Map** B2

This fine Georgian house, set in magnificent grounds leading down to Lough Conn, is full of beautiful antiques and fine art. It has a relaxed, lived-in feel. Susan Kellet, the charming owner, is a direct descendant of the original family who arrived here in the 1660s. A gracious host, she provides simply delicious country cooking. **www.enniscoe.com**

GALWAY Devondell
47 Devon Park, Lower Salthill, Galway **Tel** 091 528 306 **Rooms** 4   **Road Map** B4

Located in a residential area, this small, modern guesthouse is unremarkable from the outside but promises genuine hospitality and very good accommodation. Berna Kelly is a warm host and an excellent housekeeper. Pretty bedrooms are thoughtfully furnished, with cast-iron beds. Superb breakfasts. Open March to November. **www.devondell.com**

GALWAY Connemara Coast Hotel
Furbo, Galway **Tel** 091 592 108 **Fax** 091 592 065 **Rooms** 141   **Road Map** B4

This hotel has jaw-dropping views of Galway Bay and is ten minutes by car from the city. The Coast Club Leisure Centre is large with excellent facilities. The hotel has two restaurants, The Gallery and Daly's, along with two bars, 'Sin Sceal Eile' and Player's cocktail bar. **www.connemaracoast.ie**

Key to Price Guide see p 294 **Key to Symbols** see back cover flap

GALWAY The G Hotel
Wellpark, Dublin Rd, Galway **Tel** 091 855 200 **Fax** 091 855 203 **Rooms** 101   Road Map B4

This is a chic, five-star hotel. Interiors, designed by milliner Philip Treacy who is a native of Galway, are dark and dramatic but luxurious. Rooms are spacious and many have views of the sea. The restaurant is top class and there is also a luxury spa with a thermal suite. **www.theghotel.ie**

GALWAY Hotel Meyrick
Eyre Square, Galway **Tel** 091 564 041 **Fax** 091 566 704 **Rooms** 97   Road Map B4

In the heart of Galway, this railway hotel was built in 1845 and has been sensitively modernized, without losing its sense of historic grandeur. The tasteful interior consists of mahogany and brass features and the rooms are elegant. There is a health spa, with interesting views of the city. **www.hotelmeyrick.ie**

GALWAY Jurys Inn Galway
Quay St, Galway **Tel** 091 566 444 **Fax** 091 558 415 **Rooms** 130   Road Map B4

The best located hotel in Galway, this central three-star hotel is convenient for exploring the bustling heart of Galway. Geared towards the cost-conscious traveller, reasonably priced rooms are convenient, if basically decorated with functional, pine-coloured furniture. Breakfast and Internet access are extras. **www.jurysinns.com**

GALWAY Radisson Blu Hotel & Spa Galway
Lough Atalia Rd, Galway **Tel** 091 538 300 **Fax** 091 538 380 **Rooms** 282   Road Map B4

This contemporary hotel, overlooking Lough Atalia, is a five-minute walk to the city centre. The decor is appealing and the ambience restful. All rooms are equipped with good facilities and there's an excellent spa. Marinas restaurant serves international cuisine. **www.radissonhotelgalway.com**

INISHBOFIN ISLAND Murray's Doonmore Hotel
Inishbofin Island, Co Galway **Tel** 095 45804 **Fax** 095 45804 **Rooms** 19   Road Map A3

Situated overlooking the entrance to the island's peaceful harbour, this traditional family-run hotel is an ideal base for exploring Inishbofin Island. The restaurant serves breakfast, lunch and dinner and specializes in locally caught seafood. The welcoming bar with open fire is popular with traditional musicians. **www.doonmorehotel.com**

LEENANE Delphi Lodge
Leenane, Co Galway **Tel** 095 42222 **Fax** 095 42296 **Rooms** 12   Road Map B3

One of Ireland's most famous sporting lodges, Delphi Lodge was built by the Marquis of Sligo in the 1830s. The 600-acre estate is set in a valley surrounded by majestic mountains. Inside, there's a wonderful selection of books, antiques and fishing gear. Communal dining. Activities include fly-fishing and hiking. **www.delphilodge.ie**

LETTERFRACK Renvyle House Hotel
Renvyle, Letterfrack, Co Galway **Tel** 095 43511 **Fax** 095 43515 **Rooms** 72   Road Map A3

This historic and romantic house, on the edge of the Atlantic, is well-loved. Wooden beams, polished floors and turf fires create a relaxed atmosphere. Good food. Former guests include WB Yeats and Winston Churchill. Ideal for families. Attractions include tennis, golf, croquet and trout fishing. The outdoor pool is open May–September. **www.renvyle.com**

LETTERFRACK Rosleague Manor House Hotel
Letterfrack, Co Galway **Tel** 095 41101 **Fax** 095 41168 **Rooms** 20   Road Map A3

This wonderful 200-year-old Regency Manor is a tranquil retreat appealing to all sensibilities. Gardens planted with exotic plants and shrubs sweep down to Ballinakill Bay. Elegantly furnished, it holds great charm and character and provides relaxed luxury and panoramic views. Country house cuisine is superbly executed. **www.rosleague.com**

MULRANY Rosturk Woods
Mulrany, Co Mayo **Tel** 098 36264 **Fax** 098 36264 **Rooms** 6   Road Map B3

Set in secluded woodland and close to the sea, this stylishly furnished house is family-run and informal. Service is friendly and the en suite bedrooms are pretty. The delightful veranda overlooks Clew Bay. The host is a qualified sailing instructor and leads boating and fishing outings. Two self-catered houses on site. **www.rosturk-woods.com**

NEWPORT Newport House
Newport, Co Mayo **Tel** 098 41222 **Fax** 098 41613 **Rooms** 18   Road Map B3

This magnificent historic Georgian mansion, clad in Virginia creeper, is set in gardens that sweep down to the River Newport. Ideal for guests seeking refined comfort and gracious hospitality. The restaurant is greatly celebrated for its fresh seafood and exceptional wine list. Salmon and sea trout fishing nearby. **www.newporthouse.ie**

OUGHTERARD Currarevagh House
Oughterard, Co Galway **Tel** 091 552 312 **Fax** 091 552 731 **Rooms** 13   Road Map B3

In a tranquil spot on the shores of Lough Corrib and surrounded by woods, parkland and gardens, this romantic Victorian country house is traditionally run. Fishing is a popular pursuit in these parts: salmon, brown trout, pike and perch. Great country walks. Good home cooking using fresh local produce. **www.currarevagh.com**

OUGHTERARD Ross Lake House
Rosscahill, Oughterard, Co Galway **Tel** 091 550 109 **Fax** 091 550 184 **Rooms** 13   Road Map B3

Situated in delightful gardens, this 1850 country house provides comfortably furnished accommodation. Antiques and four-poster beds may be found in the generously proportioned bedrooms. Charming hosts. Fishing is possible on the nearby lakes and tennis on the grounds. **www.rosslakehotel.com**

PONTOON Healy's Restaurant & Fishing Lodge
Pontoon, Foxford, Co Mayo **Tel** *094 925 6443* **Fax** *094 925 6572* **Rooms** *14*   **Road Map** *B3*

In a stunning position on the shores of Lough Conn and Lough Cullen, this traditional old stone building has been refurbished, yet retains its old-world feel. Simple, neat bedrooms are reasonably priced. There's a pleasant garden on the grounds. Popular with bird-watchers and fishing afficionados. Good Irish cooking. **www.healyspontoon.com**

RECESS Ballynahinch Castle Hotel
Recess, Co Galway **Tel** *095 31006* **Fax** *095 31085* **Rooms** *40*   **Road Map** *A3*

This Victorian castle, once the home of an Indian maharajah, Ranjit Singh, is known as a fishing destination and is set in 180 ha (450 acres) of beautiful woodland and gardens on the banks of the River Ballynahinch. The elegant Owenmore restaurant, overlooking the winding river, features Connemara lamb and fresh fish. **www.ballynahinch-castle.com**

RECESS Lough Inagh Lodge Hotel
Recess, Co Galway **Tel** *095 34706* **Fax** *095 34708* **Rooms** *13*   **Road Map** *A3*

This charming country retreat is situated on the shores of Lough Inagh, one of Connemara's most beautiful settings. The bedrooms are simple and elegant and the hotel is a perfect base for fishing enthusiasts as well as for cyclists. There is an 18-hole golf course nearby. Open March to December. **www.loughinaghlodgehotel.ie**

ROSCOMMON Abbey Hotel Conference & Leisure
Galway Rd, Roscommon **Tel** *090 662 6240* **Fax** *090 662 6021* **Rooms** *50*   **Road Map** *C3*

Set on its own grounds and gardens, this four-star hotel takes its name from a 13th-century Dominican abbey, whose ruins may still be seen. It provides decent accommodation and a friendly atmosphere. En suite bedrooms are reasonably furnished and are equipped with modern facilities. **www.abbeyhotel.ie**

ROUNDSTONE The Anglers Return
Toombeola, Roundstone, Co Galway **Tel & Fax** *095 31091* **Rooms** *5*   **Road Map** *A3*

This 18th-century sporting lodge is now a charming guesthouse. It has an uncluttered interior, furnished by occasional antique pieces, whitewashed walls and wooden floors. Open fires and fresh flowers add to the quiet ambience. Beautiful gardens overlook the river. **www.anglersreturn.com**

WESTPORT Ardmore Country House Hotel
The Quay, Westport, Co Mayo **Tel** *098 25994* **Fax** *098 27795* **Rooms** *13*   **Road Map** *B3*

This small, family-run hotel offers a degree of hospitality that is difficult to resist. The accommodation is luxurious and some rooms have views over Clew Bay. Fabulous breakfasts with fresh fruit and home-baked bread. Nine of the rooms have Internet access. Open March to December. **www.ardmorecountryhouse.com**

WESTPORT Carlton Atlantic Coast Hotel
The Quay, Westport, Co Mayo **Tel** *098 29000* **Fax** *098 29111* **Rooms** *85*   **Road Map** *B3*

This modern hotel is disguised behind the traditional stone façade of an old mill. The spa has nine treatment rooms along with a hydrotherapy bath and dry flotation tanks. The Blue Wave Restaurant and Fishworks Café and Bar combine good food with great beer and a nice selection of wines. **www.atlanticcoasthotel.com**

WESTPORT Knockranny House Hotel
Westport, Co Mayo **Tel** *098 28600* **Fax** *098 28611* **Rooms** *97*   **Road Map** *B3*

Log fires, warm colour schemes and antique furniture enhance the inviting ambience of this four-star hotel overlooking the town of Westport. Rooms are bright and airy with comfortable beds. Excellent contemporary Irish cuisine is served. A health spa is on site. **www.khh.ie**

WESTPORT Westport Plaza Hotel
Castlebar St, Westport, Co Mayo **Tel** *098 51166* **Fax** *098 51133* **Rooms** *87*   **Road Map** *B3*

This contemporary hotel offers a leisure centre and spa treatments. It is the perfect family getaway in the middle of the town, with friendly, attentive staff and a swimming pool which is very popular with kids. A wonderful base for exploring the beautiful County Mayo. **www.westportplazahotel.ie**

NORTHWEST IRELAND

ARDARA The Green Gate
Ardvally, Ardara, Co Donegal **Tel** *074 954 1546* **Rooms** *4*   **Road Map** *C2*

Efficiently run by its opinionated French owner, Paul Chatenoud, this is one of the best B&Bs around. The beautiful landscape adds to its fantastic reputation. The accommodation is spread over three low thatched-roof cottages. The rooms are primitive but pleasant, with tweed coverlets on the simple beds. **www.thegreengate.eu**

ARDARA Woodhill House
Wood Hill, Ardara, Co Donegal **Tel** *074 954 1112* **Fax** *074 954 1516* **Rooms** *13*   **Road Map** *C2*

The ongoing restoration of this country house has been a labour of love for its owners who have been working on the property since 1987. On offer are en suite rooms varying in size and character, either in the main house or in the converted coach house. The restaurant uses local produce. **www.woodhillhouse.com**

Key to Price Guide *see p294* **Key to Symbols** *see back cover flap*

BUNDORAN Great Northern Hotel

Bundoran, Co Donegal **Tel** 071 984 1204 **Fax** 071 984 1114 **Rooms** 108

Road Map C2

In a dramatic location with excellent views of the Atlantic and set in 50 ha (130 acres) of parkland with an 18-hole golf course, the Great Northern is ideal for relaxed, family holidays. There is often live music at the hotel and the leisure centre has a swimming pool. **www.greatnorthernhotel.com**

DONEGAL Atlantic Guest House

Main St, Donegal, Co Donegal **Tel & Fax** 074 972 1187 **Rooms** 16

Road Map C2

This family-run guesthouse provides friendly accommodation in the heart of Donegal Town. Well-priced rooms are spacious, if a little sparse, and each one has a colour TV and coffee-maker. Some rooms share a bathroom. Staff are courteous. Only a minute's walk from the bus stop. **www.atlanticguesthouse.ie**

DONEGAL Ard Na Breatha

Drumrooske, Donegal, Co Donegal **Tel** 074 972 2288 **Rooms** 6

Road Map C2

Theresa and Albert Morrow's farm guesthouse is now situated in a largely residential area – a knock-on effect of the property boom. It achieved an EU Flower award for eco tourism. There are soothing views of the Bluestack Mountain from the residents' lounge and the restaurant serves organic produce from the farm. **www.ardnabreatha.com**

DOWNINGS Rosapenna Hotel

Downings, Co Donegal **Tel** 074 915 5301 **Fax** 074 915 5128 **Rooms** 60

Road Map C1

The wild northwest coast of Donegal is home to this hotel and golf resort situated beside the Old Tom Morris and Sandy Hills Links courses. The rooms are functional but the seaview suites are tastefully decorated and have private balconies. The restaurant favours seafood. **www.rosapenna.ie**

DUNFANAGHY The Mill

Figart, Dunfanaghy, Co Donegal **Tel & Fax** 074 913 6985 **Rooms** 6

Road Map

With a beautiful location on the New Lake shore, The Mill was once home to the current owner's grandfather. The rooms have some nice touches, with good beds and antique furnishings. Relax at the conservatory overlooking the lake. The guesthouse is attached to the excellent Mill Restaurant. **www.themillrestaurant.com**

DUNKINEELY Castle Murray House

St John's Point, Dunkineely, Co Donegal **Tel** 074 973 7022 **Fax** 074 973 7330 **Rooms** 10

Road Map C2

Stunningly located with views of McSweeney Bay, this is a wonderful place to stay. The decor is simple, but each room is individually decorated. The restaurant offers a delicious menu, with head chef Remy Dupuy specializing in seafood with a French flair. **www.castlemurray.com**

LETTERKENNY Radisson Blu Hotel Letterkenny

Loop Road, Letterkenny, Co Donegal **Tel** 074 919 4444 **Fax** 074 919 4455 **Rooms** 114

Road Map C1

Only a five-minute walk from the town centre, this four-star establishment is one of the highly-rated Radisson group. The atrium-style lobby creates a contemporary ambience that exists throughout the hotel. Disabled bedroom facilities as well as ample parking are provided. **www.radissonblu.ie/hotel-letterkenny**

LOUGH ESKE Harvey's Point

Donegal Town, Lough Eske, Co Donegal **Tel** 074 972 2208 **Fax** 074 972 2352 **Rooms** 71

Road Map C2

A Swiss-style hotel on the banks of Lough Eske, Harvey's Point has neat, modern furnishings, an excellent restaurant and many sports facilities. Most rooms overlook the lake and are airy and comfortable. The Superior Rooms have four-poster beds and are located slightly away from the main hotel complex. **www.harveyspoint.com**

MOHILL Glebe House

Ballinamore Rd, Mohill, Co Leitrim **Tel** 071 963 1086 **Fax** 071 963 1886 **Rooms** 10

Road Map C3

B&B accommodation on a grand scale is available in this early 19th-century former rectory, set in 20 ha (50 acres) of parkland, woods and farmland. It's peaceful and attractive with extensive gardens to wander in. There is special pricing for senior citizens and children. **www.glebehouse.com**

MOHILL Lough Rynn Castle

Mohill, Co Leitrim **Tel** 071 963 2700 **Fax** 071 963 2710 **Rooms** 42

Road Map C3

This beautiful castle hotel has old world charm and elegance in abundance. Rooms have views over the 120-ha (300-acre) estate with its two lakes, and there is an 18-hole championship golf course. The restaurant is excellent. A spa and leisure centre are due to open in 2012. **www.loughrynn.ie**

RATHMULLAN Rathmullan House

Rathmullan, Co Donegal **Tel** 074 91 58188 **Fax** 074 91 58200 **Rooms** 32

Road Map C1

Renowned for its excellent cuisine, Rathmullan is an award-winning country house set on the shores of Lough Swilly with mature trees, shore walks and plenty of gardens to enjoy. There are lovely sitting rooms with open fires to relax in after dinner, and there is also a spa and indoor swimming pool. **www.rathmullanhouse.com**

RIVERSTOWN Coopershill House

Riverstown, Co Sligo **Tel** 071 916 5108 **Fax** 071 916 5466 **Rooms** 8

Road Map C2

This is a very civilized, elegant 17th-century house surrounded by a vast estate. Rooms are decorated with tasteful antiques. Elegantly furnished bedrooms are huge, with four-poster or canopy beds. Open log fires and personal attention combine with the historic atmosphere to make it a real joy. Excellent food. **www.coopershill.com**

ROSSES POINT Yeats Country Hotel

⊞⏸≋⌘♨📺ⓦ   €€€

Rosses Point, Co Sligo **Tel** *071 917 7211* **Fax** *071 917 7203* **Rooms** *98*   **Road Map** *B2*

At the foot of Ben Bulben and looking out to the Atlantic, this hotel is an ideal base for exploring Yeats country. En suite rooms, though ordinary in decor, are equipped with a TV, direct dial telephone, hairdryer and coffee-maker. Access to Internet in lobby. Look out for a wide range of events held here. **www.yeatscountryhotel.com**

ROSSNOWLAGH Heron's Cove

⏸♨ⓦ   €€

Rossnowlagh, Co Donegal **Tel** *071 982 2070* **Fax** *071 982 2075* **Rooms** *10*   **Road Map** *C2*

This is a lovely guesthouse near Creevy pier. There is an attractive dinner and duvet special aimed at keeping guests overnight after dinner at the steak and seafood restaurant. All the bedrooms are en suite and the breakfast is unmissable. **www.heronscove.ie**

ROSSNOWLAGH Sand House Hotel

⏸♨📺ⓦ   €€

Rossnowlagh, Donegal Bay, Co Donegal **Tel** *071 985 1777* **Fax** *071 985 2100* **Rooms** *55*   **Road Map** *C2*

An imposing, white castellated building, right on a sandy beach at Donegal Bay, this long-established hotel is very comfortable and well decorated and has a relaxed atmosphere. Originally a fishing lodge, it now has many beautiful rooms, some with four-poster beds. The Marine Spa is a real treat. **www.sandhouse.ie**

SLIGO Clarion Hotel Sligo

⊞⏸≋♨📺📺ⓦ   €€

Clarion Rd, Sligo **Tel** *071 911 9000* **Fax** *071 911 9001* **Rooms** *162*   **Road Map** *C2*

This is an impressive hotel in its own grounds on the edge of Sligo Town and with great views of Ben Bulben mountain. There's a choice of restaurants, a kids' club and a leisure centre with a gym and swimming pool. Family suites are also available. Diners cards are not accepted. **www.clarionhotelsligo.com**

THE MIDLANDS

ATHLONE Hodson Bay Hotel

⊞⏸≋♨📺📺ⓦ   €€€

Hodson Bay, Athlone, Co Westmeath **Tel** *090 644 2000* **Fax** *090 644 2020* **Rooms** *182*   **Road Map** *C3*

In the centre of Ireland, on the shores of Lough Ree, this cheerfully decorated hotel is adjacent to Athlone Golf Club. Spacious bedrooms have been refurbished and many of them enjoy great views of the lake. Located 90 minutes from Dublin and Galway. Activities include cruising on the River Shannon. **www.hodsonbayhotel.com**

ATHLONE Wineport Lodge

⊞⏸♨📺ⓦ   €€€

Glasson, Athlone, Co Westmeath **Tel** *090 643 9010* **Rooms** *29*   **Road Map** *C3*

A romantic, lakeside lodge on the shores of Lough Ree, Wineport has bright and spacious rooms, with each one named after a different wine. Many rooms have lakeshore decks. Food and wine is excellent and there is an outdoor cedar hot tub on the roof. **www.wineport.ie**

BALLYCONNELL Slieve Russell Hotel, Golf & Country Club

⊞⏸≋♨📺ⓦ   €€€

Ballyconnell, Co Cavan **Tel** *049 952 6444* **Fax** *049 952 6046* **Rooms** *222*   **Road Map** *C3*

Taking its name from the nearby mountain, this hotel is set in 120 ha (300 acres) of landscaped gardens and lakes. It is very much a focus for business and social activity in the area. Bedrooms are spacious, with good bathrooms. The excellent leisure facilities include an 18-hole golf course, spa and treatment centre. **www.slieverussell.ie**

BELTURBET International Fishing Centre

⏸♨   €€

Loughdooley, Belturbet, Co Cavan **Tel** *049 952 2616* **Fax** *049 952 2616* **Rooms** *18*   **Road Map** *C3*

Frenchman Michael Neuville offers residential fishing holidays at this delightfully tranquil waterside place. Individual wooden chalets, on the edge of the River Erne, can accommodate up to five people, making it ideal for a family holiday, whether fishing or not. For enthusiasts, coarse and pike fishing await. **www.angling-holidays.com**

BIRR The Stables Town House & Restaurant

⏸♨   €€

6 Oxmantown Mall, Birr, Co Offaly **Tel** *057 912 0263* **Fax** *057 912 1677* **Rooms** *6*   **Road Map** *C4*

On a tree-lined mall in the centre of the town, this Georgian house is a long-established B&B with a popular restaurant. The comfortable, old-world bedrooms are en suite and either overlook the mall or the courtyard. Pets are allowed. Its central location makes it an ideal base to explore this heritage town. **www.thestablesbirr.com**

CARLINGFORD Beaufort House

♨   €€

Ghan Rd, Carlingford, Co Louth **Tel** *042 937 3879* **Rooms** *6*   **Road Map** *D3*

This is one of only fourteen guesthouses in Ireland that have earned a Michelin Bib Hotel award for high standards at affordable prices. The rooms are beautifully appointed and the hotel enjoys a shoreside location with fine sea and mountain views. The owners also run a sailing school and yacht charter service. **www.beauforthouse.net**

CARLINGFORD McKevitt's Village Hotel

⏸♨📺ⓦ   €€€

Market Square, Carlingford, Co Louth **Tel** *042 937 3116* **Fax** *042 937 3144* **Rooms** *17*   **Road Map** *D3*

This popular family-run country village inn is located in the town centre. Bedrooms are bright, clean and pretty, with adequate bathrooms. The bar, lounge and dining room of Schooners restaurant combine old-world charm with modern comfort. Occasional special offers are available. **www.mckevittshotel.com**

Key to Price Guide *see p294* **Key to Symbols** *see back cover flap*

CLONES Hilton Park
Clones, Co Monaghan **Tel** 047 56007 **Fax** 047 56033 **Rooms** 6
Road Map C2

One of Ireland's greatest country houses, this magnificent mansion overlooks 80 ha (200 acres) of woodland and green pastures. A romantic and cinematic setting with lakes, a lover's walk and formal gardens. In the charming Madden family since 1734, the house is beautifully furnished and exudes a relaxed grandeur. **www.hiltonpark.ie**

CLOVERHILL Olde Post Inn
Cloverhill, Co Cavan **Tel** 047 55555 **Fax** 047 55111 **Rooms** 6
Road Map C3

Originally a post office, this pretty stone building has been a popular inn since 1974. The ambience is rustic, with wooden beams and exposed walls. En suite rooms are modest but cosy. The superb restaurant uses regional produce. Service is efficient. Hiking, horse-riding and fishing nearby. **www.theoldepostinn.com**

COLLINSTOWN Lough Bishop House
Derrynagara, Collinstown, Co Westmeath **Tel** 044 966 1313 **Rooms** 3
Road Map C3

This attractive Georgian house is nestled into a south-facing slope overlooking Bishop's Lough and rolling countryside. It offers appealing rooms in peaceful surroundings. Bedrooms have lovely views. Good country cooking using seasonal produce is served for dinner by advance notice. **www.derrynagarra.com**

CROSSDONEY Lisnamandra Country House
Lisnamandra, Crossdoney, Co Cavan **Tel** 049 433 7196 **Rooms** 6
Road Map C3

This restored and modernized 17th-century farmhouse is ideal for those looking for simple but good accommodation at a reasonable price. The pastoral setting is relaxing. Bedrooms have en suite facilities. It is run by the Neill family, who are welcoming hosts. Open May to October. **lisnamandra@eircom.net**

DROGHEDA Boyne Valley Hotel & Country Club
Drogheda, Co Louth **Tel** 041 983 7737 **Fax** 041 983 9188 **Rooms** 71
Road Map D3

Surrounded by gardens and woodland, this much-extended 18th-century manor house, though refurbished with modern furnishings, preserves its traditional feel. It offers good leisure facilities and capable service. Bedrooms in the old building have more character, while the newer ones provide better facilities. **www.boyne-valley-hotel.ie**

DUNBOYNE Dunboyne Castle Hotel & Spa
Dunboyne, Co Meath **Tel** 01 801 3500 **Fax** 01 436 6801 **Rooms** 145
Road Map D3

Set in 8 ha (21 acres) of woodland and gardens, 16 km (10 miles) from Dublin city centre, Dunboyne is the sister hotel of the Dylan in Dublin 4. The guest rooms are modern with garden views, and with the Seoid Spa's 18 treatment rooms and hydrotherapy pool, this elegant hotel is the perfect place to rejuvenate. **www.dunboynecastlehotel.com**

KILMESSAN Station House Hotel & Restaurant
Kilmessan, Co Meath **Tel** 046 902 5239 **Fax** 046 902 5588 **Rooms** 20
Road Map D3

The last passenger train made its final stop in Kilmessan in 1947. A nostalgic reminder of a bygone era, this Victorian station building is now a cosy hotel with upgraded bedrooms featuring modern facilities. The bar overlooks very pleasant landscaped gardens, where fresh flowers feature within the hotel. **www.thestationhousehotel.com**

KINNITY Ardmore House
The Walk, Kinnity, Co Offaly **Tel** 05791 37009, 086 278 9147 (mobile) **Rooms** 4
Road Map C4

This sensitively restored Victorian house, set in its own garden, is located in the picturesque village of Kinnity, at the foot of the Slieve Bloom Mountains. The turf fire, home cooking and relaxed atmosphere add to the old-fashioned feel of the house. Bedrooms are tastefully decorated, if free of many modern amenities. **www.kinnitty.net**

LONGFORD The Longford Arms Hotel
Main St, Longford **Tel** 043 334 6296 **Fax** 043 334 6244 **Rooms** 66
Road Map C3

Located in the heart of Longford town, this is a popular family-run hotel, furnished in traditional style. All bedrooms are en suite and comfortable. Food is served all day in the coffee shop until 8pm. The restaurant serves evening meals. Health and leisure centre on site. **www.longfordarms.ie**

LONGFORD Viewmount House
Dublin Rd, Longford **Tel** 043 334 1919 **Fax** 043 334 2906 **Rooms** 12
Road Map C3

This 1750s Georgian house, on the outskirts of Longford town, was originally owned by the Earl of Longford and has been restored with flair and sensitivity. The wooded gardens create an elegant and welcoming atmosphere. The stables have been converted into the VM restaurant. **www.viewmounthouse.com**

MOATE Temple Country House & Spa
Horseleap, Moate, Co Westmeath **Tel** 05793 35118 **Fax** 05793 35008 **Rooms** 23
Road Map C4

Set in rolling parkland, this beautiful 250-year-old country house is a haven of relaxation and well-being. Meticulously maintained bedrooms are bright, airy and stylishly decorated. Delicious home cooking. Variety of spa treatments available. Attractions include nature walks, horse-riding and cycling. **www.templespa.ie**

MOUNTNUGENT Ross House Equestrian Centre
Mountnugent, Co Cavan **Tel** & **Fax** 049 854 0218 **Rooms** 6
Road Map C3

On the shores of Lough Sheelin, this old manor house enjoys a peaceful location amidst gardens. Reasonably priced accommodation comes with a range of outdoor pursuits. Bedrooms are comfortable, some with their own conservatories or fireplaces. Good home cooking for each meal. Packed lunches available. **www.ross-house.com**

MOUNTRATH Roundwood House   🚶 W   €€
Mountrath, Co Laois **Tel** *05787 32120* **Fax** *05787 32711* **Rooms** *10*   **Road Map** *C4*

This impressive 18th-century Palladian house, set in mature parkland, is surrounded by beech, lime and horse chestnut trees. Rooms are comfortable, well-proportioned, and six have Internet access. The Kennan family are delightful hosts. Enjoy good home cooking and delicious breakfasts. Communal dining. **www.roundwoodhouse.com**

MULLINGAR Bloomfield House   🏊 🍴 🛋 🚶 🛎 W   €€
Mullingar, Co Westmeath **Tel** *044 934 0894* **Fax** *044 934 3767* **Rooms** *111*   **Road Map** *C3*

Situated 5 km (3 miles) outside the town of Mullingar, this hotel overlooks the peaceful waters of Lough Ennell. Lovely parkland surrounds this former dower house, with a comfortably furnished interior and well-equipped bedrooms. Staff are helpful. Leisure centre on site. **www.bloomfieldhouse.com**

MULLINGAR Greville Arms   🍴 🚶   €€
Pearse St, Mullingar, Co Westmeath **Tel** *044 934 8563* **Fax** *044 934 8052* **Rooms** *39*   **Road Map** *C3*

In the heart of Mullingar, this three-star traditional country town hotel caters for local clientele and tourists. Bedrooms are comfortable and neat. There's a large and welcoming bar, Ulysses, and a nightclub, Le Louvre. Former patrons include James Joyce who immortalized the bar in his book *Stephen Hero*. Food served all day. **www.grevillearmshotel.ie**

MULTYFARNHAM Mornington House   🍴 🚶   €€€
Mornington, Multyfarnham, Co Westmeath **Tel** *044 72191* **Fax** *044 72338* **Rooms** *5*   **Road Map** *C3*

Home to the O'Hara family since 1858, this charming Victorian house lies close to Lough Derravarragh. Warm colours, open fires, period furniture and paintings create a classic Irish country house. The gardens are a delight. Canoes, boats and bicycles for hire. A variety of horse-based activities are available. **www.mornington.ie**

OLDCASTLE Lough Crew House   🚶   €€€
Oldcastle, Co Meath **Tel** *049 854 1356* **Fax** *049 854 1921* **Rooms** *10*   **Road Map** *D3*

Lying in the heart of this archaeologically rich area, this B&B is set in 40 ha (100 acres) of woodland and lakes. Fine furniture, paintings and log fires exude elegance. The creative Naper family, when not graciously hosting guests, are busy organizing the summertime garden opera or running the school of gilding. **www.loughcrew.com**

PORTLAOISE Ivyleigh House   W   €€
Bank Place, Church St, Portlaoise, Co Laois **Tel** *05786 22081* **Fax** *05786 63346* **Rooms** *5*   **Road Map** *C4*

This lovingly restored 1850 house is probably the best B&B in town. Thoughtfully furnished with comfort and grace in mind, it combines the ancient with the modern. Bedrooms are large and very comfortable. Breakfasts are excellent and cooked using the finest of local and seasonal produce. **www.ivyleigh.com**

SLANE The Mill House   🍴 W   €€€
Slane, Co Meath **Tel** *083 364 1612* **Rooms** *11*   **Road Map** *D3*

Nestled on the river bank in the heart of the Boyne Valley, the rooms in this 18th century Georgian manor are elegantly decorated with four-poster beds, free-standing baths and luxurious silks and velvets. Massages and various other treatments are available in the Millhouse spa, and guests have use of a pool and gym nearby. **www.themillhouse.ie**

TULLAMORE Annaharvey Farm   🚶   €€
Tullamore, Co Offaly **Tel** *05793 43544* **Fax** *05793 43766* **Rooms** *7*   **Road Map** *C4*

Equestrian activities are the main attraction at this restored grain barn with pitch-pine floors and beams and open fires. En suite bedrooms are provided. Horse-riding tuition is available in indoor and outdoor arenas. Cross-country riding and trekking can be organized. Cycling, walking and golf close by. **www.annaharveyfarm.ie**

NORTHERN IRELAND

ANNALONG Glassdrumman Lodge   🍴 🚶 🍷 W   €€
Mill Rd, Annalong, Co Down, BT34 4RH **Tel** *028 4376 8451* **Fax** *028 437 67041* **Rooms** *10*   **Road Map** *D2*

Set deep in the "Kingdom of Mourne", the hotel looks out on the region's famous dry-stone walls. Guests can enjoy the library, drawing room and gardens, and open log fires create a relaxed atmosphere. The restaurant specialises in fresh oysters from Dundrum Bay. **www.glassdrummanlodge.com**

ARMAGH Armagh City Hotel   🏊 🍴 🛋 🚶 🛎 🍷 W €€
2 Friary Rd, Armagh, BT60 4FR **Tel** *028 375 18888* **Fax** *028 375 12777* **Rooms** *82*   **Road Map** *D2*

The Armagh City Hotel may be lacking in character but the rooms are practical and well-equipped with modern services such as broadband (for an extra fee). There are also conference, business and leisure facilities, as well as the Friary restaurant. There is live music on Monday, Friday and Saturday nights. **www.armaghcityhotel.co.uk**

BALLYCASTLE Whitepark House   W   €€
Ballintoy, Ballycastle, Co Antrim, BT54 6NH **Tel** *028 2073 1482* **Rooms** *3*   **Road Map** *D1*

Bob and Siobhan Isles provide a warm welcome at this award-winning guesthouse in an old house with beautifully manicured gardens. The bedrooms are large and en suite. Breakfast is served in a big, comfortable conservatory. The full Irish breakfast is superb. **www.whiteparkhouse.com**

Key to Symbols *see back cover flap*

BALLYGALLY Hastings Ballygally Castle

274 Coast Rd, Ballygally, Co Antrim, BT40 2QZ **Tel** *028 2858 1066* **Fax** *028 2858 3681* **Rooms** *44* **Road Map** *D1*

Reputedly haunted, the four-star castle showpiece is the Ghost Room, a tiny old tower bedroom with a macabre legend. Original beamed ceilings and antique pine furniture make these rooms extremely appealing, though they are suitably equipped since the extensive refurbishment. **www.hastingshotels.com**

BALLYMENA Galgorm Resort & Spa

136 Fenaghy Rd, Ballymena, Co Antrim, BT42 1EA **Tel** *028 2588 1001* **Fax** *028 2588 0080* **Rooms** *75* **Road Map** *D1*

The River Maine sweeps past this converted gentleman's residence, enhancing the view from many of the rooms. All rooms are en suite and luxurious, and service is excellent. There are also six self-catering cottages for families and six log cabins. Fishing and other pursuits are available on the magnificent 153-acre estate. **www.galgorm.com**

BANGOR Cairn Bay Lodge

278 Seacliff Rd, Bangor, Co Down, BT20 5HS **Tel** *028 91 467636* **Rooms** *5* **Road Map** *E2*

This turn-of-the-19th-century B&B, situated on the shores of Ballyholme Bay, is a rare treasure set in its own mature gardens. Inside, there are elegant lounges decorated with a Victorian touch. Meals are served in the oak-panelled lounge overlooking the gardens and the proprietress offers beauty and natural therapies. **www.cairnbaylodge.com**

BELFAST An Old Rectory

148 Malone Rd, Belfast, Co Antrim, BT9 5LH **Tel** *028 9066 7882* **Rooms** *5* **Road Map** *D2*

This former Church of Ireland rectory is part of the Malone conservation area. It retains many of the original Victorian features, including stained-glass windows. The rooms are individually decorated and named. Organic produce forms the ingredients of the healthy breakfast. **www.anoldrectory.co.uk**

BELFAST Ash Rowan

12 Windsor Ave, Belfast, Co Antrim, BT9 6EE **Tel** *028 9066 1758* **Fax** *028 9066 3227* **Rooms** *5* **Road Map** *D2*

In the leafy southside of the city, Ash Rowan is a luxury guesthouse providing elegant rooms, furnished with luxurious Irish linen sheets and complimentary snacks. The tasteful decor features beautiful antiques. Nine different gourmet breakfasts are served here, all excellent.

BELFAST Avenue House Guesthouse

23 Eglantine Ave, Belfast, Co Antrim, BT9 6DW **Tel** *028 9066 5904* **Fax** *028 9029 1810* **Rooms** *4* **Road Map** *D2*

This refurbished Victorian town house is located in the leafy suburbs of the University area. Old and new blend well, and while all the original features have been retained, wireless Internet is available as are internet facilities in the lounge. Bedrooms are large and elegant. Fresh bread and scones baked daily. **www.avenueguesthouse.com**

BELFAST Hastings Stormont Hotel

587 Upper Newtonards Rd, Belfast, Co Antrim, BT4 3LP **Tel** *028 9065 1066* **Rooms** *110* **Road Map** *E2*

Close to the airport and overlooking the gardens of Stormont Castle, this modern and functional hotel is excellent for business people. Rooms are luxurious and tastefully decorated in muted tones, with spacious desk areas and en suite facilities. There is a charge for Internet use. **www.hastingshotels.com**

BELFAST Belfast Hilton

4 Lanyon Place, Belfast, Co Antrim, BT1 3LP **Tel** *028 9027 7000* **Rooms** *198* **Road Map** *D2*

This gigantic, sumptuous hotel in the docklands is just a five-minute walk from the city centre and its attractions. The Executive Rooms on the top four levels provide spectacular views of the city. The superb Sonoma restaurant is worth visiting. **www.hilton.co.uk/Belfast**

BELFAST Europa Hotel

Great Victoria St, Belfast, Co Antrim, BT2 7AP **Tel** *028 9027 1066* **Fax** *028 9032 7800* **Rooms** *292* **Road Map** *D2*

An imposing building in the heart of the Golden Mile, Europa is one of Belfast's best hotels, ideal for business people and tourists. Bill Clinton has stayed here during his visits to the city. Guests can make use of fitness facilities nearby. The Grand Opera House and Waterfront Hall are within walking distance. **www.hastingshotels.com**

BELFAST Malmaison Belfast

34–38 Victoria St, Belfast, Co Antrim, BT1 3GH **Tel** *028 9022 0200* **Fax** *028 9022 0220* **Rooms** *64* **Road Map** *D2*

This chic design hotel in Belfast was created in a restored seed warehouse and has some interesting features. It is an ideal location for city shopping and sightseeing. Rooms are stylish and luxurious and there is a spacious bar and brasserie restaurant. **www.malmaison.com**

BELFAST Merchant Hotel

35–39 Waring St, Belfast, Co Antrim, BT1 2DY **Tel** *028 9023 4888* **Fax** *028 9024 7775* **Rooms** *64* **Road Map** *D2*

The Merchant is an elegant five-star hotel in the historic Cathedral Quarter of the city. The ornate building dates back to 1857 and has been tastefully restored. Rooms are luxurious and stylish. There is a choice of bars, some of which have won awards, excellent dining options and a luxury spa. **www.themerchanthotel.com**

BUSHMILLS Bushmills Inn

9 Dunluce Rd, Bushmills, Co Antrim, BT57 8QG **Tel** *028 2073 3000* **Fax** *028 2073 2048* **Rooms** *41* **Road Map** *D1*

This is a cosy and charming traditional coaching inn in the village of Bushmills, with open fires and lots of nooks and crannies to hide away and relax in. Dining is excellent, with plenty of local produce. There is often live music in the Gas Bar. **www.bushmillsinn.com**

€ under £50 €€ £50–100 €€€ £100–150 €€€€ £150–200 €€€€€ over £200

CARNLOUGH Londonderry Arms Hotel

20 Harbour Rd, Carnlough, Co Antrim, BT44 0EU **Tel** *028 2888 5255* **Rooms** *35*   **Road Map** *D1*

Winston Churchill once owned this ivy-covered inn next to the harbour of Carnlough, a breathtaking setting at the foot of Glencloy. It is owned and managed by the O'Neill family, one of Ireland's longest-established hotelier families, giving the hotel a genuine warmth of welcome. Music on summer weekends. **www.glensofantrim.com**

COLERAINE Camus House

27 Curragh Rd, Castleroe, Coleraine, Co Londonderry, BT51 3RY **Tel** *028 7034 2982* **Rooms** *3*   **Road Map** *D1*

This listed country house was built in 1685 and overlooks the River Bann. An elegant pebble driveway is offset by an ivy-covered façade. Tastefully decorated rooms are non-smoking and furnished with TV and coffee-maker. Bathrooms are not en suite. Regional Galtee Irish Breakfast award winner.

CRAWFORDSBURN The Old Inn at Crawfordsburn

Crawfordsburn, Co Down, BT19 1JH **Tel** *028 9185 3255* **Fax** *028 9185 2775* **Rooms** *30*   **Road Map** *E2*

One of Ireland's oldest hostelries, this thatched 16th-century inn offers quality and comfort with roaring log fires and four-poster beds in some rooms. Each en suite room is individually decorated in a tasteful fashion and named after local landmarks, historic houses and wildflowers. **www.theoldinn.com**

CUSHENDALL Glendale

46 Coast Rd, Cushendall, Co Antrim, BT44 0RX **Tel** *028 2177 1495* **Rooms** *6*   **Road Map** *D1*

Generously proportioned rooms and a warm welcome make Glendale a cut above the other B&Bs in Cushendall. Coffee-maker, biscuits and TV are provided in each colourfully decorated bedroom. Bathrooms are en suite and there's also a TV lounge. The rates are reasonable and offer good value for money. **mary.glendale@btinternet.com**

DOWNHILL Downhill Hostel

12 Mussenden Rd, Downhill, Co Londonderry, BT51 4RP **Tel** *028 7084 9077* **Rooms** *9*   **Road Map** *D1*

This beautiful backpackers' hostel has a beach in front, cliffs at the rear and a rocky stream flowing just past it. There are laundry facilities, a guest kitchen, and a barbecue area, as well as a working pottery studio. Private rooms are available as well as dormitories with high bunks, hand-sewn quilts and full-sized beds. **www.downhillhostel.com**

DOWNPATRICK Denvir's Hotel

14–16 English St, Downpatrick, Co Down, BT30 6AB **Tel** *028 4461 2012* **Fax** *028 4461 7002* **Rooms** *6* **Road Map** *E2*

Built in 1642 by Thomas McGreevy, this is a listed building. Restoration revealed a number of interesting features, and the hotel has been well converted for modern purposes. En suite bedrooms are spacious. An atmospheric restaurant serves local specialities. **www.denvirshotel.com**

DOWNPATRICK Pheasants' Hill Country House

37 Killyleagh Rd, Downpatrick, County Down, BT30 9BL **Tel & Fax** *028 4461 7246* **Rooms** *3*   **Road Map** *E2*

Right in the middle of the wild Down countryside and lapped by Strangford Lough, this luxurious country house has its own grounds and is surrounded by the Quoile Pondage National Nature Reserve. The on-site farm provides the breakfast ingredients. Each room is decorated in a different style. **www.pheasantshill.com**

DUNGANNON Grange Lodge

7 Grange Rd, Dungannon, Co Tyrone, BT71 7EJ **Tel** *028 8778 4212* **Fax** *028 8778 4313* **Rooms** *5* **Road Map** *D2*

This lovely old Georgian house, set in pleasant surroundings, is known for its Ulster home-style cooking and warm hospitality. The proprietress, Norah Brown, has been creating award-winning culinary delights on her Aga stove for over 25 years. There's a spacious drawing room as well as a TV lounge. **www.grangelodgecountryhouse.com**

ENNISKILLEN Railway Hotel

32–34 Forthill St, Enniskillen, Co Fermanagh, BT74 6AJ **Tel** *028 6632 2084* **Rooms** *20*   **Road Map** *C2*

This convenient family-run hotel should appeal to more than just trainspotters. Across the road from the old Great Northern Railway station, this cheery yellow hostelry has a number of nicely decorated rooms, all en suite with TV and coffee-maker. The big rooms come with private baths. **www.railwayhotelenniskillen.com**

ENNISKILLEN Killyhevlin Hotel

Killyhevlin, Enniskillen, Co Fermanagh, BT74 6RW **Tel** *028 6632 3481* **Rooms** *70*   **Road Map** *C2*

The grounds of the hotel sweep down to Lower Lough Erne and many bedrooms look out on the lake, but you will need to pay extra for the view. Outstanding natural beauty in a terrific location. Great hospitality. There is a spa and health club. Chalets are also available. **www.killyhevlin.com**

ENNISKILLEN Manor House Resort Hotel

Killadeas, Enniskillen, Co Fermanagh, BT94 1NY **Tel** *028 6862 2200* **Rooms** *81*   **Road Map** *C2*

On the shores of Lough Erne, this country hotel has a rich interior, with antiques and paintings as well as a friendly staff. Rooms are tastefully decorated and there's a wide range of choice from deluxe doubles to interconnecting family suites. Some rooms have canopied four-poster beds. **www.manorhousecountryhotel.com**

HOLYWOOD Hastings Culloden Hotel

Bangor Rd, Holywood, Co Antrim, BT18 0EX **Tel** *028 9042 1066* **Fax** *028 9042 6777* **Rooms** *105* **Road Map** *E2*

A superb hotel, set in gardens and woodland by Belfast Lough, this was originally the palace of the Bishops of Down. It retains its opulence, visible in the fine antiques and valuable paintings. Many of the rooms have exquisite views of the lough and beautifully tended gardens. All of them are pleasantly decorated. **www.hastingshotels.com**

Key to Symbols *see back cover flap*

KILKEEL The Kilmorey Arms Hotel
🏠 🅰 🏃 📺 🌐 ££

41–43 Greencastle St, Kilkeel, Co Down, BT34 4BH **Tel** 028 4176 2220 **Rooms** 24   Road Map D3

An excellent base for the Mourne area, this hotel has well-furnished and simple rooms, with full en suite facilities that include coffee-maker and direct-dial phones. Service is friendly and efficient. Golf, tennis, pony trekking and a host of other leisure activities are all locally available. **www.kilmoreyarmshotel.co.uk**

LONDONDERRY Saddlers House
🌐 £

36 Great James St, Londonderry, BT48 7DB **Tel** 028 7126 9691 **Fax** 028 7126 6913 **Rooms** 7   Road Map C1

A ten-minute walk from the city walls, cosy Saddlers House serves fantastic breakfasts. The Victorian terrace boasts a walled garden and a placid British bull dog. Around the corner is the regal Merchant's House, where the spacious, airy rooms have been tastefully furnished with antiques. **www.thesaddlershouse.com**

LONDONDERRY Beech Hill Country House
🏠 🅰 🏃 📺 🌐 ££

32 Ardmore Rd, Londonderry, BT47 3QP **Tel** 028 7134 9279 **Fax** 028 7134 5166 **Rooms** 27   Road Map C1

Good service and food and a real "home from home" atmosphere. Some of the bedrooms have beautiful Victorian furniture, giving the feel of a grand old country house. Guests can walk through the hotel's 12-ha (32-acre) woodland and gardens. Massage, reflexology and reiki treatment are available. **www.beech-hill.com**

LONDONDERRY City Hotel Derry
🏠 🅰 🏃 🏨 📺 🌐 £££

Queens Quay, Londonderry, BT48 7AS **Tel** 028 7136 5800 **Fax** 028 7136 5801 **Rooms** 146   Road Map C1

On the banks of the River Foyle, this large hotel offers comfortable, well-equipped rooms and excellent facilities in a convenient location for exploring the historic city walls. The health and fitness club has a pool, steamroom and Jacuzzi. Dining options include a restaurant and lounge bar. **www.cityhotelderry.com**

LONDONDERRY Everglades Hotel
🏠 🅰 🏃 📺 🌐 £££

Prehen Rd, Londonderry **Tel** 028 7132 1066 **Fax** 028 7134 9200 **Rooms** 64   Road Map C1

This magnificent imposing four-star hotel, set on the banks of the River Foyle is the perfect base to explore 17th century Derry City. The bedrooms are beautifully decorated, luxurious and spacious. Satchmo's Restaurant uses fresh local ingredients and the Library Bar provides a more informal setting for light snacks. **www.hastingshotels.com**

NEWCASTLE Hastings Slieve Donard
🅰 🏨 🅰 🏃 📺 🌐 ££

Downs Rd, Newcastle, Co Down, BT33 0AH **Tel** 028 4372 1066 **Fax** 028 4372 4830 **Rooms** 178   Road Map D2

This stunning Victorian redbrick building overlooks the beach and the Royal County Down Golf Course. A central tower rises from the hotel, complementing the magnificent eponymous mountain behind it. Most rooms have spectacular views and 24-hour room service is available. **www.hastingshotels.com**

NEWCASTLE Burrendale Hotel and Country House
🅰 🏨 🅰 🏃 📺 🌐 ££

51 Castlewellan Rd, Newcastle, Co Down, BT33 0JY **Tel** 028 4372 2599 **Rooms** 68   Road Map

This hotel is an excellent base for climbing, horse-riding and golf. All bedrooms are very well equipped, while some have spectacular views of the Mourne mountains. Some of the Ambassador rooms have Jacuzzi baths. There's a cosy bar and the excellent restaurant, Vine. Also on site is a country club and spa. **www.burrendale.com**

NEWTOWNARDS Strangford Arms Hotel
🏠 🅰 📺 🌐 ££

92 Church St, Newtownards, Co Down, BT23 4AL **Tel** 028 9181 4141 **Rooms** 39   Road Map E

The town's only hotel, this family-run, three-star Victorian building has been home to the famous rose-growing Dicksons of Hawlmark and the headquarters of the North Down Militia. A friendly atmosphere prevails, particularly in the Horseshoe Lounge Bar, which has live music at weekends. **www.strangfordhotel.com**

PORTADOWN Cherryville Luxury House
🅰 🌐 £

180 Dungannon Rd, Portadown, Co Armagh, BT62 1JR **Tel** 028 3885 2323 **Rooms** 3   Road Map D2

Warm hospitality is assured at this large two-storey house, standing in its own grounds. Modern lines, fax and photocopier facilities are available. Bright, airy rooms are en suite, with TV and coffee-maker. Excellent and varied breakfasts brighten up the morning. **www.cherryvillehouse.com**

PORTADOWN Seagoe Hotel
🏠 🅰 🏨 📺 🌐 ££

Upper Church Lane, Portadown, Co Armagh, BT78 1R3 **Tel** 028 3833 3076 **Rooms** 34   Road Map D2

This hotel is found in the orchard county of Armagh. Its decor is simple and contemporary, as reflected in the rich fabrics and use of space. The Avanti Restaurant is pleasant and the café bar overlooks a tranquil Japanese garden terrace. The two purpose built ground floor rooms are perfect for disabled guests. **www.seagoe.com**

PORTAFERRY Portaferry Hotel
🏨 📺 🌐 ££

The Strand, Portaferry, Co Down, BT22 1PE **Tel** 028 4272 8231 **Fax** 028 4272 3999 **Rooms** 14   Road Map E2

This waterside inn on the Ards Peninsula overlooks Strangford Lough, in a designated conservation area. Many of the rooms have lovely water views and all are peaceful and pleasantly decorated. A wide range of activities are available locally. **www.portaferryhotel.com**

PORTRUSH Clarmont House
🅰 ££

10 Landsdowne Crescent, Portrush, Co Antrim, BT56 8AY **Tel & Fax** 028 7082 2397 **Rooms** 11   Road Map D1

A spacious period town house, with a beautiful white exterior, Clarmont House is located on the seafront. Panoramic views of the Skerries Islands and the Causeway coastline are the biggest draw. Booking early is recommended in this family-run place. **www.clarmont.com**

£ under £50   ££ £50–100   £££ £100–150   ££££ £150–200   £££££ over £200

RESTAURANTS, CAFÉS AND PUBS

Although the highest concentration of top gourmet restaurants is in Ireland's main cities, equally fine cuisine can be found in some very unlikely, remote locations around the country. Good, plain cooking is on offer at moderately priced, family-style restaurants all over Ireland. The restaurants listed on pages 324–45 are recommended for their high standards of service, quality of food and value

Restaurant sign
in Kinsale

for money. To supplement these listings, look out for the *Dining in Ireland* booklet published by Fáilte Ireland, the Irish Tourist Board. Pub lunches are one of Ireland's top travel bargains, offering generous portions of fresh vegetables and prime meats, and can often serve as the main meal of the day for a very reasonable price. Light meals, bar food and a variety of take-out dishes are also widely available.

IRISH EATING PATTERNS

Traditionally, the Irish have started the day with a huge breakfast: bacon, sausages, black pudding, eggs, tomatoes and brown bread. In Northern Ireland this, plus potato cakes and soda farls *(see p322)*, is known as an "Ulster Fry". The main meal, dinner, was served at midday, with a lighter "tea" in the early evening.

Although continental breakfasts are now available, you will be hard-pressed to escape the traditional breakfast, which is included in most hotel and bed-and-breakfast rates. Increasingly, however, even the Irish settle for a light salad or soup and sandwiches at midday and save their main meal for the evening. Vestiges of the old eating patterns remain in the huge midday platefuls still served in pubs.

Enjoying breakfast at Adare Manor Hotel *(see p307)*

Arriving at a café in Kinvarra *(see p212)*

TIPS ON EATING OUT

Elegant dining becomes considerably more affordable when you make lunch your main meal of the day. In many of the top restaurants, the fixed-price lunch and dinner menus offer much the same, but lunch will usually come to about half the price. House wines are quite drinkable in most restaurants and can reduce the total cost of your meal. If you are travelling with children, shop around for one of the many restaurants that provide a less expensive children's menu.

Lunch is usually served between noon and 2:30pm, with dinner between 6:30 and 10pm, although many ethnic and city-centre restaurants stay open later, particularly in Temple Bar. Bed-and-breakfast hosts will often provide an ample home-cooked evening meal, and many will serve tea and scones in the late evening at no extra charge.

In top restaurants, men are expected to wear a jacket, though not necessarily a tie, and women to wear a dress or suit. Elsewhere, the dress code is pretty informal, stopping short of bare chests and very short shorts.

Visa and MasterCard are the most commonly accepted credit cards. Fewer restaurants accept American Express and Diners Club, although most now accept debit cards. In rural areas, especially in small cafés and pubs, be prepared to pay with cash.

GOURMET AND ETHNIC DINING

This once gourmet-poor land now sports restaurants that rank among Europe's very best, with chefs trained in outstanding domestic and continental institutions. There is a choice of Irish, French, Italian, Chinese, Indonesian and even Russian and Cuban cuisines, with styles ranging from traditional to regional to *nouvelle cuisine*. Locations vary as widely as the cuisine, from hotel dining rooms, town house basements and city mansions to castle hotels and tiny village cafés. The small County Cork town of Kinsale has established itself as the "Gourmet Capital of Ireland". Outstanding chefs also reign over the gracious houses listed in *Ireland's Blue Book of Country Houses and Restaurants*, available from tourist offices.

Selection of cakes served at Bantry House café *(see pp168–9)*

BUDGET DINING

It is quite possible to eat well on a small budget wherever you are in Ireland. In both city and rural locations, there are small cafés, tea rooms and family-style restaurants with inexpensive meals. Even if a café or tea room is at a main tourist attraction, such as Bantry House, you can still expect good, home-made food and freshly baked bread and cakes. Sandwiches are usually made with thick, tasty slices of cheese or meat (not processed); salad plates feature smoked salmon, chicken, ham, pork and beef; and hot meals usually come with large helpings of vegetables, with the beloved potato often showing up roast, boiled and mashed, all on one plate.

PUB FOOD

Ireland's pubs have moved into the food field with a vengeance. In addition to bar snacks (soup, sandwiches and

so on), available from noon until late, salads and hot meals are served from midday to 2:30pm. Hot plates all come heaped with mounds of fresh vegetables, potatoes in one or more versions, and good portions of local fish or meat. Particularly good bargains are the pub carveries that offer a choice of joints, sliced to your preference. International staples such as spaghetti, lasagne and quiche have also appeared on pub menus. For a list of recommended pubs, see pages 346–51.

FISH AND CHIPS AND OTHER FAST FOODS

The Irish, from peasant to parliamentarian, love their "chippers", immortalized in Roddy Doyle's novel *The Van*, and any good pub night will end with a visit to the nearest

Cafe sign at Baltimore

fast food shop. At virtually any time of day, however, if you pass by Leo Burdock' in Dublin, there will be a long queue for this international institution *(see p32)*. With Ireland's long coastline, wherever you choose, the fish will usually be the freshest catch of the day – plaice, cod, haddock, whiting or ray (a delicacy). The many other fast-food outlets include a host of familiar international names, such as McDonald's and Kentucky Fried Chicken, as well as a wide variety of burger and kebab shops. Relatively new arrivals are several quite good pasta and pizza chains, such as Pizza Express, which is called Milano in the Republic.

PICNICS

Ireland is glorious picnic country. Farmhouse cheeses and flavoursome tomatoes are picnic treats, or stop by one of the many small shops that offer sandwiches made with fresh local ingredients. As for where to picnic, the long, indented coast is ringed with sandy beaches and over 400 forest areas, many with picnic tables; great views add to the pleasure of mountainside picnics, and there are often places to pull off the road in scenic spots. Turn off a main road onto almost any lane and you will find a picnic spot by a lakeside, riverbank or the shady edge of a field.

Empty kegs outside a pub in Kinsale

The Flavours of Ireland

Boxty, barm brack, champ, coddle, cruibins, colcannon – the basic dishes that have nourished Ireland are spiced with fancy names. But the secret of their success is their ingredients, which are nurtured in a warm, damp climate on lush hills that brings them flavour. Beef and dairy cattle can stay out all year and they make abundant butter, cheese and cream. Pork and pork products, such as ham and bacon, are a mainstay, though lamb is traditional, too. Potatoes, the king of vegetables, turn up in soup, pies, cakes, bread and scones that are piled on breakfast and tea tables. And the rivers, lakes and shores are rich in seafood.

Oysters

A chef in Connemara displays traditional Irish cuisine

THE BASIC DISHES

Irish stews are thick and tasty, traditionally featuring lamb or mutton, onion and potatoes, while beef and Guinness make a darker casserole, sometimes with addition of oysters. Carrots and turnips are the first choice of vegetables for the pot. Pork is the basis of many dishes. Trotters, called cruibins or crubeens,

are sometimes pickled, while bacon can be especially meaty. Dublin coddle, a fill-me-up after the pub on a Saturday night, relies on sausages and potatoes as well as bacon. Ham is sometimes smoked over peat and, for special occasions, it is baked with cloves and brown sugar and served with buttered cabbage. Cabbage is the basis of colcannon, cooked and chopped with mashed potato and onions,

sometimes with the addition of butter and milk. Boxty is a bake of raw and cooked potato mashed with butter, buttermilk and flour; champ is potatoes mashed with milk, butter and onions.

FISH AND SEAFOOD

The Atlantic Ocean and Irish Sea have a rich variety of shellfish, from lobsters and Dublin Bay prawns to mussels and oysters,

Barm brack **White soda bread** **Brown soda bread** **Potato bread**

Wheaten bread

Potato farls

Selection of the many traditional Irish breads

IRISH TRADITIONAL FOOD

Gubbeen cheese

If your heart is up to it, start the day with an Ulster Fry. This breakfast fry-up includes thick, tasty bacon, plus black pudding, soda farls and potato cake. A "lady's breakfast" will have one egg, a "gentleman's" two. Gooseberry jam will be spread on fried bread, and mugs of tea will wash it down. Irish stews traditionally use mutton, not so common today, while Spiced Beef uses up brisket, which is covered in a various spices then left for a week before being cooked slowly with Guinness and vegetables. A high tea in the early evening is the major meal in many homes; a main course will be followed by a succession of breads and cakes.

Irish Stew *Traditionally, neck of mutton, potatoes, carrots and onions are slowly cooked together for hours.*

Delivery in time-honoured style at Moore Street Market, Dublin

porter cake is made with Guinness or other stout. White, brown and fruit scones will never be far from tea and breakfast tables.

DAIRY PRODUCTS

Butter, usually salted, is used generously, on vegetables and in sauces as well as in puddings and on bread. Cream, too, is used in cooking, stirred into soups and whipped for puddings. The variety and quality of Irish farmhouse cheeses is impressive, although a medium Cheddar produced by a large manufacturer was hailed "Best Irish Cheese" at the 2005 World Cheese Awards.

scallops, clams and razor-shells. Herring, mackerel, plaice and skate are brought in from the sea, while the rivers and lakes offer up salmon, trout and eels, which are often smoked. Galway salmon has the best reputation and its oyster festival is famous. Salmon is usually smoked in oak wood kilns. Along the shore, a red seaweed called dulse is collected and mixed with potatoes mashed in their skins to make dulse champ.

BAKED GOODS

Bread and cakes make up a large percentage of the Irish diet. Unleaven soda bread is ubiquitous (it's great with Irish cheeses). In Northern Ireland, brown soda bread is called wheaten bread. Potato bread is fried or eaten cold, as cake.

Farls ("quarters") are made with wheat flour or oats, bicarbonate of soda and buttermilk, which goes into many recipes. Fruit breads include barm brack, traditionally eaten at Hallowe'en and on All Saint's Day, while rich

Sea trout, plucked fresh from the Atlantic Ocean

IRISH CHEESES

Carrigaline Nutty-tasting, Gouda-like cheese from Cork.

Cashel Blue The only Irish blue cheese. Soft and creamy. Unpasteurized; from Tipperary.

Cooleeny Small, Camembert-style unpasteurized cheese from Tipperary.

Durrus Creamy, natural-rind unpasteurized cheese from West Cork. May be smoked.

Gubbeen Semi-soft washed-rind cheese. Rich, milky taste.

Milleens Soft, rich rind-washed cheese. Unpasteurized; from the Beara peninsula, Cork.

St Killian Hexagonal Brie-like creamy cheese from Wexford.

Dublin Coddle *This is a comforting mixture of sausages, bacon, potatoes and onions, stewed in ham stock.*

Galway Salmon *Top quality fish can be simply served with an Irish butter sauce, watercress and colcannon.*

Irish Coffee Pudding *This is a chilled soufflé of coffee, cream and Irish whiskey, topped with crushed walnuts.*

Choosing a Restaurant

These restaurants have been selected for their good value, food and location. They are listed by region, starting with Dublin, and then by price. Price bands for Northern Ireland are given on pages 343 and 345. Map references refer either to the Dublin Street Finder on *pp116–17*, or the road map on the inside back cover.

PRICE CATEGORIES
For a three-course meal for one, half a bottle of wine, and all extra charges. These categories are for the Republic, where the euro is the currency.
€ under €25
€€ €25–35
€€€ €35–50
€€€€ €50–70
€€€€€ over €70

DUBLIN

SOUTHEAST DUBLIN Steps of Rome   €
1 Chatham St, Dublin 2 **Tel** *01 670 5630*   **Map** *D4*

This tiny Italian café, selling great coffee, is invariably abuzz with people coming and going to collect tasty slices of pizza. The reasonably priced menu includes pastas and bruschetta. Service is brisk, if a little brusque. Popular with students and fast-moving shoppers pausing for breath. Open all day and into the evening.

SOUTHEAST DUBLIN Avoca Café   €€
11–13 Suffolk St, Dublin 2 **Tel** *01 672 6019*   **Map** *D3*

Climb to the top floor of the renowned Irish craft shop, Avoca, and be rewarded with creative, wholesome and colourful cooking in a bright and airy room. The queues get lengthier during peak lunch hour. Such popularity is testament to the delicious salads, panini, hot dishes and wonderful desserts. Open daytime only.

SOUTHEAST DUBLIN Cornucopia   €€
19 Wicklow St, Dublin 2 **Tel** *01 677 7583*   **Map** *D3*

Small and often crowded, Cornucopia is one of the few exclusively vegetarian restaurants in the city, serving breakfast, lunch and dinner. This melting pot of bookworm bachelors and earthy students serves delicious, cheap, wholesome food. The menu includes salads, soups, pastas, casseroles and quiches.

SOUTHEAST DUBLIN Dunne & Cresenzi   €€
14 South Frederick St, Dublin 2 **Tel** *01 677 3815*   **Map** *E4*

This delightful Italian wine bar or *enoteca* serves authentic food and wine in a stylishly rustic atmosphere. Enjoy the excellent minestrone, antipasti platters, bruschetta, panini, pasta, delicious fruit tartlets and excellent coffee. There's a superb collection of wines, also served by the glass. Open all day and into the evening.

SOUTHEAST DUBLIN Gotham Café   €€
8 South Anne St, Dublin 2 **Tel** *01 679 5266*   **Map** *D4*

This lively and colourful spot is always abuzz. Offering bistro-style food at affordable prices, and with covers of *Rolling Stone* lining the walls, it is popular with the young and young-at-heart. Known for tasty and imaginative pizzas, it also serves pastas and salads.

SOUTHEAST DUBLIN Balzac   €€€
35 Dawson St, Dublin 2 **Tel** *01 677 8611*   **Map** *D4*

Formerly known as La Stampa, this is one of the city's most impressive and glamorous dining rooms, with full-length mirrors and an ornate ceiling. The restaurant is styled on a French brasserie theme, with top-class food and wines to match. A great dining experience, with a good value three course *table d'hote* menu for €25.

SOUTHEAST DUBLIN Coppinger Row   €€€
Off South William St, Dublin 2 **Tel** *01 672 9884*   **Map** *D4*

This laid-back and popular dining space serves fresh, simple Mediterranean-themed dishes at reasonable prices. Wild mushrooms on toast with truffle *aioli* is just one example of a starter, while mains include dishes such as roast pheasant with borlotti beans and bacon. Many dishes are designed for sharing, so it is ideal for small groups.

SOUTHEAST DUBLIN Ely Winebar & Café   €€€
22 Ely Place, Dublin 2 **Tel** *01 676 8986*   **Map** *E5*

Erik and Michelle Robson's unusual wine bar and café, just off St Stephen's Green, offers exceptional wines (many available by the glass) and an imaginative menu, which features cheese dishes, fish cakes, Kilkee oysters, lamb stew and home-made sausages. Organic meats come from the family farm in Co Clare. The atmosphere is cosy and lively.

SOUTHEAST DUBLIN Fallon & Byrne   €€€
11–17 Exchequer St, Dublin 2 **Tel** *01 472 1000*   **Map** *D3*

This excellent restaurant is in an impressive building which also incorporates a ground-floor food hall and basement wine bar, both worth a pre-dinner visit. The menu offers delicious, unhurried French-style cooking, including smoked sea trout as a starter and milk-poached pork belly as a main.

Key to Symbols *see back cover flap*

SOUTHEAST DUBLIN La Maison
15 Castle Market, Dublin 2 **Tel** *01 672 7258*

Map D4

This smart *boulangerie* has a stylish and intimate room upstairs, where high-quality snacks are served. French onion soup, home-baked breads, *tartines* (open gourmet sandwiches), salads, a hot special and delicious pastries are on the menu. Takeaway is available from the downstairs shop. In fine weather, sit outside and watch the world go by.

SOUTHEAST DUBLIN L'Gueleton
1 Fade St, Dublin 2 **Tel** *01 675 3708*

Map C4

This charming, lively French restaurant is decorated in bistro style and full of atmosphere. It serves excellent French specialities, with everything from snail and Roquefort *pithivier* (filled puff pastry) to Challans duck with sweetened chicory. The wine list is short but all French. Bookings are not accepted so queues form at busy times.

SOUTHEAST DUBLIN Trocadero
3–4 Andrew St, Dublin 2 **Tel** *01 677 5545*

Map D3

This much-loved restaurant has been in operation since 1956. A haunt of actors and the literati, it has deep-red walls lined with black-and-white images of the notables who have passed through its doors. Traditional classics include rack of lamb, steak, Dublin Bay prawns and tempting desserts. Service is intimate and welcoming.

SOUTHEAST DUBLIN Dobbins Wine Bistro
15 Stephen's Lane, Dublin 2 **Tel** *01 661 9536*

Map F5

Popular since 1978, this cheerful bistro has a warm and pleasing ambience, with red-and-white checkered tablecloths and the floor scattered with sawdust. Given the good wine list, it is a popular spot for a leisurely liquid lunch. Menu includes smoked fish cakes and prime sirloin of beef.

SOUTHEAST DUBLIN Pearl Brasserie
20 Merrion St Upper, Dublin 2 **Tel** *01 661 3572*

Map D4

This basement brasserie exudes a cool, contemporary French ethos. It combines charming service with good food at affordable prices. Seafood features prominently. The separate Oyster Bar offers lighter fare, including a fish platter. The impressive wine list is heavy on French wines. Lunch is particularly good value.

SOUTHEAST DUBLIN Peploe's Wine Bistro
16 St Stephen's Green, Dublin 2 **Tel** *01 676 3144*

Map D4

Located in the basement of a Georgian building, this is a glamorous, cosy and immensely popular restaurant. Always rushed, due to the high-quality and consistently good food. It provides an extensive wine list – over 30 are served by the glass. Book in advance.

SOUTHEAST DUBLIN Unicorn
12B Merrion Court, Dublin 2 **Tel** *01 662 4757*

Map D4

Situated around St Stephen's Green, and with a beautiful terrace, Unicorn has maintained an excellent standard since it opened in 1938. Its casual atmosphere is unparalleled and is enhanced by the friendly staff. The Italian-Mediterranean food served here is delicious and the veal is particularly appetizing. Children are welcome up to 9pm.

SOUTHEAST DUBLIN L'Ecrivain
109a Lower Baggot St, Dublin 2 **Tel** *01 661 1919*

Map F5

One of the best restaurants in the city, L'Ecrivain combines classic formality with contemporary cool. Authentic French cuisine with an Irish flavour includes delicacies such as Galway Bay oysters and caviar. Seasonal game and seafood as well as tasty desserts and cheeses also figure on the menu. Service is great.

SOUTHEAST DUBLIN Shanahan's on the Green
119 St Stephen's Green, Dublin 2 **Tel** *01 407 0939*

Map D5

The most succulent steaks in Dublin are to be found in this renowned steakhouse set in an elegantly furnished Georgian house. Though steeply priced, the food is consistently of the highest quality and the portions gargantuan. Skip starters if you hope to finish your main. Seafood, too, is available at this superbly managed establishment.

SOUTHWEST DUBLIN Café Fresh
Powerscourt Townhouse Centre, South William St, Dublin 2 **Tel** *01 671 9669*

Map C4

Located on the top floor of the historic Powerscourt Centre, this vegetarian café offers a dizzying selection of hearty salads, sandwiches, juices and hot dishes to choose from. The staff are very friendly, and organic ingredients are used wherever possible. Closed Sundays.

SOUTHWEST DUBLIN Leo Burdock's
2 Werburgh St, Dublin 8 **Tel** *01 454 0306*

Map B4

The patrons of Leo Burdock's, the oldest fish-and-chip takeaway in Dublin, include the ordinary folk of Dublin and the stars. Fresh fish and chips are made from top-grade Irish potatoes. There's a wide choice of fish including scampi, smoked cod, haddock and lemon sole goujon. Service is efficient. Branches on Liffey Street and in Phibsborough too.

SOUTHWEST DUBLIN Queen of Tarts
4 Cork Hill, Dame St, Dublin 2 **Tel** *01 670 7499*

Map C3

Opposite Dublin Castle and Dublin City Hall, this charming little café is cosy and welcoming. Apart from fresh soups, sandwiches and hot savoury tarts, there's a dazzling array of mouthwatering desserts such as chocolate fudge cake and fruit tarts. Ideal for a quick and reasonably priced snack. There are also branches at Temple Bar and Cow's Lane.

SOUTHWEST DUBLIN Odessa

13–14 Dame House Court, Dublin 2 **Tel** 01 670 7634   **Map** D3

Best loved for its cool and relaxed weekend brunches with fancy fry-ups and bellinis, the stylish, retro-look Odessa has also upped its game in the evenings with well-priced tapas-style sharing plates and an extended early-bird menu. Its a la carte menu caters for many tastes with *mezze* plates and *tagines*, alongside fillet steak and fish dishes.

SOUTHWEST DUBLIN Port House

64a South William St, Dublin 2 **Tel** 01 677 0298   **Map** D4

Port House is a traditional tapas bar housed in a candle-lit, brick-lined wine cellar. An array of Basque dishes are on offer, including *paella*, marinated prawns and meatballs, alongside an eclectic list of wines, ports and sherries. The restaurant gets very busy, so book ahead.

SOUTHWEST DUBLIN Chez Max

1 Palace St, Dublin 1 **Tel** 01 633 7215   **Map** C3

Located right outside the gates of Dublin Castle, this Parisian-themed restaurant serves up excellent *moules frites*, steaks, duck and fish specials, with delicious tartlets and risottos for vegetarians. There are a few outdoor tables overlooking the cobbled entrance to the castle.

SOUTHWEST DUBLIN Eden

Meeting House Square, Temple Bar, Dublin 2 **Tel** 01 670 5372   **Map** C3

With an outside terrace on the Square, this split-level restaurant is bright and modern in design, with cool-blue tiled walls and an open kitchen. It is known for its sirloin steaks, cleverly-contrived fish dishes and imaginative use of seasonal vegetables. The early-evening menu is good value.

SOUTHWEST DUBLIN Elephant & Castle

18 Temple Bar, Dublin 2 **Tel** 01 679 3121   **Map** D3

Very lively and ever popular, this American-style brasserie, in the heart of Temple Bar, is invariably busy. Have the mouthwatering chicken wings to start. Good omelettes, steaks, hamburgers and salads are available at affordable prices. Weekend brunches are also popular. Telephone bookings are not accepted.

SOUTHWEST DUBLIN Good World Chinese Restaurant

18 South Great George's St, Dublin 2 **Tel** 01 677 5373   **Map** C4

This restaurant's popularity with the Chinese community attests to the good quality of food on offer. The dim sum selection is a popular choice. Authentic beef, chicken and fish dishes are served, along with the standard Westernized dishes. Friendly and efficient service.

SOUTHWEST DUBLIN Jaipur

41 South Great George's St, Dublin 2 **Tel** 01 677 0999   **Map** C4

Often acclaimed as the best Indian restaurant in the city, Jaipur offers high-quality, innovative dishes. The decor, stylish with a contemporary feel, features warm, tasteful colours. It is superbly managed by a well-informed and charming staff. Vegetarians are well catered for. Branches also in Malahide, Dalkey, Ongar and Greystones.

SOUTHWEST DUBLIN Lord Edward

23 Christchurch Place, Dublin 8 **Tel** 01 454 2420   **Map** B4

The oldest seafood restaurant in the city, Lord Edward is located above a cosy and traditional pub, which serves lunch downstairs. It has changed little over the years and maintains an old-fashioned feel. Long-established waiters are known for their charming service.

SOUTHWEST DUBLIN Monty's of Kathmandu

28 Eustace St, Dublin 2 **Tel** 01 670 4911   **Map** C3

This friendly Nepalese restaurant serves tasty and interesting fish, chicken and lamb dishes at affordable prices. Vegetarians are well catered for. Try the dumplings or the tandoori butter chicken in a deliciously creamy sauce. Upstairs is more cheerful than the basement dining room. Service is good and the atmosphere relaxed. Rathgar has another branch.

SOUTHWEST DUBLIN Rustic Stone

South Great George's St, Dublin 2 **Tel** 01 707 9596   **Map** C4

Award-winning chef Dylan McGrath is in charge of the kitchen at Rustic Stone. The emphasis here is on tasty, healthy, innovative cuisine made using local, seasonal ingredients (including plenty of superfoods). The menu lists the nutritional value of every dish and meat and fish are served on hot volcanic stone, for guests to cook themselves.

SOUTHWEST DUBLIN Les Frères Jacques

74 Dame St, Dublin 2 **Tel** 01 679 4555   **Map** C3

This elegant restaurant is French in style, cuisine, atmosphere and service. Seafood and game feature prominently on the well-balanced seasonal menus. Try the grilled lobster fresh from the tank or the roast duck *magret* with chocolate sauce. Classic desserts are on the menu. Good wine list favours French bottles.

SOUTHWEST DUBLIN The Tea Room

The Clarence Hotel, 6–8 Wellington Quay, Dublin 2 **Tel** 01 407 0800   **Map** C3

The Clarence Hotel is owned by rock band U2. Come in by the Essex Street entrance, opposite the Project Theatre, and savour excellent cuisine served in this stylish dining room. High ceilings and large windows create a bright and airy atmosphere. Menus are innovative and seasonal. The lunch menu is particularly good value

Key to Price Guide see p324 **Key to Symbols** see back cover flap

NORTH OF THE LIFFEY Panem

Ha'penny Bridge House, 21 Lower Ormond Quay, Dublin 1 **Tel** *01 872 8510*

Map C3

This tiny café and bakery offers freshly prepared Italian and French food, using high-quality ingredients. The menu includes delicious croissants and *focaccia* with savoury fillings, sweet brioches with chocolate, home-baked biscuits and good coffee. The mouthwatering hot chocolate is made from dark Belgian chocolate. Nice staff.

NORTH OF THE LIFFEY The Cobalt Café

16 North Great Georges St, Dublin 1 **Tel** *01 873 0313*

Map D3

This daytime café offers a range of homemade soups, sandwiches and cakes, as well as vegetarian specials such as chickpea curry or spicy mixed bean stew. The café doubles as a gallery exhibiting the work of up-and-coming Irish artists and consequently is a popular venue for art lovers. It is also hired out as a musical venue in the evenings.

NORTH OF THE LIFFEY The 3rd Still

Old Jameson Distillery, Bow St, Dublin 1 **Tel** *01 807 2248*

Map A2

This restaurant is a part of the Old Jameson Distillery, which lies on the site of the original 18th-century distillery. At lunch time the legal eagles from the nearby Courts swoop in here to savour the daily changing à la carte menu of meat and fish dishes or delicious sandwiches and soups.

NORTH OF THE LIFFEY 101 Talbot

100–102 Talbot St, Dublin 1 **Tel** *01 874 5011*

Map E2

Mediterranean styles reflected in the decor as much as the cuisine at 101 Talbot, livening up the rather drab street on which it is located. The early-bird menu is good value and attracts many theatre-goers. Vegetarians are spoilt for choice. Dietary needs may be met.

NORTH OF THE LIFFEY Bar Italia

Quartier Bloom, 26 Lower Ormond Quay, Dublin 1 **Tel** *01 874 1000*

Map C3

The popular Bar Italia, specializing in Italian fare, is a hive of activity around lunch time, when patrons stream in for freshly prepared antipasti, risotto, grilled vegetables or the pasta specials. Desserts are also an attraction, as is the excellent espresso.

NORTH OF THE LIFFEY The Winding Stair

40 Lower Ormond Quay, Dublin 1 **Tel** *01 872 7320*

Map C3

This charming old café, gallery and bookshop won favour with the Michelin Guide in 2008, earning the Bib Gourmand Award for good food at excellent value. The food is simple – dishes like bacon and cabbage with parsley sauce – and is made with care, using locally sourced ingredients.

NORTH OF THE LIFFEY Chapter One

18–19 Parnell Sq, Dublin 1 **Tel** *01 873 2266*

Map C1

In the cellar of the Dubh in Writers' Museum, Chapter One is often cited by critics as the best restaurant north of the Liffey. Relish the imaginative European cuisine, with an Irish twist, in a dining room of character and comfort. The pre-theatre menu is a favourite among regulars who frequent the nearby Gate theatre.

FURTHER AFIELD Green 19

19 Camden St, Dublin 2 **Tel** *01 478 9626*

A cool café-bar offering dishes such as corned beef with cabbage, chicken hot pot, bangers and mash and succulent pork belly with a chorizo and white bean *cassoulet*, each for only €10. Desserts are €5 each. It's always busy for both lunch and dinner, so it's advisable to book ahead.

FURTHER AFIELD Olive

86a Strand St, Skerries, Co Dublin **Tel** *01 849 0310*

Resting on a wide pavement which allows for outside tables, Peter and Deirdre Dorrity's specialist food shop and café serves a range of freshly made soups, paninis and home-baked cookies. There is also pesto, hummus, dips and salads to suit every palate. An ideal stop for an al fresco lunch.

FURTHER AFIELD Abbey Tavern

Abbey St, Howth, Co Dublin **Tel** *01 839 0307*

Open fires, linen-clad tables, fresh flowers and a slightly old-fashioned atmosphere define this restaurant on the first floor of a characteristic old pub. Good, uncomplicated fish and meat dishes are served. The traditional cabaret evening downstairs, featuring set dinners is popular with visitors.

FURTHER AFIELD Expresso Bar Café

1 St Mary's Road, Ballsbridge, Dublin 4 **Tel** *01 660 0585*

This small restaurant is decorated in a minimalist style. Open from breakfast time, it is popular for lunch and weekend brunches. The Californian–Italian fare, featuring chicken and fish dishes, salads and pastas, uses high-quality ingredients. The bread-and-butter pudding is delicious. Children are welcome up to 5pm.

FURTHER AFIELD Hartley's

1 Harbour Rd, Dun Laoghaire, Co Dublin **Tel** *01 280 6767*

Road Map D4

This is an elegant restaurant set in the old Kingstown train station, a small stone building beside Dun Laoghaire harbour. Everything, from the food to the decor, is simple yet top class. Mains include organic meats and seafood with steaks a speciality. There is a substantial wine list. Amex and Diners credit cards are not accepted.

FURTHER AFIELD Ivans Oyster Bar and Grill

17–18 West Pier, Howth, Co Dublin **Tel** *01 839 0285*

Road Map D3

Set on the West Pier of Howth Harbour, in a picturesque fishing village, this oyster bar and grill is renowned for top-quality seafood. Platters of oysters are a speciality – the selection includes Carlingford Lough and Clarenbridge oysters, or try an oyster shot flavoured with Nam Jim. The dinner menu also features organic meats and poultry.

FURTHER AFIELD Johnnie Fox's

Glencullen, Co Dublin **Tel** *01 295 5647*

About 30-minutes' drive south of the city, on the way up to the Dublin mountains, this friendly pub has good Irish food, open fires, traditional music and dancing. Pan-seared scallops, dressed crab salad, smoked salmon sirloin steak are on the menu. The "Hooley Night", featuring dinner and a traditional show, attracts overseas visitors. Book ahead.

FURTHER AFIELD Nosh

111 Coliemore Rd, Dalkey, Co Dublin **Tel** *01 284 0666*

In the heart of Dalkey village, Nosh is contemporary in style, with light wood furniture. Well-balanced menus feature good fish and vegetarian dishes as well as succulent steaks. Cod and chips, pea and asparagus risotto, and seared scallops are also on the menu. Home-made desserts are good. The weekend brunch menu is very popular.

FURTHER AFIELD Rasam

18–19 Glasthule Rd, Dun Laoghaire, Co Dublin **Tel** *01 230 0600*

Road Map D4

A smart, modern Indian restaurant in Dublin's southside suburbs, Rasam serves a selection of dishes from around the sub-continent put together with creative flair. Starters include *papri chaat* (crispy-fried dough wafers) or *achori* (spicy bean patties) from Rajasthan. Among the mains are *manshahari thali*, a lamb, prawn and chicken dish from Mumbai.

FURTHER AFIELD Aqua Restaurant

1 West Pier, Howth, Co Dublin **Tel** *01 832 0690*

This first-floor restaurant, with lovely views over the sea and harbour, was formerly a yacht club, now converted into a bright contemporary space. Prominent on the menu are steaks as well as fish and chicken dishes. The cuisine betrays a Californian-Italian influence. Set menus are good value. Sunday brunch is accompanied by live jazz.

FURTHER AFIELD Caviston's Seafood Restaurant

59 Glasthule Rd, Dun Laoghaire, Sandycove, Co Dublin **Tel** *01 280 9245*

Stunning seafood, prepared with simple flair. Book early and reserve the last sitting so that you can enjoy a leisurely afternoon lingering over coffee and dessert. The adjoining delicatessen sells delicious fare, which is great for a picnic. Open for lunch Tuesday to Thursday and for lunch and dinner on Friday and Saturday.

FURTHER AFIELD King Sitric Fish Restaurant & Accommodation

East Pier, Howth, Co Dublin **Tel** *01 832 5235*

Named after the medieval Norse king of Dublin, this restaurant is acclaimed for good seafood and game. The dining room is stylishly modern, with scenic views. Specialities are crab bisque, Balscadden Bay lobster, black sole meunière and fillet steak with forest mushrooms. Excellent wine cellar.

FURTHER AFIELD The Lobster Pot

9 Ballsbridge Terrace, Ballsbridge, Dublin 4 **Tel** *01 660 9170*

This long-established upstairs restaurant deservedly commands a loyal following. High-quality food is well presented by professional, charming waiters. Specialities feature dressed Kilmore crab, Dublin Bay prawns in Provençal sauce, generously-sized sole on the bone, delicious steaks, chicken and game dishes.

FURTHER AFIELD Roly's Bistro

7 Ballsbridge Terrace, Ballsbridge, Dublin 4 **Tel** *01 668 2611*

In the heart of Ballsbridge, this lively, bustling bistro offers reliable, colourful and delicious food. Try the Kerry lamb pie or the Dublin Bay prawns Provençal. Other specialities include fish and game dishes and succulent steaks. Sit upstairs if possible. Take home the delicious home-made breads which are on sale. Reservations are advised.

FURTHER AFIELD Bon Appetit

9 St James Terrace, Malahide, Co Dublin **Tel** *01 845 0314*

Situated in a renovated Georgian terrace near the marina, this well-respected restaurant is inviting, with its warm colours, art collection and excellent seafood. Popular dishes in the fine dining restaurant include *foie gras*, ravioli of rabbit and sea trout. Desserts are equally tempting. Book in advance. There is also a brasserie on the lower floor.

SOUTHEAST IRELAND

BALLYMACARBRY Hanora's Cottage

Nire Valley, Ballymacarbry, Co Waterford **Tel** *052 613 6134*

Road Map C5

This celebrated family-run riverside restaurant draws patrons across long distances. The Walls are charming hosts and excellent cooks. The cosy dining room, overlooking lovely gardens, has won many awards and showcases local artisan produce where possible. Try the delicious roast rack of lamb when in season. Reservations advised.

Key to Price Guide *see p 324* **Key to Symbols** *see back cover flap*

BALLYMORE EUSTACE The Ballymore Inn
Ballymore Eustace, Ballymore, Co Kildare **Tel** 045 864 585   **Road Map** D4

Run by the O'Sullivan family, The Ballymore Inn has garnered a wonderful reputation for producing consistently good food. Ingredients, organic as much as possible, are carefully sourced. Home-made soups are served with home-baked breads. Regulars on the menu are sirloin steak with smoked paprika, pastas and fish.

BLESSINGTON Grangecon Café
The Old Schoolhouse, Kilbride Rd, Blessington, Co Wicklow **Tel** 045 857 892   **Road Map** D4

Set in a lovingly restored building in the centre of Blessington, this tastefully decorated café is a delightful spot to visit. Good, honest and wholesome cooking features salads, quiches, savoury tarts, sandwiches on home-made bread, delicious farmhouse cheese and chutneys. Organic juices as well as home-baked desserts are available

CAMPILE The Georgian Tea Rooms
Great Island, Campile, Co Wexford **Tel** 051 388 109   **Road Map** D5

Located in Kilmokea Country Manor & Gardens, a charming Georgian house set in its own magnificent gardens, the Tea Rooms offer delicious home-made fare and light lunches in the bright and spacious conservatory. Views over the walled garden and on to the River Barrow. Open daily from March to November and for dinner on Friday and Saturday

CARLOW Lennon's Café Bar
Visual Centre for Contemporary Arts, Old Dublin Rd, Carlow **Tel** 059 917 9245   **Road Map** D4

Contemporary in design, this daytime café bar is expertly run by the Byrnes who offer keenly-priced wholesome food. Try the delicious home-made soups such as the Cashel Blue and bacon and courgette, open sandwiches on home-baked breads, gorgeous salads and a selection of hot dishes. Don't miss the lovely home-made desserts

CARLOW Reddy's
67 Tullow St, Carlow **Tel** 059 914 2224   **Road Map** D4

This restaurant and bar has been in the Reddy family since 1768. Traditional Irish food is prepared with an international flair, using day-fresh ingredients. The Reddy family and their staff are warm and friendly. A wide range of steak and fish dishes feature on the menu.

CARNE The Lobster Pot Seafood Bar
Carne, Co Wexford **Tel** 053 913 1110   **Road Map** D5

The Lobster Pot, an award-winning seafood bar, is housed in a well-maintained 19th-century building. Home cooking and warm rural hospitality create a relaxing atmosphere. The restaurant is famed for its ultra-fresh fish including a delicious chowder, crab-meat salad and smoked salmon platter. Children are welcome up to 5pm.

CELBRIDGE La Serre
The Village Lyons Demesne, Celbridge, Co Kildare **Tel** 01 630 3500   **Road Map** D3

Located in the Village at Lyons Demesne, an innovative architectural restoration project encompassing the Georgian Grand Canal. Dine in a beautiful Turner designed conservatory or in the lovely courtyard. The crisp pork belly, pan-fried turbot and braised halibut are nothing short of delightful.

DUNGARVAN The Tannery Restaurant
10 Quay St, Dungarvan, Co Waterford **Tel** 058 45420   **Road Map** C5

The superbly designed, award-winning Tannery Restaurant is located in an old leather warehouse, which has been ingeniously converted with great flair and imagination. High-quality furnishings and artwork complement the outstanding and highly innovative contemporary cuisine, creating a memorable meal. There is also a cookery school.

ENNISKERRY Poppies Restaurant
The Square, Enniskerry, Co Wicklow **Tel** 01 282 8869   **Road Map** D4

This small café restaurant is a cosy and vibrant place, serving good country cooking at reasonable prices. Try the leek and blue cheese tart or the beef and Guinness pie. Other dishes include soups, sandwiches, salads and baked potatoes. Desserts are worth savouring. Vegetarians are well catered for. Open daily until 6pm.

GOREY Marlfield House
Courtown Rd, Gorey, Co Wexford **Tel** 053 942 1124   **Road Map** D4

Possibly the best in the region, this wonderfully romantic dining room is elegantly furnished and runs into a stunning conservatory. Enjoy the excellent cooking in a warm and welcoming ambience. Organically grown vegetables come from the garden. There's an extensive wine list. Staff are well-informed and personable. Reservations advised.

GREYSTONES The Hungry Monk
Church Rd, Greystones, Co Wicklow **Tel** 01 287 5759   **Road Map** D4

This delightful first-floor restaurant is well-established and regarded as a sure bet for food, wine and good fun. The theme of cheerful robed monks is apparent throughout. It has possibly the best wine list in the country. Favourite dishes include venison with Toulouse sausage in a rich game jus, as well as locally-caught seafood specials.

KILDARE The Silken Thomas
The Square, Kildare **Tel** 045 522 232   **Road Map** D4

Named after an extravagantly dressed Lord of Kildare who led an uprising against Henry VIII, this purpose-built establishment houses three bars, a restaurant and a nightclub. The main lounge bar serves food from 11am to 9pm. The restaurant offers a carvery lunch and evening meals.

KILKENNY Marble City Bar

66 High St, Kilkenny **Tel** *056 776 1143*   **Road Map** *C4*

This historic bar has great character and a lively atmosphere. European-style bar food, including breakfast, is served all day from 10am, when the good breakfast menu is on offer. Cod in a beer batter with chips, Thai fish cakes and home-made burgers with cheese, bacon and relish are on the menu.

KILKENNY Campagne Kilkenny

The Arches, 5 Gashouse Lane, Kilkenny **Tel** *056 777 2858*   **Road Map** *C4*

Serving modern, French food using local and artisan produce, Campagne is a Kilkenny favourite. The menu includes mouth-watering dishes made with organic salmon, veal, venison and free-range chicken and pork, and both the restaurant and chef have won awards. The decor includes some striking modern art. Closed Monday and Tuesday.

KILKENNY Ristorante Rinuccini

The Parade, Kilkenny **Tel** *056 776 1575*   **Road Map** *C4*

Located on the fine terrace that faces Kilkenny Castle, this popular Italian restaurant has drawn crowds for many years. Traditional dishes such as minestrone soup, antipasti and decadent lobster spaghetti are cooked with flair, and there is an impressive Italian wine list. Children are welcome up to 8pm.

KILKENNY Zuni

26 Patrick St, Kilkenny **Tel** *056 772 3999*   **Road Map** *C4*

Also offering stylish accommodation, Zuni has become a by-word for contemporary chic and superb food in this delightful medieval town. The cuisine is worldly in style, with influences from Morocco to Southeast Asia. A well-designed restaurant, it has great atmosphere and tasteful furnishings. Try the tasty risottos, salads and pastas.

KILMACANOGUE The Sugar Tree Café

Kilmacanogue, Co Wicklow **Tel** *01 286 7466*   **Road Map** *D4*

Located at the Avoca mill complex, this café has long been popular for its rustic, wholesome hot dishes, salads and quiches. It offers great breakfast choices and is always buzzing at lunchtimes. Another option here is the Fern House Restaurant, which is suitable also for lunch and dinner. Leave time to browse in the excellent crafts shop.

KILMACOW The Thatch

Grannagh Castle, Kilmacow, Co Waterford **Tel** *051 872 876*   **Road Map** *D5*

This cosy, quaint thatched pub is located opposite the lovely Grannagh Castle. Owner David Ryan offers good, reliable, freshly prepared bar food – soups, open sandwiches, salads, steak and fish dishes. Hot dishes include home-made fish pie.

LEIGHLINBRIDGE Lord Bagenal Inn

Leighlinbridge, Co Carlow **Tel** *059 972 1668*   **Road Map** *D4*

Housed in a well-established family-run hotel, on the banks of the River Barrow, this bright riverside restaurant offers classical and traditional dishes with a contemporary twist. There's an award-winning wine list. Popular carvery lunch is served in the bar.

LISMORE The Glencairn Inn & Pastis Bistro

Glencairn, Lismore, Co Waterford **Tel** *058 56232*   **Road Map** *C5*

This is an homage to a time gone by, as Stephane and Fiona Tricot have created an old world feel in their French bistro. Local produce is put to good use on a menu filled with delicious main dishes like *cassoulet* of monkfish and slow roasted lamb shank.

ROUNDWOOD The Roundwood Inn

Roundwood, Co Wicklow **Tel** *01 281 8107*   **Road Map** *D4*

In Roundwood, supposedly Ireland's highest village, this 17th-century inn is a good stopping-off point after a walk in the Wicklow Hills. Its slightly formal restaurant, with a welcoming open fire and traditional furnishings, serves excellent bar food all day. Menu includes crab bisque, smoked salmon, Irish stew and smoked trout.

THOMASTOWN The Lady Helen

Mount Juliet Conrad Hotel, Thomastown, Co Kilkenny **Tel** *056 777 3000*   **Road Map** *D5*

Enjoy classic cuisine in an elegant, high-ceilinged room with beautiful views over the gardens, which provide fresh vegetables and herbs. Wild salmon from the nearby River Nore and chicken breast with fennel stuffing in a red pepper sauce are real treats. Reservations advised. The adjacent Kendal's restaurant is less formal.

TRAMORE Rockett's of the Metal Man

Westown, Tramore, Co Waterford **Tel** *051 381 496*   **Road Map** *D5*

This is a throwback to simpler times in Ireland. Big open fires and a warm, homey ambience await. Generous, hearty portions of food include boiled bacon, spare ribs, colcannon, and the house speciality crubeens (pig's trotters). Step back in time and enjoy the experience. Call ahead for opening times. Closed Christmas to Easter.

WATERFORD Fitzpatrick's Restaurant

Manor Court Lodge, Cork Rd, Waterford **Tel** *051 378 851*   **Road Map** *D5*

In a listed stone building on the outskirts of the city, this bright and colourful fine-dining restaurant is reputed for its classical cuisine with a French influence. Linen-clad tables with fresh flowers and candles create a welcoming atmosphere. Try the roasted sea bass. Staff are courteous and attentive. Reservations are recommended.

Key to Price Guide *see p324* **Key to Symbols** *see back cover flap*

WATERFORD The Gingerman
€€

6–7 Arundel Lane, Waterford **Tel** *051 879 522* **Road Map** D5

Located in the Norman part of the city this pub is to be found in a pedestrianized lane, just off Broad Street. Welcoming fires and friendly staff make this an enjoyable spot for daytime food. Reasonably priced menu features home-made soup, sandwiches, panini and baked potatoes. Tasty hot dishes and daily specials are also on the menu.

WATERFORD Bodega!
€€€

54 John St, Waterford **Tel** *051 844 177* **Road Map** D5

The exclamation mark in the title hints at the vibrant atmosphere of this popular eatery. Inside, it is cheerfully decorated in heart-warming colours, with wooden tables and ever-changing artwork. Sunday brunch is available, while the dinner menu features fresh *foie gras*, steaks and sea bass.

WATERFORD La Bohème
€€€€

2 George St, Waterford **Tel** *051 875 645* **Road Map** D5

Waterford's beautiful chamber of commerce building is an unlikely setting for this restaurant which is housed in the basement. White tablecloths, silverware and flower-adorned tables are a reflection of the elegant French food. The crab brûlée is particularly recommended.

WEXFORD La Dolce Vita
€€

6/7 Trimmers Lane, Wexford **Tel** *053 91 70806* **Road Map** D5

This restaurant lays claim to being the best Italian restaurant in Ireland. Roberto Pons's home-made Italian bread, risotto and Tuscan salad are sumptuous and reasonably priced. The grilled seabass and Italian sausage with lentils is hard to beat. Arrive early for lunch. Open daily for lunch, and for dinner from March to November.

CORK AND KERRY

BALLYCOTTON Nautilus Restaurant
€€€

Pier Rd, Ballycotton, Co Cork **Tel** *021 464 6768* **Road Map** C6

Nautilus offers simple, wholesome French cooking in a harbour-side location in this small, off-the-beaten-track fishing village in East Cork. Fish and chips are a speciality. Take time for a short pier walk and to admire the island views. The restaurant is part of the Inn by the Harbour, which is ideal for a pre-dinner drink.

BALLYCOTTON Bayview
€€€€

Ballycotton, Co Cork **Tel** *021 464 6746* **Road Map** C6

This fine restaurant is located within a four-star manor. The chef prides himself on balancing flavour and texture, as well as presentation of the dishes. Pan fried duck, seared fillets of salmon and free range pork belly are among the mains, accompanied by a wide range of wines.

BALLYDEHOB The Pothouse
€€€

Main St, Ballydehob, Co Cork **Tel** *028 37292* **Road Map** B6

Good, wholesome food is on the menu at The Pothouse. Seafood is the speciality and dishes include roast fillet of monkfish with *ratatouille* and pesto mash, scallops with black pudding and crispy bacon and prawn orzo with chilli gremolata. There are also daily specials and an excellent apple crumble with ice cream for dessert.

BALTIMORE Chez Youen
€€€€

The Square, Baltimore, Co Cork **Tel** *028 20600* **Road Map** B5

Established since 1979. Youen Jacob's restaurant has quite a following of regulars and visitors following warm recommendations. Seafood is the star attraction and the dishes are beautifully presented. The Shellfish Platter is a delight and a work of art in itself. Try the turbot in a black butter sauce. There's an excellent wine list.

BANDON Blue Geranium Café
€

Hosfords Garden Centre, Enniskeane, Bandon, Co Cork **Tel** *023 883 9159* **Road Map** B6

Set within a wonderful garden centre, this daytime café focuses on seasonal fare, which uses local Irish artisan and organic ingredients. Quiches, sandwiches and salads as well as a more substantial menu are on offer. The interior is a summertime combination of glass and pale wood, liberally decorated with flowers.

BANTRY O'Connor's Seafood Restaurant
€€€

The Square, Bantry, Co Cork **Tel** *027 50221* **Road Map** B6

Situated in the heart of the town, this long-running restaurant serves lunch and dinner and specializes in seafood. Also on the menu are fine fillet steaks, local mountain lamb, chicken and game. Mussels are a particular speciality. Live lobsters and oysters in a fresh seawater tank are indicative of the freshness of the produce.

BANTRY Blair's Cove House & Restaurant
€€€€

Durrus, near Bantry, Co Cork **Tel** *027 61127* **Road Map** B6

This waterside restaurant enjoys a stunningly romantic setting, overlooking Dunmanus Bay. The main candlelit dining room has great character with its stone walls and black-beamed ceilings, chandelier and grand piano. The superb hors d'oeuvre buffet is a star feature.

BLARNEY Blair's Inn

Cloghroe, Blarney, Co Cork **Tel** *021 438 1470*
Road Map *B5*

Immaculately maintained and very inviting, this pretty whitewashed riverside pub has hanging flower baskets and a lovely garden outside. Inside, open fires and a charming interior are complemented by reliably good food. Traditional dishes include steak, corned beef, monkfish and salmon with a modern twist. There's live music on Mondays during the summer.

CASTLETOWNSHEND Mary Ann's Bar

Castletownshend, Skibbereen, Co Cork **Tel** *028 36146*
Road Map *B6*

A landmark restaurant in the heart of a picturesque village, the bar dates back to 1846 and retains a cosy and unique character. The welcoming charm is most appealing. Consistently superb food is the real draw. Seafood specialities include chowders, seared scallops and Dover sole. There's also an excellent cheeseboard.

CORK Crawford Gallery Café

Emmet Place, Cork **Tel** *021 427 4415*
Road Map *C5*

Located in the old Customs House, the Crawford Municipal Art Gallery is home to one of the city's best daytime eateries. Crawford Gallery Café is a bright and delightful spot to enjoy freshly prepared country house cooking and excellent home-baked desserts.

CORK Farmgate Café

The English Market, Princess St, Cork **Tel** *021 427 8134*
Road Map *C5*

Farmgate Café is located upstairs in the gallery over the bustling English Market, from where many of the ingredients are sourced. It's a lively restaurant, split between a self-service section and the restaurant proper. Wooden tables and black-and-white tiles create a down-to-earth yet stylish ambience. Honest home cooking is the main draw.

CORK Café Paradiso

16 Lancaster Quay, Western Rd, Cork **Tel** *021 427 7939*
Road Map *C5*

Undoubtedly the best vegetarian restaurant in Ireland, Café Paradiso attracts even the most committed carnivores. The ever-changing seasonal menus are imaginative and consistently good. Cheerfully decorated in a contemporary and eclectic style, its intimate atmosphere is lively and welcoming. Desserts are exquisite.

CORK Isaacs Restaurant

48 MacCurtain St, Cork **Tel** *021 450 3805*
Road Map *C5*

Housed in an 18th-century red-bricked warehouse, this informal, yet stylish, restaurant provides reliably good bistro-style cooking. The fairly-priced menu features signature dishes such as fish cakes, panfried prawns and potato cakes with black pudding. Wine list is extensive and descriptive. Friendly and efficient service.

CORK Jacobs on the Mall

30a South Mall, Cork **Tel** *021 425 1530*
Road Map *C5*

This highly acclaimed restaurants is set in the former Turkish baths. Decorated in a charming contemporary style, it has a unique ambience. Creative and colourful dishes include scallops and crab cakes with mango salad and a hot-and-sour dressing. Home-made ice creams are irresistible.

CORK The Ivory Tower

The Exchange Buildings, 35 Prince's St, Cork **Tel** *021 427 4665*
Road Map *C5*

One of Ireland's most creative chefs, Seamus O'Connell, sources the best-quality ingredients, all organic, creating unusual and delicious combinations of flavours and produce. The Crozier cheese soufflé served in an artichoke is a favourite signature dish, as is the aphrodisiac of tropical fruits.

DINGLE The Chart House

The Mall, Dingle, Co Kerry **Tel** *066 915 2255*
Road Map *A5*

This award-winning restaurant is informal in style with exposed stone walls, warm colours and wooden floors. Ebullient and attentive hosts create a welcoming atmosphere. High-quality ingredients are used to outstanding effect. Classic dishes include roast fillet of cod with fennel risotto; and Kerry lamb with red onion and feta.

DINGLE The Half Door

John St, Dingle, Co Kerry **Tel** *066 915 1600*
Road Map *A5*

Decorated in a pretty cottage style, this charming little restaurant is well known for a good, seasonal seafood menu. Try the seafood platter which is available either hot or cold and features crab claws, lobster, oysters, mussels, scallops and prawns. There are tasty desserts and a good selection of farmhouse cheeses. Portions are generous.

DINGLE Lord Baker's Restaurant & Bar

Main St, Dingle, Co Kerry **Tel** *066 915 1277*
Road Map *A5*

Believed to be the oldest bar in Dingle, this welcoming hostelry, with an open fire, serves delicious bar food such as home-made soups, crab claws in garlic butter and smoked salmon and capers. The restaurant is more formal. Specialities include classic seafood mornay and monkfish wrapped in bacon.

DINGLE Out of the Blue

Waterside, Dingle, Co Kerry **Tel** *066 915 0811*
Road Map *A5*

Interestingly named, this seafood restaurant and deli serves the freshest of fish. The decor is uncluttered and the food excellent. Try the John Dory with garlic eggplant, sole on the bone with a mond cream or crayfish. The lobster is well priced. There's a well-assembled wine list.

DURRUS Good Things Café

Ahakista Rd, Durrus, Co Cork **Tel** *027 51426*

Road Map B6

This intimate café-restaurant has created a real stir among Irish foodies. Its menu has been described as reading like a road map of the region's acclaimed artisan producers. Specialities include West Cork fish soup and smoked haddock with Desmond cheese. Open April to September, but it's worth calling ne to check.

GOLEEN Heron's Cove

The Harbour, Goleen, West Cork **Tel** *028 35225*

Road Map B6

Fresh fish and excellent wine are served here beside a lovely little harbour on the Mizen Peninsula in West Cork. Starters might include local Bantry Bay mussels or Heron's Cove crab cakes, while mains include local seafood and meats. Service is relaxed and friendly, and there are comfortable guest rooms above the restaurant.

KENMARE The Purple Heather

Henry St, Kenmare, Co Kerry **Tel** *064 664 1016*

Road Map B5

A traditional bar and restaurant, The Purple Heather was one of the first to establish Kenmare as a culinary town. Consistently good home-cooked food features soups, pâtés, breads and desserts. Also on the menu are lovely seafood salads, smoked salmon and open sandwiches with crab meat.

KENMARE The Lime Tree Restaurant

Shelbourne St Kenmare, Co Kerry **Tel** *064 664 1225*

Road Map B5

Though this charming stone building dates from the 1830s, its unique character is retained throughout. With an open fire and upstairs contemporary art gallery it enjoys a special atmosphere. Excellent local seafood, roast Kerry lamb and delicious desserts are served by friendly staff. Open Easter to October, and Saturdays from November to March.

KENMARE Mulcahy's

36 Henry St, Kenmare, Co Kerry **Tel** *064 664 2383*

Road Map B5

Bruce Mulcahy is one of Ireland's leading young chefs, whose experience and imagination attract not only locals and visitors, but other chefs and restauranteurs as well. The room is decorated in a tasteful contemporary style and exudes a friendly and intimate ambience. The selections of pasta, fish and meat dishes use organic ingredients.

KENMARE Packie's

Henry St, Kenmare, Co Kerry **Tel** *064 664 1508*

Road Map B5

This well-established and highly regarded restaurant enjoys a devoted following of regulars and return visitors. The emphasis is on local seafood and organic produce, yet Mediterranean and contemporary flavours also find their way into the imaginative cooking. Welcoming ambience.

KILLARNEY Jam

Old Market Lane, Killarney, Co Kerry **Tel** *064 663 7716*

Road Map B5

James Mulchrone's triumvirate bakery-delicatessen-café provides an attractive and well-priced stop-off for snackers and those eating on the go. The food is home-made and the ingredients are all locally produced. Friendly staff and three dining areas to choose from if you are eating in.

KILLARNEY Gaby's Seafood Restaurant

27 High St, Killarney, Co Kerry **Tel** *064 663 2519*

Road Map B5

A member of the World Master Chefs Society and one of Ireland's longest established seafood restaurants. Gaby's reputedly offers the best seafood in town. Cooking is imaginative and of a high standard with a carefully chosen wine list. A real treat is the lobster 'Gaby' with cognac and cream. Desserts are exquisite.

KILLARNEY Treyvaud's

62 High St, Killarney, Co Kerry **Tel** *064 663 3062*

Road Map B5

Brothers Paul and Mark Treyvaud have designed a daytime menu to satisfy both the busy passer-by and the stay-a-while foodie. The seafood chowder, fish cakes and the beef and guinness pie are tasty. In the evening, organic Kerry lamb, pan-fried ostrich fillet and various seafood plates make for an equally varied selection.

KILLARNEY The Garden Room Restaurant

Malton Hotel, East Avenue Road, Killarney, Co Kerry **Tel** *064 663 8000*

Road Map B5

This Victorian dining room is located within the Malton Hotel and overlooks the beautifully landscaped gardens. Traditional recipes are given a modern twist by head chef John O'Leary. Peppers, another restaurant located within the hotel, makes a good and less formal à la carte alternative.

KILLORGLIN Nick's Seafood Restaurant & Piano Bar

Lower Bridge St, Killorglin, Co Kerry **Tel** *066 976 1219*

Road Map A5

Renowned for its succulent meats as much as its seafood, this is one of Ireland's much-loved restaurants. Intimate ambience prevails, with open fires and an accompanying pianist. Try the Lobster Thermidor or the Valencia scallops mornay.

KINSALE Crackpots

3 Cork St, Kinsale, Co Cork **Tel** *021 477 2847*

Road Map B6

An unusual restaurant-wine bar selling home-made pottery as well as imaginative cuisine. The seafood – lobster, seared scallops and prawns – are excellent quality, as are the duck and steak options. The menu is wide-ranging and eclectic with a good selection for vegetarians.

KINSALE Fishy Fishy Café

€€€

Crowley's Quay, Kinsale, Co Cork **Tel** *021 470 0415*   **Road Map** *B6*

This outstanding fish restaurant is renowned for the freshness of its fare and the ingeniously simple manner of preparation. Informal in atmosphere, it is immensely popular but there is a no-reservations policy for lunch. The scampi with potato wedges, tartare sauce and pesto is tempting. They run an excellent fishmonger and deli nearby.

KINSALE Man Friday

€€€

Scilly, Kinsale, Co Cork **Tel** *021 477 2260*   **Road Map** *B6*

The oldest restaurant in Kinsale, Man Friday is nationally regarded for its excellent cuisine, unique atmosphere and friendly service. A recipient of numerous awards, it comprises a number of adjoining rooms of character and a garden terrace, lovely on a summer's evening. There's a great choice of comfort food and a superb seafood platter.

KINSALE Max's Wine Bar

€€€

48 Main St, Kinsale, Co Cork **Tel** *021 477 2443*   **Road Map** *B6*

For three decades, this bustling wine bar and eatery has been in the forefront of Kinsale's gourmet restaurants. Offering light lunches, early-evening meals and full dinner menus, it is a charming little spot, with great character. Wooden tables, exposed stone walls and a small conservatory add to its charm.

KINSALE The Spaniard Inn

€€€

Scilly, Kinsale, Co Cork **Tel** *021 477 2436*   **Road Map** *B6*

This is one of those quaint, rustic Irish pub-restaurants that draws punters in for the nightly music and friendly ambience and pleases them with tasty bar food (seafood chowder, mussels). The evening restaurant takes the culinary experience up a notch.

LISTOWEL Allo's Restaurant, Bar & Bistro

€€€€

42 Church St, Listowel, Co Kerry **Tel** *068 22880*   **Road Map** *B5*

This charming bar successfully combines traditional with modern Irish cooking. Dating back to 1859 it is traditionally furnished and has a wonderful character and welcoming atmosphere. Dishes include the Dover sole with caper and herb butter or the sirloin of Irish beef in puff pastry.

MALLOW Presidents' Restaurant

€€€€€

Longueville House, Mallow, Co Cork **Tel** *022 47156*   **Road Map** *B5*

Portraits of Irish presidents line the walls of this elegant dining room, which opens into a beautiful Victorian Turner conservatory, making it one of the most romantic restaurants in the country. Much of the fresh produce, which is expertly prepared and presented, comes from the farm on the estate and the walled vegetable garden.

MITCHELSTOWN O'Callaghan's Café & Delicatessen

€

19–20 Lower Cork St, Mitchelstown, Co Cork **Tel** *025 24657*   **Road Map** *C5*

In the heart of the busy market town, this café offers delicious quiches, panini, sandwiches, soups and tasty *focaccia* bread with melted cheese and char-grilled vegetables. Fish kebabs and garlic mussels are good. Home-baked breads, house preserves and chutneys are also available for sale. Eat in or take away. Service is warm.

MOLL'S GAP Avoca Handweavers

€€

Moll's Gap, Co Kerry **Tel** *064 663 4720*   **Road Map** *B5*

Spectacularly located on a high rocky ridge overlooking the mountain lakes of Killarney, the restaurant within the high-quality craft shop, is a good stop-over point. Wholesome home cooking is on offer, from soups and freshly prepared salads to hot dishes and appetizing home-baked desserts. Open daytime, from March to mid-January.

MONKSTOWN The Bosun

€€€

The Pier, Monkstown, Co Cork **Tel** *021 484 2172*   **Road Map** *B5*

On the banks of the River Lee, this well-known bar and restaurant serves tempting seafood. Main attractions include baked garlic mussels, stuffed fillet of trout, medallions of monkfish and wild smoked salmon. For meat-eaters, the menu offers fillet steaks, lamb cutlets and venison sausages. Tasty desserts are well worth trying.

SHANAGARRY Ballymaloe House

€€€€€

Shanagarry, Midleton, Co Cork **Tel** *021 465 2531*   **Road Map** *C6*

This nationally renowned culinary institution is acclaimed for excellent country-house cooking, served in elegant dining rooms. Much of the produce is organically grown in the walled garden. The five-course dinner menu is imaginatively conceived and expertly realized. The Allen family also run a well-known cookery school nearby. Live music most Saturdays.

TRALEE The Oyster Tavern

€€

The Spa, Tralee, Co Kerry **Tel** *066 713 6102*   **Road Map** *B5*

This is a lovely bar and restaurant 6 km (4 miles) outside Tralee where, unsurprisingly, seafood is a speciality. There's also a huge choice of meat and poultry dishes and diners have great views across the bay. The atmosphere is friendly and relaxed, and children are welcome. There is live music on Saturday night and Sunday lunch is popular.

YOUGHAL Ahernes Seafood Restaurant & Townhouse

€€€

163 North Main St, Youghal, Co Cork **Tel** *024 92424*   **Road Map** *C5*

This award-winning seafood restaurant, now in the hands of the third generation of the Fitzgibbon family, spells warm hospitality and relaxing atmosphere. Savour the finest fish from the day's catch in Youghal Harbour, locally reared beef and lamb, seasonal vegetables as well as home-baked breads and delicious desserts.

Key to Price Guide *see p324* **Key to Symbols** *see back cover flap*

THE LOWER SHANNON

ADARE The Wild Geese Restaurant

Rose Cottage, Main St, Adare, Co Limerick **Tel** *061 396451*

Road Map B5

Housed in a beautiful cottage in the picture-postcard village of Adare, this seafood restaurant has garnered an award-winning reputation for its fine dining, extensive wine list and friendly service. All products are sourced locally, some are organically grown. Superb desserts.

BALLINDERRY Brocka-on-the-Water Restaurant

Kilgarvan Quay, Ballinderry, Co Tipperary **Tel** *067 22038*

Road Map C4

A long-standing family affair, the highly respected Brocka-on-the-Water is particularly gorgeous on a fine day. Its open fires, tasteful furnishings, imaginative cuisine and warm hospitality make this immaculately maintained restaurant a perennial favourite. Seasonal menus are exceptionally good. Book in advance.

BALLINGARRY The Mustard Seed at Echo Lodge

Ballingarry, Co Limerick **Tel** *069 68508*

Road Map B5

Set in a Victorian residence, The Mustard Seed is one of the prettiest restaurants in the country. It is renowned for impressive service and excellent cooking. The menu, a mix of classical and modern Irish cuisine, prominently features local fillet of beef and pan-fried sea bass. The charming hosts create a warm atmosphere.

BALLYVAUGHAN Monks

Ballyvaughan, Co Clare **Tel** *065 70 77059*

Road Map B4

This well regarded pub-restaurant is widely known for its seafood chowder and fish cakes with salad. The mussels steamed in garlic, crab claws and seafood platter are also a sheer delight, especially taken outdoors in the summer sunshine. There's live music at weekends in summer and on Saturdays in winter.

BIRDHILL Matt the Thresher Pub & Restaurant

Birdhill, Co Tipperary **Tel** *061 379 227*

Road Map C4

This traditional country pub, located off the Birdhill exit 27 from the M7, is a frequent stopping-off point for travellers. Food is served through the day into the evening. Fresh scampi, chicken and mushroom pie and fillet steaks are a good step up from regular bar food.

BUNRATTY Gallagher's Restaurant & JP Clarke's Pub

Bunratty, Co Clare **Tel** *061 363 363*

Road Map B4

This is a great seafood restaurant and rustic country pub in one, so there is a choice of dining experiences. Located right in Bunratty, both venues are friendly and relaxed. Gallagher's offers a superb selection of seafood in a restaurant setting while JP Clarke's has a more informal bar food menu.

CAHIR Cahir House Hotel

Cahir House Hotel, Cahir, The Square, Co Tipperary **Tel** *052 744 3000*

Road Map C5

Cahir House Hotel is a hub of social and economic activity in the area. The restaurant specializes in traditional Irish cooking, using fresh produce from local growers and producers. The sirloin steak and baked fillet of salmon are particularly good. Open for dinner.

CARRON Burren Perfumery Tea Rooms

Carron, Co Clare **Tel** *065 708 9102*

Road Map B4

Ireland's first perfumery, set up over 30 years ago, is a family-run enterprise with an organic herb garden, distillation room and shop. The simple and pretty tearooms offer excellent home-made soups, quiches, sandwiches. Fresh juices as well as traditional home-baked cakes and scones are also available. Open Easter to September.

CASHEL Café Hans

Moore Lane, Cashel, Co Tipperary **Tel** *062 63660*

Road Map C5

A sister of the celebrated Chez Hans restaurant, this tiny contemporary café is one of the best in the county. For those travelling from Dublin to Cork, it provides an ideal break point on a road with a dearth of good eateries. Choose from a variety of delicious salads, open sandwiches, hot dishes and celebrated home-made French fries.

CASHEL Chez Hans Restaurant

Moore Lane, Cashel, Co Tipperary **Tel** *062 61177*

Road Map C5

Since 1968, patrons have been travelling from all over the county to savour the excellent cooking here. Housed in a converted church, it has become a veritable temple for food-lovers. Dishes showcase succulent Tipperary beef and lamb. Sole on the bone is particularly good. The early-bird dinner is good value. Reservations advised.

CLOGHEEN The Old Convent Gourmet Hideaway

Mount Anglesby, Clogheen, Co Tipperary **Tel** *052 7465565*

Road Map C5

Hailing from Connemara, chef Dermot Gannon uses local artisan ingredients and meats to create a cornucopia of flavours. The eight course tasting menu changes daily. Dinner is served Thursday to Saturday and on Sundays of bank holiday weekends. Accommodation is also available.

CLONMEL Befani's

6 Sarsfield St, Clonmel, Co Tipperary **Tel** 052 6177893   **Road Map** C5

This is a great Mediterranean and tapas restaurant in a restored listed building near the quays in Clonmel. The dinner menu is varied and includes local organic produce where possible. The sizzling tapas menu features plenty of vegetarian options. There is also a small guesthouse.

DOONBEG Morrisseys Seafood Bar & Grill

Doonbeg, Co Clare **Tel** 065 905 5304   **Road Map** B4

Housed in a handsome grey building is this fourth generation family-run bar and restaurant that sits in the centre of the pretty village of Doonbeg. The informal restaurant serves mainly seafood and meat grills but also offers dishes such as crab chowder and Thai green curry.

DOOLIN Cullinan's Seafood Restaurant and Guest House

Doolin, Co Clare **Tel** 065 707 4183   **Road Map** B4

Overlooking the River Aille, this cheerfully decorated and popular restaurant specializes in locally caught seafood and is reasonably priced. Mains include pan-seared scallops, roast loin of Burren lamb, pan-fried John Dory and Doolin crabmeat. Lovely desserts include cardamon brulée. Friendly and efficient team.

ENNIS Town Hall Café

O'Connell St, Ennis, Co Clare **Tel** 065 689 2333   **Road Map** B4

Situated in the well-restored town hall, and part of the Old Ground Hotel, this elegant café offers informal, bistro-style cooking. Open for lunch and dinner, dishes could include fillet of beef with grain mustard, sea bass with couscous and roast rack of lamb. Desserts include Bailey's parfait and hazelnut brownies. Reservations recommended.

KILLALOE Cherry Tree Restaurant

Lakeside, Ballina, Killaloe, Co Clare **Tel** 061 375688   **Road Map** C4

This delightful waterside purpose-built restaurant, with an impressive and colourful interior, has a reputation for outstanding contemporary cooking. One of the best in the region, it uses carefully sourced local ingredients. Specialities include seafood and butter roasted fillet of beef. Desserts are luscious.

LAHINCH Barrtra Seafood Restaurant

Lahinch, Co Clare **Tel** 065 708 1280   **Road Map** B4

A few miles south of Lahinch, this whitewashed house overlooking Liscannor Bay boasts a superb and long-established award-winning restaurant. It is decorated in a simple cottage style, with lovely sea views from the window tables. Food is of a consistently good standard. Wonderful hospitality. Closed January and February.

LIMERICK Aubars Bar Bistro & Nightclub

49–50 Thomas St, Limerick **Tel** 061 317799   **Road Map** B4

Located on a pedestrianized street, this modern establishment offers a bar, bistro and nightclub rolled in to one. The decor is contemporary and stylish, while the cuisine errs on the side of traditional. Portions from the grill are large and the rib-eye steak with béarnaise sauce and chunky chips is a firm favourite.

LIMERICK Copper and Spice

2 Cornmarket Row, Limerick **Tel** 061 313620   **Road Map** B4

The stylish Copper and Spice is decorated in a bright contemporary style and offers an interesting and extensive menu, featuring Indian and Thai cuisine, with the former being more authentic. Combination platters are popular, with an opportunity to taste dishes such as meat samosa, dim sum and chicken satay. Vegetarians are well catered for.

LIMERICK Hampton Grill

Henry St, Co Limerick **Tel** 061 609325   **Road Map** B4

Situated in the heart of historic Limerick, the Hampton Grill is a convenient place to stop for lunch after visiting King John's Castle or the Limerick Museum on nearby Nicholas Street. The menu focuses mainly on grilled meat – steaks, lamb and veal – although there are some pasta and salad dishes available too.

NENAGH The Pepper Mill

27 Kenyon St, Nenagh, Co Tipperary **Tel** 067 34598   **Road Map** C4

Mairead and Robert Gill moved to these larger premises so as to accommodate all of their patrons, eager to sample their strongly accented Irish menu. The chicken in a creamy cider sauce, Clonakilty black pudding and lamb shank with colcannon are all recommended and served in hearty portions.

NEWMARKET-ON-FERGUS Earl of Thomond Restaurant

Dromoland Castle, Newmarket-on-Fergus, Co Clare **Tel** 061 368144   **Road Map** B4

Excellent for fine dining, this elegant room is opulently decorated with rich fabrics and chandeliers and enjoys views over the nearby lake. A traditional Irish harpist accompanies five-course evening meals. Try the pan-fried fillet of sea-bass with mussel risotto. Full lunch is available on Sundays.

TERRYGLASS The Derg Inn

Terryglass, Nenagh, Co Tipperary **Tel** 067 22037   **Road Map** C4

A short stroll from the harbour, this superb gastro-pub is a favourite among boating enthusiasts and locals. The menu includes award-winning steaks and Southern-fried chicken served with a spicy dipping sauce. Try the succulent fresh fish and chips, caught on nearby Lough Derg. There are traditional music sessions every Sunday evening.

Key to Price Guide see p324 **Key to Symbols** see back cover flap

THE WEST OF IRELAND

ACHILL ISLAND The Beehive
€
Keel, Achill Island, Co Mayo **Tel** *098 43134*
Road Map A3

Overlooking Keel Beach, this informal, self-service daytime restaurant and craft shop offers high-quality, home-made food such as heart-warming soups, seafood chowder and home-baked brown scones. Sandwiches, farmhouse cheese plate, as well as a lovely selection of traditional cakes, tea-bracks and fruit tarts, are also made in-house.

ACHILL ISLAND Ferndale Restaurant & Guest Accommodation
€€
Crumpaun, Keel, Achill Island, Co Mayo **Tel** *098 43908*
Road Map A3

Ferndale Restaurant and Guest Accommodation enjoys a lovely location on an elevated site above the village. The restaurant commands sweeping views of the sea and island. The menu which bits a range of international influences, from the Mongolian barbecue to more traditional dishes.

BALLINA Gaughan's
€
O'Rahilly St, Ballina, Co Mayo **Tel** *096 70096*
Road Map B2

In the same family since 1936, this restaurant has a charming character and an old-world feel. Old-fashioned cooking includes hot roasts, such as baked ham and roast chicken, as well as fish pies, meat loaves, salmon and fresh crab meat. Lighter snacks available include open sandwiches and soups.

BALLYCASTLE Mary's Bakery & Tea Rooms
€
Main St, Ballycastle, Co Mayo **Tel** *096 43361*
Road Map B2

In the centre of the village, this charming restaurant offers domestic cooking in a warm atmosphere, with an open fire. On the menu are home-made soups, sandwiches and fresh salads as well as a selection of hot dishes. Try the delicious quiches, or locally caught smoked salmon and crab meat. Good home-baked bread and desserts.

BARNA O'Grady's on the Pier
€€€
Seapoint, Barna, Co Galway **Tel** *091 592223*
Road Map B4

Commanding wonderful views across the sea to the distant mountains, O'Grady's is renowned for simply prepared, high-quality seafood. Tastefully blending the contemporary with charming traditional features of the house, it enjoys a cosy atmosphere. The superb seafood platter is immensely popular.

CLEGGAN Oliver's Bar
€€€
Cleggan, Co Galway **Tel** *095 44640*
Road Map A2

Situated overlooking the working pier and the harbour where boats leave for Inishbofin, Oliver's Bar is very popular with locals and island day-trippers for its ultra-fresh seafood – served all day and into the evening. The menu offer wild smoked salmon, chowder, Connemara lamb and prime beef.

CLIFDEN Ardagh Hotel & Restaurant
€€€
Ballyconneely Rd, Clifden, Co Galway **Tel** *095 21384*
Road Map A2

This award-winning restaurant, situated on the first floor of the hotel, has lovely views of the sea, particularly at sunset. The modern dining room is pleasantly furnished and welcoming, with linen tablecloths, candles, fresh flowers and an open fire. On the menu are lobsters from the on-site sea tank, locally caught seafood and prime meats.

CLIFDEN Mitchell's Restaurant
€€
Market St, Clifden, Co Galway **Tel** *095 21867*
Road Map A3

The delightful family-run Mitchell's Restaurant offers consistently good food in a very warm and friendly atmosphere. Exposed stone walls and a fireplace give it a lovely, welcoming character. Keenly priced menus offer tasty home cooking, such as seafood chowder, excellent crab-meat salad, home-made brown bread and Irish stew.

CONG The George V Dining Room
€€€€€
Ashford Castle, Cong, Co Mayo **Tel** *094 954 5003*
Road Map B3

One of Ireland's most beautiful dining rooms, the George V has wood panelling and Waterford crystal chandeliers. Chef Stefan Matz used organic ingredients to create dishes such as duckling with orange-scented vinaigrette of asparagus and strawberries and lamb with a Mediterranean vegetable crust and reduced jus. There is also a five course dinner menu.

GALWAY Goya's Coffee Shop
€
2–3 Kirwan's Lane, Cong, Galway **Tel** *091 567010*
Road Map B4

This contemporary corner café and bakery is open during the day and is a lively spot. Elegantly decorated, it offers home-made soups, pâtés, salads, toasted sandwiches, as well as hot speciality dishes such as chicken, leek and mushroom pie. It is known for its wonderful home baking. Don't miss the traditional porter cake.

GALWAY Homeplate
€
Mary St, Galway **Tel** *091 561475*
Road Map B4

Homeplate boasts one of the best breakfasts in town as well as tasty vegetarian options. The cramped interior somehow lends itself to the relaxed ambiance and the fried potatoes are just the job the morning after a long night out in Ireland's party town.

GALWAY McDonagh's Seafood Bar

€€

22 Quay St, Galway **Tel** *091 565001*

Road Map *B4*

This renowned Galway institution is a must for anyone seeking delicious high-quality traditional fish and chips and super-fresh seafood. Situated on the most lively and atmospheric streets of the city, it comprises a takeaway section with wooden benches and tables on one side and an intimate and colourful restaurant on the other.

GALWAY Ard Bia at Nimmos

€€€

Spanish Arch, Long Walk, Galway **Tel** *091 561114*

Road Map *B4*

A café by day and a restaurant at night, Ard Bia serves a selection of wholesome and tasty dishes. The café is great for a hearty breakfast or lunch and the restaurant serves delicious meat, seafood and poultry dishes, such as slow braised shoulder of pork or chorizo and seafood casserole. There is also a limited bar.

GALWAY Kirwan's Lane Restaurant

€€€

Kirwan's Lane, Galway **Tel** *091 568266*

Road Map *B4*

Located in an appealing stone building, the restaurant is contemporary in decor and cuisine. The tasteful furnishings exude a warm and friendly ambience. Menus display clear Asian influences and offer bistro-style dishes. The more informal "Seafood at Kirwan's" restaurant is on the ground floor.

GALWAY Owenmore Restaurant

€€€€€

Ballynahinch Castle Hotel, Connemara, Galway **Tel** *095 31006*

Road Map *B3*

The Owenmore, located in the Ballynahinch Castle Hotel, has splendid views over the Ballynahinch River. The seasonal menu might include Connemara salmon or Cleggan lobster, as well as locally-sourced meats, game, fish and oysters. Reservations are essential for anyone not staying at the hotel. Open for dinner only. Closed February.

INISHMORE Pier House

€€€

Kilronan, Inishmore, Co Galway **Tel** *099 61811*

Road Map *B4*

The wonderful view of Kilronan Harbour cannot help but inspire brothers Damien and Ronan O'Malley, originally from Clifden. They open their doors everyday from mid-March to mid-October. Specialising in modern Irish fare, the menu features local fresh seafood and Connemara lamb shank.

INIS MEÁIN Inis Meáin Restaurant

€€€

Inis Meáin, Aran Islands, Co Galway **Tel** *086 826 6026*

Road Map *B4*

On one of Galway's Aran Islands, Inis Meáin is a unique restaurant serving great locally sourced food which is either grown or caught on the island. The modern building, which also includes guest accommodation suites, makes the most of its beautiful surroundings, with panoramic sea views. Advance reservations are advisable.

KILCOLGAN Moran's On The Weir

€€€

The Weir, Kilcolgan, near Clarinbridge, Co Galway **Tel** *091 796113*

Road Map *B4*

Now in the seventh generation of the Moran family, this seafood restaurant specializes in oysters. The original picturesque thatched cottage, with a simple decor, has been extended to accommodate a larger clientele. Menu features crab, lobster, dressed prawns, organic smoked salmon, garlic crab claws and mussels.

KINVARA The Pier Head Bar & Restaurant

€€

The Quay, Kinvara, Co Galway **Tel** *091 638188*

Road Map *B4*

Located in the harbour of this scenic fishing village, The Pier looks out over Kinvara Bay and Dunguaire Castle. It is the best restaurant in the area where seafood is the main attraction. Warm colours exude a friendly atmosphere. Lobster is a speciality and so is prime fillet steak. Live music is often played here.

LEENANE Blackberry Café

€€

Leenane, Co Galway **Tel** *095 42240*

Road Map *B3*

Situated at Killary Harbour, this charming little café and restaurant offers lovely home cooking during the summer months from noon until 9pm. Home-made soups, sandwiches, panini, fresh oysters, smoked salmon, traditional Irish stew, seafood salads. Finish with a delicious dessert such as the rhubarb tart.

LETTERFRACK Kylemore Abbey Restaurant

€€

Kylemore, Letterfrack, Co Galway **Tel** *095 41448*

Road Map *A3*

This self-service restaurant is set in the grounds of Kylemore Abbey, which enjoy a stunning mountainside setting, overlooking a peaceful lake. The industrious Benedictine nuns run gardens, a craft shop and a pottery studio as well as this popular self-service eatery. Good wholesome cooking includes soups, sandwiches, casseroles and quiches.

LETTERFRACK Pangur Bán Restaurant

€€€

Letterfrack, Co Galway **Tel** *095 41243*

Road Map *A3*

The elegant Pangur Bán is housed in a beautifully restored 300-year-old stone cottage. Good home cooking with influences from the Orient make for an interesting and imaginative menu. Try the char-grilled breast of chicken with black pudding on garlic and *wasabi* mash with tomato *jus*. Advanced booking advised.

MOYCULLEN White Gables

€€€

Moycullen, Co Galway **Tel** *091 555744*

Road Map *B4*

Housed in an old 1920s stone cottage, this intimate restaurant serves traditional cuisine with a focus on seafood. Classics include poached halibut Veronique and scallops mornay. Among the meat options are favourites such as roast duckling with orange sauce and Connemara lamb.

Key to Price Guide *see p324* **Key to Symbols** *see back cover flap*

PORTUMNA Castlegates Restaurant
Shannon Oaks Hotel, Portumna, Co Galway **Tel** *090 974 1777*
€€
Road Map C4

The bright Castlegates Restaurant serves evening meals in its warm, coloured dining hall. Its menu comprises classic and fusion dishes using the finest local produce, fish and meats. The bar serves a carvery lunch and informal food during the day. In summer, the nearby River Shannon keeps the place pleasantly breezy.

ROSCOMMON Gleeson's Restaurant & Townhouse
Market Sq, Co Roscommon **Tel** *090 662 6954*
€€€
Road Map C3

This well-restored 19th-century house overlooks the historic town square. The café and restaurant offer delicious home cooking in a warm and welcoming atmosphere. The menu focuses on traditional Irish ingredients that have been locally sourced; try the signature dish, Roscommon lamb stew.

ROUNDSTONE O'Dowd's Seafood Bar & Restaurant
Roundstone, Co Galway **Tel** *095 35809*
€€€
Road Map A3

In business since 1906, O'Dowd's has a warm and welcoming atmosphere, with its wood panelled walls and open fires. Bar food is served until 9:30pm. The slightly more formal restaurant serves good seafood – chowder, fresh oysters, hot buttered lobster and mussels – and home-made chicken and mushroom pie. Reservations required.

WESTPORT McCormack's at The Andrew Stone Gallery
Bridge St, Westport, Co Mayo **Tel** *098 25619*
€
Road Map B3

McCormack's butcher shop has been in operation since 1847 and is now in the sixth generation of the family. Upstairs lies this daytime, simply decorated restaurant. Family recipes are used for the home-made dishes such as seafood chowder, savoury tarts and meat casseroles. Sample the mouthwatering home-baked desserts.

WESTPORT The Lemon Peel
The Octagon, Westport, Co Mayo **Tel** *098 26929*
€€€
Road Map B3

This lively, modern bistro-style restaurant serves popular contemporary dishes. The no-frills decor creates a warm atmosphere, complemented by a pleasant staff. Start with baked crab, Cajun blackened shrimp or Caesar salad. Follow with traditional roast duck in Grand Marnier. Great desserts. The early-bird menu is very good value.

NORTHWEST IRELAND

ANNAGRY Danny Minnie's Restaurant
Teach Killindarragh, Annagry, Co Donegal **Tel** *074 954 8201*
€€€€
Road Map C1

A romantic candlelit dinner can be had in this elegant restaurant, housed in a luxurious family-owned B&B in the heart of the Gaelic-speaking Gaeltacht. Danny Minnie's is beautifully decorated with hanging prints, tapestries and paintings, and there are two fireplaces. Seafood and Irish meats figure heavily on the menu. Reservations required.

ARDARA Nancy's
Ardara, Co Donegal **Tel** *074 954 1187*
€
Road Map C1

Owned by the seventh generation of the same family, Nancy's is well-known for its good-value bar meals and snacks that are simple, yet very satisfying. Star attractions include the chowder as well as Charlie's Supper – prawns and smoked salmon warmed in garlic and chilli sauce. The atmosphere is exhilarating.

BALLYSHANNON Nirvana
The Mall, Ballyshannon, Co Donegal **Tel** *071 982 2369*
€€€
Road Map C2

This is an appealing contemporary restaurant, wine bar and café in deepest Donegal. The local chef uses quality ingredients in his classic modern European dishes – all of which taste as good as they look. It's also a good option for lunch, with pizzas, salads, soups and toasted sandwiches on offer.

CARRICK-ON-SHANNON Oarsman Bar & Boathouse Restaurant
Bridge St, Carrick-on-Shannon, Co Leitrim **Tel** *071 962 1733*
€€€
Road Map C3

This attractive pub is owned by Conor and Ronan Maher, who are the seventh generation of their family in the hospitality industry. The brothers' legacy is reflected in the bar's easy-going ambience and the restaurant's superb food, prepared by a talented kitchen staff.

CASTLEBALDWIN Cromleach Lodge Country House
Castlebaldwin, Co Sligo **Tel** *071 916 5155*
€€€€
Road Map C3

Fabulous views of Lough Arrow and the Bricklieve Mountains form a backdrop for gourmet dining in this hilltop country house. Moira Tighe is an innovative chef who carefully sources local ingredients to conjure modern Irish dishes, such as fresh Killybegs monkfish coated in Parmesan cheese served with clam chowder and salsa verde.

DONEGAL The Olde Castle Bar and Restaurant
Tirconnell St, Donegal, Co Donegal **Tel** *074 972 1252*
€€€€
Road Map C

The exterior of this bar and restaurant may look old-fashioned and traditional, but the dishes served here have a modern Irish twist. The emphasis is on local ingredients and seafood is the speciality; choose from Donegal Bay mussels in a white wine and cream sauce, fresh Donegal Bay oysters or Connemara salmon.

DUNKINEELY Castle Murray House

St John's Point, Dunkineely, Co Donegal **Tel** *074 973 7022*

Road Map C2

With wonderful views across the bay and spectacular surroundings, this relaxed restaurant makes a perfect setting for enjoying classic French dishes. The house speciality is prawns and monkfish in garlic butter, but the menu's seasonal with more of an emphasis on red meats in winter.

GLENTIES Highlands Hotel

Main St, Glenties, Co Donegal **Tel** *074 955 1111*

Road Map C1

Considered by many to be the centre of town life, this upbeat restaurant and bar has great steak. Other attractions include vegetarian curry and stir-fry. Local seafood is also available. The gigantic lunches are great value. The friendly staff extend great hospitality. There's also a small gallery here.

GREENCASTLE Kealy's Seafood Bar

The Harbour, Greencastle, Co Donegal **Tel** *074 938 1010*

Road Map C1

Right by the harbour, Kealy's uses fresh seafood and organic farm produce to create its award-winning cuisine. House specialities include baked Atlantic salmon with a wholegrain mustard crust and baked fillet of hake on braised fennel with a tomato and saffron buttered sauce. All dishes are healthy, yet delicious.

KINCASSLAGH Iggy's Bar

Kincasslagh, Co Donegal **Tel** *074 954 3112*

Road Map C2

This great little pub is a popular haunt for locals and visitors alike. Ann and Iggy Murray serve simple pub food with the emphasis on seafood. The sandwiches and soups are particularly appetizing. The crab sandwich goes very well with a pint of Guinness.

LETTERKENNY The Beetroot Restaurant

41 Port Rd, Letterkenny, Co Donegal **Tel** *074 912 9759*

Road Map C1

Modern decor and a variety of European dishes with sizzling grills, meat, poultry and fish add up to a pleasant dining experience in the town centre. The menu features tasty dishes such as chorizo chicken melt, seared fillet of organic salmon or beetroot and goats' cheese risotto. Open for lunch Monday to Friday.

LETTERKENNY Castle Grove Country House Hotel

Ballymaleel, Letterkenny, Co Donegal **Tel** *074 915 1118*

Road Map C1

This part of the Castle Grove group is in keeping with the style of the rest of the house. The restaurant combines ingredients from the hotel garden with Gallic flair to create beautiful dishes. A particular favourite on the four-course menu is pan-fried fillet of beef with grilled horseradish polenta and caramelized chicory.

RATHMULLAN Weeping Elm

Rathmullan Country House, Co Donegal **Tel** *074 915 8188*

Road Map C1

Liam McCormick, known for his imaginative Donegal churches, designed the tented ceiling of this lovely gourmet restaurant. Sample the unusual seaweed-based dessert of carrageen moss with stewed fruits. Yogurt and carrageen pudding is also on offer at the excellent buffet-style breakfasts.

ROSSES POINT Waterfront Bar and Restaurant

Rosses Point, Co Sligo **Tel** *071 917 7122*

Road Map B2

The brightly coloured pub exterior belies the quality of the cuisine in this excellent restaurant. It offers simple delicious bar food alongside an innovative à la carte menu. Seafood is the speciality here, with mussels, clams, monkfish, seabass and cod all on the menu. Sunday lunch is popular.

SLIGO Davis's Restaurant @ Yeats Tavern

Drumcliff Bridge, Sligo **Tel** *071 916 3117*

Road Map C2

With the refurbishment of its interior, Davis's Restaurant @ Yeats Tavern has evolved into an award-winning bar and eaterie. It is a popular stop-off point for locals and tourists in the Northwest. The menu features traditional and international dishes, including irresistible garlic mussels and sweet chilli prawns.

SLIGO Montmartre

1 Market Yard, Sligo **Tel** *071 916 9901*

Road Map C2

This establishment is a favourite amongst locals and is often referred to as Sligo Town's best restaurant. As the name suggests, the menu is French influenced. Stephane Magaud creates imaginative dishes using the best local ingredients, from seasonal game to seafood dishes, including lobster.

SLIGO Coach Lane Restaurant

1–2 Lord Edward St, Sligo **Tel** *071 916 2417*

Road Map C2

This is a Sligo favourite with a varied European-style menu which includes lots of fresh fish, such as monkfish, clams and organic salmon, meat and poultry dishes, as well as pasta and vegetarian options. There is a friendly bar on the ground floor and live traditional music on Sunday night.

STRANDHILL Bella Vista

Shore Rd, Co Sligo **Tel** *071 912 2222*

Road Map C2

It would be difficult for the food to measure up to the breathtaking view of Strandhill's shore front. The simple, but high-quality, sandwiches, pasta, soup and pizza work a treat. The evening menu is more extensive with an emphasis on seafood and steak.

Key to Price Guide *see p324* **Key to Symbols** *see back cover flap*

TOBERCURRY Killorar's Traditional Restaurant

Teeling St, Tobercurry, Co Sligo **Tel** *071 918 5679*   Road Map B3

As the name suggests, this restaurant is ideal for authentic Irish fare. Boxty (potato pancakes), crubeens (pig's trotters) and Irish stew are on the menu on Irish music nights in June and August. There's also fresh salmon caught from the River Moy. Snacks and full meals are served all day. A great place for traditional music and food.

THE MIDLANDS

ATHLONE The Left Bank Bistro

Fry Place, Athlone, Co Westmeath **Tel** *090 649 4446*   Road Map C3

Situated in the heart of Old Athlone, this stylishly designed restaurant is the essence of soulful minimalism. Creative and delicious food is served in a relaxed, informal atmosphere. Lunches feature soup, chicken fajitas, vegetable tartlets and focaccia sandwiches. Extensive dinner menu includes steaks and seafood.

ATHLONE Wineport Lodge

Glasson, Athlone, Co Westmeath **Tel** *090 643 9010*   Road Map C3

This delightful lakeside lodge boasts an award-winning restaurant with a diverse menu that combines fresh local produce with international flavours. Try the buttered crab claws with hoi sin pancakes or the loin of rabbit with mint and chorizo risotto. The turf smoked lamb is a favourite starter. A separate children's menu is available.

BIRR The Thatch Bar & Restaurant

Crinkill, Birr, Co Offaly **Tel** *057 912 0682*   Road Map C4

This beautiful traditional thatched pub, with white washed walls, cobblestones and fresh flowers, is situated just outside the town. In the same family for the last 200 years it offers genuine, warm hospitality and good, imaginative food. Try the delicious roast pheasant with fresh herbs and fruit stuffing.

BLACKLION MacNean House & Bistro

Main St, Blacklion, Co Cavan **Tel** *071 985 3022*   Road Map D2

Neven Maguire, one of Ireland's leading chefs, has drawn huge national attention with his excellent cooking. His family-run guesthouse has earned him numerous awards. Local artisan produce features in imaginative menus. Sea scallops with crab and saffron risotto is a winning recipe. The game dishes are excellent. Closed Monday and Tuesday.

CARLINGFORD Ghan House

Carlingford, Co Louth **Tel** *042 937 3682*   Road Map D3

A natural stop-off point between Dublin and Belfast, this 18th-century county house can be found on the edge of Carlingford village. The menu is based on home-grown and local produce with oysters, mussels and lobster fresh from the sea. The Cooley lamb and beef are good options for meat-lovers.

CARLINGFORD Kingfisher Bistro

Darcy McGee Court, Dundalk St, Carlingford, Co Louth **Tel** *042 937 3716*   Road Map D3

This cosy little restaurant at the heritage centre is perhaps the best in the area. It offers reliably good food at reasonable prices. Set in a stone building, with warmly coloured walls, it offers Continental cuisine with an occasional Southeast Asian flavour. Tasty steaks and fish dishes. Vegetarians are well catered for.

CARRICKMACROSS Nuremore Hotel & Country Club

Carrickmacross, Co Monaghan **Tel** *042 966 1438*   Road Map D3

The restaurant at the scenic Nuremore Hotel is regarded as one of the best in the area. Elegantly furnished, it boasts an immensely talented chef who is attracting patrons from around the country. Try the signature tiar of Annagassan crab. Worth a detour.

CLOVERHILL The Olde Post Inn

Cloverhill, Co Cavan **Tel** *047 55555*   Road Map C3

This restaurant is in a lovely old post office and its superb, classical cooking has won it many awards. The five-course dinner menu includes mains such as braised suckling pig, stuffed loin of rabbit or herb-crusted loin of venison, with excellent starters and homemade desserts. There is also accommodation.

COLLON Forge Gallery Restaurant

Collon, Co Louth **Tel** *041 982 6272*   Road Map D3

The leading restaurant in the area, this is an immaculately maintained venue of great character. It is adept at combining French and Irish cooking to delicious effect. Local seafood and game feature prominently on the seasonal menus.

DUNDALK Quaglino's

The Century Bar, 19 Roden Place, Dundalk, Co Louth **Tel** *042 933 8567*   Road Map D3

Housed on the first floor of an attractive listed building dating to 1902, the award-winning Quag Inc's offers high-quality meals. Baked Carlingford oysters in an herb and garlic butter is a house speciality. The Century Bar has great character and retains many of its period and historic features. There's a good early dinner menu.

KELLS The Ground Floor Restaurant
Bective 52, Kells, Co Meath **Tel** *046 924 9688*

Road Map D4

The off-beat paintings lend to the youthful atmosphere of this contemporary restaurant. The menu features popular dishes from around the world such as Mexican quesadilla and sizzling fajitas. Other choices include steaks, pastas and pizzas all of which are produced with flair. The early-bird dinner is great value.

KELLS The Vanilla Pod
Headfort Arms Hotel, Kells, Co Meath **Tel** *046 924 0084*

Road Map D3

Part of the hotel, this hip bistro-style restaurant is contemporary in design, with oak tables, dim lighting and stylish table settings. The food is modern, with a variety of global influences. Try the grilled goat's cheese *crostini* (thin slices of toasted bread) with plum chutney. The chocolate fondue is a treat. Kids eat free between 5:30–6:45pm daily.

LONGFORD Aubergine Gallery Café
Ist Floor, The White House, 17 Ballymahon St, Longford **Tel** *043 334 8633*

Road Map C3

This bright and stylish first-floor restaurant, with interesting artwork, serves international fare with a Mediterranean and modern Irish slant. Succulent steaks, good seafood, poultry and tasty vegetarian dishes are served, all at a reasonable price. Try the sirloin steak with whiskey and pepper cream.

MONAGHAN Andy's Restaurant
12 Market St, Monaghan **Tel** *047 82277*

Road Map D2

The immaculately maintained, family-run Andy's Restaurant is located in the heart of town and has been the recipient of many awards. The cheerful old-fashioned atmosphere draws a regular clientele. Quality ingredients are used in its good cooking. Informal food is available downstairs in the lovely traditionally-styled bar.

MULLINGAR Ilia Tapas Restaurant
37 Dominick St, Mullingar, Co Westmeath **Tel** *044 934 5947*

Road Map C3

This is a smart tapas bar which serves a selection of tasty meat and seafood morsels with a creative twist. Tapas offerings include carpaccio of beetroot, haddock and scallion croquettes and baby squid stuffed with prawn mousse. A good selection of wines is available. There are also early-bird, à la carte and takeaway menus.

MULLINGAR The Belfry Restaurant
Ballinegall, Mullingar, Co Westmeath **Tel** *044 934 2488*

Road Map C3

Formerly a church, now a wonderfully designed restaurant, the Belfry is tastefully furnished, well-lit and has a welcoming atmosphere. The expertly cooked and appealingly presented food is a blend of modern Irish and traditional French cuisine. Open from Wednesday to Sunday.

PORTLAOISE The Kitchen & Foodhall
Hynds Sq, Portlaoise, Co Laois **Tel** *057 866 2061*

Road Map C4

This delightful self-service bistro and delicatessen is a landmark establishment in the centre of town. It has earned a reputation for delicious home cooking. Terrines, quiches, home-baked breads, freshly prepared salads, wholesome hot dishes and wonderful desserts are on the menu. Open daytime only.

TRIM Franzini O'Brien's
French's Lane, Trim, Co Meath **Tel** *046 943 1002*

Road Map D3

Set in a lovely location, overlooking Trim Castle, this smart and spacious eaterie is well designed with easy parking. It offers well-informed, friendly service and international cuisine at affordable prices. The atmosphere is informal and lively. Menu features delicious fajitas and soups. There's a very good wine list. Open evenings only.

NORTHERN IRELAND

ARDGLASS Aldo's
7 Castle Place, Ardglass, Downpatrick, Co Down BT30 7TP **Tel** *028 4484 1315*

Road Map E2

This Italian restaurant has been owned and managed by the Vinaccia family since 1973. The service is very good and friendly, with a menu of antipasti, pasta, fresh fish and meats. Vegetarians are well catered for and, with prior notice, an extensive selection can be provided. Open from Thursday to Sunday.

ARMAGH Manor Park Restaurant
2 College Hill, The Mall, Armagh BT61 9DF **Tel** *028 3715 353*

Road Map D2

Located in an attractive Georgian house next to the Planetarium, Manor Park specializes in inventive, modern British and Irish cuisine. Particular highlights of the menu are the roasted fillets of monkfish wrapped in Black Forest ham, the fricassee of lobster and scallop and the lamb shank served with champ and a thyme and rosemary sauce.

BALLYCASTLE The Cellar Restaurant
11B The Diamond, Ballycastle, Co Antrim, BT54 6AW **Tel** *028 2076 3037*

Road Map D1

Hearty portions of delicious local seafood are served with warmth in the cosy surroundings of this town centre haven. The surf-and-turf with Rathlin lobster and charred baby beef fillet steaks is a tasty option and offers superb value for money. Steaks are cooked to perfection, service is excellent and the staff are friendly.

Key to Symbols *see back cover flap*

BELFAST Archana Balti House

53 Dublin Rd, Belfast, Co Antrim, BT2 7HE **Tel** *028 9032 3713*   Road Map D2

One of the best Indian restaurants in Belfast and one of the first on the island, Archana serves up a mouth-watering selection of curries and Balti dishes. It's particularly noted for its vegetarian options, even catering widely for vegans. The Thali lunch is particularly good value. Fully licensed to serve alcohol.

BELFAST Castle Cellar Restaurant

Antrim Rd, Belfast, Co Antrim, BT15 5GR **Tel** *028 9077 6925*   Road Map D2

With a strikingly romantic setting, the Castle Cellar Restaurant offers one of the best views in Belfast. The decor is in keeping with the grandeur of the castle's design. The star attractions include peppered fillet of venison and pan-fried salmon. Open for lunch daily and dinner everyday except Monday and Tuesday.

BELFAST Crown Liquor Saloon

46 Great Victoria St, Belfast, Co Antrim BT2 7BA **Tel** *028 9027 9901*   Road Map D2

Crown Liquor Saloon is a real Belfast landmark which dates back to 1848. The bar's snug-like booths include able space for a bowl of Irish stew and champ – a local speciality of potatoes, spring onions and butter. It's well worth a visit if only for a pint and a look around at the fascinating Victoriana.

BELFAST Mourne Seafood Bar

34–36 Bank St, Belfast, Co Antrim, BT1 1HL **Tel** *028 9024 8544*   Road Map D2

This is a complimentary marriage between restaurant and fish shop. Customers pass through the shop of stocked fish into a long bar and restaurant. The menu varies depending on the local fresh fish caught that day. Oysters, mussels and cockles are farmed from Mourne's own shellfish beds, which also supply branches in Dundrum and Newcastle.

BELFAST Shu

253 Lisburn Rd, Belfast, BT9 7EN **Tel** *028 9038 1655*   Road Map D2

A contemporary dining space in a restored Victorian building, Shu is a bright and buzzing restaurant serving fine, seasonal food with a French influence. Game and seafood feature heavily, and treats such as game consommé, smoked haddock lasagne and roast partridge might feature on a typical menu.

BELFAST Alden's

229 Upper Newtownards Rd, Belfast, Co Antrim, BT4 3JF **Tel** *028 9065 0079*   Road Map D2

A city favourite, Alden's has a tasty selection of meat, seafood and poultry dishes made using simple, high-quality ingredients. A set menu is available for lunch and dinner (Monday to Thursday only), which offers great value for money. There is also an interesting wine list with some good-value options.

BELFAST The Barnett Room

Malone House, Barnett Demesne, Belfast, Co Antrim, BT9 5LH **Tel** *028 9068 1246*   Road Map D2

Housed in a graceful late-Georgian mansion, the Barnett Room is renowned for its excellent cuisine. Only the best-quality Ulster produce is used in the brasserie-style menu served at this local favourite. Vegetarian dishes are often the house special. Open for lunch only.

BELFAST Bourbon

60 Great Victoria St, Belfast BT2 7BB **Tel** *028 9033 2121*   Road Map D2

The plush red and burgundy interior is matched by an elegant menu, which has clearly been designed to entice the customers. The venison and crispy duck are tempting in a restaurant with enough variety to suit most palates. A pre-theatre menu is available Monday to Saturday.

BELFAST Metro Brasserie

13 Lower Crescent, Belfast, Co Antrim, BT7 1NR **Tel** *028 9032 3349*   Road Map D2

This is a trendy modern version of the traditional brasserie housed in the beautiful Crescent Townhouse. The interior design is striking and unusual and gives the place a sophisticated but relaxed atmosphere. There's a separate vegetarian menu as well as an extensive selection of cocktails.

BELFAST Zen

55–59 Adelaide St, Belfast, Co Antrim, BT2 8FE **Tel** *028 9023 2244*   Road Map D2

As the name suggests, Zen is a restaurant with the calmness and serenity of a rock garden. The beautiful elegant surroundings are matched only by the presentation of the food. Extensive menu of sashimi, sushi, tempura, maki rolls and other Japanese specialities. Try the dinner set.

BELFAST Cayenne

7 Ascot House, Shaftesbury Sq, Belfast, Co Antrim, BT2 7DB **Tel** *028 9033 1532*   Road Map D2

Celebrity chefs Paul and Jeanne Rankin opened this restaurant in 1999, and serve a delicious mix of Thai, Japanese and other Asian-influenced dishes. Exotic and innovative mains, such as spiced breast of duck with Shanghai noodles, sprouting broccoli, oyster mushrooms and black bean sauce are typical.

BELFAST Deane's Restaurant

36–40 Howard St, Belfast, Co Antrim, BT1 6PF **Tel** *028 9033 1134*   Road Map D2

You have a choice here of a seafood bar on the first floor, or an informal French brasserie on the ground floor. Chef Michael Deane has a superb reputation, so it is hardly surprising that you will find excellent food in whichever of the two you choose to eat in.

€ under £15 €€ £15–25 €€€ £25–35 €€€€ £35–50 €€€€€ over £50

BELFAST James Street South

21 James St South, Belfast, BT2 7GA **Tel** *028 9043 4310*   **Road Map** *D2*

This is one of the city's best and most stylish restaurants. Housed in an old linen mill, the dining room and bar have a cool and contemporary feel. Cuisine is classical French style, using the best Northern Irish produce, and the wine list is extensive. Service is also top class.

BELFAST Nick's Warehouse

35–39 Hill St, Co Antrim, Belfast, BT1 2LB **Tel** *028 9043 9690*   **Road Map** *D2*

Nick and Kathy Price's converted warehouse, tucked away in the cobbled backstreets of central Belfast, gets top marks for atmosphere. The menu includes Nick's latest culinary innovations made from produce sourced from the best suppliers.

BUSHMILLS Bushmills Inn

9 Dunluce Rd, Bushmills, Co Antrim, BT57 8QG **Tel** *028 2073 3000*   **Road Map** *D1*

Originally an old coaching inn, this popular hostelry is only a few miles from the Giant's Causeway and close to the Bushmills Distillery. It overlooks the garden courtyard making for a lovely view and wonderful atmosphere. Food is a combination of classical and new Irish.

DUNDRUM The Buck's Head

77 Main St, Dundrum, Co Down, BT33 OLU **Tel** *028 4375 1868*   **Road Map** *E2*

Open fires and hospitable, friendly service make this a preferred stop for lunch, high tea or dinner. The cuisine is a mix of traditional and modern, made from local produce. Seafood particularly features fresh catch, such as oysters from Dundrum Bay. The atmosphere is pleasant and the large attractive dining room overlooks a walled garden.

DUNGANNON Viscount's Restaurant

10 Northland Row, Dungannon, Co Tyrone, BT71 6AP **Tel** *028 8775 3800*   **Road Map** *D2*

A Victorian church has been converted into a medieval-style banqueting hall with the emphasis on fun as much as food. The decor is almost Arthurian with maroon drapes, heraldic banners and beautiful stained-glass windows. The "Viscount's Fayre" dinner menu caters to all appetites. Good carvery.

ENNISKILLEN Franco's

Queen Elizabeth Rd, Enniskillen, Co Fermanagh, BT74 7DY **Tel** *028 6632 4424*   **Road Map** *C2*

This lively Italian restaurant has a bustling atmosphere. The wide choice of pizza and pasta dishes sit alongside organic salmon and lobster, as well as other Mediterranean influenced dishes. The staff here are efficient and friendly. An eatery known for being good value.

ENNISKILLEN The Sheelin Tea Shop

Bellanaleck, Enniskillen, Co Fermanagh, BT92 2BA **Tel** *028 6634 8232*   **Road Map** *C2*

On the shores of Lower Lough Erne, the Sheelin is a thatched cottage with great home-cooking and traditional Irish dishes on the menu. T-bone steak and Guinness beef pie are specialities as are the delicious home-baked buns and scones. Alcohol is not served.

ENNISKILLEN Belleek Restaurant

Manor House Country Hotel, Killadeas, Enniskillen, Co Fermanagh, BT94 1NY **Tel** *028 6862 2200*   **Road Map** *C2*

Around 11 km (7 miles) outside of Enniskillen is the delightful Belleek Restaurant, part of the Manor House Country Hotel *(see p318)*. The restaurant has wonderful views over Lough Erne – ask for a table in the conservatory. Fresh local produce is used to create delicious, traditional dishes, and the set menu offers good value for money.

FLORENCE COURT Arch House

59 Marble Arch Rd, Florence Court, Co Fermanagh, BT92 1DE **Tel** *028 6634 8452*   **Road Map** *C2*

Beside Marble Arch caves, this farm restaurant offers great food and service. Produce fresh from the farm is used, with wild salmon and Lough Erne trout on offer too. Desserts such as lemon soufflé and fresh fruit pavlova are a speciality. Closed October to Easter. Accommdation is also available. Reservations are essential.

HILLSBOROUGH Hillside Bar & Bistro

21 Main St, Hillsborough, Co Down, BT26 6AE **Tel** *028 9268 9233*   **Road Map** *D2*

This attractive country-style pub and restaurant has an excellent seasonal menu. There's an informal bistro as well as a more formal restaurant, open for special occasions, and live music on weekends. The bar serves a good selection of real ales, while mulled wine is available on cold winter nights.

HOLYWOOD Bay Tree Coffee House

118 High St, Holywood, Co Down, BT18 9HW **Tel** *028 9042 1419*   **Road Map** *E2*

This is a very popular café and bakery – the cinnamon scones are legendary. Lunch is served daily, with an emphasis on fresh fish, vegetarian food and organic salads. Dinner is served five nights a week (not on Tuesday or Sunday), and the café is also open on Sundays for takeaways. Booking is advised.

LIMAVADY The Lime Tree

60 Catherine St, Limavady, Londonderry, BT49 9DB **Tel** *028 7776 4300*   **Road Map** *D1*

Right on the main street of the attractive town, The Lime Tree is small and quite simply decorated. The impressive menu offers unusual and subtle tasting dishes put together with local ingredients. There are excellent options for meat eaters such as Sperrin lamb with Moroccan spiced sauce and roasted stuffed saddle of rabbit.

Key to Symbols *see back cover flap*

LONDONDERRY Badger's Bar & Restaurant
16–18 Orchard St, Londonderry, BT48 6EG **Tel** *028 7136 0763*
Road Map C1

Attracting an older type of clientele for chat, pints and conviviality, Badger's Bar & Restaurant is a charming pub specializing in steaks, salad and afternoon tea. Guinness casserole is particularly recommended, although its liquid form doesn't appeal to everyone's taste.

LONDONDERRY Brown's Bar & Brasserie
1 Bonds Hill, Londonderry, BT 47 6DW **Tel** *028 7134 5180*
Road Map C1

Look past the rather unremarkable façade of the building and you'll discover some of the best-value food in the city. A modern European menu, relying on fresh and often organic ingredients, is complemented by minimalist yet warm decor. Lunch Tuesday to Friday, and Sunday, dinner Tuesday to Saturday. Live music on Friday nights.

LONDONDERRY The Metro Bar
3–4 Bank Pl, Londonderry, BT48 6EA **Tel** *028 7126 7401*
Road Map C1

Shadowed by Derry's city walls, the Metro is a local favourite. Although it only dates back to the 1980s, it has a formidable presence in the area. The food, from soup and sandwiches to Guinness beef stew, is first-rate. Service is very good with friendly staff. The lovely views can be enjoyed over a pint. Open for lunch only.

LONDONDERRY Quay West Wine Bar & Restaurant
Boating Club Lane, Londonderry, BT48 7QB **Tel** *028 7137 0977*
Road Map C1

Quay West is a cool and smart urban dining space in the city, with a great menu full of spicy specialities with a large selection of fish, meat, poultry and vegetarian options. There is a great wine list, service is friendly and relaxed, and prices offer good value for money.

NEWCASTLE Seasalt
51 Central Promenade, Newcastle, Co Down, BT33 0AA **Tel** *028 4372 5027*
Road Map D2

Situated on a seafront terrace facing the water, Seasalt has a great range of dishes, from seafood chowder and pasta to meat, fish and steaks. The views are wonderful and there's a casual, friendly atmosphere here. The restaurant is not licensed to sell alcohol, but allows you to bring your own.

OMAGH Grant's Restaurant
29 George's St, Omagh, Co Tyrone, BT78 2EY **Tel** *028 8225 0900*
Road Map C2

Named after Ulysses S Grant, this restaurant offers a good selection of dishes. The menu features fresh seafood, pasta, burgers and steak along with a selection of creative vegetarian options. Sunday lunch is very popular so it is advisable to book in advance.

PORTBALLINTRAE Porthole Bar & Restaurant
Bay View Hotel, 2 Bayhead Rd, Portballintrae, Co Antrim, BT57 8RZ **Tel** *028 2073 4100*
Road Map C1

Part of the Bay View Hotel, this restaurant has stunning views over the Atlantic and a relaxed, friendly atmosphere. The menu focuses on locally-sourced ingredients, such as seafood, fresh fish and delicious steaks. There's regular live music at the weekends and a comfortable lounge area where you can enjoy coffee after your meal.

PORTRUSH The Harbour Bistro
The Harbour, Portrush, Co Antrim, BT56 8DF **Tel** *028 7082 2430*
Road Map D1

The Harbour is probably the nicest place in town. The traditional pub area on the ground floor has roaring fires and a great atmosphere. The restaurant is also informal and offers a good selection of à la carte dishes. Food is traditional Irish with a twist and there is a good wine selection.

PORTSTEWART Morellis
53 The Promenade, Portstewart, Co Londonderry, BT55 7AF **Tel** *028 7083 2150*
Road Map D1

Opened in 1911 as an ice cream parlour, Morellis is also an Italian-style café. The menu includes hot food, such as authentic Italian pasta, sandwiches and paninis, as well as a long coffee list. Home-made pastries and desserts are a delight, especially the ice creams. Lovely location on the Promenade with a view of the bay.

RICHHILL Stonebridge Restaurant
74 Legacorry Road, Richhill, Armagh, BT61 9LF **Tel** *028 3887 0024*
Road Map D2

This is an à-la-carte restaurant, carvery and brasserie all in one, with great-quality food and excellent, locally sourced produce used in the cooking, which has won awards. Family-run, the eatery is located in a former listed building. A great restaurant for breakfast, lunch or dinner.

STRANGFORD The Cuan
4 The Square, Strangford, Downpatrick, BT30 7ND **Tel** *028 4488 1222*
Road Map E2

This is a family-run pub and restaurant with accommodation (nine rooms) in Strangford on the shores of Strangford Lough, with warm and friendly service. The dining menu features lots of seafood and a wide choice of meat dishes and roasts. The Cuan is also a popular venue for lunch.

WARRENPOINT Restaurant 23
23 Church Street, Warrenpoint, Co Down, BT34 3HN **Tel** *028 4175 3222*
Road Map E2

The young chef and owner of this stylish and contemporary restaurant is Trevor Cunningham, who is well known in Northern Ireland and has won awards for his simple, classical cooking. Seafood and game feature on the menu – a sample dish might be Fermanagh old spot pig with apple chutney celeriac purée, black pudding beignet and calvados jus.

Pubs in Ireland

The archetypal Irish pub is celebrated for its convivial atmosphere, friendly locals, genial bar staff and the "craic" – the Irish expression for fun. Wit is washed down with whiskey or Guinness, the national drinks. Irish pubs date back to medieval taverns, coaching inns and she-beens, illegal drinking dens which flourished under colonial rule. In Victorian times, brewing and distilling were major industries. The sumptuous Edwardian or Victorian interiors of some city pubs are a testament to these times. Snugs, partitioned-off booths, are another typical feature of Irish pubs. Traditional pubs can be boldly painted, thatched or "black-and-white" – beamed with a white façade and black trim. Some rural pubs double as grocers' shops. All pubs across Ireland are now smoke-free, but many have beer gardens where smoking is permitted.

Good pubs are not evenly distributed throughout the country: in the Southeast, Kilkenny is paradise for pub-lovers, while Cork and Kerry possess some of the most picturesque pubs. The Lower Shannon region is noted for its boisterous pubs, especially in County Clare where spontaneous music sessions are common. The West has an abundance of typical Irish pubs, and the many tourists and students guarantee a profusion of good pubs in Galway. The listings below cover a selection of pubs throughout Ireland; for Dublin pubs, see pages 110–11.

SOUTHEAST IRELAND

Brittas Bay: *Jack White's Inn*
Jack White's Cross, Co Wicklow.
Road map D4. **Tel** 0404 47106.
A typical Irish country pub perfectly situated off the N11, which runs from Dublin to the Southeast. Simple but tasty pub fare is served until 9pm. A real local legend, this pub is mired in controversy, due to a murder committed here in 1996. 🍴 🍷 ♿ ♫

Carlow: *Teach Dolmain*
Tullow St, Co Carlow.
Road map D4. **Tel** 059 913 0911.
This multi-award winning pub, in Carlow's town centre, has a curious collection of unique pottery and ancient artifacts from the town's and Ireland's history. This pub has an excellent menu and is ideally suited for large groups. 🍴 🍷 ♿ ♫

Dungarvan: *Quealy's*
82 O'Connell St, Co Waterford.
Road map D5. **Tel** 058 24555.
This is a relaxed, friendly and popular pub situated just off Dungarvan's main square. It stands out for its modern menu of surprisingly good quality bar food, which makes the most of locally sourced ingredients Prices are reasonable, presentation is good, service is smooth and a lively atmosphere pervades. 🍴 ♿

Enniscorthy: *The Antique Tavern*
14 Slaney St, Co Wexford.
Road map D5. **Tel** 053 923 3428.
This traditional, timbered, black-and-white pub is charming. The dark, intimate bar contains relics such as pikestaffs from Vinegar Hill, the decisive battle in the 1798 uprising that was fought outside town. Pub lunches and local chat are on offer. In good weather, you can sit on the balcony and enjoy the pleasant views of the River Slaney. 🍴 🍷 ♿ ♫

Enniscorthy: *Holohan*
Slaney Place, Co Wexford.
Road map D5. **Tel** 053 923 5743.
At the back of the Castle Museum, this is essentially an evening only pub with few pretensions. Its unusual location makes it worth a visit for a pint or two – it is built right into the base of an old quarry and a vertical cliff forms part of the back wall of the bar. ♫

Kilkenny: *The Left Bank*
High St, Co Kilkenny. **Road map** C4. **Tel** 056 775 0016.
Encompassing a sports' bar, an outdoor bar and a cocktail bar, this venue in an impressive old city centre bank is vast yet hospitable. There are plenty of nooks for quiet chat, as well as every option to be in the thick of it with room to dance and a sociable smoking area. 🍷 ♿

Kilkenny: *Hibernian*
1, Ormonde St, Co Kilkenny.
Road map C4. **Tel** 056 777 1888.
Sited in an old bank and part of the Hibernian Hotel, this rather formal pub, popular with a mixed age crowd, still has its original decor. Modern Irish food is available and live Irish music every Tuesday year round. 🍴 🍷 ♿ ♫

Kilkenny: *Kyteler's Inn*
27 St Kieran's St, Co Kilkenny.
Road map C4. **Tel** 056 772 1064.
In good weather you can sit in the courtyard of this historic coaching inn and cellar bar. Food is available all day, and meals are served daily until 9pm (last orders). An effigy of a witch sits in the window frame, a reminder of the story of a former resident, Dame Alice Kyteler. In 1324, Alice and her maid were pronounced guilty of witchcraft after four of Alice's husbands had died in mysterious circumstances; although pardoned, Alice was again accused but escaped, leaving her maid Petronella to burn at the stake. 🍴 🍷 ♿ ♫

Kilkenny: *Langton's*
69 John St, Co Kilkenny.
Road map C4. **Tel** 056 776 5133.
Langton's is noted for its black-and-white exterior, Edwardian ambience and the stylish glass interior at the back. The front bar is cosy with a low ceiling. Pub food is on offer, and there's music and dancing at least one night a week during the summer; Tuesday, Thursday and Saturday are club nights. 🍴 🍷 ♿ ♫

Kilkenny: *Marble City Bar*
66 High St, Co Kilkenny.
Road map C4. **Tel** 056 776 1143.
Marble City Bar, the most famous pub in town, is named after the local limestone, which becomes black when polished. This four-storey building has an Art Deco façade. A busy café-bar with no reservations. Bar food till 9pm. 🍴 🍷 ♿

Kilkenny: *Tynan's Bridge House Bar*
2 John's Bridge, Co Kilkenny.
Road map C4. **Tel** 056 772 1291.
This is the most genuine old-world pub in town, with an intimate interior lit by charming lamps. Quaint relics of the former grocery store and pharmacy are on display, from a set of old scales to the drawers labelled with names of nuts and spices. No music, no TV; as the publican puts it, this is "a chat bar". An outdoor smoking area has been added. 🍷

Kilmore Quay: *Kehoes*
Co Wexford. **Road map** D5.
Tel 053 912 9830.

This maritime-themed pub is known for its seafood dishes that are made up of the catch of the day, brought direct from the quay. Last orders are at 8.30pm and children are welcome. 🍴 � 🎵

Leighlinbridge: *The Lord Bagenal Inn*
Co Carlow. **Road map** D5.
Tel 059 972 1668.

This pub is a well-known stop-off point for those travelling south from Dublin. Set in a small, peaceful village in County Carlow the Lord Bagenal overlooks a picturesque marina on the River Barrow. It boasts award-winning food and has a children's crèche. Accommodation is available in the hotel here. � 🍴 🎵

New Ross: *Corcoran's Pub*
Irishtown, Co Wexford.
Road map D5. *Tel 051 425920*

Head here if you crave fresh home-made food. Having had five generations of continuous ownership, Corcoran's is one of the oldest pubs in town and has a friendly atmosphere. Card games are played every Monday with music sessions on weekends, including Irish music, singing and dancing. 🎵 🍴 � 🎵

Waterford: *Henry Downes*
8–10 Thomas St, Co Waterford.
Road map D5 *Tel 051 874118*

Dating from 1759, this unusual pub located in County Waterford bottles its own whiskey. It is dark and cavernous with a chequered history. This makes it a fine stop for a good pint and a chat with the locals.

Waterford: *Jack Meade's Pub*
Cheekpoint Rd, Co Waterford.
Road map D5. *Tel 051 850950.*

Situated under an old stone bridge 7 km (4 miles) south of town, Jack Meade's provides a quiet and quaint atmosphere. In the summer, musicians play outdoors and children can amuse themselves in the playground. Drop by for the setting and some lunch. 🍴 � 🎵

Waterford: *T and H Doolin*
George's St, Co Waterford.
Road map D5. *Tel 051 841504.*

Set in the city's most charming pedestrianized street, this traditional, 18th-century black-and-white pub offers an intimate atmosphere and good "craic". Traditional folk music sessions are held every night. 🍴 � 🎵

Wexford: *Centenary Stores*
Charlotte St, Co Wexford.
Road map D5. *Tel 053 912 4424.*

Tucked away in a converted warehouse, this dimly lit pub is the most popular in Wexford. The friendly bar staff and a mixed local and bohemian crowd chat in the wood-panelled bar. Drinkers are entertained with sessions of traditional music every Sunday morning, and it's open until late on Friday and Saturday nights. 🍴 � 🎵

Wexford: *Macken's*
Bull Ring, Co Wexford.
Road map D5. *Tel 053 912 2949.*

This pub has a prime location on one of the corners of the historic bull ring. It's an excellent place to stop for a pint or two and watch the world go by. If you're lucky, there might even be some live music. 🎵

CORK AND KERRY

Baltimore: *Bushe's*
Co Cork. **Road map** B6.
Tel 028 20125.

Famous in County Cork, this pub serves the best ales and pints in the village and is well used to visitors dropping by. Sit outside in the summer and gaze out onto the islands or watch the beautiful sunset. 🍴 � �=

Cahirciveen: *The Point Bar*
Valentia Harbour, Co Kerry.
Road map A5. *Tel 066 947 2165.*

Best to save this one for the summer months. With its variety of ultra-fresh seafood dishes and stunning views of Valentia Island, the Point Bar is considered by many to be one of Kerry's greatest. 🍴 � �=

Castletownshend: *Mary Ann's*
Co Cork. **Road map** B6.
Tel 028 36146.

Since opening in 1846, Mary Ann's has maintained excellent service and a great reputation for quality home-made food. Full of interesting antiques, this is one of the best examples of a traditional pub in Ireland. 🍴 � �=

Clonakilty: *De Barra's*
Co Cork. **Road map** B6.
Tel 023 33381.

This is one of the best-known pubs in West Cork, with a traditional folk club open most nights; many musicians come from the Gaeltacht *(see p229)*. The bar is true to its origins, with hand-painted signs and traditional whiskey jars. Simple snacks and full lunches are served from noon to 4pm. 🍴 � 🎵

Cork: *Bodega*
46–47 Cornmarket St, Co Cork.
Road map C5. *Tel 021 427 2878.*

This bright, modern pub and restaurant was once a warehouse. The high ceilings create a feeling of openness; the huge wall-spaces are taken up by art, much of it for sale. Soup and sandwiches in the afternoon give way to an international menu in the evening. On Saturdays, the open air market outside adds to the hustle and bustle. 🍴 � �=

Cork: *Chateau Bar*
St Patrick's St, Co Cork.
Road map C5. *Tel 021 427 0370.*

This bar in the heart of the city occupies a striking building that was once on the quayside. Founded in 1793, this elegant pub has a stylish Victorian interior and offers good quality bar fare. 🍴 � �=

Cork: *Clancy's*
15–16 Princes St, Co Cork.
Road map C5. *Tel 021 427 6097.*

One of Cork's oldest pubs, Clancy's has been open since 1824. It has one of the longest continuous bars in Ireland and has live music performances from May to September. Food is available in the Lunchtime Carvery or Steak Restaurant where the emphasis is on quality Irish cuisine. � 🍴 �= 🎵

Cork: *The Gables*
32 Douglas St, Co Cork.
Road map C5. *Tel 021 431 3176.*

This traditional Irish pub combines good food and live music. The menus, both food and wine, are an alternative to typical pub food and are well worth sampling. Food is served from 12:30 to 3pm and 5 to 9pm. Traditional live music on Wednesday and Sunday complements this already atmospheric pub. 🍴 🎵

Cork: *Henchy's*
40 St Luke's Cross, Co Cork.
Road map C5. *Tel 021 450 785.*

This traditional pub dates from 1884 and has retained much of its Victorian ambience, enhanced by the mahogany bar and stained glass. It has long been associated with artists and is where young hopefuls come to show their work to a largely sympathetic audience. � �=

Cork: *The Long Valley*
10 Winthrop St, Co Cork.
Road map C5. *Tel 021 427 2144.*

Located just off Patrick Street, this pub has a sense of the unexpected. It attracts all sorts of characters from chancers to professionals. It is well known for its smooth pints of Murphy's, which any self-respecting local will choose over Guinness. 🍴 � 🎵

Dingle: *Ashes*
Main St, Co Kerry. **Road map** A5.
Tel 066 915 0989.
An old-world style bar dating back to 1849. The charming traditional frontage sets the tone for the cozy and inviting atmosphere found within. Pop in for a casual drink or light snack in the day or an informal and good-value seafood meal in the evening. ▯

Dingle: *Dick Mack's*
Green St, Co Kerry.
Road map A5.
This individualistic spot is part shoe shop, part pub, and retains the original shop and drinking counters. The pub is a haunt of local artists, eccentrics and extroverts. In the evening, regulars often congregate around the piano.

Dunquin: *Krugers*
Ballyferriter, Co Kerry.
Road map A5. *Tel 066 915 6127.*
Situated close to the quays for the Blasket Islands, this well-known family pub is also a guesthouse from March to September. The pub is decorated with family memorabilia and stills from the famous films made in the area, such as *Ryan's Daughter* and *Far and Away.*
▯ ▯

Glencar: *The Climber's Inn*
Co Kerry. **Road map** B5.
Tel 066 976 0101.
This family run pub is a famous landmark on the way to the Kerry highlands. It boasts an open fire and serves up great home-cooked meals with interesting vegetarian options. Chat with other hikers and climbers after a day's trekking. ▯ ▯

Killarney: *Buckley's Bar*
College St, Co Kerry.
Road map B5. *Tel 064 643 1037.*
This oak-panelled bar is noted for its regular traditional music sessions and its filling meals. The pub was opened in 1926 when Tom Buckley, a homesick emigrant, returned from New York. Bar food is served until 4pm.
▯ ▯ ▯

Killarney: *The Laurels*
Main St, Co Kerry. **Road map** B5.
Tel 064 643 1149.
This claims to be Killarney's liveliest pub and is popular with young locals and tourists. It has been run by the O'Leary family for almost a century and provides excellent bar snacks and meals (steak, mussels, oysters, fish) in a separate restaurant area. ▯ ▯ ▯

Killorglin: *The Village Inn*
2 Upper Bridge St, Co Kerry.
Road map A5. *Tel 066 976 2337.*
If it is hospitality you are after, this traditional spot is the place for you. It is found on the narrowest street in the centre of Killorglin. Irish music is played on Thursday and Saturday evenings in summer.
▯ ▯ ▯

Kinsale: *Kieran's Folk House Inn*
Guardwell, Co Cork. **Road map** B6.
Tel 021 477 2382.
This convivial corner of old Kinsale draws locals and visitors alike. The interior is snug and welcoming, with live music every night during the season. The inn also houses a pleasant guesthouse and a noted restaurant – the Shrimps Seafood Bistro, open for lunch and dinner all year. ▯ ▯ ▯

Kinsale: *The Lord Kingsale*
Main St, Co Cork. **Road map** B6.
Tel 021 477 2371.
This beamed, old-fashioned pub attracts a quiet, genteel crowd. It is several hundred years old but the interior is, in part, a clever fake. In summer, live music is performed every night. Bar food is served from noon to 3pm.
▯ ▯

Scilly: *The Spaniard Inn*
Kinsale, Co Cork. **Road map** B6.
Tel 021 477 2436.
Set on a hairpin bend in the village of Scilly, this popular fishermen's pub has the air of a smugglers' inn. There is often live traditional music in one of the bars most nights during the summer and it is particularly popular at weekends. The restaurant and bar offer simple, but excellent fare. ▯ ▯ ▯

Sherkin Island: *The Jolly Roger*
Co Cork. **Road map** B6.
Tel 028 20379.
Island atmosphere pervades this cozy pub, which serves outstandingly good-value lunches. In summer you can sit outside and admire the view of Baltimore Harbour and the bay. ▯ ▯ ▯

THE LOWER SHANNON

Annacotty: *Finnegan's*
Co Limerick. **Road map** B5.
Tel 061 337338.
Originally a 17th-century coach stop, history and folklore permeate this renowned establishment in County Limerick. Finnegan's specializes in steaks and freshly caught seafood. Cosy and extremely friendly. ▯ ▯

Ballyvaughan: *Monk's Pub*
The Pier, Co Clare. **Road map** B4.
Tel 065 707 7059.
This quaint pub is situated beside the pier, overlooking Galway Bay. Inside, country furniture and peat fires are matched by local seafood including chowder. There is also traditional Irish music performed. Ring for details.
▯ ▯ ▯ ▯

Bunratty: *Durty Nelly's*
Co Clare. **Road map** B4.
Tel 061 364861.
Set beside Bunratty Castle, this extremely commercialized pub appeals to locals as well as tourists. The 17th-century atmosphere is sustained by the warren of rooms, inglenook fireplaces and historical portraits. Traditional music is performed most evenings, and wholesome food is available both from the bar and from the two restaurants. ▯ ▯ ▯

Doolin: *McDermott's*
Roadford, Co Clare. **Road map** B4.
Tel 065 707 4328 or 707 4700.
No Clare pub is complete without a traditional music session and McDermott's does not disappoint. It has live music every night from St Patrick's Day until late October. A warm welcome and a cold pint are guaranteed by the staff. The original 1867 tiled floor is still in place. ▯ ▯ ▯

Doolin: *Gus O'Connor's*
Co Clare. **Road map** B4.
Tel 065 707 4168.
This famous pub is known to lovers of traditional music the world over. The pub has been in the O'Connor family for over 130 years and combines an authentic grocery store with a lively pub. This is the place for spontaneous music, simple bar food, young company and great "craic".
▯ ▯ ▯ ▯

Ennis: *The Cloister*
Abbey St, Co Clare. **Road map** B4.
Tel 065 682 9521.
This historic pub is situated by the famous Ennis Friary *(see p189)*. The pub's cozy, atmospheric interior is complemented by a patio in summer, and by traditional music on some nights. ▯

Ennis: *Queen's Front Bar*
Abbey St, Co Clare. **Road map** B4.
Tel 065 682 8963.
This historical pub, refurbished in 2009, lies beside the impressive ruins of Ennis Friary *(see p189)*. It serves superb, traditional Irish food. Good for families, the Queen's welcomes all ages.
▯ ▯ ▯

Killaloe: *Goosers*
Ballina, Co Clare. **Road map** C4.
Tel 061 375791.

This delightfully picturesque waterfront pub on the Ballina side of the river has a thatched roof, traditional interior and a welcoming atmosphere. Noted for its cuisine, Goosers serves reasonably priced seafood in the restaurant and satisfying "pub grub" in the rustic bar. 🍴 🚗 ♿ ♫

Kilrush: *Crotty's Pub*
Market Square, Co Clare.
Road map E4. *Tel* 065 905 2470.

This popular and award winning pub was once run by one of the foremost exponents of the concertina, Lizzie Crotty (1885–1960). Today it hosts live traditional music three nights of the week in summer. Tasty bar food is available all day Monday to Saturday. 🍴 🚗 ♿ ♫

Limerick: *The Locke*
3 George's Quay, Co Limerick.
Road map B4. *Tel* 061 413733.

Set on a quay on the Shannon, this is a typical black-and-white pub. In summer, it is a favourite port of call for riverside strollers. In winter, blazing fires and snugs make it a cozy spot. Traditional music is played from Sunday to Thursday nights. The restaurant is open all day. 🍴 🚗 ♿ ♫

Limerick: *Nancy Blake's*
19 Upper Denmark St, Co Limerick.
Road map B4. *Tel* 061 416443.

Limerick's best-known bar, Nancy Blake's has much to offer in the way of good "craic" and traditional music. If you prefer rhythm and blues, try the adjoining Outback Bar. The cozy main bar serves soup and sandwiches at lunchtime. Music is played on Monday, Wednesday, and Saturday. 🚗 ♫

THE WEST OF IRELAND

Aran Islands: *Ti Joe Mac's*
Kilronan, Inishmore, Co Galway.
Road map B2. *Tel* 099 61248.

This pub stands straight in front of visitors as they leave the boat. It serves soup and sandwiches. 🍴 🚗 ♫

Clarinbridge: *Moran's Oyster Cottage*
The Weir, Kilcolgan, Co Galway.
Road map B4. *Tel* 091 7961 3.

Set in a thatched cottage, this bar was a regular port of call for crews from passing "hookers' (traditional ships). Nowadays, you can sample all kinds of seafood here, though Moran's (see p333) is best known as the most famous oyster bar in Ireland – the owner holds the local speed record for shelling oysters. 🍴 🚗 ♿

Clarinbridge: *Paddy Burke's Oyster Inn*
Co Galway. **Road map** B4.
Tel 091 796226.

Founded in 1835, this authentic thatched pub has leaded window-panes and a charming beamed interior. Apart from the renowned Clarinbridge oysters and buffet lunches, gourmet menus are also available at lunch and dinner. 🍴 ♿

Clifden: *EJ Kings*
The Square, Co Galway.
Road map A3. *Tel* 095 21330.

This spacious, bustling pub is situated on several floors, with the ground floor the most appealing. Seafood platters or varied pub fare can be enjoyed by the peat fire. In summer live music is often on offer, especia ly folk and ballads. The staff are exceptionally friendly. 🍴 🚗 ♫

Galway: *Busker Brownes*
Cross St Upper, Co Galway.
Road map B4. *Tel* 091 563377.

This barn-like city pub occupies several storeys, including the shell of a 16th-century convent on the top floor. The Slate House, the pub next door is under the same management, and both are popular with local students. There are jazz sessions on Sundays. 🍴 🚗 ♿ ♫

Galway: *Cooke's Thatch Bar*
Cooke's Corner, 2 Newcastle Rd,
Co Galway. **Road map** B4. *Tel* 091 582959.

Situated on the outskirts of Galway, this traditional thatched inn has passed into new owner-ship after seven generations in the same family, but is still renowned for its friendliness. The pub includes an off-licence with over 20 wines on sale as well as beer and spirits. 🚗

Galway: *Dew Drop Inn*
Mainguard St, Co Galway.
Road map B4. *Tel* 091 561070.

Locally known as Myles Lee, this is an intimate, vintage pub that encapsulates Galway's Bohemian traditions. The authentic low level lighting makes this pub a comfy place, especially on cold nights when the log fire is crackling. The Dew Drop serves one of the best pints of Guinness in town

Galway: *The King's Head*
15 High St, Co Galway.
Road map B4. *Tel* 091 566630.

Founded in 1649, this historic pub is adorned with a bow-fronted façade. The homely interior contains 17th-century fireplaces. Simple lunch snacks are served in the main bar. In the back bar, various live bands playing in the evenings attract a youthful crowd. 🚗 ♿ ♫

Galway: *McSwiggen's*
Eyre St, Wood Quay, Co Galway.
Road map B4. *Tel* 091 568917.

In the centre of the city, the snug, relaxing bar has terracotta floors and comfortable seats. 🍴 ♿

Galway: *The Cottage*
79 Salthill Lower, Co Galway. **Road map** B4. *Tel* 091 526554.

This pub in County Galway has recently been refurbished. A quiet and intimate atmosphere prevails, making it a good place for a natter and a drink. On the downside, it is located in somewhat of an urban no man's land, halfway between Salthill and the city centre. 🍴

Galway: *The Quays*
Quay St, Co Galway. **Road map** B4.
Tel 091 568347.

The Quays was originally a small thatched cottage but the building was knocked down to make way for this three-storey bar. The top floor is a circular mezzanine that overlooks the rest of the bar. A good venue for music, the traditional music nights are Friday and Sunday evening. Hearty lunches are served daily. Outside seating during the summer months. 🍴 🚗 ♿ ♫

Galway: *Tigh Neachtain*
Quay St, Co Galway.
Road map B4. *Tel* 091 568820.

Set in the "Latin Quarter", this 18th-century town house boasts a distinctive oriel window. Inside, a musty wood interior is home to old-world snugs and friendly service. Traditional music can often be heard here, and upstairs is Arc Bia restaurant. 🍴 🚗 ♿ ♫

Killala: *Golden Acres* Co Mayo.
Road map B2. *Tel* 096 32163.

This comfortable pub is located near the major activity centres of the area. Deep-sea fishing, golf and boat trips are all within walking distance of this homely country bar. It features good pub food. 🍴 ♿ ♫

Oughterard: *The Boat Inn*
Conremara, Co Galway.
Road map B3. **Tel** 091 552196.
This hotel, bar and restaurant is
located next to Lough Corrib
on the edge of Connemara. The
lively boat-shaped bar serves bar
food and snacks. Local musicians
perform at weekends and
weekdays during the summer.
🏠 🍴 ♿ 🎵

Westport: *The Asgard Tavern*
The Quay, Co Mayo. **Road map** B3.
Tel 098 25319.
This old inn facing the pier and
Clew Bay is decorated with a
nautical theme. Both the main
downstairs back bar and the
upstairs restaurant provide
excellent seafood and salads.
The small downstairs front bar,
known as the snug, is the most
atmospheric. 🍴 ♿ 🎵

Westport: *Matt Molloy's*
Bridge St, Co Mayo. **Road map** B3.
Tel 098 26655.
Founded by the flautist from the
traditional Irish folk band The
Chieftains, this deceptively
spacious pub is designed along
equally traditional lines. There
is live music in the back room
every evening, when the pub is
packed. 🎵

NORTHWEST IRELAND

Burtonport: *The Lobster Pot*
Co Donegal. **Road map** C1.
Tel 074 954 2012.
This cosy pub lies near the pier.
The old timber surrounds of the
interior are used as a backdrop to
an incredible selection of Gaelic
sporting memorabilia. The
seafood is renowned as the best, but other
good dishes are served as well.
🍴 ♿ 🎵

Crolly: *Leo's Tavern*
Menaleck, Co Donegal.
Road map C1. **Tel** 074 954 8143.
Owned by the father of modern
folk musicians Clannad and of
the singer Enya, this friendly pub
attracts locals and tourists for its
sing-songs round the accordion,
and traditional music nights.
🍴 🏠 ♿ 🎵

Culdaff: *McGrory's*
Co Donegal. **Road map** C1.
Tel 074 937 9104.
On the idyllic Inishowen
Peninsula *(see pp226–7)*, this is
a place of quality food and drink.
McGrory's restaurant caters for up to
60 diners in a comfortable yet stylish
setting. The Backroom Bar, also
located in the pub, is a top music
venue, featuring live music of all
kinds. 🍴 🏠 ♿ 🎵

Donegal: *O'Donnell's*
The Diamond, Co Donegal.
Road map C2. **Tel** 074 972 1049.
This middle of the road venue has
a small bar. A larger lounge in the
back is used for live performances
and karaoke nights. Local
musicians entertain here on any
given night.
🏠 🎵 ♿

Dromahair: *Stanford Village Inn*
Main St, Co Leitrim.
Road map C2.
Tel 071 916 4140.
Set in a picturesque village, this
traditional pub has been in the
same family for generations. The
tiny, quaint Biddy's Bar remains
unchanged, adorned with family
portraits and old grocery jars.
The main bar has mellow brick-
work and flagstones from a
ruined castle. Delicious food
is on offer all day in the summer
and there are often impromptu
evening music sessions.
🍴 🏠 🎵

Sligo: *Osta*
Stephen St, Sligo. **Road map** C2.
Tel 071 914 4639.
This airy wine bar is located on
the bank of the Garavogue river.
The wines have been handpicked
by those in the know. It's also a
good stop for a bite to eat.
🍴

Sligo: *Hargadons*
4 O'Connell St, Co Sligo. **Road map**
C2. **Tel** 071 915 3709.
This is an old world pub that
sports an authentic interior to
match. Tasty bar food is available
along with a warm atmosphere.
Take advantage of the popular
summer beer garden on balmy
nights.
🍴 🏠

Strandhill: *Strand House Bar*
Strandhill, Co Sligo. **Road map** C2.
Tel 071 916 8140.
The turf fire here warms the
surfers from the nearby beach,
while the snugs make for perfect
one-to-one conversations over a
pint or some food. 🍴

Sligo: *Shoot the Crows*
Grattan St, Co Sligo. **Road map** C2.
This authentic, old world pub
attracts all kinds of colourful
characters and has a great atmosphere. Music is ambient jazz and
traditional Irish. 🎵

THE MIDLANDS

Abbeyleix: *Morrissey's*
Main St, Co Laois. **Road map** C4.
Tel 05787 31233.
If driving through County Laois,
it is worth stopping at this
genuinely traditional pub. The
18th-century inn was remodelled
in the Victorian era and has stayed
the same ever since. The grocery
section survives while the plain
and unpretentious bar serves
simple bar snacks. 🍴 🏠

Carlingford: *PJ O'Hare's
Anchor Bar*
Tholsel St, Co Louth. **Road map** D3.
Tel 042 937 3106.
Known locally as PJ's this atmos-
pheric pub and grocery store is
popular with sailors and locals alike.
A friendly and often eccentric
welcome is matched by bar food
such as oysters and sandwiches.
Music is played in the summer.
🍴 🏠 ♿ 🎵

Crinkill: *The Thatch*
Birr, Co Offaly. **Road map** C4.
Tel 05791 20682.
Mooted as *the* traditional pub,
the Thatch is one of the oldest
pubs in South Offaly and as its
name suggests, has always been
thatched. It has won All Ireland
Pub of the Year five times
and certainly lives up to its
reputation. Children are
welcome. 🍴 🏠

Dundalk: *The Jockeys*
47 Anne St, Co Louth.
Road map D3. **Tel** 042 933 4621.
This friendly pub offers home-
cooked lunches daily at very
reasonable prices. The walls are
covered in Gaelic Athletic
Association mementos *(see p29)*,
portraying its proud Gaelic sports'
tradition. This pub has been in
existence, in one guise or another,
since 1799. Live music on Friday
nights. 🍴 ♿ 🎵

Kilbeggan: *Locke's Distillery
Museum*
Mullingar, Co Westmeath.
Road map C3. **Tel** 05 93 32307.
As well as being the oldest licensed
pot still distillery in the world
(established in 1757) this historic
complex has a whiskey bar – the
ideal place to sample a few brands
before buying *(see p49)*. There is
an adjoining restaurant. 🍴 ♿

Kilnaleck: *The Copper Kettle*
Co Cavan. **Road map** C3.
Tel 0494 33623.
This lively family-run pub has
a wonderful atmosphere. It is
well known for its wholesome,

home-cooked meals, served all day. There's entertainment every Saturday night all year round. 🍴 ♿ 🪑 🎵

Kinnitty: The Dungeon Bar
Birr, Co Offaly.
Road map C4. **Tel** 05791 37318.
Sited in the basement of medieval Kinnitty Castle, less than a mile from Kinnitty village, this candle-lit bar is not quite as spooky as it sounds. Historic Irish memorabilia covers the walls and the food and drinks are well presented. There's traditional Irish music every Friday and Saturday night. 🍴 🪑 🎵

Longford: Edward
Valentine's Main St, Co Longford.
Road map C3. **Tel** 043 334 5509.
Relax in Edward Valentine's wonderful, warm, old-world atmosphere. There is a lively atmosphere at the weekends in what is otherwise a home away from home. ♿ 🪑 🎵

Portlaoise: O'Donoghues
Market Sq, Co Laois. **Road map** C4.
Tel 057 862 1199.
Leave the modern world behind and enjoy the traditional atmosphere of this award-winning, old style pub. This is the perfect spot for a quiet pint or a snack. The Seasons Restaurant is located overhead. ♿

Portlaoise: Tracey's Pub and Restaurant
The Heath, Co Laois.
Road map C4. **Tel** 05786 46539.
This charming thatched cottage pub and restaurant is 6 km (3 miles) outside of the town, but is well worth the journey. It is the oldest family-run pub in these parts, and there is a good range of pub grub (roasts, fish, salads) as well as prime steak at amazingly reasonable prices. 🍴 🪑

NORTHERN IRELAND

Ardglass: Curran's Bar & Seafood Steakhouse
83 Strangford Rd, Chapeltown, Co Down. **Road map** E2.
Tel 028 4484 1332.
This charming pub and restaurant is in the Curran ancestral home, which dates from 1791. Expect warm service and the freshest catch. A good choice for families with its play area and beer garden. 🍴 🧒 ♿ 🪑

Bangor: Jenny Watt's
41 High St, Co Down. **Road map** E2.
Tel 028 9127 0401.
Likable and very popular, this bar with Victoriana trimmings is found in the centre of town. The walls are adorned with local photos and memorabilia. There's live jazz at Sunday lunch times, and more music on Tuesdays Wednesdays and Thursdays. Bar food is served, and there's a beer garden. 🍴 🪑 🎵

Belfast: Crown Liquor Saloon
46 Great Victoria St, Co Antrim.
Road map D2. **Tel** 028 9027 9901.
This Victorian gin palace ranks as one of the most gorgeous bars in Ireland (*see p277*). Lunch includes several local specialities, such as Irish stew and champ, but the Strangford Lough oysters really do stand out. Robinson's, the pub next door, is particularly lively in the evening. 🍴

Belfast: Irene and Nans
12 Brunswick St, Co Antrim.
Road map D2. **Tel** 028 9023 9123.
Conveniently located close to the Grand Opera House, this stylish bar echoes with the spirit of the 1950s. The superb cocktail list and great menu make this the perfect place to be seen, with evening entertainment on Friday and Saturday. The staff are well-trained and courteous. 🍴 ♿ 🪑

Belfast: Lavery's
2–14 Bradbury Place, Co Antrim.
Road map D2. **Tel** 028 9087 1106.
Yet another of Belfast's fine old gin palaces. Bar food served at lunch and discos in the evenings. It is popular with students from Queen's University. 🍴 ♿ 🪑 🎵

Belfast: White's Tavern
Winecellar Entry, Co Antrim.
Road map D2. **Tel** 028 9024 3080.
Just one of several daylight-free pubs tucked away in the Entries (*see p277*) sector of Belfast city that are best at lunch time when decent, reasonably priced pub food is served. White's lays claim to be the oldest tavern (1630) in the city. Other pubs in this series of alleys that are worth a look include the Morning Star. 🍴 ♿ 🪑 🎵

Broughshane: The Thatch Inn
57 Main St, Co Antrim.
Road map D2.
Tel 028 2586 2727.
This old-thatched pub in the ancient village of Broughshane exudes charm, character and warmth. The Thatch Inn is well known for great food, warm welcomes and live music. 🍴 ♿ 🎵

Bushmills: Bushmills Inn
9 Dunluce Rd, Co Antrim.
Road map D1.
Tel 028 2073 2339.
Set in an old coaching inn, this cosy bar is lit by gaslights. There is also an excellent restaurant on the premises 🍴 🪑 ♿

Enniskillen: Blake's of the Hollow
6 Church St, Co Fermanagh
Road map C2.
Tel 028 6632 0918.
One of a number of popular town-centre pubs, Blake's dates back to Victorian days and has many of its original fittings. 🍴 ♿ 🎵

Hillsborough: Plough Inn
The Square, Co Down.
Road map D2.
Tel 028 9268 2985.
This typical village pub, dating from the 1750s, has wooden ceiling beams and a selection of crockery, china and other ornaments on the walls. There's a bistro upstairs open during the day, serving international dishes. The Hillside, just down the main street, is also worth a visit. 🍴 🪑 ♿ 🎵

Killylea: Digby's Bar & Restaurant
53 Main St, Co Armagh. **Road map** D2. **Tel** 028 3756 8390.
This friendly, traditional village inn, decorated with old photographs of local places and people, is family-run. It boasts an extensive menu with some good wines and is a relaxed, enjoyable venue for families. 🍴 🧒 ♿ 🪑

Londonderry: The Park Bar
35 Francis St, Co Londonderry.
Road map C1. **Tel** 028 7126 4624.
A warm, welcoming, family-run bar close to the city centre and adjacent to St Eugene's Cathedral. The usual choices of European lagers and Guinness are on tap.

Omagh: The Mellon Country Hotel
134 Beltany Rd, Co Tyrone.
Road map C2.
Tel 028 8166 1224.
Just 1 mile from the Ulster American Folk Park, this country inn is a popular stopping-off point. Set in the foothills of the Sperrin mountains, the inn overlooks the Strule River. A rustic interior is a reminder of the building's corn milling past. A casual, comfortable place with friendly service. 🍴

SHOPPING IN IRELAND

Ireland offers a wide range of handmade goods, usually regionally based and highly individual. Its most renowned products include chunky Aran sweaters, Waterford crystal, Irish linen, handloomed Donegal tweed and tasty farmhouse cheeses. The thriving crafts industry is based on traditional products with an innovative twist. Typical of contemporary Irish crafts are good design, quality craftsmanship and a range spanning

Linen shirt and tweed waistcoat

Celtic brooches, bone china, knitwear and designer fashion, carved bogwood and books of Irish poetry. Kitsch souvenirs also abound, from leprechauns and shamrock emblems to Guinness tankards and garish religious memorabilia. In the directory on page 355, a map reference is given for each address. Dublin shopping is covered in detail on pages 104–107. Road map references are to the towns and cities on the inside back cover.

Fruit and vegetable market in Moore Street, Dublin

WHERE TO SHOP

The choice of places to shop in Ireland ranges from tiny workshops to large factory outlets, and from elegant boutiques to high-street chain stores. Bargains can often be had at bric-a-brac shops and local markets, although the banter is sometimes the best thing on offer. This guide lists market days for every town featured. Sometimes the best produce or products are to be found off the beaten track; locals are always happy to let you know where.

WHEN TO SHOP

Most shops are open from Monday to Saturday, 9am to 5:30 or 6pm. In shopping centres and large towns, shops tend to have at least one late-night opening, usually on Thursday or Friday (Thursday in Dublin). In tourist areas, craft shops are generally open on Sundays too. Shops are closed at Easter and Christmas

and on St Patrick's Day but are open on most other public holidays. In Killarney, Ireland's tourist capital, most shops are open until 10pm in summer.

HOW TO PAY

Major credit cards are generally accepted in department stores and larger retail outlets, but smaller shops prefer cash. Most traveller's cheques are accepted in major stores with a passport as identification.

SALES TAX AND REFUNDS

Most purchases are subject to VAT (sales tax) at 21 per cent, included in the sales price. However, visitors from outside the European Union (EU) can reclaim VAT prior to departure. When shipping goods overseas, refunds can be claimed at the point of purchase. If taking your goods with you, look for the CashBack logo in shops, fill in the special voucher, then visit CashBack offices at Dublin or Shannon Airport.

BOOKS

Reading is a national passion in Ireland, so bookshops are generally very good. In bigger shops expect solid sections on Irish archaeology and architecture, folklore, history, politics and cuisine. **Eason and Son** is one of the country's most widespread bookstore chains with a large collection of Irish literature and newspapers. Seek out the smaller, "Irish Interest" shops too. In Galway, **Kenny's Books**, hidden away in an industrial area, is packed with both new and second-hand books.

MUSIC

Traditional musical instruments (see pp24–5) are made in many regions, especially County Clare, also known as the "singing county". Handmade harps are a speciality in Mayo and Dublin. Instruments such as handcrafted *bodhráns*, uillean pipes, tin whistles

A traditional fiddle maker in his workshop in Dingle

Colourful bric-a-brac shop in Kilkenny

and fiddles are on sale throughout Ireland. There are several specialist record shops that sell traditional Irish recordings. **Golden Discs** is a chain of music stores, and stocks a good selection of traditional Irish music.

FOOD AND DRINK

Markets have become a popular way to shop for food in Irish cities. Most of what's on offer is produced locally under organic conditions. Smoked salmon, home-cured bacon, farmhouse cheeses, soda bread, preserves and handmade chocolates make perfect last-minute gifts.

Guinness travels less well and is best drunk in Ireland. Irish whiskey is hard to beat as a gift or souvenir. Apart from the cheaper Power's and Paddy brands, the big names are Bushmills *(see p266)* and Jameson *(see p179)*. Rich Irish liqueurs include Irish Mist and Baileys Irish Cream.

CRAFTS

Crafts are a flourishing way of life in rural Ireland, and the distinctive products can be purchased from either city department stores or work-shops and individual vendors. The **Crafts Council of Ireland** has branches in Dublin and Kilkenny, and can recommend good small-scale outlets in the country. Tourist offices also provide lists of local workshops, where you can watch the production

process. Craft shops, such as the **Kilkenny Design Centre** and **Bricín**, sell good examples of different crafts. In Cork and Kerry there is an abundance of workshops, mainly in Kinsale and Dingle. The *Guide to Craft Outlets* is available at local tourist offices. Distinctive products from this area are traditional tiles based on designs found in Kilkenny Cathedral and nearby medieval abbeys. Further west, green Connemara marble is made into "worry stones", small charms traditionally exchanged between families as marks of long-lasting friendship. Also in Connemara, **Roundstone Music** makes "bodhrans" in front of interested tourists.

Other crafts include metalwork, leatherwork and carpentry. Local woods are used for ash or beech furni-ture, blackthorn walking sticks and sculptures made of 1,000-year-old bogwood – petrified wood salvaged from Ireland's unique boglands during turf cutting.

Kylemore Abbey teapot

CRYSTAL AND GLASSWARE

In the wake of Waterford Crystal *(see p147)*, the brand leader comes countless fol-lowers. The price depends on reputation, the quantity of lead used in the glass and the labour-intensiveness of the design. **Tipperary Crystal** offers a range of lines and **Galway Irish Crystal** is another elegant brand.

In Kilkenny, the famous Jerpoint Abbey inspires local designs by **Jerpoint Glass**. Decorated with simple yet stylish motifs, the small vases, candlesticks, jugs and bowls make pleasing gifts. Most stores will pack and send glassware overseas for you.

Crystal from around Ireland can be found in most craft and design shops, but if you want to see how glass is made it's best to visit a factory.

CERAMICS AND CHINA

Although more renowned for crystal, Ireland also has many reputable producers of ceram-ics and china. Established in 19th-century Ulster, Belleek Pottery *(see p269)* produces creamy china with a lustrous sheen and subtle decorative motifs, including shamrocks and flowers. In Galway, **Royal Tara China** is Ireland's leading fine bone china manufacturer, with Celtic-influenced designs, while Kylemore Abbey *(see p208)* specializes in exquisite handpainted pottery. **Louis Mulcahy's Pottery**, in Bally-ferriter, is noted for fine decorative glazes, while in Bennettsbridge, **Nicholas Mosse Pottery** produces hand-painted designs. Enniscorthy in Wexford is another centre for ceramics.

Pottery display in Kilkenny Design Centre

Old sign for the linen department at a former Brown Thomas store

LINEN

Damask linen was brought to Armagh by Huguenot refugees fleeing French persecution during the late 17th century. As a result, Belfast became the world's linen capital. Ulster is still the place for linen, with sheets and double-damask table linen on sale in Belfast – at **Smyth's Irish Linen**, for example – and in other towns. Linen, embroidered by hand, is made in Donegal. Linen-making can be seen at Wellbrook Beetling Mill (*see p268*).

KNITWEAR AND TWEED

Aran sweaters are sold all over Ireland, particularly in County Galway and on the Aran Islands themselves. One of Ireland's best buys, these oiled, off-white sweaters used to be handed down through generations of Aran fishermen. Legend has it that each family used its own motifs. If a fisherman died at sea and his body

was unidentifiable, his family could recognize him by his sweater.

Given the Irish experience of wet weather, warm and waterproof clothes are generally of good quality, from waxed jackets and duffel coats to sheepskin jackets. Knitwear is on sale all over Ireland. **Avoca Handweavers** and **Blarney Woollen Mills** are the best-known outlets. Good buys include embroidered sweaters and waistcoats as well as hand-woven shawls, hats, caps and scarves.

Donegal tweed is a byword for quality, and is noted for its texture, tension and subtle colours (originally produced by dyes made from lichens and minerals). Tweed caps, scarves, ties and suits are sold in outlets such as **Magee of Donegal**.

Interior of Avoca Handweavers in Kilmacanogue

JEWELLERY

In its golden age, Celtic metalwork was the pride of Ireland (*see pp32–5*), and many contemporary craftspeople are still inspired by traditional Celtic designs. Handcrafted or factory-made silver, gold and ceramic jewellery is produced in a variety of designs. The Claddagh ring from Galway is the most famous Celtic design – the lovers' symbol of two hands

cradling a crowned heart. **Cahalan Jewellers** in County Galway is one of the most renowned and has a huge range of unique Irish and antique jewellery. For heraldic jewellery, try **James Murtagh Jewellers** in County Mayo.

FASHION

Inspired by a predominantly young population, Ireland is fast acquiring a name for fashion. Conservatively cut tweed and linen suits continue to be models of classic good taste, though young designers are increasingly experimental, using bold lines and mixing traditional fabrics.

A-Wear is a good value chain of stores that features funky, young designs for women and has branches in most cities. At the long-established **Brown Thomas** on Grafton Street and in many small boutiques, you will find clothes designed by the best Irish designers, including Quin and Donnelly, Paul Costelloe, John Rocha, Louise Kennedy and Mariad Whisker.

Some designers, such as Pauric Sweene, Eilish Kennedy and Heidi Higgins, have eschewed traditional Irish textiles and forged fresh styles in new materials.

Ladies' fashion and the hottest trends can be found in **O'Donnell's** in Limerick, while up north, there are many outlets of **Clockwork Orange** and **Fosters Clothing**. For a unique boudoir-style shoe shopping experience, try **The Pink Room** near Carlingford Lough.

For budget clothing Dunnes Stores and Penneys have branches throughout the Republic and Northern Ireland. Clothing and shoe sizes are identical to British fittings.

Selection of hand-knitted sweaters at a craft shop in Dingle

DIRECTORY

BOOKS

Eason and Son
113 Patrick's St, Cork, Co Cork. **Road map** C5. *Tel 021 427 0477.* www.easons.ie

Kenmare Bookshop
Shelburne St, Kenmare, Co Kerry. **Road map** B6. *Tel 064 41578.*

Kenny's Books
Kilkerrin Pk, Liosban, Tuam Rd, Galway, Co Galway. **Road map** B4. *Tel 091 709 350.* www.kennys.ie

McLoughlin's Books
Shop Street. Westport, Co Mayo. **Road map** B3. *Tel 098 27777.*

MUSIC

The Dingle Record Shop
Green St, Dingle, Co Kerry. **Road map** A5. *Tel 087 298 4550.* www. dinglerecordshop.com

Golden Discs
Eglinton St, Galway, Co Galway. **Road map** B4. *Tel 091 565688.*

Hickey's Music Shop
Clonakilty, Co Cork. **Road map** B5. *Tel 023 36666*

FOOD AND DRINK

McCambridges
38–39 Shop St, Galway, Co Galway. **Road map** B4. *Tel 091 562259.*

Spillane Seafoods
Lackabane, Killarney, Co Kerry. **Road map** B5. *Tel 064 31320.*

CRAFTS

Bricín
26 High St, Killarney, Co Kerry. **Road map** B5. *Tel 064 66 34902.*

Crafts Council of Ireland
Castle Yard, Kilkenny, Co Kilkenny. **Road map** C4. *Tel 056 776 1804.*

Doolin Crafts Gallery
Ballyvoe, Doolin, Co Clare. **Road map** B4. *Tel 065 707 4309.* www.doolincrafts.com

Geoffrey Healy Pottery
Rocky Valley, Kilmacanogue, Co Wicklow. **Road map** D4. www. healy-pottery.com

Kilkenny Design Centre
Castle Yard, Kilkenny, Co Kilkenny. **Road map** C4. *Tel 056 7722118.* www. kilkennydesign.com

Roundstone Music
Roundstone, Connemara. **Road map** B4. *Tel 095 35875.* www.bodhran.com

The Wicker Man
44–46 High St, Belfast, Co Antrim. **Road map** D2. *Tel 028 9024 3550.*

West Cork Craft
Rossnagoose, Skibbereen, Co Cork. **Road map** B6. *Tel 028 21890* www. westcorkcraft.org

CRYSTAL AND GLASSWARE

Connemara Marble Factory
Moycullen, Co Galway. **Road map** B4. *Tel 091 555102.*

Galway Irish Crystal
Merlin Park, Galway Co Galway. **Road map** B4. *Tel 091 757311.*

Jerpoint Glass
Stoneyford, Co Kilkenny. **Road map** D5. *Tel 056 772 4350*

Sligo Crystal
2 Hyde Bridge, Sligo, Co Sligo. **Road map** C2. *Tel 071 914 3440.*

Tipperary Crystal
Ballynoran, Carrick-on-Suir, Co Tipperary. **Road map** C5. *Tel 051 640543.*

CERAMICS AND CHINA

Louis Mulcahy's Pottery
Clogher, Ballyferriter, Dingle, Co Kerry. **Road map** A5. *Tel 066 915 6229.*

Michael Kennedy Ceramics
Bolands Lane, Gort, Co Galway. **Road map** B4. *Tel 091 632245.* www.michaelkennedy ceramics.com

Nicholas Mosse Pottery
Bennettsbridge, Co Kilkenny. **Road map** D5. *Tel 056 772 7505.* www.nicholas mosse.com

Royal Tara China
Tara Hall, Mervue, Co Galway **Road map** B4 *Tel 091 705602.* www.royaltara.com

Treasure Chest
31–33 William St, Galway, Co Galway. **Road map** B4. *Tel 091 567237.*

LINEN

Forgotten Cotton
Savoy Centre St Patrick's St, Cork, Co Cork. **Road map** C5 *Tel 021 427 6198.*

Smyth's Irish Linen
65 Royal Ave, Belfast, Co Antrim. **Road map** D2. *Tel 028 9024 2232.*

KNITWEAR AND TWEED

Avoca Handweavers
Kilmacanogue, Co Wicklow. **Road map** D4. *Tel 01 286 7466.*

Blarney Woollen Mills
Blarney, Co Cork. **Road map** B5. *Tel 021 438 5280.*

Magee of Donegal
The Diamond, Donegal, Co Donegal. **Road map** C2. *Tel 074 972 2560.*

Quills Woollen Market
1 High St, Killarney, Co Kerry. **Road map** B5. *Tel 064 66 32277*

Studio Donegal
The Glebe Mill, Kilcar, Co Donegal. **Road map** B2. *Tel 074 973 8194.*

JEWELLERY

Cahalan Jewellers
Main St, Ballinasloe Co Galway. **Road map** B2. *Tel 09096 42513.*

Hilser Brothers
Grand Parade, Cork Co Cork. **Road map** C5. *Tel 021 427 0382.*

James Murtagh Jewellers
14 Bridge St, Westport, Co Mayo. **Road map** B3. *Tel 098 25322.*

O'Shea's Jewellers
24 Main St, Killarney, Co Kerry. **Road map** B5. *Tel 064 66 32720.*

FASHION

A-Wear
Grafton St, Dublin 2. **Road map** D3. *Tel 01 472 4960.* www. awear.com

Brown Thomas
2 Grafton St, Dublin 2. **Road map** D3. *Tel 01 605 6566* www. brownthomas.com

Clockwork Orange
Victoria Square, Belfast, Co Antrim. **Road map** D2. *Tel 028 9032 0298.*

Fosters Clothing
5 Strand Rd, Londonderry, Co Londonderry. **Road map** C1. *Tel 028 7136 6902.*

O'Donnell's
11 Catherine St, Limerick, Co Limerick. **Road map** B4. *Tel 061 415932.*

The Pink Room
Dundalk St, Carlingford Co Louth. **Road map** D3. *Tel 042 9383 669.*

What to Buy in Ireland

St Brigid's cross

Hundreds of gift and craft shops scattered throughout Ireland make it easy to find Irish specialities to suit all budgets. The best buys include linen, tweeds and crystal from factory shops which invariably offer an extensive choice of good quality products. Local crafts make unique souvenirs, from hand-made jewellery and ceramics to traditional musical instruments. Religious artifacts are also widely available. Irish food and drink are evocative reminders of your trip.

Traditional hand-held drum (*bodhrán*) and beater

Connemara marble "worry stone"

Traditional Claddagh ring

Enamel brooch

Bronzed resin Celtic figurine

Modern jewellery and metalwork *draw on a long and varied tradition. Craftspeople continue to base their designs on sources such as the Book of Kells (see p64) and Celtic myths. Local plants and wildlife are also an inspiration. County Galway produces Claddagh rings – traditional betrothal rings – in gold and silver as well as "worry stones".*

Fuchsia earring from Dingle

Celtic-design enamel brooch

Donegal tweed jacket and waistcoat

Tweed skirt and jacket

Clothing *made in Ireland is usually of excellent quality. Tweed-making still flourishes in Donegal where tweed can be bought ready-made as clothing and hats or as lengths of cloth. Knitwear is widely available all over the country in large factory outlets and local craft shops. The many hand-knitted items on sale, including Aran sweaters, are not cheap but should give years of wear.*

Tweed cap

Tweed fisherman's hat

Aran sweater

Irish linen *is world-famous and the range unparalleled. There is a huge choice of table and bed linen, including extravagant bedspreads and crisp, formal tablecloths. On a smaller scale, tiny, intricately embroidered handkerchiefs make lovely gifts as do linen table napkins. Tea towels printed with colourful designs are widely available. You can also buy linen goods trimmed with fine lace, which is still hand-made in Ireland, mainly in Limerick and Kenmare.*

Set of linen placemats and napkins

Nicholas
Mosse
plate

Nicholas
Mosse
cup

Belleek
teapot

Fine linen handkerchiefs

Irish ceramics *come in traditional and modern designs. You can buy anything from a full dinner service by established factories, such as Royal Tara China or the Belleek Pottery, to a one-off contemporary piece from a local potter's studio.*

IRISH PROVERBS

ILLUSTRATED BY
KAREN BAILEY

Book of Irish Proverbs

Books and stationery *are often beautifully illustrated. Museums and bookshops stock a wide range.*

Irish crystal, *hand-blown and hand-cut can be ordered or bought in many shops in Ireland. Visit the outlets of the principal manufacturers, such as Waterford Crystal and Jerpoint Glass, to see the full range— from glasses and decanters to elaborate chandeliers.*

**Celtic-design
cards**

**Waterford crystal tumbler
and decanter**

Food and drink *will keep the distinctive tastes of Ireland fresh long after you arrive home. Whiskey connoisseurs should visit the Old Bushmills Distillery (see p265) or the Jameson Heritage Centre (see*

p179) to sample their choice of whiskeys. Good regional food can be found at local shops all over Ireland. Try the dried seaweed, which is eaten raw or added to cooked dishes.

| Jameson | Bushmills | Fruit cake made | Jar of Irish | Packet of dried |
| whiskey | whiskey | with Guinness | marmalade | seaweed |

ENTERTAINMENT IN IRELAND

If there is one sphere in which Ireland shines, it is entertainment. For details about entertainment in Dublin, see pages 108–15. Elsewhere in Ireland, nightclubs and concerts by international entertainers tend to be concentrated in large cities, but many other events including theatre, arts festivals, traditional music and dance, cultural holidays and even medieval banquets take place all over the country. Most towns and cities also have one or two cinemas showing the latest movies on release.

Morris Minor van advertising the Clonakilty Folk Club

Not to be overlooked is the free entertainment (planned or spontaneous) provided by a night in a pub. For more active forms of entertainment, covered on pages 362–7, the list is even longer, from golf to pony trekking and cycling to scuba diving. Those who prefer their sports sitting down can go along as spectators to Ireland's famous horse race meetings, as well as Gaelic football, hurling, soccer and rugby matches. A happy mix of these activities can easily be put together with almost any itinerary.

Ulster Symphony Orchestra at the Ulster Hall in Belfast

INFORMATION SOURCES

The tourist board for the Republic, **Fáilte Ireland**, and the **Northern Ireland Tourist Board** (see p371) both publish a yearly *Calendar of Events* that lists major fixtures around the country, and all the regional tourist offices have information about happenings in each locality. To supplement these listings, check regional newspapers and inquire locally.

BOOKING TICKETS

Tickets can usually be bought at the door on the day or evening of most events. Advance booking is a must, however, for popular concerts and plays. Many cultural and arts festivals require tickets only for the key performances, but for internationally famous festivals, such as the Wexford Opera Festival, you will need to book well in advance through the festival office for all performances.

Credit-card bookings for plays, concerts and other events around Ireland can be made by telephone through **Keith Prowse Travel (IRL) Ltd** and **Ticketmaster** in Dublin.

MAJOR VENUES

In many Irish cities, the main theatres host a huge variety of events. In Cork, the **Opera House** presents predominantly Irish plays during the summer, with musical comedy, opera and ballet at other times of year. The city's **Everyman Palace Theatre** stages plays by local and visiting companies interspersed with concerts of both classical and popular music. Sligo's **Hawks Well Theatre**, Limerick's **Belltable Arts Centre** and Carlow's **George Bernard Shaw Theatre** are venues for drama and concerts. In Belfast, the **Grand Opera House, Waterfront Hall** and **Lyric Theatre** present Irish and international plays, experimental drama, pantomime and opera.

THEATRE

From international tours to amateur productions, there is excellent theatre to be seen in virtually every location in Ireland. In Galway, the **Druid Theatre** specializes in avant-garde plays, new Irish plays and Anglo-Irish classics, with frequent lunchtime and late-night performances, while Gaelic drama, Irish music, singing and dancing have all thrived at the **Taibhdhearc Theatre** since 1928. Waterford boasts its resident Red Kettle Theatre Company which performs at the **Garter Lane Theatre**, while the **Theatre Royal** brings amateur drama and musicals to the city.

Keep an eye out for small theatre groups performing in local halls around the country. Many of them are superb and they have spawned several of Ireland's leading actors.

Home of the Druid Theatre Company in Galway (see p210)

The Moscow Ballet at Belfast's Grand Opera House *(see p276)*

CLASSICAL MUSIC, OPERA AND DANCE

Major venues for classical music include the **Crawford Art Gallery**, Opera House and Everyman Palace in Cork; the Theatre Royal in Waterford; the Hawks Well Theatre in Sligo; and the Belltable Arts Centre in Limerick. Belfast's **Ulster Hall** hosts concerts from rock bands to the Ulster Symphony Orchestra.

Opera lovers from around the world come to Ireland for the **Wexford Festival of Opera** in October and November and the **Waterford Festival of Light Opera** in late September and early October. At Wexford, neglected operas are revived, while Waterford selects more mainstream operas and musicals. Elsewhere, opera is performed in Cork's Opera House and in Belfast's Grand Opera House.

Ireland has no resident ballet or avant-garde dance companies, but leading international companies perform occasionally at the major venues around the country.

ROCK, JAZZ AND COUNTRY

When international music stars tour Ireland, concerts outside Dublin are held at large outdoor sites. **Semple Stadium** in County Tipperary and Slane Castle *(see p255)* in County Meath are popular venues. Tickets and information are available from Ticketmaster.

Musical pubs *(see pp346–51)* are your best bet for good rock and jazz performed by Irish groups. Check local tourist offices and newspapers for rock and jazz nights, which usually take place midweek, with country and traditional music at weekends. For some

of Ireland's "big band" jazz music, keep an eye out for Waterford's Brass and Co who play at dances around the country. Jazz lovers have a field day at the **Cork Jazz Festival** in late October, when music pours from every pub and international jazz greats play in the city's theatres.

Pub scene at Feakle Traditional Music Weekend, County Clare

TRADITIONAL MUSIC AND DANCE

The country pub has helped keep Irish music alive and provided the setting for the musical revival that began in the 1960s. Today, sessions of informal or impromptu music are still commonplace. In pubs, traditional music embraces ballads and rebel songs, as well as the older *sean-nos* – unaccompanied, understated stories, often sung in Irish.

Nights of Irish music and song are scheduled in many pubs, such as The Laurels and the Danny Mann in Killarney, the Yeats Tavern in Drumcliff, near Sligo, and An Brog in Cork. In Derry, the Gweedore Bar, Castle Bar and Dungloe Bar are among the cluster of musical pubs along Waterloo Street. Wherever you are, a query to the locals will send you off to the nearest musical pub. For more pub listings, *see pages 346–51*.

In Tralee, **Siamsa Tíre**, the National Folk Theatre, stages marvellous folk drama incorporating traditional music, singing and dance. The Barn, in Bunratty Folk Park, is the setting for a traditional Irish night during the summer months.

Comhaltas Ceoltóirí Éireann, in Monkstown *(see p102)* has branches around the country and organizes traditional music and dance nights all year. Traditional Irish dancing can be stylish step dancing or joyous set dancing. Visitors are usually encouraged to join in the fun.

The Fleadh Cheoil (national traditional music festival) is a weekend of music, dance, song and stage shows that spill over into colourful street entertainment. It takes place at the end of August in a different town each year and attracts large crowds. Earlier in August, the **Feakle Traditional Music Weekend** in County Clare is a more intimate celebration of traditional music, song and dance

A large audience for open-air music at the Cork Jazz Festival

Knappogue banquet at Knappogue Castle, County Clare

Most famous are the medieval banquets – the one at Bunratty Castle (see pp192–3) was the first and is the liveliest, with year-round performances. From April to October, there is a medieval banquet at Knappogue Castle (see p189), and at Dunguaire Castle (see p212) there is a quieter, more intimate programme of music and poetry. From March until November, the highly enjoyable Killarney Manor Banquet, held at the stately manor on the Loreto road just south of Killarney, creates an early 19th-century atmosphere.

FESTIVALS

The Irish are experts at organizing festivals, staging a week of street entertainment, theatre, music and dance to celebrate almost everything under the sun (see pp48–51).

In mid-July the lively town of Galway is host to the **Galway Arts Festival**, one of the largest festivals in Ireland. Here you will find Irish and international theatre and music, street entertainment and events for children. Taking place over one week in late July and early August is the **Boyle Arts Festival**. The events here include art exhibitions, poetry and drama performances as well as classical, traditional, folk and jazz concerts. Creative workshops are run for both adults and children.

Kilkenny Arts Festival in August, another major festival, features poetry, classical music concerts, movies and a range of crafts. The **Cork Film Festival** takes place within the first two weeks of October when international feature, documentary and short films are screened at venues all over the city. The **Belfast Festival at Queen's** is held for two weeks in October to late November. The lively and cosmopolitan programme includes a mixture of drama, ballet, comedy, cabaret, music and film. These take over the Queen's University campus plus theatres and other venues throughout Belfast.

In May, June, and July the **County Wicklow Gardens Festival** entices gardening enthusiasts to wander around

the county's most beautiful gardens. In mid-June, the **Music in Great Irish Houses** festival opens the doors to many of Ireland's historic homes to which the public seldom has access, with classical music performed by top-rate musicians. Venues include Mount Stewart House (see pp282–3) and University College, Cork.

Kilkenny Arts Week street theatre

TRADITIONAL BANQUETS WITH ENTERTAINMENT

Ireland's banquets have gained international fame and are great fun. Each of the banquets features costumed waiters and performers, as well as traditional food and drink of the chosen period.

CULTURAL BREAKS

A break in Ireland focused on any one of the cultural aspects of Irish life is enriching as well as fun. Choose from a variety of cultural topics and study courses: Irish music and literature, great houses and gardens, Irish language and folklore, crafts and cookery.

One of the most fascinating possibilities is the exploration of Ireland's 5,000-year history as revealed in the many relics strewn across the landscape. The **Achill Archaeological Summer School** in County Mayo, for example, runs a course that includes the active excavation of ancient sites.

To learn the secret of Irish cooking, there is no better place than the **Ballymaloe School of Cookery** in County Cork; it is run by Darina Allen, Ireland's most famous cook.

For literature enthusiasts, the **Yeats International Summer School** studies the works of Yeats and his contemporaries, while **Listowel Writers' Week** brings together leading writers for lectures and workshops.

Folk dancers in traditional Irish costume

DIRECTORY

BOOKING TICKETS

Keith Prowse Travel (IRL) Ltd
Irish Life Mall, Dublin 1.
Tel 01 878 3500.
www.keithprowse.com

Ticketmaster
Grafton House,
70 Grafton St, Dublin 2.
Tel 01 648 6060.
www.ticketmaster.ie

MAJOR VENUES

Belltable Arts Centre
69 O'Connell St, Limerick.
Tel 061 319866.
www.belltable.ie

Everyman Palace Theatre
MacCurtain St, Cork.
Tel 021 450 1673.
www.everymanpalace.com

George Bernard Shaw Theatre
Old Dublin Rd,
Carlow, Co Carlow.
Tel 059 917 2400.
www.gbshawtheatre.ie

Grand Opera House
Great Victoria St, Belfast.
Tel 028 9024 1919.
www.goh.co.uk

Hawks Well Theatre
Johnston Ct, Sligo.
Tel 071 916 1518.
www.hawkswell.com

Lyric Theatre
55 Ridgeway St, Belfast.
Tel 028 9038 5685.
www.lyrictheatre.co.uk

Opera House
Emmet Place, Cork.
Tel 021 427 0022.
www.corkoperahouse.ie

Waterfront Hall
2 Lanyon Place, Belfast.
Tel 028 9033 4400.
www.waterfront.co.uk

THEATRE

Druid Theatre
Chapel Lane, Galway.
Tel 091 568660.
www.druidtheatre.com

Garter Lane Theatre
22A O'Connell St,
Waterford.
Tel 051 855038.
www.garterlane.ie

Taibhdhearc Theatre
Middle St, Galway.
Tel 091 562024.
www.antaibhdhearc.com

Theatre Royal
The Mall, Waterford.
Tel 051 874402.
www.theatreroyal.ie

CLASSICAL MUSIC, OPERA AND DANCE

Crawford Art Gallery
Emmet Place, Cork.
Tel 021 490 7855. www.crawfordartgallery.ie

Ulster Hall
Bedford St, Belfast.
Tel 028 9032 3900.
www.ulsterhall.co.uk

Waterford Festival of Light Opera
Theatre Royal, Waterford.
Tel 051 874402.
www.waterfordfestiva.com

Wexford Festival of Opera
Theatre Royal, High St, Wexford.
Tel 053 912 2144.
www.wexfordopera.com

ROCK, JAZZ AND COUNTRY

Cork Jazz Festival
20 South Mall, Cork
Tel 021 427 0463.
www.corkjazzfestival.com

Semple Stadium
Thurles, Co Tipperary.
Tel 0504 22702.

TRADITIONAL MUSIC AND DANCE

Comhaltas Ceoltóirí Éireann
32 Belgrave Sq,
Monkstown, Co Dublin.
Tel 01 280 0295.
www.comhaltas.com

Feakle Traditional Music Weekend
Maghera, Caher, Co Clare.
Tel 061 9243885.
www.feaklefestival.ie

Siamsa Tíre
National Folk Theatre,
The Town Park, Tralee,
Co Kerry.
Tel 066 712 3055.

The Traditional Irish Night
Bunratty Castle and Folk Park, Bunratty, Co Clare.
Tel 061 360788. www.shannonheritage.com

FESTIVALS

Belfast Festival at Queen's
Festival House, 25 College Gardens, Belfast.
Tel 028 9097 1197.
www.belfastfestival.com

Boyle Arts Festival
King House Main St,
Boyle, Co Roscommon.
Tel 071 966 3085.
www.boylearts.com

Cork Film Festival
Emmet House, Emmet Place, Cork. Tel 021 427 1711.
www.corkfilmfest.org

County Wicklow Gardens Festival
St Manntan's House,
Kilmantin Hill, Wicklow.
Tel 0404 20070.

Galway Arts Festival
Black Box Theatre, Dyke Rd, Terryland, Galway.
Tel 091 509700. www.galwayartsfestival.com

Kilkenny Arts Festival
9/10 Abbey Business Centre, Kilkenny.
Tel 056 775 2175.
www.kilkennyarts.ie

Music in Great Irish Houses
29 Rose Pk, Dun Laoghaire, Co Dublin.
Tel 01 664 2822. www.musicgreatirishhouses.com

CULTURAL BREAKS

Archaeology
Achill Archaeological Summer School
Folk Life Centre, Dooagh, Achill Island, Co. Mayo.
Tel 098 43564. www.achill-fieldschool.com

Gerard Manley-Hopkins Summer School
Great Connell,
Newbridge, Co. Kildare.
Tel 045 433613. www.gerardmanleyhopkins.org

Cookery
Ballymaloe School of Cookery
Shanagarry, Midleton,
Co Cork.
Tel 021 464 6785.
www.cookingisfun.ie

Houses, Castles & Gardens of Ireland
16A Woodlands Pk,
Blackrock, Co Dublin.
Tel 01 298 3714.
www.gardensireland.com;
www.castlesireland.com

National Trust
Rowallane House,
Saintfield, Ballynahinch,
Co Down.
Tel 028 9751 0721.
www.ntni.org.uk

Irish Language
Conversation Classes
Oidhreacht Chorca Dhuibhne, Ballyferriter,
Co Kerry.
Tel 066 915 6700.

Literary
Goldsmith Summer School
Rathmore, Ballymahon,
Co Longford
Tel 043 667 1423.
www.goldsmithfestival.ie

James Joyce Summer School
University College Dublin,
Belfield, Dublin 4.
Tel 01 716 8159.

Listowel Writers' Week
24 The Square, Listowel,
Co Kerry. Tel 068 21074.
www.writersweek.ie

William Carleton Summer School
Dungannon District Council, Circular Rd,
Dungannon, Co Tyrone.
Tel 028 8772 5311.

Yeats International Summer School
Yeats Society, Yeats Memorial Building,
Douglas Hyde Bridge, Sligo.
Tel 071 914 2693.
www.yeats-sligo.com

Music
Willie Clancy Summer School
Miltown Malbay, Co Clare. Tel 065 708 4148.

Sports and Outdoor Activities

Sign outside a fishing tackle shop in Donegal

Even in the largest Irish cities, the countryside is never far away, and it beckons alluringly to every lover of the great outdoors. Topping the list of spectator sports is Ireland's famous horse racing, followed by hurling, Gaelic football and soccer, which also make for very exciting viewing. Those who want to do more than just watch, can choose between fishing, golf, horse riding, sailing, cycling, walking and water sports. Entire vacations can be based around any of these activities. In addition to the contacts on pages 366–7, Fáilte Ireland in the Republic, the Northern Ireland Tourist Board and all local tourist offices have information on spectator and participant sports. For details of main events in the sporting calendar, see pages 28–9.

Steeplechase at Fairyhouse Racecourse

SPECTATOR SPORTS

The Irish passion for horse racing is legendary. **The Curragh** (*see p129*), where the Irish Derby is held, is a leading racecourse. **Fairyhouse**, the venue for Ireland's Grand National, is a popular spot year round, but especially around Christmas when Dubliners descend to lay bets on the annual races. **Punchestown**, in County Kildare, has been a fixture of the racing scene for more than 150 years and has a capacity of 80,000 people. **Leopardstown** in Dublin is also a well-liked track and has year round racing.

Many smaller racecourses, with exciting, informal atmospheres, are found throughout Ireland. Galway Race Week in late July is a great social event. A racing calendar for the whole of Ireland, available from **Horse Racing**

Ireland, lists National Hunt and flat race meets, which occur on 230 days of the year.

There are also 18 recognized greyhound stadia operating in the Republic. The best known are Dublin's **Shelbourne Park** and **Harold's Cross Stadium**, both of which have excellent dining facilities.

Croke Park hosts Gaelic football and hurling matches. International rugby and soccer matches are usually held at the **Aviva Stadium**, Ireland's most impressive sports stadium. For soccer tickets, contact the **Football Association of Ireland**. Rugby enthusiasts should get in touch with the **Irish Rugby Football Union**.

For golfers, the annual highlight is the Irish Open Golf Championship in July. The venue varies from year to year. For tickets and information, contact the **European Tour**.

FISHING

With its abundant coastline and some of the cleanest stretches of freshwater found in all of Europe, Ireland is a paradise for anglers. Coarse, game and sea fishing are all very popular. The lakes and rivers are home to bream, pike, perch and roach. Coastal rivers yield the famous Irish salmon, along with other game fish. The sea trout and brown trout also offer anglers a challenge.

Flounder, whiting, mullet, bass and coalfish tempt the sea angler, while deep-sea excursions chase abundant supplies of dogfish, shark, skate and ling. You can plan sea-angling trips from many different places – the Cork and Kerry coastline is a highly favoured starting point.

Clonanav Fly Fishing Centre near Clonmel, County Waterford, is popular with both novice and experienced anglers as it has superb accommodation, as well as a reliable, experienced staff. Regarded as the best fishing river in the east, River Slaney has many fisheries along its banks. **Ballintemple Fishery** is a good choice, and offers angling equipment for hire, and instruction is needed. **Mike's Fishing Tackle** in south Dublin is also a good place to buy tackle. Live bait is available for purchase.

Information on the required permits can be obtained from

Fishing in the canal at Robertstown, County Kildare (*see p128*)

Walking in the Gap of Dunloe, Killarney *(see p163)*

the **Central Fisheries Board**
in the Republic, and from
Inland Fisheries, Department
of Culture, Arts and Leisure,
Northern Ireland. Contact
the **Irish Federation of Sea
Anglers** for useful tips, or
in order to book sea fishing
trips or courses.

Maps and other information
on fishing locations can be
obtained from Fáilte Ireland
in the Republic, and from the
Northern Ireland Tourist Board
(see pp370–71). It is also worth
consulting the **Irish Angling
Update** website, which posts
helpful and regularly updated
reports on angling conditions
throughout Ireland.

WALKING AND MOUNTAINEERING

A walking holiday puts you in
the very middle of the glorious
Irish landscape. The network
of waymarked trails all over
the country cut through some
truly breathtaking and lovely
areas. Information on long-
distance walks is available
from Fáilte Ireland
and the

Northern Ireland Tourist
Board. The loveliest routes
include Wicklow Way *(see
p139)*, Dingle Way, Kerry
Way, Munster Way and Barrow
Towpath. Each of these may
be split into shorter sections
for less experienced walkers
or those short of time. The
800-km (500-mile) Ulster Way
encircles Northern Ireland,
taking in the
spectacular
scenery around
Giant's
Causeway *(see
pp262–3)* and
the peaks of the
mountains of Mourne
(see pp284–5).

Irish Ways offers walking
holidays in the Republic. To
find out about organized
walks in Northern Ireland,
contact the **Ulster Federation
of Rambling Clubs**.

An Óige Hill Walkers Club
organizes a hike each Sunday
or the Wicklow and Dublin
mountains for experienced
walkers. Once a month, the
club's programme includes an

introductory hard hike which
allows novices to try out more
rigorous hiking.

The award-winning **Michael
Gibbons' Walking Ireland
Centre** specializes in half-day
walks and full-day tours in
summer that guide walkers
through the landscape and
heritage of Connemara.

Skibbereen Historical Walks
enables visitors to learn about
Ireland's past via Skibbereen, a
small town largely associated
with the Famine.

Contact the **Mountaineering
Council of Ireland** for more
details about mountaineering
and rock climbing holidays.
For any hike, remember to go
well-equipped for the highly
changeable Irish weather.

CYCLING

With the exhilarating range of
countryside to be explored,
and the largely traffic-free
roads, cycling is a pleasure in
Ireland. Several organizations
such as **Celtic Cycling** offer
planned itineraries as well as
accommodation.
**Premier Cycling
Holidays** have
several bicycle
tours, which
seem to have
been expertly
designed to maximize the
thrill of cycling.

Cycling Ireland is the
governing body of cycling in
Ireland, and its website
provides information on
cycling routes and amenities
throughout the country.

You can transport your bike
fairly cheaply by train or by
bus. For bike rental, try **Neill's
Wheels** depots, which can
be found in both Northern
Ireland and the Republic,
or the **Cycleways** outlet in
Parnell Street, Dublin.

Sign for the Ulster Way, the
trail around Northern Ireland

Cycling through the Muckross House estate near Killarney *(see p159)*

Golfers at Portstewart in Northern Ireland (see p260)

GOLF

Out of the 300 or more golf courses spread throughout Ireland, over 50 are championship class. Many of the most beautiful greens verge on spectacular stretches of coast, and are kept in top condition.

In County Kilkenny, the internationally acclaimed golf course, **Mount Juliet**, was designed by golfing legend Jack Nicklaus. County Kildare's **K Club** is home to two superb 18-hole championship golf courses. Arnold Palmer designed both, but each has its own characteristics and special set of challenges. Champion golfer Christy O'Connor Junior designed **Galway Bay Golf Club**. This difficult course, a must for all keen golfers, is dotted with historic ruins dating back to the 16th century.

Acknowledged as one of the truly great links courses, **Portmarnock Golf Club** is situated to the north of Dublin, about 19 km (12 miles) from the city centre. Its quality and location have made it a splendid venue for some of the game's most celebrated events. On the Atlantic coast, **Lahinch Golf Club** in County Clare is a must for devoted golfers, and is a recognized Mackenzie course.

Northern Ireland's best-known courses are **Royal Portrush Golf Club** and **Royal County Down Golf Club**.

The **Golfing Union of Ireland**, the **Irish Ladies Golfing Union** and the tourist boards have information on courses, conditions and green fees all over the country. Equipment can be hired at most clubs, but most golfers prefer to bring their own.

HORSE RIDING AND PONY TREKKING

The Irish are rightly proud of their fine horses. Many riding centres, both residential and non-residential, offer trail riding and trekking along woodland trails, deserted beaches, country lanes and mountain routes. Dingle, Donegal, Connemara and Killarney are all renowned areas for trail riding – post-to-post and based. Post-to-post trails follow a series of routes with accommodation in a different place each night. Based trail rides follow different routes in one area, but riders return to stay at the same location each night.

Aille Cross Equestrian Centre in Connemara offers horseback trail riding for both experienced and novice riders. Riders spend four to six hours a day on Connemara ponies or hunting horses. Further south, **Killarney Riding Stables** is located just 2 km (1 mile) from the heart of Killarney town. Adventurous riders can start the four- or six-day Killarney Reeks Trail here.

Horse riding in Killarney

The **Mountpleasant Trekking and Riding Centre** can be found within 2,000 acres of forestry and rolling countryside around Castlewellan in County Down. The centre caters for both novice and experienced riders.

Five Counties Holidays provides vacations that include horse riding in different areas of the north-west of Ireland. Also, many riding centres, such as **Equestrian Holidays Ireland** based in Co Cork offer guidance and lessons to beginners as well as to more advanced riders. They also provide lessons in show jumping.

WATER SPORTS

With a coastline of over 4,800 km (3,000 miles), Ireland is the perfect venue for water sports. Surfing, windsurfing, scuba diving and canoeing are the most popular activities, as there are ample facilities along the entire Irish coastline.

Conditions in Sligo are the best in Ireland for surfing, but many other coastal locations offer good conditions. The **Irish Surfing Association**, the national governing body for surfing and related activities such as knee boarding and body surfing, has plenty of information about surfing in all 32 Irish counties. Windsurfing centres in Ireland are

Surfing at Bundoran, Donegal Bay (see p230)

mainly found near Dublin, Cork and Westport.

Diving conditions are variable but visibility is particularly good on the west coast. The **Irish Underwater Council** will put you in touch with courses and facilities. **DV Diving** organizes scuba diving courses and offers accommodation near Belfast Lough and the Irish Sea where there are a number of historic wrecks to be explored.

Inland, Lower Lough Erne (see pp270–71) and Killaloe by Lough Derg (see p190) are popular holiday centres. The **Lakeland Canoe Centre** between Upper and Lower Lough Erne gives canoeing courses and also organizes canoeing holidays (with overnight camping), including one down the charming Shannon-Erne Waterway (see p235). From March, **Atlantic Sea Kayaking** organizes one-day outings, as well as two- to eight-day trips around Castlehaven, Baltimore and beyond.

There are several areas all around the coast that are safe for experienced swimmers. Ask locally for details. In Dublin, the popular 40 Foot in Sandycove is a favourite haunt of dedicated sea swimmers. Children are quite safe in the sandy waters inside the harbour while adults can enjoy the deeper waters on the seaward side of the harbour wall. Contact the **Dublin Tourist Office** for more details.

CRUISING AND SAILING

A tranquil cruising holiday is an ideal alternative to the stress and strain of driving, and Ireland's 14,000 km (900 miles) of rivers and some 800 lakes offer a huge variety of conditions for those who want a waterborne holiday. Stopping over at waterside towns and villages puts you in touch with the Irish on their home ground. Whether you opt for Lough Derg or elsewhere on the Shannon, or the Grand Canal (see p101) from Dublin to the Shannon, a unique view of the Irish countryside opens up all along the way.

Yachting off Rosslare, County Wexford (see p151)

Running between Carrick-on-Shannon in Country Leitrim and Upper Lough Erne in Fermanagh, is the **Shannon-Erne Waterway** (see p235), a disused canal reopened in 1993. From here it is simple to continue through Upper and Lower Lough Erne (see pp270–71) to Belleek. **Emerald Star** has a fleet of cruisers for use on the waterway.

Shannon Castle Line runs a modern and high-quality fleet of cruisers on the Shannon. **Silver Line Cruisers**, which also operates on the Shannon, is barely 2 kms (1 mile) from the grand canal, and promises relaxed, uncrowded cruises.

The coast between Cork and the Dingle Peninsula is a popular sailing area. The **International Sailing Centre** near Cork offers tuition. The **Irish National Sailing School** in County Dublin provides lessons at all levels.

More experienced sailors can charter a yacht and sail up the dramatic Irish shore to the western coast of Scotland.

HUNTING AND SHOOTING

Ireland's hunting season runs from October to March, and although fox-hunting tends to predominate in the Republic (it is banned in Northern Ireland), stag and hare hunts also take place. Contact **The Irish Master of Foxhounds Association** in the Republic, and the **Countryside Alliance** in Northern Ireland.

Duck shooting is also available. The shooting season is from September to the end of January. Clay-pigeon (year round) and pheasant shooting (November to January) are also popular. **Mount Juliet Estate** offers guns for hire and supplies cartridges. **Colebrook Park** in County Fermanagh offers deer-stalking outings and lodging. Northern Ireland's **National Countrysports Fair**, usually held in May, is a major attraction for game enthusiasts.

The **National Association of Regional Game Councils** will provide you with details of permits required for hunting.

SPORTS FOR THE DISABLED

Sports enthusiasts with a disability can obtain details of facilities for the disabled from the **Irish Wheelchair Association**. Central and local tourist boards and many of the organizations listed in the directory also advise on available facilities. The **Share Village** provides a range of activity holidays for both disabled and able-bodied people.

Boats moored at Carnlough Harbour on the Antrim coast (see p257)

DIRECTORY

SPECTATOR SPORTS

Aviva Stadium
62 Lansdowne Rd,
Dublin 4. *Tel 01 238 2300.*
www.avivastadium.ie

Croke Park
Dublin 3. *Tel 01 819 2300.*
www.crokepark.ie

Curragh Racecourse
The Curragh, Co Kildaire.
Road map D4.
Tel 045 441 205.
www.curragh.ie

European Tour
www.europeantour.com

Fairyhouse
Rataoth, Co Meath.
Road map D3.
Tel 01 825 6167. www.
fairyhouseracecourse.ie

Football Association of Ireland
80 Merrion Sq, Dublin 2.
Dublin map F4.
Tel 01 703 7500.
www.fai.ie

Harold's Cross Stadium
Harold's Cross Rd, Dublin 6.
Tel 01 497 9023.
www.igb.ie

Horse Racing Ireland
Ballymany, The Curragh,
Co Kildaire. **Road map**
D4. *Tel 045 455 455.*
www.hri.ie

Irish Rugby Football Union
62 Lansdowne Road,
Dublin 4.
Tel 01 647 3800.
www.irishrugby.ie

Leopardstown
Foxrock, Dublin 18.
Tel 01 289 0500.
www.leopardstown.com

Punchestown
Naas, Co Kildaire.
Road map D4.
Tel 045 897 704.
www.punchestown.com

Shelbourne Park
Pearse Street, Dublin 2.
Tel 01 202 6621.
www.
shelbournepark.com

FISHING

Ballintemple Fishery
Ardattin, Co Carlow.
Road map D4.
Tel 059 915 5037.
www.ballintemple.com

Central Fisheries Board
Swords.
Tel 01 884 2600.
www.cfb.ie

Clonanav Fly Fishing Centre
Ballymacarbry,
Co Waterford.
Road map C5.
Tel 052 36765.
www.flyfishingireland.com

Inland Fisheries
Interpoint,
20–24 York St, Belfast.
Road map D2.
Tel 028 9025 8825.
www.dcalni.gov.uk

Irish Angling Update
Tel 01 884 2600.
www.cfb.ie

Irish Federation of Sea Anglers
Mr Hugh O'Rorke,
67 Windsor Dr,
Monkstown, Co Dublin.
Tel 01 280 6873.
www.ifsa.ie

Mike's Fishing Tackle
Patrick St,
Dun Laoghaire, Co Dublin.
Road map D4.
Tel 01 280 0417.

WALKING AND MOUNTAINEERING

An Óige Hill Walkers Club
61 Mountjoy St, Dublin 7.
Dublin map C1.
Tel 01 830 4555.
www.anoige.ie/activities

Irish Ways
Belfield Bike Shop,
University College Dublin,
Dublin 4.
Tel 01 260 0340.
www.irishways.com

Michael Gibbons' Walking Ireland Centre
Market Street, Clifden,
Co Galway.
Road map A3.
Tel 095 21379.
www.walkingireland.com

Mountaineering Council of Ireland
13 Joyce Way, Parkwest
Business Park, Dublin 12.
Tel 01 625 1115.
www.mountaineering.ie

Skibbereen Historical Walks
Skibbereen Heritage Ctr,
Skibbereen, Co Cork.
Road map B6.
Tel 028 40900.
www.skibbheritage.com

Ulster Federation of Rambling Clubs
12B Breda Hse, Drumart Dr,
Belfast. **Road map** D2.
Tel 028 9064 8041.
www.ufrc-online.co.uk

CYCLING

Ardclinis Activity Centre
High St, Cushendall,
Co Antrim. **Road map** D1.
Tel 028 2177 1340.
www.ardclinis.com

Celtic Cycling
22 Ballybricken,
Waterford.
Road map D4.
Tel 051 850 228.
www.celticcycling.com

Cycleways
185–6 Parnell St, Dublin 1.
Dublin map C3.
Tel 01 873 4748.
www.cycleways.com

Cycling Ireland
619 North Circular Rd,
Dublin 1.
Tel 01 855 1522.
www.cyclingireland.ie

Neill's Wheels
Tel 085 153 0648.

Premier Cycling Holidays
Portland, Nenagh, Co
Tipperary. **Road map** C4.
Tel 090 974 7134.

GOLF

Galway Bay Golf Club
Renville, Oranmore,
Co Galway. **Road map** B4.
Tel 091 790 711.
www.galwaybaygolf
resort.com

Golfing Union of Ireland
Carton Demesne,
Maynooth, Co Kildare.
Road map D3. *Tel 01
505 4000.* www.gui.ie

Irish Ladies Golfing Union
1 Clonskeagh Sq, Dublin
14. *Tel 01 269 5544.*
www.ilgu.ie

The K Club
Straffan, Co Kildare. **Road
map** D4. *Tel 01 601 7200.*
www.kclub.com

Lahinch Golf Club
Lahinch, Co Clare. **Road
map** B4. *Tel 065 708
1100.* www.lahinchgolf
hotel.com

Mount Juliet
Thomastown, Co Kilkenny.
Road map D5
Tel 056 777 3044.
www.mountjuliet.ie

Portmarnock Golf Club
Portmarnock, Co Dublin.
Road map D3 *Tel 01 846
2968.* www.portmarnock
golfclub.ie

Professional Golf Association
Dundalk Golf Club,
Blackrock, Dundalk,
Co Louth. **Road map** D3.
Tel 042 932 193.
www.pga.co

Royal County Down Golf Club
36 Golf Links Rd,
Newcastle, Co Down.
Road map E2. *Tel 028
4372 3314.* www.
royalcountydown. org

Royal Portrush Golf Club
Dunluce Rd, Portrush, Co
Antrim. **Road map** D1.
Tel 028 7082 2311.
www.royalportrush
golfclub.com

DIRECTORY

HORSE RIDING AND PONY TREKKING

Aille Cross Equestrian Centre
Loughrea,
Co Galway.
Road map B4.
Tel 091 841216.
www.aille-cross.com

Association of Irish Riding Establishments
Beech House, Naas
Co Kildare.
Road map D4.
Tel 045 854 518.
www.aire.ie

British Horse Society
House of Sport,
Upper Malone Rd,
Belfast.
Road map D2.
Tel 028 9268 3801.
www.bhsireland.com

Equestrian Holidays Ireland
Whispering Pines
Crosshaven, Co Cork.
Road map C6.
Tel 021 483 1950.
www.ehi.ie

Five Counties Holidays
Ardmourne House,
Castlederg, Co Tyrone.
Road map C2.
Tel 028 8167 0291.
www.five-counties-holidays.com

Killarney Riding Stables
Ballydowney,
Killarney, Co Kerry.
Road map B5.
Tel 064 66 31686.
www.killarney-riding-stables.com

Mountpleasant Trekking and Horse Riding Centre
Bannonstown Rd,
Castlewellan, Co Down.
Road map D2.
Tel 028 4377 8651.
www.mountpleasant centre.com

WATER SPORTS

Atlantic Sea Kayaking
The Abbey,
Skibbereen, Co Cork.
Road map 36.
Tel 028 21058.
www.atlanticseakayaking com

Baltimore Diving and Watersports Centre
Baltimore, Co Cork.
Road map B6.
Tel 028 20300.
www.baltimorediving.com

Dublin Tourist Office
www.visitdublin.com

DV Diving
138 Mountstewart Rd,
Newtownards. Co Down.
Road map E2.
Tel 028 9186 1686.
www.dvdiving.co.uk

Irish Surfing Association
Easkey Surf and
Information Centre,
Easkey, Co Sligo.
Road map B2.
Tel 095 49428.
www.isasurf.ie

Irish Underwater Council
78a Patrick St,
Dun Laoghaire, Co Dublin.
Road map D4.
Tel 01 284 4601.

Lakeland Canoe Centre
Castle Island, Enniskillen,
Co Fermanagh.
Road map C2.
Tel 028 6632 4250.

CRUISING AND SAILING

Athlone Cruisers
Jolly Mariner, Athlone,
Co Westmeath.
Road map C3.
Tel 090 647 2892.

Charter Ireland
Galway City Marina.
Road map B4.
Tel 087 244 7775.
www.charterireland.ie

Emerald Star
The Marina,
Carrick-on-Shannon,
Co Leitrim.
Road map C3.
Tel 071 962 7533.
www.emeraldstar.ie

International Sailing Centre
East Beach
Cobh, Co Cork.
Road map C6
Tel 021 481 1237.
www.sailcork.com

Irish National Sailing School
Dun Laoghaire,
Co Dublin.
Tel 01 284 4195.
www.inss.ie

Lough Melvin Holiday Centre
Garrison, Co Fermanagh.
Road map C2.
Tel 028 6855 8142.
www.melvinholiday-centre.com

Shannon Castle Line
Williamstown Harbour,
Whitegate, Co Clare.
Road map C4.
Tel 061 927042.
www.shannoncruisers.com

Silver Line Cruisers
The Marina,
Banagher, Co Offaly.
Road map C4.
Tel 05791 51112.
www.silverlinecruisers.com

Tara Cruisers
Unit 12, Market Yard
Centre, Carrick-on-
Shannon, Co Leitrim.
Road map C3.
Tel 071 962 2266.
www.taracruisers.ie

HUNTING AND SHOOTING

Colebrooke Park
Brookeborough,
Co Fermanagh.
Road map C2.
Tel 028 8953 1402.
www.colebrooke.info

Countryside Alliance
Larchfield Estate
Balliesmills Road,
Lisburn, Co Antrim.
Road map D2.
Tel 028 9263 9911.
www.caireland.org

The Irish Master of Foxhounds Association
www.imfha.com

Mount Juliet Estate
Thomastown,
Co Kilkenny.
Road map D5.
Tel 056 777 3000
www.mountjuliet.ie

National Association of Regional Game Councils
Castle Street, Cloghan,
Co Offaly.
Tel 090 645 7757.
www.nargc.ie

National Countrysports Fair
Moira Demesne,
Lisburn, Co Antrim.
Road map D2.
Tel 02392 662306.
www.irishfieldsports.com

SPORTS FOR THE DISABLED

Irish Wheelchair Association
Blackheath Dr,
Clontarf, Dublin 3.
Tel 01 818 6400.
www.iwa.ie

Share Village
Smith's Strand, Lisnaskea,
Co Fermanagh
Road map C2.
Tel 028 6772 2122.
www.sharevillage.org

SURVIVAL
GUIDE

PRACTICAL INFORMATION

Although Ireland is quite a small island, visitors should not expect to see everything in a short space of time, since many of the country's most magnificent attractions are in rural areas. In remote parts of the island the roads are narrow and winding, the pace of life is very slow and public transport tends to be infrequent. However, although the Republic of Ireland remains one of Europe's most unspoiled destinations, it has a

Ireland
Tourist Board logo

very well-developed economy. Any decent-sized town in the Republic is likely to have a tourist information centre which offers a full range of facilities to help the visitor, including maps and leaflets to take away, as well as staff on-hand to offer advice. Northern Ireland has its own tourist board which also has offices in most towns. The level of hospitality is first-rate across the whole of the country.

Shop at Shannon Airport

VISAS AND PASSPORTS

Visitors from the EU, US, Canada, Australia and New Zealand require a valid passport but not a visa for entry into the Republic or Northern Ireland. All others, including those wanting to study or work, should check with their local Irish or British Embassy first. UK nationals born in Britain or Northern Ireland do not need a passport to enter the Republic of Ireland but should take one with them for car rental, medical services, cashing of traveller's cheques or if travelling by air.

CUSTOMS INFORMATION

When you arrive at any of Ireland's airports you will find three queues for immigration. Since Ireland is a member of the European Union, any citizen from other EU countries can pass directly through the blue channel – but random checks are still

carried out to detect any prohibited goods. Travellers entering from countries outside of the EU, as well as those coming from the Channel Islands and Canary Islands, are still required to

pass through customs. Go through the green channel if you have nothing to declare and use the red channel if you have goods to declare or are uncertain of the customs allowance.

TOURIST INFORMATION

In both the Republic and Northern Ireland there is an impressive network of tourist information offices. In addition to providing lots of free local information, the tourist offices in large towns sell maps and guide books and can reserve accommodation for a nominal charge. There are also tourist information points in some of the smaller towns and villages. The opening hours

LANGUAGE

The Republic of Ireland is officially bilingual – almost all road signs have place names in both English and Irish. English is the spoken language everywhere apart from a few parts of the far west, called Gaeltachts (see p229), but from time to time you may find signs written only in Irish. Here are some of the words you are most likely to come across from the ancient language.

Sign using old form of Gaelic

USEFUL WORDS

an banc – **bank**
an lár – **town centre**
an trá – **beach**
ar aghaidh – **go**
bád – **boat**
bealach amach – **exit**
bealach isteach – **entrance**
bus – **bus**
dúnta – **closed**
fáilte – **welcome**
fir – **men**
gardaí – **police**
leithreas – **toilet**
mná – **women**
oifig an phoist – **post office**
oscailte – **open**
óstán – **hotel**
siopa – **shop**
stop/stad – **stop**
ticéad – **ticket**
traein – **train**

The Heritage Service-run Parke's Castle in County Leitrim (see p233)

can be somewhat erratic and many are open only during the summer season. The local museums and libraries can be another useful source for a selection of tourist literature.

Before leaving for Ireland you can get brochures and advice from **Tourism Ireland**, which has information on both Northern Ireland and the Republic. Their offices can be found in major cities all over the world. **Fáilte Ireland** (the Irish Tourist Board) and the **Northern Ireland Tourist Board** (NITB) can also supply you with maps and leaflets. For more local information on sights, accommodation and car rental, it's worth contacting the regional tourist offices in Dublin, Cork, Galway and Limerick.

If you pick up a list of places to stay in a tourist office, it's worth noting that not every local hotel and guesthouse will be included – these lists recommend only those establishments that have been approved by the Tourist Board.

ADMISSION CHARGES

Most of Ireland's major sights, including ancient monuments, museums and national parks, have an admission fee. For each place of interest in this guide, we specify whether or not there is a charge. The entrance fees in the Republic of Ireland are normally between €3 and €8, with some offering discounts for students and seniors.

The Irish Heritage Service manages and maintains national parks, museums, monuments and gardens. At most Heritage Service sites you can buy a Heritage Card, which allows unlimited, free admission to all sites managed by the service for a year. At €21 for adults, €16 for senior citizens, €8 for children and students, and €55 for a family ticket, the card is a particularly good investment. Popular Heritage Service sites include Céide Fields (see p204), Cahir Castle (see p195) and the Blasket Centre (see p158).

Entrance fees in Northern Ireland are about the same as in the Republic, also with discounts offered to students and senior citizens. North of the border the **National Trust** has a scheme similar to the Heritage Card, but membership is more expensive (€48.50 per annum per person or €84.50 for a family ticket). Although there are fewer sites to see, these include Mount Stewart House (see p282–3) and Carrickfergus Castle (see p275). The card, however, only represents good value for money if you are also planning to visit National Trust sites across the water in Great Britain.

Heritage Card giving access to historic sites

DIRECTORY

TOURISM IRELAND OFFICES ABROAD

United Kingdom
For the whole of Ireland:
Tourism Ireland UK, Nations House, 103 Wigmore St, London W1U 1QS.
Tel 0800 039 7000.
www.tourismireland.com
www.discoverireland.com

United States
345 Park Avenue, New York, NY 10154.
Tel 1 800 223 6470.
www.tourismireland.com

TOURIST BOARD OFFICES IN IRELAND

Fáilte Ireland and
Baggot St Bridge, Dublin 2.
Tel 01 602 4000.
www.failteireland.ie

Northern Ireland Tourist Board
59 North St, Belfast BT1 1NB.
Tel 028 9023 1221. Belfast Welcome Centre: 47 Donegall Place.
Tel 028 9024 6609.
www.discovernorthernireland.com

OTHER CONTACTS

National Trust
Tel 028 9751 0721.
www.nationaltrust.org.uk

The Heritage Service
Tel 01 647 5000.
www.heritageireland.ie

OPENING TIMES

Opening hours are usually between 10am and 5pm, though some sights close for lunch. Few places are open on Sunday morning. Some museums shut on Mondays.

From June to September all the sights are open but crowds are at their biggest. July is the marching season in the North (see p49) but tensions have eased in peace time Belfast and Derry, many shops and restaurants still choose to close at this time.

Some attractions close for winter, while others keep shorter hours. Many places open for public holidays, such as Easter, and then close again until summer.

Interpretative centre at Connemara National Park *(see p208)*

INTERPRETATIVE CENTRES

Many of Ireland's major sights are ruins or Stone Age archaeological sites, which can be difficult to fully appreciate. However, interpretative or visitors' centres, which explain the historical significance of sites, are widely available. Entry to the site may be free, but you have to pay to visit the interpretative centre.

In areas of natural beauty, such as Connemara National Park *(see p208)*, an interpretative centre acts as a useful focal point. The centre provides information leaflets and has reconstructions of sights. There are 3D models and displays, as well as an interesting audiovisual presentation on the development of the local landscape over the last 10,000 years. There is also a shop selling postcards, books and posters.

RELIGIOUS SERVICES

Ireland has always been a deeply religious country and churchgoing is still an important way of life for many. The Republic of Ireland is 87 per cent Roman Catholic, which means that finding a non-Catholic church may sometimes be difficult. In the Republic and Northern Ireland, the tourist offices, hotels and B&Bs all have a list of local church service times available.

STUDENT TRAVELLERS

Students with a valid ISIC card (International Student Identity Card) benefit from reduced admission to museums, concerts and other forms of entertainment. It also procures over 15 per cent reduction on the Bus Éireann network. ISIC cards can be obtained from branches of **USIT** travel in Dublin, Belfast and other college towns. To find out where your nearest issuing office is, visit www.isic.org. USIT will also supply under 26s with an EYC (European Youth Card) for discounts on air fares, and in restaurants, museums, shops and theatres. The card is recognized in over 20 European states.

European Youth Card

An ISIC card no longer obtains rail travel reductions in Ireland. In the Republic, Irish Rail produces its own Student Travelcard for a good discount on Irish Rail (also known as Iarnród Éireann), DART, Dublin Bus and Luas fares. Cards cost €12 and are issued by post or in person at one of the listed card centres at www.studenttravelcard.ie. Bring along the completed online form and a signed letter from your university. Similarly in the North, discounts on NI Railways, Ulsterbus and Metro (the Belfast bus service) are available with the Translink Student Discount Card. See www.translink.co.uk for further details.

FACILITIES FOR THE DISABLED

Most sights in Ireland have access for wheelchairs. This book gives basic information about disabled access for each sight, but it's worth phoning to check details. The **Citizens Information Board** provides information for the Republic, publishing county guides to accommodation, restaurants and amenities. In the North, **Disability Action** can advise on accessibility, while **ADAPT** provides information and a book on disabled access to over 400 venues in the cultural sector. Both tourist boards also have guides to accommodation and amenities.

TRAVELLING WITH CHILDREN

Ireland has a large young population, and children are made welcome in hotels and restaurants. However, note that in the Republic those under the age of 18 can visit a pub only if accompanied by a parent or guardian, and then only until 9pm. There are often great deals or discounts available to families. Many sights offer a discount admission to children and under-5s usually get in free. School holidays are obviously peak times for travelling with children, and there are many activities available to cater for families. Some hotels offer a special family deal, which includes horse-riding and fishing among other things.

Families relaxing, Kinsale Harbour, County Cork

Black Abbey in Kilkenny has disabled access

ELECTRICITY

The standard electricity voltage in both parts of Ireland is 230 volts AC, 50 Hz. The standard plug is the three-pin IS 411 (BS 1363), as used throughout Great Britain. Adaptors are readily available in airport shops. Before using appliances from other countries, always make sure that they are compatible with the Irish system; it might be that you need to use a power converter or power transformer.

IRISH TIME

The whole of Ireland is in the Western European Time zone, the same as Great Britain, that is five hours ahead of New York and Toronto, one hour behind Germany and France, and ten hours behind Sydney. In both the North and the South, clocks go forward one hour for summer time.

CONVERSION CHART

Imperial to Metric
1 inch = 2.5 centimetres
1 foot = 30 centimetres
1 mile = 1.6 kilometres
1 ounce = 28 grams
1 pound = 454 grams
1 pint = 0.6 litres
1 gallon = 4.6 litres

Metric to Imperial
1 millimetre = 0.04 inches
1 centimetre = 0.4 inches
1 metre = 3 feet 3 inches
1 kilometre = 0.6 miles
1 gram = 0.04 ounces
1 kilogram = 2.2 pounds
1 litre = 1.8 pints

GREEN IRELAND

Ireland has long been known as the Emerald Isle, but this has more to do with the small population and a lack of industrialisation than any official environmental initiatives. However, the Green Party joined a coalition government in the Republic in 2007, and building standards have been tightened; motor tax has been revised to favour cars with lower emissions; second homes are now taxed, and a carbon tax was introduced in 2010.

The land of Ireland is still predominantly in agricultural use. Organic food produce is becoming popular and farmers' markets are held regularly in most large towns. There are vast areas of unspoilt coastline, lakes, mountains and forests. Pollution from agriculture and sewage can be a problem, but the situation is improving and the water quality in coastal bathing areas is good.

Ecotourism is on the increase and organizations such as **The Organic Centre** and the **Centre for Environmental Living and Training (CELT)** run courses on such topics as beekeeping, sustainable house design, and organic gardening. Agritourism is also more widespread with working farms offering guestrooms throughout the country; these can be booked through **Irish Farmhouse Holidays**.

For more information on green issues, the Sustainable Ireland website (*www.sustainable.ie*) is an indispensible resource.

Personal Security and Health

Ireland is probably one of the safest places to travel in Europe. Petty theft, such as pickpocketing, is seldom a problem outside certain parts of Dublin and a few other large towns. Tourist offices and hoteliers gladly point out the areas to be avoided. In Northern Ireland security measures have been relaxed in the light of the peace accord. In the Republic, however, crimes against the individual are on the increase, but rates still tend to be lower than in other parts of the UK and Europe.

Pearse Street Garda Station, Dublin

POLICE

The police, should you ever need them, are called the Garda Síochána (Gardaí, for short) in the Republic of Ireland and the Police Service • Northern Ireland (PSNI) in the North. The PSNI is the only territorial police force in the UK that is routinely armed.

Both police forces are working together to tackle the issue of organised cross-border crime.

Garda   **PSNI policeman**

PERSONAL SAFETY IN THE REPUBLIC

Violent street crime is relatively rare but it is still advisable to take suitable precautions, such as avoiding poorly lit streets in the cities and larger towns. Poverty and a degree of drug addiction in central Dublin have been known to cause a few problems, and Limerick isn't the most inviting of places after dark. There have also been a number of racist attacks in Dublin, connected with an increase in immigration. But if you take sensible precautions, avoiding back-streets at night and keeping to the popular and busy areas, there should be little cause for concern.

In some of the larger towns you may be approached in the street by people asking for money. This rarely develops into a troublesome situation, but it is still best to avoid eye contact and leave the scene as quickly as possible.

PERSONAL SAFETY IN NORTHERN IRELAND

Even at the height of the Troubles in Northern Ireland, there was never a significant threat to the tourist, and travelling around the province was deemed to be as safe as in the Republic. As long as peace prevails, no extra precautions need to be taken here but first-time visitors should be prepared for certain unfamiliar situations, no better or worse than in the South. When driving, if you see a sign that indicates you are approaching a checkpoint, slow down and use dipped headlights. To keep fuss down to a minimum in these situations, it is a good idea to keep a passport or some other form of identification close at hand. If you are walking around the city centres of Belfast and Londonderry, you may notice a strong police or military presence. This is unlikely to inconvenience you.

During July, visitors may find themselves in slow-moving traffic behind an Orange march *(see p49)*. Tensions between local communities can be higher at this time, but the affected areas are easily avoided.

PERSONAL PROPERTY

As pickpocketing and bag-snatching can be a problem in the larger towns, it's best not to carry around your passport or large amounts of cash. Most hotels have a safe; or consider using traveller's cheques *(see p376)*. When out and about, use a bag that can be held securely, and be alert in crowded places and restaurants. A money belt may be a good investment.

Garda station

PSNI badge

If travelling by car, ensure that all valuables are locked in the boot and always lock the car, even when leaving it for just a few minutes. If Northern Ireland, do not leave any bags or packages unattended, as they may result in a security scare.

LOST PROPERTY AND BAGGAGE ROOMS

Report all lost or stolen items at once to the police. In order to make a claim against your insurance company you need to send in a copy of the police report. Most train and bus stations in the Republic operate a lost-property service but there is no such service in Northern Ireland.

If you wish to do a day's sightseeing unencumbered by baggage, most hotels and some main city tourist offices, both in the Republic and Northern Ireland, offer baggage storage facilities. Ensure all luggage is locked.

IN AN EMERGENCY

In the Republic and Northern Ireland, the emergency phone number for Police, Ambulance or Fire Brigade is 999 or 112 from a mobile, which should only be used if really necessary. In a medical emergency which does not require an ambulance, you should visit a general practitioner (GP) or the outpatients, accident and emergency or casualty department of the nearest public hospital. In the Republic, if you are not referred to the hospital by a GP you may be asked to pay a fee of €100.

If you find yourself in difficulties, with no money, or unwell and not speaking the language, call the nearest police station for practical advice. Tourist offices will also be able to help. Public hospitals are used to providing translation for patients of many nationalities.

Dublin ambulance

Dublin fire engine

Garda patrol car

HOSPITALS AND PHARMACIES

Residents of countries in the European Union, the European Economic Area and Switzerland can claim free medical treatment in Ireland with an European Health Insurance Card (see below.) Also, be sure to let the doctor know that you want treatment under the EU's social security regulations. In Northern Ireland, British citizens need no documentation.

Non-EU travellers should either have their own travel insurance or be prepared to pay up front for treatment.

A wide range of medical supplies is available over the counter at pharmacies. However, many medicines are available only with a prescription authorized by a local doctor. If you are likely to require specialized drugs during your stay, ensure you bring your own supplies and a copy of the original prescription. You can also ask your doctor to write a letter with the generic name of the medicine you require. Always obtain a receipt for insurance claims.

TRAVEL AND HEALTH INSURANCE

Before travelling, make sure that your possessions are insured; it might be difficult and more expensive to get insurance in Ireland. It is also worth noting that travel insurance for the UK may not cover you in the Republic so make sure you have an adequate policy.

Private health insurance policies may include a certain level of travel coverage. US visitors in particular should check before leaving home whether they are covered by their insurance company for medical care abroad. They may

Small rural health centre in County Donegal

have to pay first and reclaim costs later; if so, be sure to get an itemized bill.

Holders of a European Health Insurance Card are entitled to free treatment. Cards can be applied for online and take about a week to be sent to your address. They are free of charge and valid for five years.

DIRECTORY

USEFUL ADDRESSES

Police, Fire, Ambulance and Coastguard Services
Tel Dial 999 or 112 in both the Republic and Northern Ireland.

Police Exchange
For non-emergency police assistance in Northern Ireland.
Tel 028 9065 0222.

Beaumont Hospital
Beaumont Road, Dublin 9
Tel 01 809 3000.

City Hospital
Lisburn Road, Belfast BT9 7AB.
(offers emergency dental treatment)
Tel 028 9032 9241.

Dublin Dental Hospital
Lincoln Place, Dublin 2.
Tel 01 612 7200.

European Health Insurance Card
www.ehic.org

Hickey's Pharmacy
55 Lr O'Connell St, Dublin 1
Tel 01 8730427.

Royal Victoria Hospital
Grosvenor Road, Belfast BT12
6BA. *Tel 028 9024 0503*

Banking & Local Currency

The Republic and Northern Ireland have different currencies. The euro is the currency in the Republic and the pound sterling is the currency in Northern Ireland, the same as in Great Britain. When travelling between Northern Ireland and the Republic, there's no shortage of money-changers in towns near the border. Check online or in the daily newspapers for the standard rate of exchange to give yourself a guideline. Some tourist attractions offer money-changing facilities but for the best exchange rates use the banks or *bureaux de change*.

First Trust Bank logo

BANKS AND BUREAUX DE CHANGE

Banks throughout Ireland generally provide a very good service, although opening times can vary significantly. Both north and south of the border, there are fewer bank branches in small towns than there once were, so it's advisable to do your banking in the bigger towns if possible.

In the Republic of Ireland, retail banks include the Bank of Ireland, the Allied Irish Bank (AIB), the Ulster Bank, the National Irish Bank and the Permanent tsb. The usual banking hours are Monday to Friday from 10am to 12:30pm and from 1:30 to 4pm, but most branches now stay open during lunch time. There is extended opening (until 5pm) on one day of the week. In Dublin, Cork and most other cities and towns, late opening is on Thursdays. Branches of the Permanent tsb remain open at lunch time and up to 5pm on weekdays. Some rural areas are visited once or twice a week by a mobile bank. Check locally for days and times.

In Northern Ireland there are four retail banks: the Ulster Bank, the Bank of Ireland, the Northern Bank and the First Trust Bank. Most are open from 10am till 4pm, though a few close for a lunch hour at 12:30pm. In both the Republic and in Northern Ireland, all banks close on public holidays, some of which differ from North to South *(see p51)*. In addition to the foreign exchange counters at the main banks, there are some private *bureaux de change* in large towns and cities. As with most other exchange facilities, *bureaux de change* stay open later than banks. Check their rates first before undertaking any transactions.

Northern Bank logo

ATMS

Automated teller machines (ATM), or cash dispensers, are common in most towns in Ireland, in and outside of banks on main streets, in large shops and at shopping centres. Using these machines is the most convenient way to manage your money while on holiday, and exchange rates are good. Cards in the Plus, Link, Cirrus and Maestro networks, and Visa and MasterCard credit cards, can be used in most ATMs. Be careful to protect your PIN number at all times and avoid using ATMs that appear to have been tampered with.

CREDIT CARDS AND TRAVELLER'S CHEQUES

Throughout Ireland you can pay by credit card in most hotels, petrol (gas) stations and large shops. Keep in mind that you will need your PIN. VISA and MasterCard are the most commonly accepted; fewer businesses take American Express and Diners Club cards. Traveller's cheques are the safest way to carry large amounts of money. These can be bought before setting out at American Express, Travelex, or your own bank. In Ireland they can be purchased and exchanged at banks and *bureaux de change*.

WIRING MONEY

The cheapest way to get money from home is to have your own bank wire funds to a bank in Ireland. This process is very slow, often taking several days; it's much faster, though expensive, to get money sent through a company such as Western Union (tel: 1800 395395).

BUREAUX DE CHANGE

Joe Walsh Tours
69 Upper O'Connell St. Dublin 1.
Tel 01 872 2555.
www.joewalshtours.ie

Thomas Cook
Belfast Park S.C.
Tel 028 7166 47053.

Travelex
Belfast International Airport.
Tel 028 9444 7500.
www.travelex.com

Ornate post office and *bureau de change* in Ventry, County Kerry

CURRENCY IN NORTHERN IRELAND

Northern Ireland uses British currency – the pound sterling (£), which is divided into 100 pence (p). As there are no exchange controls in the UK, there is no limit to the amount of cash you can take into and out of Northern Ireland. In addition to the British currency, four provincial banks issue their own banknotes (bills), worth the same as their counterparts. To tell them apart, look for the words "Bank of England" on British notes. It is best to use the provincial banknotes in Northern Ireland rather than in Britain – some shops may be reluctant to accept notes that are unfamiliar to them.

Banknotes
British banknotes are issued in the denominations £50, £20, £10 and £5. Always carry small denominations as some shops may refuse the £50 note.

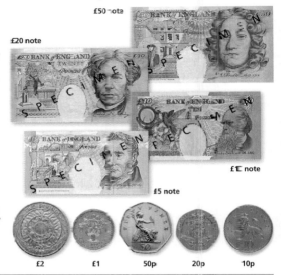

£50 note

£20 note

£10 note

£5 note

Coins
Coins come in the following denominations: £2, £1, 50p, 20p, 10p, 5p, 2p and 1p. All have the Queen's head on one side and are the same as those elsewhere in the UK, except that the pound coin has a different detail – a flax plant – on the reverse side.

£2 £1 50p 20p 10p

THE EURO

The Republic of Ireland was one of 12 countries which adopted the euro in 2002. EU members using the euro as sole currency are known as the eurozone. Several EU members have opted out of joining this common currency.

Euro notes are identical throughout the eurozone, each featuring designs of fictional architectural structures and monuments. The coins have one side identical (the value side), and one side with an image unique to each country. Notes and coins are exchangeable in each of the participating euro countries.

€50 note

€20 note

€10 note

€5 note

Banknotes
Euro banknotes, each a different colour and size, have seven denominations. The €5 note (grey in colour) is the smallest, followed by the €10 note (pink), €20 note (blue), €50 note (orange), €100 note (green), €200 note (yellow) and €500 note (purple).

€2 coin €1 coin 50 cents 20 cents 10 cent

Coins
The euro has eight coin denominations: €2 and €1 (gold and silver); 50 cents, 20 cents, 10 cents (gold); 5 cents, 2 cents and 1 cent (bronze).

Communications & Media

eircom
phonebox

Both parts of Ireland are well served for national daily and Sunday newspapers, and there are many Irish magazines. The TV and radio are dominated by the state broadcasters RTE and BBC, but independent local radio thrives all over Ireland.

The postal system is reliable and there are post offices in every small town. The Irish are big users of mobile phones, and as a result, public telephones are less used now. Prepaid phonecards, however, remain good value. Most large towns have an Internet café, and Wi-Fi points are becoming more common.

PUBLIC TELEPHONES

The Republic's national telephone company, eircom, once ran all the telephone services in the country, but other companies now also provide public phones. Eircom's service includes coin, card and credit card telephones that provide an efficient service. For those intending to spend more than €5 on calls during their stay, it is worth using a phonecard, as these offer discounts.

Northern Ireland uses British Telecom (BT) public phones, which accept either coins, cards or credit cards. Both BT and eircom phonecards are available from post offices, supermarkets and other retail outlets.

PHONING FROM THE REPUBLIC OF IRELAND

Cheap call rates within the Republic and to the UK are from 6pm to 8am on weekdays and all day at weekends. Off-peak times for international calls vary depending on the country you call, but are generally as above.
• To call Northern Ireland: dial 048, followed by the 8-digit number.
• To call the UK: dial 00 44, the area code (minus the leading 0), then the number.
• To call other countries: dial 00, followed by the country code (for example, 1 for the USA, 61 for Australia), the area code (minus the leading 0), then the number.
• Credit cards issued in certain countries including the USA, Australia and Canada

are accepted as payment for calls to the country in which the card was issued.

PHONING FROM NORTHERN IRELAND

Cheap call rates within and from the Province are the same as for the Republic.
• For calls within Great Britain and Northern Ireland: dial the area code and the number required.
• For calls to the Republic of Ireland: dial 00 353, then the area code minus the first 0, then the number.
• For international calls: dial 00, then the country code (for example, 1 for Canada, 64 for New Zealand), then the area code minus the first 0, then the number.

All phone numbers in Northern Ireland have an area code of 028, followed by an 8-digit local number.

MOBILE PHONES

Mobile phones are as popular in Ireland as they are elsewhere, both for making calls and sending text messages. Vodafone, O2, 3 Mobile and Meteor are the main service providers. Before travelling, check on your provider's roaming charges for making and receiving calls. It may work out more economical to buy an Irish SIM card if your phone is not blocked. Alternatively, you could consider buying a cheap pre-pay phone with its own SIM card. The Irish network uses the 900 or 1800 GSM system, so visitors from the US (where

the system is 800 or 1900 MHz band) will need to acquire a tri- or quad-band set.

RADIO AND TELEVISION

Ireland has three state-controlled television channels, RTE One, RTE Two and Irish-language TG4, as well as two privately run channels, TV3 and 3e. Other channels, including five British terrestrial ones are available. There are six national radio stations.

Daily newspapers of the Republic

NEWSPAPERS AND MAGAZINES

The Republic of Ireland has six national daily papers and five Sunday papers. Quality dailies include the *Irish Independent*, the *Examiner* and *The Irish Times*, the latter being well known for its journalistic excellence. The North's top local paper is the *Belfast Telegraph*, which has morning, afternoon and late editions. The Province's morning papers, the *News Letter* and *Irish News*, are less rewarding. Ireland's daily tabloids are the *Star*, *Irish Sun* and *Irish Daily Mail*.

To find out what's on and where, the broadsheets are a useful source of information and most towns have a local or regional paper with listings.

In larger towns throughout Ireland, British newspapers (including *The Times*) are on sale, as well as US publications *Newsweek*, *USA Today* and *Time* magazine.

Coffee and computers at the
Central Cyber Café in Dublin

THE INTERNET AND FAX

The main cities in the Republic
and Northern Ireland have
plenty of access to computers
and the Internet. Public facilities are available free of
charge from public
libraries, but you may
have to book in
advance. The easiest
and fastest way to
access the Internet is
at one of the Internet
cafés found in major
towns and cities.
The cafés often
charge by the half-
hour for computer
use, so costs can
build up quickly
especially if printing pages.
Internet access is often
cheaper during off-peak times
so check charges beforehand.

Fax is not widely used but
machines can be found in
stationary and photocopy
shops and Internet cafés.

POSTAL SERVICES

Main post offices in the
Republic and Northern
Ireland are usually open from
9am to 5:30pm during the
week and from 9am to around
1pm on Saturdays, although
times do vary. Some smaller
offices close for lunch on
weekdays and do not open on
Saturdays. Standard letter and
postcard stamps can also be
bought from some newsagents.

The Republic of Ireland
does not have a first- and
second-class system, but
sending a postcard is a few
cents cheaper than a letter.
Though it is improving all the
time, the postal service in the
Republic is still quite slow –
allow three to four days when
sending a letter to Great
Britain and at least
six days for the
United States.

In Northern
Ireland, letters to
other parts of the UK
can be sent either
first- or second-class,
with most first-class
letters reaching their
UK destination the
next day. The cost of
a letter from North-
ern Ireland is the
same to all EU countries.

Both postal services offer
the faster option of couriers,
which offer delivery from the
next working day for the
UK and Europe.

POSTBOXES

Postboxes in Ireland come in
two colours – green in the
Republic and red in the
North. Many of Ireland's postboxes are quite historic. Some
of those in the Republic even
carry Queen Victoria's monogram on the front, a relic
from the days of British rule.
Most towns and villages have
a postbox, from which the
mail is collected regularly.

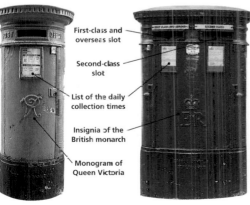

Postbox in the Republic

Northern Ireland double postbox

POST OFFICE

Northern Ireland
Post Office sign

post

Republic of Ireland
Post Office logo

First-class and
overseas slot

Second-class
slot

List of the daily
collection times

Insignia of the
British monarch

Monogram of
Queen Victoria

DIRECTORY

USEFUL NUMBERS
REPUBLIC OF IRELAND

Emergency Calls
Tel 999.

Directory Enquiries
Tel 11811 (Republic and
Northern Ireland).
Tel 11818 (all other countries).

Operator Assistance
Tel 10 (Ireland and Great
Britain). Tel 114 (international
calls).

USEFUL NUMBERS
NORTHERN IRELAND

Emergency Calls
Tel 999.

Directory Enquiries
Tel 118118 (UK, Republic of
Ireland and all other counties).
Tel 153 (all other countries).

Operator Assistance
Tel 100 (UK).
Tel 114 (all other countries).

INTERNET CAFÉS

Claude's Cafe
4 Shipquay St, Derry
Tel 028 7127 9379.
www.claudescafe.co.uk

Global Internet Café
8 Lower O'Connell Street,
Dublin
Tel 01 878 0295.
www.globalcafe.ie

**Revelations Internet
Café**
27 Shaftesbury Square, Belfast.
Tel 028 9032 0337.
www.revelations.co.uk

POST OFFICES

**General Post Office
(Dublin)**
O'Connell Street, Dublin 1.
Tel 01 7057600
(customer services).

**Bloomfield Post Office
(Belfast)**
346 Beersbridge Road
Tel 028 9045 0501.

TRAVEL INFORMATION

Ireland's three main airports, Dublin, Shannon and Belfast, are well served by flights from Britain, the United States and an increasing number of countries around the world. If you are travelling by sea from  the UK, there is a very good choice of ferry routes from ports in Britain to both the Republic and Northern Ireland. Instead of buying separate tickets, you can purchase combined coach/ferry and rail/ferry tickets from almost all of the towns in mainland Britain. The slowly improving public transport systems in both the North and South reflect the rural nature of the island. With this in mind, travelling around Ireland is probably best enjoyed if you embrace the Irish way of thinking and just take your time.

Aer Lingus Airbus in flight

GREEN TRAVEL

There is a well-established railway infrastructure throughout Ireland, and train travel is becoming an increasingly attractive option, particularly on the Dublin–Cork and Dublin–Belfast routes. The rail network may have received little funding in recent years, with greater investment in the national system of motorways, but there have been improvements in the rolling stock and the frequency of services. The bus network is also good, offering comfortable services to all parts of the country (*See pp390–91*).

If you are interested in car sharing, the Northern Ireland Roads Service operates a scheme. Their website (www.carshareni.com) can provide you with further information.

In the cities, public transport is plentiful but hampered by the abundant use of private cars. There are discussions underway regarding the introduction of a congestion charge in Dublin and Belfast. Elsewhere, walkers are well catered for with waymarked trails. There is also good cycling on an extensive network of minor roads.

FLYING TO THE REPUBLIC OF IRELAND

Flights from most of the major European cities arrive at **Dublin Airport** which is Ireland's busiest airport. Regular services to the Republic depart from London's five airports (Heathrow, City, Gatwick, Luton and Stansted) and other cities in

The exterior of Dublin International Airport

Britain, plus the Channel Islands and the Isle of Man.

The major airline operating scheduled flights between Britain and the Republic is **Aer Lingus**. However, **Ryanair** is a fierce rival, with cheap fares from several airports in Britain and all over Europe. **Aer Arann** offers flights within Ireland and to the UK.

Aer Lingus and **United Airlines** fly direct from the US to Dublin Airport and **Shannon Airport**, ten miles outside Limerick. **Delta Air Lines** fly direct to Shannon and then on to Dublin.

Cork Airport is served by flights from London (Heathrow and Stansted), Birmingham, Manchester, Bristol, Plymouth, Cardiff, Leeds, Glasgow, Paris, Amsterdam and Dublin. No airlines fly direct to Ireland from Australia or New Zealand, but there are plenty of connections via London and other capitals.

The Republic's other airports have fewer flights. There are many charter flights for pilgrims to **Ireland West**

Airport sign in English and Gaelic

Airport Knock in Co Mayo, which also has flights from Dublin, London (Stansted) and Manchester. There are flights into Kerry from Dublin, Luton and Stansted airports, and Waterford Airport has flights from both Manchester and Luton. Galway is well served with five daily flights from Dublin.

AIRPORT CONNECTIONS IN THE REPUBLIC

The Republic's three main airports are all served by regular bus services. Dublin Airport is accessible by over 700 buses and coaches daily, including direct services between the airport, the city's main rail and bus stations and the city centre every 15 to 20 minutes, from early morning to around midnight. The trip takes 30 minutes to an hour. At Cork, the Bus Éireann service takes 25 minutes from the airport into the city. Buses run every 45 minutes on weekdays and hourly at the weekends. At Shannon Airport, Bus Éireann runs a regular service into Limerick which takes 30 to 45 minutes to the city centre. In addition, several buses a day go to the town of Ennis, about 20 km (12 miles) away. The Republic's smaller airports depend mainly on local taxi services.

All airports in the Republic have both long- and short-stay parking facilities.

FLYING TO NORTHERN IRELAND

Aer Lingus operates flights from Heathrow as well as regional UK airports to **Belfast International Airport**. There are also flights every two hours, operated by **British Midland**, from London Heathrow to **George Best Belfast City Airport**.

This airport is used by smaller aircraft, but is favoured by many because of its location just 6.5 km (4 miles) from the city centre. The airport also has more flights from the UK – around 15 cities plus London Gatwick, Stansted and Luton – than Belfast International. The City of Derry Airport is Northern Ireland's smallest and handles flights from Stansted, Manchester and Glasgow.

AIRPORT CONNECTIONS IN NORTHERN IRELAND

The airports in Northern Ireland are generally well served with transport links. The Belfast International Airbus service will take you from the airport to the Europa Buscentre via Oxford Street Bus Station and Centra Railway Station. This runs every half hour and takes about 40 minutes from end to end. The Airport Express 300 runs from Belfast International to the city centre every 10 minutes.

At Belfast City Airport the Airport Express 600 runs every 20 minutes throughout the day. There are also trains

Information signs in the main concourse of Shannon Airport

from the airport to Central Station about every 30 minutes. Derry's airport is on local bus route number 143, which goes into the city centre once an hour (less frequently at weekends). All airports in Northern Ireland have taxi ranks and both long- and short-term parking facilities.

TICKETS AND FARES

Airline options between the United States and Ireland have increased in the last few years, with frequent flights now from both the East and West coasts. It's quite easy to get a round-trip flight to Shannon from the East Coast for under US$700. The best bargains are on flights with fixed dates. Air fares from the US are at their highest in the peak season which runs from July to September.

Many UK airports serve Ireland and airlines offer a host of options on fares. It's not difficult to get a round-trip flight from mainland UK to Dublin for well under £100. The cheapest place to fly from is usually London, especially Luton and Stansted airports. Prices are fairly constant all year except at Christmas, during summer and on public holidays, when there are few discounted fares.

Many airlines offer discounts to under 25s, while USIT (*see p373*), Campus Travel and specialist travel agents often have cheaper rates for students and under-26s.

One of the Airlink buses which take passengers from Dublin Airport into the city centre

DIRECTORY

MAJOR AIRPORTS

Belfast International
Tel 028 9448 4848.

Cork Airport
Tel 021 431 3131.

Dublin Airport
Tel 01 814 1111.

George Best Belfast City Airport
Tel 028 9093 5093.

Ireland West Airport Knock
Tel 094 9368100.

Shannon Airport
Tel 061 712000.

AIRLINES

Aer Lingus
Tel 081 836 5000 (Ireland).
Tel 1 800 474 7424 (US).
Tel 0870 876 5000 (UK).
www.aerlingus.com

Aer Arran
Tel 0818 210 210 (Ireland).
Tel 020 474 7747 (Netherlands).
Tel 0870 876 7676 (UK).
www.aerarann.ie

British Midland (bmi)
Tel 01 407 3036 (Ireland).
Tel 0870 607 0555 (UK).
www.flybmi.com

Cityjet
Tel 01 870 0100 (Ireland).
www.cityjet.com

Delta Air Lines
Tel 01 407 3165 (Ireland).
Tel 1 800 241 4141 (US).
Tel 0845 600 0950 (UK).
www.delta.com

easyJet
Tel 0870 600 0000 (UK).
www.easyjet.com

Qantas
Tel 01 407 3278 (Ireland).
Tel 13 13 13 (Aus). Tel 1 800 227 4500 (US). www.qantas.com.au

Ryanair
Tel 01 812 1212 (Ireland).
www.ryanair.com

United Airlines
Tel 1 800 864 8331 (US).
www.united.com

Arriving by Sea

Travelling by ferry is a popular way of getting to Ireland, especially for groups or families intending to tour the country by car. Nine ports in Great Britain and two in France provide ferry crossings to Ireland's six ports. Nowadays, all ferries are of the modern drive-on/drive-off variety with lounges, restaurants and shops. There are also a greater number of crossings and shorter journey times available. Prices vary largely depending on the time of year.

Logo of Irish Ferries

Stena HSS on the Dun Laoghaire to Holyhead crossing

FERRIES TO DUBLIN AND DUN LAOGHAIRE

There is a good choice of ferry services running between Holyhead in Wales and Ireland. **Irish Ferries**, the country's largest shipping company, operates on the Holyhead–Dublin Port route and has up to five crossings a day. The high-speed service takes 1 hour 49 minutes, while the conventional ferry takes about 3¼ hours. **Stena Line** also operates four ferry crossings each day on the same route.

The service from Holyhead to the Dublin suburb of Dun Laoghaire is operated by Stena Line. This route is served by the Stena HSS (High-speed Sea Service) and takes 1 hour 49 minutes. As the largest ferry on the Irish Sea, the HSS has the same passenger and vehicle capacity as the conventional ferries but its jet-engine propulsion gives it twice the speed.

P&O Irish Sea offers an eight-hour crossing from Liverpool to Dublin. **Norfolkline** makes the same journey in approximately 7 hours, and offers one daytime and one nightime service daily. Note that on Sundays and Mondays there is only a night crossing available.

Vehicle loading and unloading times on the fast ferries are considerably shorter than with other ferries. Passengers requiring special assistance at ports or on board the ship should contact the company they are booked with at least 24 hours before the departure time. Passengers travelling with bicycles should mention this when booking – most ferry companies allow bicycles free of charge. Companies generally operate throughout the year with the exception of Christmas Day and Boxing Day.

FERRIES TO ROSSLARE

Rosslare, in County Wexford, is the main port for crossings

Irish Ferries ship loading up at Rosslare Harbour

from South Wales to Ireland. Stena Line runs a service from Fishguard in South Wales using both the conventional ferry and the speedier Sea Lynx catamaran-style ferries. Those intending to take a car on Sea Lynx should make sure the measurements of their vehicle, when fully loaded, are within those specified. The maximum dimensions allowable per vehicle are 3 m (10 ft) high by 6 m (20 ft) long and up to 3 tonnes.

Irish Ferries operates two daily crossings to Rosslare from Pembroke in South Wales (3 hrs 45 mins), with 14 crossings weekly, as well as a service from Roscoff in France (17 hrs 30 mins), with three crossings weekly. Irish Ferries and P&O also run regular services to Rosslare from Cherbourg (18 hours). Cabins and berths are available on all crossings to Rosslare and should be booked well in advance.

FERRIES TO CORK

There is only one route per week direct to Cork from Roscoff in France operated by **Brittany Ferries**. The ferry leaves from Cork on a Saturday and from Roscoff on a Friday. The service is only available from April to October and the crossing time is 14 hours. Cabins and berths are available on routes to Cork but need to be booked well in advance in high season.

Fastnet Line operates a service between Swansea in England and Cork (11hrs 30mins). There are six crossings a week, alternating between Swansea and Cork. Note that departure times may vary due to tidal restrictions, check the website for more information.

Dun Laoghaire terminal

PORT CONNECTIONS IN THE REPUBLIC

All Ireland's ports have adequate bus and train connections, as well as taxis waiting to meet arrivals.

At Dublin Port, Bus Éireann buses meet ferry arrivals and take passengers straight into the city centre.

From Dun Laoghaire, DART trains run into Dublin every 10 to 15 minutes calling at Pearse, Tara Street and Connolly Stations. These go from the railway station near the main passenger concourse. Buses also run to Eden Quay and Fleet Street in the city centre every 10 to 15 minutes.

For those requiring car hire, Hertz has a desk at Dun Laoghaire. However, anyone arriving at Dublin Port will have to rent from the city centre. There is an Avis office at Old Kilmainham and a Hertz office on South Circular Road, both in the city centre.

TRAIN AND BUS THROUGH-TICKETS

It is possible to travel from any train station in Great Britain to any specified destination in Ireland on a combined sea/rail ticket, available from train stations throughout Britain.

Eurolines, a subsidiary of Bus Eireann, runs a through-bus service from about 35 towns in Britain to over 100 destinations in the Republic. **Ulsterbus/Translink** offers the same service to destinations in Northern Ireland. Tickets for both these bus companies can be booked through **National Express**, which has over 2,000 agents in Great Britain. Travellers from North America, Australia, New Zealand and certain countries in Asia can buy a Brit Ireland pass. As well as including the return ferry crossing to Ireland it allows unlimited rail travel throughout Great Britain and Ireland on any five or ten days during one month.

Directions for ferry passengers

FERRY ROUTES TO THE REPUBLIC OF IRELAND	OPERATOR	LENGTH OF JOURNEY
Roscoff–Rosslare	Irish Ferries	17hrs (Oscar Wilde)
Fishguard–Rosslare	Stena Line Stena Line	3hrs 30min (Stena Europe) 1hr 50min (Festcraft)
Holyhead–Dublin	Irish Ferries Stena Line	1hr 49min (Jonathan Swift) 3hrs 15min (Stena Adventurer)
Holyhead–Dun Laoghaire	Stena Line	1hr 49min (Stena HSS)
Liverpool–Dublin	Norfolkline P&O Irish Sea	8hrs 8hrs (Norbay)
Cherbourg–Rosslare	P&O Irish Sea Irish Ferries	18hrs (Normandy) 18hrs (Normandy)
Pembroke–Rosslare	Irish Ferries	3hrs 45min (Isle of Inishmore)

FERRIES TO BELFAST AND LARNE

Stena Line operates two of their HSS Stena Voyager ferries between Stanraer in Southwest Scotland and Belfast. This journey takes 2 hours and the service runs five times daily.

A Liverpool to Belfast service is run by **Norfolkline**, leaving Liverpool (Birkenhead) every evening and six mornings a week, and taking approximately 8 hours to reach Belfast. Note that on Mondays there is only a night crossing available. Crossing the Irish Sea with the **Isle of Man Steam Packet Co** lets you visit the Isle of Man en route. Leaving from Liverpool, this service provides the added advantage of allowing you to disembark at Dublin and return from Belfast or vice versa.

There are three routes from Britain to Larne (north of Belfast): from the Scottish ports of Cairnryan (1 hour 45 minutes) and Troon (1 hour 50 minutes); and from Fleetwood in Lancashire (8 hours). The services from Cairnryan and Troon are operated by **P&O Irish Sea**, who sail both conventional ferries and the high-speed Superstar Express on the Larne–Cairnryan route. This service runs from mid-March to early October and takes just under 2 hours. During the week there are up to seven sailings a day to Cairnryan. The services from Fleetwood and Larne, on the other hand, are run by **Stena Line** and run daily.

Cars and lorries disembarking at Larne Port

PORT CONNECTIONS IN NORTHERN IRELAND

Belfast Port is located 1.5 km (1 mile) from the city centre, and can be easily reached by bus, taxi or on foot. Flexibus shuttles also operate to the city centre via the Europa Buscentre and Central Railway Station. From Larne Harbour, a regular bus service connects to the town's bus station, and from here, buses run every hour into Belfast city centre. There are also trains to take ferry passengers from Larne Port to Belfast's Yorkgate and Central train stations.

FARES AND CONCESSIONS

Fares on ferry crossings to Ireland vary dramatically according to the season – prices on certain days during the peak period of mid-June to mid-September can be double those at other times of the year. Prices increase greatly during the Christmas

and New Year period, too. It is advisable to book your journey both ways before setting out. Those travelling to ports without a reservation should always check availability before setting out. Check the ferries' websites for special offers and discounts.

Often, the cheapest way for families or groups of adults to travel is to buy a ticket that allows you to take a car plus a maximum number of passengers. At certain times of the year on particular routes, the return ticket for a car and two adults (two children count as one adult) can cost less than €120. The cheapest crossings are usually those where the passenger must depart and return within a specified period. Fares are normally reduced for mid-week travel and early-morning or late-night crossings. Ferry companies offer discounts for students with a student travel card *(see p372)* and some have cut-price deals for those with InterRail tickets *(see p389)*.

FERRY ROUTES TO NORTHERN IRELAND	OPERATOR	LENGTH OF JOURNEY
Cairnryan–Larne	P&O Irish Sea	1hr 45min (European Causeway)
	P&O Irish Sea	1hr (Superstar Express)
	P&O Irish Sea	1hr 45min (European Highlander)
Fleetwood–Larne	Stena Line	8hrs (Stena Pioneer)
		8hrs (Stena Leader)
Liverpool–Belfast	Norfolkline	9hrs
Stranraer–Belfast	Stena Line	1hr 45 (Stena HSS)
		3hrs 15min (Stena Caledonia)
Troon–Larne	P&O Irish Sea	1hr 50 min (North Channel Fast Ferry)

On the Road

One of the best ways to see Ireland's magnificent scenery and ancient sites is by car. Driving on the narrow, twisting country roads can be a pleasure; often you don't see another vehicle for miles. It can also be frustrating, especially if you find yourself stuck behind a slow-moving tractor or a herd of cows. If you don't want to take your own vehicle, car rental in Ireland is no problem. All the international car rental firms operate in the Republic and are also well represented in the North. Touring by bicycle is another enjoyable way of seeing the best parts of the island at your own leisurely pace.

Irish-language road sign instructing motorists to yield or give way

WHAT YOU NEED

If you intend to take your own car across on the ferry (see pp382–4) check your car insurance to find out how well you are covered. To prevent a fully comprehensive policy being downgraded to third-party coverage, ask your insurance company for a Green Card. Carry your insurance certificate, Green Card, proof of ownership of the car and, importantly, your driver's licence. If your licence was issued in Great Britain, you should also bring your passport with you for ID.

Membership of a reputable breakdown club like the **AA, RAC** or **Green Flag National Breakdown** is advisable unless you are undaunted by the prospect of breaking down in remote parts. Non-members can join up for just the duration of their trip. Depending on the type of coverage, automobile clubs may offer only limited services in Ireland.

CAR HIRE

Car rental firms do good business in Ireland, so in summer it's wise to book ahead. Rental – particularly in the Republic – is quite expensive and the best rates are often obtained by renting in advance. Broker companies, such as **Holiday Autos**, will shop around to get you the best deal. Savings can also be made by choosing a fly-drive or even a rail-sail-drive vacation, but always check for hidden extras.

Car rental usually includes unlimited mileage plus passenger indemnity

Rural petrol pump

insurance and coverage for third party, fire and theft, but not damage to the vehicle. If you plan to cross the border in either direction, however briefly, you must tell the rental company, as there may be a small insurance premium.

To rent a car, you must show a full driver's licence, held for two years without violation. US visitors are advised to obtain an international licence through AAA before leaving the States to facilitate dealing with traffic officials should problems occur.

PETROL

Unleaded petrol (gas) and diesel fuel are available just about everywhere in Ireland. Although prices vary from station to station, fuel in the Republic is quite expensive; in Northern Ireland it costs even more. Almost all the stations accept VISA and MasterCard, although it is worth checking before filling up, particularly in rural areas.

ROAD MAPS

The road map on the inside back cover shows virtually all the towns and villages mentioned in this guide. In addition, each chapter starts with a map of the region showing all the major sights and tips on getting around. If you plan to do much driving or cycling, you should equip yourself with a more detailed map. Ordnance Survey Holiday Maps are among the best road maps. You can usually get town plans free from tourist offices (see p370–71). The tourist boards of the Republic and Northern Ireland both issue free lists of suggested routes for cyclists.

A busy Hertz car rental desk at Dublin Airport

The familiar sight of a farmer and cattle on an Irish country road

RULES OF THE ROAD

Driving in Ireland is unlikely to pose any great problems. For many, the most difficult aspect of it is getting used to overtaking on the right and giving way to traffic on the right at roundabouts (traffic circles). On both sides of the border, the wearing of seat belts is compulsory for drivers and all passengers. Rear seat belts must also be worn. Children must have a suitable restraint system. Motorcyclists and passengers must wear helmets. Northern Ireland uses the same Highway Code as Great Britain. The Republic of Ireland's Highway Code is very similar – find copies of both at bookstores. In the Republic, learner drivers display an "L" plate, and in Northern Ireland, cars carrying a red "R" plate identify "restricted" drivers who have passed their driving test within the previous 12 months and have to keep to lower speeds.

SPEED LIMITS

The maximum speeds are shown in miles in Northern Ireland and kilometres in the Republic, except in some rural areas where they are still in miles. They are much the same as those in Britain:
• 50 km/h (30 mph) in built-up areas.
• 100 km/h (60 mph) outside built-up areas.
• 120 km/h (70 mph) on motorways.
In inner-city Dublin the speed limit is 30km/h (20 mph). On certain roads, which are clearly marked, the speed limits are either 65 km/h (40 mph) or 80 km/h (50 mph). Where there is no indication, the speed limit is 95 km/h (60 mph). In the Republic, vehicles towing caravans (trailers) must not exceed 90 km/h (55 mph).

DIRECTIONS AND ROAD SIGNS

Road signs in the Republic are in both English and Irish, and distances are shown in kilometres. In the North distances are shown in miles.
One sign that is unique to the Republic is the regulatory traffic sign "Yield" ("Géill Slí" in Irish-speaking areas)

– in the UK this is worded "Give Way". Throughout the Republic and Northern Ireland, brown signs with white lettering indicate places of historic, cultural or leisure interest.

SIGNS IN THE REPUBLIC

Unprotected quay   Junction
or river ahead   ahead

Children or   Dangerous
school ahead   bends ahead

SIGNS IN NORTHERN IRELAND

Motorway direction sign

Primary route sign

ROAD CONDITIONS

Roads in Northern Ireland and the Republic are well surfaced and generally in good condition, although both have many winding stretches requiring extra caution. The volume of traffic, particularly in the South, is much lower than in rural parts of Britain. On some of the more isolated rural roads you may not come across another driver for miles.
Many sections of Ireland's national roads have been upgraded to motorways, and there has been extensive construction of two-lane carriageways across the country, including in remote areas such as County Donegal.

A rural road, Dingle Peninsula

PARKING

Finding parking in Ireland used to be easy, but this is no longer the case. Due to increased congestion, the majority of towns now have paid parking on and off street. Dublin, Belfast and a few other cities have either parking meters or (fairly expensive) parking lots. Parking on the street is allowed, though a single yellow line along the edge of the road means there are some restrictions (there should be a sign nearby showing the permitted parking times). Double yellow lines indicate that no parking is allowed at any time.

Disc parking – a version of "pay & display" – operates in most large towns and cities in the Republic and the North. Discs can be purchased from fuel stations, tourist offices and many shops.

In Northern Ireland, almost all towns and villages have Control Zones, which are indicated by large yellow or pink signs. For security reasons, unattended parking in a Control Zone is not permitted at any time of the day.

Parking disc sign

Warning sign in Northern Ireland

CYCLING

The quiet roads of Ireland make touring by bicycle a real joy. The unreliable weather, however, can be something of a hindrance. Shops such as **Kearney** in Galway, rent bikes to tourists and are usually open at least six or seven days a week. It is often possible to rent a bike in one town and drop it off at another for a small charge. You can also take bikes on buses and trains, usually for a small surcharge.

Many dealers can provide safety helmets, but it is always best to bring your own lightweight waterproof clothing to help cope with the unpredictable weather.

SECURITY ROADBLOCKS IN NORTHERN IRELAND

In the late 1960s, when the Northern Ireland Troubles began, roadblocks were introduced on to the roads, with checkpoints staffed by the army or the police. These days, the peace agreement has led to a much more relaxed attitude and if you are travelling by road, whether in the centre of Londonderry or the remote Sperrin Mountains, you are very unlikely to come across a roadblock.

In the unlikely event of your being stopped, show your driver's licence and insurance certificate or rental agreement when asked.

DIRECTORY

CAR-RENTAL COMPANIES

Alamo
Tel 0870 599 4000 (UK).
Tel 877 222 9075 (US).
www.alamo.com

Argus Rent-a-Car
Tel (0) 23 83002 (Ireland).
www.argusrentals.com

Avis
Tel 021 432 7460 (Cork).
Tel 08445 818181 (UK).
Tel 800 331 1084 (US).
www.avis.com

Budget
Tel 01 844 5150 (Dublin).
Tel 800 793159 (US).
www.budget.ie

Dan Dooley
Tel 062 53103 (Dublin).
www.dan-dooley.ie

Hertz
Tel 01 844 5466 (Dublin).
Tel 0207 026 0077 (UK).
Tel 800 654 300 (US).
www.hertz.com

Holiday Autos
Tel 0871 472 5229 (UK).
www.holidayautos.co.uk

Irish Car Rentals
Tel 1850 206088 (ROI).
Tel 0800 4747 4227 (UK).
www.irishcarrentals.com

Murrays/Europcar
Tel 01 614 2888 (Dublin).
www.europcar.ie

National Car Rental
Tel 061 206025 (Limerick).
www.carhire.ie

BREAKDOWN SERVICES

Automobile Association
Tel 01 617 9999 (ROI).
Tel Rescue No. 1800 667788.
www.aaireland.ie

Royal Automobile Club
Tel 01 412 5500 (ROI).
Tel Rescue No. 1800 535005.
www.rac.ie

Green Flag National Breakdown
Tel 0800 000111 (to enrol in UK).
www.greenflag.com

BICYCLE-RENTAL SHOPS

Kearney Cycles
Tel 091 563356.
www.kearneycycles.com

Cyclists checking their directions in Ballyvaughan, County Clare

Travelling by Train

The Republic of Ireland's rail network is run by **Irish Rail** (Iarnróc Éireann) and is state-controlled. The rail network is far from comprehensive and quite expensive, but the trains are generally reliable and comfortable and can be a good way of covering long distances. The service provided by **Northern Ireland Railways** (NIR) is more limited but fares are slightly cheaper. There is an excellent train service between Dublin and Belfast, with a journey time of approximately two hours. Fares can be as little as €36 round trip, with substantial discounts for online bookings.

The DART at Bray railway station, County Wicklow

TRAIN SERVICES IN THE REPUBLIC OF IRELAND

Although the more rural areas in the Republic of Ireland are not served by train, Irish Rail operates a satisfactory service to most of the large cities and towns. Taking the train is probably the fastest and most convenient way of going from Dublin to places like Cork, Limerick, Galway, Waterford and Sligo. However, there are glaring gaps in the network; for example, Donegal is totally devoid of train services, so if you are planning to explore the west coast of Ireland using public transport, you will have to continue westward from towns such as Sligo, Westport, Galway and Limerick using the local bus services.

The two main train stations in Dublin are Connolly Station, for trains to the north, northwest and Rosslare, and Heuston Station, which serves the west, midlands and southwest. These two stations are connected to the city centre by the No. 90 bus service which runs every 10 to 15 minutes and takes a quarter of an hour – traffic permitting. All trains in the Republic of Ireland have standard and super-standard (first-class) compartments. Bicycles can be taken on intercity trains for a small fee.

OUTER DUBLIN RAIL SERVICES

The handy electric rail service known as DART (Dublin Area Rapid Transit) serves 30 stations between Malahide and Greystones with several stops in Dublin city centre. A Rail/Bus ticket allows three consecutive days' travel on DART trains as well as Dublin Bus services. Tickets can be purchased at any of the DART stations. The Luas light rail service connects central Dublin with the suburbs. The first lines were completed in 2004, and interconnect with the DART. *(See also p392).*

TRAIN SERVICES IN NORTHERN IRELAND

The rail network in Northern Ireland is sparse, with only two main routes out of Belfast. One line travels west to Londonderry via Coleraine (for the Giant's Causeway) and the other provides Ireland's only cross-border service, operating a high-speed link between Belfast and Dublin eight times a day. There is also an express service out to Larne Harbour and a commuter line to Bangor.

All trains leave from Central Station, which is not in fact in the centre, but has regular links to Great Victoria Street station in the heart of the city's business and shopping district. There are no baggage rooms at any of Northern Ireland's train or bus stations.

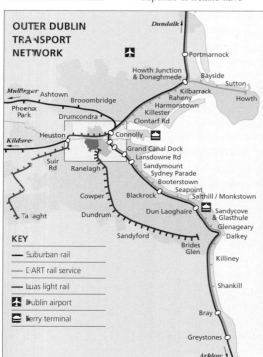

OUTER DUBLIN TRANSPORT NETWORK

Dundalk

Portmarnock

Howth Junction & Donaghmede

Bayside

Sutton

Mullingar   Ashtown

Kilbarrack

Raheny

Howth

Brooombridge

Harmonstown

Phoenix Park

Killester

Drumcondra

Clontarf Rd

Kildare

Heuston

Connolly

Grand Canal Dock

Lansdowne Rd

Suir Rd

Sandymount

Ranelagh

Sydney Parade

Booterstown

Seapoint

Cowper

Blackrock

Salthill / Monkstown

Tallaght

Dundrum

Dun Laoghaire

Sandycove & Glasthule

Glenageary

Sandyford

Dalkey

Brides Glen

Killiney

Shankill

KEY

— Suburban rail

— DART rail service

— Luas light rail

✈ Dublin airport

⛴ Ferry terminal

Bray

Greystones

Arklow

TICKETS AND FARES

Throughout Ireland, train tickets are generally quite expensive, but discounts are available for students and there are lots of bargain incentives and concessionary passes. Most of these include bus travel, so you can get virtually anywhere in Ireland on one ticket.

One of the best tickets available is the Open-Road Pass which allows unlimited travel on all Bus Éireann services from periods of three days (€54) to 15 days (€234) An 8-day Irish Explorer ticket, which costs €245, is valid on all Irish Rail and Bus Éireann services throughout the Republic; travel in Northern Ireland is not included.

Both passes cover many local services, including transport in Cork, Waterford, Limerick and Galway.

The ticket office at Belfast Central Station

CONCESSIONS

Good concessions for students are available with cards issued by Irish Rail and Translink for use in the South and Northern Ireland respectively (see p372).

An InterRail Youth Global Pass allows unlimited travel for a continuous period of 22 days or one month, or for a flexible duration of 5 or 10 days in the Republic and 30 other European countries. It is available for European citizens only. Older travellers can get InterRail Adult passes costing slightly more. Similar passes are offered by Eurail for non-Europeans.

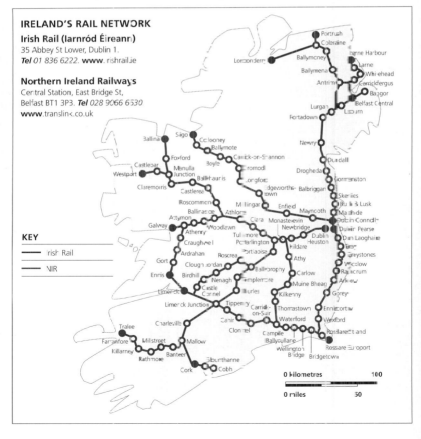

IRELAND'S RAIL NETWORK

Irish Rail (Iarnród Éireann)
35 Abbey St Lower, Dublin 1.
Tel 01 836 6222. www.irishrail.ie

Northern Ireland Railways
Central Station, East Bridge St,
Belfast BT1 3P3. *Tel* 028 9066 6630
www.translink.co.uk

KEY

—— Irish Rail

—— NIR

0 kilometres 100

0 miles 50

Travelling by Bus and Taxi

The bus services throughout Ireland are generally quite good, for such a rural island. However, longer journeys often involve changing buses en route so extra travelling

Logo on Bus Éireann local and express buses

time should be allowed. Touring by bus is also a good way to see Ireland – local tourist offices have details and prices of the numerous tours available and they often take bookings. Taxi services are available in all major cities and towns in Ireland. In the Republic, taxis are identified by a yellow light on the roof. In the North, cities like Belfast and Londonderry have both mini-cabs and London-style black cabs.

Boarding a bus at the Europa Buscentre in Belfast

GETTING AROUND BY BUS

The Republic of Ireland's national bus company, **Bus Éireann**, operates a country-wide network of buses serving all the cities and most of the towns. In Dublin, the main bus station is the Busáras on Store Street, a short walk from O'Connell Street.

There are a number of private bus companies which either compete with the national network or provide services on routes not covered by Bus Éireann. In rural Donegal, for example, there are several private bus services. Some are not fully licensed, so check whether you would be covered in the event of an accident. Local tourist offices should be able to point out the most reputable firms.

Ulsterbus runs an excellent service throughout Northern Ireland including express links between all the major towns. Belfast has two main bus stations – the Europa Buscentre off Great Victoria Street and Laganside Station. Check before setting out that you are going to the right one. Note that for reasons of security, there are no baggage rooms at any of the stations in Northern Ireland.

TICKETS AND FARES

In the Republic, long-distance buses are about half the price of the equivalent train trip. If you are making the return trip on the same day, ask for a day-return ticket, which is much cheaper than the normal round-trip fare. Under 16s pay approximately half the adult fare and student travelcard holders also get a healthy reduction. For those intending to do a lot of travelling it is cheaper to buy a "Rambler" ticket. This allows unlimited bus travel throughout the Republic for a certain number of days in a set period, for example, 15 days' travel out of 30 consecutive days. A variety of other tickets are also available.

A "Freedom of Northern Ireland" ticket gives you unlimited travel on all Ulsterbus routes for either a day or a week. Ulsterbus also offers cheap day-return tickets. Students are eligible for a 15 per cent discount by showing a Translink Student Discount Card. There are also a number of period passes available that combine bus and rail travel (see p389).

BUS TOURS

While the bus services in Ireland are generally adequate for getting from town to town, using public transport isn't a very practical way of exploring specific areas or regions in great detail, unless you have a lot of time on your hands. If you find yourself in a remote area like Connemara (see pp206–8) but have only a very limited amount of time in which to see its main attractions, a local guided tour of the area is a good idea. For about €25 per adult you can do the picturesque "figure of eight" circuit by bus, starting from Galway and taking in Spiddal, Kylemore, Letterfrack, Oughterard and then returning to Galway (summer only). The bus sets out at 10am and returns at about 5:30pm, making regular stops at places of interest. The price does not include admission

Express service bus in Northern Ireland

fees or lunch. Book in advance or on the day at Galway Tourist Information Centre. Four-hour or one-day tours such as this are available in many of Ireland's main tourist areas. Other popular tours of rural Ireland include Glendalough *(see pp140–41)*, Donegal *(see pp224–31)* and the Ring of Kerry *(see pp164–5)*.

In Dublin and other cities in the Republic, Bus Éireann and some local companies run half- and one-day excursions. **Dublin Bus** (Bus Átha Cliath) runs a Dublin City tour, which leaves from O'Connell Street Upper. This guided tour takes in the city's most famous sights.

In northern Ireland, Ulsterbus operates tours from the Europa Buscentre in Belfast to all the major places of interest. These tours include the Causeway Coast *(see p261)*, the Glens of Antrim *(see p267)* and the Ulster-American Folk Park *(see p269)* near Omagh. Ulsterbus prefers bookings to be made in person at their Belfast office. In summer, **Translink** operates up to two guided bus tours per day around Belfast; in winter tours run on Thursday and Saturday only.

A city bus from the Republic of Ireland's national company, Bus Éireann

LOCAL TRANSPORT

Local bus services throughout the Republic are generally well-run and reasonably priced. **Dublin Bus** runs the bus services in the Greater Dublin area *(see p392)*. The on-street light rail service, **Luas** *(see p392)* provides an easy way to reach suburban areas previously only accessible by bus. The Luas lines connect with the DART rail service *(see p392)* at Connolly Station and will eventually link to a proposed Metro system.

In the rest of the Republic the bus services including city buses in Galway, Limerick, Waterford and Cork, are operated mainly by Bus Éireann; a timetable is available at tourist offices and bus stations. Some bus routes connecting towns and villages are served by private companies as well as Bus Éireann. For bus times (and stops) in more remote areas, try asking the locals.

Northern Ireland's bus network is run by **Ulsterbus/ Translink**, including in Belfast where the local service is called **Metro** *(see p393)*. Regional timetables are available at bus stations.

TAXIS IN THE REPUBLIC

With the exception of the Republic's most rural places, there is usually a local taxi service. Apart from in Dublin, where they are plentiful cruising taxis are a rarity, and the best places to find taxis are at train or bus stations, hotels and taxi ranks – your hotel or B&B will also be able to provide details. Four- or eight-seater taxis are available and prices are usually based on metered mileage; if not, it is always best to confirm the fare to your destination before travelling.

TAXIS IN NORTHERN IRELAND

Taxis in Northern Ireland are reasonably priced; journeys within the centre of Belfast will usually cost no more than £6 by mini-cab or black cab. In most decent-sized towns in the North you will find at least one taxi office or a rank where you can wait for a cab. Otherwise, ask for the number of a taxi firm at a local hotel or B&B. A taxi plating scheme is in place, with large plates front and rear of the vehicle, which helps identify legal taxis. Tipping taxi drivers is customary but not obligatory.

Cars wait in line at a Dublin taxi rank

Travelling within Cities

The historic centres of Dublin and Belfast are compact and very easy to navigate. Both are well served by public transport, whether by bus, commuter train or, in the case of Dublin, tram. Each city can be explored in a leisurely fashion on foot – a little less so by bicycle. Both cities offer plenty to see in a small area, as well as easy access to the mountains.

Travelling within Dublin

BUS

A Dublin Bus double-decker is still the best way to see the city. You can buy prepaid tickets including a one-day pass for €6) in newsagents, or pay as you board. It is best to have the correct fare, otherwise you will be given a receipt for the excess amount, which can only be cashed in at Dublin Bus HQ in O'Connell Street. Fares start at €1.15 and depend on how far you travel. Buses run from about 6am to 11.30pm; Nitelink buses run through the night at weekends. Bus routes and timetables are displayed at each bus stop. For bus tours *see p390.*

LUAS

The Luas (luas is the Irish word for speed) light rail system, completed in 2004, is a comfortable and speedy way to get around. There are two on-street lines connecting the city centre with the suburbs. The two lines do not connect with one another and it is a 15-minute walk from the St Stephen's Green stop on the

Green line to the Abbey Street stop on the Red line. The Red line connects with the railway stations Heuston and Connolly, and with the DART at Connolly. Payment is made at ticket machines at Luas stops, and a return fare starts from €2.90.

DART

The electric rail commuter system DART (Dublin Area Rapid Transit) serves 30 stations along the coast from Malahide and Howth on the north side to Greystones on the south, with several stops in the city centre. DART stations have ticket machines and booking offices. They also sell the rail timetable (€3) which contains maps and schedules for DART and mainline rail services. Avoid rush hour if you want to get a great view of the bay from the train.

DART and Luas tickets

TICKETS AND FARES

There is a complicated system of concession tickets for travelling on Dublin Bus, DART trains and Luas trams. So far there is no ticket that combines all three, but you can get one-day or three-day tickets for DART (€8.30 and €17.80) or bus and DART (€10.20, €20). You can also get a one-day ticket for DART and Luas (€9.50) or bus and Luas (€7.50). A three-day Rambler ticket for Dublin Bus costs €13.30; five days cost €20. Tickets are on sale from newsagents, the Dublin Bus office in O'Connell Street, and machines at Luas stops and DART stations.

DRIVING IN DUBLIN

Driving a car in Dublin's congested city centre is best avoided. The short distances are more easily covered on foot, or by bus or Luas. If you do need to drive, there are plenty of multi-storey car parks, and a system of pay-and-display on-street parking which costs €2–€5 per hour, depending on the zone. Costs are shown on the ticket machines in the street. Make sure you return to your car on time as clamping is common.

The M50 ring road around Dublin is a barrier-free, no-cash toll road. Tolls must be paid online within 48 hours (www.eflow.ie).

CYCLING IN DUBLIN

Dublin has many cycle lanes, and ever more people travel to work by bike. **Dublinbikes** is a self-service bike rental scheme with 40 hire stations around the city. The first 30 minutes of hire are free.

A good place for the uninitiated cyclist is along the paths on either side of the River Liffey below the Custom House. Local shops, such as **Cycle Ways**, rent bikes to tourists. Alternatively, **Neill's Wheels** in Dublin offers city cycle tours with a local guide.

Luas light rail station, Dublin

WALKING IN DUBLIN

The outer suburbs of Dublin may sprawl for miles, but the city centre is very small and makes for a pleasant amble on foot. A walk east along the river from stately Heuston Station to the far end of the south quays near the sea will take less than an hour, and a walk between Dublin's two Georgian squares Parnell Square on the north side to St Stephen's Green on the south, takes little more than half an hour. St Stephen's Green itself is pleasant for a relaxed stroll.

Travelling within Belfast

Belfast Metro Bus

BUS

Metro, Belfast's local bus service, is a great way to see the city and its environs. Prepaid tickets are on sale in shops displaying the Metro sign or at the Metro kiosk in Donegall Square West. These need to be placed on the electronic reader next to the driver when you board. Alternatively, pay the driver in coins. The fare depends on how far you travel, starting at £1.20. Maps showing the bus routes are available on www.translink.co.uk.

TICKETS AND FARES

The handy Metro Day Ticket (£2.70 for use after 10am, or £3.50 before), allows unlimited travel all day on the Metro bus system. There are multi-journey tickets from £6 for people staying more than a few days.

Metro prepay ticket

DRIVING IN BELFAST

As with any other small city centre, there is no great advantage in driving a car in

Belfast Public transport is good, the distances are easily covered on foot and the black taxis are cheap. There is even a black taxi tour of the city.

For those who do wish to drive around the city there is little traffic congestion. Ample car parking can be found in the centre of the city with multi-storey car parks and on-street pay-and-display parking (see p387). Make sure you get back to your car on time to avoid a fine.

CYCLING IN BELFAST

Belfast is becoming more cycle-friendly, with a good network of cycle lanes and tracks. The many parks are ideal for cycling and walking, and a number of traffic-free cycleways connect Belfast with other towns. For further details, visit www. sustrans.org.uk. All bicycles are carried free of charge on Translink (the overall transport authority) buses and trains, and there is covered bicycle parking at many

stations. Bikes are available for hire from local shops such as **McConvey Cycles.**

WALKING IN BELFAST

Belfast is a peaceful city these days, and visitors can walk around without need for concern. The city centre is small and easily negotiated on foot. It's a 20-minute walk from the centre to Queen's

Sign for cycle and pedestrian path

University, the Titanic Quarter or West Belfast. Walking tours leave from the Belfast Welcome Centre, Donegall Place. These include the general tour, **Historic Belfast**, and the **Blackstaff Way**, which visits the streets around the city centre. Both cost £6.

General Index

Acknowledgments

Dorling Kindersley would like to thank the following people whose contributions and assistance have made the preparation of this book possible.

Main Contributors

Lisa Gerard-Sharp is a writer and broadcaster who has contributed to numerous travel books, including the *Eyewitness Travel Guide to France*. She is of Irish extraction, with roots in County Sligo and County Galway, and a regular visitor to Ireland.

Tim Perry, from Dungannon, County Tyrone, writes on travel and popular music for various publishers in North America and the British Isles.

Additional Contributors

Cian Hallinan, Eoin Higgins, Douglas Palmer, Audrey Ryan, Trevor White, Roger Williams.

Additional Photography

Peter Anderson, Joe Cornish, Andy Crawford, Michael Diggin, Steve Gorton, Anthony Haughey, Mike Linley, Ian O'Leary, Stephen Oliver, Magnus Rew, Clive Streeter, Rough Guides/Mark Thomas, Matthew Ward.

Additional Illustrations

Richard Bonson, Brian Craker, John Fox, Paul Guest, Stephan Gyapay, Ian Henderson, Claire Littlejohn, Gillie Newman, Chris Orr, Kevin Robinson, John Woodcock, Martin Woodward.

Additional Picture Research

Miriam Sharland.

Editorial and Design

MANAGING EDITORS Vivien Crump, Helen Partington
MANAGING ART EDITOR Steve Knowlden
DEPUTY EDITORIAL DIRECTOR Douglas Amrine
DEPUTY ART DIRECTOR Gaye Allen
PRODUCTION David Proffit, Hilary Stephens
PICTURE RESEARCH Sue Mennell, Christine Rista
DTP DESIGNER Adam Moore
MAPS Gary Bowes, Margaret Slowey, Richard Toomey (ERA-Maptec, Dublin, Ireland)
MAP CO-ORDINATORS Michael Ellis, David Pugh
Marion Broderick, Margaret Chang, Martin Cropper, Guy Dimond, Fay Franklin, Yael Freudmann, Sally Ann Hibbard, Annette Jacobs, Erika Lang, Michael Osborn, Polly Phillimore, Caroline Radula-Scott.

Relaunch – Editorial and Design

EDITORIAL Fay Franklin, Anna Freiberger, Bhaswati Ghosh, Kathryn Lane, Susan Millership, Mani Ramaswamy, Alka Thakur, Asavari Singh
FACTCHECK Des Berry
DESIGN Maite Lantaron, Baishakhee Sengupta, Shruti Singhi
PICTURE RESEARCH Ellen Root
DTP Vinod Harish, Jason Little, Shailesh Sharma
CARTOGRAPHY Uma Bhattacharya, Casper Morris, Kunal Singh

Index

Hilary Bird.

Special Assistance

Dorling Kindersley would like to thank all the regional and local tourist offices in the Republic and Northern Ireland for their valuable help. Particular thanks also to: Ralph Doak and Egerton Shelswell-White at Bantry House, Bantry, Co Cork; Vera Greif at the Chester Beatty Library and Gallery of Oriental Art, Dublin; Alan Figgis at Christ Church Cathedral, Dublin; Labhras ó Murchu at Comhaltas Ceoltóirí Éireann; Catherine O'Connor at Derry City Council; Patsy O'Connell at Dublin Tourism; Tanya Cathcart at Fermanagh Tourism, Enniskillen; Peter Walsh at the Guinness Hop Store, Dublin; Gerard Collet at the Irish Shop, Covent Garden, London; Dónall P Ó Baoill at ITE, Dublin; Pat Cooke at Kilmainham Gaol, Dublin; Angela Shanahan at the Kinsale Tourist Office; Bill Maxwell, Adrian Le Harivel and Marie McFeely at the National Gallery of Ireland, Dublin; Philip McCann at the National Library of Ireland, Dublin; Willy Cumming at the National Monuments Divison, Office of Public Works, Dublin; Eileen Dunne and Sharon Fogarty at the National Museum of Ireland, Dublin; Joris Minne at the Northern Ireland Tourist Office, Belfast; Dr Tom MacNeil at Queen's University, Belfast; Sheila Crowley at St Mary's Pro-Cathedral, Dublin; Paul Brock at the Shannon Development Centre; Tom Sheedy at Shannon Heritage and Banquets, Bunratty Castle, Co Clare; Angela Sutherland at the Shannon-Erne Waterway, Co Leitrim; Máire Ní Bháin at Trinity College, Dublin; Anne-Marie Diffley at Trinity College Library, Dublin; Pat Maclean at the Ulster Museum, Belfast; Harry Hughes at the Willie Clancy School of Traditional Music, Miltown Malbay, Co Clare.

Additional Assistance

Emma Anacootee, Lydia Baillie, Claire Baranowski, Des Berry, Nadia Bonomally, Kathleen Crowley, Rory Doyle, Sylvia Earley, Nicola Erdpresser, Anna Freiberger, Rhiannon Furbear, Yvonne Gordon, Peter Hynes, Ciara Kenny, Delphine Lawrance, Jude Ledger/Pure Content, Therese McKenna, Alison McGill, Caroline Mead, Kate Molan, David O'Grady, Mary O'Grady, Madge Perry, Marianne Petrou, Tom Prentice, Pete Quinlan, Rada Radojicic, Susana Smith, Aine Toner, Dora Whitaker.

Photography Permissions

The publisher would like to thank all those who gave permission to photograph at various cathedrals, churches, museums, restaurants, hotels, shops, galleries and other sights too numerous to list individually.

Picture Credits

a - above; b - below/bottom; c - centre; f - far; l - left; r - right; t - top.

Works of art have been reproduced with the permission of the following copyright holders: © ADAGB, Paris and DACS, London 2011 90tr. The publisher would like to thank the following individuals, companies and picture libraries for permission to reproduce their photographs:

ABBEY THEATRE: Ros Kavanagh 115tl; AER LINGUS/AIRBUS INDUSTRIE: 380tc; Akg, LONDON: National